Date: 2/12/21

BIO JACOB
Warren, Rosanna,
Max Jacob : a life in art and
letters /

Further praise for *Max Jacob*

"Rosanna Warren's eloquent chronicle of the life and times of painter-poet Max Jacob brilliantly revives the lost 'new world' of Modernism's beginnings, and takes in the full landscape of her subject's mercurial, magnanimous soul. Warren's Jacob is a man of astonishingly reconciled contradictions—Jew and Catholic, provincial and cosmopolitan, lover and loner, harlequin and bard—who boldly practiced and preached an 'art of controlled discontinuity' through two world wars and made an art of sacred ritual until his tragic last days."

—Megan Marshall, Pulitzer Prize–winning author of
Margaret Fuller: A New American Life

"Rosanna Warren's biography of Max Jacob, one of the pioneers of French Modernism, offers a penetrating and beautifully researched portrait of this complicated and troubled figure—a Jew turned devout Catholic, practitioner of a loopy version of the Kabbalah, and, with all this, a promiscuous homosexual prone to infatuation with often dubious young men. Jacob was an intimate of Picasso, Apollinaire, and other Modernists in painting and literature, and the book conveys a vivid and detailed sense of the Modernist movement in its heyday in the early twentieth century. This is a major achievement."

—Robert Alter, author of *The Hebrew Bible*

"There are run-of-the-mill biographies not very different from gossip columns and there are great biographies, which we put on the shelf next to books by eminent historians. So is this volume—a fascinating history of French and European Modernism with Max Jacob, Jew and Catholic, poet, painter, and friend of the most famous artists, as the central figure. We are confronted here with the noble hubris of Modernism as it collides with the despicable crimes of the last century. The tragic ending of Max Jacob's life will stay with us for a long time, will make us wonder once again: how was it possible. Rosanna Warren tells us how many years, how many decades she needed to write this major book, so rich in detail, so intelligent. We, the grateful readers, can only say—it was worth it!"

—Adam Zagajewski, author of *Asymmetry*

"The friends of Max Jacob were, as he said, his 'native land.' What friends they were—main inventors not just of 'bohemia,' but of the twentieth century imagination! In Rosanna Warren, Jacob has another astonishing friend—his preternaturally meticulous, eloquent biographer. Warren honors Jacob with a fiercely truthful account, reckoning with his eccentric genius as well as with his *fautes*, his sins. Her empathetic tenderness, combined with tough-minded analysis, quickens Jacob's art, his tragedy, and the convoluted depth of his faith. Warren elevates his stature, his greatness. Max Jacob is passionately alive in this book, and its reader, too, will inevitably discover him as a complex but treasured friend, a compatriot."

—James Carroll, author of *The Cloister*

"This is a gripping biography of Max Jacob, the now largely forgotten French poet and painter whose prose poems once influenced poets all over the world. It brings to life Paris in the years when it was the capital of the avant-garde in literature and modern art and where its practitioners all knew each other. Both as a story of one remarkable man and a portrait of an epoch, it is brilliant and immensely entertaining."

—Charles Simic, author of *The Lunatic*

Max Jacob

Max
Jacob

A
LIFE IN
ART AND
LETTERS

ROSANNA WARREN

W. W. NORTON & COMPANY
Independent Publishers Since 1923

For information about permission to reproduce selections from this book, write to
Permissions, W. W. Norton & Company, Inc., 500 Fifth Avenue, New York, NY 10110

For information about special discounts for bulk purchases, please contact
W. W. Norton Special Sales at specialsales@wwnorton.com or 800-233-4830

Manufacturing by LSC Communications Harrisonburg
Book design by Chris Welch Design
Production manager: Julia Druskin

Library of Congress Cataloging-in-Publication Data

Names: Warren, Rosanna, author.
Title: Max Jacob : a life in art and letters / Rosanna Warren.
Description: First edition. | New York, N.Y. : W. W. Norton & Company, [2020] |
     Includes bibliographical references and index.
Identifiers: LCCN 2020017722 | ISBN 9780393078855 (hardcover) | ISBN
     9780393247374 (epub)
Subjects: LCSH: Jacob, Max, 1876–1944. | Poets, French—20th century—Biography. |
     Cubism and literature—France. | French poetry—Jewish authors.
Classification: LCC PQ2619.A17 Z94 2020 | DDC 841/.912 [B]—dc23
LC record available at https://lccn.loc.gov/2020017722

W. W. Norton & Company, Inc., 500 Fifth Avenue, New York, N.Y. 10110
www.wwnorton.com

W. W. Norton & Company Ltd., 15 Carlisle Street, London W1D 3BS

1 2 3 4 5 6 7 8 9 0

For Katherine and Chiara

CONTENTS

How did the story of Max Jacob's life become the story of my life? I have often asked myself. I didn't mean to write this book. To my French friends, I call it *une biographie involontaire*. It was a case of possession.

At age twenty, still in university, I was trying to make myself into a painter. I spent that summer in Paris studying art in the New York Studio School program, in the mornings painting at their studio on the Boulevard Raspail, and in the afternoons translating and editing the studio notebooks of the painter André Derain. I had stumbled into this occupation. My teacher, the painter Leland Bell, was crazy about Derain and often lectured on him, but his French wasn't good, so he and Robert Stoppenbach, Derain's dealer, arranged for me to work in the Bibliothèque Littéraire Jacques Doucet, one of the great research libraries of France, to produce an English text of Derain's notes. At that time, the notes hadn't been edited or published in French, so in my innocence I sat at the massive beechwood table, poring over the painter's scrawls on notebook pages stained, here and there, with turpentine. It felt like a séance. And among the papers I found notes about the poet Max Jacob, and about the woodcuts Derain had made to illustrate Jacob's collection of poems, *Les Oeuvres burlesques et mystiques de Frère Matorel, mort au couvent*, published in 1912 by Daniel-Henry Kahnweiler, the master dealer of Cubist art.

I had never heard of Max Jacob. The figure intrigued me. He was Jewish, from Brittany. He was homosexual. He was Picasso's first French friend, his initiator into French culture when the Spanish painter appeared in Paris just as he turned nineteen and hardly spoke French. At the conglomeration of studios in Montmartre known as the Bateau Lavoir, as Picasso (and Braque and Gris) reinvented painting, Jacob helped to reinvent poetry, and with his compressed, hard-edged ironic prose poems and synapse-skipping verse lyrics, he showed Apollinaire and many others the way out of the Symbolist haze. He lived in poverty, hand to mouth, reading palms, preparing horoscopes, and selling his gouaches. In 1909 he saw a vision of Christ on the wall of his shabby room in Montmartre; in 1915 he converted formally to Roman Catholicism with Picasso as his godfather. In 1921 he withdrew to live as a lay associate of the Romanesque Benedictine monastery of Saint-Benoît-sur-Loire near Orléans, and stayed there until 1928, when he hurled himself back into worldly life in the capital. He was famous, friends with Cocteau, Coco Chanel, Prince and Princesse Ghika, and a gaggle of aristocrats. In 1936 he retreated once again to Saint-Benoît, and it was there that the Gestapo arrested him on February 24, 1944. He died of pneumonia on March 5 in the concentration-transit camp of Drancy outside Paris, thereby being spared transport to Auschwitz, where his brother and sister had already perished.

In those days I lived in a fever of poetry and painting. I walked each morning from my *chambre de bonne* in an attic in the seventh arrondissement up the Boulevard Raspail, chanting Mallarmé and Apollinaire, so oblivious to traffic that I several times risked being run over. One weekend I rented a car and drove to Saint-Benoît, my ostensible purpose being to draw the Romanesque capitals of the basilica. But Max Jacob waylaid me. In the dusty village of Saint-Benoît where the eleventh-century church surges up from wheat fields, the spirit of the campy, mystical poet-painter took hold of me, and as if a ghostly hand had gripped mine, I found myself writing poems inspired by Jacob, to Jacob, in the pages of my drawing pad. When I returned to the United States that fall, I typed them up. They were among the first poems I ever published, and they helped tilt my lifework from painting to writing. That turn, too, was involuntary.

When my first book of poems came out a few years later, it contained the poems I'd written for Max Jacob. I remember, with electrical clarity, the phone call from my editor, Kathleen Anderson, suggesting that I write a biography of Jacob. In the sublime arrogance of youth, I replied that I'd never write a biography, that it was "a low, mimetic mode." (Lord knows, I've been sufficiently chastened since then.) I hung up. A few minutes later it came to me with the force of revelation that *of course* I would write the life of Max Jacob. He had already chosen me. I called Kathy back.

That telephone call led to the work of three decades. I had no idea, when I pranced off to France in 1985 on a Guggenheim fellowship with a baby, a toddler, and a gallant young babysitter, what scale of work I had taken on. I thought the book was to be about French Modernist poetry. But the more I burrowed into the Bibliothèque Nationale (in the grand old building on the Rue Richelieu), the Bibliothèque Littéraire Jacques Doucet, and other libraries, and interviewed people who had known Jacob, the more it dawned on me that this book also had to be about Jewish life in France, and I set myself to reading French newspapers and literary journals from the Dreyfus Affair onward. Even though I had spent part of my childhood in France, I hadn't paid much attention to French anti-Semitism before Jacob's story forced me to confront it. I realized, also, that nationalist, antidemocratic ideas like those of Charles Maurras and Léon Daudet have not been a fringe mania in France but have been, at times, respectable.

I also came to see that this was a story about homosexuality. Jacob suffered for his passions. Homosexuality has not been a criminal offense in France since Napoléon's laws, but persecution of homosexuals continued in the nineteenth century and into the twentieth under other laws. Same-sex love was considered morally and medically deviant and socially shameful; gay people were often arrested for "disturbing the peace" or corrupting minors, and gay bars and dance halls were raided.[1] As a Catholic, Jacob was convinced that his loves would lead to damnation. Yet he was powerfully attracted to young men, and for years he ricocheted back and forth between erotic encounters and the confessional. In his sprightlier moods, he believed that the sacrament of confession would cleanse his soul and ensure his salvation (leaving him free to indulge his sexual appetites); more often he experienced torment and shame, torn between his physical and spiritual desires. Usually his sexual escapades were fleeting, but in several cases he fell truly and masochistically in love, thus suffering not only Catholic guilt but emotional ravages: he tended to fall for decadent and selfish men, the worst of whom, Maurice Sachs, turned out to be a vengeful parasite, possibly a psychopath. (Sachs ended up working for the Nazis and died—murdered either by fellow prisoners or by guards—on a forced march from a work camp in Germany in 1945.)

Max Jacob's suffering would be nothing more than material for gossip were it not for the remarkable poems it produced. Out of his anguish, he spun lyrics of startling originality, a dissonant art mixing folk songs, advertising jargon, slang, Romantic pastiche, melody, melancholy, puns, and aphorisms. He also wrote plays, experimental novels, and still more experimental short fiction, but it is especially the story of his poetry in verse and prose I hope this book will tell, and I have threaded the poetry through the narrative.

ARRIVING IN PARIS in 1985, I was able to interview a number of people who had known Jacob. By now they are long dead. My quest led me to Versailles, to the modest apartment of Henri Dion and his wife. Dion, the treasurer of the Association des Amis de Max Jacob, worked in the tax department in Versailles and met Jacob in 1942. Passing through the Dions' front door, I entered another century. This elderly couple lived in a brilliant shrine to the Virgin Mary: every square inch of wall was covered in a paper mosaic of Byzantine splendor, a bedazzlement of scarlet, ultramarine, emerald, and gold, with figures of the Virgin in various sizes nested in every nook and cranny. There was barely room for the heavy, old-fashioned wooden dining table. Henri Dion spoke with a mystic, sparkling sweetness.

Another day brought me to the entirely different realm of the Marxist sociologist and philosopher Henri Lefebvre. Known for his many tomes, including *Everyday Life in the Modern World* (1968) and *The Production of Space* (1974)—works still influential today—Lefebvre received me in his apartment near what was then the fairly new Centre Pompidou. He lived in a shrine, not to the Virgin Mary, but to intellect: the tall windows shed light into a high, airy room lined with bookshelves. As a young man, in the early 1920s, Lefebvre had known Jacob around Saint-Benoît and Orléans in association with the journal *Philosophies*, which Lefebvre helped to edit. The aged professor resembled a hawk: he sat tensely upright in his chair; he was thin and energetic, with white hair tossed back from his high, pale, angular forehead; he had a sharp nose and crystalline blue eyes. I must have seemed unusually innocent that day, a young mother trying to look respectable in a prim white suit and pink blouse. Lefebvre leaned toward me and said, "You are a strange person to be writing about Max Jacob." "Why?" I asked. He leaned closer and rasped, "Max Jacob was *perverted*."

Yet another surprise greeted me with Maurice Morel, a priest who had known Jacob at the Hôtel Nollet from 1928 to 1936 and who was passionate and learned about painting. I was to visit him in the Catholic nursing home where he lived in Neuilly. After being admitted through the tidy garden, I climbed three flights of dull, institutional, oyster-gray stairs and proceeded down a dim hallway to his room. The door opened upon his bedroom, a private gallery of masterworks of modern art, all given to Abbé Morel by the artists, his friends: Picasso, Braque, Giacometti . . . And several drawings of horses leaping across a field, by Max Jacob. Abbé Morel's right arm was paralyzed so he could no longer draw and could barely write; his voice was weak, his skin gray, his face swollen as if with cortisone. Yet a kindly intelligence flashed from his eyes, and as he spoke of Jacob and his painter friends, his round face ripened into smiles, a joyous wisdom. (I wondered what insurance he had for his astounding collection of art.)

I came closest to Jacob through the composer Vittorio Rieti. I had known Vittorio slightly in New York, but Jacob brought us together in a friendship that would last until Vittorio's death in 1994. An Italian Jew born in Alexandria, Vittorio composed ballet music for Balanchine, and in the 1930s he lived in Paris at the Hôtel Nollet, where Jacob also lodged. He was friendly with the composers Henri Sauguet and Darius Milhaud, and he circulated in the same world of artists and wealthy patrons of the arts in which Jacob also flourished in those years. He knew Picasso, Chanel, *tutti quanti*, and told me endless stories about them. He introduced me to Madeleine Milhaud and took me to visit the shabby Hôtel Nollet, pointing out where the various characters had lived and describing the teeming communal life in that hive of artists. And he introduced me to Henri Sauguet.

We visited Sauguet, a jowly, sharp-eyed man, at his apartment, where he sat in a comfy armchair with books stacked on the floor and overflowing from the worktable. We then went out to a long lunch at a *bistrot*, Vittorio and Sauguet pingponging reminiscences back and forth. Vittorio managed to escape to New York in 1940, but Sauguet remained in France. He spoke at length about Jacob. He was deeply fond of him, and at the news of the poet's arrest, it was he who went with Pierre Colle to Picasso's studio on the Rue des Grands Augustins to try to persuade him to sign an appeal to the German authorities for Jacob's release. Picasso replied, "Max is an angel; he can fly over the wall by himself." Since Vittorio's death, his son, the painter Fabio Rieti, has generously shown me letters his father wrote in the 1930s describing life with Jacob at the Hôtel Nollet.

A natural pedagogue, Jacob influenced a number of writers who went on to make names for themselves. One was the noted poet, the Egyptian Jew Edmond Jabès. I visited Jabès and his wife in their book-laden apartment on the Rue de l'Épée de Bois, a tiny street near the Jardin des Plantes. Deep-eyed and courteous, Jabès recounted how, in his youthful enthusiasm, he had sent a manuscript of poems to Jacob, and how, when he visited the master, Jacob simply dropped the whole packet into the wastebasket and said they could start from there. Since Jabès returned to Egypt, his relationship to Jacob developed mainly through letters, a record of literary apprenticeship that Jabès later published. His own mystical sense of the depths of meaning beckoning from within each letter has a great deal to do with Jacob's Kabbalistic language games.

Jacob was Breton, and never forgot it. His Catholicism arose, imaginatively, from his childhood in Quimper, a cathedral town, and the colorful, folkloric Catholic culture there, everywhere visible and audible in tales, songs, and festivals. My quest led, of course, to Quimper, and to the surrounding countryside with its rocky coastline, harsh fields, steep wooded hills, stone chapels, and carved granite calvary scenes, *calvaires*, at rural crossroads. Jacob knew this country intimately and painted it all his life. There I met with the Breton folklorist, playwright, and scholar Pierre

Jakez Hélias, author of the best-selling *Le Cheval d'orgueil* (The Horse of Pride). The child of peasants, Jakez Hélias managed to scrabble an education and became a noted presence in theater and radio. (He was also active in the Resistance.) He knew Jacob from the 1930s and spoke to me of the poet's quicksilver charm.

Max Jacob, a Breton Jewish Catholic who certainly qualified as Jewish for the Gestapo, felt it part of his mission to convert others—Jews, Protestants, and atheists—to the Catholic faith. One of those he converted was Dr. Robert Szigeti, a young Jewish doctor from Montargis, near Orléans, whom Jacob knew during his last days at Saint-Benoît. When I met Dr. Szigeti, he lived in Paris. Slender, gentlemanly, he made it clear that he owed the spiritual and intellectual shape of his life to Jacob; he was one of the group of faithful younger friends sustaining the poet in his last years. Another of that circle was the poet Marcel Béalu, whom I also met in Paris, at the small bookshop he ran near Saint-Sulpice. Like so many people who had known Jacob, Béalu was still, to some degree, under his spell, and spoke ardently of Jacob's generosity, brilliance, and quirkiness. When life at Saint-Benoît felt cramped, Jacob often visited Béalu and his wife Marguerite in their modest house in Montargis, visits Béalu recorded in his book *Dernier visage de Max Jacob* (Max Jacob's Last Face).

Jacob had strained relations with many members of his family, but one cousin devoted years of his life and considerable resources to preserving the memory of his famous relative. Didier Gompel was the son of the feminist lawyer Yvonne Netter, and grandson of Gustave Gompel, the magnate of the department store Paris-France where Jacob worked in his early days in Paris. Max Jacob had long ago outraged his cousin Noémie, Gustave Gompel's wife, with an impertinent dedication and was banished, but the Gompels' daughter, little Yvonne, evidently a strong-willed person, continued to see her cousin in private, and in the 1930s her son Didier, a young man with artistic curiosity, took to visiting Jacob at the Hôtel Nollet. For him, the hotel represented a realm of bohemian freedom and inspiration, and Jacob was its presiding magus. After the war, as Didier Gompel prospered, he was able to build up a substantial collection of Jacob's correspondence, manuscripts, and paintings. When I visited him, he allowed me to stay for several hours making sketches of Jacob's paintings. Gompel edited and published several volumes of Jacob's letters, and the originals may now be consulted in the Bibliothèque Nationale de France.

Jacob spent his last years at Saint-Benoît, and I owe some of my sense of that time to conversation with Roger Toulouse, the young painter from Orléans whom Jacob befriended. I spent a day walking around the basilica and the village with Toulouse, hearing his stories, and together we visited the poet's grave in the local cemetery: his remains had been transferred there in 1949. I also met and talked with Abbé Hatton, vicar of Saint-Benoît during Jacob's last years there, and with the author and Resistance fighter Jean Rousselot, another friend from the poet's old age.

To follow the thread of Max Jacob's life is to be led into the maze of the twentieth century in France, its artistic majesty, spiritual torment, and political fractures. I found no Minotaur in this labyrinth, but I did have to figure out how to plot my path around giants, all of them closely bound up with Jacob: Picasso, Apollinaire, Cocteau. The challenge was to let them play their parts without letting them take over the story. Max Jacob was not a giant, but he was a larger force in the creation of modern French literature than has been recognized. He exerted a profound influence on key writers whom he advised, chief among them Michel Leiris, Edmond Jabès, Louis Guilloux, and Raymond Queneau. I hope this book will make that case and at the same time suggest new lines of sight on an artistic world and on heroic figures we thought we knew well.

Max Jacob

Part I

CHAPTER I

BRITTANY

I.

O n July 12, 1876, a French Jewish baby, Max Jacob Alexandre, was born in an apartment next door to his family's comfortable house on the quay of the Odet River in
Quimper; his mother had retreated there to have her fourth baby in peace.[1]
In the center of the Cornouaille region in the southwestern corner of Brittany, Quimper sits placidly with its pottery works, its Gothic cathedral, its
sixteenth-century half-timbered houses, and its cobblestone streets about
twenty kilometers up the Odet River from the southern coast.

The town attracted tourists, and as an administrative center, it was
protected from the poverty of the surrounding farms and fishing villages
with their thatched cottages. Brittany is a land rich in folklore. According to one legend, the town was founded in the fifth century by Gradlon,
the king of Is. The city was engulfed by the sea when the king's demonic
daughter Dahut betrayed it: the king escaped to build a safer city inland,
and Dahut became a mermaid. A statue of the king on his horse still dominates the cathedral roof.

Whatever the town's origin, Max Jacob was steeped in its fables but
also in its modern life. "Quimper. Pretty town, 20,000 souls. The houses
amongst the foliage look like polished jewels on fields of green silk," he
noted in the story "The Traveling Actor."[2] The visiting aviator in Jacob's
novel *Le Terrain Bouchaballe* (The Bouchaballe Lot, 1923) describes his
entry by train: "In a generally medieval suburb, tanneries confront a

solitary line of chestnut trees comfortably stationed at the foot of a line of beeches whose trunks seemed to me to be made out of glove leather. The train station was a stain of rust and blood against picturesquely terraced gardens."[3]

The cathedral of Quimper seems to soar out of the bedrock of legend. Its crooked nave, mysteriously skewed to incorporate an eleventh-century chapel into the twelfth-century choir and the fifteenth-century nave and transept, suggests pagan energy still pressing on orthodox forms. It is dedicated to the Virgin and to Saint Corentin, another friend of Gradlon's, a hermit who fed the king on a magically reviving fish.

The cathedral bells still ring out the hours over the steeply pitched slate rooftops today as they did in Jacob's childhood. As a boy, looking from his bedroom window, Max admired the Gothic spires, golden at twilight, white in moonlight at night.[4] On saints' days, the narrow streets were jammed with processions of the faithful in their embroidered and brocaded suits, bearing banners for the saint and chanting Breton hymns. Max's grandfather and parents sold traditional Breton costumes and furniture in the family stores. But when the Jacob family, successful citizens of Quimper, were preparing to attend a wedding in the cathedral, their landlord, Canon Rossi, informed them that as Jews they were not welcome.[5] And when young Max went to meet his music teacher, the town organist, in the organ loft of the cathedral, his father forbade him to return to the alien sanctuary, saying, "Our place is not there."[6]

There were few Jews in Brittany in 1876, almost none in Quimper. Max Jacob's family was known as "Jacob" but called "Alexandre" on documents until 1888, when they made "Jacob" official. The paternal side had migrated from Prussia, shortly after 1808, when Napoléon liberalized religious worship in France. Considerable obscurity surrounds the names of many European Jews in the eighteenth and nineteenth centuries; surnames were often bureaucratically imposed, and "Alexandre" seems to have been one of those artificial names to which the family had no real attachment. Even before Max's family officially took the name "Jacob," his mother's maiden name, they were known in Quimper as *les Jacob juifs* to distinguish them from the numerous Christian Breton Jacobs.

In 1876 the inhabitants of Quimper hardly knew any Jews except "their" Jacobs, the decorous family of Lazare Alexandre and his wife, Prudence Jacob Alexandre. The household in the elegant building at 8 rue du Parc included the paternal grandparents Samuel and Mirté-Léa Alexandre, Lazare's younger brother Maurice, and the four children of Lazare and Prudence: Delphine, aged four; Maurice, two; Gaston, one; and the baby, Max. Two more children would follow: Jacques in 1880, and Mirté-Léa in 1884. The Jacobs had a long lease on the ground floor with its shop and workshops, the courtyard (now Cour Jacob), the large second floor and balcony, and some attic rooms. A small one-story house in the back courtyard was rented to the family of a postman. Above the Jacobs lived Baron Charles Louis Richard with his family and two maids. Max's Alsatian grandfather Samuel had started a substantial business as a tailor and merchant of Breton antiques, among them carved peasant box beds and chests (many of which he hired local craftsmen to fabricate). The family ran two nearly adjacent establishments on the Rue du Parc, the fashionable, chestnut-shaded street along the quay: La Belle Jardinière furnished fine clothes and furniture to the bourgeoisie of Quimper, and Au Bon Marché provided more proletarian customers with ready-made garments.

Samuel, Max's grandfather, seems to have been the most emphatic personality of the household. He was born sometime between 1813 and 1818 in Neunkirchen in Prussia.[7] The family left soon after the Napoleonic invasion, settling first in Alsace, then in Paris, where Samuel met and married Max's paternal grandmother, Mirté Mayer. Before moving to Quimper, the young couple lived for a while in Paris, then in Tours (where their son Lazare, Max's father, was born in 1847), then for a few years in Lorient, on the southern coast of Brittany, where a cousin had already opened a shop. Max later recounted his family history with considerable fantasy: he told his biographer Robert Guiette that his grandfather had wandered starving in Alsace, digging up potatoes and carrots from the frozen earth with his sister, "Aunt Julie, who would become the mother of Jean-Richard Bloch, the mother-in-law of Sylvain Lévi, and the grandmother of many millionaires."[8] In Max's account, his grandmother Mirté Mayer was a lace-maker from Avignon and a person of such admirable piety that she "edified" the whole region by washing the feet of the poor and giving away half of every meal. Her death in Quimper in 1884, when Max was eight, was supposed to have elicited bundles of letters of sympathy from convents, priests, and a bishop.[9]

Jacob's biographer Pierre Andreu established that Max had no grandmother from Avignon. Both grandmothers were Parisian, and neither seems to have been distinguished by piety. The mythical grandmother from Avignon has historical importance, however: she turns up in the imaginative web that Picasso's friends wove around *Les Demoiselles d'Avignon,* the painting in which one of the whores was known as "Max's Granny." Andreu speculates that the lady in question may have been Max's maternal great-grandmother, the mother of Léon Jacob (David), a merchant of gold and silver lace trimmings, father of Prudence, Max's mother, who would marry Lazare Alexandre in Paris on July 25, 1871, in the wake of the Commune.

II.

IN FRANCE, in the late nineteenth century, there were proportionally fewer Jews than in most European countries. Jewish yearbooks of the time cite a population of 80,000, with 50,000 centered in Paris.[10] At Max Jacob's birth in 1876, French Jews, though they could not know it, were enjoying the last years of almost a century of comfortable assimilation and relative freedom from harassment, and synagogues throughout France celebrated in 1889 the centenary of the French Revolution, which had established the rights of citizenship for Jews in 1791.[11] Observant French Jews imitated Catholic rituals of baptism and confirmation, dressing their children as for the Catholic rite, and after 1856 rabbinical dress was almost indistinguishable from that of Catholic priests. Max Jacob's family was nonobservant; except for some vestiges of faith among the grandparents, the ethos of the Jacob/Alexandre household was secular and "voltairean." The family even celebrated Christmas, but in the spirit of secular gift-giving; the holiday was folded in with festivities for Prudence Jacob's birthday on December 22, a brother's birthday on December 27, and New Year's Day, the traditional day for the exchange of gifts in France.[12] "You know, as for me, I don't give a hoot about God!" Max later had the character he invented for his mother exclaim.[13]

This period of comfort for French Jews had always been something of an illusion, and it ended around 1881 with publications like the newspaper *L'Antijuif.* Max's childhood would coincide with the spreading hostility, which gathered in intensity with the appearance of Édouard Drumont's infamous book *Jewish France* in 1886 and his newspaper *La Libre parole* (Free Speech); with the death in 1892 of the young Jewish army officer Armand Mayer in a duel provoked by Drumont's articles; and with the hysteria over the Dreyfus Affair in 1894.

The Aryan myth had been flourishing in France for years, thanks to the Breton philosopher Ernest Renan, who admired Joseph Arthur de Gobineau's *Essay on the Inequality of Human Races,* a threnody for the dissipating purity of Aryan blood.[14] Renan's racial theory promoted the primitive Breton Celts to pure Aryan visionaries: he saw his saints as "the true rishis," essential Aryans, "solitary masters of the nature, dominating it through asceticism and the force of will."[15] Renan was vastly popular in his day, lamenting the modernity of the Third Republic, a materialist age dominated by "businessmen, industrialists, the working class (the most selfish of all classes), Jews, English of the old school and Germans of the new."[16] The association of Jews with the vulgarity of commerce was commonplace. But for Max Jacob, the Jewish son of a storekeeping family, the constant reminders must have stung. That they left their scars is only too evident: as an adult convert to Roman Catholicism, he occasionally parroted generalizations about the materialism of "the Jews."

In 1876, Max Jacob was an infant, and news of Aryan supremacy did not disturb his cradle. Nor would most *quimpérois* have been reading Renan or Gobineau. More familiar to most of them, literate and illiterate, would have been the medieval image of the wicked Jew as preserved in ballads, like the song (or *gwerz,* in Breton) "Izabell ar Iann" ("Isabelle LeJean") collected by the folklorist F. M. Luzel, whose work Jacob would ransack,

later, for his own Breton poems. In "Izabell ar Iann" the Jew buys a girl
from her brother Louis:

> My dear little mother, if you love me,
> Protect me from the Jews;
> Protect me from the Jews,
> Put me in a room locked with a key . . .
> Tell me, my brother Louis,
> Do I have to go with the Jew?
> —Yes, you have to go with the Jew.
> Since he's paid the price;
> Four hundred *écus*, in good cash,
> Your mother and your father received,
> And your brother Louis just as much,
> For promising you to the Jew.[17]

III.

THE JACOB HOUSE stood between the fashionable Café de l'Épée, frequented by the military officers whose parade ground lay just across the
river, and the equally fashionable Pâtisserie Lafolye. The public entrance
of the house, 8 rue du Parc, gave access to the family store, La Belle
Jardinière, and in the workshop the Jacob children scurried among the
antique box beds, dressers, chests, and pottery while the workmen sang
Breton ballads as they embroidered traditional costumes.

The Rue du Parc was a continuous spectacle. Even before he was
allowed to run about the streets, Max observed picturesque *quimpérois*
from the balcony. Next door to La Belle Jardinière, the well-to-do con-
gregated after mass on Sunday at the *pâtisserie*. The street, a charming
saunter along the river, funneled gossip into the Jacob household, where
at least two members received it eagerly: Max, and Prudence Jacob, his
mother, whom Max later depicted, in many works, as the fictional character Madame Gagelin, a snob and a meddler.

Max's boyhood friends remembered his mother as a hard and irascible woman.[18] "Hard," *dur*, was the epithet Max Jacob would use for his own persona in the novel *Filibuth*. When Max narrated his life to Robert Guiette, he described his mother as "exhausting herself in recriminations to keep order among her children," while the jovial father "had only to appear, smiling, in their midst to quiet the horrendous wrangling and battles of this army."[19] Prudence Jacob was seen as "irritable and impatient," and Max, who was small for his age, was frequently beaten, not only by his mother but also by his older brothers. He claimed to have received his last clout from his mother at the age of twenty-four, for a spelling error. For all her cantankerousness, Madame Jacob didn't lack zest; she presided over a tumult of card games, charades, and hide-and-seek, and as a child Max entertained his family and his brothers' friends with puppet shows. It was from his mother that he imbibed his love of comic opera and his music hall repertoire, his store of lyrics from Offenbach and Hervé that would serve him well in his war against Symbolist poetry.

IF JACOB SPENT years compiling a brief against his mother, his silence in regard to his father is almost deafening. In the memoir he semidictated to Guiette, the chapter on Quimper and his family is dominated by the grandfather Samuel and his "pious" wife. Max's father enters only in the brief final paragraph that reads, in its entirety: "Max retained a delightful memory of his father. He was the soul of dignity joined with the most radiant gaiety."[20] One might imagine that Lazare Jacob had died early in his son's life. In fact, he died in 1917, when Max was forty-three. But the Jacob household was ruled first by the patriarch Samuel, and after his death by his vigorous daughter-in-law, Prudence. Lazare appears briefly in the Guiette memoir in the chapter on Max's youth as "the poor father" in his shop, surrounded by English and American tourists, while the ceilings rattle beneath the herd of his children and their friends in the apartment above. He was known as an excellent tailor; Max's school fellow Abel Villard later boasted about the "superb suit" with pants, vest, and frock coat that Monsieur Jacob had made him for one hundred francs.[21]

Grandfather Samuel, the Prussian-Alsatian immigrant, was a man of remarkable energy. Not content with his success as a tailor and as a merchant of antiques, he invented ointments and a hair lotion. At age eighty, in perfectly good health, he simply decided not to walk anymore, insisted on being carried up and down stairs, and had himself wheeled through town in a little carriage, stopping to chat with fellow citizens. Max remembered him with fondness and spoke of his death in 1889, when Max was thirteen, as the first grief of his life: "I loved this grandfather who didn't beat me, he and only he, who used to bless me and say, 'He'll go far, this one.' "[22]

It was not quite true that the grandfather was the only member of the family to spare the boy. Max's aunt Delphine, his mother's sister, was also fond of him. Her only child, Henri, was fourteen years older than Max, and she had maternal affection to spare for her sister's children. Nor was Max's childhood unrelievedly bleak. His mother's and brother's birthdays coincided with Christmas and New Year's Day, and the festivities filled the house with chocolates and candied chestnuts, culminating in a frenzy of gift-giving on New Year's Eve. A crate of presents would arrive each year from an uncle in Saint-Servan, and the children tore open the gilded packages it yielded.[23]

Most often, however, Jacob in later accounts stressed the beatings he received and his own rage, so great that once he bit his own hand until it bled. He defended himself by entrancing his siblings with puppet shows and ditties, like this incantation for spooky stairwells:

Gentlemen cats and gentlemen thieves,
If there are cats and if there are thieves,
Gentlemen cats, don't scratch me!
Gentlemen thieves, don't frighten me![24]

School provided no refuge from physical punishment. At the lycée, which he entered at age eleven, Max was known as *le juif* and ignored during recess except when he was being punched. Abel Villard, son of the art teacher, remembered the schoolyard hazings and described Max's curling in upon himself, arms raised, whenever someone approached. Abel himself roughed Max up several times until he and his brother René became disgusted by the bullying and took the pariah under their protection. In René Villard, Max found a lifelong friend, and the two were soon joined by Raoul Bolloré.

IV.

RENÉ AND RAOUL were a year older than Max and in the class ahead of him (though they became classmates in the rhetoric class when Villard and Bolloré had to repeat). The friendship developed in the schoolyard during recess and on Sundays when the boys met, sometimes in René's house and often *chez les Jacob*. The formidable Madame Jacob entertained her son's friends amiably enough: in her salon they could count on a snack of cakes from the Pâtisserie Lafolye. They were intoxicated readers, ransacking the municipal library as well as the little book rental shop. Max, who was reprimanded by the shocked librarian when he tried to check out *Madame Bovary*, later embedded the scene in *Le Terrain Bouchaballe*: "*Madame Bovary!* . . . He wants *Madame Bovary*! Get out of here, you little wretch, before I tell the principal! As if I were here to pander to their appetites!"[25]

By the age of thirteen, Max was reading the foreign Romantics, "Edgar Poe," Hoffmann, and Achim d'Arnim. Their erudite professor of literature, Monsieur Parturier, introduced the boys to the then little-known sixteenth-century poet Maurice Scève, whom Max later pronounced "the ancestor of modern poets."[26]

Raoul, René, and Max carried their literary excitements beyond the Jacobs' salon and with two other boys launched a literary magazine, *La Cigogne* (The Stork). Max's contribution was a fantastical tale inspired by Hoffmann, and Raoul Bolloré, who had been secretly poring over his grandfather's issues of the racy Parisian journal *Gil Blas*, provided a bawdy story in what he took to be the tone of the Parisian boulevards. No issues of *La Cigogne* survive, but in his reminiscences, René Villard, later a professor at the lycée of Saint-Brieuc, recalls that certain titles were "suggestive" and that the contributor-editors "seemed rather taken by the fair sex, which is natural for that age."[27] Unfortunately the principal had daughters and banned the fledgling journal as soon as he discovered it. The young editors reorganized as Le Club Universel. But Max, frightened by the prohibition, refused to participate.

René Villard has left both physical and psychological descriptions of his friend. The physical portrait affects a quasi-clinical objectivity, displacing Jacob's Jewishness to "white Negro" and "Assyrian": "I visualize him again with the black, frizzy hair of a white Negro, a rounded slightly bumpy forehead, his asymmetrical jaws converging on an oblique chin which a fine Assyrian beard would cover for years. The nose, though quite prominent, was thin then; the lips were narrow, but the mouth large; and his eyes, almost always half-shut, had a metallic glint in which malice and subtlety sparkled as they do today."[28]

Small and precocious, Max loved his classes and excelled in them, gaining the admiration of his teachers.[29] A pattern emerges: that of the physically weak child, unappreciated at home, who combines a need for approbation with a defensive instinct for sarcasm and malice. As an adult, Jacob baffled his friends by his oscillation between hypersensitive timidity and sarcastic assault; his friendships followed a rhythm of complaint, offense, and agonized reparation.

Max's friendship with Villard and Bolloré remained strong despite his defection from Le Club Universel, and Villard preserved a record of their shared adolescence in a notebook, *Le Cahier des maximes*. Several other boys joined the triumvirate in these interspersed reflections. Years later Max remembered René Villard as "a noble boy, a generous character, straight and honest, a Breton from the old days."[30] Villard wrote long poems in alexandrines, but it was Raoul Bolloré who was, according to Max, "a kind of Rimbaud," a "thirteen-year-old poet who had genius."

WHO WAS THIS young Rimbaud to whom Max was so devoted? At the lycée, Raoul Bolloré carried off many of the first prizes; only in his last two years did Max rival him in *prix d'honneur* and *prix d'excellence* in subjects as various as French composition, German, history, physics, and natural sciences. To the end of his life, Max reproached his mother (and the fictional Madame Gagelin) for the obsession with prizes, intensified by the competitive lycée system. Bolloré, the acknowledged leader, seems to have felt the competition more keenly than his friend; Bolloré called their neck-and-neck achievements "the bolloréo-jacobine joust."[31]

The excerpts by Bolloré in the *Cahier des maximes* show a boy of lively mind, adept at the hair-splitting analyses fostered in philosophy classes, and at the same time imbued with Romanticism: "I would want to die in a cradle of foliage, hanging in a hammock filled with rose petals, with a little cool stream beneath me giving off a venomous perfume."[32] Max's entries follow similar oscillations, with more irony; to Hippolyte Piouffle's Baude-lairean cigar reveries, Max replied, "This thought seems to me all the more subtle because I had it yesterday, just like you."[33] But Max himself was not above evoking a Romantic suicide ("On a stormy day, I let a fragile boat drift, and embracing my beloved, I let the waves carry me off"),[34] and when asked about his preferred rapture, he replied, "To die." When Raoul did die two years later, drowning himself in the Vilaine River at Rennes, it was, Max wrote to René Villard in 1938, "the irreparable act for which I have mourned all my life."[35]

The friends had witnessed a drowning several years earlier. On a warm afternoon, Raoul, René, Max, and several others had gone swimming in the Odet, outside town, accompanied by their teacher, Abbé Hamelin. One of the children, Émile Thomas, was dragged out into the current and sank. The boys screamed, and the *abbé* threw himself into the river, cas-sock and all. He managed to dive in spite of the cumbrous garment, but when he brought Émile to shore, the boy was no longer breathing. This was no voluptuous extinction: Max reacted with hysteria, fleeing across the fields, shrieking, his arms raised, tears pouring.[36]

||

FROM HIS EARLY days in the lycée, Max was drawing and taking piano lessons. It would have astounded his art teacher to be told that Max would one day make his living by selling his paintings. Since he was nearsighted, he couldn't see the plaster casts from which students were supposed to copy in the art class taught by Monsieur Villard, his friend's father, and his charcoal renditions were so smudged and off-kilter that Villard would explode in insults in an exaggerated Alsatian accent.[37] The teacher's temper was not improved by the fact that Max often hid his classical figure behind an enormous tree, which would become not just a habitual symbol but a mystic sign for him in adult life.[38]

But the aspiring artist was not discouraged. He doodled female nudes in his geometry notebook, to the consternation of the math teacher who discovered them and threatened to report them to his father. Kindly Monsieur Jacob was not perturbed; shown the offending sketches that evening at the club to which he and the math teacher belonged, he merely chuckled, "Well, well! Not bad at all! I didn't realize my son Max had talent."[39]

In his first few years of lycée, Max was a nervous and moody child. He defended himself in the schoolyard by biting, and at home he was increasingly racked by migraines. He told Robert Guiette that he had noticed that his suffering mollified his normally ferocious mother, and he speculated that he had half-invented the headaches to gain his mother's sympathy. Invented or not, the nervous symptoms alarmed his parents so much that they took him to Paris in 1890 to see the famous Dr. Charcot, and Max spent the winter in a Parisian sanatorium for "girls and boys with growing pains."[40]

Jean-Martin Charcot, at the age of sixty-three, was at the height of his glory. A cold and imposing man, the founder of modern neurology and a pioneer in the study of multiple sclerosis and hysteria, he held the chair in the clinical study of nervous illnesses at the medical school in Paris, and he counted among his patients the Emperor of Brazil, the Queen of Spain, and the Grand Dukes of Russia. His public lectures at the Salpêtrière Hospital drew an audience from around the world. Freud, studying with him in 1885–86, wrote to his fiancée that "Charcot, who is one of the great physicians, a genius and a sober man, simply uproots my views and intentions. After some lectures I walk away as from Notre-Dame, with a new perception of perfection."[41]

Charcot was celebrated for his open-mindedness. In 1865, for instance, he chided the German anthropologist Rudolf Virchow for his patriotic distortions of science in the pursuit of German Aryan purity.[42] At the same time, Charcot believed in a "Jewish neuropathy" of "travelling and nomadism." To him, the Wandering Jew embodied "this irresistible need to move around, to travel without being able to settle anywhere,"[43] and he launched one of his assistants on a doctoral dissertation on the subject. Freud described an evening reception at Charcot's grand house with complicated testiness: "Thank God, it's over"; in a political discussion that night, Freud identified himself as "neither Austrian nor German" but as a Jew.[44]

What did the fourteen-year-old Breton Jewish boy make of the great doctor? He left little record of the experience. The meager evidence suggests that the sanatorium with its chic clientele made a deeper impression than Freud's hero. But the encounter is not hard to imagine, since all of Charcot's outpatient consultations (except for foreign royalty) took place in the doctor's eighteenth-century residence. Prudence Jacob accompanied Max to the august consulting room, which occupied a separate wing of the mansion and was designed to suggest a holy sanctuary with its vast ceiling, built-in library, somber paintings, and stained-glass windows. The suppliants, screened by a secretary, had to walk the length of the room to approach Dr. Charcot at his massive desk. The doctor had a high, "antique" forehead, deep-set eyes, and long white hair brushed back behind his ears. His biographer writes that "visitors and patients were all intimidated by the atmosphere, not least by the impenetrable mask of the Doctor."[45]

The visit seems to have been in no way traumatic for Max. It may even have been somewhat exalting. He had succeeded in forcing his mother's hand, and Paris now lay open to him. The main elements in Charcot's treatment for hysterical and neurasthenic symptoms ("change of milieu, separation from weak and indulgent parents, . . . discipline, moral and intellectual hygiene")[46] granted him a temporary freedom; he was "separated" from his (none-too-indulgent) parents, and the new milieu was indeed a change. Max would be the smartest and healthiest of her children, the doctor assured Madame Jacob.[47] In 1919, Max Jacob included Charcot as a figure typical of the era in the comic poem "1889" in *La Défense de Tartufe* (Tartufe's Defense): "Charcot uses mood-enhancement to treat kidney disease. / Pozzi uses anesthesia when removing ovaries."[48] From all we can tell, Charcot treated Max's neurasthenia by a change of "mood."

Max later described himself, in this debut in Paris, as "a wild little Breton, either lymphatic or too exuberant."[49] The city cured him. He absorbed Wagner, Debussy, Beethoven; haunted the Opéra and the Comédie-Française; and frequented his sophisticated cousins. Julie Bloch, his father's sister, had daughters who had made prominent marriages, Noémie marrying the department-store magnate Gustave Gompel, and Désirée marrying Sylvain Lévi, a renowned professor of Sanskrit at the Collège de France. Julie's son Richard Bloch was a respected engineer, a graduate of the École Polytechnique. Max further amused himself by flirting with a young lady at the sanatorium. When he returned to Quimper for his last three years of lycée, his migraines had subsided, and he was ready to conquer the world, swaggering with his new knowledge of the capital and carrying off awards in school. This was the period of the *Cahiers des maximes* with its precocious cynicism and Romantic fantasy. Max crowned his glory by winning eighth honorable mention (*huitième accessit*) in the national philosophy exam in 1894, the year of his graduation. Since only two prizes and ten honorable mentions were given in the entire country, the award was cause for acclaim in the local newspaper and jubilation in the Jacob household.

It must have appeared to the elder Jacobs that Dr. Charcot had worked wonders on their troubled son. They anticipated for him a "brilliant" career, no doubt academic, to be nursed in that princely institution, the École Normale Supérieure: a fellowship for preparation for the École Normale was reserved for Max at the prestigious Lycée Lakanal in Paris, and he seemed to be on the way to joining Sylvain Lévi and the Blochs in earning renown for the family. But Max had his own ideas. Nor had the magic of Dr. Charcot or Paris erased his deepest discomfitures. Several times, in adolescence, he half-heartedly tried to kill himself. When he was seventeen, the year before his graduation, he tried again. As he recalled the scene: "His father found him hanging by his necktie from the window hasp. It was dinnertime. He said, 'Aren't you ashamed of fooling around like a child?' His mother added, 'There's always time to kill yourself.' "[50] When Max left for Paris in October 1894 to continue his studies, he enrolled not at the Lycée Lakanal but at the École Coloniale, the school for colonial administration, which seemed to promise romance and adventure.

CHAPTER 2

THE GATES OF THE CITY

I.

Max Jacob arrived in Paris in October 1894, after a seven-hour train trip from Quimper. He signed up not only at the École Coloniale, but also at the Faculté de Droit, the law school. The hotel where he spent his first days, on the tiny Rue Corneille, placed him in the heart of the sixth arrondissement, squeezed between the Théâtre de l'Odéon and the Jardin du Luxembourg, a few streets away from the intersection of the two feverish boulevards of the Left Bank, "Boul' Mich" and the Boulevard Saint-Germain. It was, and still is, the neighborhood of students, dominated by the fortresses of French education and professional privilege: the Faculté de Médecine, the Collège de France, the Sorbonne, the École des Mines, the École Normale Supérieure, and the Faculté de Droit.

Jacob soon found a room in a boardinghouse on the far side of the Jardin du Luxembourg at 12 rue de la Grande Chaumière, a narrow street in a quarter renowned more for studios, paint shops, and artists than for students. Right across the street, the Alsatian Charlotte Futterer fed painters and poets in her *crémerie*, where Gauguin held court in the autumn of 1894. Another inhabitant of Jacob's boardinghouse would soon be August Strindberg; the tormented Swedish playwright took refuge there in January after his separation from his wife and the triumphant premiere of his play *The Father* at the Théâtre de l'Oeuvre. There is no evidence that Jacob met him, but they lived in the same building for a few months; while

Jacob studied law half-heartedly, Strindberg pursued alchemical experiments with sulfur, crucible, and Bunsen burner until his hands were raw and bleeding.[1] In 1936 Jacob used Strindberg as a symbolic figure for the 1890s in his memoir *Chronique des temps héroïques* (Chronicle of Heroic Days): "The North was in fashion because of Ibsen. Strindberg was in fashion because of the North. And chemistry was in fashion because of Strindberg who was decomposing sulfur in Montparnasse (historical)."[2]

Not many documents describing Jacob's early student days in Paris survive. One is a pencil sketch by a sidewalk artist in a café from the fall of 1894. It portrays a young dandy in profile with a bowler hat, pince-nez, hint of mustache, starched shirt collar, cravat, and wide-lapeled jacket. Perched high, the hat exposes, under its flaring brim, a head of neatly cropped hair, in one of the few hirsute pictures of a skull that would soon be famously bald. The eighteen-year-old in this drawing has made a strenuous effort to get himself up as a man of the world. From the descriptions of Max in the lycée, we can imagine him entering the capital with a mixture of trepidation and swashbuckling academic precocity. He was versed in the myth of the conquest of Paris: the heroes of Stendhal, Balzac, and Flaubert had led the way. The city itself had been imagined as a spawning ground of crime and despair as well as of fortune, throughout Balzac's *Comédie humaine*, in the novels of Eugène Sue, in the poems of Baudelaire, in the stories *Scènes de la vie de bohème* by Henri Murger (which Puccini converted into the opera *La Bohème* two years after Jacob's arrival in Paris).

Coming to Paris, Jacob entered not so much a geographical area as a heavily charted literary terrain. In a novel published in 1924, *L'Homme de chair et l'homme reflet* (The Man of Flesh and the Reflected Man), Jacob described a young man stepping into the capital, and translated Parisian bohemia into a reading list. The authorial voice breezily advises, "You should consult, on the subject of the Latin Quarter, various scholarly authors and my masters Jules Vallès and Maurice Barrès. . . . Also consult Murger, forever and still true to life, the *Memoirs* of George Sand and *tutti quanti*."[3]

In entwining the portrait of the hesitant hero, Maxime Lelong (who suffers from a miserly mother, *née* Gagelin), with sardonic expostulations to his past, the narrator flashes us a glimpse of Jacob's own youth. One must be cautious in using fiction as biographical evidence. But in his fictions, Jacob drew freely on his own life, and his novels are kinetic essays in group portraiture, with the kaleidoscopic self-portraits in highest color. This scene from *L'Homme de chair et l'homme reflet* presents a multiple exposure of identities: of the hero, of the narrator, and of Max Jacob the author:

> Then, in the train, Maxime wept because he was a failure; he was just a little over eighteen years old. . . . And I who write here! . . . and you who write here . . . remember your exalted youth, your dismal youth. O my youth! my dear and detested youth! O my past! my useless past! O the inexorable past which will not return, which will never return. . . . "Nevermore!" . . . At least if you'd managed to describe a young man from before the war.[4]

II.

THE "YOUNG MAN from before the war," who would soon bark at Apollinaire's poems, "Still too Symbolist!" arrived in Paris at the peak of Symbolism. A literary vogue rather than a doctrine, Symbolism grew up as a fin de siècle reaction against Romantic verbosity, the expository clarity of Parnassian poetics, and the descriptive claims of Naturalism. Inspired by Stéphane Mallarmé and Villiers de l'Isle Adam, its adherents cultivated a private language of vagueness and reverie.

Symbolism was never a school, and it shared a permeable cell wall with the Decadents, the casual name for those writers grouped around Paul Verlaine in the Latin Quarter. The scruffy, limping Verlaine and Mallarmé, the retired schoolmaster, were old friends and had published poems together in *Le Parnasse contemporain* before their obscurities distanced them from the Parnassians, the group dedicated to classicism and formal order. The two poets honored each other, and their devotees floated back and forth between cliques and between the banks of the Seine.

The Symbolists' strength can be measured by the attacks they drew, and by the number of journals that ran Symbolist colors up the mast.[5] *Mercure de France*, *L'Ymagier* (launched by Remy de Gourmont and Alfred Jarry in October 1894, just as Jacob arrived in Paris), and *La Revue blanche* attracted powerful writers and reproduced the paintings of Bonnard, Vuillard, Munch, and Lautrec. It was in the pages of *La Revue blanche*, in April 1894, that Mallarmé, at the crest of his fame, published a version of his lecture from Oxford and Cambridge, "Music and Literature," carrying news of revolutionary poetics abroad: "Indeed, I bring news. Most extraordinary news. Verse has been tampered with."[6] Jacob's obscure debut in Paris coincided with Mallarmé's publication of meditations on his English trip and on literary patrimony, a survey from the man who now embodied French poetry in its purest form.[7]

Max Jacob and his companions André Salmon, Guillaume Apollinaire, Pierre Reverdy, and Blaise Cendrars would declare their mission, a decade later, to be a rupture with Symbolism. "I wanted to fight against the Symbolist antiquarian claptrap," Jacob explained years later,[8] and the violent rhetorical styles of these younger writers became a standard feature of avant-garde movements of the new century.

After the deaths of Verlaine and Mallarmé, minor talents reproduced Symbolist effects with mechanical regularity, and Symbolism contracted into an airless cult. "My God! My God! When will we have rain, / And snow and wind in the house!" Maeterlinck cried in the title poem of his appropriately named collection, *Hothouses*, in 1889.[9] The year after Jacob's arrival in Paris, André Gide would publish *Paludes* (Swamps), a prose account of fin de siècle stagnation. Soon Jacob's friend Jules Romains would lead his own revolt: "The Symbolists have shown, in regard to reality and to life, a sort of neuropathic detachment. Their successors all proclaimed . . . a return to mental health, which requires the recognition of reality."[10]

Such was the ferment in French letters into which Max Jacob stepped in 1894. It was a year that saw the emergence of two writers who would break from Symbolist to Modernist aesthetics, paving the way for Jacob. Exactly Jacob's age but more precocious, the Parisian Léon-Paul Fargue published his "Tragic Overtures" in *L'Art littéraire* in January–February

1894, to be followed in the May–June issue by prose pieces by his twenty-one-year-old friend Alfred Jarry. A quasi-Breton from Laval, just over the eastern border of Brittany, Jarry had spent his adolescence in Paris at the Lycée Henri IV, where the philosopher Bergson taught. Soon to astonish the world with the play *Ubu Roi,* Jarry crowned 1894 with his sadistic dream-play *Haldernablou,* a not-so-veiled account of his affair with Fargue. Fargue and Jarry spiced the formulas of Symbolism to a cutthroat brew: ambiguity, contorted syntax, neologisms, archaisms, ellipsis, incantatory repetition, and dense alliteration.

At age eighteen, Jacob already sensed the changes. Mallarmé he would judge affected and obscure.[11] Emerging from his schoolboy cocoon, however, Jacob was more familiar with the worldly wit of *Gil Blas* than with *La Revue blanche,* and he knew Symbolism through its morbid Belgian practitioner Francis Poictevin rather than through its masters.[12] Poictevin was committed to a lunatic asylum in 1894, the year Max Jacob entered the city to search for his own words.

III.

HE CAME JUST as crisis exploded. On October 15, Captain Alfred Dreyfus, a Jew, was arrested for espionage after the discovery of an anonymous memo in a scrap basket in the German embassy. The military authorities committed themselves to the theory of Dreyfus's guilt, and by the end of October, Drumont's *La Libre parole* was whipping up an anti-Semitic furor and preventing any reconsideration of the case. The trial was held quickly, in December, as Jacob was adjusting to student life in the capital. With the help of testimony from an imaginative handwriting specialist and forgeries provided only to the prosecution, the high command obtained the desired result: on December 22, Captain Dreyfus, to his astonishment, was convicted of treason and sentenced to deportation to Devil's Island. Hardly anyone doubted his guilt. The prominent men who would defend him several years later now called for his head: Jean Jaurès, a deputy in the Assembly, thought he should have been condemned to death, and Georges

Clemenceau described Dreyfus as "a foul soul, an abject heart."[13] Three weeks after the trial, Captain Dreyfus was stripped of his epaulettes, military buttons, and braid, and his sword was broken before a jeering crowd in the courtyard of the Invalides. Two weeks later he was on a ship, in manacles, heading for French Guyana.

French Jews, during the tumult of the trial, remained silent. No evidence of the guilt of the real spy, Commandant Ferdinand Esterhazy, had as yet come to light. These liberal, patriotic Jews owed their well-being and civil status to the French Republic. Bernard Lazare, the young Jewish writer who would soon become Dreyfus's first great defender, had just published his book *Anti-Semitism, Its History and Its Causes*, endorsing the view that the Jews were a "refractory" people, impeding social progress.[14] In the year of Dreyfus's conviction, Lazare predicted that with total assimilation, anti-Semitism would disappear. In 1894, French Jews had no desire to appear "refractory" in defending a Jewish traitor.

MAX JACOB WAS too busy adjusting to his new life to concern himself with Jewish identity. The Latin Quarter and Montparnasse are contiguous neighborhoods and flow into each other, just as student bohemia overflowed into artistic bohemia in the 1890s. Passing back and forth between his lectures and his rented room, Max would have found himself caught in the eddies of the rebellious city culture that had known itself as "bohemia" since the 1840s. In Paris in 1894 he found himself for the first time in the midst of a "counterculture." He responded confusedly: his grades dropped, and at the end of his first year of study, in the spring of 1895, he failed his examinations both in law and at the École Coloniale.

In *The Origins of Contemporary France*, Hippolyte Taine described the shock of transition experienced by the typical student promoted to advanced studies in the capital:

> Now in France, no university police intervenes, as in Bonn or Göttingen, in Oxford or Cambridge, to watch over his conduct and reprove his infractions, either in his living quarters or in public places; in the schools of medicine, law, pharmacy, art, paleography and library sci-

ences, Oriental languages, the Sorbonne, the École Centrale, the student's emancipation is total and sudden. When he leaves his secondary school to enter an institution of higher learning, he does not pass, as in England or Germany, from a restricted liberty to a less restricted liberty, but from a claustral discipline to total independence. In a furnished room, in the promiscuity and anonymity of a banal hotel, barely escaped from boarding school, the twenty-year-old novice discovers all about him the innumerable temptations of the street, the bars, little restaurants, dance halls, obscene publications, chance encounters, vulgar attachments. . . . He yields to the occasion, to example; he follows the current, he floats randomly, he lets himself go.[15]

Thin, hypersensitive, and showing no apparent interest in the opposite sex, Jacob was hardly able to take up the challenge of so many temptations, but his poor grades suggest that the transition from family life to independence in the capital distracted him mightily.

It is hard to imagine a more brilliant contrast to Quimper than the Left Bank in the 1890s. Law students flaunted velveteen caps and jackets; aspirants to the arts slouched between café and studio in smocks and berets; blacks from Martinique studying law and medicine wore silk top hats, white waistcoats, white spats, kid gloves, and jewelry; alluring women, from shopgirls and artists' models to the various classes of demimondaines, drank freely in the cafés, cabarets, and dance halls and sauntered the streets, shoulder to shoulder with vendors crying wares: flowers, roasted chestnuts, newspapers, olives, and crawfish. William Chambers Morrow, an American visitor, described delightedly for the folks back home the bustle of handcarts (often piled high with someone's entire worldly fortune), art students, vagrants, laundresses, and workmen hauling portable bathtubs complete with hot water for the baths city-dwellers of modest means could rent by the hour.[16] With an eye for the sentimentally naughty and little sense of the grim class strife France was suffering, Morrow dwelled particularly on the life of art students. They specialized in comic outrage; Max Jacob would have seen them in April, in fantastic costumes, parading their floats across Paris from the École des Beaux-

Arts in the Latin Quarter to the Bal des Quat'z'Arts at the Moulin Rouge in Montmartre. They roared back again at dawn, commandeering street cleaners' brooms, ragpickers' sacks, and horse-drawn cabs, interrupting the drill of the Garde Municipale in the courtyard of the Louvre, and sacrificing to the Seine, from the Pont du Carrousel, the papier-mâché statue from the victorious float.

BEYOND THE BORDERS of bohemia, and oblivious to the distress of the working class, the Belle Époque pursued its pleasures. Recovered from the defeat by Prussia and the agony of the Commune in 1871, Paris in the 1890s was taking full advantage of the stage set created by Baron Haussmann and the entrepreneurs of Napoléon III's regime. The new boulevards, parks, department stores, and cafés opened up a theater for the display of fortunes recouped or newly seized. The Universal Exposition of 1889, which thrust the Eiffel Tower into the Parisian skyline, had turned the city into a vast show-and-tell; Egyptian and Javanese dancers made colonial adventure look sexy, and exhibits of electricity and engineering in steel promised a future of technological conquest. The whole extravaganza expressed the temper of a nation that had paid off its debt to the conqueror and now celebrated the centenary of its own revolution. Everyone wanted to show off.[17] And just in 1894 Auguste and Louis Lumière, aptly named, were outpacing Edison and preparing to shoot the first film: motion pictures would open up a whole new dimension of display.

The courtesans, *cocottes* or *grandes horizontales,* who preyed upon the new fortunes embodied spectacularly this spirit of exhibition. In a city famous for expertise in sex, the Third Republic raised the system to monumental scale. Like her rivals Méry Laurent (Mallarmé's friend) and Laure Hayman (a model for Proust's Odette), Max's future friend Liane de Pougy lived in a veritable palace, a fantasy of oriental luxury complete with highly publicized pearls and, after her marriage to Prince Georges Ghika, a retinue of three Mauritanian "slaves." Liane's amorous exploits and suicide attempts kept her in the news. In appearances at the Folies Bergère, on posters, in the fashionable magazines of London and Paris, at the races, at the Bois de Boulogne, she imprinted a type of ethereal beauty on the imagination of the epoch. All this Parisian drama would enter Jacob's work.

IV.

IN 1894 SYMBOLISM seemed triumphant. Villiers de l'Isle Adam's play *Axël* was recited at the Théâtre Montparnasse in April, five years after its author's death. In August, Verlaine, ill and indigent, was crowned Prince des Poètes in one of the literary banquets typical of the day. In September, Debussy completed "Prélude à l'après-midi d'un faune." In October, as Jacob signed the registry of the École Coloniale, Remy de Gourmont and Alfred Jarry published the first issue of *L'Ymagier;* and Édouard Vuillard was completing the panels of the "Public Gardens" to decorate the dining room of Alexandre Natanson, one of the founders of *La Revue blanche.* From Vuillard's reveries of charmed public space, foliage, cottony sky, lawns, children's games, and patterned cloth, one would never suspect that France was in an industrial recession, that bombs were exploding all over Paris, and that Sadi Carnot, the president of the Republic, had been stabbed to death by an Italian anarchist. If 1894 was a rich year for Symbolism, it also marked the peak of anarchist violence and bourgeois reaction in France. Many leading writers and artists, including Mallarmé, Gustave Kahn, Signac, and Pissarro, more or less openly supported the anarchist cause.[18]

French workers had earned the official right to strike only ten years earlier, but the right meant little, since strikes were still suppressed by the police, who often fired on protesters. Concepts such as an eight-hour workday or a six-day week were chimerical. Haussmann had destroyed working-class neighborhoods, exiling the poor to the fringes of the city, where they lived in squalor, drawing no benefit from the grandiose new systems of sewers, gas, electric lights, and clean water that transformed life within the capital. With grim working conditions, unemployment, high food prices, and housing shortages, many of the poor turned to violence. Max Jacob's later obsession with the word *bour-*

geoisie and its permutations derives more from social comedy than from politics, and veils a private war against his mother, but his vocabulary touches on serious class conflict. In 1885 the anarchist newspaper *La Varlope* was advertising "antibourgeois products,"[19] and *Le Drapeau noir* in 1884 promoted the use of poison by an anarchist league to reduce the bourgeois population.[20]

The league's successes were probably fanciful. More effective were the bombs, which became such an epidemic between 1892 and 1894 that newspapers carried special "Dynamite" columns. The famous Ravachol, who gave his name to a revolutionary song, was guillotined on July 11, 1892, for a series of murders and bombings. On December 9, 1893, a workman named Vaillant sent a bomb spinning from the visitors' gallery into the Chamber of Deputies where it shot nails in all directions, wounding a number of dignitaries. Vaillant died on the guillotine on February 5, 1894, shouting "Death to bourgeois society and long live anarchy!"[21] He was a hero with the intelligentsia; in praising his act, the poet Laurent Tailhade remarked, "Who cares about the victims if the gesture is handsome!"[22] A week after Vaillant's death, a well-educated young man, Émile Henry, threw a bomb into the Café Terminus in the Gare Saint-Lazare, killing one person and wounding twenty; he later claimed responsibility for a bomb that had killed five people in a police station in 1892. Henry was executed on May 21, 1894, with Clemenceau and Maurice Barrès among the many spectators sympathetic to the criminal. The rest of the year brought a long list of attacks, including the explosion on April 4 in a restaurant in which Laurent Tailhade lost an eye. (Did he consider that gesture "handsome"? one wonders.)

As Max Jacob began his Parisian life, the government responded to the wave of violence by enacting the "vicious laws" clamping down on freedom of the press, of speech, and of association, and it rather lamely wound up the proceedings of the "Trial of the Thirty," a prosecution of a large number of suspect intellectuals and a few thieves. Only the thieves were convicted, but the trial marked the conclusion of the terrorist attacks. In their search for anarchists, the police even descended upon the rickety jumble of studios in Montmartre at 13 rue Ravignan, which would soon become famous as "Le Bateau Lavoir." They found no weapons or bombs but so disturbed the artists that several moved out.[23]

One hysteria gave way to another. France had just emerged from the collapse of the Panama Canal Company in 1892, a financial scandal that Drumont fanned to a blaze in *La Libre parole*. The anarchist interlude and the recession had not soothed tempers on any side. When Dreyfus was arrested, pandemonium broke out again, and French society began to crack along the fault lines of anti-Semitism in a seismic disturbance that would shake families, salons, and electoral alliances.

Max Jacob came to manhood at a time when older orders—political, social, and aesthetic—were fracturing. Class warfare had erupted in actual violence, and anti-Semitism and journalistic abuse would soon provoke anti-Jewish riots around the country. As a Jew, as a homosexual, and as a rebellious son of the bourgeoisie, Jacob would find himself at the confluence of the major struggles of his time. He would transpose those conflicts into aesthetic and erotic realms, choosing his own fields of battle and his own weapons, preferring privacy to politics.

V.

MAX JACOB TOLD Robert Guiette in 1928 that he had chosen the École Coloniale because "my guardian angel indicated in that manner that my life would unfold in a country other than that which seemed mine. I mean a moral country."[24] His older brother Maurice, less successful in school than Max, joined the army and left for French West Africa in 1895 as a sergeant; he would spend much of his life as a civil servant in Senegal and come to be known in the family as "The African." In this career he joined many others of his generation as France consolidated its hold on Indochina as well as on Algeria, Tunisia, Senegal, French Guinea, Madagascar, and the French Congo.

Jacob's studies in the École Coloniale included "general, Indochinese, and penitentiary" courses.[25] It is hard to imagine that the nervous poet-to-be ever saw himself as a colonial officer, and it is in the experience of estrangement rather than of domination that colonial themes would later seep into his poems and novels.

The sense of the foreign as metaphysically and not just geographically "other" permeates many of the prose poems of *Le Cornet à dés* (The Dice Cup), Jacob's famous book from 1917. "Poem" is fairly typical, and in its puns (*cartes* can be playing cards or maps, while *un tour* can be a circular movement, a turn, or a magic trick), it refuses any literal reality:

> When the boat had arrived at the islands of the Indian Ocean, it was observed that there were no maps (*cartes*). We had to disembark! That's when we saw the passengers: there was the bloodthirsty man who gives his wife tobacco and takes it back again. The islands were dotted all around. On top of the cliff, we saw little negroes with bowler hats: "Maybe they'll have maps!" We took the cliff path: it was a rope ladder; all along the ladder, maybe there were maps! Even Japanese maps! We kept climbing. Finally, when there were no more rungs (ivory crabs, somewhere), we had to climb using our wrists. My brother the African managed very well, as for me, I found rungs where there weren't any. At the summit, we're on a wall; my brother jumps. I'm at the window! I'll never bring myself to jump; it's a wall of red planks: "Go around," my brother the African calls to me. There are no more terraces, or passengers, or boat, or little negro; there's the turn (*le tour*) I have to make. What round? It's discouraging.[26]

If the École Coloniale taught Jacob anything, it was his own alienation from practical politics. Paul Claudel and Saint-John Perse, his near contemporaries, composed their poems within the ramparts of careers in the French foreign service. For Max Jacob, the foreign territory would be the landscape of his own soul; and for studies in domination, he would look closer to home, within the family. In the spring of 1895, as Claudel embarked for Shanghai, we find Max Jacob as that common creature, a miserable student in Paris. He had failed his examinations in law and at the École Coloniale, and he was staggered by the news of the suicide of his best friend, Raoul Bolloré, the idol of his lycée days.

VI.

ON MARCH 4, 1895, Raoul Bolloré threw himself into the Vilaine River in the Breton city of Rennes, where he and René Villard had gone to continue their studies. Villard supposed the motive to be disappointment in love. Not much is known about the reasons for the act, which the schoolboy musings on romantic death in the lycée *Cahier* hardly seem to predict or explain.[27] Raoul had been the anointed genius of the class, the hero of Max's boyhood, and his death left a void that would not be filled until the eruption of Picasso into the poet's life. Raoul's charismatic power was such that his younger brother Armand followed him, two years later, into the fateful river; the boys are buried together in the family tomb in Quimper.

The scholar Yannick Pelletier speculates that Raoul Bolloré's death accounts for Jacob's neglect of his studies in Paris and his decisive turn toward a life in the arts, as if to realize his dead friend's ambitions.[28] But Jacob had already given signs of his artistic nature; nor did he turn, all of a sudden, to art in 1895. Pelletier's explanation simplifies the workings of grief and the slow clarification of vocation. What we do know is that in 1938 Max Jacob wrote to René Villard that Bolloré's death had marked him deeply: "Poor dear boy, who committed the irreparable act for which I have mourned all my life. The only irreparable act."[29] We also know that, according to Max, his admiration for Raoul had had the intensity of piety. In the spring of 1895, ill at ease in Paris as he prepared for a profession that would satisfy his family, he must have felt a solitude verging on despair.

||

GRIEVING AND CONFUSED, Jacob spent the summer of 1895 at home and then scrambled through another academic year in Paris, pulling himself together sufficiently to earn passing grades, both in law school and at the École Coloniale. But he had no sooner started his courses the following fall, 1896, than he was summoned for military service in the 118th Regiment in Quimper. If Jacob was finding academic life rebarbative, he found military life impossible. An old black man who worked in the library of the École Coloniale had already predicted Jacob's failure: he used to say to him, "Jacob, when you get to heaven, all the angels will play on their trumpets: 'Max, ah qu' t'es rigolo / dans ton costume de tringlot' " (Max, what a joke you are, in your soldier's outfit). Jacob lasted three months in the barracks. He was so weak and puny, he was put under observation in the military hospital, then discharged as a "confirmed hysteric."[30]

The Dreyfus excitement was gathering in intensity as the captain's brother accumulated evidence of the accused man's innocence and of a cover-up at the highest level in the War Office. French Jews were charged more than ever with being unpatriotic and were protesting with growing vigor. Jacob's discharge occurred at a time when the presence of Jews in the army, and the very nature of Jewish citizenship, were matters of furious debate, and in the story touching on his military adventure, "Surprised and Delighted," from *Le Roi de Béotie* (1921), his ironic periphrasis suggests the humiliation he felt at the rejection:

> Let me confess that my attempts to take part in barracks drills were so ineffectual that those whose task it was to direct such drills eventually found their patience exhausted. And when after six weeks the kindly vigilance of the military authorities put an end to my labors in order to spare me further fatigue, I was more successful in concealing my shame at being relieved of my responsibilities than were my superiors in concealing their joy at having discharged theirs.[31]

Released from the army in January 1897, Jacob returned to his family, the school year being too advanced for him to rejoin his classes in Paris. In "Surprised and Delighted" he declares, "Military discharge meant holidays, and on holiday I still am."[32] For several months he was free to scribble, draw, play the piano, and roam the countryside.

"I had discovered my Brittany," Max Jacob declared to Guiette. The exaltation led directly to his having a room of his own within the family house, and a ripening sense of vocation. What was "his" Brittany? "This is a country of eclipses, by turns harsh under the Romans, dark, plague-ridden in the Middle Ages, revived by the monks," he wrote to Michel Levanti in 1938.[33] It was also a land of stubborn poverty, stony soil, Atlantic storms, and except in the larger towns, a peasant culture of primitive Roman Catholicism and lingering Royalist sympathies, a politics defined more by resistance to modernity and to the French nation, now associated with the Revolution, than by any allegiance to kingship or to France itself. One could hardly imagine a more remote imaginary *patria* for an urban middle-class Jew. Yet through its songs and stories, which Jacob had heard since childhood, folkloric Brittany penetrated his being, and the boy who had been assailed as a "dirty Jew" in the schoolyard would in turn repossess that land through song, story, and painting. And that land would provide him with his own version of the Modernist primitivism that Picasso would seek in African and ancient Iberian sculpture, and Derain in medieval woodcuts and folk pottery.

Even as a schoolboy Max had enjoyed rambling outside town, some-times hiking for days in summer, turning up at the Villard family's sum-mer house on the coast. Closer to home, he loved the pond at the Color Mill, so named because the Quimper ceramics workers used it for rinsing dyes off the terra-cotta.[34] In the months of liberty after his army discharge, Jacob resumed his rural explorations, and Brittany became "my Brittany." The severe beauties of the landscape, the steep wooded hills and windswept plains, instilled in him a mania for sketching. Painting these views would ensure him his modest living for most of his adult life. It is rare, however, to find a Jacob drawing or gouache of unpopulated landscape; most often he was drawn to human scenes: the granite chapels, ossuaries, and freestanding *calvaires* of this region haunted by legends of death, scenes of rural labor, and the ritual processions of village pardons with the women in their elaborate lace *coiffes* and the men in embroidered vests. By "my Brittany," Jacob meant a deeply human and storied landscape.[35]

In his letter to Michel Levanti, as in the playful preface to *La Côte* (1911), his first collection of Breton poems ("Finally, here's a preface! I wanted to write a preface! a real preface ... !"),[36] Jacob offhandedly displays an intimate acquaintance with the literature on Brittany. His story "The Golden Cross" in *Le Roi de Béotie* adapts the archaic clerk's romance, a subject of innumerable songs and tales in which a young seminarian falls in love, usually with fatal consequences. In Jacob's modern prose version, the daughter of shopkeepers tempts the seminarian Savinien with the prospect of an annual income of seven thousand francs. Savinien calculates (wrongly) that an ecclesiastical career would be still more profitable and rejects Hortense. In the ironic conclusion, "he was subjected to a frightful tongue-lashing from his family and in order to justify his behavior had to demonstrate a piety which became real."[37]

Max Jacob delighted in such permutations of class and motivation. He found them in the past as well as in the present. In Jacques de Cambry's *Voyage dans le Finistère* from 1799, he dug up treasures of geographical, economic, and cultural observation. With a stylistic flair and curiosity unusual in a government functionary of any epoch, Cambry had reported on public fountains, child rearing, infanticide, church going, architecture, diet and alcohol consumption, agriculture, roads, and manners: Max Jacob noted with glee in Cambry's book that the inhabitants of Quimper in the late eighteenth century were known for their passion for card-playing, amateur theatricals, and improvisational society verse.

But the deeper strata of Cambry's work, as of Max Jacob's imagination, lie in peasant culture, in both its piety and its poetry: "Imagination rules them; their language is figurative, full of metaphors and boldness."[38] In its origins and at its core, Brittany is—or was, until the era of highways and television—a bardic stronghold. In the Brittany that Max Jacob took to heart, singers still wandered from town to town, performing at pardons and wherever else they could collect an audience and find food and lodging. Among the earliest bards was Hyvarnion, who came from England in the sixth-century Celtic migration, as recounted by the priest Albert le Grand, the seventeenth-century author of *Lives of the Saints* that Jacob loved.[39] In his poem "The Girl of the Fountain," Jacob would blend the tale of Saint Y Sulio with that of Hyvarnion, who dreamed of a virgin and found her the next day by a fountain; she was Rivanone, herself a famous singer, and their son Hervé, born blind, became a bard and a saint.[40] In that winter of 1897, wandering the country roads on his bicycle and covering the walls of his attic room with scrawls and sketches, Max Jacob entered his own bardic dream.

VII.

JACOB'S STORY "SURPRISED and Delighted," about being discharged from the army, is a tale of abuse of confidence by the hero, a young would-be *littérateur*, and his consequent expulsion from friendship and home. First published in June 1914, it incorporates factual information in an imaginary action. The discharge, the description of his "vacation" in his native city, the retired policeman turned librarian, the intrigue concerning the *amours* of a young doctor, can all be corroborated from other biographical documents.[41] It would be a gross error, however, to locate the story's power in its documentation, or to suppose that Max Jacob actually gave his father the stroke with which the narrative concludes. It is a symbolic structure, a miniature expulsion from Eden, and its subject is the birth of the artist.

From a biographical point of view, "Surprised and Delighted" and Jacob's account to Guiette are of interest for the ways in which they diverge from ascertainable fact. In both cases, the divergences concern guilt and the tension between the prodigal artist and the bourgeois family. The detective plot—the young writer spying on his doctor friend—combines many elements from the actual life of Quimper. The dénouement, however, involving the deciphering of handwriting and the reconstruction of the amorous adventures of others, makes the narrator responsible for his father's medical crisis and compounds the writerly guilt with an imaginary punishment seen as having lifelong consequences. The story ends with the father's fit and the mother throwing the son out of the house.

In fact, Jacob's break with his family could not have occurred in that winter of 1897. And his father had no stroke. Several more years of fumbling would intervene before Jacob adopted the bohemian life that would alienate his clan. By the early spring of 1897, he had returned to Paris and was performing well at both schools; he earned his baccalaureate law degree in July; it was not until December 1897 that he dropped out of the École Coloniale, and not until 1899 that he announced his intention of becoming a painter, at which point his family decreed that he had gone crazy.[42]

The fiction tells the deeper truth, however. From Jacob's point of view, his betrayal of his family stemmed from that quickening of his artistic and literary impulses in the winter of 1897, and the awakening brought in turn a guilt that swelled toward patricide in the son's imagination. Lazare Jacob, Max's good-natured father, had been ailing for some time and died in 1917, a few years *after* the composition of the story. The military discharge, far from being a random detail deposited by life, establishes the essential pattern of expulsion and guilt that structures the story and, to some extent, Jacob's life. Similarly, in his account to Guiette, Max Jacob telescoped several years of hesitant detachment from his family into three swift paragraphs that once again involve guilt, this time against his mother:

> I remained with my family, because classes had already begun at school. I spent my days bothering the whole household by playing Beethoven symphonies as badly as possible, or singing *La Damnation de Faust* off key.
>
> My main activity consisted in filling sketchbooks with pencil scribbles representing Bretons and landscapes. I had discovered my Brittany and I drew it with passion if not with talent. It became an obsession. I was given an attic room in the house, and I covered its walls with exalted inscriptions.
>
> One fine day, I left for Paris, in the month of February, with no trunk and no overcoat, having stolen 29 francs from my mother's desk drawer. Which corresponded to the price of the trip.[43]

The crime of theft, which recurs often in Jacob's works, probably has some origin in fact.[44] Its interest lies in its intimate appropriateness as an assault on the money-conscious mother, and in the laconic gesture of self-justification. Whether represented as the father's collapse or as theft from the mother, the departure for Paris—for a life of art—remained a defining moment in Max Jacob's myth of himself: he had to steal his life from his family and wound them in doing so. That voyage beyond the borders of tightly knit clan was no small achievement.

||

WHEN HE TOOK the train from Quimper to Paris in the spring of 1897, whether he had stolen the money for the fare from his mother or desperately provoked his father, Jacob had in his heart already betrayed his family's trust. In the several years that followed, he wriggled and scratched within his chrysalis; the period has all the incoherence of the usual passage from youth to adulthood, with narrative order imposed only in hindsight. Plunging back into the capital, Jacob nursed his Breton persona. In a fanciful autobiography provided in 1911 for Kahnweiler, his first publisher, he pretended to have spent five years in the navy.[45] Writing in 1924 to his friend the painter Moïse Kisling, Max evoked his student days with a good dose of self-pity:

> At twenty, I was at the mercy of odd jobs, harassed by my family,
> surrounded by so-called protectors who protected me only
> when they saw me or not at all. I was fairly wretched, feeling the
> disgrace of poverty and not yet having perceived the star: I mean
> the reason for this poverty, the goal of our privations, since I had
> absolutely no idea that I might one day have some success, or the
> appearance of talent if not the real thing. I was a toy in the hands
> of the bourgeoisie, a stranger to myself, and no destiny beckoned
> me from the horizon. . . .
>
> So, in that period, a Jew raised in a Voltairean family, I lived
> at the Quai aux Fleurs, and as I passed Notre-Dame, I went in—
> oh! not right up to the choir stall! just to the entrance of the nave
> where I knelt in shadow:
>
> "My God!" I said, "if you exist! Look on my distress!
> Help me!"[46]

It is hard to situate the scene precisely. If Jacob is really describing himself at twenty, the episode predates his military humiliation. The sense of privation, abandonment, and religious longing, however, colors the entire period. As for the bourgeoisie, Jacob probably had in mind not only his various employers but the successful Parisian cousins, the Blochs and the Gompels who, sensing his bohemian tendencies, held him at arm's length, though Gustave Gompel "protected" him to the extent of eventually finding him a clerkship in his department store.

Returning to Paris, Jacob continued his courses in law and at the École Coloniale. His parents must have had him on a punitively restricted stipend: to Guiette, he mentioned staying with an impoverished Breton friend, "the admirable and stouthearted Madec," also enrolled at the École Coloniale.[47] Madec helped Jacob find a room at 112 boulevard Arago, a depressing part of the thirteenth arrondissement; no down payment was required, and Jacob slept in a borrowed hammock until he procured a couch for eight francs.

After lodging came the problem of funds. Jacob tried to turn his shaky if vivacious musical talent to account, renting a piano and giving lessons. His principal student was a young Italian opera singer preparing a debut at La Scala: she howled and tossed her hair so energetically that Jacob could only dash along in an improvised accompaniment. Her older sister soon arrived from Italy, however, and fired the accompanist, who was in turn evicted from his room for making so much noise. He moved along to the Rue Denfert-Rochereau, to "a damp, black and sinister room where I tasted truly sad days."[48]

||

SOMEHOW DURING THIS dark period, Jacob managed to pass his law exams in June, to spend the summer of 1897 in Quimper, and to return to his courses in Paris in the fall. There Bernard Lazare, now a convert to the cause of Dreyfus, published his broadside addressed to the Chamber of Deputies, "A Judicial Error: the Truth of the Dreyfus Affair," provoking

a new spasm of defense in the army and the government, and more passionate calls by Dreyfus's defenders for review of the sentence. If Jacob
paid any attention to the developing *affaire,* he left no record of it. On
December 4, 1897, he resigned formally from the École Coloniale and
blundered along in poverty as a law student for the following year. At one
of his lowest points, when he was hungry and sick on New Year's Day
1898, a young friend, the painter Fernand Alkan, brought him a gift of
raw chestnuts: "Here are some not-yet-candied chestnuts," he said, and
advised Max to be an art critic, "like everybody else."[49]

Meanwhile anti-Semitic riots erupted across France and Algeria in the
wake of the novelist Émile Zola's dramatic open letter to the president,
"J'accuse," on January 13, 1898, denouncing the army and the government for suppressing the truth of Dreyfus's innocence. Zola was tried for
defamation in February and convicted (and later escaped to England). In
Paris, Nancy, Rennes, Bordeaux, Montpellier, Marseille, Rouen, and many
other cities, huge crowds marched, rampaged, attacked Jewish shops, and
burned Dreyfus in effigy. In Quimper, on January 22, police broke up
an anti-Semitic demonstration that erupted among youths waiting for the
results of the military lottery.[50] In Paris, Max Jacob must have taken care
to remain inconspicuous as Jules Guérin, a nationalist organizer, patrolled
the Latin Quarter, the large boulevards, and the area around the Palais
de Justice with a private army, largely uninhibited by the police, carrying
signs demanding "Zola to the gallows" and "Death to the Jew," breaking shop windows, and beating up people who appeared Jewish. Many of
the rioters were students, from the law school, the Sorbonne, the École
Normale Supérieure, and the Parisian lycées; some of Max's classmates
from the law school must have been out roaring around the streets while
he stayed indoors.

In May a municipal councilor in Quimper campaigned for local elections by plastering the town with posters proclaiming "We need a Republic delivered from connections to international Jewry and Freemasonry."[51]
The agitation continued over the summer as a captain in the Ministry of
War accidentally discovered Colonel Henry's major piece of evidence
against Dreyfus to be a forgery. Henry confessed and the next day cut

his own throat in prison. Esterhazy, the real spy, fled to England, but the mounting evidence of Dreyfus's innocence only infuriated the anti-Dreyfusards, who claimed that Henry had been murdered by Jews. Charles Maurras, the nationalist writer, commended Henry's "patriotic forgery." In November 1898, Max Jacob quietly received his law degree while Paris was disrupted by a general strike and by fear of civil war, and Guérin's Ligue Antisémitique once more roamed the streets shouting "Down with Jews!" On October 25, a mob tried to storm the gates of the National Assembly, cavalry blocked the streets and took over the Tuileries, and Prime Minister Henri Brisson lost the vote of confidence in his government. The anti-Semitic turmoil continued far into the night.

VIII.

THE LAW DEGREE Jacob received in the midst of these convulsions was a useless document for the artistic destiny he had vaguely in mind, and he seems rarely to have tried to use it. It took him months to work up the courage to follow Alkan's suggestion about art criticism. Another friend pushed him into it in the turbulent fall of 1898. "After all," he said, "do you or do you not have your high school diploma?"[52] With the friend's letter of recommendation in hand, Jacob called on Roger Marx, the inspector general at the Beaux-Arts who held court on Sunday mornings. Marx, who had a flowing beard and slippers, sent Jacob off with a letter to Arthur Meyer, editor-in-chief at the influential newspaper *Le Gaulois*. Meyer, a Jewish convert to Catholicism, had been pilloried some years earlier by the Catholic polemicist Léon Bloy as "the liege man of the legitimist party, one of the most appalling figures of the high society of that era."[53] Guy de Maupassant had used Meyer as a model for the stereotyped avaricious Jew, Walter, a newspaper editor in his novel *Bel-Ami*. When Max Jacob met this figure who had attracted such hostile attention, Meyer also was wearing slippers and appeared "grimy"; he passed the young man along to Maurice Méry, a journalist at *Le Gaulois* and editor of a small weekly, *Le Moniteur des Arts*. Jacob presented his sample, an article on the Breton painter Lucien Simon. Méry measured it with a string, accepted it, and paid Jacob the princely sum of twenty francs. Emerging into the street, Max Jacob thought he had conquered the capital.

Jacob's stint in journalism lasted one year. That year may be considered his last stab at pleasing his family. Signing his articles "Léon David" (his mother's family surname), he darted about the city in a waistcoat and top hat, grew a beard, carried a briefcase, and consorted with successful (and now forgotten) painters who praised and pampered him. One finds no hint, in his memoirs or his correspondence, of the Dreyfus Affair or the serious national violence of that year, 1898–99.

In two poems published in *La Défense de Tartufe* in 1919, however, the painful politics of the fin de siècle are exorcised by being turned into music hall lyrics. "1889" evokes the Universal Exposition and the bourgeois culture that created it:

> Loïe Fuller, what a wench,
> With a bim, with a bang, with a bounce off the bench,
> But Rodin's no-go,
>> He's zero!
>> Otéro!
> Now there's a gal to steal the show![54]

After a canter past cultural and medical highlights of the period, colonial politics and attempted *coups* whirl by like carousel horses: "They say he's made it all the way to Timbuctu; / that's somewhere in Africa, who knows if it's true." By the end, Drumont himself, the high priest of anti-Semitism, swings by as simply one more symptom of the age, neutralized by rhyme and comically opposed by the Eiffel Tower:

> Every morning, the peasant junk dealer Édouard Drumont
> In his paper announces the revolution.
>> But!
> The universe will be saved by
> That iron tower in the sky.

In the companion poem, "1900," the Dreyfus Affair is similarly swept along in doggerel couplets, the tragic and the trivial linked by rhyme: "Our only politics were the Affair. / Oh! The iced drinks served in the luxury liner bar!"[55] But to balance Drumont at the end of "1889," Dreyfus becomes the emblematic figure of sacrifice concluding "1900," a poem written during World War I:

> Man's intelligence had grown so bold
> That the human animal went into revolt.
> And history records: poor Dreyfus, meanwhile,
> Took the sin upon himself in his Devil's Isle.
> Angel and demon, wrestle on! The match lasts today
> With millions of deaths tallied in the fray.
> > No more billiards!
> > Just Biard cafés.

The poem concludes with *sprezzatura,* plunging from "millions of deaths" to comic contraction in the "cafés Biard," a chain of cheap, popular cafés all over Paris.[56] Only obliquely do we see Jacob's response to the political horrors of the age. Nor is it clear for what collective sin Dreyfus suffers. In these poems composed during the throes of Jacob's later conversion and published in a volume subtitled "Ecstasies, Remorse, Visions, Prayers, Poems, and Meditations of a Converted Jew," Jacob has drawn Dreyfus into a plot involving the revenge of the "human animal" against a too-highly evolved rationality. A version of the old Christian story of "salvation through the Jews" seems to be reenacted here, with the Jew sacrificed to redeem a secular world that has abandoned faith for reason.[57]

WHILE JACOB THOUGHT about tonal values and the picturesque peasantry, the Dreyfus case bounced around the different chambers of the Ministry of Justice, President Félix Faure collapsed in a coma during a tryst with his mistress in the Presidential Palace, and the nationalist Paul Déroulède took the occasion of Faure's funeral to try to launch a coup d'état. In June, after the High Court of Appeal reopened the Dreyfus case, the new president,

Émile Loubet, was attacked with a cane at the races by a royalist baron. The forces loyal to the Republic responded with a huge demonstration at Longchamps, one hundred thousand people marching and singing the Marseillaise. The prime minister fell from power the next day, making way for the ministry of Waldeck-Rousseau, who would institute the regime known to the anti-Dreyfusards as the "government of treason" since he restored national order, supported the retrial of Dreyfus in August, and helped engineer a pardon for the captain in September, when the second verdict, in spite of all the evidence, was returned by the military court in Rennes as "guilty with extenuating circumstances."

Taken up in his new career as an art critic, Max Jacob seems to have remained as detached as possible from the furor. The kindly Maurice Méry invited him to dinner at his home, and in the summer of 1899 he appointed Jacob editor-in-chief of the new format of *Le Moniteur, La Revue d'art*. For the first time since his triumph in the lycée philosophy exam, Jacob found approbation at home and in his native city. From a vacation in Quimper in July 1899, he wrote Méry of distributing announcements of *La Revue d'art*: "All these good people know me and keep their eye on me, more or less closely; they hope to see my statue in the town square one day, and a plaque on my house."[58] Some of the same "good people" would, two months later, paste anti-Dreyfusard posters demanding "Down with Jews!" and "Frenchmen! Buy nothing from Jews!" across the Jacob family stores, but this was writing on the wall that Max Jacob would not take seriously until 1939.

In later life, Jacob rarely referred to his year of art journalism. He became intoxicated with his success, he told Guiette.[59] One can imagine Jacob, the mature stylist, wincing at such larded passages as this description of Charles Cottet: "a painter with rich, invisible brushstrokes, with harmonious and simple color in the human figures, truly sincere in his landscapes, translating into a sober and classical language his sense of grave poetry, sad philosophy, his deep love of terrifying nature and the rough people of the sea."[60] But the articles reveal more than juvenile pomposity. The thirty-three pieces signed by Léon David show that Jacob had not been wasting his time in Paris. At the age of twenty-three he covered the Post-Impressionist art scene with authority; he displayed a wide field of reference, including Pascal, Ruskin, and the Rosicrucian magus Sâr Péladan; most importantly, he presented a coherent aesthetic stance taken from Baudelaire, Delacroix, and the Symbolists and lucidly criticized the official salons.

Already, in his young art criticism, Jacob used the "primitive" as a weapon in skirmishes with academic art, as Gauguin was doing at about the same time. Against the École des Beaux-Arts and the salon system, Jacob reiterated paeans to naiveté, originality, and the bizarre. He praised James Ensor for being "wise enough to break with the Academy at a time when nothing but recipes is taught there."[61] Of Lucien Simon, he said, "No Gérôme has spoiled the beautiful exactitude of his color, his sincerity in drawing."[62] Again and again he insisted on the nonrepresentational nature of modern art, accusing the painters of mountain scenery of "Alpine pedantry."[63] He celebrated Cézanne, and in the official salons he lamented the absence of Monet, Pissarro, Signac, and Vuillard. In Puvis de Chavannes he admired the Symbolist refusal of realism,[64] but one senses his impatience with the art of the fin de siècle in his resistance to what Delacroix called "the infernal facility of the brush"[65] and in his rallying cry from Baudelaire, "These days, we paint too well."[66] By the time he published his last article for *La Revue d'art* in January 1900, Max Jacob was ready for Picasso.

He was also ready to drop his career in journalism. A remark from "someone"—perhaps Sylvain Lévi—punctured the illusion: "You're enjoying success!—Really? So that's success? . . . Well, well! You could write a little better, all the same!"[67] "I resolved," Max told Robert Guiette, "to learn to write in French." That resolution closed off to him the last official profession of which his family might have approved. They withdrew all support. He was twenty-three years old, alone in Paris.[68]

CHAPTER 3

MEETING PICASSO

I.

After giving up his job as an art critic, Jacob seems to have moved from his room at Notre-Dame des Champs in Montparnasse to attic lodgings on the Quai aux Fleurs on the Île de la Cité.[1] There, in the neighborhood of the bird market and almost in the shadow of the Cathedral of Notre-Dame, he balanced his lonely hunch about his future against the disapproval of his family and the indifference of the city. The room was a little citadel; as described by a friend who knew him at the time, "The tiles of the bedroom and kitchen were always freshly waxed; you could see yourself reflected as in a mirror and skate there as if at the Ice Palace. And from the window there was a fine view of the Seine and the Île Saint-Louis. 'I do my own housework,' he liked to say, rubbing his hands which were as finely cared for as the tiles."[2]

Having spent the previous year consorting with painters, Jacob entertained briefly the notion that he, too, might be an artist. His family was flabbergasted. In 1920, in the preface to the catalogue of his first show, Jacob described their shock. "One female relative told me, 'Goodness! We never had such a thing in the family!' A Parisian cousin, however, took it differently: 'Well, well. I hope we'll have a Prix de Rome soon.' "[3]

His family expected worldly success. They had already tasted it in the commercial triumph of Gustave Gompel, the owner of the wholesale department store, and in the scholarly eminence of Sylvain Lévi. The academic Prix de Rome represented the antithesis of the art Jacob admired; when he was decorated chevalier de la Légion d'honneur in 1933, his characteristic and ironic comment was that it would make his mother happy.[4]

Bohemia carried the day. Jacob enrolled in the Académie Julian, a popular studio often used by aspiring painters as preparation for the École des Beaux-Arts. It was not simply an antechamber to official art: many modern painters enjoyed its relative freedom and its eight-hours-a-day sessions of drawing from the model. At the time Jacob attended, Jean-Paul Laurens and Benjamin Constant were the masters who descended from on high to review student work. In this hermetic little world near the Bourse, Max Jacob began a new course in humiliation. As he described it later,

> An elegant young man asked me if I were selling pencils; this gentleman wasted his wit and his time, I was so dazed with timidity that I understood his insolence only a long time later, thinking back on it. M. J.-P. Laurens stared at me from my feet to my head with his arching eyebrow and small diligent eye; he took my pencil and voluptuously extended the line of a leg to correct it. I never saw M. J.-P. Laurens again. M. Benjamin Constant talked through his nose and talked of gray-blue poetry. Since he looked no more like a painter than I did, he had perhaps a touch of sympathy for me, but he didn't show it. I was sad and poor.[5]

Even while he studied drawing, the ex-philosophy student, ex-law student, ex-art critic tried his hand at verses. Drafts for some of these poems can be studied at the Doucet Library in Paris. A visionary character, the fashion designer Jacques Doucet helped many artists and writers, and later bought a number of manuscripts from Jacob. The manuscript entitled "Le Christ à Montparnasse: Poèmes 1905–1916" (Christ in Montparnasse: Poems 1905–1916) contains poems that Jacob would later apportion into three books. In spite of the subtitle, several of the poems represent work from as early as 1900.[6] Next to the title of the first section, "Le Mauvais garçon" (The Bad Boy), Jacob wrote, "These are my first verses." Practically scratched out, straining toward form, sometimes written on notebook pages with occult symbols on the back, the drafts show a young man dramatizing his separation from home. They show, as well, the struggle to wrest a fresh style from the conventions of French verse.

Perhaps the earliest—certainly the most naïve—of the poems in "Le Mauvais garçon" is one Jacob never finished or published. Untitled, it exists only in a fragmentary draft in the Doucet manuscript.[7] The manuscript shows him groping toward a shapely language:

I've lost the apple trees which . . .

I've lost my apple trees and I've lost my faith.

I've lost the wheelbarrow, tipped over by the furrow
The mud-spattered barrow with its axle cracked . . .

It concludes:

And Paris has made a pimp of my honest heart.
Give me back my homeland, that old opera tune,
Or let me die!

In rough, half-rhyming alexandrines (the official twelve-syllable line of French verse), the poem harps on loss. The speaker, presented first as a "bourgeois" fresh out of school, merges by the end into a symbolic peasant. In its uneasy oppositions, the poem looks forward to themes Jacob would play upon in his later work; this draft merely testifies to the young man's disorientation. Since the foyer at home had never been edenic, his prodigal emotions crystallize momentarily around one homely object, the wheelbarrow. The anxieties gather into naïve exclamation, giving way to comic inflation and, by the end, to parody, as if a poem by Lamartine should conclude in an Offenbach libretto, "an old opera tune."

This lament resembles a later poem, "A Thousand Regrets," composed partly in August 1912 and placed third in the Doucet manuscript. But instead of starting with loss, "A Thousand Regrets" begins, "I've found

Quimper again." Whereas "I've lost the apple trees" stages a provincial's alienation in Paris, "A Thousand Regrets" explores the alienation of the prodigal son finding himself no longer welcome in his native town: "I've found Quimper again where my first fifteen years were born / And I haven't found my tears again."[8]

Most of the poems in the section "Le Mauvais garçon" in the Doucet manuscript flail between these poles of home (seen sometimes as Eden, sometimes as oppression) and the capital (seen alternately as disillusionment and as liberation).

AT HOME

We aren't little girls anymore
It's about time to learn to make hats
And as for you, brother ? . . . Ah! the cheat!
Leave me alone, Mother! He has to be told.
I'll look straight up from the head of the table.
Don't you have five fingers like us, your sisters?
Don't you have five limbs, including your head?
Don't you have five senses, vision, taste,
Smell, hearing? The mother tried. . . .
At the head of the table where the four sat
The mother, daydreaming, considered her rings.

What a large table! It's the Day of the Dead
The room is brilliant, the day is not white
Upon your elder brother rests a star.[9]

A fluctuating voice without quotation marks, "At Home" observes its material from an eerie distance and is sophisticated in its compression, mobility of perspective, and simple diction. The tongue-lashing sounds like those administered by Jacob's elder sister Delphine, who would eventually take over the family store with Gaston.[10] But the poem preserves a cool surface. And like so much else in Jacob, it may be more or less fictional. In the last four lines, the controlling consciousness withdraws from the sister, past the detached mother, to the afflicted son/brother, and out beyond to some external voice that addresses him: "Upon your elder brother rests a star." However deftly "At Home" objectifies its raw material, family life here is seen as a Day of the Dead, and the light emanating from that life resembles the aura of a migraine. When one knows Max Jacob as the pioneer of abstraction in the prose poems of *Le Cornet à dés* (The Dice Cup) of 1917, it is startling to discover how closely linked these early drafts are to the poet's personal life. But these poems dramatizing the home front laid the groundwork, as well, for Jacob's later social satire in verse and prose. What no member of the family could have foreseen was that the Jacob sons and daughters, as adults, would wear quite a different star, the yellow star identifying them as Jews under the Nazi occupation.

The poem placed first in "Le Christ à Montparnassse," and giving its name to the section of the manuscript, is "The Bad Boy's Lament."[11] Like "I've lost the apple trees," it is situated in a "here" that is clearly the capital with its vice and freedom, and it expresses a similar nostalgia for childhood. Both poems start with the first-person pronoun and recall the lost world. But "The Bad Boy's Lament" is far more assured.

THE BAD BOY'S LAMENT

I remember summer's shutters latched shut
The shutters, which the roses regret
Ah! the great white fish on the tablecloth of glass
Catherine, the maid! and young Nicholas!
On the pond behind the gas works, the sun
It's the sickness of love
That keeps me here with different desires
Among the demons and the streetwalking girls
    Ah! let's chug another down
Another girl's hauled off in the paddy wagon now!

Jacob is playing, here, not with *vers libre*, but with *vers libéré*, "freed verse." From the first tremor of metrical nonconformity in line two, to the shock of the bald statement, "It's the sickness of love," to the slur in the last line between thirteen and fourteen syllables in the French, the poem maintains a sly nostalgic relationship to the alexandrine.

It's a compact, complex, and mysterious poem. In a series of oppositions—past/present, province/city, interior/exterior, female/male—it builds up pressure released not in a resolution but in an exclamation. The first line leads one to imagine the dim interior space of a dining room shuttered from summer heat, and the image of the tablecloth encourages that reading. But the "great white fish" metamorphose from a poached lunch to clouds reflected in the glassy surface of the pond that appears in line five. The poem refuses to resolve such ambiguities.

Love enters the poem midway, as a rupture in the time and place of memory, and a rupture in meter. The image associated with it by French rhyme, the crossroad or intersection (*amour/carrefour*), suggests love's conflicted presence: this public, salable, "different" love is at cross-purposes with the innocence of the poem's beginning. Jacob prefigures here one of the major paths his verse will take as it finds shapes for the pain of desire, and especially the pain of "different" desire.

The last line introduces an institution that will recur throughout Jacob's work: the police. He was as fascinated by codes of social order and their enforcement as he was by codes of prosody, and he would acknowledge and subtly undermine these structures of authority all his life. Though not illegal, the homosexual "different desires" he must have been feeling by then were shameful and often persecuted by the police. And just as Jacob found the shapes for much of his poetry within the hierarchical rules of verse, so even now, or perhaps within a very few years when he had come to understand himself better, he found—with what perverse humor we may imagine—many of his sexual partners in the ranks of the police and the Republican Guards who could have arrested him.[12]

II.

IN 1924, MAX Jacob recalled having prayed in Notre-Dame, "My God! If you exist! Look on my misery! and help me!"[13] In the event, it was the kindly Maurice Méry, publisher of the *Revue d'art* from which Jacob had resigned, who gave practical help. For a while in 1900, Jacob worked on layout at Méry's new comic weekly journal, *Le Sourire*. Here he undoubtedly came into contact with the editor-in-chief Alphonse Allais, the noted humorist and a regular at the Montmartre café Le Chat Noir.[14]

Le Sourire makes painful reading, so virulent are its anti-Semitic and racist cartoons. One wonders what constant mental deflection Max Jacob, or any Jewish or black reader, would have had to make not to feel annihilated. A typical cover, from November 18, 1899, shows a couple in evening dress, the middle-aged woman with hard, masculine features and beaklike nose followed by an oaf of a man. The caption identifies them as "M. le Duc de Bouvines et Mme la Duchesse, née Issachar-Dan," the joke being that a bovine aristocrat has replenished his bank account by marrying a hideous Jewess. With the Exposition of 1900, attention focused on blacks. Innumerable gags turn on the question of interracial sex. "Nasty black," a white woman exclaims. "Beat it! I don't want any little pickaninnies from you!"[15]

The drawings reflect a society permeated with anti-Semitism and racism. Turning the pages of *Le Sourire* in the knowledge that Jacob designed many of those layouts, one begins to imagine the complex set of defenses he must have developed to live in that society, let alone to participate in amusing it. For many Jews, as for Bernard Lazare before the Dreyfus Affair, the answer was assimilation. Max Jacob's mad humor and cockeyed puns may be a version of going one better than assimilation: it was a form of seizing the controls.

Working in the command center of Parisian humor, Jacob did more than cultivate his wit. He was furthering his poetic education. The tradition of cabaret poetry ran strong in the Latin Quarter and in Montmartre; in the 1880s and '90s, Allais loomed large on the scene. He had been associated with the legendary café Le Chat Noir since its founding;

he contributed articles to the café's newspaper, advocating policies such as the assassination of mothers-in-law (under the name of the eminent critic Francisque Sarcey); he became the editor-in-chief of the paper in 1891 and took over also as the leader of the band of pranksters known as "Les Fumistes."

Most important for Jacob, the caustic verse composed in this milieu provided an antidote to Symbolism. Where the latter could verge on solemn nonsense, Allais and his followers specialized in blasphemous nonsense, assaulted all pretensions, and through puns and crazy rhymes turned poetic conventions on their heads. The verbal textures for which Max Jacob became famous—lexical and phonetic sleights, mimicry, and clash of tones—have at least part of their origin in the verse of the cabarets and especially in Allais.

III.

THE YEAR 1900 must have seemed grim to Jacob as he polished the tiles in his attic room, scrambled from one job to another, and muttered his prayers in Notre-Dame. Paris, meanwhile, was speeding up and spreading out. Signing a pardon for Captain Dreyfus in September 1899, President Émile Loubet tried to turn the country's attention to the future. That meant the Universal Exposition of 1900, which was to celebrate the wealth, power, and unity of the Republic. Two massive railroad stations, the Gare d'Orsay and the newly rebuilt Gare de Lyon, were completed, and a new bridge, the Pont Alexandre III, linked the Esplanade des Invalides to the two new major permanent buildings of the exposition on the Right Bank, the neo-Baroque Grand Palais and its more gracious neighbor, the Petit Palais.[16] Motorized trams now shared the streets with horse-drawn omnibuses, private carriages, and pedestrians. The first Métro line was inaugurated in July 1900, rumbling along the Right Bank from Vincennes to Porte Maillot, and bicycles skimmed through the streets and parks. Architecture was changing too: Art Nouveau, the "style 1900" whose sinuosities would come to symbolize the soul of the Métro, animated private and public buildings with its thistles and bulges, mosaic tiles and squirming cornices. Up near the Panthéon, the Sorbonne was nearing the completion of its sixteen-year renovation in a far more prosaic style. Jacob roamed the city, observed it, and made it his own.

LAYING OUT COPY for *Le Sourire* was not Jacob's only employment in this bustling year. At some point he was hospitalized in the Hôtel-Dieu for pneumonia,[17] weakness of lungs being a problem from which he would suffer all his life. Perhaps to convalesce, he returned for a while to Quimper and spent enough time there to try being an apprentice to a carpenter. One can hear, in his remarks to Guiette, his sense of his family's disappointment: "How many people have I disappointed in my life, which has been so full of hopes and unconscious lies. The protectors of my childhood expected a scholar or an honest civil servant: I gave them some kind of ignorant artist. To the protectors of my youth who expected a painter, I gave a writer, and vice versa. To others I gave nothing at all."[18]

Quimper, meanwhile, was suffering the political commotions that Jacob later transformed in the novel *Le Terrain Bouchaballe*. Urbain Couchouren, a wealthy lawyer who died in 1893, had left to the city an orchard by the riverbank for the construction of a municipal old age home. Thus began schemes and counterschemes involving everyone in town. Not till 1897 did a presidential decree permit official acceptance of the inheritance; not till 1899 did the mayor present his proposal to the town council to substitute a theater and park for the old age home, enraging both the Catholic Right and the Socialists. Yet another topic of furious debate arose in 1900: the proposal by a mining company to prospect for coal right in the town and in the surrounding woods, meadows, and farmlands. With a Flaubertian eye for the grotesque, Jacob was already dreaming of a novel that would capture this panorama of the Third Republic.[19]

Finding that carpentry didn't suit him, he tried to use his law degree and worked for a while as a law clerk in Quimper.[20] The job enlarged his sense of sorrow and vice and provided ideas for fiction but no career, and soon enough we find him back in Paris angling for work. One idea, natural enough given his literary tastes, was to work in the Bibliothèque Nationale. Armed with a letter of recommendation, he presented himself to the director, Omont, who promised to arrange "something."[21] The dénouement was bizarre: having been invited to a masquerade dinner at his cousins' house several days later, Jacob went to an antique shop to rent a fez and silver spectacles to disguise himself as a Levantine Jew. The shop's only mirror was set out on the sidewalk; as Jacob stepped out to admire his costume, Omont happened to walk past in all his austere dignity. And that was the end of Jacob's candidacy for a job at the library. "But that didn't prevent Max Jacob from using the library," he added.[22] This vignette suggests yet again the complexity of Jacob's relation to Judaism. Right in the aftermath of the Dreyfus Affair, when Degas banished Jewish friends from his house and would cross the street in order not to have to pass his neighbor, the art dealer Berthe Weill, on the Rue Victor Massé,[23] Jacob accepted and deflected the identity by making a costume party joke of it.

In 1901, Jacob found yet another job in Paris. While the nation simmered—the first major congress of Radicals and Radical Socialists, Prime Minister Pierre Waldeck-Rousseau pushing his anticlerical proposals into law[24]—Jacob worked as a secretary for a "philanthropic lawyer" who was organizing an exhibit on "The Child through the Ages" at the Petit Palais.[25] It was probably around this time that he wrote a children's story for his mother, "The Tale of the Bell That Doesn't Go to Rome." The story bears no date, but in a later note accompanying the gift of the manuscript to the library in Quimper, he explains, "For a children's magazine— It must date from the turn of the century—My mother wanted to enter a contest for an Easter story and asked me to write her one. I sent her this."[26]

The tale gives a glimpse of relations between this difficult mother and her difficult son. For all their reciprocal tension, the mother has asked a literary favor, and her son has obliged. There is no record of the story's having won a prize. It is of interest partly for its lyrical style and partly for the idealized fiction of Frenchness and of relations between mother and child. The opening paragraph, like the poems Jacob was writing around this time, recalls a childhood house; but in the story the nostalgia extends back to immemorial generations in the house, suppressing all the struggle of Jewish emigration:

Far away, far away, in the depths of Quercy, and near the house where I was born, there's a handsome pointed steeple. Old house where I was born! It's also the house where my mother still lives! and where my grandmother died and many of my great-grandparents and their grandparents died. I can't think about it without a surge of emotion.

The story, recounted to the child by the bell-ringer to explain the destiny of the cracked bell, involves the imperfect conversion of a wicked lord who even in his reformed state commits a crime of arrogance and is killed by the very bell he has had cast as a sign of his faith. "And that is the story of the bell that can't go to Rome," concludes the tale,

And it's just this way that the bell-ringer of Grail-en-Quercy told it to me and I went right away to repeat the legend to my mother, trembling. And my mother caressed my blond, curly locks and said, "This proves, you see, my child, that piety is nothing without virtue."

Even granting that a tale for a children's magazine might be expected to be saccharine, this one suggests something about Max Jacob's inner world and the eventual logic of his own conversion. Like the child in the tale, Max grew up in the sight of a beautiful steeple; and like that child, he felt himself to be thoroughly French. His own conversion would consecrate that dream of belonging, and it led to a life of faith in which he imagined himself to be constantly threatened by demons, like the lord in the story.

IV.

IN 1901 THE shabby poet-secretary-artist was not imagining his own conversion. What he *was* doing would have appalled any good parish priest. In long sessions in the Bibliothèque Nationale, he was studying magic. In this he was not alone. For a generation, Paris had been bubbling with occult activities, rumors of which spread across the Channel and attracted the attention of figures such as W. B. Yeats and the poet

AE. In the mystical atmosphere of French Symbolism, the otherworldly rites, incantations, and incense fumes rising from various little sects blended naturally with transcendental poetics. Disgust with politics after the defeat by the Germans in 1870 and the violence of the Commune in 1871 may have contributed to this withdrawal into magical spirituality. Hardly an artist, writer, or musician in Paris was immune to the lure.[27] Later, in the 1920s, Max Jacob's friend the painter André Derain would fill his studio notebooks with ideas about the mystical power of numbers derived from occult sources.[28] These notebooks, teeming with Egyptian hieroglyphics and Hebrew letters, are typical of the generation that came of age in 1900 and closely resemble the exercises in Jacob's notebooks. Jacob concentrated on the Kabbalah, the Tarot, astrology, and the sort of syncretic occultism that had fascinated Gérard de Nerval back in the 1830s and '40s. Jacob's early notes are riddled with these researches as he annotates the numerical values of Hebrew letters and attempts to interpret Roman deities as astrological powers through Hebrew numbers. It's a hybrid system, an attempt to reduce the world to a unifying order of numbers, and an attempt to gain magical control over reality. In some Kabbalistic theory, the person who has realized inwardly the fusion of the ten superior worlds of the spirit with the ten parallel elements, or Envelopes (Keliphoth) of the inferior worlds, can find a magical power that can "influence God."[29]

As he pored over occult treatises, Jacob felt personally powerless in the face of the vast materialistic society of the Third Republic. His only power lay in his intelligence, his wit, and his dreams of poetic and spiritual authority. But some of his occult studies proved to be of practical value: he began to earn pocket money by casting horoscopes and advising people on propitious gems and colors. His younger cousin Pierre Abraham (Bloch), brother of the writer Jean-Richard Bloch, left a mean-spirited portrait of Jacob's activities in those days. The animus with which Pierre Abraham describes Max's visits to his family—visits that occurred more than half a century before the composition of the memoir—suggests a degree of tension between Max Jacob and this branch of his father's family. Max's Aunt Julie had married a M. Bloch, and their son, the engineer Richard Bloch, was the father of the three brothers—Pierre, Marcel, and Jean-Richard—described in Pierre Abraham's memoir. Part of Pierre's hostility may have been due simply to divergence in temperament between the cousins. The engineer's family was straitlaced, and Pierre Abraham states that he disliked "the breeziness, verging on impertinence, with which [Max Jacob] dissociated himself from the common concerns of all those who work for a living."[30] Part may be due to the boy's jealousy of Max's friendship with the literary elder brother, Jean-Richard. Part, however, seems to have sprung from religious resentment. Pierre Abraham's father, a graduate of the prestigious École Polytechnique, was the only one of Aunt Julie's many children to observe the formal practices of Judaism. Though Pierre Abraham insisted that what he called "the very small event" of Max's conversion in no way contributed to his bitterness, his tone suggests otherwise.[31] "Max," wrote Pierre Abraham,

> was my cousin from Quimper, come to "seek his fortune" in Paris, and who, dragging his gaiters from table to table, sang for his supper by telling good fortunes with the aid of decans, occultations, and astral conjunctions. This behavior had little success in a milieu as strict [as the Bloch household]: the stars were meant to stay politely in their places and not meddle in our business.
>
> Max's presence in our house was not assiduous, more from his doing than because of my parents. Each time, his visit was marked by a constraint as palpable as the odor of ether reeking from his shabby jacket, which I perceived more than anyone since I sat next to him.
>
> His columnar forehead, his premature baldness emphasized by his remaining black hair, his broad and sensual nose, his lower face as elastic as those of old ham actors on tour, all this seemed to have been covered with some sort of transparent varnish: it was the first face that ever evoked for me, in its entirety, the word "glabrous."[32]

Max Jacob did earn dinners by telling fortunes. More seriously, in astrology, he found a system of classification of character types that would provide the underlying structure for his fiction. But it was the Kabbalah, generally considered in France of that period as merely one of various occult systems, that made the most enduring impression.[33] For one thing, it gave him oblique access to a spiritual dimension of Jewish heritage that his family almost completely ignored. For another, it opened up a vision of a poetic world: a world conceived as emanating from the power of language, with the secret doctrine of the Bible hidden in the numerical values of the letters of the alphabet. Max Jacob was neither the first nor the last poet to feel the grandeur of a vision in which God manifests Himself in the Word. "In the beginning was the Dot *which is not God*," he later explained to Michel Levanti, "then there was the Voice. Then there was articulation, or letters. The world is *the book of God*. This is not an image. Everything is letters or number. From that follows the importance of the name! the name of the Lord is sacred and all existence is attached to the name: to name is to create. So that I add that to spell is a magical operation. Diction!!!"[34] Truth, in Kabbalah, lies behind veil after veil, and can be approached only through long initiation.[35] "The literal sense of Writing is that envelope; and woe to him who takes this envelope for the Writing itself!"[36]

Jacob read the *Sepher Ha-Zohar* (The Book of Splendor) from the Kabbalah in the translation of Jean de Pauly. Though Jacob sometimes had vicious things to say about Jews, rather in the spirit of a family quarrel—they think they're martyrs, they want revenge, their successes seem to punish others, they and their children are all future Ph.D.'s[37]—and though, after his conversion, his confessors instructed him to leave impieties alone, he persisted in pondering the Kabbalah all his life, and saw no contradiction between its revelations and the Christian order. In 1937 he wrote excitedly about Paul Vulliaud's *La Kabbale juive*, and in 1938 he declared, "I am Jewish and quite a Kabbalist from time to time (and, deep down, very much a Kabbalist . . . yes indeed!"[38] He told the poet Yvon Belaval that the Kabbalah was "in my view the only true philosophy."[39]

V.

THE MAN WHO would prove the most formidable friend of Jacob's life, Pablo Ruiz Picasso, was eighteen years old in 1900. He would soon drop the paternal surname Ruiz. That February he had his first serious show in Barcelona, where his family was established, and he was already building a reputation as one of the forceful painters of Catalan *modernisme*. Even conservative critics praised his precocious talent.[40] Quite a few of the drawings sold, and Picasso's large work *Last Moments* was chosen to be among the Spanish paintings sent to the Universal Exposition in Paris in the spring. Now the young artist set his heart on the European capital of art. Throughout the spring and summer of 1900, he painted Spanish scenes to sell in Paris, and he scraped together money for the trip by doing magazine illustrations, trying his hand at posters, and wheedling funds from his family and the parents of his traveling companion, the painter Carles Casagemas. In late October 1900, Picasso and Casagemas arrived at the Gare d'Orsay and settled in the studio of the Catalan painter Isidre Nonell, high up on the Butte Montmartre, nestled under the church of Sacré-Coeur at 49 rue Gabrielle, the same narrow street where Max Jacob would one day live.

During his first two months in Paris, Picasso lived in Nonell's studio, not only with Casagemas and Manuel Pallarès, another Catalan painter, but also with three obliging models who attached themselves to the young men. The Spaniards explored brothels and cabarets on the Rue de Clichy; they haunted galleries and museums and visited the Exposition; Picasso and Pallarès, at least, enjoyed the city's erotic liberties; and they painted. Picasso, who had just turned nineteen, painted with prodigious energy: in oils and pastels, with broad, powerful strokes and dramatic chiaroscuro, he recreated the embracing lovers, morphine addicts, dance halls, and street and bedroom scenes of the city of art and love. His sketchbooks from this period are full of rapid drawings of whores and cabaret dancers with sharp, angular features and legs aggressively thrust out: Paris was a city for the taking in more ways than one.[41]

And he sold his work. Pere Mañach, a Catalan dealer, sold three of Picasso's pastels to Berthe Weill, a tiny, determined Jewish art dealer in Montmartre. She immediately resold Picasso's bullfight scenes for a profit. Mañach put Picasso on a monthly stipend and sent collectors to his studio. Unfazed by Picasso's prank of hiding in bed when she had climbed the six flights of stairs to visit his studio, Weill bought more work and arranged the sale of Picasso's ambitious *Moulin de la Galette* (1900)—fiercely chiaroscuro, with sloe-eyed vamps and flaring gas lamps—to an important collector of modern art, the publisher Arthur Huc.[42] By the time Picasso returned to his family in Barcelona for Christmas, he had made his mark in Paris and had begun to absorb, not only its bohemian scenery but the lessons of its recent masters: Gauguin, Toulouse-Lautrec, Manet, Van Gogh, and Degas. He was troubled and frightened, but not thrown off track, by the news of Casagemas's suicide in Paris in February 1901. Picasso would return to Paris in the spring of 1901 for his first French one-man show, and through that show he would meet Max Jacob.

JACOB LATER CALLED the encounter with Picasso in late June 1901 "the great event of my life."[43] The painter had arrived in Paris in mid-May. In a Montmartre apartment he shared with his dealer Mañach, he painted feverishly to prepare for the show due to open June 24 at Ambroise Vollard's gallery on the Rue Lafitte, a few blocks south of Berthe Weill's gallery. Weill detested Vollard and accused him of botching Picasso's opening.[44] But Vollard was an important dealer, so it was a *coup* for Mañach to have arranged an exhibit on the Rue Lafitte. Despite Weill's dire account, the show did well: of the sixty-four paintings, pastels, and watercolors—many of them dashed off, at the rate of two a day, in the few weeks since Picasso's arrival—over half sold, and Picasso was called "the brilliant newcomer" in *La Revue blanche*.[45]

"Picasso was born in Malaga, October 24, 1881," began Jacob in *Cahiers d'art*. Oddly, the astrologically sensitive Jacob was off by a day; Picasso was born on October 25.[46] Picasso was a Scorpio, and Jacob, in the book on astrology he wrote with Claude Valence (the pseudonym of Conrad Moricand), described the Scorpio as exhibiting "firmness in planning and sang-froid in action." Its emblem is a man gutting a wolf. Its elementary nature, Jacob and Valence went on to say,

> is reptilian. It symbolizes the greatest procreative power, intra-atomic energy, seminal energy, and Sex. The sexual and passional harshness of the Scorpio is indicated by its poisonous sting, but two other attributes are less well known: the eagle and the dove, which signify, respectively, the flight of thought (which remains inaccessible); and the Holy Spirit. It is at this last stage only that the Scorpio appears human and no longer terrifies. The Scorpio is a principle of life and death. Its dispositions are extreme and contradictory. The spirit is revolutionary, with a penchant for destruction, in order to rebuild afterwards and strengthen itself. The Scorpio symbolizes "silver."

Scorpio's good qualities, Jacob (and presumably Valence) continued, are "logic, willpower, and resistance." Its defects are cruelty, jealousy, intransigence.[47]

This portrait of Scorpio, composed in the late 1930s, owes much to Jacob's knowledge of Picasso. The Scorpio appears here as a god of destruction and creation, as well as a fount of dark sexual energy, and that is indeed how the painter appeared to Jacob: he could unleash his powers not only on art but on friends and lovers.

Jacob refrained, on the whole, from writing memoirs about his hero. To Picasso's annoyance, however, he did publish glimpses of the life they shared, first in stories in *Le Roi de Béotie*, then in several brief accounts in magazines.[48] In 1927 he remembered the painter as a young man: "When I knew him in 1899 [*sic*],[49] he was eighteen years old; he was beautiful to perfection, with a face like ivory, without a wrinkle, from which his eyes gleamed, much larger than now, with a black crow's wing of his hair across his forehead as across a jewel chest."[50] In 1923 Jacob wrote,

> He looked like a child. His large black eyes which have an expression so intense when he looks at you, so mocking when he speaks,

so tender when he is moved, shone with life beneath his wide, low, categorical forehead. His hair was thick, unbrushed, glossy. . . . One or two silver strands gleam in that black mass now. At that time, his face was of ivory and of the beauty of a young Greek; irony, reflection, and effort have added delicate lines to the waxen face of this small man who resembled Napoléon.[51]

With a lover's acuity, Jacob remembers the physical impression made on him by the man who became his *daimon*. The contrast of black and white, the mesmerizing eyes, the forehead bespeaking genius, all contribute to the idealized portrait. The first vision he received, however, was not of a man but of paintings. Keeping up his habits from his days as an art critic, Jacob visited Vollard's shop from time to time ("One didn't yet say 'gallery,' " he informed his audience at Nantes in 1937),[52] and this day in late June, at Picasso's show, he was so amazed at the work that he left a note for the painter.[53] In his speech at Nantes, Jacob noted the influences of Lautrec, Vuillard, and Van Gogh but insisted on the young painter's powers of transformation, and on the shock his work administered even to the avant-garde modes in Paris. "I knew all about that scene," declared Jacob.

Picasso imitated everyone, a little, including the literary Lautrec. . . .
He imitated all that but his imitations were carried away in such a
whirlwind of genius that in that whole exhibition of countless paintings, one felt only the explosive force of an entirely new and original
personality.[54]

Mañach responded to Jacob's note with a visiting card and an invitation to meet Picasso at the apartment they shared. Dressed up in his art critic outfit—top hat, elegant jacket, white gloves, and monocle[55]—Jacob presented himself. Picasso, he said, welcomed him, "both hands extended, as if he had always known me, and showed me, jabbering half in Spanish and half in French, even more canvases than there had been at Vollard's. We clasped hands with that fire of friendship one no longer experiences after one's twentieth year."[56] (Jacob was on the verge of his twenty-fifth birthday but evidently did not lack in ardor.) Ten or so fellow Spaniards were sitting around in the studio and invited Jacob to share their dinner of beans cooked over an alcohol burner, washed down with swigs of wine from a a terra-cotta jug. They stayed up late talking, singing, and listening to the guitar. The next day, Jacob recalled, "the whole gang came to visit me, 13 Quai aux Fleurs, and Picasso painted my portrait in the midst of my books and papers. I read to him all night long, not, certainly, pieces of art criticism, but the poems I had been scribbling since my childhood along with my crossings-out, and Picasso wept and embraced me and said I was the only French poet of the age."[57]

However touching, this scene of poetic consecration probably conflates a number of occasions. In 1927 in *Cahiers d'art*, Jacob mentioned that Picasso painted his portrait that first night but located the poetic affirmation three years later, when Picasso was settled in the Bateau Lavoir and could understand French more easily.[58] The lecture at Nantes was delivered a decade later than the article in *Cahiers d'art* and in several other ways contracts events in telescopic hindsight.[59] In symbolic terms, however, Jacob's account at Nantes tells an essential truth: his recognition of Picasso's genius was accompanied by a reciprocal recognition of his own poetic destiny. In 1931, in the autobiographical sketch he wrote for a dictionary of contemporary artists, he said, "In 1898 [*sic*] I met Picasso; he told me I was a poet: it's the most important revelation of my life except for the revelation of the existence of God."[60] Less histrionically, Jacob wrote in *Cahiers d'art* that around 1904 he was writing poetry "because Picasso found I had talent, and I believed in him more than in myself."[61]

Most accounts of that first night at Jacob's room corroborate the painting of the poet's portrait. Jacob, in 1927, thought the portrait long since lost or painted over, just as he feared the friendship had been obscured by the passage of time. But Hélène Seckel observes that the portrait of Jacob revealed by X-ray beneath Picasso's painting from late 1901, *Crouching Woman and Child*—now in the Fogg Art Museum at Harvard—may well be the lost work. It certainly dates from the first months of their friendship, if not from the first session at the Boulevard Voltaire.[62] Jacob also remembered having given Picasso some of his treasures that night, a woodcut by

Dürer and all the Daumier lithographs he owned. "I gave him all that, I think he must have lost them," Jacob wrote wistfully in 1927. "That night all the Spaniards left except Mañach who was dozing in an armchair, but Picasso and I spoke in sign language until morning."[63]

After that night, Picasso and Jacob saw each other every day until December, when Jacob went to Quimper and Picasso returned to Barcelona. Jacob may have felt small and poor when he compared himself to his Parisian cousins. But in his vicissitudes he had been absorbing Parisian culture, and he had learned the city inside out. He could move like a chameleon from one setting to another, adapting himself to each environment with his fabulous mimicry, passing swiftly from the salons of the *haute bourgeoisie* to the dives of Montmartre. Five years older than Picasso, he was elegant, worldly, shabby, fanciful, witty, malicious, tender, vulnerable, and erudite. For Picasso, who until now had spent his time in Paris in the company of fellow Spaniards, Max Jacob was his first and intimate guide to France: French poetry, French lore, the French *comédie humaine*, and the occult. Jacob showed him the streets and buildings, too, and their artistic fauna, like the satirical painter Willette, something of a star at the time, whose "Wagnerian profile" Jacob pointed out to Picasso, the "energetic little adolescent."[64] Picasso's imagination was infinitely absorptive, Jacob unstintingly generous in nourishing that imagination.

Picasso's friend from Barcelona, the failed sculptor and poet Jaime Sabartés, has described the literary hijinks produced by Max Jacob for his new friend and the Spanish entourage. Not surprisingly, Verlaine is the poet whose work Jacob performs: Verlaine, whose sincerity, poverty, and self-laceration haunt Jacob's novel *Saint Matorel*. Sabartés remembered Jacob reciting Verlaine, calling up the mood Jacob and Picasso were indulging and exorcising in these days of struggle, when Picasso was entering his Blue Period, painting the whores in the Saint-Lazare Prison and having trouble selling these mournful works. "Max Jacob began to read the poem from the book he had brought," wrote Sabartés.

> At first he fit the cadence of his voice to the pace of the lines. He would read slowly and deliberately. He brought the weight of sound to bear

on a parenthesis to emphasize the rhythm. Bit by bit he would grow excited. As if the feelings drawn up from a previous reading which he wanted to communicate to his hearers poured into his memory, suddenly he would stop, gesture, leaf violently through the book; each time he started a new poem he raised his voice, made gestures to suit his modulations, to mark the pauses, to emphasize the weight of a word or accentuate the rhyme. In pitch darkness he began to read "A Great Black Sleep," seeming to draw the lines up from the shadow of a distant memory. He certainly knew them by heart. Now he recited slowly in a deeper voice; he prolonged cadences; his enunciation interrupted by silences sometimes seemed to leave the lines suspended. . . . At the end of the last stanza he suffocated the words "silence . . . silence" in a sigh, and lay down on the floor.[65]

Jacob also threw himself into the promotion of Picasso's work. The painter was under contract to Mañach. But it was often Jacob who carried Picasso's work to Vollard and to other dealers;[66] it was probably in this period that Jacob arranged the sale of Picasso's portrait of Bibi-la-Purée, an old ham actor, to his cousin Gustave Gompel.[67] One wonders what Gompel, whose success his nephew Pierre Abraham attributed to his "thick-headed good sense and solid stupidity," made of the wicked old face grinning out at him from Picasso's impasto.[68] Probably not much: when he bought Picasso's *Two Saltimbanques* several years later at Max's urging and hung it in his study, he would ask Pierre Abraham, "You like that? I don't. I don't see anything in it. It's Max who made me buy it."[69]

||

AS THE AUTUMN of 1901 deepened, so did the financial difficulties of the two friends. The painter found himself more and more at odds with Mañach, and Jacob's job with the "philanthropic lawyer" came to an end. By mid-December, Jacob retreated to Quimper. It rained heavily, the whole town was muddy, and the countryside was dark, he told his new acquaintance, the novelist Charles-Louis Philippe. After complimenting his correspondent with news of an admirer of Philippe's recent novel *Bubu de Montparnasse,* Jacob announced that he was awaiting news of "an administrative career."[70]

The fact that Jacob was on such terms—slightly formal but friendly—with Charles-Louis Philippe tells us something of the literary life he had temporarily left in Paris. Two years older than Jacob, Philippe was the son of a shoemaker from the Auvergne and earned his living as a bureaucrat in the Hôtel de Ville in Paris. When *Bubu* appeared to some acclaim in 1901, Philippe had already brought out a volume of short stories and two novels at his own expense. Jacob liked *Bubu,* responding to the frankness and simple elegance of the style, as well as to its milieu of shopkeepers, whores, and pimps. He wrote the author, who turned up at Jacob's door soon afterward, dressed, Jacob remembered, "as a sort of delivery man, wearing a smock-like jacket and a big lorgnon of the sort that sold for one franc twenty-five at the Bazar of the Hôtel de Ville."[71] Philippe was a modest man who kept to his small circle of friends (which now included Francis Jammes and Gide); he had in common with Jacob a short stature and slight physique, a provincial background, and a love of Dostoyevsky. The two men were practically neighbors, Philippe living in a sixth-floor room on the Île Saint-Louis, Quai Bourbon, and Jacob still on the Quai aux Fleurs.

Philippe asked his host if he wrote poems. As Jacob later recalled, " 'Oh no!' I told him, and then, since he insisted, I showed him a stack of the little poems I wrote in those days. He found them impressive. 'I'm going to take them right over to *La Plume,*' he said. I remember the gesture I made then. Placing my hand on my manuscripts, I looked at him steadily and told him, 'Not yet!' "[72]

Max Jacob had released one poem from his stack, but not to the Symbolist fortress of *La Plume.* Nor does "The Burial" seem designed for a refined literary public. On December 21, Jacob's old place of employment, *Le Sourire,* published the piece, structured like a child's song to satirize the participants in an ostentatious funeral, including the corpse: "Here's the parents' carriage . . . Here's the priest's carriage . . . Here's the stockbroker's carriage." The cabaret verse of "The Burial" is hardly a chef-d'oeuvre, though it does have a crude vitality; it feels like an exercise in the mode of Alphonse Allais.[73] But in its last stanza, spoken by the dead son, one might hear the protest of the living son, the author, struggling to assert his right to life:

> But the most annoyed of everybody
> Was the dead body:
>> "It would be
>> Really
>> Very scary
>> If they buried
> Me alive!"

||

THE EFFORT, WHATEVER it was, that Max Jacob made in December 1901 in Quimper to secure "an administrative position" came to nothing. The parental house can hardly have been welcoming; it was made more miserable by the cold, dark weather, and even worse by the attack on the house by a crowd of peasants infuriated by the new anticlerical laws, "as if the worthy gentleman [Max's father] were responsible for the misfortunes of the Church," his son later said.[74]

In all his memoirs, Max Jacob slides quickly over the year 1902. It was a hand-to-mouth business of patching together odd jobs in Paris, writing poetry, and studying occult arts.[75] Back in the capital, there was some question of his being hired as a secretary at the Musée Carnavalet. That project evaporated,[76] and Jacob fell back on tutoring or, as he said, being a nanny for a boy in a wealthy family.

One of the only documents surviving from 1902 is a letter to Max Jacob from Picasso, now living in his family's house in Barcelona. In highly hispanicized French, Picasso describes his impatience with his friends, who (he said) were writing lousy books and painting idiotic paintings.[77] Besides a sketch of Picasso posing in front of a bullring, the letter includes a description of the painting he was working on, one of the Saint-Lazare pictures of a sad whore and a young mother holding an infant.[78]

In Paris, Berthe Weill continued the shows of young artists she had started the previous December. In March she managed to sell a painting by Picasso for the fairly good sum of 160 francs;[79] in April she showed paintings by Picasso and by an imitator of Renoir. That show inspired Félicien Fagus of *La Revue blanche* to write another admiring article in which he launched the challenge to Spanish painters: "Which one—the time is ripe—will become their Greco?"[80] Weill scheduled another show, to include Picasso and three other painters, for November 15.

Picasso arrived with two friends on October 29. Right from the start, everything went wrong. He had no money. After a week in Montmartre sleeping on the floor of his traveling companion's hotel room, he moved to a cheap room of his own in the Latin Quarter. But the dealers were not biting: Durand-Ruel turned him down; he was no longer on speaking terms with Mañach; if he saw Vollard, nothing came of it; even Berthe Weill was too poor to pay for the pastel of two mothers with babies he produced as a potboiler.[81] Weill recalled not having been able to support Picasso at this stage, and how he held it against her;[82] she was just recovering from a serious injury and had barely reopened her gallery.

When Max Jacob, with his young pupil in tow, visited Picasso, the painter had been forced to leave his hotel room and take refuge in the attic room of a sculptor called Sisket in the Hôtel de Maroc on the Rue de Seine.[83] This seems to have been the darkest time in Picasso's life. Sabartés reports that he "could not stomach some grotesque incidents and the pettiness of persons known to him and Max. Picasso refused to speak about this matter and the vile and repugnant egoism of the individuals concerned, preferring not to stir the mud with which he was besmirched."[84] In a letter to Jacob the following year, Picasso wrote: "I become sad as I think with disgust of those Spaniards of the Rue de Seine."[85] He could no longer afford canvas, paint, or even a lamp but was drawing scenes of lamentation on paper. His wretchedness shocked Jacob:

> It was winter. He had with him some sort of sculptor named Sisket who wore a red woolen belt and workmen's trousers. They lived in a garret at the Hôtel du Maroc, rue de Seine, and stayed in bed

because there was only room for the iron bedstead. This bed was covered with huge drawings and a great black portfolio. . . . Neither the sculptor nor Picasso could afford to eat. I was a tutor at the time and I visited Picasso with my pupil. I think that handsome gentleman will remember, all his life, this scene of poverty and genius. I became a store clerk and quite naturally Picasso came to live in my room, Boulevard Voltaire, on the fifth floor.[86]

With all the overlapping and sometimes conflicting accounts, the precise chronology of events is difficult to work out, particularly since records show that Jacob did not start work at the Paris-France store owned by Gustave Gompel until February 5, by which time it is generally thought that Picasso had returned to Barcelona.[87] Jacob's effort at employment, however, seems linked in his memory with the project of helping to support Picasso, and he probably took the step of applying to his rich cousin for help with the idea of a longer sojourn with Picasso in mind. It was at this juncture, probably in early December 1902,[88] that Jacob moved from the Quai aux Fleurs to the larger room the two would share on the Boulevard Voltaire, off in the eleventh arrondissement beyond the Place des Vosges and far from the artistic communities of Montmartre and the Latin Quarter. Since all his accounts mention working in the store right across the boulevard while Picasso slept during the day in their one bed, one wonders if he had a trial period in the store in January when he was not officially on the books of Paris-France.

Jacob described the scene of moving his tiny household with subtly combined reproach and nostalgia in his story "The Voltaire Warehouse" in *Le Roi de Béotie*:

He who didn't abandon me during my hardships before his own took him away from a friend and from his studies, P.P. whose paintbrush has become an instrument of glory, if he remembers the appalling look with which we stared, one evening, from the height of a hotel window, at the sidewalk on the Boulevard Voltaire, will not have the strength to smile at the memory of the carriage [*fiacre*, a name

Picasso later wanted Jacob to adopt] that carried me toward the suburbs, far from my apartment at the Quai aux Fleurs, holding on our
knees a metal tub and an oil lamp, the same lamp that illuminates
this page; or at the memory of the dinner of rotten fish and gassy
sausage we ate, standing up, on the Rue de la Roquette.[89]

Picasso, too, remembered their modest meals, though the menu he
described is less revolting. The following summer, writing Jacob from Barcelona, he recalled "the room on the Boulevard Voltaire and the omelettes
the beans and the Brie and the fried potatoes."[90] The suicidal thoughts
recur a number of times in Jacob's memoirs: "The room had a vast balcony over the Boulevard Voltaire," he told his audience at Nantes, "and
one evening when we were leaning from it, he took my arm and broke the
silence: 'Let's go in, we shouldn't think such things.' "[91] The anecdote was
passed along later to Louis Aragon, who incorporated it in his novel *Anicet
ou le Panorama*.[92] Whatever their thoughts, the friends worked themselves
up by reading the stoical poems of Alfred de Vigny: the verses made them
weep, Jacob recalled.[93] Vigny's "Moses," in particular, that exaltation of
solitary heroic genius, so struck Picasso that he noted the reference on
several drawings.[94]

It was a lonely time for them both, too poor to frequent cafés and cabarets. But they sustained each other. Jacob read to Picasso the poems he
hardly showed to anyone else. And he struggled to care for his protégé;
looking back, in *Chronique des temps héroïques* (Chronicle of Heroic Days),
he compared Picasso to Napoléon and himself to Constant, the emperor's
privileged *valet de chambre*: "I waxed the shoes [of Picasso] when shoes
were still waxed around 1900, little thinking that I was entering History with a black brush in my hand."[95] He rustled up enough money to
drag Picasso to see Puccini's opera *La Bohème* and revel in its romantic
depiction of artistic sacrifice.[96] Picasso's first great love, Fernande Olivier,
described Jacob's generosity: "After a trip to Spain, it was Max Jacob who
allowed Picasso, penniless, to live and work. . . . Of Max's goodness and
generosity to him, I know only what Picasso himself has said. But he owes
him much. It was Max Jacob who sustained, encouraged, and helped him

when he suffered deep difficulties in his youth."[97] The friends fortified each other by telling each other's fortunes. Picasso preserved, all his life, the two sketches of Jacob's reading of his palms (indicating a "superb" line of the heart, promising many and intense affections as well as disillusionments).[98] For his part, Picasso, just before his departure for Barcelona in mid-January, drew a comic strip of Max Jacob's literary glory, "Clear and Simple Story of Max Jacob and His Glory or Virtue Rewarded," dated January 13, 1903: Jacob is shown scribbling at his table by the light of the famous oil lamp, carrying a manuscript to a publisher, having the work greeted with enthusiasm ("Ole! Ole!"), banqueting with two ladies at Maxim's, receiving a laurel crown and a ham from Athena, and having a monument to his glory erected by Rodin near the Arc de Triomphe.[99]

"Finally, " Jacob wrote in *Cahiers d'art*, "Picasso sold a pastel one day to a Mme Bernard and with the money he returned to Barcelona."[100] The lady was probably his paint merchant's wife.[101] But Picasso did not leave without entertaining himself with *another* lady, one who had just entered his friend's life.

CHAPTER 4

ROMANCE

I.

Max Jacob's first sexual union with a woman came as such a revelation, it was rivaled only by the apparition of a divine presence on his wall in 1909.[1]

Cécile Acker, as Jacob identified her on several drawings and in one memoir, or Germaine Pfeipfer, as he identified her to Guiette, first struck him as "a tall skinny woman."[2] In his two pen and ink portraits of her, she usurps most of the page and appears massive and terrifying. In both drawings, front face and profile, she is wearing a dark, squashed, looming hat; her nose is important and predatory; front face, her eyes are large and heavily lidded, in profile darkly blank. She seems to emerge from the stratum of Jacob's imagination that produced Madame Gagelin and all the aggressive, lubricious, miserly, atheistic females who people his fiction. He sometimes imagined hell as female: describing it in a meditation, he wrote, "Have you known women lushes, thieves, gold-diggers, obese matrons?"[3] In the poem "At the Boiler!" he writes, "Satan's wallet / is made of the skin of female loins."[4] He suggested that *abîme*, "abyss," a masculine noun, should take the female gender, and in 1904 he remarked in a notebook on a female spider devouring her mate.[5] Looking at his drawings of Cécile/ Germaine, one could well believe that a kiss would be the "surgical operation" he described in an early prose poem: "What gave this kiss its intriguing quality was that Madame meant nothing to me and could be nothing to me. It was only an experiment! Something like a surgical operation. It was a matter of bringing the corner of her mouth in contact with mine, attending successively to each part of her lips, in order to rub, slowly, the surface of our epidermises, and open one's mouth at the same time!"[6] Yet this is the woman who made him so happy, the first night they spent together, that he opened the window and sang and improvised verses to the sky, and he wrote on his profile drawing of her, "Cécile—the only violent passion of my life."[7]

Cécile or Germaine (or Geneviève, according to Picasso) was probably not a fellow employee at Paris-France, as Andreu assumes,[8] but her husband seems to have worked there, and it was in the crowded restaurant where the clerks and workmen ate lunch that Max Jacob met the enterprising lady. She was eighteen years old. One of the men alerted Jacob: "You know, Pfeipfer is jealous, seems you've been making eyes at his wife." "What wife?" Jacob asked. "There, the tall skinny one." Jacob looked over where the man pointed and found, he said, "nothing remarkable" in her.[9]

As the workers bustled out after lunch, Jacob lingered and apologized to Madame Pfeipfer for having inconvenienced her: he hadn't even noticed her, he insisted. "She began to laugh and replied, 'We'll see, we'll see.' "[10] So began the great love that allowed Max Jacob for a few months to possess, in terrestrial form, the goddess, the red Venus, in the magnitude and triviality of her mystery. Victor Matorel, the author's self-projection in *Saint Matorel*, hallucinates after his affair with Léonie: "No! No! I have seen the scarlet woman! I have seen the woman of blood! I have seen the thighs of the true Venus! I have seen her Phrygian bonnet."[11] The Phrygian bonnet alludes not to the red cap worn by Marianne, the symbol of the Revolution and the Republic, but to the *bonnet d'ordonnance* worn by the prostitutes in the Saint-Lazare Prison, where Picasso had found his models the year before.[12] Jacob's Venus seems to be an apotheosized whore. But so were many of the women in Picasso's paintings of this period, and the allusion leads to delicate questions of chronology and of Picasso's relations with Max Jacob's lover.

That Picasso knew her is clear. He referred to her in a letter written to Jacob the following September as if he had seen and judged her: "O love! . . . love is easy promises are breezy & you are so in love with your *not beautiful* and *not very elegant* married woman! O love!"[13] Furthermore, he drew a dark, sensual torso-length portrait of her in the nude, annotated on the back, "Geneviève amie de Max Jacob vers 1903," and he gave John Richardson to understand that he, too, had slept with her.[14] On the other hand, Jacob told Guiette that he was already living at 33 boulevard Barbès when the affair started: that is, no longer sharing the room with Picasso on the Boulevard Voltaire. Perhaps Picasso stayed on in Paris longer than is generally thought, which would have given him more time to observe the romance, and to meddle in it. It may even be possible that André Salmon was *not* mistaken when he asserted that Picasso had shared a lodging with Jacob in the little room on the Boulevard Barbès.[15]

The deeper logic of the situation is more interesting than fussing with undocumented dates. There's no record of Jacob's sexual experiences before this date, but in the highly autobiographical *Saint Matorel*, the author (called "I, Matorel") states that he had already "known love with a gentle horror—Must I confess that I was a sodomite, without joy, it's true, but with ardor?"[16] Jacob must have suffered desperate confusion and frustration living with the beloved young genius who was a vigorous, cynical womanizer. In spite of their differences, the two men were linked at this stage by their contempt for women. If Picasso did sleep with Cécile, it must have been a contemptuous gesture, since he hardly admired her; it could also have been some form of offhand macho bravado and one-upmanship to his older friend and protector, Max Jacob. The women in Picasso's early paintings seethe with demonic sexuality and look either diseased or inflamed; the year before, in a page covered with scribbles dedicated to "Monsieur Max Jacob Stockholder in Thought," Picasso had drawn stocky whores and scrawled misogynistic slogans like "God is good he gives us women who bug the shit out of us."[17]

Who knows with what diabolical amusement Picasso observed his friend falling into the hands of a married woman who, though she may have been skinny, still exhibited generous breasts in Picasso's smoky drawing? Jacob's dedication of *Saint Matorel* to Picasso suggests much and explains nothing: "To Picasso—for what I know he knows / for what he knows I know." And one can only speculate about the forces motivating Jacob in his affair: a desire to impress Picasso? Sexual curiosity overcoming timidity? Chronology tells the most poignant story. At two crucial moments in his life when he felt abandoned by Picasso, Max Jacob turned to a mighty form of compensatory love. His affair with Cécile must have been in its infancy when Picasso broke up the little bachelor ménage on the Boulevard Voltaire and left for Barcelona in late January or early February; Jacob consoled himself in a nine- or ten-month interlude with an insistent woman. Seven years later, when Picasso moved from the Cubist intimacy of Le Bateau Lavoir to the Boulevard de Clichy, Jacob experienced an even more powerful form of consolation: Christ seemed to appear on the wall of his room on the Rue Ravignan, on September 28, 1909, at five in the afternoon.[18]

JACOB'S AFFAIR WITH Cécile coincided with a period he felt to be one of the most degrading, but instructive, in his life: his eight months as a clerk at Paris-France.[19] In *Saint Matorel,* Paris-France has become "La Maison Cheiret et Cie," the neighborhood of the Boulevard Voltaire has become the equally depressing Faubourg Saint-Antoine, and Jacob divides his persona between the narrator, "Monsieur Max," a janitor at the store, and the visionary hero Victor Matorel.

If Paris-France provided Jacob with rich material, it was also the backdrop for disillusionment in love. In *Saint Matorel,* Léonie, the Cécile figure, dominates chapter two in harebrained dialogue that reveals her as callow, calculating, promiscuous, and roughly good-natured. "Victor was so delicate! When he was fired, after the episode of the trunk, he took his whole month's pay, he told me, 'Get out since you're cheating on me, and take all this!' "[20] Matorel prays to be delivered from the memory of Léonie: "I've got other things to do than bother myself with carnal love. It was on the Boulevard Barbès in a room for 100 francs. We had only a little iron-frame bed."[21] In the story "The Voltaire Warehouse," also based on the episode with Cécile, the clerk Léonce Moineau (Sparrow) loses his job at the store because of his distraction in love; even worse, his fiancée, having tricked him into marriage with false assurances of her lucrative job in fashion design, becomes an outright whore.[22]

Jacob's own story was less melodramatic. The day after his apology to Madame Pfeipfer, he dallied in the restaurant after lunch. She waited for him and led him out for a walk, during which she told him the sad tale of her life, especially about her drunken husband and his friend who never took her out to the country. Whereupon Max Jacob offered to take her to the country the very next day, and they made a rendezvous.

"The next day, at noon, I was sitting at the terrace of a café by the Barbès Métro stop with an old Spanish tenor who had lost his voice. All of a sudden I jumped to my feet. My glass fell and smashed. And I said, 'There she is!' The old tenor laid his hand on my arm: 'But you're in love, my good fellow.' I replied, in all innocence, 'Is that what it's like, being in love?' "[23] During the train ride to the country, Madame Pfeipfer told him about her thirteen lovers and her taste for silk stockings and for the illustrated supplement of *Gil Blas;* on the return to Paris she visited his room and admired the portrait of her he had made from memory. She sat on his bed, "folding her skirt carefully, and said, 'I'll tell you when it's time.' "[24]

For the next few weeks the affair progressed in clandestine meetings in the evening in the bistros and side streets.[25] Jacob also cultivated the friendship of Cécile's husband and let it be known that, slight though he was, he'd been a champion boxer, sword fighter, and marksman. At a certain point he tried to drop her by writing her that he needed his solitude in order to work on his art. The declaration had the opposite effect: Cécile not only consummated the affair physically on Jacob's narrow bed (prompting him to sing in triumph from his open window) but, shortly thereafter, moved in with him. He shouldn't worry, she reassured him, she wouldn't cost him anything. She earned money by knitting dolls' clothes.[26]

In Jacob's narration to Guiette, he passes quickly over the actual affair, though it dragged on until the following November, when he lost his job at Paris-France. He and Cécile hardly had much in common: she used his manuscripts as stuffing for cushions (if we can believe Matorel), and she seems eventually to have taken up again with her husband and perhaps even with his friend Georges. By the end of September, Jacob confessed the awkwardness of his situation to Picasso, who responded in a letter of worldly advice: "O love! You tell me you don't want to distress her and you must distress her a great deal and not only that way it will be over more quickly."[27]

By late November, not even Jacob's family ties with the august Gustave Gompel could persuade the supervisor to keep him on at Paris-France. In impeccable administrative jargon, the manager reported to the boss that Jacob was drawing portraits of women co-workers "with packing pencils on paper, ditto."[28] Jacob was fired. That rupture permitted his break with Cécile. They had to separate, he told her; he'd return to his girlfriend poverty, and she to her husband. When she wept, he persisted: " 'Besides, you've been cheating on me for days now. . . . In the evening your hair is fixed differently, and your petticoat fastened differently. Just like murderers who hang around the house of their victim, you told me you'd had an apéritif with your husband. . . . That apéritif you took with him is the same one you take with me at night.' "

When she protested, he "fired off a great accusation: 'If it's not your husband, it's Georges.' She cried again. And I wrote the first prose poem of my life: 'She was so weary that even the buttercups on her hat seemed to wilt.' "[29]

Though Jacob later insisted that he, too, wept at the separation, and that he had been motivated primarily by the desire to spare Cécile a life of "dark poverty,"[30] in the Guiette version his personification of poverty as a girlfriend and the culmination of the tale in the production of a prose poem—the genre that was to be his most original contribution to French literature—suggest a deeper level of satisfaction with the trade-off. Failed love is resurrected as art. Never again did Max Jacob seek love with a woman, unless we count a boast to Apollinaire, in 1909, about a mistress who was a dancer (of whom there is no evidence), and a mysterious engagement in the spring of 1913 to an Indochinese woman alluded to in letters to Jean-Richard Bloch, Apollinaire, and André Billy.[31] A prose poem in *Les Oeuvres burlesques et mystiques du Frère Matorel* (1912), "The Poet's Marriage," expresses his choice: "Verboten! Verboten! / Ah! Everything prohibited and the streets are blocked! Blocked! / Verboten! Verboten!"[32] The plot in *Saint Matorel* leads clearly away from Léonie and the Red Venus to a more transcendent form of love: "Of the Red Venus one can know only her crimson thighs. I know naked shoulders also and I shall know the face and eyes of the eternal Virgin."[33] While some of his earthly loves would take decidedly less ethereal form (like young policemen), poverty would indeed keep Max Jacob company most of his life; and with the publication of the collection of prose poems, *Le Cornet à dés* in 1917, he came into his own as a writer who had recreated a genre.

CÉCILE DID NOT disappear without a trace. Jacob told Guiette and Béalu that he entered paintings in the Salon des Indépendants around 1907 with the sole purpose of attracting her attention, and she apparently did attend the opening. When she appeared, Jacob said, he was with Picasso and Braque, and he couldn't keep from laughing; he found her grotesque. But his friends, he later claimed, found her "very beautiful."[34] Nor was this her last appearance. She turned up, sumptuously dressed, accompanied by some "gentlemen" on the Boulevard Rochechouart. Calling to Jacob on the sidewalk, she told her companions that Jacob had "truly loved her" and would still marry her right then today if she asked him to. To which Jacob replied, "That would be the first time the hors d'oeuvre was eaten as a dessert." She visited him one last time in his room on the Rue Ravignan, with a young gigolo. He never saw her again.[35]

In these retrospects, Max Jacob presents Cécile as hideous. But he needs also to affirm that his friends found her "very beautiful." In both representations, she confirms his tenuous superiority in a society that in so many ways treated him, the Jew, the homosexual, as worthless. In the one later encounter, Cécile scarcely appears seductive. Georges Gabory tells how

one summer day, in 1919, we were sitting on the terrace of the Café Pierrots, Place Pigalle, Max, Gris, Reverdy, etc . . . the whole group; suddenly, in the midst of our discussion of literature and art, spiced with a dash of malicious gossip—a large dash—Max went pale and plunged his nose into his glass of beer muttering 'Cécile!' A fat lady in a red suit was coming down Avenue Houdon. . . . She passed near us with an absentminded air. Had she recognized Max? And did she remember the Boulevard Barbès?[36]

By the time Jacob narrated his life for Guiette, he was a figure of minor legend. His life, as presented to his scribe, had the polish of expert fiction. His heart's truth at the separation from Cécile must have been less composed. Whatever his relief at being rid of her, his feelings cannot have been simple: he had experienced one more rupture with a conventional life. An intimate attachment, however ludicrous, had been broken, leaving him once again alone. An early poem from the Doucet manuscript, written on the same notebook paper and in the same ink and handwriting as "I've lost the apple trees," and therefore probably dating back to 1901 before the episode with Cécile, suggests the core of pain in Jacob's experience of love. There is no way to gauge the degree of fiction in this draft, but it suggests a lived disappointment:

> The pain you have caused me is buried in my soul
> As the beech tree's strange fruit lies in deepest soil.[37]

The poem portrays the lover as a betrayed child, the unworthy beloved simply as "O woman":

> My crime was to love like a child at prayer
> My crime, O woman, was to have chosen you
> My crime was to have given my entire life
> To one not worth my love, unfit to be held dear.

Whatever the rejection at the source of the poem—and its "woman" may camouflage a male lover—the crisis leads, as in other early poems, to a paroxysm of nostalgia for the childhood home with its hills and farms, the family house and shop, his boyish reading and wax sculpting, the great chestnut trees with their "opulent arms," the Odet River. It concludes by turning to God:

Listen, O my Lord, in whom I trust, hear my call!
Would you console a soul, and possess it all?

II.

THROUGHOUT 1903, JACOB at least enjoyed the solace of Picasso's company in letters, which abounded in affection, wit, and news of his painting. The most frequently recurring phrase was "*Ye trabaille*" (I'm working). During the summer Picasso inquired whether Max had a vacation from Paris-France and invited him to Barcelona. In August he described, and sketched, one of that year's blue figures. Another refrain was the lack of cash, which prevented him from executing all the paintings he had in mind.

After leaving Paris-France, Max Jacob, too, had to cope with a want of cash. "So!" he told Béalu in 1943. "There I was on the floorboards of a narrow garret, at 33 boulevard Barbès at the corner of the Rue Poulet. 'What do you know how to do? Art criticism? That's over!' I had no more contacts in the world of theaters and newspapers since I'd become a department store clerk."[38] What he *did* know how to do, he thought, was to tell stories. He sat down to produce a juvenile potboiler.

Having handed over his entire month's pay to Cécile, he couldn't even afford to buy bread. Not surprisingly, the story he composed, "Histoire du Roi Kaboul Ier et du marmiton Gauwain" (The Story of King Kaboul the First and the Scullion Gauwain), revolves around gastronomy. To fuel the work, he arranged with a baker to deliver bread to his door; when she came, each morning, he wheezed that he was too sick to get out of bed and would pay for it later.[39] With this system, he nourished himself for the six weeks it took him to write his story. "I never polished my style and scratched over the *whiches* and *who's* and the commas, as I did for this tale, which had to be perfect," he told Guiette.

It is perfect, in its way. Twining the conventions of the fairytale with a parody of municipal life in the Third Republic, the story follows the rise of a talented scullion, Gauwain, through adventures culinary, amorous, diplomatic, and military, to his winning of the kingdom and the hand of Princesse Julie. Jacob's apprenticeships stood him in good stead; in its medley of styles, the story satirizes class pretensions, Republican patriotism, and grandiosity. Scratching away in his freezing room on a diet of bread and water, Max Jacob imagined royal menus: "flaky almond pastries with vanilla and cream; flowers crystallized in sugar; maraschino, raspberry, pistachio, jam, and cherry ice-creams; Peruvian chestnut jelly."[40] The tale earned him a fairytale success when he ran into an acquaintance called Gaston Courtillier who worked for the publishing house Picard and Kaan. Jacob presented his story. It was accepted on condition that all religious references be removed; in this year of fierce anticlerical legislation, a book to be used as a prize in public schools had to have "church" replaced by "town hall," "priest" by "schoolteacher," and so forth.[41] Jacob emerged with the sum of thirty francs. With this treasure, he replenished the oil in his lamp, bought tobacco, paid the baker, and went out to dinner in a restaurant, a meal that appeared to him "the best of his life." He topped off the evening at the theater.

Encouraged, Jacob produced another story, "Le Géant du soleil" (The Sun Giant). "We've already published you," they told him at Picard and Kaan; but Courtillier sent him over to a new publisher, the Librairie générale. Not only was his story accepted: he was commissioned to turn it into a book. The publisher, Gaston Bonnier (of the Academy of Sciences, noted Jacob, ever alert to pomposity), reported to him that a reader for the house had declared, "The young man who wrote this has a brilliant future."

"I wrote to my family," said Max Jacob. "They invited me to write the book in Quimper, where they received me like the prodigal son."[42]

Part II

CHAPTER 5

THE BATEAU LAVOIR

I.

The prodigal son did not linger long at home. He wrote the children's book quickly, but by the time he returned to Paris, manuscript in hand, the editor had changed his mind.[1]

While in Quimper, Jacob not only turned his story "The Sun Giant" into a book. He conceived *Le Terrain Bouchaballe*, the novel drawn from the full comic register of his native city, which was at this time roiled with controversy.[2] Two years earlier, in the local newspaper, Quimper's librarian had described gangs of royalists coming to blows in the streets with angry Republican laborers.[3] By 1904, the town erupted in battles over the Couchouren heritage, the orchard on the riverbank that had been left to the city as a site for an old people's home. The factions had been quarreling for ten years, and the scandal precipitated the mayor's early death.[4] Now the new theater—a rococo pavilion with French windows, balconies, a polychrome faience tympanum, and a quadrangular dome meant to suggest Monte Carlo or Vichy—opened in a splash of festivity. The inauguration took place with a performance of Gounod in which, the local paper remarked, the star soprano "sang each note exactly as it was written." From this stew of scandal, political intrigue, and the provincial dream of art, Jacob would create *Le Terrain Bouchaballe*.[5]

The province and the capital: these were the poles of Jacob's life. For now, the city exerted the strongest pull. By March, he was back in Paris, living with his brother Jacques, a tailor, at 33 boulevard Barbès. On March 19 the sculptor Julio González wrote to Picasso, still in Barcelona, that he had seen Jacob taking some drawings of Picasso's to a publisher.[6] Jacob was eagerly awaiting his friend's return. On March 31 he wrote inviting the painter to live in the rooms he shared with Jacques; he had a mattress ready for him on the floor. And though he had had to sell books to buy stamps for the letter, he expected money soon.[7]

The money would have been payment for his children's book, *Histoire de Roi Kaboul Ier et du marmiton Gauwain*, and for "The Sun Giant," which was coming out as a story in *Les Lectures de la semaine* even though the book contract had been withdrawn. His satirical prose piece "The Sarahmitaine's Free Gift" had just appeared in *Le Sourire*. In this vignette, a sentimental lithograph offered as a promotion in a store reveals the greed and opportunism of a whole cast of characters, from clerks to bourgeois clients to their maid to the ragpickers who live by recycling society's vanities. The aesthetic that would become known as Modernist is already visible in Jacob's assault on description: "It's beside the point to describe a winter dawn. If you care to read a description of this type of meteorological phenomenon, you'll find it in any well-made novel of manners."[8]

With a title deranging the name of the famous department store La Samaritaine into a camp allusion to the aging Sarah Bernhardt, "The Sarahmitaine's Free Gift" is a slight piece. But Jacob had already used this sort of material in dissonant and savvy poems. The poets who would soon become his companions, Guillaume Apollinaire and André Salmon, were also beginning to publish their poems; while their work at this stage was still redolent of Symbolism, Jacob was making an edgy art of satire and ventriloquism.

A good example is "Invitation to the Voyage" from 1903. Evoking and rejecting the *luxe, calme et volupté* of Baudelaire's canonical poem, Jacob's verses hew roughly to an eight-syllable line. His rhymes are equally disturbing, sometimes rhyming the same word (*couler l'eau / menthes à l'eau;* running water/ mint in water) and often rhyming a Romantic word with a technological one: *rameaux/vélos* (boughs/bicycles); *machines/aubépine* (machines/hawthorn). The last stanza is a minicritique of a whole Romantic literature of escape, filtered through the lingo of commerce and advertising that was, after all, Max Jacob's mother tongue:

> For sale: four deserts, genuine,
> With easy access to the train line.
> See owner-agent of assign
> > M. Chocarneau,
> > 18 boulevard Carnot.[9]

Years before Picasso and Braque incorporated fragments of newspapers into their paintings, Jacob recognized the flotsam and jetsam of public language as material for poetry. He recognized, also, the value of distorting convention: the deliberately clumsy rhymes and syllable counts mock nineteenth-century mellifluousness as the poem's modern modes of transport—trains, cars, bicycles, flying machines—mock Romantic and Symbolist tropical seascapes and drunken boats. Jacob dedicated "Invitation to the Voyage" to Louis Bergerot, about whom little is known except that he was a friend of both Jacob's and Picasso's and worked in a train station. Picasso, writing from Barcelona, had asked Jacob to send his greetings to the Bergerot family and had written to Bergerot at the same time asking for news of Max.[10] Bergerot turns up, touchingly, in a note on a copy of another of Jacob's poems in the Doucet manuscript of *Le Christ à Montparnasse;* on "Like Mary Magdalen," Jacob wrote, "copied by Louis Bergerot, now employed at the Gare de l'Est. My first fan."

Looking forward to Picasso's arrival, Jacob hoped to recreate the intimacy they had shared a year and a half earlier, writing that he had enough mattresses and blankets for two, but that if Picasso preferred to be on his own, he should choose a studio, not a hotel. And Jacob asked him to bring back his (Jacob's) trunk, which was convenient for storing poems.[11] This trunk would become famous.

||

THE BIRTHPLACE OF CUBISM, the Bateau Lavoir (Washerwomen's Barge), the crazy building at 13 rue Ravignan in Montmartre, has inspired an enormous literature. It is here that Picasso would live with his first great love, Fernande Olivier; here he drew together his gang of fellow creators, *la bande à Picasso*, painters and poets who would change the forms of art for the new century.

Picasso arrived in Paris on April 13 with his friend the painter Sebastià Junyer Vidal. They installed themselves in the studio just vacated by the Basque sculptor Paco Durrio. Junyer Vidal paid the rent. This time Picasso's journey was well organized, and it would be his definitive move to France.

Called "La Maison du Trappeur" (The Trapper's House), later renamed Le Bateau Lavoir by Salmon or Jacob, this ex-piano factory and ex-locksmith shop could be entered on the first floor from the Rue Ravignan, but in the rear it plunged three stories to the Rue Garreau. In the 1880s it had been a haunt for anarchists, Gauguin visited often, and the poet-dramatist Paul Fort lived there while directing his Symbolist theater across the square. Jacob, who visited every day and later lived there for a while, described it often. In 1937 he remembered:

> Picasso returned with what the dealers have called the Blue Period paintings, vaguely imitative of El Greco. He led me to the crown of the Butte Montmartre. We scorned all previous art and all the schools, and in the evenings, to amuse ourselves, we improvised plays, without spectators, which we never wrote down and which concluded in wild bursts of laughter. He lived at 13 rue Ravignan . . . , a sort of hangar made of ill-fitting boards, at once cellar and attic, poised on a kind of cliff Montmartre still hardly conceals with its huge new apartment houses. Our neighbors were quasi-laundresses, and a fruit and vegetable vendor, and those poor people complained of the noise Picasso's bitch Frika made at night with her chain.[12]

Fernande Olivier, who had been living in the building since 1901 as the mistress and model of the sculptor Laurent Debienne, recalled that the place was "an icebox in winter, a steam bath in summer."[13] The tenants shared one toilet on the ground floor and fetched their water either from the one faucet down there or from the public fountain in the middle of the Place Ravignan.

André Salmon, a poet the same age as Picasso who had been born in Paris but brought up in St. Petersburg, had returned to France for his military service and now, discharged, was knocking about Paris looking for jobs in journalism. Good-natured, boyish, and handsome, he folded easily into the bohemia of the Latin Quarter. He made his way to the Bateau Lavoir later in 1904. "Imagine a strange barracks made of boards," he wrote in his drug-drowsy novel, *Le Manuscrit trouvé dans un chapeau* (The Manuscript Found in a Hat), published in 1919 with drawings by Picasso. "Four floors on the side of the Butte Montmartre, arranged in such a way, split up among so many steep and tortuous streets, that three of the four floors of this house were actually ground floors." Salmon described the fruit and vegetable vendor, Sorieul, who sold mussels of mysterious provenance during the winter, and whose drunken son worked as a sandwich ad-man and bawled out the bohemian artists. "Oh! Strange nights of the Rue Ravignan," remembered Salmon, "the terrifying house where we found hanged men and whose roofs opened up, hurling drunkards into mysterious wells. I wrote verses while caressing my cat Zamir, the wind lifted the Butte Montmartre right up, the planks of the ark groaned. Why didn't the wind carry off the boat while M. Picasso's huge dogs barked lugubriously, shaking their chains at night?"[14]

Salmon didn't invent the deaths. A German painter plunged to his death while clearing snow off a skylight, and another German, Wiegels, hanged himself in his studio. But Salmon exaggerated the size of the dogs. Frika, a mongrel Picasso had brought from Barcelona, was hardly huge, and the modest size of Feo and Gat, dogs he acquired in Montmartre, can be judged from Picasso's drawings in Salmon's book.[15] "O Picasso and you, Max Jacob, enchanter and poet, and you, shade of my Guillaume [Apollinaire],"

Salmon apostrophized. "Do you remember our past nights? Our nights of madness, laziness, and willpower when the storm tortured the ship, from keel to prow."[16]

Junyer Vidal soon returned to Barcelona, so during Picasso's first six weeks at the Bateau Lavoir, Jacob had his friend to himself except for the company of the Catalan sculptor Manolo and a Gypsy guitarist who slept on the floor. Jacob visited every day. The complex tone of their friendship, tinged with Jacob's adoration, irony, and self-abasement, can be gleaned from this memoir the poet composed in 1931:

> It's 1904, Picasso is already strong, but his visitors are still only the picturesque Manolo and a poor little Jew (that's what Vollard called him) who doesn't believe he's a poet. I lived at Barbès. I arrived at 13 rue Ravignan early in the morning. To my own bare bed, and my dark little worktable, I preferred this doorway that had pretensions to grandeur a hundred years earlier, and Picasso's narrow door decorated with bits of practical advice. It was at the end of a catwalk corridor, above the invisible cliffs of Montmartre geology, at the end of a cliff of stairs.
>
> I called out his name. Hardly awake, Picasso opened the door. I had arrived across all the stone steps of Montmartre and oceanic Paris seen from on high.[17]

The romance of friendship and of a heroic new art colors Jacob's recollection: the giddy interior heights of the studio, the mythic panorama of the city spread out below. Self-torturing Jewishness remained a vital element, one that Jacob could not forget and could not allow his reader to forget. How could he forget? Wherever he turned, he met anti-Semitism, sometimes in blandly unconscious form, as in Fernande Olivier's description of Jean Moréas, the Greek poet who reigned at the Symbolist restaurant La Closerie des Lilas and detested Jews. When a Jewish writer said, "When I die," Moréas replied, "But my dear friend, you've been dead for years."[18]

Jacob was far from craven in his relations with Picasso. Salmon remembered him in the role of elder friend, initiator, and magus, calling the young painter *mon petit.*[19] The friendship between Picasso and Jacob in this period left relics in drawing: Jacob's ink sketch of Picasso in profile, annotated in Picasso's hand, "Portrait made by Max Jacob," reveals an exaggeratedly large head of dark hair—yet another homage to genius?— an intensely focused eye, and the thin mustache that would soon disappear.[20] Picasso's portrait of Jacob, on café notepaper, shows the writer, also in profile, with a high, bald forehead; scruffy hair still adorning the back of his skull; a dark, intelligent gaze further darkened by a pince-nez; a firm, compressed mouth; and strong chin.[21] This is a portrait of power, not of pathos, and it shows that the bond between the two men was not simply a matter of subservience on the part of one and dominance by the other. There are also two self-portraits by Picasso from 1904 inscribed to Jacob. In these rapid sketches, Picasso has already shaved off the mustache, and across his forehead falls the telltale wing of black hair.[22]

Picasso's other close friend from this period, Manolo, also turns up in drawings by Jacob owned by Picasso.[23] Manolo—Manuel Martinez Hugué—was one of the most piquant of the characters who populated the Latin Quarter and Montmartre. Picasso knew him from Barcelona and from his stay in Paris in 1901. An adventurer, a not untalented artist, and an occasional thief, Manolo surprised even the worldly-wise Parisians with his pranks. Not only did he provide material for endless comic sagas, but he was the go-between in some of the crucial encounters in the formation of *la bande à Picasso.*

In Jacob's drawing, Manolo looks slyly sidewise; his face is lined, and his dark hair erupts in tufts over his temples. As Salmon recounted it, Manolo was the illegitimate son of a Spanish general and a mother Manolo never mentioned. He hardly knew his father, who was off oppressing Cuba during Manolo's youth. The boy grew up in the slums of Barcelona, where he became an accomplished thief. When he was about fourteen, his father returned, wanted to inspect his son, and had the police track him down. Manolo was hauled up before the general and endured a scolding and a dose of paternal advice, and in the farewell embrace—the last time they were ever to meet—the boy stole his father's gold watch. At some point he skipped across the border to France to avoid the draft, and he stayed

on in Paris, drawing, sculpting, and living by his wits. "I don't know anything stupider or sadder than professional thieves," he used to say, "those
thieves who think they have to steal every day or every night. There they
are, peacefully at a bistro or with a girlfriend, and the poor guys look up at
the clock and say, 'Shit! Already eleven o'clock. . . . Have to go steal.' "[24]

Manolo stole only on inspiration. Once when he was staying in Paco
Durrio's studio during the owner's absence, he sold Durrio's Gauguins
to Vollard (who later returned them).[25] He ran a chimerical lottery for
sculpture he never produced. He once sold a pawnshop ticket for what was
supposed to be a fancy camera to a stray acquaintance in a café: when the
ticket was redeemed, it yielded a stinking old mattress, but Manolo was
long gone. In spite of the Gauguin episode, he rarely stole from friends,
but he did pinch clothes from Max Jacob and Léon-Paul Fargue (returning
Jacob's trousers as too disreputable to sell). On one occasion he carried off
the wallet from Picasso's blue velvet vest that was hanging on a nail in the
studio. Picasso crossed Paris by hackney cab, tracking him to his hole of
a room in the attic of a hotel in the Latin Quarter, and menaced him with
a revolver. Jacob told the story:

> As Picasso is wise enough to demand his property back without
> exacting vengeful humiliations, he made the trembling guilty party
> climb into the cab, and having accompanied him silently back to the
> hangars, he took up his painting where he had left off, letting lad-
> ders, stretchers, easels, canvases play their docile role in this drama
> of Honor Saved. "*Cré cogne*! How about that! Just what I said! It was
> under the paper with meat scraps for the cat." Picasso contemplated
> his picture. "*Oui bienne*! Put it in the pocket of the velvet vest," he
> said, without turning around.[26]

Picasso was working his way through, and out of, his Blue Period with
its famished beggars and prostitutes. A typical work is the etching *The
Frugal Repast*, a picture of an emaciated couple that he was still refining
when Fernande Olivier first visited his studio in the summer of 1904.[27] It

was Jacob who traipsed around to dealers to try to sell these visions of destitution. He remembered:

> The dealers who boast these days about having discovered Picasso called him a madman. "Your friend has gone out of his mind," Monsieur V. [no doubt Vollard] said to me. . . . One day when Picasso was sick and I had gone to try to interest this same Monsieur V. in a landscape, . . . he said scathingly, "The bell tower is crooked" and turned his back on me. Picasso sold drawings for ten *sous* to a mattress dealer on the Rue des Martyrs, and the ten *sous* were gratefully received.[28]

The Rue des Martyrs was well named. A steep street heading up to the Butte Montmartre, its name seems emblematic for these years of struggle for artistic survival. The mattress salesman was Père Soulié, an alcoholic who dealt in pictures on the side because so many of his clients were poor painters who couldn't pay cash. Fernande Olivier suspected him of acting as a front for the editor, essayist, and underground art dealer Louis Libaude, whose pen name was Henri Delormel; depicted as a phallus by Picasso, Delormel was famous for cheating artists.[29] Jacob also knocked on Berthe Weill's door and occasionally managed to sell a drawing or gouache of Picasso's to the tightfisted Clovis Sagot, who ran a gallery on Vollard's street, the Rue Laffitte.

No longer a store clerk, Jacob was writing poetry because Picasso believed in him.[30] He told Guiette, "Picasso had come back from Spain and found Max desperate over the loss of his job. 'What kind of life is that?' Picasso asked. 'Live like the poets!' "[31] The imperative to follow a life of art extended even to physical appearance. To "live like a poet," he had to shave his beard, take off his pince-nez, and wear a monocle.[32]

In 1904 Jacob not only "lived like" a poet. He was writing groundbreaking poems. When he told Tristan Tzara in 1916 that it was only in 1905 that he "became" a poet, he must have been referring to his first serious publication, the five poems Apollinaire printed in *Les Lettres modernes* in May 1905. But by then Jacob had been writing for years. "Written in 1904," which would appear in print for the first time only in 1921 in *Le Laboratoire central*, shows him already in command of sophisticated maneuvers that we recognize in hindsight as Modernist: a mobile geography, shifting and plural pronouns and centers of consciousness, discontinuities in tone and register, nonsequiturs, abrupt juxtapositions of reference and address, and a dissonant prosody. "Written in 1904" is a fine example of this art of controlled discontinuity. Though there have been objections to the idea of Cubist poetics, the poem's disturbances do present a literary analogy to the disruptions Picasso and Braque would introduce in the depiction of objects in space—three years later.[33]

WRITTEN IN 1904
[fragments]

If I recall, the place of Pilate's tomb
Was in Vienna, or else in Draguignan
Abd-el-Kader's sons snapped photos there
To hang up as ex-votos in fresh air
Goddesses spun their silk from ocean foam
And fished for golden coinage in the ponds
Washerwomen beat the hours to pass the time
And the Loire revealed its soul at every bend. . . .
The sky squeezes two atmospheres into one stair
So patriarchs could prophesy from there
White sailors dressed in Oceanic blue
Offered Pilate's glove to lordly Baal
And telepathy in telegrams seeping through
Inspired in all the cult of Pilate's soul
The politicians and the men of Theodose
Had also taken of Pilate a mighty dose
Pantheons paralyzed for a hundred years
Are stirred by lightning and by blood besmeared.[34]

"Written in 1904" not only veers wildly in time and space, from Dra-guignan to Vienna, from biblical Jerusalem to Paris; it imagines Paris itself in motion, like a barge moving up the river. Male and female identi-ties blend: "I have the prettiest arms, you the prettiest tits / Together we'd make a perfect woman." What keeps this centrifugal poem coherent is the abstraction of poetic form: the kitsch alexandrines and rhyming couplets of the opening and closing passages provide the grid. "Written in 1904" comments comically on its own deformation of inherited form. "Double sixes! My turn to pause!" refers to a throw of the dice, an image taken from Mallarmé's radical work *Un coup de dés* (A Throw of the Dice) that Jacob would recall in the title of his collection of prose poems in 1917, *Le Cornet à dés* (The Dice Cup). But it also describes, saucily, the classi-cal, twelve-syllable alexandrine line, complete with the central caesura: "My turn to pause!" In "Written in 1904," the multiplied consciousness, the social satire, the jangling of high diction with slang, the hallucinatory geographies, the puns, all set the stage for an interpenetration of natural and supernatural realms, and the liberation of the soul from the social self. The poem maintains a comic relation to Christianity—it depicts, after all, a world devoted to Pilate—but Jesus appears as an opening between realities, and the poem concludes in a vision of worldly glory exploding in lightning and blood.

A definition of poetic modernity that Jacob later gave Marcel Béalu describes principles he adopted in 1904: "complexity in form; dominance of interior harmony over meaning; speed in the association of images, ideas, and words; love of words; surprises, willed or not; the appearance of dream or dream itself; invisible rhythms."[35] The disjunctive method permitted exploration of his perpetual themes, *humour/amour* (humor and love, a key pun in French), and his descent into the unconscious where, he came to feel, he led the way for other poets.[36]

Another early poem, "Like Mary Magdalen," more private and lyrical than "Written in 1904," presents a self-portrait, only slightly veiled. A poem of frustrated love, human and divine, in the Doucet manuscript it is called "Fortifs," slang for the old city walls. It is dedicated to Picasso.

The revisions are revealing. Picasso drops out as the acknowledged emotional source, and the later placement of the poem under the aegis of the Magdalen provides a heterosexual frame while setting the private crisis in a Christian context of repentant love. "Fortifs" / "Like Mary Magdalen," however, expresses not repentance but distress. Unlike "Written in 1904," it has a single lyric consciousness, a persona defined by deprivation: separation from God in the deserted fortress and the storm-struck ship, separation—by implication—from the human beloved.

LIKE MARY MAGDALEN

My God, you gave me a soul of solitude
And in my heart, a fort untenanted
Ramparts that the owners long since fled.
My God, you gave me a monastic soul
A soul for whom your absence is a grief
Yearning for stars, devoted to art's control
Centrifugal like the spines on the holly leaf
And you rigged my vessel for tenderness
From the high shrouds hear the long-drawn wails
It's the wind of love, Lord, in my sails
Love, my God! Say rather, storm, distress
Ship-rammed heart
Ideally starred
How broken, downcast?
By lust! Alas![37]

As Picasso's life in Montmartre gathered momentum, Jacob retreated to Quimper for a long summer. He could live cheaply there in the family house where his sister Delphine and brother Gaston now helped their parents run the shops. The arrangement felt strained: it was difficult for his hardworking relatives to see that Max's bohemian life had borne much fruit. At the age of twenty-eight, he had published almost nothing. In Quimper, he wrote for hours on end and browsed about the town, nosing out gossip.

A notebook dated June 1904 gives a sense of his preoccupations. Jottings of gossip to be used in fiction (so-and-so sleeping with a peasant woman while his lodger pretends not to notice) alternate with literary musings ("Mallarmé is a botched project") and with aphorisms ("I spend the second part of my life suffering the pains I created in the first half"). He lists rhyme words, scribbles notes for drawings, and makes the odd piquant observation, such as the fact that the female spider devours its mate after copulation. Misogyny is a recurrent theme: he notes, "X writes to me about the state of his soul, 'Je suis affemmé'" (a pun on *femme* [woman] and *affamé* [hungry]: I am bewomaned). National politics flicker into the notebook with the idea for a story about the separation of church and state, a question agitating all France at that moment.[38]

On June 28 he wrote a sibylline postcard to Picasso, "Write me, 8 rue du Parc, Quimper."[39] He could not know it, but one phase of his friendship with Picasso was closing and a new one was about to open, when the Bateau Lavoir would become the center of a feverish group of artists and poets, and Jacob would have to share his idol with rival poets and with the first serious mistress in the young painter's life.

II.

IN THE SUMMER of 1904, Picasso was amusing himself with several women, principally a haunted-looking model named Madeleine who found her way into a number of his drawings and paintings.[40] Picasso was also seeing Margot Luc, the stepdaughter of Frédé who ran the bar, the Lapin Agile, and Alice, soon to become Alice Princet when she married the actuary Maurice Princet. But the significant encounter of the summer, and the only one to affect Max Jacob, was with Fernande Olivier.

Tall, full-bodied, and sultry-eyed, with a rampart of auburn hair piled above her forehead, Fernande was already living at the Bateau Lavoir when Picasso jokingly blocked her way one stormy afternoon that August 1904. He was holding a kitten, Fernande recalled, which he handed to her, laughing. She laughed also and a moment later visited his studio. Fernande had a striking visual memory: "Picasso, short, dark, thickset, troubled, troubling, with dark, deep, piercing, strange yes, almost immobile. Awkward gestures, feminine hands, sloppily dressed, badly groomed. A thick lock of hair, black and brilliant, slashed across his intelligent and stubborn forehead. Half bohemian, half workman in his dress; his hair, too long, brushed the collar of his shabby jacket."[41] In the studio, Fernande was amazed, intrigued, and a little put off by the morbid Blue Period paintings. She remembered the mattress propped up on blocks, the cast iron stove, and a chipped yellow bowl for a washbasin with a towel and a bit of soap. The only seats were a little black trunk and a cane chair. Easels and canvases crowded the space; tubes of paint lay scattered on the floor with paintbrushes and jars for turpentine. A tame white mouse lived in the drawer of the table.[42]

Fernande began seeing Picasso frequently, often to smoke opium with him. Picasso had begun experimenting with the drug and wanted to teach her: opium showed her the real meaning of the word *love,* she remembered.[43] But she did not move right in with this new lover. She had not yet extricated herself from the affair with Debienne, and soon after meeting Picasso, she took up in a desultory way with his friend Joaquim Sunyer. Picasso, for his part, was still seeing Madeleine. But when Jacob returned in September, it was with Fernande that he had to reckon. Picasso introduced them in the Place Ravignan, and Fernande observed, she said, "with some astonishment, this skipping little man with bizarre and penetrating eyes behind his lorgnon, ceremonious, looking pleased with himself, bowing very low with his hat in his hand."[44]

Fernande Olivier was one of the few women Jacob liked, and she in turn came to feel real affection for him. His sketch of her, however, doesn't lack for undertones. In "Wartime Bohemia in 1914" in *Le Roi de Béotie*, he recalled, "The painter's companion was Valeria, a woman whose beauty, both refined and heavy, brimming over with charm and imagination and all the features of a gentle and tumultuous personality, served, in turn, to attract and drive away the lovers of the new art and the artist's friends."[45] She, for her part, remembered his distrust of women, his sensitivity, his fear of being persecuted, which would sometimes lead to his storming off in a dudgeon. Then the group would be bored without him and would go hunt him down to coax him to return and amuse them with his stories and performances of poetry and comic opera.

THE MAIN FIGURES of *la bande à Picasso* met in the autumn of 1904 or early in 1905.[46] What really matters is not the precise date but the mythic structure of these meetings, all the participants recognizing afterward that they had witnessed the birth of a new world. Jacob struck the right note, the fairytale note, in his account to Guiette: "One morning as I arrived, as usual, from my lodgings on the Boulevard Barbès, Picasso, whom I hadn't seen the night before, told me that he'd spent the evening in a bar on the Rue d'Amsterdam with an astonishing man, Guillaume Apollinaire, and that he'd take me to meet him that very night."[47]

The illegitimate son of Angelica de Kostrowitzky, a daughter of minor Polish nobility, and an unknown father,[48] Guillaume Kostrowitzky, as he called himself in France, had been brought up in Rome, the city of his birth, until the age of seven, and then in Monte Carlo, where his mother worked at the Casino, luring customers to spend extravagantly.

In 1899 Guillaume experienced one of the scapegrace adventures that would eventually fill his fiction. Madame de Kostrowitzky and her lover, an Alsatian gambler, deposited Guillaume and his younger brother in a *pension* in the little town of Stavelot in eastern Belgium, near the famous resort at Spa. With the adults off trying to repair their fortunes, the boys were left for three months on their own with increasingly ragged clothes and worn-out shoes, and the *pension* bill mounting daily. It was here that Apollinaire began to create himself as a poet. The uncertain idyll concluded when the boys, on instructions from their mother, fled the *pension* at dawn, hiked through the woods, and caught a train to Paris. Guillaume Apollinaire entered Paris as a criminal, wanted for fraud.

In the capital, he had a period of odd jobs and poetic experimentation very like Jacob's: clerical work, ghostwriting, stenography. And he wrote poems, developing a chanting alexandrine line, verging, at times, on Ronsardian fullness. In 1901 he went to work as a tutor in the household of a German viscountess on the Rhine. A year later he returned with a broken heart and a sheaf of poems that gained him entry into one of the citadels of Symbolism, the magazine *La Plume* with its soirées in a cellar café in the Latin Quarter. By 1904 he was emerging as a poetic force.

TWO IMPISH CHARACTERS, Jean Mollet and Manolo, prepared the encounter of Picasso and Apollinaire, which was the meeting not only of two darkly inspired young masters but of two worlds: Apollinaire's Left Bank of late Symbolist poetry, and Picasso's Right Bank Montmartre of experimental painting. Mollet orbited around the poet to such an extent that he was jokingly called his "secretary." Manolo was one of Picasso's closest companions. First occurred the meeting of the two go-betweens. Mollet got to know Manolo in the Left Bank restaurant La Closerie des Lilas, the bastion of Symbolism. Manolo inveigled the baron—Apollinaire's nickname for Mollet—up to the Butte with a promise of a free meal; Frédé, who had recently taken over the seedy bar Au Lapin Agile (or Lapin à Gill, after the cartoonist André Gill, who ran it in the 1880s), often fed artists for free if they turned up hungry and penniless after one a.m., as Manolo and Mollet did one night.[49] During that first visit, Mollet was so entranced by Frédé's singing and guitar playing that he drank late, passed out, and woke next morning in a strange bed with a pretty young woman asking him if he'd like some cocoa. No wonder he became a habitué. On the walls of this smoky haunt, which the local thugs (*apaches*) and their girls shared with the artists, Mollet saw paintings by Picasso—though perhaps not yet the stark, Lautrec-like *Au Lapin Agile* that Picasso would paint in 1904.

Soon after that first visit, Mollet met the artist himself at Le Lapin Agile. Manolo's surprise and joy at seeing Picasso suggest that the meeting took place in the spring of 1904, when the artist had just returned from Barcelona: "When we arrived, Manolo let out a cry, 'Pablo,' and when the effusions and embraces had calmed down, Manolo introduced me. Before me stood Pablo Picasso, about whom he had so often spoken."[50] Once again an encounter with Picasso transformed the life of the observer:

This man was not large, but thickset, very dark, and his physiognomy expressed overwhelming force of will; but his eyes, especially his eyes, had a fascinating expression; they were somewhat hard, but became extremely soft when he smiled. Everything in him drew one to him, and one felt that one must attach oneself to him, that forever after one's life would be linked to his. . . . I have had only one other great emotion in my life; it was when I heard Guillaume Apollinaire recite his poems.[51]

Mollet's gifts, one can see from this passage, were his perception of genius and his capacity for devotion. Apollinaire, who had by this time drawn Mollet and Salmon into his first editorial adventure, the literary journal the *Festin d'Esope*, had taken to holding court in Austin's Fox and the Criterion, two English bars on the Rue d'Amsterdam near the Gare Saint-Lazare, where he would catch the last train home to his mother's villa in Le Vésinet. One evening in one of these bars—Mollet and Picasso remembered it as Austin's, Jacob as the Criterion[52]—Mollet presented his prize, Picasso, to Apollinaire. Picasso described the scene to Brassaï: "It's through him [Mollet] that I got to know Guillaume Apollinaire. . . . He brought me one day to a bar near the Gare Saint-Lazare—Austin's, rue d'Amsterdam—where the poet used to go often. And it was in that same bar that I in turn introduced Max Jacob to Guillaume Apollinaire. . . . Mollet was an honest-to-God marriage-broker. . . . He loved to make matches."[53]

Picasso made the next match, bringing Jacob to Austin's. In 1937, the details of the meeting were still vivid in Jacob's memory:

Apollinaire was smoking a short-stemmed pipe and expatiating on Petronius and Nero to some rather vulgar-looking people whom I took to be jobbers of some sort or traveling salesmen. He was wearing a stained, light-colored suit, and a tiny straw hat was perched atop his famous pear-shaped head. He had hazel eyes, terrible and gleaming, a bit of curly blond hair fell over his forehead, his mouth looked like a little pimento, he had strong limbs, a broad chest looped across by a platinum watch chain, and ring on his finger. The poor boy was always being taken for a rich man because his mother—an adventuress, to put it politely—clothed him from head to toe. He was a clerk in a bank in the Rue Le Peletier. Without interrupting his talk, he stretched out a hand like a tiger's paw over the marble-topped table. He stayed in his seat until he was finished. Then the three of us went out, and we began that life of three-cornered friendship which lasted almost until the war, never leaving each other whether for work, meals, or fun.[54]

In "Souvenirs sur Picasso" and in the memoir dictated to Guiette, Jacob emphasized the initial trio. "Picasso, Max Jacob, Apollinaire," he told Guiette. "It was then [1905] that was created—but only for a few initiates—the new aesthetics. Picasso made a modern poet out of Apollinaire, who was still immersed in Symbolism. From that point on, the trio determined the poetic climate."[55] In 1927 Jacob again described Apollinaire's handshake: "He put out his hand to me, and in that instant began a triple friendship that lasted until the death of Apollinaire."[56] Two points stand out in these accounts. One is the gentle setting aside of Salmon from the original nucleus; the other is the elegiac coloring that Apollinaire's early death gives to each reminiscence.[57]

Apollinaire had, in every sense, a tiger's paw. Physically imposing, protean, and restless, already a published poet and founder of a magazine, Apollinaire dominated while Jacob could only amuse, intrigue, and seduce. To the Dadaist Tzara, Jacob later described Apollinaire as resembling "at the same time, a Farnese Hercules and an English aesthete."[58] Apollinaire had an exuberant erotic appetite, mainly heterosexual, with a taste for perversities that delighted Picasso. In a year or so the poet would compose two witty pornographic novels (*Les Onze mille verges*, The Eleven Thousand Rods, and *Les Exploits d'un jeune Don Juan*, The Exploits of a Young Don Juan) and with a couple of friends would surreptitiously catalogue the locked collection of erotica in the Bibliothèque Nationale.[59] Over the next few years Apollinaire would pick up extra money editing selections of the Marquis de Sade, translating Aretino, and writing anonymous porn novels. This erotic erudition not only amused Picasso; it opened darker worlds to him that called to forces in his own nature. With Apollinaire,

Picasso could share fantasies unappealing to Jacob; it was to Apollinaire that the painter gave the steamy 1905 gouache of lesbians making love, *The Embrace*, which the poet kept by his bed.[60] It was to Picasso that Apollinaire wrote in 1906, with manly brutality, about a girlfriend: "Maybe I'll come to Spain, but without Yette whom I've liquidated because she really laughed too much."[61]

It was not only erotic curiosity that drew Picasso and Apollinaire together. Both were emerging from Symbolism and were intrigued by figures of Harlequins and street entertainers. "It was in 1905," wrote Jacob. "Picasso and Apollinaire understood each other perfectly. Picasso was painting Harlequins and *Saltimbanques;* Apollinaire was putting them in his poems. The face of Apollinaire appears often in his [Picasso's] works. So does mine. We never left each other; we went to wait for Guillaume Apollinaire when he got off work at the bank that employed him on the Rue Le Peletier. We had lunch and dinner together."[62]

The Harlequin kinship bore almost immediate fruit. Apollinaire sent Picasso drafts of two Harlequin poems that would wind up, revised, in his book *Alcools;*[63] Picasso's first drawing of Apollinaire appears on a bookplate representing the poet as a massive king at his table holding aloft a goblet of wine.[64] Apollinaire's Rabelaisian hunger was as legendary as his restlessness and his feats of strategic farting. In his 1916 novel *Le Poète assassiné* (The Assassinated Poet), he would portray himself as a force of appetite raised to a metaphysical principle: "His eyes devoured everything they touched, and when his eyelids closed rapidly like jaws, they gulped down the universe."[65]

The insistence on the triumvirate of Picasso, Apollinaire, and Jacob obscures the fact that only eight days later Salmon entered the group.[66] It also raises questions about what we might call psychological math. From Jacob's point of view, an original pair (Jacob and Picasso) expanded to become a mythic threesome. But three is an unstable number. In histories of the period written now, one pair yields to another: Apollinaire is seen as replacing Jacob as Picasso's court poet. It is also the case that Picasso and Apollinaire won worldwide fame, whereas Jacob never had more than a specialized notoriety. Jacob's friendship with his massively talented and more worldly-wise rival would develop, over the years, in rhythms of affection, jealousy, hurt, resentment, and admiration.

Picasso and Apollinaire, at any rate, were in no hurry to leave Jacob out. Picasso's first poem seems to have been addressed to Jacob after the fateful meetings. Picasso wrote from Apollinaire's house; in witty reciprocity, the painter sent a poem to thank Jacob for a drawing, alluded to Jacob's favorite food of poverty (rice), and signed himself "Moses" in a nod to the poem by Alfred de Vigny that Jacob and Picasso had admired together on the Boulevard Voltaire. Apollinaire is given the code name "Stendhal":

> Poem to thank you for your drawing
> It's Sunday I'm at Guillaume's
> And I've put on my white velvet pants
> My big red sweater
> And my black vest
> I'm by the fire with my pipe in my hand
> And I think of you of the rice the other night of your logical lines
>
> Moses and Stendhal[67]

Here is when André Salmon enters the story. We can observe the scene both through his eyes and through Jacob's. In the Guiette memoir:

> One winter morning, as I arrived in the hallway that led to the studio, a tall thin young man asked me where Picasso lived. I asked, "Are you M. André Salmon?"
>
> He replied, "Are you M. Max Jacob?"
>
> One minute later we were sitting on the dark red mattress with no legs that served as a sofa in the studio. Salmon became Picasso's friend and mine.
>
> The group of artists was formed.[68]

Guiette went on to describe the expansion of the group and the friendships with Matisse, Braque, and Gris. Picasso was the sun at the center of this solar system. Suddenly, word got out, and studio life in Montmartre became crowded, as Paul Fort brought his Symbolists from the Closerie des Lilas, Jules Romains enticed his acolytes, and artists, writers, and artistic tourists flooded in from Spain, Holland, Germany, and Italy.[69] In this chapter dictated to Guiette, Jacob contrived to pay back whatever honor he had previously subtracted from Salmon, describing how among the poets of Montparnasse who thronged to see Picasso, Salmon was considered "the first." "He has assumed a still greater position since then," added Jacob, referring no doubt to Salmon's fecundity as journalist and art critic. To call Salmon "the first" among the Left Bank poets was a flourish: one would have to set aside Fort, Moréas, Jarry, and Apollinaire himself. But the long friendship between Jacob and Salmon would be marked by such generosities.

In 1905, at age twenty-four, Salmon was hardly "first," but he was establishing himself in Symbolist circles through his amiability and a poetic talent more facile than forceful. He had helped Apollinaire run *Le Festin d'Esope* for its nine issues and had published a number of his poems there; he had had poems in the Symbolist pages of *La Plume;* in 1905 his poems began to appear in Mécislas Golberg's *Revue littéraire de Paris et Champagne*. His friendship with Paul Fort was paying off; when the first issue of Fort's *Vers et Prose* appeared, Salmon was on the masthead as secretary; his own poems would be printed there, and in 1905 his first book of poems came out in the series Fort launched.

Salmon would be one of Jacob's most loyal friends. He portrayed Jacob sympathetically as Septime Fébur, the poet-magus, in the novel *La Négresse du Sacré-Coeur* (The Black Venus), and he later wrote a book about him, *Max Jacob, poète, peintre, mystique et homme de qualité* (Max Jacob, Poet, Painter, Mystic, and Gentleman). In a memoir, Salmon recounted the scene of their meeting at Picasso's door, seeing it in the stark light of Jacob's death:

"M. Max Jacob?"
"M. André Salmon?"
They would never abandon one another. For life, for death . . . Death![70]

Salmon had met Picasso the night before, led to the Bateau Lavoir by the indefatigable Manolo. The painter described, at length, his friend Jacob, and now during this first long day in Picasso's studio, Jacob scintillated, gossiped, and performed, leaving Salmon indeed "dazzled" but a little overwhelmed.[71] Jacob told so many malicious stories about his relatives that the next day he sent Salmon a postcard, asking him not to repeat the tales. Picasso added a "Greetings to Salmon," and Max a postscript, alerting Salmon to meet them at Picasso's show the following Monday at two-thirty "precisely."[72] To follow up that first meeting, Jacob proposed a picnic a few days later, even though it was winter. He liked the old city walls to the west rising over the Bois de Boulogne, so he and Salmon trekked from Montmartre almost halfway across Paris to the old *fortifs*, which had already given their name to Jacob's poem to Picasso. Dressed in the black frock coat tailored for him by his father, Jacob drew cream cakes, jellied meats, sausages, and bread from the basket and—as Salmon remembered—waited for his new friend to speak. This was to be Salmon's day to reveal himself. "How we strove to charm each other," Jacob recalled years later. "It was ridiculous and charming and necessary. After that, everything would come naturally."[73]

III.

COOKING WAS DIFFICULT in the studios, so the gang often rollicked down the Butte to eat at the grubby little restaurant run by Père Vernin on the Rue Cavalotti, near the Place de Clichy. Vernin sometimes charitably forgot the bills the artists ran up, and they could usually count on a coarse but hearty meal there. Actors as well as painters and writers turned up. There Jacob met the hot-tempered actor Marcel Olin, who would introduce him to the *Fantômas* mystery series and who would die in battle in World War I. And there he met Charles Dullin, who would run the Théâtre de l'Atelier from 1921 to 1929 and produce Jacob's play *Chantage*. There, also, sat Maurice Princet, the dour actuary, with Picasso's former casual girlfriend Alice, who would shortly run away with the painter André Derain.[74]

Gallivanting down the hill for yet another greasy meal at Vernin's, the companions would chant Jacob's ditty:

> I'm tired of eating at Vernin's
> But that's where everybody goes
> Because they serve wine in thimblefuls
> And helpings of cream cheese.[75]

Under this gaiety lay the somber fact of poverty. Vernin's was situated a few doors down from a pawnshop, but there were times when no one had anything to pawn. And there was the seriousness, the demanding riskiness of the work in which these young artists were engaged. Picasso never stopped for an instant, said Jacob, seeing his painting in his mind's eye, "meditating new ways to attain perfection."[76]

In a reminder of the ways in which the bohemian son remained dependent on his family, Salmon described a rare visit by Jacob's father. With the insouciant anti-Semitism characteristic of the era, Salmon mentioned that the gang laughed at "M. Abraham Jacob"—the very name "Abraham" seemed to elicit a snigger—provoking Max's wrath. Max was far from his own baptism, Salmon explained, and was sensitive to anti-Jewish slights, so much so that he exploded one day in protest when a stranger eating at Vernin's opened up Drumont's anti-Semitic newspaper *La Libre parole* in front of him.[77] His father, a man of quiet dignity, paid the large bill Max had run up at Vernin's and arranged in the future to settle periodically whatever his son had not been able to pay, with the proviso that Max could order only a prescribed set of healthy items at each meal. Jacob immediately made a private deal with Vernin to allow him to substitute items of comparable value and to treat his friends, so that Vernin could be heard shouting to the waiter, "An absinthe for M. Olin as an *hors d'oeuvre* for Max! And three *picon-curaçaos* at M. Picasso's table as veal Marengo for Max, who's fine!"[78]

When they weren't eating at Vernin's, they stayed closer to Sacré-Coeur and went to Azon, who ran a little bistro called Les Enfants de la Butte. A meal there cost only ninety *centimes*, and Azon, susceptible to the idea of literary glory, often extended credit to writers. He broke with Salmon, however, when he discovered his client really hadn't written the articles signed Paul Adam, Maurice Maeterlinck, and René Maizery, as he had claimed.[79] Some nights—not often, because Picasso usually painted from ten until dawn[80]—the group turned up at the Lapin Agile, where Frédé's wife Berthe served a substantial meal that cost two francs but that Picasso and his friends could sometimes wangle for less. Here in the shadows Picasso's painting *Au Lapin Agile* (himself as Harlequin, with Germaine, the model who had proved fatal to his friend the suicide Casagemas) hung cheek by jowl with paintings by Suzanne Valadon and others; the massive figures of a cast of Apollo and his lyre, a Javanese plaster relief of a deity, and a huge Crucifixion looked on as Frédé sang to the guitar, and clients caroused with song, poetry, and dance.[81] Dancing was provided by Jacob, famous for his jigs on tabletops. Nobody needed to pay admission to a nightclub when Max Jacob could fly into his impersonation of a barefoot female entertainer, his trousers rolled up to expose his hairy legs; his vest tossed aside; his shirtsleeves flapping and his shirt unbuttoned over his thick, crinkly, dark chest hair; his bald head and his pince-nez gleaming as he wriggled, dipped, sashayed, and pointed his toes. Or he would snatch a woman's hat and place it on his head, wrap himself in a shawl, and warble lyrics of sentimental ballads and comic opera, most memorably Hervé's "Atmospheric Lobster," until the room collapsed in laughter.[82] Yet all this entertainment had its desperate side. "How often," said the poet Henri Hertz, "have I seen Max acting the clown with the eyes of a man in despair."[83]

Frédé kept a guest book. On one of its pages, one can chart the progress of the evening in Jacob's improvised verses:

> 9 p.m.
> Finding the rhyme for Frédéric
> There's the "hic"!
> I prefer to wait to be drunk
> Before I write aboard your book.

2 a.m.

On board! Piano A. Bord.
    Ship's register, bored,
Paris, the pensive sea will bring
    Right to your door this evening
O innkeeper of the Misty Quai
    Your sheaf of spray.[84]

The Lapin Agile had its miserable side. The local *apaches* sometimes provoked fights and even wounded or killed each other, and Jacob was once attacked by two thugs outside the tavern.[85] A rival for a woman's affections shot Frédé's son dead, right at the cash register. Years later Jacob—no longer dancing on tables—described the Lapin Agile as "a very dusty, dark lair for poverty, pathetic songs, silence, and the noise of drunks. Some have tried to defend this sad and pretentious bistro, but you won't find me doing it."[86]

The violence of the *apaches* could be unnerving, but it provided raw material for writers: Jacob, his friend Pierre Mac Orlan, Francis Carco, and Salmon would all populate their novels with the roustabouts, pimps, whores, and thieves they knew from la Butte. The rough life also provided material for comedy. One night at the Lapin, someone was wounded in the stomach with a corkscrew, and Max Jacob was hauled into court as a witness. Salmon delighted in the scene:

Max Jacob had put on his frock coat from Quimper for so exalted an occasion. On the witness stand he was magnificent. . . . He of the sonorous voice could arrange to make himself inaudible when it suited his fancy. In his testimony, you could hear absolutely nothing except, once in a while, "corkscrew," enunciated as if onstage at the Odéon. Visibly irritated, the judge sent him back to his seat. Max Jacob, who could cry at will, withdrew sobbing, protesting that it was disgraceful to insult a witness—in the midst of general hilarity, in which the author of the corkscrew crime and his two guards joined even more crazily than the others.[87]

At least one of the artists mimicked this violence. Picasso was famous for carrying a revolver; he used it not only to menace thugs but, more often, to terrorize bores. Once, in a café, when some chatterbox spoke slightingly of Cézanne, Picasso placed his revolver on the marble tabletop and said, "One word more and I'll shoot." Another time, outside the Lapin Agile, he fired in the air to scare away three Germans who had just visited his studio and wanted him to "explain his aesthetics."[88] Fernande Olivier remembered him firing shots in the air as he came home with his *bande* at dawn, all of them drunk, singing, cursing, and shouting "Down with Laforgue!"[89] The revolver had, however, more symbolic than practical significance. It stood for the revolutionary force of Picasso's art, and Jacob devised a mythic genealogy for the weapon, spreading the story that it had passed ceremonially to Picasso from Alfred Jarry.[90]

It seems that Picasso never met Jarry. It is true that through his friendship with Apollinaire and Salmon, who knew and admired the inventor of *Ubu Roi,* Picasso imbibed much of Jarry's spirit and probably came close to meeting him. (The one time he and Apollinaire went to visit Jarry, he said, the master was out.)[91] In 1905 Jarry was already sick and spent long periods in his native Brittany being cared for by his sister. We must take as a fable, then, Jacob's story in the 1933 memoir "Jeunesse" and later in *Chronique des temps héroïques* that Picasso encountered Jarry in Jacob's presence at a dinner given by Maurice Raynal, that the "psychic pope Jarry" had passed on his powers to Picasso in the gift of the revolver, "the new distinguishing mark of the papacy," and that "the revolver was really the harbinger comet of the century."[92] Like any enduring myth, it contains a core of truth. Jarry would haunt Picasso's imagination, both visually in his roughly elegant drawings and woodcuts, and literarily; Picasso drew on his spirit in composing his own plays, and many years after Jarry's death, he could recite his lines by heart.[93]

BY 1905, PICASSO had emerged from his Blue Period, lightened his palette with ochres, yellows, and pinks, and was painting Harlequins and *saltimbanques.* The show at the Galerie Serrurier included—along with works by a couple of other painters—thirty paintings and some drawings and gouaches by Picasso, many depicting the circus performers he claimed as his kin. Less famished than the characters in the blue paintings, these slender adolescents and massive strongmen preserve something of the melancholy of the earlier work; they seem ethereal, called into being more through outline than through volumetric rendering; they almost float in their barren, chalky landscapes.

Ever attentive to his friend's needs, Jacob brought his wealthy cousin and former employer at the department store to Picasso's studio. Gustave Gompel had already been persuaded to buy Picasso's *Portrait of Bibi la Purée* from Vollard in 1901, and now he purchased the gouache *Saltimbanque au chien* (Entertainer with Dog). On this occasion, having asked the price of a painting and being told it cost fifty francs, he looked around the shabby studio with its stacks of canvases and exclaimed, "Well then, you're very rich!" This story became legendary. Telling it to Cocteau in 1926, Jacob painfully gave it a Jewish slant. Ever the ventriloquist, he assumed the casual anti-Semitism of the day. "The real remark," Jacob wrote Cocteau, "was made by a fat Jew, good-natured and stupid, named Gustave Gompel, who has a fortune of eighty million francs. He was holding a gouache of *Saltimbanques* in his hand, rubbed his mustache with the [other] hand, and, his eyes wide with amazement, he exclaimed, 'There's a fortune on these walls!' The Prophets were Jews."[94]

There may have been a hypothetical fortune on the walls of the Bateau Lavoir, but Picasso often couldn't afford the rent or even food. His principal dealers were Clovis Sagot and drunken old Père Soulié, and transactions could be rough. Soulié turned up at the studio one day asking for a flower painting. Picasso had none, but offered to paint one.

"But I need it tomorrow," cried le Père Soulié.

"Fine, you'll have it tomorrow, it just won't be dry."

"Never mind. I'll be careful carrying it."[95]

Picasso had no white paint left and no more credit at the paint store, but he whipped up a flower arrangement for which Soulié duly paid twenty francs. Sagot, for his part, was a well-known skinflint. When Picasso was hard up and invited Sagot to his studio, the dealer offered seven hundred francs for three paintings. Picasso refused, but returned in desperation a few days later, only to find that Sagot had lowered his offer to five hundred francs. Picasso refused again; a few days later he was reduced to accepting three hundred francs for the three works. Not surprisingly, he developed a lifelong resentment of dealers.[96]

But his reputation was growing. If Jacob was useful as an unofficial agent, Apollinaire turned out to have a knack for art journalism. He published a piece on Picasso in the first issue of *La Revue immoraliste,* the journal he started in April 1905. Responding to Charles Morice's reference, in the *Mercure de France,* to Picasso's "sterile melancholy," Apollinaire declared, "It has been said of Picasso that his paintings display a precocious disillusionment. I maintain the contrary." He praised "the mixture of the delightful and the horrible" in Picasso's work, and the plebeian grace of his characters. A month later, in *La Plume,* he devoted a longer article to his friend: "Picasso has observed the human images that floated in the azure of our memories, and participate in divinity to bring forth metaphysicians."[97] Apollinaire's dithyrambic homage hardly qualifies as art criticism and registers few visual facts about the paintings. But he does communicate the mood of Picasso's imaginary worlds with such enthusiasm, he seems to be describing his own inner world. As indeed he is: at this point, the poet and the painter of Harlequins were inspiring each other daily.

IV.

MAX JACOB, IN 1905, was hardly known as a poet. He held aloof from the Symbolist gatherings at the Soleil d'Or, and he hadn't yet appeared at the Closerie des Lilas. But through Apollinaire he was about to gain a modest public. In May, the second issue of *La Revue immoraliste,* rebaptized more soberly *Les Lettres modernes,* carried five poems by Max Jacob: "Bellybutton in the Fog"; "Tie-Rods"; "Scabies"; "Baldness of the Butte Montmartre"; and—dedicated to Picasso—"The Horse." Jacob included none of these in any book; they are minor pieces, interesting mainly for what they show of the ferment of language from which Jacob's better poems would spring. "Baldness of the Butte Montmartre" is, formally, the most conservative in its alexandrine/octosyllabic quatrains, regular rhyme, and even more in its Romantic self-pity. The first line has a flash of poetry: "Smoker of cheap tobacco in the backstage wings of dream." A touch of Chaplinesque enchantment appears in the glimpse of the mystic going down the long stairs of Montmartre: "And my hat in its nimbus of nirvana / Climbed back down, alone." "Tie-Rods" and "Scabies" are exercises in phonetic doodling. But in a few months, this nonsense, refined, would help Jacob dismantle Symbolist conventions. Jacob's liveliest poem from *Les Lettres modernes* was the offering to Picasso, "The Horse." Its satire and its dissonance, along with its tenderness, sly mystery, and echoes of Jules Laforgue, mark it as a period piece, in tune, in its way, with Picasso's Harlequin reveries.

THE HORSE

Passersby were leaving the boulevard des Capucines
Fearful of master and mistress assassins
The last automobiles, with green eyes
  Crossing the winter
  Fought with streetlamps
Now a cab-horse was waiting at the Grand Hotel
Perhaps he was dreaming of meadows, eternal afternoon teas
  Where one grazes far from stinking sewers
  Perhaps of those first country-sides
  Perhaps of the stable on Rue Campagne-Première
An animal's dream! . . . The spark beneath his eyelid
    Mystery . . .
Who can read your depths, o familiar beasts?
This one, to lullaby her boredom
—It was a white mare—
In her breathing and in the night
Hummed a love song.[98]

"Still too Symbolist!" Max Jacob used to snap at Apollinaire, when his friend peopled his alexandrines with fairies and magicians.[99] Jacob was the more radical at this point, as he urged Apollinaire and Salmon to put their language under greater strain and to register the industrial, commercial world around them. Jacob was writing far stronger poems in 1905 than the ones Apollinaire printed in *Les Lettres modernes*. Much of this work came into public view only in 1912 in *Les Oeuvres burlesques et mystiques du Frère Matorel, mort au couvent* (The Burlesque and Mystical Works of Brother Matorel, Deceased in the Convent) with illustrations by Derain. Matorel is Jacob's fictive alter ego, and the three sections of poems interspersed with commentaries present a veiled autobiography. The book opens with a group of parodies ("A Few Really National Songs"), pastiches of traditional genres (*complainte, romance,* patriotic anthem, children's ditty), and the hilarious "Grand Recitative for Salons": "Damnation! Damnation! Cursed Hilda! Die!"[100] Jacob composed these early in 1904 after losing his job at Paris-France, with the idea of selling them to a songbook publisher. The publisher sent him away, saying, "You aren't cut out for this work, Sir. You're too good for this."[101]

In *Pièces burlesques*, the "national songs" are followed by four nonsense poems. In their decomposition of surface sense, "Variation of a Formula" and "Avenue du Maine" play havoc with social as well as with semantic order. "Variation of a Formula" fiddles with a Jewish theme, taking it no more seriously than it takes the Boers who conclude the poem. The surging stock market, the stereotypical "levite" Lévy running to avoid blows, the poor brutes of Boers (who had just lost the war to the British) are all recognizable from the jokes in *Le Sourire* and from the stories crowding every Parisian newspaper. One must see the French to get the feel for the phonetic play:

La bourse houle! avis!
La bourse ou la vie!
Là bout sous la vie
(Glas! Boue!) sourd, l'ami
Glabre ours sous l'habit

Las! Bouc saoul, Lévy
Court, à court d'avis
Et vite les coups évite
A court souffle, ce lévite.[102]

The market surges! Your view!
Your purse or your life!
There purls beneath life
(Death knell! Mud!) Deaf, the bald
Friend, bear beneath his suit
Tired! Drunken scapegoat, Lévy
Flees, short on advice
And quickly dodges blows
Short of breath, this levite.

This ditty disperses an unbearable social reality into a riot of plural senses. On one level, the Jewish writer rejects identification with the caricatured Jew. On another level of self-castigating humor, he presents a self-portrait (the Jew dodging blows). The detached voice of the fictive editor of *Les Oeuvres burlesques et mystiques*, added in 1911, keeps interfering, adding yet another layer of disguise: "It's pointless to insist on the vulgarity of these exercises. . . . Let the reader remember that these humble rhymes were cobbled together in one of the grimmer districts of Paris, one farthest from intellectual centers."[103]

"The Music Lesson," which follows the editor's remark, uses nonsense less defensively. It diagnoses a "dead art" ("art mort," also a pun on Armor, the old name for Brittany): the classic French sonority of Racine and Corneille expanded into Romantic afflatus, then attenuated in Symbolism and the Parnasse. At this stage, both in verse and in prose poems, Jacob's contribution is one of de-composition, a cerebral art attacking tradition. Puns flip the sense of every line. The poem concludes:

Litige! Par le sceptre métis! L'écrit y sert.
Oh! Music! music! qu'y faire?[104]

Contest! By the half-breed scepter! Writ will serve.
Oh! Music! music! what to do?

The fictive editor in *Saint Matorel* comments, "It appears that
Matorel . . . has studied the contemporary masters. Matorel is seeking his
way as a poet."[105] It isn't clear what the editor means by the "contemporary
masters." The word games in "The Music Lesson" owe a great deal to
Mallarmé, something to Allais, Franc-Nohain, and perhaps to Jarry, Fargue, and even Rimbaud, but the poem is unlike anything else being written in France at that time. Matorel/Max Jacob was "seeking his way," but
he was also beginning to find it.[106] One form it took was the prose poem.

SINCE THE OBSCURE publication in 1842 of Aloysius Bertrand's collection
of prose poems, *Gaspard de la nuit,* this hybrid genre had offered French
poets a laboratory in which to experiment with the very idea of verse. Pictorial in Bertrand, anecdotal and allegorical in Baudelaire and Mallarmé,
the prose poem was characterized by brevity and by its critical stance
toward both verse and prose. It evolved in Symbolist practice alongside
vers libre, influenced by the versets—unlineated verse paragraphs—of the
early French translations of Whitman in the 1880s. In Rimbaud's *Illuminations,* published in 1886 in *La Vogue,*[107] one can observe the first French
free verse poems, "Marine" and "Mouvement," crawling to shore out of
the tidal pool of prose poems like new amphibious creatures. By 1905
Rimbaud was exerting an enormous influence on experimental French
poets. For Claudel, he had opened a door into the supernatural and the
spiritual;[108] for Paul Fort, the saints were Verlaine, Mallarmé, Villiers,
and Lautréamont, but Rimbaud was a god.[109] Jacob, however, considered
Rimbaud's art a symptom of Romantic disorder, and he worked to define
the prose poem as coolly objective, self-contained, and—at some level—
abstract. Rimbaud, he thought, was too "subjective"; Jacob's own prose
poems "had nothing to do with Rimbaud, who had the source of his imagery within himself, not outside himself."[110]

A few of the prose poems in *Le Cornet à dés* can be dated to 1905.[111] By
this time, Jacob had initiated his walking discipline: rambling through the

city, he forced himself, in each interval between lampposts, to come up with a new image or poetic idea or "relationship to a subject, whether a person, an object, a poster, a billboard, a postcard." If no idea appeared, he halted at the lamppost until something occurred to him and he jotted it down (sometimes on telegraph blanks filched from a post office).[112] These exercises contributed to the concentrated form of the poems. "Simultaneous Poem with Simple Superposition" (called simply "Poem" in *Le Cornet*) already has full control of pace and tone. It also has Jacob's characteristic disorientation of narrative line, speaker, and personae; his teasing between truth and falsehood; his ironic relationship to a classical past; and the geometric abstraction imposed by the title.

POEM

(originally titled "Poème simultané avec superposition simple": Simultaneous Poem with Simple Superposition)

"What do you want from me," says Mercury.
"Your smile and your teeth," says Venus.
"They're false. What do you want from me?"
"Your wand."
"I'll never give it up."
"Come bring it over here, divine mailman."

You should read this in the original Greek: it's called *Idyll*. At high school, a friend of mine who kept flunking his exams told me, "If you translated a novel by Daudet into Greek, you'd be ready for the exam! But I can't work at night. It makes my mother cry." You should read that in the original Greek also, gentlemen; it's an idyll, ειδυλλος, a little picture.[113]

||

THE YEAR STEAMED ahead with reciprocal intensities of friendship and creation at the Bateau Lavoir. A few postcards survive, flotsam from that lost world. "I need to see you tomorrow morning, Saturday: tell Max to come," Apollinaire wrote to Picasso on May 5.[114] On July 23, Picasso and Jacob joined in sending Apollinaire greetings for his name day, Saint Apollinaire.[115] Other objects offer their testimony. One evening after a visit to the circus, Picasso modeled a clay head of Max Jacob as a clown; the more Picasso worked on the head the next day, the less it resembled Jacob, so that only the chin and jaw remain of the initial portrait.[116] A further record of the intimacy of Picasso and Jacob survives in the drawings they did together. However humble Jacob was about his own art, shared sketching remained an important element of the friendship. In engravings and sketchbook pages, one finds, mingled and overlapping, Picasso's fluid horses, nude men and women, a cat, a Fernande-like profile, and Max Jacob's more angular, hesitant drawings: a woman fixing her hair, studies of a female face.[117] When a Dutch painter invited Picasso to visit Holland for a few weeks in the summer, it was Jacob who made the trip possible, borrowing money from the concierge.[118] On that trip Picasso took a notebook of Jacob's partly filled with his friend's writing; he filled the rest of it with drawings.[119] Apollinaire, too, scrounged up enough money for a short vacation that summer, in Belgium; and the young writer Maurice Raynal went off to Normandy, provoking a facetiously lyrical letter from Jacob, who stayed in Paris: "May the tides bring you golden rhymes, along with rose-colored shells."[120]

On September 3, when the gang reassembled in Montmartre, the season commenced with a public celebration of the secular tradition, the unveiling of the statue of the Chevalier de la Barre. For this Enlightenment martyr, a young nobleman tortured and executed in 1766 for refusing to doff his hat at a church procession, Jacob composed a pastiche of a patriotic song, a purée of clichés and slang he would often be asked to perform.[121] Over three thousand freethinkers turned out for the celebration. In July the radical government had passed the definitive law separating church and state, provoking strikes across the country, violence that would only worsen the following year, when the state began to make inventories of church property. For Jacob, the disruption occurred on a more intimate front: on the day of the inauguration of the statue, Fernande moved in with

Picasso. The painter was so crazy about her, he had set up a little fetishistic altar to her in the alcove above his studio.[122]

||

STILL IN OBSCURITY, Jacob was writing poetry and perhaps his novel *Le Phanérogame,* but Picasso grew in authority and power. Not only had his voluptuous mistress moved in, he was finishing a major painting, *Les Saltimbanques,* a composition he had worked and reworked since the previous spring. One of the last of the Harlequin period, *Les Saltimbanques* sets its six itinerant figures in a bare, dreamlike landscape. The entertainers are grouped around a stocky strongman, though each seems strangely alone, gazing into a private distance. The tall Harlequin on the left holding the little girl's hand is an idealized portrait of Picasso, his regard level with the horizon. The painter's horizons must indeed have seemed wider these days. The retrospectives of Manet and Ingres at the Salon d'Automne had suggested new scope for large-scale figure composition, the simplification of planes, and the treatment of rhythm, while the Fauve room at the Salon, exhibiting work by Matisse, Derain, and Vlaminck, caused an uproar in the press. Picasso had not yet met these painters, but the publicity about this new avant-garde must have stimulated him to rival them in his own way. And out of the same Salon appeared Picasso's first great patrons, the Steins.[123]

Leo Stein had been living in Paris since 1902. He was trying to become a painter, attending classes at the Académie Julian and painting in his apartment at 27 rue de Fleurus. His sister Gertrude joined him the following year, and in 1904 Michael Stein and his wife Sarah also set up a Parisian household. Leo, his eyes just opened to modern art, purchased Matisse's *Woman with a Hat* out of the Salon d'Automne 1905, and sometime that year he bought Picasso's *Harlequin's Family with an Ape* from Clovis Sagot and—after quarreling with Gertrude, who didn't want it—Picasso's nude *Girl with a Basket of Flowers.*[124] In short order, Leo visited the Bateau Lavoir and invited Picasso and Fernande for dinner at 27 rue de Fleurus, where Picasso and Gertrude Stein recognized each other as equals. Their artistic friendship ignited immediately, and the first form it took was Picasso's proposal to paint her portrait. Through the Steins, Picasso would meet his major rival, Matisse, and through Gertrude's portrait sessions in the Bateau Lavoir, which went on all through the winter of 1906, she became familiar with *la bande à Picasso*. They, in turn, often visited the Rue de Fleurus, which was rapidly becoming a center for modern art as Gertrude and Leo crowded their walls with works by Bonnard, Matisse, Cézanne, Renoir, Toulouse-Lautrec, and—not least—Picasso.[125]

From this febrile scene, Max Jacob temporarily withdrew. By Christmas 1905 he was back in Quimper, where he would stay to work on his novel until the spring. He left Paris not without wounded feelings at Picasso's intimacy with Fernande. Apollinaire, writing to a friend, reported, "We see less of Picasso. You know that Fernande's name is Bellevallée. Max, who is angry with them, calls Picasso 'the Lily of the Bellevallée.' "[126]

CHAPTER 6

TOWARD CUBISM

I.

I n 1906 and 1907, Picasso's coterie at the Bateau Lavoir would cohere into a movement that set the terms of modern art. Max Jacob was intimately involved, a daily witness to the pictorial inventions of Picasso and Braque as he himself helped reinvent French poetry.

After three and a half months in Quimper, Jacob returned to his artistic family in Montmartre. His postcard from April 15 to Picasso shows the kind of bond he felt: "My dear friend, I'm leaving tomorrow at 8 in the evening, I'll be at our house [*chez nous*] at 9 a.m. the day after tomorrow." Equally revealing is his delicate distinction between plural and singular pronouns: "What a celebration to see you all again! To see you again, my dear friend."[1] The Bateau Lavoir really was *chez nous* for Jacob. He often spent from morning until night at Picasso's studio, writing, drawing, and sharing meals. He returned in time to see a major financial and artistic coup for the painter when Apollinaire brought Vollard to the studio. The lordly dealer, who had given Picasso his first show in Paris but disdained the Blue Period, now bought twenty works for two thousand francs, more money than Picasso had ever possessed. Jacob and Salmon watched Vollard stack his horse-drawn cab so full of paintings, he had to sit in front with the driver for the return trip. Jacob's eyes filled with tears for his friend's success.[2]

The coup also brought tears of loss. Picasso's good fortune allowed him to return, with Fernande, to Barcelona and then to the Pyrenees to renew his inspiration from his own land. Barely a month after Jacob's reunion with his idol, he said goodbye to Picasso and Fernande in a raucous meal at Azon's bistro along with Apollinaire, Manolo, and Maurice and Alice Princet, after which they all dashed to the Gare d'Orléans, lugging baggage to pack the couple off on the train. Apollinaire evoked this party in rhymes he sent Picasso and Fernande a few days later: Max Jacob sang old love songs, recited a monologue, and danced a gavotte, and after the train pulled out of the station, the gang migrated to Austin's Fox, "to console that Breton / Who later got drunk on rounds of old Burton. / But the train, all of a sudden, recharged with a start / And shot off to the Iberian land like a fart."[3]

As late spring and summer unrolled for Picasso and Fernande in the spectacular mountainscape at Gosol, a village in the Pyrenees they could reach only after eight hours on muleback, Apollinaire and Jacob kept them up to date on Parisian gossip. Jacob regaled them with chronicles: the lousy plays he'd seen, the goings and comings of the women who lived across from him on the Boulevard Barbès, the sniping one-upmanship among the habitués of Vernin's bistro, chapters from *Le Phanérogame*, Manolo's shenanigans, and a report on the youth of the Quartier Latin (more impassioned by philosophy than by art these days). After describing a play about Prussian aggression, Jacob asked, in one of his few political remarks, "And when will we have colonial drama? When will we see on stage how we treat our blacks? Never," he concluded; for philistine audiences, "blacks are not interesting, *it's not agreeable to watch them die*."[4] In the jaunty, heartless tone affected by their group, he told Picasso and Fernande, "Jarry is sick: he's been carried off to Brittany. This illness will be his death or his life. Alcoholic, he could die; if he convalesces, he could return a magnificent and fresh Jarry. So watch out! But if Jarry dies, the place of Harlequin is up for grabs."[5]

Picasso painted in a euphoria of renewed contact with Spain: landscapes, still lifes, nude figures of adolescent boys, nude figures of Fernande, and portraits of their innkeeper, whose craggy face strangely resembled Picasso's own and who became a kind of model for the portrait of Gertrude Stein.[6] As usual, Picasso sent Jacob drawings. Writing with a hangover, Jacob juggled clichés and puns, and reciprocated with echoes of one of his Matorel poems: "The Spanish poverty of a noble race, it's your whole art which . . . which . . . (here topos, development, clichés I'll spare you) your thunder! Air. (There's the state of my cerebellum.)" The last line, drawn from the puns of his poem "Avenue du Maine," loses most of its sense in translation: "Déménage tes méninges, ange! Ménage et déménage." The frolic of syllables fractures logic, releasing new vision: "Clear out your cerebellum, angel, manage [save] and clear out."[7]

Picasso and Fernande returned in August, earlier than planned, in flight from an outbreak of typhoid. Jacob didn't visit his family in Quimper that summer: instead, he wangled their paying of his term's rent in Paris by writing them he would be awarded the Palmes académiques ("I didn't say when I would be awarded the Palmes académiques," he confessed to Picasso).[8] Paris was in the grip of a heat wave. But they all settled back into their familiar rhythms as Apollinaire returned from a holiday in Holland and Picasso finished the portrait of Stein from memory. The previous spring, through the Steins, he had met Matisse. Now Apollinaire introduced him to his neighbor from Le Vésinet, André Derain, a painter fresh in his Fauve glory. For a while, Picasso and Derain had much to teach each other, so much that when Derain moved to Paris, he took a studio in Montmartre.

The autumn of 1906 was a time of preparing ambitious projects, for *la bande* and especially for Picasso. Salmon went off for six weeks to act in a traveling theater company,[9] but he was already working toward his second book of poems. Jacob, "the oldest representative of the young literature," as he called himself,[10] was filling his Breton trunk with poems and scraps of stories and working on *Le Phanérogame*. The one sign that he was beginning to be known outside Montmartre occurs in two letters by the anarchist editor Mécislas Golberg to Salmon, thanking him for the introduction to Jacob and asking him to secure his friend's collaboration in Golberg's *Cahiers* and in the little satirical journal *Poliche*.[11] Picasso threw himself into important paintings; in the large *Self-Portrait with Palette*, the *Two Nudes*, and other male and female nudes, he simplified his palette and locked bodies into surrounding space. All these figures have a brooding, massive force that presses against the frame. *Les Demoiselles d'Avignon* had, in some sense, already begun.

Nineteen-hundred-seven would be a year of drama for Jacob and his companions. In art, it produced competitive, radical figure painting. Matisse showed his *Blue Nude* and Derain his *Large Bathers* at the Salon des Indépendants in March. Both paintings would challenge Picasso in the *Demoiselles*. The fact that Gertrude and Leo Stein bought the *Blue Nude* and that the German dealer Wilhelm Uhde, already friendly with Picasso, bought five of Braque's six Fauve landscapes intensified the rivalry. Jacob himself showed six gouaches in the Salon, partly (he claimed) in the hope of seeing Cécile, his erstwhile girlfriend.

Concocted with cigarette ash, coffee stains, and dust as much as with pigment, Jacob's fey renderings of Breton scenes and Parisian streets and theaters were not meant to vie with the giants of painting who were his companions. Nor could he compete with them in the field of love. Jacob was, by this time, not so discreetly homosexual, which displeased Fernande, who once asked him if he didn't fear getting arrested for his encounters with strangers.[12] Apollinaire, curious about all forms of sex, jotted gossip in his diary about Jacob being a *tante* (queer) and about who was and who wasn't queer.[13] All the more important, then, for Jacob—physically slight, known to be a *tante*—to pretend to keep up appearances with his male heterosexual friends. It was one of his many theatrical performances. Derain, Vlaminck, and Braque were all tall and square-shouldered; Derain and Braque were trained boxers, and Vlaminck imposed with his bulk, stature, and bad temper. They made heads turn when they walked down the street as a trio, Fernande said.[14] Picasso was smaller but stocky and gave the impression of physical force. Given all these tensions, there is a complex pathos in Jacob's account of his appearance in—and Cécile's appearance at—the Salon des Indépendants, when, he assured Guiette, his friends found her "beautiful."[15]

THESE TOUCHY CONCERNS about male honor broke out in challenges to two duels, one involving Jacob and the other Apollinaire. Both incidents turned to comedy but might have resulted in violence or death. Henri Delormel, the *louche* literary journalist who had funded two issues of Apollinaire's magazine (named, successively, *La Revue immoraliste* and *Les Lettres modernes*), briefly engaged Jacob as a secretary for fifty francs a month but paid him, as Apollinaire noted in his diary, "one hundred *sous* by one hundred *sous* and with grief."[16] Jacob already had reason to dislike Delormel; he had attacked Jarry and Fargue as homosexuals in a story in 1897,[17] and under the name of Louis Libaude, as an unlicensed art dealer, he preyed on poor artists. Picasso had caricatured *le gros* Lolo, as he was called, with his bald and pointy head, which Mollet thought of as a hard-boiled egg but others thought of as a prick.[18] Delormel was famously stingy. On February 26, 1907, Apollinaire jotted in his diary,

> Impelled by his avarice, he wanted to let Max go and to justify himself asserted that Max was queer (it's a bit true) but not in the usual sense because Delormel hesitated between three secretaries, Max, Bernouard, and Doury, all queers. Finally Max, having heard some of Delormel's gossip about his morality, sent his witnesses: Salmon and me, I made an appointment with Delormel but we didn't go because Salmon had taken hashish and forgot the duel. Yesterday we went to Delormel's but he wasn't there.[19]

By March 5, Jacob's duel had blown over, Delormel having attested in writing that he had never spoken ill of his secretary. But Apollinaire, perhaps sensing the possibilities of useful notoriety, tried to provoke a duel of his own. On March 2 in *Le Censeur politique et littéraire*, Max Daireaux reported on a Symbolist banquet at which Apollinaire called attention to himself by shouting for Apollinaris water. Offended, Apollinaire sent Max Jacob and Jean de Mitty—another journalist—to demand satisfaction. Apollinaire by this time was publishing articles widely and had connections throughout the milieu of Parisian journalism; his friend the writer and journalist André Billy created enough strategic delays in the encounter of the seconds to allow the poet to calm down.[20] When the seconds finally met, tempers had cooled and the affair turned to farce: Jacob borrowed

Picasso's top hat for the occasion, and while he and Mitty waited in the foyer of Daireaux's house, he noticed the valet staring at the hat, which he had removed and was holding in his hand. Only now did he notice the name PICASSO painted brilliantly inside the hat.

Mitty, a Romanian who had invented a French aristocratic lineage for himself, tried to curry favor with one of Daireaux's aristocratic seconds; he addressed the count (or baron) in his most dandyish manner. "I knew a member of your family well, M. de Saint-Gratien, in the Isère. . . ."

"Monsieur," replied the other glacially, "I have family all over France, except in the Isère."[21]

During the deliberations Apollinaire waited in Picasso's studio. All turned out peacefully: the four witnesses drew up a report testifying that no offense had been intended or given. Daireaux insisted that the affair receive no publicity, but the story ran through the city anyway. What all the memoirists remembered years later was the comic coda: Jacob presented Apollinaire with a bill. Since Jacob was very poor, and Apollinaire chronically hard up and tight with money, this bill was not entirely a joke.

First day: 9 a.m.	a little coffee for the second witness	0,10 fr
10 a.m.	a box of matches for the second witness who had left his home	0,10
11 a.m.	a bun for the witness whose lunch would be delayed	0,05
noon	a newspaper for the witness who is bored waiting	0,05
5 p.m.	the second witness offers an aperitif to the first witness	1,20
Second day	Among other things, the witness—to soften up "the enemy"—offers him an apéritif, etc. etc.[22]	

||

THE REAL STORY of the Bateau Lavoir that spring was not farcical duels but the genesis of Picasso's *Demoiselles d'Avignon* and the birth of Cubism. Jacob watched it happen, step by step. He was also frank about his incomprehension about what Picasso was trying to achieve with his crosshatched, primitive women, their anatomies yanked out of classical perspective and jammed into curtained space in three distinct styles. "Neither I nor Apollinaire understood a thing about it," he later told the writer Robert Levesque.[23]

Nobody else did either, at first. As Picasso meditated and sketched for this large composition that would revolutionize Western figure painting, he became moody and solitary. Salmon reported his preoccupation and his temporary abandonment of painting so that he could work out the preliminary problems in drawing.[24] Jacob thought the precipitating shock for the *Demoiselles* was Picasso's encounter with African art. "We were eating dinner at Matisse's one Thursday," he remembered. "Picasso, Guillaume, and I. Matisse showed us an African statuette which Picasso examined as he examines. The next morning around eight, instead of finding him in bed when I arrived at the studio where I spent from morning until night each day, I found him in front of large sheets of Ingres drawing paper, where there were heads of women, in yellow, cross-hatched to show shadow, with their mouths touching their noses." In this letter to Levesque, Jacob included drawings that indicated, quite faithfully, Picasso's early studies.[25] Every day when Jacob arrived, he found the floor littered with new drawings. "Go out and play," Picasso used to say in those days to Jacob and Apollinaire, so he could work uninterrupted.[26]

Picasso also managed to withdraw somewhat from Fernande. To allow him to concentrate on his new task, the Steins rented another studio for him downstairs at the Bateau Lavoir.[27] It was solitary work, but in several ways it was communal as well. In the first place, the painting that came to be known as *Les Demoiselles d'Avignon* emerged, like any great work, in conversation with its predecessors. African art was hardly its only begetter. Picasso in this period was absorbed by El Greco's *Apocalyptic Vision;*[28]

Picasso's whores jut up and out of a confined space modeled on the dimensions of El Greco's painting, and like El Greco's figures, they crackle against folds of electrifying drapery.[29] The *Demoiselles* also has affinities with Cézanne's *Large Bathers* and with Romanesque Catalan sculpture. More notoriously, his garish women owe something to the fifth-to-third-century-B.C.E. stone Iberian heads that Apollinaire's friend Géry Pieret obligingly stole from the Louvre and sold for a song to Picasso.[30]

This theft would come back to haunt Picasso and Apollinaire, though in 1907 it must have seemed one more bohemian prank. Picasso studied these heads voraciously and donated their staring boldness to the women in the center of the *Demoiselles* group before hiding the contraband in his studio.[31] Pieret ran off to his native Belgium and then to California. Jacob was not mistaken, however, in asserting the importance of African art to the *Demoiselles:* in these months, Picasso returned again and again to the Musée d'Ethnographie du Trocadéro, and African and Oceanic art contributed significant, if controversial, power to the two women on the right in Picasso's monumental painting.[32]

In spite of Picasso's withdrawal, Jacob and Apollinaire often ate lunch with him in the new studio,[33] and the painting's name, which Picasso always hated, arose from their joking. At first they called it *The Philosophical Brothel*, a name that would have suited early versions in which a sailor sits in the center and a medical student enters from the left holding a book or, in some drawings, a skull.[34] It was Salmon who came up with the name *Les Demoiselles d'Avignon*. And that was partly because Max's grandmother was supposed to have come from Avignon, and they thought it was funny to put her in a brothel.[35]

Max Jacob's so-called Avignonese grandmother may have been the mother of his maternal grandfather, Léon Jacob.[36] What mattered for Jacob and his friends was the myth of a pious grandmother, all the better as a candidate for a whorehouse. But Jacob may be more closely worked into the fabric of the painting: he may have served as an early model for the sailor, and he may have been, at some point, the bald medical student who was eventually transformed into a woman.[37] Whether or not he inhabited Picasso's brothel at some point, Jacob was certainly the subject of a portrait painted early in 1907 in the slashing, simplified styles of the Iberian and Romanesque portions of the *Demoiselles*. And he watched the painting evolve from beginning to end.

Picasso suffered from the incomprehension and even hostility of his companions. Salmon, Jacob reported, was "opposed to it."[38] Equally galling was the derision his new work inspired in collectors. When the Steins visited in May, they were probably not shocked, as Picasso had not yet painted the African mask on the woman on the right. But when Leo Stein saw the painting in its latest phase, he erupted in manic laughter.[39] So did Matisse, when he came to see it with the illustrious art critic Félix Fénéon.[40] It must have been small solace to Picasso, but solace all the same, that Wilhelm Uhde was sufficiently intrigued by the work to bring his friend the young Daniel-Henry Kahnweiler to see it. Kahnweiler—newly arrived in Paris to embark on his career as art dealer—did not immediately understand Picasso's monstrous women, but he bought some gouaches and would become the shepherd of Cubism as Vollard had been for Cézanne.

II.

MAX JACOB, MEANWHILE, concluded a major effort of his own: in April he finished *Le Phanérogame*. Like so much of his early work, it went into his trunk. Fiction aspiring to the condition of drama, *Le Phanérogame* unfolds as dialogue between the hero and various characters, including a committee of academicians with improbable names like Tropgrandglaïeul (Toogreatgladiola). Amusing from line to line, the novel loses momentum in the jumble of jokes. Jacob would publish it at his own expense in 1918. It is hard to believe it will ever gain a wide readership, though its daring imagination of "a third sex" might win it a contemporary audience.[41]

The novel provides a key to Jacob's preoccupations in this period. Against the lucubrations of the academicians, the Phanérogame—an "American" who flies by vibrating his thighs—erupts in spiritual assertions. When Tropgrandglaïeul declares that "genius is thus nothing more than an excess of matter," the Phanérogame replies, "They should eat Jacob's ladder."[42] The academicians' debates turn on questions of gender, power, and sexuality, and read like parodies of Remy de Gourmont's clinical accounts of the sexual instinct.[43]

"Is this to say that the war between the sexes is destined to conclude?" asks Hainabord (a name suggesting Hate-on-Board). "Yes!" replies Tropgrandglaïeul, "through the creation of a third sex, composed uniquely for pleasure and in no way implicated in our vital interests."[44] One might view *Le Phanérogame* not only as a parody of a world dominated by positivistic social science, but also as a homosexual's satirical perspective on a heterosexual world in which he must play a variety of roles in order to survive. The frantic puns and parodies seem a protective coloration. The hero's name, Phan-éro-game, suggests, in Greek etymology, a play on appearance, love, and marriage; in botany, the word means a plant with visible exterior sexual organs.[45] A third object of satire in *Le Phanérogame* is the myth of racial purity. Gobineau's *Essay on the Inequality of Human Races* and a whole pseudoscientific literature of race lie behind Hainabord's question, "Don't you think the woman who joins the superior race to the strength of her own race is a benefactor to humanity?"[46]

By the end of the novel, the Phanérogame has been interned in "the Asylum for Superior Degenerates," but he escapes, letting pages of a manuscript flutter to the ground. These pages bear traces of Jacob's occult research, and some of the meditational practices prescribed would remain constant in the author's Christian life: "Following a certain ritual . . . try to locate the best part of yourself in the moment of prayer, when man is truly a child."[47] As vulnerable, elusive, and marginal as his creator, the Phanérogame is last spotted at the source of the Zambezi River in East Africa, flying away to elude white explorers.[48]

JACOB'S POEMS, HOWEVER, were shyly making their way. The October 1907 issue of *Poliche,* a new literary gazette in Reims founded by Jean-René Aubert and co-edited by the ailing Mécislas Golberg, ran a prose poem and a poem in verse by Jacob. The prose poem, "Metempsychosis" would appear in *Le Cornet à dés* in a tightened version.

METEMPSYCHOSIS (1907 VERSION)

Shadows! an open door! The pools of blood are shaped like clouds. Bluebeard's seven wives are no longer in the darkroom. This organdy *coiffe* is the only relic of their destinies. But over there, ah! on the Ocean, there are seven slave ships, seven! . . . They're gliding now in the mountain's shadow. Seven slave ships whose rigging drags topsails in the sea, like women's braids on their shoulders. The ones in front approach as if to show off the thousand details of their huge, hollow sails.[49]

The verse poem in *Poliche*, "Hallucination," explores a different sacrificial scene, envisioning Saint Denis on a tram in the midst of a flock of sheep being driven across Paris to the slaughterhouse (not an unfamiliar sight in those days). The mixture of modern and familiar elements (the tram, the sheep) with the miraculous (the saint holding his own severed head), the tenderly awkward, even primitive feel of the poem, and its rapid transitions are purely Jacobian. Central to this vision is the desire for transformation and the Christian character of that desire:

Move along, sheep, to the slaughterhouse of La Villette!
Saint-Denis! Saint-Denis! Let's ride toward the Opera
With our old clothes, our old souls, et cetera
Sheep of the fold!
Sheep for butchery.[50]

This haunting did not come unbidden from Jacob's unconscious. Like all the members of *la bande à Picasso* at this stage, he sometimes cultivated visions chemically. Hashish and opium were their favored drugs, but Jacob preferred ether, which was cheap and whose distinctive odor sometimes hung about his clothes. At least once, he pushed his quest into a dangerous terrain when he wanted to see the Devil and drank a strong brew of wormwood. The story, when Jacob narrated it years later, assumed mythic proportions:

For three days, lying on his bed in the dark, Max suffered genuine torment and saw extraordinary things impossible to relate, for they would burn the tongue and yank the pen from the fingers. And when the door to his room finally opened, those who sought him saw the Demon and fled. Max fled also. He ran across the city like a man possessed (as indeed he was). Crowds shrank back from him to let him pass. Even policemen drew back in spite of their uniforms, and the church where he tried to take refuge emptied out in the snap of a finger. "Now," says Max, "I'm looking for the herb which helps you see heaven. But I've forgotten its name and I'll never find it."[51]

Picasso and Fernande had been smoking opium since they met. Occasionally they transformed the studio into an opium den, and in the flickering lamplight they drank lemon tea and lounged with members of *la bande* in a drowsy intimacy.[52] But there is no evidence that Picasso ever let drugs interfere with his work: he was much too driven for that. It was not until the German painter Wiegels committed suicide in the Bateau Lavoir in 1908 through a combination of overdose and hanging that Picasso and Fernande became frightened and swore off drugs. Apollinaire and Salmon, for their part, used opium and hashish frequently. Experience in Asia in the navy had initiated quite a few Frenchmen to the use of opium, and Picasso's gang also smoked at the wittily named "Union Marine de la Butte Montmartre," a "yacht club" run by the painter Georges Pigeard, where nautical discussions (and Jacob's renditions of Breton sea shanties and of "The Atmospheric Lobster") accompanied nights of reverie.[53] Apollinaire liked to smoke in a "mortuary chapel" decorated with wax tapers and an obscene crucifix.[54]

But Jacob had no taste for such props. With a dose of ether, he was happy to withdraw into his room and let his fantasy roam. Though he later claimed not to have taken ether before 1909, wanting to preserve his sacred vision of that year from the taint of drugs, it's clear that he participated earlier than that in the experiments of the whole *bande*.[55] The results were not always pretty. Francis Carco remembered Jacob, intoxicated by ether, causing a disturbance on the sidewalk, with people milling to gawp as policemen threatened to march him down to the station, "holding him solidly with one hand and with the other holding their noses."[56] Carco claimed the drug made Jacob lucid and spared him the torpor of the morning after, but Fernande remembered it differently. On days when he was penniless and wild for a dose, she would lend him small change. But the mornings after these indulgences he'd be found unconscious in the street, and she'd swear never to relent again.[57]

III.

THE LITTLE CLAN of the Bateau Lavoir made room for several newcomers in 1907. One was the wispy young painter Marie Laurencin, with whom Braque had become friendly a few years earlier. Braque may have first brought her to the Bateau Lavoir, but it was Picasso who met her at Clovis Sagot's gallery and told Apollinaire he had found a wife for him.[58]

Not everyone was charmed. Fernande thought Marie Laurencin had the face of a goat, with oddly angled eyelids and a sharp nose, and the air of "a slightly vicious little girl."[59] Fernande, Jacob, and other intimates of the Bateau Lavoir were irritated by Laurencin's affectations, which included a tendency to fluff up her hair and shriek or emit odd noises. All of a sudden, she would interrupt conversation with a piercing cry. "That's the cry of the great llama," she would explain.[60]

But Apollinaire was captivated by this girl whose eccentricities matched his own, illegitimate like himself, and like him living with a difficult mother. In spite of her apparent naïveté, she was already entertaining several lovers.[61] Coldness and self-absorption emanate from her memoirs; she would not allow herself to be moved by the art of the Bateau Lavoir, so much more powerful than her own, and when she painted the group portrait of *la bande* in 1909 in her childlike style, she pointedly left out Jacob, Salmon, and her old friend Braque. Apollinaire entertained her, adored her, introduced her into artistic milieus, and wrote about her work: he once likened her to Salome dancing before Picasso-as-John the Baptist, a comparison that cannot have pleased Picasso, who was hardly ready to lose his head.[62] She never entered into the spirit of the Bateau Lavoir; as she later said, Apollinaire

> spent his evenings at Picasso's with Max Jacob, at 13 rue Ravignan, and the three of them did nothing but quarrel, trip each other up, glare, and especially trade insults—their specialty—and then suddenly, they adored each other again. They hardly drank; they were drunk maybe once every two months and became excessively polite. I never paid any attention to them; I read love stories, Marivaux's *Marianne*, and I think I hated them, feeling them so different from me; especially their African statues, which irritated me no end.[63]

Apollinaire moved out of his mother's house and rented an apartment on the Rue Léonie (soon to be renamed Rue Henner) in lower Montmartre. Here in his cramped salon and bedroom, he served tea on Wednesdays; and here he and Laurencin would celebrate their love (though only in the armchair, never on the bed, which no one but its owner was allowed to touch).[64]

In this season of strain at the Bateau Lavoir, as Picasso fought his way into the *Demoiselles*, Fernande apparently felt more and more replaced by the wild women in his painting and seems to have tried to mend things by adopting a child. This episode does not turn up in her memoirs but left its mark in the memories of friends. Apollinaire recorded in his diary that the Picassos had taken in a nine-year-old girl whose mother was in a whorehouse in Tunis.[65] Salmon made her the heroine of his Montmartre novel, *La Négresse du Sacré-Coeur*. In his memoirs he describes how Fernande petted her and how all the members of *la bande* spoiled her, Jacob bringing her a doll, Salmon offering candy. Drawings of Raymonde turn up in Picasso's sketchpad, and that spring Picasso painted a vigorous, African-mask-like mother and child. But Fernande's temper was not maternal: she veered from pampering the child to slapping her. And as Raymonde may have been a bit older than nine—more like thirteen, as in Salmon's novel—Richardson hints that other tensions may have been at work in the household. A drawing by Picasso of Raymonde in a chair, lifting her leg to wash her foot and fully displaying her vagina, suggests as much.[66] By the end of July, the painful comedy had played itself out, but when Fernande tried to return Raymonde to the orphanage, the directress refused to take her back.[67] A concierge in Montmartre finally accepted her. As Henri Hertz recalled:

> I met Max Jacob at Apollinaire's, who lived then in an ugly little apartment on the Rue Henner, which was called Léonie in those days. With Max, there were Marie Laurencin, Picasso, his lady companion, and a little girl pouting in a corner. Max was in the middle of the room trying to arrange some toys in a cardboard suitcase that he was having a hard time snapping shut and securing with string. Absorbed in his task, his face distressed and vexed, as I saw when he turned toward me his clear, distracted eyes which gave off, in eclipses, great nocturnal beams, like lighthouses, like the moon, he offered me two fingers, the index and middle finger, a little bent, a little concave, with squarish fingertips and worn-down fingernails which I followed, so many years later, whether awkward in their domesticity among battered tools, whether agile in their elevation, holding a pen, pencil, or paintbrush. When the baggage was ready, Max took the little girl by one hand, picked up the suitcase with the other, muttered something to Apollinaire and Picasso, and left. I went with him to the threshold. He paused, and gave me a deep sad smile, the only smile of his I have ever seen.[68]

That summer brought another separation. In late August, Fernande wrote Gertrude Stein to announce that Picasso was leaving her. He was not, he said, "cut out for this kind of life."[69] While he waited for payments from Vollard to allow Fernande to move out, she hunted for lodgings, and he threw himself into paintings that extended the method of the *Demoiselles*. By mid-September, Fernande had found a room and was giving French lessons to Alice Toklas, Gertrude's friend newly arrived in Paris. Picasso and Fernande could not easily extricate their lives from each other, however, and attended Stein's welcoming dinner for Toklas together at the end of September.[70] At this delicate moment in Picasso's relationship with Fernande, Jacob moved from his lodgings on the Boulevard Barbès and rented a room a few doors down from the Bateau Lavoir at 7 rue Ravignan, "to be nearer Picasso."[71]

On the Rue Ravignan, Jacob established a domain that was inimitably his own. It was on the ground floor, with a window opening on the inner courtyard where the tenants tossed their garbage. Hardly any sunlight penetrated into his room. Of the many descriptions of this central laboratory, Fernande's stands out; she had not left the neighborhood, and she moved back in with Picasso in early December. Max, she wrote, "welcomed visitors on Monday. You could meet strange people there, silent, motionless, sitting quietly in dark corners. All sorts of people, which made the atmosphere heavy, sometimes suffocating, but truly mysterious. It was like being among conspirators. And why not? Weren't they conspiring against everything established in art?"[72]

It was a poor room, but not sad. It suggested a peculiar, personal intelligence and smelled of a mixture of cigarette smoke, oil, and incense, of old furniture and ether.[73] An idiosyncratic order reigned. Roland Dorgelès didn't know where to sit during his first visit: clothes lay on the bed, books on the chairs; "the table was covered with flasks, mugs, and tubes of paint; a bag of roasted chestnuts was stuffed into a shoe, a gouache was drying in front of the coal stove. The disorder extended even to the walls, where signs of the zodiac mingled with bizarre maxims and the addresses of friends."[74] Here Jacob created his world, which reached beyond the room into the whole neighborhood where he knew all the concierges, housewives, and shopkeepers, kept track of the gossip, collected stories, and read horoscopes.

IV.

AN OLD WORLD was dying, a new one being born. Alfred Jarry, who had already bequeathed his revolutionary revolver to Picasso—in myth if not in fact—came back to Paris that fall, still ill, still alcoholic, and still outrageous. "We will pass away precisely on All Saints Day," he announced in his lugubrious Père Ubu voice, and that was what he did, dying on November 1, 1907, of tubercular meningitis in the Hôpital de la Charité.[75] He was buried in Bagneux Cemetery, followed by a cortège that included much of literary and artistic Paris. His death, like Cézanne's the year before, could be felt not so much as an absence as an affirmation: a set of energies, possibilities, and openings.

In literature, the publication in March 1908 of Jules Romains's *The Unanimous Life* expressed the confidence of a vigorous new age: "We've stripped the flesh off the world / Fact by fact, sun after sun."[76] Romains (born Louis Farigoule) had grown up in Montmartre. This restless, brilliant young man, who dressed in workman's clothes and loved to wander the streets at all hours, was finishing his *agrégation* at the École Normale Supérieure. *The Unanimous Life* brought him immediate attention, and he became friendly with Jacob and Apollinaire. Their admiration, as usual, took a jocose form. One night as Jacob and Apollinaire sauntered through the streets, Apollinaire improvised a pastiche of *The Unanimous Life*, bellowing "I kiss on your forehead the entire human race," followed by obscenities; they collapsed laughing on a bench until a policeman moved them along.[77]

The sense of a new art emerging is palpable in the last issue of the *Cahiers de Mécislas Golberg*, entitled *Le Dernier cahier* (The Last Notebook) and published after Golberg's death in 1908. This rare document, ornamented with beautiful woodcuts, commemorates the anarchist editor, and its contrasting texts show the revolution in the making. Beside the Symbolist poems with their crowns of "scarlet roses," Max Jacob's poem "Interior Scene" (which Poulenc would later set to music) is rude and disruptive. In the same issue, poems by Romains and Salmon flex similar muscles.[78]

A CHANCE ENCOUNTER that spring brought Jacob's boyhood rushing back to him. Walking near the Panthéon, he came face to face with Eugène Parturier, his favorite teacher from the lycée, the man who had introduced him to the poetry of the Renaissance master Maurice Scève. Parturier, it turned out, was teaching in Paris, continuing his work on Scève, and painting seriously enough to show his work at the Salon des Artistes Français. Of course he remembered his gifted student. A few days later Jacob wrote him a respectful note expressing the hope of seeing again "the most sympathetic witness of my childhood."[79] The two men would correspond fitfully, but loyally, until their deaths within a month of each other in 1944.

March also brought the annual Salon des Indépendants, where Jacob showed six works in pastel and gouache, two of them (a male portrait and a landscape) lent by the dealer Sagot, and two other landscapes lent, respectively, by Apollinaire and Picasso. The fact that Sagot owned some of Jacob's work indicates that, for all his humility, Jacob was by this time something more than an amateur painter. Apollinaire had noted in his diary, the year before, his pleasure in Jacob's art: "amusing, witty, decorative."[80] The storm of attention this time centered on Derain's *La Toilette* and Braque's *La Femme,* large, blocklike compositions with three nude women, inspired by Picasso's new idiom. This salon was, therefore, a triumph by proxy for Picasso. Jacob, later, was frank in attributing a defensive strategy to Picasso; he was also unreasonably dismissive of Braque, writing, "One evening Picasso met Braque and made him his student. It was Braque who took on the responsibility of showing the first Cubist painting, for reasons I need not go into."[81] In *Chronique des temps héroïques,* Jacob casts Picasso as Christ and Braque as Saint Peter: " 'You are Peter,' said the Lord, 'and on this stone I will build my church. . . . ' Provisionally it was the shoulders of Saint Peter/Braque that carried the work of God the Creator."[82] In a first draft, Jacob explained that Picasso feared, as a foreigner, drawing hostility to himself and the new art, and so he let it rest on Braque, ex-corporal and a Frenchman.[83] In spite of his closeness to Braque in the early years of Cubism, Picasso could be snide about him. Braque was always the follower, he implied years later when he was divorcing Olga Khokhlova and snickered, "Mme Braque must be worried."[84]

IN EARLY APRIL, Jacob traveled to Quimper for the wedding of his younger sister, Mirté-Léa. He was back in Paris by the twenty-fifth, however, for a literary honor that he owed to Apollinaire. This year the Salon des

Indépendants extended its attention beyond visual art to poetry, in three lectures called "Discussions of Heroic Times." Paul-Napoléon Roinard spoke, the first week, on the dead masters, Baudelaire, Vigny, and Nerval, followed the next week by Victor-Émile Michelet on the doldrums of Symbolism, clearing the way for Apollinaire's talk, "The New Phalanx."

Apollinaire was adept at literary politics. He flattered almost everyone and was careful to insist that the innovative younger poets were extending the Symbolist tradition. He was generous to friends, praising Salmon's "exquisite novelty." When he came to Jacob, however, he had to smother a burst of laughter with his hand, a gesture Jacob took painfully to heart, though he may have misinterpreted as aggression what was only good humor.[85] Apollinaire's words were friendly enough:

> Fame will come soon to take hold of Max Jacob on his Rue Ravignan. He's the simplest possible poet, and he often seems the most bizarre. This contradiction will be easily clarified, when I have said that Max Jacob's lyricism is armed with a delicious style, cutting, rapid, brilliantly and often tenderly funny, quite inaccessible to those whose concern is rhetoric and not poetry. Max Jacob's sense of goodness and beauty will never align him with those poets who seek a wretched eloquence, and who reproach him for shunning lucidity through specious thoughts.[86]

In spite of his praise, Apollinaire seemed to predict that Jacob would never reach a large audience. The occasion, one of mingled triumph and hurt, must have been further complicated by the fact that it was Jacob's friend the actor Marcel Olin, a tall, domineering man whom Carco described as "one of Max's demons, who led him on to drink, and teased him cruelly," who declaimed several of Jacob's prose poems.[87] The lecture did grant a provisional glory. After the talk the participants withdrew to a café, where Jacob's manuscripts were passed around, and he felt, at least briefly, like a significant writer. "Afterward Apollinaire often made fun of me," he noted bitterly in 1943 in an inscription on a copy of *Le Cornet à dés*.[88]

||

APOLLINAIRE NOW MOVED more and more into the limelight. Along with poems and essays, he wrote his first preface to an art catalog; describing the work of Bonnard, Braque, Denis, Derain, and others, he celebrated what he called the "three plastic virtues"—purity, unity, and truth, terms he left vague enough to apply to all the artists in the show. One would never turn to Apollinaire for precise pictorial observation. What this preface provided was a battle cry (it was time to "be the masters," to leave the corpses of the fathers behind); and he took as the symbol of the new art that flame he had just evoked in the poem "The Brasier": "I have thrown in the noble fire . . . / This Past, these death's heads."[89]

THE SUICIDE OF Karl-Heinz Wiegels at the Bateau Lavoir cast a temporary horror among *la bande*. Alerted by the mailman, Picasso rushed into the studio to find the body hanging in the window.[90] Wiegels had, Dorgelès said, "left the party."[91] But the party continued, literally, in the outlandish cortège that followed the coffin, artists and their companions all decked out in Spanish capes, evening gowns, and matador hats, with one doped-up girl in a hackney cab taking herself for a queen in a procession and tossing flowers from the mortuary wreath into the indignant crowd.[92]

The symbolic party went on, more seriously, in the work of painting and poetry. Picasso was finishing his large canvas *The Three Women*. The poets were gathering: Romains brought together the Montmartre poets with his friends at L'Abbaye in Créteil, and Salmon moved from the Latin Quarter to the Rue Saint-Vincent, a few streets away from the Bateau Lavoir. One of his movers, a workman from the lower slopes of Montmartre, asked him what the hell he was doing moving up to Sacré-Coeur: "If you go up there, it's your business, but when you're up there, there are some people to stay away from. I mean, *la bande à Picasso*." He said he particularly loathed Max Jacob, who went horsing around giving himself airs; one day he was going to knock his top hat down over his ears.[93]

As usual, summer brought a lull. Friends scattered. Braque returned to the Mediterranean port of l'Estaque, where he painted the landscapes that would launch Cubism in the fall, and Picasso withdrew with Fernande to the village of La Rue des Bois. The party continued even here: the Dutch writer Fritz Vanderpyl and his mistress joined them; then they entertained Derain and his new mistress Alice Princet (who had run away from her actuary husband); then Jacob came to stay for several weeks. When Apollinaire wanted to visit, Fernande wrote to welcome him but warned that he'd have to share a room with Max. It would be quiet, she promised: "So much so that Max says the silence seems exaggerated."[94]

Back in Paris that fall, artistic life was marked less by the Salon d'Automne, where the jury controlled by Matisse excluded Braque's Cézanne-inspired landscapes, than by the show Kahnweiler organized for Braque to honor these inventive paintings. This show established Kahnweiler as the visionary dealer of avant-garde art, and it provoked the name "Cubism," put into circulation by the critic Louis Vauxcelles.[95] It also gave Apollinaire another chance to identify himself with the new art, though the preface he wrote for the catalog betrayed no comprehension of Braque's extraordinary spatial invention and irrelevantly concluded with an advertisement for Marie Laurencin.[96]

V.

LA BANDE À PICASSO was now in full flower of youth and fantasy, and their energy often spilled over from art into pranks. This joyous society lived by the *blague,* the joke, at once an expression of irreverence for any code outside its own, delight in disorder, and a stylish nonconformity, like Picasso's workman's garb or Braque's and Derain's proletarian chic of garish ties and checkered jackets. The young painter Jacques Vaillant, still enrolled in the Beaux-Arts, had given up to Braque his studio at the bottom of the steps to Sacré-Coeur and had taken a studio in the Bateau Lavoir. Happy-go-lucky, a *bon-vivant,* Vaillant was easily won over to the new aesthetics, though for whatever reasons—his "phlegm," his bourgeois upbringing—he couldn't give his paintings much shape. When the *bande* criticized his compositions, Vaillant didn't go hang himself like Wiegels,

Salmon said, but would explode, "You bastards, you're just saying that to make me think I'm a jerk, but you can go to hell, there's not one of you except Picasso who has the balls to pitch together on one canvas ten figures like my *Breton Wedding!*"[97]

With his middle-class parents hovering in the background, Vaillant was a perfect butt for *blagues*. His mother sent her maid over twice a month to clean his studio; word spread over the Butte, and in vain Vaillant would bluster and order his friends "to leave Mother's maid in peace." Once, when she rolled his sofa on casters out into the Place Ravignan to do a more thorough sweeping, Braque got hold of it and led a group "tobogganing" down the steep narrow streets of Montmartre with two little girls aboard, shrieking in glee; the next day Vaillant was nearly summoned to the commissariat for attempted debauch of minors. Another day, when the maid moved his furniture out onto the sidewalk to do a particularly serious cleaning, Vaillant returned to find his pals conducting a mock auction, with Jacob playing the auctioneer: "What do I hear? Twenty-five francs for this wardrobe, in genuine Norway pitch pine, twenty-five francs, fifty—any bids?" When Vaillant stormed in to repossess his belongings, he almost had to fight one vexed buyer who thought he had purchased a mattress, while Jacob remonstrated, "But Sir, you see perfectly well that M. Vaillant has returned to redeem his possessions. The sale is cancelled. Goodnight, ladies and gentlemen."[98]

In late November or early December, *la bande* gathered for an elaborate but serious *blague*, a dinner celebrating the Douanier Rousseau. So complex were the levels of humor and homage at the Bateau Lavoir, and so contradictory the opinions about Rousseau, that the controversy engendered by the banquet persists to this day. Fernande's chapter on Rousseau embodies the contradiction: Picasso decided to organize a banquet in honor of Rousseau, she says, but *la bande* was "delighted to play a joke on the *douanier.*"[99] As many memoirs of Rousseau make clear, his naïve dignity made him the target of many jokes, some of them cruel. But Picasso, in search now of versions of the primitive, had been truly intrigued by Rousseau's large painting *The Snake Charmer* at the Salon d'Automne the year before, and he had just bought Rousseau's portrait of Yadwigha, which he would keep all his life. It was partly to celebrate this purchase that he organized the banquet, which was both *blague* and serious homage. Not all were convinced of Rousseau's genius. Derain, who stayed away, asked Salmon, "So what's going on? The triumph of the imbeciles?"[100] But for Picasso, Salmon, Uhde, and Robert Delaunay, among others, Rousseau was a giant, though an innocent one; and Jacob remembered that Apollinaire wouldn't mock the old man, "because Picasso wouldn't have allowed it."[101]

Jacob was not present for the dinner itself, being in a huff with Picasso, but he lent his room as an adjunct kitchen, and his curiosity overcame him so he joined the party in its last, drunken stage.[102] Picasso had decorated the studio with green drapes and lanterns to resemble the Douanier's own ceremonial evenings of art, music, and poetry; the portrait of Yadwigha held pride of place on an easel; a banner proclaimed "Honor to Rousseau," and the artist himself was seated on a dais, so pleased that he scarcely noticed the hot wax dripping on his head from a taper fixed to the wall. Jacob wasn't there to witness the scurrying around to replenish provisions when the catered food didn't arrive, or tipsy Marie Laurencin falling into the pies and being sent home by Apollinaire, and he probably didn't hear Apollinaire's and Salmon's recitations of their poems to Rousseau. He may have been there after the delighted and sleepy old man had been sent home in a horse-drawn cab his admirers paid for, when Salmon and Vaillant simulated attacks of delirium tremens, writhing on the floor and foaming at the mouth with soap bubbles (to the consternation of Gertrude Stein, who took it seriously).[103] "Rousseau was charming in his weakness, his naïveté, his touching vanity," wrote Fernande. "For a long time he remembered, with deep emotion, this reception, which the good man took in good faith as an homage to his genius."[104] Picasso later told Geneviève Laporte, "You know, it was really a joke. Nobody believed in his talent. He was the only one who took it seriously, he cried with joy. We couldn't turn back."[105] But Picasso had watched every stroke of Rousseau's brush when he visited his studio.[106] Salmon was probably not far off the mark when he concluded, "In organizing the banquet of the Rue Ravignan, Picasso, Fernande Olivier and their friends wanted to please Rousseau who was to die two years later, and for whom this was one of the last joys of his life." [107]

VI.

THE YEAR 1909 brought new artistic surges: the founding of *La Nouvelle Revue française;* the publication of Romains's *First Book of Prayers;* a row stirred up by the soon-to-be Futurist Filippo Tommaso Marinetti's play *Le Roi Bombance* (King Bombance); the publication of Apollinaire's masterpiece, the long poem "The Song of the Ill-Beloved" in the *Mercure de France;* and Kahnweiler's publication of Apollinaire's first literary book, *L'Enchanteur pourrissant* (The Rotting Sorcerer) in collaboration with Derain. For Jacob, it was a year of continued writing and painting, almost no publication, a wrenching quarrel, separations, and a mystical apparition.

Père Soulié, the old art dealer, died in April, as if to punctuate one period of Picasso's life; with the patronage of the Steins, the support of Vollard and Kahnweiler, and his growing reputation, Picasso was about to step beyond the bohemia of the Bateau Lavoir. For Jacob, the separation started in early May, when Picasso and Fernande set out for another summer in Spain, the destination this time being the mountain village of Horta de Ebro. Jacob, back in Paris, wrote to complain that Apollinaire was acting, he said, like a lout. [108]

Jacob's hypersensitivity seems to have been at the origin of this quarrel. A rumor went about that Apollinaire felt slighted by Jacob, who responded with the full force of his hurt feelings, accusing Apollinaire of avoiding him and laughing at him. [109] More contretemps followed, a missed appointment for which Apollinaire apologized, and a renunciation of friendship by Jacob. By late June, feelings had calmed, and Jacob wrote in his old playful tone a visionary letter to Apollinaire that described, in the image of an onion, the interpenetration of spiritual and physical universes in rings within rings, and anticipated a spiritual revolution for which Jacob seems to have been hungering. For all the joking, the onion metaphor really did represent Jacob's Kabbalistic view of reality. What he would gain from conversion to Christianity was a single mediating figure who could connect sacred and earthly spheres and embody a supreme love impossible in merely human connection. Jacob concluded this letter by assuring Apollinaire of his "adhesive friendship."[110]

Adhesive the friendship may have been, but cracks were appearing in the tight little world of the Bateau Lavoir. Fernande Olivier would feel the fracture in 1912 when she and Picasso separated for good.[111] But a preliminary dispersal occurred in 1909. Apollinaire had already moved to the suburb of Auteuil-Passy to be closer to Laurencin. On July 13, Salmon married and moved with his bride out of Montmartre to the Left Bank: Apollinaire celebrated them in a poem honoring both Memory and the Future (which rhyme in French: *souvenir* and *avenir*), evoking his meeting with Salmon in the "infernal cellar" of the tavern where they had read their youthful poems.[112] The poem praises love, friendship, and poetic solidarity, but the day-to-day reality would be that from now on neither Apollinaire nor Salmon could breeze so easily in and out of the Bateau Lavoir.

The harsher blow fell in September when Picasso and Fernande returned from Horta and moved from the Bateau Lavoir to a large apartment on the top floor of 11 boulevard de Clichy. Jacob skips over this move in a one-sentence paragraph in his memoir from 1927: "Around 1910, Picasso had become very well off; he went to live at the Boulevard de Clichy, 32 or 24."[113] (Jacob got the address wrong.) In his memoirs for Guiette, he suppressed the move entirely. Fernande said that Picasso made up his mind to move on his return from Spain "reluctantly, because he left behind in that house on the Rue Ravignan the few most beautiful memories of his life."[114]

The Boulevard de Clichy was not far from the Butte—it is the boulevard separating lower Montmartre from the ninth arrondissement—but it represented a definite change of social world. The building was owned by a former government minister. The few pieces of rickety furniture brought from the Bateau Lavoir went into a maid's room in the new establishment, and into the maid's room also went a maid, complete with cap and apron, to serve regular meals and to spare Fernande the little housekeeping she might have been inclined to do. Picasso's father sent an Italian cabinet and Hepplewhite chairs; Picasso and Fernande filled the rooms with mahogany tables and chests, a real brass bedstead instead of the old mattress propped on blocks off the floor, a piano, and a sofa. "Picasso Becomes Bourgeois," Fernande titled this chapter in her memoir.[115] The apartment had a large studio that Picasso furnished with old oak furniture, African masks and statuettes, bric-a-brac from junk stores, bits of old tapestry, musical instruments, and a huge sofa covered in violet velvet and gold buttons. Frika the dog, three Siamese cats, and a new companion, the monkey Monina, completed the household.

The excitement of the move was accompanied by an artistic event. Picasso and Fernande had barely unpacked in the Boulevard de Clichy when Picasso held a *vernissage* there to show his summer's work, paintings and drawings that were by now frankly Cubist: boxy landscapes, mountainous cleft portraits of Fernande, and anthropomorphic mountains. His admirers approved: the Steins bought three pieces, Kahnweiler bought gouaches and drawings, and Vollard purchased most of the paintings that were left.

Alone on the Rue Ravignan, separated from his idol—separated from the figure who, he said, had been the great encounter of his life, and the figure who "is not, but [who] creates himself, as Vico said of God"[116]—Max Jacob had the only possible greater encounter. One afternoon late in September he came back from the Bibliothèque Nationale. He put down his briefcase and looked for his slippers. When he raised his head, a sacred figure was glowing against the red cloth hanging on his wall. "It was the great event of his life," said Guiette. "He told the story, in prose of blood, tears, and love."[117]

CHAPTER 7

CHRIST AND THE DRUIDS

I.

The Being who appeared on Max Jacob's wall against the red cloth was masculine and young, with hair flowing down to his shoulders.[1] He wore a yellow silk robe with blue trim. Jacob first saw him from behind, but the Being turned his head, revealing his forehead, brow, and mouth in a peaceful and radiant face. He was standing in a landscape Jacob himself had painted. In an instant, the poet later claimed, his flesh fell to the ground, and he was "undressed by lightning." Two words echoed in his brain: "To die, to be born."[2] The apparition set off a flood of colorful images and a chorus of voices that kept Jacob awake all night. In the scene that most impressed him, six monks resembling him carried the corpse of another monk into the room, and a woman appeared with serpents twined in her hair and arms.

This experience has been accepted by Jacob's readers as the "real" account of his vision, as contrasted with the fictive versions he presented in *Saint Matorel* in the months immediately following the event. He crafted this supposedly factual version for the autobiographical work *La Défense de Tartufe: Extases, remords, visions, prières, poèmes et méditations d'un Juif converti* (Tartufe's Defense: Ecstasies, Remorse, Visions, Prayers, Poems, and Meditations by a Converted Jew), a mixture of poems, documentary confession, and diary extracts published ten years after the vision. The account from *Tartufe* is the one installed in Guiette's biography. In 1939 Jacob dictated a more extended version of the apparition, as requested by a priest, Abbé Foucher.[3] It relates the same story he had written in *La Défense de Tartufe:* the figure on the wall against the painting, the poet falling into rapture, the vision of the monks and the woman with snakes. This is the story he erected as his official truth.

And here the problems start. In his different retellings, Jacob gave different dates. Sometimes he claimed that the Revelation occurred on September 28, 1909. This is the date in the earliest surviving record, a letter to Jules Romains from October 1909, just a few weeks after his vision;[4] in a manuscript draft for *La Défense de Tartufe* entitled "Different States of Mind, or Portrait of the Author at Work" dated June 1917;[5] and in an interview in the journal *Minotaure* in 1933.[6] In three places in *La Défense de Tartufe,* the date appears as September 22 (with the further precision, in one of these passages, that it occurred at four p.m.).[7] In his "Account of My Conversion" he said simply that the vision came in September 1909, as he did in several meditations composed in the late 1930s.[8] Elsewhere October was preferred. In November 1914, in a letter to Maurice Raynal, he named October;[9] he specified October 7, 1909, in the poem "Christ at the Movies" in *La Défense de Tartufe;*[10] and he named October 28 in a letter written in January 1915 to his cousin Jean-Richard Bloch.[11]

Why all these different dates? Some scholars simply note the discrepancies and don't make much of them.[12] Others, like the Jesuit priest André Blanchet in *Literature and the Spiritual* and in his edition of *La Défense de Tartufe,* don't remark on the problem at all.[13] Still others, like John Richardson and Didier Gompel-Netter, choose a date arbitrarily without providing compelling evidence. But it is a problem, and a serious one, since the apparition marked a turning point in Jacob's life. And thinking about it illuminates Jacob's central drama of identity in relation to the sacred.

It is useful to follow Blanchet in comparing the documentary versions of the experience in *La Défense de Tartufe* and the much later "Account of My Conversion" to the fictive versions in *Saint Matorel*. As Blanchet noted, the freshest material, closest in time to the experience, was recorded in the story, dialogues, and prose poems of *Saint Matorel*, composed in the immediate aftermath of the vision. The supposedly literal account in *La*

Défense de Tartufe wasn't composed until seven years later. The "realistic" account of God appearing on the wall, with the details of the return from the library and the slippers, is a much more literary artifact than the fiction of *Matorel,* which describes a hallucinatory experience and depicts the hero's fever lasting for days.

Matorel has traveled across Paris to find a mysterious blind man. Images of blindness, death, and birth recur in rapid episodes involving a black woman giving birth to twins, one dead and one alive, and Matorel (eight days after the search for the original blind man) assisting a blind beggar-woman. Then Matorel falls ill, and on the second day of his fever, he has the central visionary experience. And it doesn't include the apparition of the elegant long-haired Being at all:

> The second day of his illness, Matorel had two visions, different in intensity from the usual visions of madness: the first was of himself as a beggar woman, with curly hair, eyes bright as burning coals, circling around a white marble statue; the second was of six monks resembling him and carrying his corpse; at the same time, he heard a tremendous noise in his room; clouds covered the ceiling, red thunder shot out of the clouds; a woman in a white dress appeared, treading on a serpent, and a thousand voices Matorel understood to be from demons and angels spoke in turn.
>
> The Angel
>
> Lie down on your bed and pray.
>
> Matorel
>
> I was lying down when I saw the clouds and the thunder; the sun was red, the backs of the clouds were white and spherical.
>
> The Angel
>
> You have seen God![14]

The six monks and the woman with the serpent reappear in later accounts, but the divine in the Matorel story has no human shape: it's just visible thunder. This part of *Saint Matorel* spreads out in music hall dialogue, with demons and planets chattering along with the angel and even God, mixing Kabbalistic, theosophical, and zodiacal imagery. Only at the end of the third chapter of part two does God appear shaped as a man:

—*Open the door! Let the light in.*
—*Wait! I beg you, let me get dressed.*
—*Don't get dressed, open the door.*
—*My God! My God! Who are you? Oh! Poor man!*
—*Look at my bleeding face, look at my weeping face, libertine. Do you know this robe?*
—*What? It's you? It's you, my Lord Jesus Christ.*[15]

After brief stage business about how to fit the cross through the door, Jacob bursts into Kabbalistic numerology: Christ explains that his Cross is the form of the Hebrew letter *T*, which corresponds to the number nine: two times four plus one, reason and will.[16]

Saint Matorel is a hybrid fiction, but it contains hallucinatory material that suggests the actual messiness of Jacob's life in the fall of 1909. His official accounts in *La Défense de Tartufe* and in "Account of My Conversion," texts composed to be read by devout Catholics, present, on the contrary, artificial reconstructions of visionary experience. The much later "Account" gives still more naturalistic detail: Jacob claimed that the morning of his vision, the landlord had sent two workmen to his dark room in the lower courtyard, one to let in more light by opening a skylight in the roof, and one to let in more air by installing a movable pane in the window. Jacob later took these apertures as signs of the grace that would soon break open his life.[17]

Let us return to the question of dates. Bearing in mind the ten days, at least, in the Matorel narrative, we find in three other documents evidence of visionary experience extending over more than ten days and confirming the essential truth of the Matorel story. The first is the letter Jacob wrote Jules Romains only a few weeks after his crisis. The second is the draft for *La Défense de Tartufe* entitled "Different States of Mind," dated June 1917.

The third is Jacob's article entitled "The Key to Dreams," published in *Philosophies* in 1925.[18]

The letter to Romains clears up the mystery. Writing in October 1909 in the first flush of excitement, Jacob described a sequence of visions that corresponded pretty closely to the story he would give his hero, Matorel: "Thirteen days after the apparition of the Thunder of 28 September, the apparition of Jesus confirmed me in my faith."[19] This claim accounts both for the vision of thunder in *Matorel* and for an encounter with Christ; it explains why Jacob sometimes referred to his apparition as having occurred in late September 1909 and sometimes in early October; and it suggests how he progressively fashioned his experience into an artifact whose simplified lineaments could more easily capture the imaginations of his audience (and perhaps his own).

"Different States of Mind" fills out the picture even further. This essay, in neat handwriting identified by Jacob's scrawl on top of the page as belonging to a "copyist," describes a state of mystical waiting preceding an encounter with God. The Gallic rationalism contrasts amusingly with the occult subject matter. Subtitled "Portrait of the Author at Work," it does indeed offer a self-portrait. He distinguishes "waiting" from attention since this mystical waiting is involuntary.[20] The person waiting for vision is subject to vague regrets and sorrows. The waiting may be interrupted by distractions that sound very much like Jacob's life in Paris: brilliant chatter in public places. In a later stage, a highly associative state of mind can delude the seeker into thinking himself illuminated. Physiological changes occur: visual and auditory illusions; creativity; and heightened receptivity to grace. Finally Jacob shifts to first-person confession: "It is, on the occasion of a living apparition by which the Lord deigned to make me believe in Him, 28 September 1909, the mystical state which preceded and followed it." This mystical state continued for weeks, perhaps months. The reader will find a portrait of his crisis in his book *Saint Matorel,* he advises. The central encounter resembles the one in *La Défense de Tartufe:* the beautiful Christ wearing a yellow and blue robe. In the article in *Philosophies,* Jacob similarly described months of "unconscious waiting" preceding a visionary experience.[21]

||

DOES THE EVIDENCE of literary fabrication mean that his vision was a lie? Just one more Montmartre farce, as many of his friends supposed? One more performance by the Harlequin poet, whose whole life we might nowadays consider performance art? Putting the various texts together, it seems that his years of occult studies, combined with the shock of Picasso moving away, precipitated days of illness and hallucination resulting in two particularly intense visions, one of thunder, and one, thirteen days later, of a Christ figure. The question to ask is, what did Jacob make of these visions, and what did they make of him?

Like Yeats's dalliance with spirits, Jacob's vision emerged from years of meditative practice, and this eruption had the practical consequence of directing his writing more and more along Christian lines. It had the more extended consequence of changing his entire life. That he chiseled his days of hallucination down to one dramatic anecdote seems a writerly device: but the anecdote became his reality, and he made it real by adapting the rest of his life to a theology and to a myth of himself. To prove this reality and to make it concrete, he drew a circle in blue chalk on the wall where the Lord had appeared.[22]

At times, Jacob feared that he had deceived himself. His stand-in, Matorel, asks in "Doubt," "And what if all my daytime and nocturnal enchantments were lies!"[23] Years later, in "Mystical Poems," Jacob worried at the same question. Addressing the God of the wall, he declared, "I am a witness of the Invisible. The one I saw from the crown of his hair to the hem of his robe was not of this earth. Will you believe me? ... Am I crazy enough to have invented for myself a God on a wall? And if this God wasn't a God, how could he have converted me?"[24]

II.

IMMEDIATELY AFTER THE apparition, Jacob went in search of a priest at a local church, Saint-Jean-l'Évangéliste in Montmartre, hoping for baptism.

Hearing the tale, the priest just smiled. In his pastoral duties in bohemia, he must have been used to hearing about a wide spectrum of miseries and delusions. He was also wary, he told Jacob years later, of jokes played by journalists.[25] In any case, he didn't offer to baptize this excited Jewish poet-ragamuffin, who went home and wrote a bitter complaint in rhyming couplets. "To a Priest Who Refuses to Baptize Me" concludes:

> Those who please God won't always please you, Sirs!
> Adieu! I must keep silent, it appears,
> At this new insult suffered. I won't rail:
> My mouth, addressing you, regains its smile.[26]

Disappointed but undaunted, Jacob incorporated his vision into his daily life. He began attending mass at Sacré-Coeur, not taking communion but praying. He went about in a hypersensitive state, enjoying the visions of angels and demons he thought God continued to send to him.[27] He read the Old and New Testaments, and he kept up his researches in the Bibliothèque Nationale, now more than ever ransacking books of symbolism for help in interpreting the images parading through his mind. His struggle to reconcile esoteric exegesis with a new conception of religious practice left strong traces in *Saint Matorel* and in *La Défense de Tartufe*. The prose poem "Significations" in *Tartufe* asks, "Is it better to understand than to pray, or better to pray than to understand?"[28] A philosopher to whom he narrated his experience introduced him to a lady who examined him with her lorgnon, saying, "I wouldn't have believed it," but sent him to see her pious daughter. This young lady gave him her copy of Saint François de Sales's *Introduction to the Devout Life* and warned him that humans never saw God or His Son but only guardian angels.[29]

In the following weeks, Jacob entertained his friends with the story. Picasso, at least, took him seriously, or that was how Jacob remembered it in a letter he wrote to his hero twelve years later as he was leaving for his first extended stay in the monastery.[30] As he told Guiette, God had intoxicated him.[31]

||

CHRIST'S MOST IMMEDIATE effect on Max Jacob was to stimulate his writing. Jacob had drawn increasingly close to Jules Romains in the last few years, and in an article in the recently founded *La Nouvelle Revue française*, Romains cited two prose poems by Jacob, "My Flowers in My Hands" and "The Bay at the Beach," admiring their evocation of the "soul in the real."

Elliptical, tender, verging on the sinister, they show Jacob's new art of suggestion and nonsequitur.

MY FLOWERS IN MY HANDS

We went our separate ways, my older brothers and I, near the ditches; "Here, take the knife!"

We were under the pine trees, it was all meadow and flowers. "Ah! Watch out for the water!"

Every now and then we approached each other, holding a flower: "It's fool's parsley!"

But when it came to finding a vase at home to hold the harvest, that was another story!

The naval officer was sleeping in his bed, his back to the door.

The cousin was cleaning house, with the sheets hanging over the chairs.

My sisters sang in the attic and I stood there like a small child, my flowers in my hands, on the steps of an endless staircase.[32]

"My Flowers in My Hands" presents an allegory of the poet half in and half out of his family, his offering rejected. (The offering itself is suspect: *ciguë-rose*, in English fool's parsley or cowbane, is a kind of water hemlock, a poisonous plant.) Romains went on to laud Jacob in a lecture at the Salon d'Automne, calling him one of the "rare sincere poets who use their soul as an organ of perpetual revelation."[33] These appreciations encouraged the diffident poet, but the figure in the blue and yellow robe on his wall now plunged him into a period of sustained creation.

Almost as a magical confirmation of Jacob's new powers, a publisher appeared at his door. This was Daniel-Henry Kahnweiler, the young German art dealer who collected Picasso and who was about to publish Apollinaire's Symbolist dream tale *L'Enchanteur pourrissant* (The Rotting Sorcerer) with illustrations by Derain. In 1943 Jacob would describe Kahnweiler's visit as a direct result of his vision: God was taking care of him.[34] To Guiette, Jacob would explain that in his mystical state, he simply gathered his prose poems and notes of visions and turned them into *Saint Matorel*.[35] He claimed that Kahnweiler bought the manuscript for 150 francs and demanded, as part of the bargain, a four-panel screen painted by Picasso. No evidence of this screen has turned up.[36]

SAINT MATOREL COULDN'T have been composed in a few days, but it did include material written earlier, and Jacob finished it by the time he went to Quimper six months later in April 1910. Even before *Matorel*, his conversion bubbled up in a Breton tale he published in *Pan* in December 1909, "Vulcan's Crown." There "Our Lord Jesus Christ" appears from a cooking pot to the little lame hunchbacked tailor Toulic. This unlikely hero— a version of the poet—is sent off on a quest on the ship of Cocambo, the King of the Sun, to steal the crown of King Levanaël, King of the Cheeses. Toulic is promised good fortune if he accomplishes this feat, as Jacob imagined good fortune attending the appearance of Our Lord Jesus Christ on his wall. The tale unfolds in a spoof on professional folklorists, citing the innkeeper as the source of the tale: "So he said, said he." The strands Jacob would twine together in his larger works were all visible in this tale: a divine apparition, a visionary journey, Breton folklore, the satire of modern life, and even three prose poems and a pseudo-Breton lyric.[37]

But it was into *Saint Matorel* that Jacob poured the first, large-scale account of his vision. "A masterpiece (I swear) of mysticism, sorrow, and meticulous realism," he claimed in a letter to Tzara in 1916.[38] Much later he would express doubts about it: in a copy he annotated for Paul Bonet in 1943, he wrote, "This book amazes me! What a salad of visions truly seen, of small observations noted in low and vulgar circles, ungenerous, hardly universal. It all smells of Montmartre of 1900, soiled with the habits of petty clerks."[39] Yet to Jean-Jacques Mezure, in 1941, he described *Saint Matorel* as the story of his conversion.[40]

Mixing prose narration, rhymed dialogue, and prose poems, *Saint Matorel* breaks the frame of realist storytelling as self-consciously as Picasso had broken conventions of pictorial illusion in *Les Demoiselles d'Avignon*. At the same time, it's one of Jacob's most revealing pieces of autobiography. He dramatized his experiences of the whole previous decade: his ineffectual labors in his cousin's department store, here called La Maison Cheiret & Cie.; his affair with Cécile/Germaine, here called Léonie; his occult theories and commerce with angels and demons; his encounter with God. Except for the short final section ("The End of the Prologue"), which drags a bit, it's a vivacious, original work. It shows the hierarchies of reality as Jacob understood them, from the grim minutiae of daily life to celestial visions.

Jacob projected himself into two characters, the narrator, "Monsieur Max," a janitor at Cheiret & Cie., and the goofy hero Victor Matorel, a ticket collector in the Métro, formerly a clerk at Cheiret & Cie.[41] From the first few words, we know we're not going to follow a linear plot. We start with Matorel on his deathbed talking to Satan. The narrator remarks, "Maybe this Prologue should have been kept for an Epilogue. . . . Victor Matorel, in religion Brother Manassé, is dead. . . . But the forms are eternally immobile and mobile in heaven and God respects no chronological order. Thus, Prologue."[42] (Tongue in his metafictional cheek, the narrator exclaims, as he introduces Matorel's prose poems, "And what more, I ask you, can one demand from a realist author?")[43] The living Matorel enters the story in chapter one, making cockeyed puns and describing his philosophy of intersecting realities: spiderwebs in the absolute, love on earth, the cube and the circle, demons and angels, and the need to skin men's backs to sensitize the openings in the spine.[44] Later, in his tour in a gypsy caravan to sell cheap garments in the provinces, Matorel explains, "Heaven is the nape of Man's neck; but Man is only one heaven: there are others."[45] Still later, in the Ball of the Spirits following the revelation of God to Matorel, Saturn declares, "Have you ever thought of the question of doors, wrists are doors, ankles are doors. . . . The waist is a door. Learn Hebrew."[46]

This corporeal spirituality would remain a constant for Jacob. It allowed him to unite mysticism, erotic love, and an increasingly incarnational poetics, especially after his formal conversion when he focused more and more on the wounded body of Christ.[47] *Saint Matorel* displays, not the body of Christ, but a phantasmagoria of spirits. The profane body makes humiliating love. Léonie rattles on, crude, ignorant, selfish, and promiscuous: "These high-society guys are like the rest: The little piggie! The little piggie! . . . They live only for the little piggie!" She's describing Jacob and his experience with Cécile when she says of Victor Matorel that he was sensitive, but a screwball who opened the window and began singing the first night they made love.[48] In chapter three Matorel confesses: "My God, deliver me from the atrocious and delicious image of Léonie," remembering making love with her on the narrow little bed. The angel asks, "Didn't God intend you to die of joy while loving?" to which "I, Matorel" replies that he has been a sodomite.[49]

Saint Matorel recounts Matorel's friendship with the cynical womanizer Émile Cordier (a slant version of Picasso or Apollinaire?); an encounter with God; Matorel's conversion of Cordier; and Matorel's retreat to the monastery of Saint Teresa of Àvila in Barcelona, where he suffers temptations (including the cupid who turns out to be a demon). Matorel becomes prior of the monastery and dies "in the odor of sanctity." The resumed Prologue, concluding it all, takes the souls of Matorel and Cordier, both dead, on a wild horseback ride through the zodiac and pitches them back to earth as injured angels where they are imprisoned by the demon Barbazel and rescued by God through machinations involving "a terrible Italian canon who resembled Mirabeau"—a reappearance of the Canon Rossi from Jacob's childhood in Quimper. A touch of realism in the "End of the Prologue" recalls the floods that had just torn through Paris in January 1910.[50]

All of *Saint Matorel* shines with the light of Jacob's apparition, stylized as opéra bouffe. Impudent, heretical, and sincere, inventing an aesthetic we would now call camp, Jacob embeds his experience in the tale of Matorel. To Cordier, Matorel explains, "We are the living dead. We must die unto ourselves, in our moral poverty we each have a child in us, that's why the Child God is in the manger."[51] In a mirror-game of fictive and real identities, Matorel/Jacob prays to a Jewish/Christian God: "Adonaï Sabaoth, in the name of your Son, whom I know as I know your name and as I know myself, replace what is matter in me by spirit."[52] How *did* Max Jacob ever know himself, would become the critical question of his life.

WORKING ON *SAINT MATOREL,* Jacob had much in mind Kahnweiler's publication of Apollinaire's *L'Enchanteur pourrissant* with woodcuts by Derain. When his own manuscript was complete, he showed it to Derain and asked if he would illustrate it. Derain demurred, explaining that the work was so disconcerting, it left no room for an artist. He promised, however, to illustrate another book of Jacob's in the future.[53]

When he still thought Derain might provide art for *Saint Matorel,* Jacob seems to have had a nasty falling out with Picasso.[54] Whatever the fight was about, Jacob's description to Marcel Olin makes bitter reading and shows a Max Jacob both wounded and uncharacteristically vicious. He had sold some drawings of Picasso's, he told Olin, because he had no money and he had to eat, and he stated, with wild unreasonableness, that Picasso had "been against him his whole life." The book, he explained, would be illustrated by Derain (not Picasso).[55]

III.

JACOB'S ANGER DIDN'T last long. By mid-April, he had set up shop back in Quimper, where a stream of letters to friends shows him hard at work on a play about Matorel's adventures in the afterlife (*Le Siège de Jérusalem,* The Siege of Jerusalem) and gathering the poems that would go into *Les Oeuvres burlesques et mystiques de Frère Matorel.* He apologized to Salmon for being a lout and leaving Paris the very day they had agreed to meet;[56] to Kahnweiler, he reported on his new work and on the plans for *Saint*

Matorel. On April 19 he still hoped that Derain would illustrate it; ten days later he had heard—evidently from Kahnweiler—that Picasso would provide the art. In a further sign of reconciliation with *la bande à Picasso*, he dedicated the book to Apollinaire. In May he complimented Salmon on his new book of poems, comparing it to Halley's Comet, visible over France on May 18. "Ah! You're no longer a Symbolist!" Jacob exulted.[57]

Jacob stayed five months with his family in Quimper. Relations were not easy. In his illuminated state, Jacob worked hours a day in his childhood bedroom, a sweet room, he wrote Salmon, but dark.[58] He was also annotating Ovid's *Metamorphoses*, and when he was tired, he fooled around downstairs in the living room on the piano, *rouillé* (rusted), he said, by the sap of his adolescent playing, or *vérouillé* (bolted shut). All this activity by the thirty-four-year-old unemployed son didn't impress his parents, and for a while the situation grew so strained that he worked during the days at the house of his aunt Delphine and uncle Raphaël, the genial couple who had often taken him in during his adolescence.[59] But home base remained the Rue du Parc, where he felt like "the cursed son."[60]

He hardly had time to brood over it, his writing kept him so busy. So did his delighted reacquaintance with his town. When he wasn't polishing Matorel's poems, he fashioned anecdotes about Quimper into stories that would find their way into *Cinématoma, Le Roi de Béotie*, and *Le Terrain Bouchaballe*. "I write about a story a week," he reported to Kahnweiler, "and not goat shit, but sweet stuff!"[61] He eagerly anticipated visits by friends; Salmon thought of coming, and so did Henri Hertz and Jules Romains. Jacob lamented to Kahnweiler that his family wouldn't allow him to invite Salmon to lunch—"so painful for a gentleman!"[62] In August, Romains arrived, Baedeker in hand, and Jacob proudly escorted the famous young author through town, ignoring the students who dogged their steps.[63]

Jacob's effervescence spilled into a new literary friendship. Through his friend the poet Joseph Savigny, Jacob met another literary *quimpérois*, Pierre Allier. Eleven years younger than Jacob, Allier was the son of Jacob's old history professor from the lycée. He had grumpily obeyed his parents and enrolled in medical school; after completing the thesis, he left medicine for law, but his true bent was literary, and when Jacob met him in the summer of 1910, he was studying law and writing Breton songs, stories, and newspaper articles.

The day he met Allier, Jacob invited him and Savigny back to his room, where he pulled out his manuscripts and read them bits of the play about Quimper, *Le Terrain Bouchaballe,* and the local stories he was amassing. He dazzled them, Allier remembered, with his writing, his Parisian sophistication, his theories of style, his accounts of his apparition, his occult lore, and his manic imitations. He soon drew the younger men into his work. After days at the library, Jacob would meet Allier and Savigny and the trio would make the rounds of the taverns of Quimper, recording dialogue, tales, and songs in the manner of the folklorist François-Marie Luzel, material that would nourish Jacob's work for years.[64]

Seeing each other almost every day, Jacob and Allier shared adventures that would wind up in *Le Terrain Bouchaballe,* such as a lavishly advertised aviation "meeting."[65] The first airplanes ever seen in Quimper arrived in pieces, by train, and were assembled on the horseracing track in front of an enormous crowd. The spectators, who had paid a high price for their tickets, waited three days for the aeronautical demonstration to begin while the pilots lounged in the refreshment booth getting drunk on champagne. By the end of the third day, a mob poured onto the field threatening to burn the planes and throw the pilots in the river, which provoked one little buzz over the field by each plane. The incident provided Jacob with an entire chapter of *Le Terrain Bouchaballe,* with Allier as the minor character Hélary.[66]

The persistent theme in Jacob's correspondence in the summer of 1910, however, is Kahnweiler's preparation of *Saint Matorel.* Having secured Picasso's collaboration, the dealer asked Jacob to prepare a prospectus for the book. The flustered author protested that he hardly knew who he was and couldn't praise himself; he appended a fantastical biography, presenting himself as a Breton sailor whose voyages have taken him to Asia and Australia, and whose later life in Paris initiated him into the life of art.[67] As he did so often, Jacob communicated his truth in a fable: this portrait of Breton origins, supernaturalism, irony, and urban sophistication describes him quite accurately.

Picasso, who was spending the summer in Spain, set to work on the etchings in August. Unfazed by Jacob's fragmented narrative, the painter used the assignment as a way to pursue his own experiments with Cubist renditions of the human figure ("Mademoiselle Léonie" and "Mademoiselle Léonie sur une chaise longue"); still life ("La Table"); and landscape ("Le Couvent"). Their sober dignity doesn't exclude an element of playfulness suited to the story of Matorel. In no way illustrative, Picasso's plates maintain a parallel life that complements Jacob's text. These companions who had sustained each other through ten difficult years in creating revolutions in their arts collaborated at a distance, but in instinctive sympathy, on what would become a masterpiece and a milestone in art history: the first illustrated Cubist book.[68] Kahnweiler liked it so much, he named the little sailboat he shared with Vlaminck the *Saint-Matorel*.[69]

IV.

IN LATE SEPTEMBER, still in Quimper, Jacob received the proofs of *Saint Matorel*, and by October 1 he reestablished himself in the Rue Ravignan for a season of publications of poetry and prose, anticipation of the appearance of *Saint Matorel*, and decisive new friendships.

Of these, the most consequential would be the encounter with the poet Pierre Reverdy. A southerner, son of a Socialist winegrower and town councilor who had lost his land in the phylloxera crisis in the vineyards, Reverdy arrived in Paris in October and soon met Jacob through a common friend.[70] In his 1917 novel *Le Voleur de Talan* (The Thief of Talan), Reverdy depicted himself as a young provincial frightened by the metropolis and Jacob as Le Mage Abel, a magician who claims, "I taught the birds to sing, / The poets to use stars and glowworms [worms/verses: *des vers luisants*] without mixing them up / I juggled with the sun / and the moon."[71]

Eager to absorb the new art, Reverdy began visiting Jacob's room— "as deep and dark as a well"—on the Rue Ravignan,[72] and he made friends with Juan Gris, who lived up the street. He met Picasso one night when Gris fetched the fellow Spaniard to help rescue Max Jacob, staggering drunk or high on ether, from a gang of hollering urchins.[73] As Gris shadowed Picasso, learned from him, and became the third Cubist in Kahn-weiler's troupe, so Reverdy adopted from Max Jacob a radical poetics, especially the experimental form of the prose poem, an imitation that would later give rise to heated rivalry.

JACOB'S NEW CONFIDENCE radiates in a letter to the poet Charles Vil-drac. Mostly an appreciation of Vildrac's recent book of poems, the letter announces that Jacob has been back in Paris for a month; he's written a play and a book of stories.[74] In late October, *Nouvelles de la république des lettres* published three of Jacob's poems: "Closing Time," "History," and "Parenthesis." "Closing Time" is a comic glimpse of bohemia, where the names of the characters probably correspond to Jacob's acquaintances, but without enough clues to permit much identification: "Népomucène" must be Picasso, since that is one of the painter's many middle names.[75] "His-tory" is a joking parable of anticlerical violence. The third poem, "Paren-thesis," is none other than the ditty, first named "Sadness," that Jacob had given to Picasso in October 1905, as a protest at the painter's having set up house with Fernande.[76]

Other fruits from his summer appeared in the publication in *Pan* of the first stories with the *Terrain Bouchaballe* material, using the name "Guichin" for Quimper. Entitled "Guichin Stories," the two vignettes present Jacob's perpetual tension between secular and sacred. The first, "The Prisoners' Story," recounts in the voice of the innkeeper the tale of a wily prison warden who outwits a tobacco smuggler and keeps the contra-band tobacco for himself. The second story, "The Repentant Mother and Daughter," reworks a devotional tale about prostitution and saintliness in an anonymous tale-teller's voice, catching the lilt and repetitive structure of oral narration.[77] This kind of material would not only fill up his play and novel *Le Terrain Bouchaballe* but would very shortly translate into the pseudo-Breton poems in *La Côte* and, years later, the more personal mas-terpiece, the poems of Jacob's alter-ego Morven le Gaélique.

IN DECEMBER, AS Jacob waited for the publication of *Saint Matorel*, Picasso received another tribute: Vollard showed his Blue and Rose period Picassos and even a few Cubist works. And Apollinaire received a comeuppance that must have pained and perhaps secretly relieved Max Jacob: he didn't win the Prix Goncourt for his stories, *L'Hérésiarque et Cie* (The Arch-Heretic & Co).

Saint Matorel was published on February 11, 1911. On Picasso's copy, Jacob wrote, "It's you who light up the stars at night—Saint Mathorel [*sic*] to Picasso."[78] On Kahnweiler's copy, he wrote an off-rhyming, punning couplet: "To HK, mainstay of French art and companion of the lily / of Ulysses. I offer you this bouquet you gathered for yourself."[79]

The bouquet, at first, did not find many admirers, and it was expensive. Produced only as a deluxe edition, this historic book initially had only eight subscribers, including Picasso's patron, the state councilor Olivier Sainsère, and Jacob's friend, the fashion designer Paul Poiret.[80] But for Max Jacob, the book represented a major step forward and a public connection of his art with that of his hero.

Apollinaire welcomed the book with a pat of his tiger's paw. Perhaps jealous since Picasso wouldn't illustrate his next book, *Le Bestiaire ou le cortège d'Orphée* (The Bestiary or the Procession of Orpheus), he wrote several versions of a quatrain congratulating his friends. The more printable one runs:

Jacob and Picasso live companionably
One painting canvases, the other in delirium
Pablo pisses off his pictures and Max wipes my bum
One after his fashion, the other frenziedly.[81]

A draft of the quatrain drops the third line and concludes: "Don't call Jacob queer / He dislikes cunt."[82]

||

FOR THE NEXT four years, Jacob led a frenetic double life. He dashed around Paris playing the clown, entertaining friends in cafés, studios, and his own enchanted room, or earning his supper by amusing guests in the wealthy salons where he began to be invited. At the same time, he meditated, prayed, and pored over the Bible. Whether in the dim chambers of concierges and housewives of Montmartre or in elegant drawing rooms, he was in demand for reading horoscopes, telling fortunes, and advising about the magical properties of gems and colors. Paul Poiret, already one of the most fashionable clothing designers in France, devotedly followed Jacob's advice in dressing himself: a green tie on Mondays, blue on Wednesdays, and brown on Saturdays, with matching cufflinks.[83] At parties in *le beau monde,* Jacob rippled away on the piano performing Mozart or opéra bouffe, imitated famous writers, mesmerized the guests, and then slipped downstairs to have a drink at the corner bar with the chauffeurs of the rich. He would confound his audience at the bar: when they scoffed at the idea that he'd just been upstairs at the Duchess So-and-So's, he described the interior of the apartment and the exact livery of the servants in such detail that they were flabbergasted and took him for a master burglar like the popular fictional character Fantômas.[84]

The regime was exhausting, and in early March Jacob fell ill. Worried at not having seen him for several days, Picasso tracked him to his lair and found him huddled in bed. Only after intense persuasion did Jacob agree to move down to the Boulevard de Clichy to stay with Picasso and Fernande. His convalescence took at least two weeks, during which he proved to be a patient both "charming and execrable," entertaining them even in his weakness but refusing to eat anything he didn't like. When he had recovered, Fernande said, they realized how much they loved him from the degree of anxiety they had felt.[85]

THROUGHOUT THE SPRING of 1911 Jacob prepared his collection of Breton songs, *La Côte* (The Coast), and he had Brittany intensely in mind. The Celtic druids, for him, were just another manifestation of the universal sacred, and in some ways an extension of his apparition; at this stage, Jacob was a long way from orthodox Catholicism. Writing to Bloch, he declared that his Druid School is a "reasoned and silent application of the Occult Sciences," and he described the work of the Unanimists, and of Bloch in particular, in terms he had just used in *Saint Matorel*, as inspiration from the planet Mars.[86] A few weeks later he returned to his druidical/zodiacal schemes. At this point, Jacob still imagined that Romains's Unanimist group might participate in the Cubist revolution, and he praised their work: "In 1909 there was a revolution in the cosmos! The planet Mars came near the earth. Now Mars influences the moon and the moon means all artists worthy of the name. That's why we had *L'Inquiète! L'Armée dans la ville! La Lumière!*"[87]

JACOB PRESENTED HIS Breton poems in *La Côte* as both a pastiche and a love letter to his native land. These apparently simple songs allowed him to approximate, in verse, the freshness and "primitive" boldness of form that Picasso had incorporated from African sculpture and that Derain was adapting from medieval art and old woodcuts; these anomalous Breton poems aligned perfectly with the Modernist celebration of "the primitive."

La Côte is divided into two sections. In the first, Jacob plays it fairly straight with his pared-down versions of traditional songs accompanied by *en face* translations in a Breton that linguists have identified as a "subdialect of the *haut-vannetais*"[88]—that is, the Breton spoken in the region around Vannes, not in Cornouailles, the region of Quimper—a wretched mélange of demotic Breton supplied by Jacob's collaborator Julien Tanguy. Jacob hardly knew any Breton, and the Breton text is so bad, the scholar Pierre Jakez Hélias surmises that the collaborator/translator must have been illiterate and that Jacob had transcribed his oral translation.[89]

In these Breton poems Jacob, ever the mimic, took on a disguise at odds with his Montmartre sarcasm. *La Côte* is tonally at cross-purposes with itself. In this self-division, it resembles its author. At times, Jacob borrowed a song from the folklorist F. M. Luzel, shortened it, and arranged Luzel's prose in flexible meter and rhyme. Most of the poems in *La Côte*, however, invented new songs from traditional Breton themes, not unlike the way the Jacob family business refashioned traditional Breton costumes and furniture.[90] In these songs, some in verse, some in cadenced prose, Jacob made something whole within himself, resurrecting the tales and melodies of his childhood and the pagan Christianity of the Breton saints whose shrines he had visited in his youth. But more than the content of the tales, it was a language he made his own, simple, direct, and concrete:

> Mother, my mother-in-law
> Watch over my baby dear
> I'm going to the graveyard
> To join my husband there . . .
> ("Le Seigneur Comte")[91]

Pierre Jakez Hélias wrote of *La Côte* that it is characteristic Jacob, "a mixture of pastiche/parody/clowning on the one hand, and on the other of an authentic emotion joined with aesthetic pleasure." That seems as good a description as any. So does Hélias's remark that "one has to look for Max Jacob's truth under his fireworks . . . a truth, by the way, always to be understood as plural."[92] To Tristan Tzara, in 1916, Jacob downplayed *La Côte* as a little book written to make fun of Paul Fort.[93] A few months later he wrote in a similar vein, sending copies of *La Côte* to two young soldiers at the front, Jean Paulhan and Albert Uriet, referring to "This *Côte* which you'll understand as a comic work aimed against the infatuation with 'folk poetry,' 'folk criticism,' etc."[94]

But in 1924, Jacob would write to the Breton philosopher Jean Grenier that *La Côte* was "the purest expression of my inner life."[95] He went on to argue that Brittany resembled Russia in its mists and violent colors, its drunken binges, irony in suffering, and mystical visions, and he wound up observing: "I wrote *La Côte* at the height of the Cubist crisis when everyone expected me to write *Le Cornet à dés,* which didn't come out until five years later." As Hélias suggests, both of Jacob's claims are true of *La Côte:* it *is* a parody of Paul Fort's folklorism, and at the same time a tender tribute to his native land and an experiment in a spare poetic language.

It would take years for this simplicity to return to Jacob's poetry, and when it did, it would be in the poems of his imaginary Breton alter ego Morven le Gaélique, whose work began appearing in print in 1927 and wasn't collected in a book until long after the real poet's death.

V.

IN JUNE 1911 the newspaper *Paris-Midi* announced the forthcoming publication of *La Côte*, presenting it as the work of "the modest mechanic" Jules Tanguy with a "heart of mistletoe" (signifying his Celtic-druidic origins), supposedly inspired by Max Jacob and "translated" into French by him. Jacob must have dictated the piece to the journalist, his friend André Billy, since it reproduces the precise terms of Jacob's hoax.[96] Just as *La Côte* appeared, Picasso and Apollinaire were caught up in a judicial nightmare, a drama whose reverberations reached Jacob in Brittany.

Having helped nurse Jacob back to health in March, Picasso missed the Bateau Lavoir so much that he rented another studio there, not only to have more space in which to work but also, Richardson suggests, so that he could carry on affairs outside Fernande's line of sight. The couple was suffering strains. In July, Picasso departed by himself for Céret, a town of strong Catalan culture in the eastern Pyrenees, just north of the Spanish border. Fernande wrote to Gertrude Stein that she was thinking of taking a holiday in Holland, though she changed her mind and joined Picasso in Céret in mid-August.[97]

A jocose letter Jacob sent to Picasso in Céret makes sense in light of the painter's temporary separation from his lover. On the back of the envelope, Jacob drew a heart pierced by an arrow and a banner bearing the comically deformed Latin tag SI VIS AMOREM, PARA PLUIE.[98] The standard Latin saying is *Si vis pacem, para bellum* (If you desire peace, prepare for war). Jacob turned the Latin imperative verb *para* (prepare) into the French noun *parapluie* (umbrella): If you desire love, *para pluie* (prepare for rain). It seems a covert acknowledgment that his friend was scouting for new love and risking bad weather with his old love.

La Côte appeared on August 31, just as crisis erupted into the lives of Picasso and Apollinaire: their implication in the theft of the *Mona Lisa* from the Louvre. The painting was stolen on August 21, a Monday, when the museum was closed. Apollinaire and Picasso were dragged into the affair by Apollinaire's friend Géry Pieret. Pieret, who had returned in

April flush from four years in the American West, rapidly ran through his money and attached himself to Apollinaire, squatting in his apartment and drawing a meager salary as his "secretary." It was he who had stolen the two ancient Iberian stone heads from the Louvre in 1907 and sold them to Picasso. Picasso still had the heads in his studio. Now Pieret, hard up for cash, stole a third head and placed it on Apollinaire's mantelpiece. At this point things ceased being funny.

When Apollinaire asked Pieret to leave his apartment in late August, the very day the *Mona Lisa* was stolen, Pieret sold the story of his thefts to *Paris-Journal* and also sold them the recently stolen Iberian head, boasting about how easy it was to loot the Louvre. The newspaper published its scoop on August 29. Even though Pieret was not named, Apollinaire must have been frightened and summoned Picasso and Fernande back from Céret. They returned on September 3 or 4, just about the time Jacob left for Brittany.

Apollinaire and Picasso packed the two remaining Iberian heads in a suitcase and tried, and failed, to throw them into the Seine at night, after which Apollinaire dropped them off anonymously at *Paris-Journal*. Someone denounced Apollinaire to the police; his apartment was raided, and incriminating letters from Pieret were discovered; and Apollinaire was locked up in the prison, La Santé, from September 8 to 12. Picasso, too, was hauled in for questioning. He and Apollinaire, in their terror, incriminated each other, and according to some accounts, Picasso denied even knowing Apollinaire. If true, such a betrayal was a prelude to another betrayal, when he would refuse to sign a petition to release his old friend Max Jacob from the prison camp at Drancy in 1944.[99]

Picasso and Apollinaire were resident aliens in France and terrified of being deported. The days of imprisonment and the public humiliation shook Apollinaire to the core. The experience prompted the anguished short lyrics "À la Santé," which he would publish in *Alcools* in 1913; it also plunged him into depression and inspired his friends to rally to cheer him up, founding a new literary journal to occupy him: André Billy, René Dalize, André Salmon, and André Tudesq raised the money and launched *Les Soirées de Paris*. The first issue came out in February 1912, with Apollinaire's article, "Of Subject Matter in Modern Painting," which made the not surprising argument that subject matter no longer mattered. More enduringly, that issue carried Apollinaire's masterpiece, the lyric lamenting his loss of Marie Laurencin, "Le Pont Mirabeau." For though in October 1911, just after his release from prison, he moved from his apartment on the Rue Gros in Auteuil to an apartment on Marie's street, she was slipping away from him, and his poems mourning her loss, "Marie" and "Le Pont Mirabeau," ring in the same cadences and with some of the same imagery as the poems from prison.[100]

||

WHILE HIS FRIENDS were suffering, Max Jacob was propelled into a world of luxury in the villa that his patron Paul Poiret had rented on the Île Tudy, off the southern coast of Brittany. The fashion designer Poiret had earned his sobriquet Poiret le Magnifique by masterminding extravagant soirées at his mansion in Paris, fantastic costume parties with fireworks, exotic dancers, and food from the Arabian Nights. For his holidays he packed friends on houseboats for cruises down French rivers or, as in September 1911, rented a villa for days and nights of banqueting, charades, dancing, and music. Poiret not only relied on Jacob to read his horoscope and advise him on colors and gems; he adored his conversation and for this holiday "kidnapped" the poet and paid him to give a lecture to his houseguests.[101] (Poiret so admired Jacob's intelligence that when Isadora Duncan said she "was good at making babies" but needed a brilliant man to father them, Poiret thought of Max Jacob, but then reflected that it probably wouldn't work.)[102]

After two weeks on Île Tudy, Jacob settled at the family house in Quimper for a visit that would last all autumn. Having lost his room at 7 rue Ravignan in Paris ("for abuse of ether")—the room in which God had appeared to him—he was eager to find new lodgings in Montmartre and hoped his friend Maurice Raynal would let him take over his room at 53 rue du Chevalier de la Barre.[103] Jacob also told Raynal that he was tired from fifteen days of partying with the Poirets. A few days later he renewed his request to take over Raynal's room. As Raynal didn't confirm the plan, Jacob complained to Kahnweiler that on his return to Paris in early December, he'd be sleeping under bridges.[104]

With copies of *La Côte* in hand, Jacob promoted his Druid School in Brittany, the land of Druids, and the press picked up the story, not always flatteringly. An anonymous article from the Parisian *Les Hommes du jour* sneered:

> The "poet" Max Jacob isn't satisfied with fooling around with the writers and men of letters who surround him. He's just founded a school of which he's the unrivaled head and the only disciple: the Druid School.
>
> Let us recall in this context a couplet making the rounds of the *salons* and literary circles:
>
> "Hégiton, Max Jacob, an idyllic fop,
> Arranges to be bugg—ed by a cop."[105]

The journalist may have been Octave Béliard, who signed an equally hostile article on Jacob and his "Druidism" employing the same expression, "an idyllic fop," a few weeks later in the same newspaper.[106] The paper must have been hard up for news, since an adjacent column pursued the druidic theme, announcing that "M. Max Jacob, founder of the Druid School, cubist, and professor of Kabbalah, has just published a volume of Celtic poems in collaboration with M. Julien Tanguy," and it reprinted Jacob's plea from his preface for a household to employ Tanguy as a chauffeur.

MOST OF WHAT we know about Jacob's life in the autumn of 1911 comes from his letters to Kahnweiler. He described his progress on the third Matorel volume, *Le Siège de Jérusalem;* discussed the impending publication of *Les Oeuvres burlesques et mystiques de Frère Matorel, mort au couvent;* and regaled his correspondent with gossip. From a letter dated October 6, we learn that a painting had been stolen from the museum in Quimper. Since Jacob was still in Paris when the *Mona Lisa* disappeared in August, he exclaimed: "Someone has stolen a painting from the Museum; I think if I lived in Perpignan, they'd have stolen it from the Perpignan Museum."[107] What for Apollinaire and Picasso had been an agony, Jacob turned into a joke, and his quip became famous: "Va-t'en te faire Homolle, ô Guey" (Go make yourself Homolle, O Guey, "homol-ogous"). Jean-Théophile Homolle was the director of the Louvre who had just been fired over the scandal of the *Mona Lisa* and the Iberian heads; Fernand Guey directed the Museum of Quimper from which a Boucher disappeared in early October. A local newspaper reported of Guey that "the street urchins assailed him with the latest wisecrack from Max Jacob, the cubist druid vacationing in the town of his birth, 'Va-t-en te faire Homolle, ô Guey.' Half the town shouts, 'He'll go!', the other half, 'No he won't!' "[108]

In almost every letter, Jacob complained that Picasso hadn't written to him. One can well imagine that Picasso had his hands full, though by late September an article on him by Salmon in *Paris-Journal* shows that Picasso had gotten back to work.[109] He and Apollinaire repaired their friendship, but it would never quite recover its old freedom, and Apollinaire began courting the second-rate imitators of Cubism, Albert Gleizes, Jean Metzinger, and Henri Le Fauconnier. Picasso and Braque refused to exhibit in those salons, and Kahnweiler had nothing but contempt for the parvenu Cubists who claimed the movement for themselves.[110]

Apollinaire and Salmon, however, made their livings as journalists and throve on the fray.[111] Neither was an acute art critic, to say the least. Salmon, in his account of Cubism after the salons of 1911, made a terrific muddle, claiming that "Picasso was never a Cubist" and calling Metzinger the leader of Cubism.[112] Apollinaire was more circumspect: already in his article on the Salon des Indépendants in April 1911, he acknowledged "the influence" of Picasso on modern art, but he celebrated the exuberance of Robert Delaunay, treated Le Fauconnier's bloated *Abondance* as a serious work, and claimed that "Metzinger is here the only practitioner of Cubism properly speaking."[113] Soon he would be trumpeting the Futurists and Robert Delaunay's Orphism in an attempt to maintain his position as the premier impresario of poetic and artistic avant-gardes.[114]

In 1911, as Picasso and Braque began to bathe in that mysterious aura, celebrity, they inevitably attracted envy, imitation, and competition. Modernism was born in serious revisions of the formal possibilities of making art, but it was accompanied by furious power plays and a war of manifestoes and publicity. Painters and poets became newly conscious of the press as a weapon, a dangerous force that could defend and promote one's art but by which one could just as easily be wounded. Marinetti, after surviving a car wreck, raised the volume by publishing the first Futurist Manifesto in *Le Figaro* in 1909, celebrating speed, machines, war ("the world's only hygiene"), and scorn for women and calling for the destruction of museums, libraries, and academies.[115] Jacob, worried about the writer Francis Carco, wrote to Salmon in affected slang to ask him to watch out for Jacob's own reputation: "It seems little Carco's writing about me. Keep an eye on this, huh?"[116]

Among the giants of modern art, Jacob was finding his modest place.

CHAPTER 8

BOHEMIA RISING

I.

J acob's place in modern art had everything to do with his revolutionary poems, and one of his major endeavors in 1911 was the construction of the manuscript of his Matorel poems for Kahnweiler. This volume was distinct from the novel *Saint Matorel*. On pages scrawled with revisions, often containing notes to his benefactor Jacques Doucet, we can follow his poetic evolution, and we can also see the importance of wealthy patrons in sustaining and promoting the new art.

FROM THE HOARD of the Doucet manuscript, Jacob took much of the work for his three early books: *Les Oeuvres burlesques et mystiques de Frère Matorel*, *La Défense de Tartufe*, and *Le Laboratoire central* (The Central Laboratory). The manuscript is subtitled "Poèmes 1905–1916," but some of the poems date from as early as 1900 or 1901.[1] Already the previous April, Jacob had begun to sort through the contents of the trunk to cull poems for Kahnweiler. On April 28, 1910, he wrote that he had prepared three volumes: "Burlesque poems" (which would become the first part of *Les Oeuvres burlesques et mystiques*); "Poems of the Orient and Brittany" (which would become *La Côte*); and "The Book of Enigmas," "a suite of colorful Persian poems I made to impress people with my genius, if I may say so." These would become the second section of *Les Oeuvres burlesques et mystiques*.[2]

In 1911 Jacob left a parcel of poems with Kahnweiler and relied on his publisher to do some of the choosing and ordering. On October 4 he wrote instructing Kahnweiler to take what he wanted, as Jacob trusted his taste.[3] But he insisted on keeping many of the burlesque pieces, declaring the next day that the book depended on the contrast between the burlesque and the mystical.[4]

Along the way, Jacob changed his mind about the order. He had at first entitled the work *Les Oeuvres mystiques et burlesques de Frère Matorel*.[5] But in the prospectus he reversed the order to *burlesques et mystiques*, reflecting the progression in Matorel/Jacob's religious and poetic life.[6]

Though he left some choice to Kahnweiler, Jacob had a firm hand in the book's architecture. It is strikingly *not* a miscellany. Like *Saint Matorel*, except in poetic form, *Les Oeuvres burlesques et mystiques* traces the story of Jacob's Parisian life: his years of obscurity, his search for God, his apparition. The fictive editor's comments stitch the pieces into yet another oblique autobiography. The collection moves from early pieces like "Electoral Lament: Le Chevalier de la Barre," through imitations of folk songs, romances, and bourgeois parlor pieces like "Discreet Confession: Piano and Vocal Tune for Boarding Schools." The very titles wink at the genres, like "Grand Dramatic Recitative for Drawing Rooms."[7]

Jacob placed here his experiments with controlled phonetic delirium, poems such as "Variation on a Formula," "The Music Lesson," and "Avenue du Maine," whose puns had spilled over into a letter to Picasso in 1906: "Les manèges déménagent" (The merry-go-rounds are moving out).[8] "Matorel the poet is finding his way," the editor declares of these early pieces. One of the most revealing is "Cracked Statue."[9] In its thirteen lines, it's a cracked sonnet, conjuring but not conforming to traditional form. Cracked in many ways, it alludes to and jars with Baudelaire's famous sonnet "The Cracked Bell"; it's missing a line; it's in rhyming couplets instead of quatrains and tercets; its first line doesn't rhyme with anything; and its dense play of assonance and dubious syntax is well-nigh incomprehensible even to a native French speaker. Yet the poem presents a legible self-portrait to anyone familiar with Jacob. The adjective *bréhaigne* (sterile) often refers to an androgynous creature: it signals Jacob's ambiguous sexuality. *Pépie* means "chirps": the multicolored (*versicolore*) mutable poet utters no grand statement, but "chirps" a bird-like, marginal new poetry. This new art is fully aware of crude, commercial modernity ("Let's Americanize"), while the older art, the grandpa, expires in a corner. The poem turns suddenly intimate as it shifts to the second-person singular ("the shadow leans on your footsteps") and then to the vulnerable, first-person confession of the poet waiting for the divine to enter his life.

> A third party's neglectful friend erupts in sterile chirps.
> Rainbow-colored! He weeps, adorned in bows,
> Mourning the dull year as it goes.
> Who is this lord? The land of commerce has a fever:
> Let's Americanize the pleasure of our zither!
> Let the old grandpa cry by himself in a corner!
> His death distresses no sister or brother.
> The shadow leans on your footsteps, black and frail:
> It's like a ripe grape beaten down by hail.
> But on the bright altar broad daylight stays alert
> To declare at large the emptiness of my heart
> And say no clay is so dry in its ancient clods
> As my heart, my heart, my heart lacking for gods.

Jacob organized *Les Oeuvres burlesques et mystiques* in three sections. The first contains an ebullient mixture of satiric verses and radical prose poems. Some reflect a quest for God; many chart a quest for poetry itself. "In his excursion into modern literature, has Matorel retrieved only one name and one life work: the name and work of Arthur Rimbaud?" asks the editor. "We cannot be sure. Where does this clerk-poet's irony begin, and where does it end?"[10] (Jacob's absorption and rejection of Rimbaud would vex him for years.) The penultimate piece in section one, "The Situation of Writers," puts the perilously comic, comically perilous "situation" of the experimental writer into high relief. In this prose poem, a millionaire lectures the poet fatuously about Oscar Wilde and Mallarmé, then kicks him out when he refuses a task of menial copying (refusing to reproduce art for philistines). The editor remarks, "Matorel reflected that the profession of writers isn't a profession. Poor Matorel! He wasn't so crazy!"[11]

The second section moves through hallucinatory prose poems and verse, including scenes of erotic experiment and longing, a sense of the self as doubled, and the eruption of mystery, as in this glimpse from 1907 of a horse (always a totem animal for Jacob): "Wild and merry, the horse / Strikes the ground with his hoof."[12]

Increasingly, the poems shift perspective: "The city is behind the night"; or "The fish are eyes which forget. / The boats are eyes. The eyes are boats carrying the haystack of sun. The eyes are boats whose eyelashes are oars."[13] Mirrors distort; colors and forms blend and separate; the reader experiences severe optical disorientation. The final section, entitled "Victor Matorel's Mystical Crisis," shorter than the others, plunges into dialogue with angels and spirits. The book concludes with a confession of doubt—what if all the visions have been a delusion?—and with Matorel's farewell in rhyming couplets: a farewell to poetry and to his *cortège* of familiar spirits, genies, and Harlequins as Matorel prepares to enter the convent.

MATOREL, LIKE RIMBAUD, bade farewell to poetry, but Max Jacob decidedly did not. Perhaps because they were hidden by the frame story of Matorel, or by Jacob's own performances as the Harlequin of Montmartre, or perhaps because Kahnweiler published *Les Oeuvres burlesques et mystiques de Frère Matorel* in a very limited edition, the remarkable poems in this collection were hardly noticed at the time except by a small circle of connoisseurs. Even later, when *Le Cornet à dés* in 1917, *La Défense de Tartufe* in 1919, and *Le Laboratoire central* in 1921 made Jacob famous, most readers seemed unaware that he had already, in 1912, published one of the key collections of innovative French poetry of the twentieth century. He had done it the year before Apollinaire published *Alcools*.

II.

IN THE FALL of 1911, Jacob labored to complete the third Matorel volume, the play *Le Siège de Jérusalem*. It proceeded alongside his commentary on the Gospels and notes for a lecture on the Gospel of Saint Luke that Poiret had commissioned. In October, Jacob wrote Kahnweiler that he'd "finished the Gospels," and he even had the unrealistic notion of having them published by a Catholic house connected to the cathedral in Quimper.[14] The two projects, the esoteric biblical commentary and the play, are closely linked, to the detriment of the play. Long before the apparition in 1909, and for the rest of his life, Jacob tried to cram all his occult researches, Greco-Roman mythology, astrology, Kabbalah, and Christianity into a single symbolic system. One might see this as the effort by a person who experienced himself as plural to make himself whole: to be Jewish and Catholic, Breton and Parisian, worldly and ascetic, manly and womanly.

Jacob's notebooks abound in sketches of this fantastical unity, and his letters, even late in his life, often mention his dream of completing a book on the symbolism of the Gospels.[15] Not content with amalgamating the Hebrew Bible into Christian Scripture, Jacob sought a further integration into systems of astrology and Greco-Roman mythology. In notes for the essay "Religious Anatomy," he lined up the signs for the zodiac— Aries, Taurus, Gemini, Cancer, and so forth—with the twelve tribes of Israel— Dan, Reuben, Judah, Manasseh; and in turn, he aligned these with gems thought to have magical powers: sapphire, cornaline, ruby, agate . . . As he had in *Saint Matorel*, he filled *Le Siège de Jérusalem* with these allegories. But whereas the fiction of *Saint Matorel* maintained its energy from the character of Victor Matorel and his adventures as a poor clerk and employee of the Métro, the play removed all that tension between the real and the fantastic.

THE ACTION IN *Le Siège de Jérusalem* takes place in Matorel's afterlife and maintains a monotonous uniformity of music hall gags and ditties. Since

Matorel has already died, the plot revolving around his second death, staged as an imitation of Christ, feels feeble. Nor does the hero exhibit any character to speak of. His sanctity being a premise, he moves mechanically toward his fate. The weight of unassimilated reading drags the play down: partly a knock-off of Goethe's *Faust*,[16] partly a comic version of the Revelation of Saint John the Divine and its zoology, partly a spoof of Offenbach, *Le Siège de Jérusalem* lumbers from start to finish.

Jacob had high hopes for his play, as his inscription on the final version testifies: "This manuscript was completed in Quimper on Wednesday 8 November 1911 with the gracious gratitude of the author to the Lord creator of the world, to Jesus Christ His son, the Savior of the world, and to the angels who protect his pen."[17] After that outburst, he dug into the archives of Quimper, unearthing material for his novel *Le Terrain Bouchaballe* and for the stories in *Cinématoma* and *Le Roi de Béotie*. He described them as "A Dance of the Dead and the Living."[18]

Life in the family house remained stressful. His elder brother Maurice, who had returned from colonial administration in Senegal, made disparaging remarks about "people who drag poverty around with them. . . . And there's moral poverty—the worst!"[19] Jacob began suffering from a raging toothache, which he tried to calm with ether, running up his father's bill at the pharmacy and alarming his mother, who threatened to send him to a dentist and have him treated as an addict.[20] On December 8 he left for Paris, where Picasso and Fernande took him in at the Boulevard de Clichy. By January, he had set up house in a room at the Bateau Lavoir, with his tooth still hurting but his spirits restored.[21]

III.

JACOB'S STUDIO AT the Bateau Lavoir was right under Picasso's, and by day at least, the communal artistic-poetic life jogged along. Desperately poor, Jacob hawked copies of *La Côte* around the cafés. As he confessed later to Tzara, his copies of *La Côte* constituted "a daily bread, like a Host";[22] to Michel Leiris, in 1921, he would describe the humiliation of selling subscriptions to his books in cafés and salons as a form of beggary only slightly disguised.[23] He still made a modest living composing horoscopes, and sometimes he earned dinner by entertaining guests at evening parties. He wasn't too poor, however, to give a copy of *La Côte* to Apollinaire with an affectionate dedication: "To my dear Wilhelm, who already has his street in Auteuil and an empire in my heart."[24]

In March, Jacob's cousin Jean-Richard Bloch published a collection of short stories, *Lévy*, with the Nouvelle Revue Française. Jacob complimented him but complained that he found the style gritty.[25] Bloch's prose verges on crudeness, and his polemical designs are overbearingly obvious, with the title story presenting a fairytale of successful assimilation and idealizing the Jewish characters as "noble." Jacob may have had complicated feelings, too, about his younger cousin's being published by a prestigious press while he himself was peddling *La Côte* privately and selling *Saint Matorel* and *Les Oeuvres burlesques et mystiques* by subscription through Kahnweiler, and having trouble securing a publisher for his new collection of stories, *Cinématoma*.

IN FEBRUARY, THE newly fledged Futurist painters Giacomo Balla, Umberto Boccioni, Carlo Carrà, Luigi Russolo, and Gino Severini, led by the poet and publicist Marinetti, held their first Parisian exhibit, provoking tart articles by Apollinaire. The tiresome jockeying for the lead in the avant-garde intensified. The Italians were only weak imitators of Picasso and Derain, Apollinaire declared in *L'Intransigeant;*[26] in *Le Petit Bleu* he quoted their claim "to have taken the lead in the movement of European painting" and replied, "It's idiotic. . . . One hardly dares pronounce a judgment on such stupidity."[27]

Apollinaire continued to unfurl his columns in various newspapers, retailing gossip about the arts, visiting royalty, and oddball characters, with now and then a dash of anti-Semitism. In April 1911, he recounted with amusement a nasty episode he had witnessed, of a man driving a Jew away by making the gesture of an ass's ears at him during an anti-Semitic street demonstration; now in February 1912, in Yiddish-inflected French, he served up a joke about the "end" of a Jew's phallus being yards away from a tailor's shop, in the synagogue.[28] Apollinaire himself, with his unknown father, was often derided as a Jew and defended himself indignantly, even challenging the pugilist poet Arthur Cravan to a duel.[29]

JACOB, MEANWHILE, CONTINUED on his merry way. Ardengo Soffici, an Italian painter and art critic and (initially) enemy of the Futurists, admired Picasso and often visited the Bateau Lavoir. On one of those visits, in the early spring of 1912, he saw a louche-looking man with long black hair knocking at Jacob's door. When he asked Picasso about it, Picasso snickered and said it must be Jacob's current boyfriend. A little later Jacob appeared in the studio, his bald head and his ears glowing a rosy red. As Soffici described the scene:

> "And so?" asked Picasso.
>
> Jacob smiled his gap-toothed smile with an expression of bliss; then he pressed his lips together like someone tasting a delicious liqueur, and looking straight at us both, "Ah, what lovely buttocks my friend has!" he exclaimed in ecstasy, his eyes turned heavenward.
>
> How amazing life is![30]

In April, Jacob must have been pleased at the sympathetic review of *La Côte* by his old friend Henri Hertz in *La Phalange*. A versatile poet and journalist, Hertz praised the play of wit and sincerity in *La Côte* and concluded, "It's dangerous, these days, to be serious and touching while seeming to fool around. Even Voltaire wouldn't try it."[31] And on April 20, 1912, *Les Oeuvres burlesques et mystiques de Frère Matorel, mort au couvent,* appeared in an edition of one hundred copies, printed, like *Saint Matorel,* by Paul Birault. Derain had made sixty-six woodcuts, faux-naif versions of medieval emblems, images from popular almanacs, and kitsch religious art. His bold, simple forms—birds, beasts, Matorel praying and reading—stood out starkly in black and white. Like *Saint Matorel, Les Oeuvres burlesques et mystiques* is a rare treasure, a masterpiece of modernist book art.

||

WHILE DOMESTIC UPHEAVALS were about to change the lives of both Picasso and Apollinaire, Jacob suffered a crisis on a smaller scale, one of the hideous gaffes he made from time to time. He had sent out a batch of subscription forms for *Les Oeuvres burlesques et mystiques*. The form mailed to Jean-Richard Bloch was returned from Poitiers with the brutal stamp, "Refused." Jacob went into one of his paranoid fits, thinking his cousin had spurned his book. He fired off a letter to Bloch, meant to be comic but containing the slogan resounding often on French streets, "Down with Jews." Bloch, naturally, was shocked, and the episode threw Jacob into a paroxysm of remorse and shame as he fell over himself in apologies when he realized that the subscription form had been rejected, not by his cousin, but by the post office for insufficient postage. He explained the sorry tale in several hysterical letters to Bloch.[32] In one of these missives he mentioned that his elder cousin, the scholar Sylvain Lévi (Bloch's uncle), had called Jacob "a sick man," which was just what he felt like in this affair. In a footnote, he said he might be sent to Africa to join his brother Maurice in the civil service, a highly improbable scenario.

This storm passed, displaced, possibly, by the drama in Picasso's life. Trouble had been building between the painter and Fernande for several years, but in the last few months their mutual alienation had increased. Picasso was carrying on a well-disguised affair with Marcelle Humbert (also known as Eva Gouel), the slender mistress of the Polish painter Lodwicz Markus (called Marcoussis by his friends). Fernande, for her part, seduced a young Italian painter named Ubaldo Oppi, who had been led by Severini into Picasso's circle. Fernande relied on her trusted friend Marcelle/Eva to cover for her rendezvous with Oppi, but Eva, who had her own plans, kept Picasso fully informed. Picasso and Eva were so secretive that the only people who knew of their love were Kahnweiler and Braque (though Jacob may have suspected, so sensitive was he to Picasso's moods).

On May 16, two days before the explosion, Picasso wrote Apollinaire claiming that he felt ill and couldn't come to dinner the next evening, but suggesting—as if all were normal—that Apollinaire dine with him and Fernande soon.[33] On May 18, Picasso announced to Fernande that he knew about her affair with Oppi; that he was leaving her for Eva; and that because he wanted her out of the apartment (which was in her name), Kahnweiler would sublet it from her. Picasso wrote Braque that Fernande "had run off with a Futurist."[34] The next day he and Eva left for Céret.

Artistic Montmartre was flabbergasted. Severini, who felt responsible for having introduced Oppi into the group, would recount the drama in his memoir.[35] It was left to others to clean up the wreckage, and Max Jacob became Fernande's principal comforter.[36] Kahnweiler guarded Picasso's privacy, giving his address in Céret to no one; he removed paintings from the Bateau Lavoir studio for safekeeping in the gallery; he sent his prize painter everything he asked for—money, old tubes of paint, his palette and brushes (even the dirty ones), easel, sheets, pillows, his kimono—and supervised the dismantling of the studio, having to deal all the time with an angry and volatile Fernande.[37]

In June, Picasso and Eva fled Céret because Fernande threatened to arrive there with friends. Moving east from the Languedoc region into Provence, Picasso rented a villa in the town of Sorgues, north of Avignon. There Braque and his wife Marcelle—the *other* Marcelle—joined them in August, when the two painters would work together, challenging each other and pushing Cubism into what would later be called its synthetic phase. For Picasso, erotic renovation was forcefully associated with artistic renewal.

APOLLINAIRE, MEANWHILE, SUFFERED a romantic drama of his own. Marie Laurencin finally put a brutal end to their affair that summer of 1912. He was so distraught, he left his apartment in Auteuil and moved in with his friends the Russian painter Serge Férat and his "foster sister" (one who had shared the same wet nurse), Baroness Hélène d'Oettingen, at their apartment near the Gare Saint-Lazare. (Férat's real name was Serge Jastrebzoff, which Picasso always pronounced "G. Apostrophe.")[38] Only in November did Apollinaire settle into his new apartment at 202 boulevard Saint-Germain.[39]

Max Jacob was also peripatetic. On July 9 he moved from the Bateau Lavoir to the room he had been coveting for months, Maurice Raynal's old lodging on the Rue du Chevalier de la Barre, just a few streets away from the Bateau Lavoir. Braque helped him move, reporting to Picasso that it had taken an immense effort. Jacob, in a letter to Braque, praised his "heroism."[40] One imagines endless boxes filled with Jacob's bric-a-brac—his oil lamps, screens, and drapes; battered chairs, pots and pans, materials for gouaches and magic amulets; his considerable library; and his shabby dandy's wardrobe, all piled to the ceiling of some modest horse-drawn cab or perhaps onto handcarts. (Neither Jacob nor Braque gave details of the transport.) Whereupon Jacob fled to Brittany.

As he reported to Bloch, he tore himself away from Paris "like an animal fighting its way out of a thorn bush."[41] The thorns he escaped had just been made pricklier by the announcement of the forthcoming publication of the tendentious book *Du cubisme* by the salon Cubists Albert Gleizes and Jean Metzinger.[42] Back in Quimper, Jacob dug into his Breton novel and worked, as well, on the odd story or poem. His friendship with Bloch regained its equilibrium. His letters to his cousin sparkle with news of his writing, literary gossip, and compliments: everyone is praising Bloch, Jacob writes, "everything echoes your name and intoxicates me with the joy of belonging to your blood, your race, your heart."[43]

For weeks, not knowing where Picasso was hiding, Jacob complained to Kahnweiler about his friend's silence. Picasso, for his part, sent curt messages to Max through Kahnweiler—"Give Max an affectionate hello" (May 31); "Tell Max I love him a lot and if I don't write it doesn't matter" (July 4).[44] Jacob pestered Kahnweiler for news.[45] At this point, Jacob didn't know that Braque had joined Picasso or that they were in Sorgues. He described his labors on *Le Terrain Bouchaballe,* "which has to be the most beautiful book of the twentieth century, something better than the hydroplane, the movies, color photography, and mercury lighting." His mother was not impressed. " 'You take so much trouble,' says Mme Jacob my mother, 'and for so little.' "[46]

In a refrain that would become habitual later in letters from Saint-Benoît, he claimed that he was bored . . . and not bored. Friends passed through Quimper: Salmon, Henri Hertz, Duhamel and his wife, the Poirets, Louis Latourette (one of two adherents to Jacob's Druid School, the other being the poet Louis de Gonzague Frick).[47] And as usual, he reported tensions with his family: the household had been enlarged by a brother-in-law, Lucien Lévy, his younger sister Mirté-Léa's husband, and their three-year-old son. He referred glancingly to Fernande, calling her "our famous widow," saying she had written to him from a resort on the English Channel where she was visiting friends.

Kahnweiler must have scolded Jacob about leaving Paris in a rush, because in a subsequent letter Jacob defended himself. More interesting is another reference to Fernande: "Are you mad at me for having taken care of and still taking care of the 'Merry Widow'? Poor girl! I don't think she is [so merry]. *Don't repeat this nickname!*"[48] By this time, Jacob had heard from Braque, in Sorgues, and we learn that Braque had been sending Jacob postcards as subjects for his gouaches. But Jacob wasn't painting; he was utterly "possessed" by literature. This letter also narrates one of Jacob's few heterosexual temptations, a visit by some cousins, a young actor from the Comédie-Française, his sister, and another young woman. They made Jacob show them Quimper, clambering up the tower of the Episcopal palace and then the cathedral and Mont Frugy. The adventure produced a cousinly kiss with Eva in the garden of Mont Frugy. "The hardened old bachelor that I am, after having settled Mlle. Eva in the train (she's eighteen!) and having confirmed that she didn't dislike me, reflected that it was really charming to live with such birdies and almost fell in love. That's the most momentous event of my monastic holiday."[49]

From August 20 to September 28, Jacob was again drawn into the Poirets' frenetic parties on Île Tudy. While he was there, Kahnweiler wrote to ask for a prospectus for *Le Siège de Jérusalem*. At this point they expected Derain to illustrate the play; Derain later backed out, and Picasso stepped into the breach, producing three etchings, classic Cubist works: *Woman with a Guitar*, *Still Life with a Skull*, and *Portrait of a Woman*—that have no bearing on the plot of the play.

IV.

THE PREVIOUS NOVEMBER Jacob had spent days in the archives of Quimper quarrying material for stories. He completed the manuscript (now entitled *Mémoires apocryphes*, Apocryphal Memoirs) during the year, and on leaving Paris he gave it to Poiret, who promised to take it to the publisher Fasquelle. Fasquelle turned it down; Poiret then entertained the idea of publishing it himself; by December, Jacob had retitled it *Cinéma Thomas* and hoped for a publication sponsored by Poiret, "the Discreet Tailor."[50] Perhaps because Poiret's attention was taken up by his fashion empire, perhaps because war intervened, the book finally titled *Cinématoma* wouldn't appear until 1920 from Cendrars's Éditions de La Sirène.[51] It is one of Jacob's most original works and, according to an interview he gave in 1924, his favorite.[52]

Jacob didn't call the pieces in *Cinématoma* "stories." He called them "characters," recalling the literary portraits immortalized by La Bruyère in the seventeenth century. But just as he refashioned the nineteenth-century prose poem, Jacob reinvented the character sketch. Years later he told Marcel Béalu he thought of them as exercises in "comparative astrology" and claimed to correlate the vocabulary of his personages with their stars.[53] Astrological or not, into these chapters he poured his gift of mimicry, presenting a map of French society in a set of vocal performances. It's an incomplete map, excluding the aristocracy, but still astonishing in its range, with voices of Breton peasants; provincial petit-bourgeois; a Parisian whore and her husband, a small-time crook; lawyers; and struggling journalists and bluestockings. Jacob's letters to Picasso and Kahnweiler abound in such mockingbird exercises. Though he considered the "characters" of *Cinématoma* to be minor work, these short prose pieces and those of the later collections *Le Roi de Béotie* and *Le Cabinet noir* have proven to be his richest contribution to the art of French fiction.[54]

It is in *Cinématoma* that we first meet Jacob's portrait of his mother as Madame Gagelin. She holds a place of honor (or dishonor) as the first "character" in the book; one imagines the glee with which Jacob performed this exorcism, parroting his mother's voice and displaying her snobbism, pettiness, and vengefulness. However unjust to Prudence Jacob, Madame Gagelin at times echoes Madame Jacob directly, as when she exclaims "I'm a Republican, I am, a Voltairean!"[55] Madame Gagelin prides herself on her "chic," on being "a woman of the world," and imagines that with her gifts and education, she should have married a politician rather than a horse dealer. She describes her dead husband as a boor and an imbecile; she calls her children cretins and slaps and spanks them. Her taste in art is pathetically philistine; she justifies hypocrisy as "a worldly necessity"; she's penny-pinching and scheming—so much so that her cousins threaten to sue her over an inheritance.[56] Written as a letter to her detested son-in-law to be opened on her decease, Madame Gagelin's testament is galvanically alive. She was never a beauty, she claims, but she had, "as they say, '*du chien*,' the devil's beauty"; she who had studied piano with the celebrated Ravina "wasn't going to beat a retreat in front of a three-franc-an-hour twit"; her family thinks they can "worm her secrets out of her."[57] She has an extravagant vocabulary for idiots and fools. Each of Jacob's characters is a triumph of voice, rhythm, and phrasing. It's a performative art that works well in short bursts but that he never managed to adapt perfectly to the longer form of the novel.

In *Cinématoma*, Max Jacob is a petit-bourgeois Proust in miniature, an ethnographer of minutely recorded hierarchies. "Extracts from the Memoirs of a Lady Journalist" parodies a self-deluding woman writer in the tawdry milieu of Parisian journalism and portrays her lover, Édouard, a cad and parasite. In "A Gentleman Traveling First Class for the First Time," a department store clerk indulges in dreams of luxury, taking a train trip in first class thanks to a ticket purloined for him by a friend; he suffers agonies observing his traveling companions, fearing at each gesture to betray his social ignorance.

In "Memoirs of a Gentleman and a Lady, Followed by Albert's Notes," a story about a whore, a burglar, and a pimp, Jacob embedded a piece of his own life. The scene where the woman leaps from her café chair at the arrival of the man she has a crush on replicates Jacob's own experience with his lover Cécile/Germaine in 1902: he'd been sitting at a café with his friend the old tenor and leaped up when she appeared, breaking his glass.[58] The tenor speaks chapter four, "Memories of an Old Tenor, Gone Mad." In his dissociative speech and mystical visions, he's yet another mask for Jacob, proto-Surrealist and visionary: "All the pianos are dead, eaten up by rats"; "Nobody sees the angels passing by, but they recognize each other"; "Hell is just as close to man as Paradise is."[59]

Cinématoma transcends the genre of social satire. In its depictions of the suffering poor it touches Dostoyevskian depths, nowhere more than in chapter two, "The Woman Who Found a Husband," a piece shocking in its frankness. Taking up a tale of infanticide, already the subject of several poems in *La Côte* and a motif that runs throughout Breton folklore, Jacob speaks in the voice of a peasant girl, Marie LeBolloch, who has gotten pregnant. But Jacob didn't have to turn to old books for this story: a version of it occurred when he was a child, in the family of the postman whose family rented the one-story house in the Jacobs' back courtyard.[60] A whole rough world of poverty, village meanness, and earthy realism comes to life in Marie's ungrammatical speech.

These are dramatic monologues, leaving it to the reader to make emotional and moral sense. Throughout the cast of characters in *Cinématoma*, one great character is almost missing: God. He appears only in the anomalous story about the conversion of a late Roman emperor.[61] Jacob, who thought he had been touched by grace, depicts in this book an orphaned modern world left to the grimness and sorrow of its appetites.

BY THE TIME he returned to Quimper from the Poirets' house party at the end of September, Jacob reported to Kahnweiler that he'd at last heard from Picasso. (Picasso and Eva had left Sorgues and moved into an apartment on the Boulevard Raspail in Montparnasse, thus shifting the center of the art world from the Right to the Left Bank.) Jacob also wrote that the mayor of Quimper had resigned, and everything was turning out in Quimper just as in his "futile" novel.[62] Jacob's younger sister, he added, had at last found a maid by going to the welfare office and paying a premium: in essence, buying a slave.[63] He'd heard from Picasso that "Wilbourg" Braque was still in Sorgues (as Picasso baptized Braque, the heroic "aviator" of Cubism, after the death of Wilbur Wright in May 1912). Jacob signed off with a flourish: "There's only one country, the country of the Heart!! God! How bored I am!!!"

Jacob spent the fall writing his novel, and the life of the town flowed continuously into it. On October 23 Quimper elected a new mayor, a Socialist, and Jacob narrated to Braque the debates that stirred the town, controversies that even Flaubert couldn't have invented about public urinals and the sewer system in the girls' lycée.[64] We get a more private glimpse of him in drafts of poems in the manuscript *Le Christ à Montparnasse*. The scribble entitled "Quimper 1912," an anguished cry to God, starts in rhyming couplets and scatters into free verse jottings. "I feel as small as a slug in a field," it begins. The untitled draft on the following page in the manuscript bears the note "Made in Quimper in 1912" and transforms its irritability into jest: "Everything unnerves and crushes me, and gives me pain. / Carry me off to Nice, to Le Havre, to Charenton."[65]

In this mood of alienation, he wrote a poem called "A Thousand Other Regrets" that survives in three states. He sent an early version in August to his friends the Hertzes with a letter in which he complained of missing their group: the Hertzes, Charles Vildrac, and Jean-Richard Bloch. His postscript to Emma Hertz, a talented pianist, is intensely affectionate: "My dear friend, your taste is more precious to me than that of the crude and ignorant crowd."[66]

In supple *vers libre* and loose rhyme, "A Thousand Other Regrets" recalls Jacob's adolescence in Quimper and mourns his adult feeling of estrangement. A sidewise, seriocomic couplet rhyming *lourd* (heavy) with *amours* (loves) suggests love as one source of the poem's torment and fear of being hated. In this early version, the poem has the freshness of the pieces in *La Côte;* it practices none of the phonetic hijinks of *Les Oeuvres burlesques et mystiques:*

Before, when I drew near your small white houses at the outskirts of
    town,
Quimper, I cried so hard I couldn't see the trees.

I've again found my earliest fifteen years,
But I can't find my tears.
Now everything's ugly, the summer's made of stone.

On the back of the notebook page, Jacob doodled Hebrew letters, alchemical signs for moon demons out of Cornelius Agrippa's book of magic, a grid for a magic square, and a drawing of the Moon Goddess with a crescent moon on her head and a crescent moon in her hand: whatever his new Christian orientation, he continued to practice magic.[67]

CHAPTER 9

ART WARS

I.

The two years leading up to the Great War saw the flowering of modern art in the work of Stravinsky, Proust, Picasso, and Apollinaire, and Jacob's poems are part of this story. As Jacob and his friends declared war on older conventions of the arts, they also declared imaginary war on one another, not anticipating that these battles might be displaced by real military assaults.

HOLED UP IN Brittany in the autumn of 1912, Jacob missed the most tempestuous season in the history of Cubism. In October, the young painter Jacques Villon, along with Gleizes, Metzinger, and Picabia, organized an enormous, supposedly Cubist exhibit, showing their own work and that of Villon's brothers Marcel Duchamp and Raymond Duchamp-Villon, along with many others, including Fernand Léger and Juan Gris. They called the show "The Golden Mean." Apollinaire opened it with an idiotic lecture entitled "The Dismemberment of Cubism." He "dismembered" Cubism into "scientific cubism," "orphic cubism," "physical cubism," and "instinctive cubism," performing rhetorical contortions in order to praise his new friend Robert Delaunay. The critic Maurice Raynal, in the single issue of the journal *The Golden Mean* launched with the show, claimed that it was "the first complete grouping of all the artists who ushered in the twentieth century, with works clearly representative of the tastes, trends, and ideas that characterize it overall." This, of a show in which Picasso and Braque refused to participate![1]

Max Jacob avoided being drawn into the melee. As he told Picasso, he had not taken up the invitation to submit work to the journal: "I want to be neither my friends' mouthpiece, nor their *de facto* interviewer."[2]

In December, Jacob wrote Picasso from Quimper, narrating tales from his town and asking his friend's advice on a title for his novel. He listed thirteen possibilities, of which number five, *Le Terrain Bouchaballe*, would prevail. A few days later he wrote Kahnweiler to say that he had almost finished his book, that his father had read it and made no comment, and that his family seemed "furious" with him. He stayed on with them through Christmas, however, and into the new year. It was to Quimper that Picasso, back in Céret with Eva, sent a postcard greeting to Max on December 23.[3] The year 1912 concluded with the founding, in Italy, of a new avant-garde journal that would be hospitable to Max Jacob; in late December, Soffici wrote Picasso to announce the birth of *Lacerba* in Florence and to ask his help in securing contributions from the poet.[4]

||

JACOB RETURNED TO Montmartre in early January, occupying Raynal's old room on the Rue Chevalier de la Barre. He was anxious about publication. *Cinématoma* (still called *Apocryphal Memoirs*) was in Poiret's hands, and Jacob had sent *Le Terrain Bouchaballe* to the publishing house the Mercure de France. He had schemed for at least a year to interest the Mercure in the book; months earlier he had squabbled with Apollinaire about it, accusing his friend of not helping him meet privately with Rachilde, the influential novelist and wife of the Mercure's director.[5]

Life in Montmartre lurched along. Modigliani, never a close friend of Jacob's but close enough to paint several portraits of him, collapsed from illness, fatigue, and alcohol and retreated to his family in Livorno to convalesce.[6] Reverdy moved with his companion, the seamstress Henriette Bureau, from the Bateau Lavoir to the nearby Rue Cortot, an apartment beneath the lodging of the drunken painter Utrillo, his mother the painter Suzanne Valadon, and her companion Utter, a ménage whose brawling resonated up and down the street.[7] When the Salon des Indépendants opened in February, Apollinaire reviewed it in *Montjoie!*, reporting the arrival of "Orphism, pure painting, simultaneity" in the work of Robert Delaunay, in which the poet took a proprietary interest: "It is the first manifestation of this movement which I foresaw and announced."[8] Laurencin's large decorative painting *The Elegant Ball* inspired his enthusiasm, "one of the strongest and freest of the Salon."[9] On February 17, Max Jacob was still living on the Rue Chevalier de la Barre, but by the end of the month he moved several streets away to a room on the Rue Gabrielle that would be his den until he left Paris for the monastery of Saint-Benoît-sur-Loire in 1921.[10] His friend the actor Sylvette Fillacier (wife of Marcel Olin) helped him move and remembered traipsing up and down the aptly named Rue du Calvaire (Calvary Street) carrying Max's "broken oil lamp, a chipped platter, a battered basin, a bottle of oil, a dented pitcher, a leaky bucket, a wobbly chair, and a turtle which, you said, kept the bedbugs away."[11]

His change of lodgings coincided with the painful news that the Mercure de France had rejected *Le Terrain Bouchaballe*. Writing to Bloch, for once Jacob was too hurt to joke. "They accuse me of preciosity, of a weak plot (a novel I made into a play!), they insult my style (try working on style for fifteen years). It's a real sorrow," he complained.[12] The refusal must have wounded all the more, following Fasquelle's rejection of *Cinématoma* and coming just as Apollinaire's collection of poems, *Alcools,* was due to appear from the Mercure and as Ollendorff was about to publish Salmon's *Gentle Rascals,* a book of stories about petty criminals in the Quartier Latin.[13] (Salmon's chatty and lurid stories hardly rise above the level of newspaper gossip.) Jacob's closest literary friends were finding established publishers while he, for all his brilliance, seemed shut out. Apollinaire sent *Le Terrain Bouchaballe* to a publisher in Lausanne; nothing would come of that attempt, and Apollinaire may not have tried very hard. In this somber mood, Jacob declared to Bloch, "I want to change my life," and fired off the surprising news that he planned to get married after visiting Picasso for a couple of months in Céret.

Hardly anything is known of this romance of Jacob's. Many years later he told the painter Roger Toulouse that he had been in love for some months in 1914–15 (*sic*) with a woman from Indochina.[14] Given his general feelings about women and his strong attraction to men, this project of marriage sounds more like an extension of his plan to "change his life" than an expression of committed love. It somewhat resembles his fantasy of finding wholeness and stability in the Catholic Church. But who can tell?

JACOB'S PLAN TO visit Picasso and Eva in Céret had a more serious foundation. He had been seeing a lot of them in spite of Picasso's having moved across the river to Montparnasse. Picasso wrote Apollinaire anxiously on February 27, saying that Max had told him that at the offices of the Mercure, he'd seen the proofs of Picasso's portrait for the frontispiece of *Alcools* reproduced in blue. It should be printed in black, Picasso insisted. A few days later he wrote Apollinaire, inviting him to dinner "with Monsieur Max Jacob."[15]

Picasso and Eva left for Céret on March 10, a week before the publication of Apollinaire's long-announced book on modern painting, *Méditations esthétiques: Les Peintres cubistes.* The book is a patchwork of Apollinaire's art journalism. Stimulated by the controversies over Cubism, facing competition from the team of Gleizes and Metzinger and from Salmon, and inspired by Robert Delaunay to emphasize Orphic color over Cubist geometry, Apollinaire compiled his volume hastily. His publisher skewed its focus by printing the subtitle, *Les Peintres cubistes,* in large type, whereas Apollinaire started his argument with a hymn to light, flame, and purity in terms that had nothing to do with Cubism. Not surprisingly, the book irritated Kahnweiler, who regarded Apollinaire as an irresponsible muddler in art criticism.[16]

Picasso had long since stopped paying attention to Salmon, but he cared about Apollinaire and seems to have maintained a charitable silence with him in regard to this book. He was not so reticent with Kahnweiler, to whom he wrote from Céret that he had received Apollinaire's book and was "disappointed with all this chatter."[17] Apollinaire, for his part, sent an extraordinarily aggressive letter to his old friend Kahnweiler, accusing him of trying to "destroy" him and claiming to be "the only one able to lay the foundations for future artistic understanding." He threatened, "He who seeks to destroy shall be destroyed. . . . Let this be the simple warning of a poet who knows what must be said, and knows what he is and what others are in matters of art."[18]

Picasso wrote Kahnweiler on April 11, asking him to give Jacob the money for his trip to Céret and to put it on Picasso's "account." This was neither the first nor the last of the generous acts with which Picasso honored his friendship with Jacob. The painter had signed an exclusive contract with Kahnweiler in December, being paid far more than the other artists in the gallery. Jacob, by contrast, earned next to nothing. Kahnweiler must have given Jacob the funds immediately, because a few days later Picasso reported that Max had arrived in Céret.[19] Thus began one of the happiest chapters in Jacob's life, though it coincided with a fairly dark one for Picasso.

Picasso and Eva were installed in a large apartment in the house Picasso had occupied during his earlier stay in Céret. Jacob's letters to Kahnweiler, Apollinaire, and Bloch are ecstatic. This was his first trip to the South of France. He marveled as the train skimmed past Toulouse, Carcassonne, and the mountains of the Voirons, and he flew into panegyrics about Céret: its "precipices," the rugged countryside, and scents of thyme, lavender, and rosemary. It was raining so heavily he couldn't see Mont Canigou, but it didn't matter; an intense shared life went on inside the house, and Picasso and Eva spoiled and petted him. He would rise at six, he told Kahnweiler, and write a prose poem or two to get himself going. Picasso brought him his breakfast—hot chocolate and a croissant—at eight, glancing "indulgently" at Jacob's paintings before withdrawing. After breakfast, Jacob read *The Lives of the Saints* and other dusty volumes he found in the attic, worked at his watercolors and drawings, and wrote poems. It was a "cellular" life, he said: he, Picasso, and Eva spent the days, each in a "cell" working, but gathered for lunch and dinner, which they prepared at home, a diet based on artichokes and salad. Loyal though he was to Fernande, Jacob clearly liked Eva and praised her housewifely virtues, her devotion to Picasso, and her indulgence of him—a "dirty and phlegmatic guest when he wasn't acting crazy or witless."

Jacob painted a good deal during this visit and even worked up the nerve to try some "Cubist" scenes, geometrically simplified gouaches and ink drawings of the landscape of Céret with its staggered houses, cliffs, and Mont Canigou looming behind. The drawings have a naïve charm, though he confessed to Kahnweiler that his Master didn't approve of his Cubist attempts. The postscript of this letter is telling in its brevity: "I'm in very bad relations with my family, my marriage is off."[20] It is as if, having temporarily found his ideal family with Picasso and Eva, he could weather criticism from his biological family and cast off the fantasy of creating a family of his own through marriage.

IN BARCELONA, PICASSO's father's health was failing. His son had spent a few days there at the end of March; now, on May 3, he received word that his father was dying, and he hurried back to attend the deathbed. A few days later he rejoined the little household in Céret and was hard at work. The letters from the three inhabitants of the house in Céret reveal quite a spectrum of feelings. Jacob's are exuberant, though not insensitive to his host's bereavement: in letters to Kahnweiler, Apollinaire, and Bloch, Jacob mentioned Picasso's grief and, in passing, the fact that Eva had been ill, kept in bed for days by bronchitis (in fact an early sign of the cancer that would kill her). But mainly Jacob described the landscape, their "cellular" life, excursions across the Pyrenees into Spain to see bullfights, and on one occasion a village dance they attended at the frontier. Jacob became so enthused with the picturesque scene (and perhaps with the wine) that he whirled around with a blond Spanish woman and then a young brunette, before "the silence and sadness of night in the mountains fell over us again."[21] He remarked flippantly to Apollinaire on the many "pederasts and etheromanes" hanging out in the cafes of Céret, carefully dissociating himself from those figures.[22]

Eva's letter of May 14 to Gertrude Stein reflected a darker mood. Not only did she report her illness and Picasso's mourning; she told Stein that Picasso's beloved dog Frika was seriously ill and would have to be put down. Eva didn't relate the details, but Picasso paid a local gamekeeper to shoot Frika in the head, and his grief for the dog seems to have mingled with grief for his father in ways he would never forget. Even in old age, Picasso mourned for Frika.[23] Picasso, who rarely expressed emotion directly, wrote to Kahnweiler at his father's death, "You can imagine the state I'm in."[24]

Jacob claimed not to be writing much poetry in Céret, but the incantatory experience of the village dance in Figueras, Spain, inspired one of his best poems. "Honor of the Sardana and the Tenora" poured out like a lyric extension of his letter. Starting in rhyming couplets, interrupted by a prose commentary on the Catalan wind instrument the tenora, and concluding in rhyming quatrains, the poem ardently transforms the scene into a chain reaction of metamorphoses, a mix of wit, gaiety, extravagant rhymes, and melancholy that maintains a wild momentum. It begins:

> The sea's the Aegean Sea that flows past Alicante.
> Oh! it's an income of twenty-five thousand I want!

The nasal, piercing sound of the tenora—something like a clarinet—and the whirling rings within rings of the dance carry the poem along:

> The shock of yellow on red entails,
> O tenora, your onion-scented scales.
> It's made me drunk like alcohol.
> It's snuffed out like a candle
> Its memory always I'll recall.[25]

Apollinaire's collection *Alcools* was published at the end of April, and the household in Céret waited impatiently for a copy. On May 16 Picasso wrote Apollinaire, partly to express sympathy for the illness of Marie Laurencin's mother, partly to report that he was "still very sad" but beginning to work again, but mainly to request a copy of *Alcools*, which bore his portrait of the poet as its frontispiece.[26] Around the same time, Jacob reported to Apollinaire on life in Céret, adding his own plea for a copy of *Alcools*. In this letter, which contained news of Eva's illness, Jacob slipped in a delicate reference to his hopes for the publisher in Lausanne to whom Apollinaire had sent *Le Terrain Bouchaballe;* he asked Apollinaire to return the manuscript if it seemed clear that the attempt would come to nothing.[27] One feels Jacob's sensitivity—the crosscurrents of this friendship, his excitement at his friend's achievement, and worry about his own.

A few days later, Jacob reported to Kahnweiler, Picasso's copy of *Alcools* arrived. It was too fancy to touch, but not as fancy as Kahnweiler's beautiful editions, Jacob remarked; he was afraid to read it for fear of soiling it with ash from his cigarette.[28] He would, of course, read it, with all the rivalrous intensity his old comrade's masterpiece would naturally excite. Apollinaire had composed the book with poems going as far back as 1901, interspersed with poems Jacob had seen since the early days of their friendship. Three of the newest poems, "Le Pont Mirabeau," "Marie," and "Hunting Horn," commemorate his wounded love for Laurencin. The book opens and closes with major new poems—"major" in length but also in artistic daring, a new rapidity in association of ideas and images, radical discontinuities, and fluid interplay between lyric cadences and free verse. This lush harmonizing of the old and new arts of poetry is a key to Apollinaire's genius and is evident in the lines of "Zone" that open the book:

> Finally you're tired of this ancient world
> Shepherdess O Eiffel Tower the flock of bridges bleats this morning[29]

The first line, professing weariness with the old world (and by implication, its old poetry) is a classic alexandrine with a central caesura, the verse of that old world.[30] The second line lengthens to sixteen syllables to declare its independence from the old system. The poem's mobile geography carries it all over Europe and through Paris, through centuries and through oscillating pronouns, but also through a single night into a sacrificial dawn in the brutal final line with its play on words, "Soleil cou coupé" (Sun neck cut), where the word for "neck," *cou,* is cut from *coupé,* the word for "cut." Apollinaire added this magnificent poem in November 1912 to the first proofs of the book at the same time that he astonished his editors by removing all punctuation from the volume, a revolution in typography and poetics.[31]

APOLLINAIRE ACKNOWLEDGED HIS friendship with Jacob by dedicating to him one of the older poems. "Palace," first published in 1905, mixes Symbolist dream imagery with whimsical obscenity ("Lady of my thoughts with ass of purest pearl . . .").[32] But Jacob was soon drawn into a controversy about *Alcools*. In a vituperative review in the *Mercure de France*, Georges Duhamel took revenge on Apollinaire for attacking his comrades Romains and Chennevière a few years earlier. Apollinaire was caught by surprise, as he had long published in the *Mercure*, and as *Alcools* had appeared with the Mercure publishing house. Apollinaire's book was a junk shop, declared Duhamel; he compared the poems to "a jumble of faked paintings, exotic patched pieces of clothing, bicycle parts, and more or less unmentionable toilet articles." As for the poet, "he looks like a mixture of Levantine Jew, South American, Polish squire, and *facchino* [Italian porter]."[33] To add insult to injury, Duhamel accused Apollinaire of swiping effects from Max Jacob.

Apollinaire was beside himself and wanted to challenge Duhamel to a duel. To calm him down, Louise Faure-Favier kept him to dinner with André Billy and René Dalize at her house and distracted him sufficiently that by the end of the evening he dropped the idea of a duel, but the group decided to enlist Jacob to protest Duhamel's claim about influence.[34] Jacob complied, sending this formal, absurd, and untruthful letter to the editor of the *Mercure:*

> Monsieur Guillaume Apollinaire has been publishing poetry continuously since 1898. In 1905, I wasn't writing anything, in prose or verse, and my first collection of poems appeared in 1911.[35]

||

IN CÉRET, PICASSO threw himself back into work, one of his tasks being to illustrate Jacob's final Matorel book for Kahnweiler, *Le Siège de Jéru-*

salem. He and the dealer-publisher wrote back and forth about the business; *Le Siège* would be published with three etchings that had even less to do with the plot than Picasso's illustrations for *Saint Matorel*.[36] They followed the line of Picasso's own concerns: two densely worked images of women (whereas there are almost no female characters in the play), and a still life with a skull, a *memento mori* that arose out of the artist's mourning for his father and his dog. The etchings of women play straight lines against voluptuous, curving arcs, and *Nude Woman with Guitar* flaunts two distinct, round breasts with budding nipples, quite at odds with the angular geometries from which they spring; they seem an homage to Eva's erotic power.[37]

THE PREVIOUS DECEMBER, Soffici had announced the birth of the journal *Lacerba*. He had come to blows with the Futurists two years earlier when Boccioni, Marinetti, and several friends took the train from Milan to Florence to punch Soffici, whom they had never met, as he sat in a café, in retaliation for his criticism of Futurism in the journal *La Voce*. But while arguing aesthetics at the police station where they'd been dragged in front of the mystified commissioner, they found surprising common ground.[38] Now Soffici and his old collaborator Giovanni Papini quit *La Voce* and joined forces with Marinetti in launching *Lacerba*, meant to lead a cultural revolution in Italy. Full of fire and brimstone, *Lacerba* sent contradictory signals about French art, on the one hand attacking it and asserting Futurist supremacy, on the other publishing writers in French (like Jacob and Apollinaire) and constantly referring to French writers, artists, and theories. The awkward fact was, Modernism *had* begun in France.[39]

Jacob was only too happy to accept Soffici's invitation, which reached him in Céret. He wrote in April and again in May, sending verse and prose poems and securing Kahnweiler's permission to reprint excerpts from *Saint Matorel*.[40] His first publication in *Lacerba*, the poem "Establishment of a Commune in Brazil," followed a couple of pages later by a drawing by Picasso, appeared in mid-June, just as Picasso, Eva, and Jacob took another trip to Spain to see bullfights before returning to Paris. The poem is one of Jacob's most legible, an allegory of a utopian Catholic commune in the Brazilian jungle, where wild animals become mystically tame before the settlement is massacred by savages. So, concludes the poem's speaker, he had been living a life of innocent love, piety, and prayer,

> But cruel laugher, the worries heaped on me,
> Money and scandal and others' stupidity
> Have turned me into the hard bourgeois whose signature you see.[41]

It was not one of Jacob's best poems, but it reveals another version of the mythic self he was evolving; the sense of himself as hardened (*dur*) would reappear a few years later in Monsieur Dur, the hero of his novel *Filibuth, ou la montre en or* (Filibuth, or the Golden Watch).

In the same issue as Jacob's poem, Marinetti published an important statement of Futurist poetics, "The Wireless Imagination and Words at Liberty," amplifying his literary manifesto of the previous year. Already in "Technical Manifesto of Futurist Literature" in 1912, using the phrase "words at liberty," which both Apollinaire and Jacob would take up, Marinetti had called for the destruction of syntax (in syntactically correct sentences); the suppression of adjectives, adverbs, and conjunctions; the elimination of the "I"; the replacement of intelligence by "divine intuition"; and the creation of "the mechanical man with interchangeable parts."[42] Now, in *Lacerba,* he let loose a torrent of Futurist demands: for acceleration, novelty, destruction of the past, and glorification of the machine, in the service of "a violent and dynamic lyricism."[43]

In this hysterical context, Soffici introduced Max Jacob, conveying with three anecdotes the already stylized persona of Jacob the mystical Harlequin of Montmartre. One tale relates the Virgin's scolding Max; she appears outside Sacré-Coeur to tell him, "Oh! My poor Max, what a loser you are." Jacob had run around the cafés of Montmartre for years entertaining listeners with versions of this encounter. Soffici's second story mythologizes what must have been a humiliating experience and not an uncommon one for a homosexual who found his partners by cruising. Jacob was arrested one evening as he emerged from a café, Soffici relates, and dragged down to the police station, where the commissioner berated him for "the vices everyone knew him to indulge." The commissioner was preparing to throw him in jail when the poet opened his mouth. "We never found out exactly what he said, but his words were so sweet, so celestial, full of such virtue, that the commissioner and even his constables had their hearts softened, tears poured down their faces, and they fell to their knees at his feet to adore him."[44] (As many of his friends intimated, Jacob had run-ins with the police from time to time, though in the turn-and-turn-about world of official hypocrisy and actual sexual mores, he often found his sexual partners in the ranks of the police.)[45] Soffici concluded his introduction with one of Jacob's fantastical autobiographical sketches, with the poet claiming to have been a sailor before becoming a Parisian writer and dandy.

PICASSO, EVA, AND Jacob started back to Paris on June 20, stopping in Toulouse to visit the museum. At home, Picasso and Eva would soon have to contend with Picasso's falling sick, variously diagnosed with "a little typhoid fever" or Malta fever, but in any case he was so debilitated that doctors were called. The newspapers reported his illness (he had now attained such fame), and Matisse visited every day bringing gifts of flowers and oranges.[46] Picasso recovered quickly, and in early August he and Eva returned to Céret. Jacob felt reassured enough about his friend's health to joke about it to Bloch in a parody of journalistic style: "In the elegant dining room sumptuously decorated in a barbaric style and pale in the livid light of the gas jet, the painter strolled with his own equally livid pallor. Monsieur Picasso was ill."[47]

JACOB NOW BEGAN to publish a good deal, not only in *Lacerba* but also in *La Phalange, Les Soirées de Paris,* and *Montjoie!.* Grateful though he was for the welcome in *Lacerba,* he was never an ally of the Futurists. His work was at home there only in that he was dismantling literary conventions, but his tone had nothing of the stridency of Marinetti, Papini, or Boccioni. The first issue of *Lacerba,* dated January 1, 1913, struck a Nietzschean note, with Papini calling for "freedom" and a morality of the superman, "in which everything is permitted and legitimate."[48] Marinetti's paeans to war and machinery, Boccioni's assertions that all modern painting (Cézanne, Degas, Picasso, Braque) was only a prelude to Futurism,[49] Papini's call for a "Massacre of Women"—all this swashbuckling created an odd context for Jacob's whimsy.[50]

Apollinaire, feeling the need to consolidate his position as leader of the avant-garde, seized on the Futurist rhetoric with opportunistic enthusiasm. Whereas a few months earlier he had derided Marinetti and Boccioni, now he leaped on their bandwagon, publishing his own manifesto "THE FUTURIST ANTITRADITION" as a pamphlet in June 1913 before bringing it out in *Lacerba* in September.[51] Taking up Marinetti's eye-catching graphics and expressions (WORDS AT LIBERTY, PLASTIC DYNAMISM), Apollinaire repeated the cry for the suppression of syntax, punctuation, history, and so forth; flung MERDE (shit) at critics, pedagogues, philologists, and other devotees of the past; and presented ROSES to himself and to the avant-garde artists of whom he approved—Marinetti, Picasso, Boccioni, Jacob, Metzinger, Gleizes, Laurencin, Matisse ... The list is a desperate attempt to herd the Italians and the French into the same corral, to reconcile Futurism with Cubism, Orphism, and all the other emerging "isms," and to position himself as master of ceremonies.

MAX JACOB HAD no such ambitions, but he did want to see his work in print, and *Lacerba* gave him that forum. He was grateful, too, for the twenty francs he was paid for the suite of mini-prose poems, "Monsieur Max Jacob's Divan," that would appear in the July, August, and September issues.[52] In calling his suite a "divan," he was alluding to classical collections of Persian poetry and also to Goethe's *West-Eastern Divan*. In these snippets he extended his inspiration from the Persian poems in *Les Oeuvres burlesques et mystiques*. The new pieces are less imagistic and mysterious than the Matorel Persian poems, and he never reprinted them, but they have epigrammatic economy: "In the harbor of my heart, there's no sandbar or riptide: enter, vessels, you'll be sheltered in pools of tenderness."[53]

In August, *La Phalange* published five poems of Jacob's, including "A Thousand Other Regrets"and "Prayer," composed the previous summer in Quimper.[54] It was Henri Hertz who took Jacob's poems to this Symbolist journal where Apollinaire had published for years. To Hertz's astonishment, Apollinaire threw a tantrum. He may have been still smarting at Duhamel's taunt that he imitated Jacob. Hertz wondered,

> Didn't he know of Max's secret work? Didn't he know what that beehive of poverty and exaltation contained, just a few hundred meters from where he lived, the cubbyhole of the Rue Ravignan? I don't know if he ever went there. I never encountered him there. Didn't he know what was on the shelves, dusty even in the draughts, above the bed frame propped up on bricks: the fraying shirts lined with fluttering scraps of paper where this teeming poetry hatched and shivered, whose wings took fire at the slightest gesture, the slightest glance, and made the whole room sing?[55]

II.

AT THE END of September, artistic Paris gathered for a celebration that was at once a consecration of Modernism and a family occasion: the Futurist painter Gino Severini married Paul Fort's black-eyed, dark-ringletted sixteen-year-old daughter Jeanne, who had grown up in the Symbolist hothouse of the Closerie des Lilas and was known as "the Princess of the Closerie."[56] Now that Fort was *prince des poètes* and the Futurists had been successful in their clamorous public relations, the event was treated as a "royal wedding" in the French and even in the international press.

Severini's fellow Futurists in Milan at first threatened to expel him from the group ón antimatrimonial principle, but recognizing the value of the publicity of the rite, they changed tactics, and Marinetti sped to Paris in his white Bugatti to be one of Severini's witnesses at the ceremony at the town hall of the fourteenth arrondissement. The groom's other witness was Apollinaire, and the Franco-American poet Stuart Merrill and Alfred Vallette, editor of the *Mercure de France*, stood up for the bride. Marinetti even lent the newlyweds his magnificent car for a day and night of honeymoon.

For the feast, the wedding party repaired to a revered Symbolist meeting place, the Café Voltaire behind the Théâtre de l'Odéon. The guest list combined an honor roll of old Symbolists and the new avant-garde: the novelist Rachilde; Salmon; the *soi-disant* Cubists Gleizes and Metzinger; Léger; and young Francis Carco, who buttonholed Rachilde and managed in that way to have his novel of Parisian low life, *Jésus-la-Caille*, accepted by the Mercure. Max Jacob put on a performance even more spectacular than usual. After a bout of fast punning and repartee with Paul Fort, he seized a bottle and announced that the plaster cast of the Victory of Samothrace, a wedding gift from an Italian cast-maker, was an "old work" and "made no sense in an assembly of Futurists," and smashed it to pieces.[57]

In hindsight, the wedding seems an emblem of the high spirits and joyous, innocent destructiveness of Modernism, the Dionysian party preceding a real slaughter. Diaghilev had shaken Paris in May with his production of Stravinsky's *Le Sacre du printemps* danced by Nijinsky. In November, Grasset published *Du côté de chez Swann*, the first volume of Proust's revolutionary novel. Jacob rose with this tide of invention. Every issue of *Lacerba* that autumn carried his work: in September, Soffici ran the "Mademoiselle Léonie" section from *Saint Matorel;* in October appeared another section, "The Conversion of Émile Cordier"; in November *Lacerba* published his new poem "Chinese Republic and Revolutions." This incoherent poem mixes a cocktail of revolutionary fervor, wisecracks, puns, and sententious colonialist advice. Inspired by the Boxer Rebellion followed by Sun Yat-sen's revolution in October 1911 and the establishment of the Republic of China, Jacob—ex-student of the École Coloniale— fantasizes that the Marseillaise now floats across China, and he lectures the new republicans on maintaining peace and neutrality. Politics were never Jacob's strong point; he didn't reprint this poem.[58]

When Jacob wrote Bloch at the end of September, he had recovered from the disappointment of his novel's rejection by the Mercure. One reason for his improved humor was financial. The Austrian dealer Adolphe Basler was buying his gouaches at five francs apiece, and Jacob began to earn more from his painting than from his writing, setting a pattern that would endure for the rest of his life. Something of the old communal world of the Bateau Lavoir was taking shape in Montparnasse. Jacob still lived on the Rue Gabrielle in Montmartre but increasingly carried on his social life across the river: Picasso and Eva moved at the end of September to an immense studio apartment overlooking the Montparnasse cemetery, rue Schoelcher, 5 bis, just off the Boulevard Raspail; Paul Fort and the crowd from the *Mercure de France* still presided at the Closerie des Lilas; Serge Férat and Hélène d'Oettingen had brilliantly revived *Les Soirées de Paris* on the Boulevard Raspail and at their apartment a few doors down. A *carte pneumatique* from Jacob to Bloch dated October 8 gives a glimpse of this hectic world: trying to make a date with Bloch, Jacob explains that he'll be at home until four, when he'll take a young painter to meet Apollinaire, and that he'll dine later that evening with the Picassos at their new place.[59]

Jacob still made part of his modest living selling copies of *La Côte*, and during one of these commercial expeditions he met the young playboy Conrad Moricand, who in those days dabbled at painting, spending his father's money freely, and hanging out with Kisling, Cendrars, and Salmon. Moricand, a demonic character who would become a professional astrologer and a good friend of Jacob's, remembered being introduced to Jacob by Kisling at the Rotonde in the summer of 1913. Dressed in a deliveryman's cap, a smart jacket, red socks, and a monocle, Jacob carried copies of his book in a briefcase and performed a stylized version of himself for the clients of the café, mingling his parents' skill as shopkeepers with his role of bohemian entertainer. Moricand was struck by Jacob's eyes, with their sidewise glances and their mixture of dark and light, of brilliance and humidity. Under Jacob's dandyism lay immense sadness, Moricand felt, and sensed that Jacob was always on the edge of some crisis—of remorse, tenderness, or despair.[60]

IN NOVEMBER APOLLINAIRE opened the first issue of the resurgent *Soirées de Paris* with a chronicle of the new Salon d'Automne in Berlin and the Parisian salon. This hymn to "simultaneity," "Orphism," and Robert Delaunay would provoke a pointed response from the Futurists in *Lacerba*. Even more than *Orphism*, the word *simultaneous* seemed to possess coveted market value. In this historic issue, flanked by black and white reproductions of Picasso's constructions, Jacob published three poems. Two are verse poems composed around 1900 and recalling Quimper: "The Bad Boy's Lament" and "At Home"; the third is a mini-self-portrait in a prose poem, "Merry Joker." Max Jacob wouldn't reprint this piece in a book, probably because it wasn't abstract enough, but for that very reason it's useful for the biographer:

> It's me, the merry joker.
>
> The smallest pince-nez on a mustache stops me in my tracks, and not to find my name on a letter not addressed to me surprises and wounds me. But if someone organizes a farandole, I know how to sing and run at the same time. The other day I was singing "The Little Hunchback" in a farandole and I noticed there was a hunchback there. I wondered if I should stop the song or continue it. I had the wit not to sing all the verses. It's me, the merry joker.[61]

On December 15 appeared the second issue of the new *Soirées de Paris*, sumptuously illustrated with reproductions of paintings by Laurencin, Gleizes, and Matisse. Apollinaire and "Jean Cérusse"—the punning name for the team of Serge Férat and the Baroness d'Oettingen, "C'est Russe" (It's Russian) or "Ces Russes" (Those Russians)—had turned the magazine into a leading art journal. But *Les Soirées de Paris* was as rich in writing as in visual art. The December issue ran Apollinaire's "simultaneist" poem "Monday Rue Christine," a free verse "found" poem composed of fragments of talk overheard in a bar, a bold step forward even from the experimental poems in *Alcools*.

Max Jacob's three poems directly follow Apollinaire's. The first, "The Costume Ball," seems a response to the new "simultaneist" style his friend was developing in poems such as "The Windows," which contains this line: "We'll send it by a *message téléphonique*."[62] "The Costume Ball" starts: "The buffets' crystal in telegraphic style." Apollinaire and Jacob were both excited by the new technologies of communication as metaphors for a poetics of immediacy.

Dense in wordplay, puns, and rhymes, "Le Bal masqué," "Malvina," and "Marsupiau" would all take their place in *Le Laboratoire central*. They are hardly translatable, they so multiply senses out of the jostle of sounds. This is a dreamlike art constantly unmaking and remaking sense. "Marsupiau" winks at Jacob's disguised sexuality: "Am I a woman or a boy?" asks Marsupiau.[63] Jacob crystallized that uncertainty in a deformation of language. "Marsupiau" is a false singular form of the plural noun for marsupials in French, *marsupiaux*: the correct singular form would be *marsupial*. Jacob's character is not quite masculine or feminine, neither singular nor plural, and he wears a fictitious skin, since *piau* is a nonsense word combining *peau* (skin) and the verb *piauler* (to whine or make cheeping noises).[64]

Max Jacob wound up the year 1913 in a joyous mood. His poetry was appearing in print in France and Italy, and he was celebrated as the life of the party in bohemian Paris. That month the *Mona Lisa* was recovered in Florence, but the restoration of a classic mattered less to Jacob and his friends than the invention of new forms.

III.

AVANT-GARDE WRITERS, PAINTERS, and sculptors were spoiled by years of peace, and many of them—like the Futurists—were spoiling for a fight on aesthetic if not on nationalist grounds. (Marinetti did have some experience of real war, having covered Italy's war with the Ottoman Empire to seize Libya in 1911. He found battle exhilarating.) In Paris, Picasso, Braque, Derain, and Gertrude Stein developed a passion for boxing, and the archaic practice of dueling provided another form of ritualized violence. In June 1914 two Polish painters, Jacob's friend Moïse Kisling and Leopold Gottlieb, settled a point of honor, meeting at dawn in a park: they attacked first with pistols and then with sabers, fighting so violently they had to be separated. Both were superficially wounded, Gottlieb on the chin and Kisling on the nose. Kisling called his wound "the fourth partition of Poland."[65]

Simultaneism now became the new battle cry. In his chronicles of November 1913 in *Les Soirées de Paris*, Apollinaire had celebrated the Simultaneism of Robert Delaunay, and though he granted that Delaunay had borrowed the term from the Futurists, he asserted the supremacy of the French in the new art.[66] Try as he might, Apollinaire would find it impossible to maintain allegiances with Delaunay and the Futurists at the same time, and he would eventually break with Delaunay, having thrown in his lot with Marinetti with his own manifesto, "THE FUTURIST ANTI-TRADITION." Acutely conscious of the value of Apollinaire's adherence, the Futurists reasserted their proprietorship of Simultaneism while flattering Apollinaire.[67]

But Apollinaire now had to defend himself on another flank. The young Swiss poet Blaise Cendrars (whose real name was Frédéric-Louis Sauser) burst into Paris in September 1912 after a stint in New York and some years in Russia where he was apprenticed to a Swiss watchmaker. That month Cendrars published a free-floating revolutionary poem, "Easter in New York." Apollinaire may or may not have been inspired by its mobile geographies when he composed his free-floating "Zone" that same month to add to the proofs of *Alcools*. A year later Cendrars, who now lived near the Delaunays and seemed to be displacing Apollinaire in their affections, published an extraordinary scroll poem-painting in collaboration with Sonia Delaunay, "La Prose du Transsibérien et de la Petite Jehanne de France," advertised as "the first Simultaneist book."[68]

Seven years younger than Apollinaire, Cendrars (whose nom de plume is rich in suggestions of burning, cinders, and the philosopher Blaise Pascal) was an inventive and combative poet. In "La Prose du Transsibérien" he quoted Apollinaire's radical poem "The Betrothal," suggesting that he had absorbed its lessons and surpassed it.[69] Now Cendrars confronted the elder poet head-on with a free verse poem-portrait of his rival:

Apollinaire
1900–1911
For twelve years the sole poet in France.[70]

II

LE SIÈGE DE JÉRUSALEM came out on January 21, 1914, in the same sober format as Kahnweiler's editions of Jacob's other Matorel books. Paul Poiret and his former master in fashion design, the great Jacques Doucet, were among the subscribers. At the same time, more and more of Jacob's poems were appearing in journals; he was no longer just the joker of Montmartre.

Not that he gave up his pranks. Louise Faure-Favier remembered a dinner at Laurencin's blue apartment in Auteuil, where Jacob began reading fortunes in the palms of the guests. He predicted to Laurencin that she would live for a long time abroad—which Marie, a thorough Parisian, protested. (She would, in fact, soon live abroad, when she married a German, the Baron Otto von Waëtjen, thus losing her French citizenship and going into exile in Spain during World War I.) Jacob informed René Dalize that he would die earlier than anyone in the room. (Dalize would indeed die first, killed in action May 7, 1917.) Reading Apollinaire's palm, Jacob said, "You will enter neither the *Revue des deux mondes*, nor the Académie Française. I foresee a short life and glory after your death. I see"—and at this point he had to duck to avoid the blow Apollinaire aimed at his head. Apollinaire stormed out of the apartment to pace up and down the hallway outside, while Jacob predicted that Faure-Favier would "climb very high, and preside at the tables of ministers." She excused herself to lure the angry poet back from the corridor, only to have Jacob offend him again by assuring him, "The gods are early to summon those whom they protect," at which Apollinaire exploded with an obscenity and the dinner party broke up. "Now this happened six months before the war," Faure-Favier declared, implying that Jacob had, indeed, eerily predicted his friends' fates.[71]

Whatever their quarrels, Apollinaire kept publishing Jacob in *Les Soi-rées de Paris*. The February issue featured paintings by Derain, a major "Simultaneist" poem by Apollinaire, letters by Jarry, and three poems by Jacob. In his editorial, Apollinaire continued his chauvinist diplomacy with the Futurists, batting the formulas back and forth ("words at liberty," "simultaneity," "telegraphic style") and insisting on French priority while trying to placate Marinetti. It was quite a performance, especially since Marinetti, after all, had launched the key phrase "words at liberty."[72] Apollinaire repaired his old quarrel with Jules Romains by crediting him with the first "simultaneous" poem, and criticized the extreme application of Marinetti's "words at liberty." This is the traditionalist Apollinaire, the craftsman of verse, not the flame-throwing revolutionary of "THE FUTURIST ANTITRADITION."

In July, Apollinaire would fight in another Simultaneist controversy, this time with Henri-Martin Barzun, but these polemics grew more and more absurd. Jacob, for one, was writing prose poems with abstract titles like "Simultaneous Poem with Simple Superposition" and "Simultaneous Poem with Two Turning Cylinders." No one had a copyright or patent on these ideas.[73]

OF JACOB'S THREE poems in *Les Soirées de Paris* in February, the prose poem "La Rue Ravignan de Montmartre" would become famous. It would appear (under the shorter title "La Rue Ravignan") in *Le Cornet à dés*, and it has often been quoted. Beatrice Hastings, Modigliani's fiercely liberated South African lover who wrote under the name Alice Morning, contributed to the poem's renown by printing a translation in the London journal *The New Age* in 1915. (Hastings gave this ultramodern poem an antiquarian cast by using the archaic pronoun *thou* in addressing the Baudelairean ragpicker, whereas Jacob uses the familiar *tu*. She also introduced new characters: Talleyrand, Louis XIII.) This is her version:

> One never bathes twice in the same stream, says Heraclitus. However, they are always the same who come up the steep street at the same hour.
>
> Each evening I see them, gay or sad. I, who watched from behind the window, with the science of the past amid the present—I have given names of the historic dead to all these passers-by. See, here is Agamemnon, there Madame Hanska. Patroclus is at the bottom of

the hill, Clytemnestra close by me. Talleyrand is a beggar, Ulysses is a milkman. Castor and Pollux are the genteel ladies of the fifth floor. Louis XIII is a barber; Pharoah, a tripe-seller.

But thou, old ragpicker, thou comest with the fairy morning—at the moment when at last I put out my good lamp—to sort the box of débris, débris still fresh—thou, unknown, mysterious and wretched ragpicker, I name thee Dostoyevsky.[74]

By now Jacob had perfected his version of the prose poem, refashioning the anecdotes of Baudelaire and Mallarmé, and the radical but Romantic sallies of Rimbaud. If Jacob is known today outside France as a writer, it is due to his renovation of the prose poem: his cool abstraction, his elliptical constructions, his lucid manipulation of the absurd, his send-up of sentimental conventions in fiction and poetry. "La Rue Ravignan" shows the poet at his magical work, turning the sordid street in Montmartre into a scene of classical nobility (Agamemnon, Ulysses, Patroclus). The short opening sentences debouch into the final long sentence with its incantatory repetitions culminating in the talismanic name, Dostoyevsky—that wild Christian imagination to whom no human perversity or perversion was alien.[75]

IV.

ON MARCH 2, Jacob attended the historic auction of modern art at the Hôtel Drouot organized by his friend André Level. Ten years earlier Level had founded a group called The Bear's Skin to invest in modern art with the promise to sell it a decade later. (The name referred to a fable of La Fontaine in which a bear taunts a hunter who has sold his skin before catching the prey.) A connoisseur, Level bought works by the forward-looking artists of his time but hadn't risked any truly shocking pieces. His calculations paid off. The sale was widely advertised, and the press attended in force along with *tout Paris*, including Proust's friend Prince Antoine Bibesco, Jacob's patron Paul Poiret, and a host of dealers. Apollinaire, Salmon, and

Raynal came in their capacity as art critics. Picasso and Matisse stayed away. This was the test of the market, the first time a collection of modern art had been sold, and the market rendered an enthusiastic verdict. Picasso's works sold for far more than their estimated value.[76]

Picasso, in the spring of 1914, playfully incorporated allusions to Jacob in his work. Two of the *papiers collés* from early in the year include ripped pages from *Lacerba,* and the subscription bulletin for *La Côte* dominates Picasso's *Still Life with Glass and Game of Cards (Homage to Max Jacob).*[77] Jacob was seeing a good deal of his friend. On April 14, he visited Suresnes with Picasso, Eva, and the Catalan sculptor Pau Gargallo, and together they wrote a greeting to Apollinaire.[78] Another day Jacob arranged to introduce the sculptor Jean Arp to Picasso, and arriving late at the bistro where they were to meet, he found them already in conversation because Picasso had become fascinated by the stranger's unusual tie clip, a little copper box with colored glass rattling inside it, and the stranger (Arp) had given it to him. "But you told me you didn't know Picasso!" exclaimed Jacob.[79]

Though the spring of 1914 was a season of camaraderie, it didn't lack in difficulties. On March 20, Jacob wrote Marcel Olin that he was so poor, he'd had trouble buying the stamp for the letter, and that in order to eat, he had to cadge invitations from fancy hostesses. He reported that Apollinaire was cobbling together old novels to sell for a few francs, and that Jacob's patron Basler, who had been buying his paintings, had no more money. To make matters worse, Jacob quarreled with Jean Royère, editor of *La Phalange:* Royère had asked Jacob for art criticism; Jacob asked to be paid in meals; Royère refused. Nor was *Lacerba* sending payments. There's a sense, in this letter, of the pressure of international politics on the daily life of the arts in Paris.[80]

Picasso, meanwhile, suffered from Eva's continued illness. He and Eva kept it secret, but it's clear that she was seriously sick, perhaps with cancer of breast or lung, and she had an operation in the spring of 1914.[81] Another disruption came in the dissolution of the Stein household. Leo Stein, who had never liked Cubism (he called it "an utter abomination") and who disliked Alice Toklas, moved to Italy in April 1914. He and Gertrude dismantled their collection by selling three valuable Picassos to Kahnweiler and dividing the rest, Gertrude keeping the remaining Picassos, and Leo the Renoirs and the Matisses, while they split the Cézannes.[82] The fame these artists had attained can be measured by the report in the *New York Sun*: "One of the world's finest collections of four living French masters, Cézanne, Picasso, Matisse and Renoir, will be disintegrated with the departure from Paris of Leo Stein."[83]

MAX JACOB NOW began to publish at a much greater rate. Some of the poems were older, some new, but all show mastery. *Lacerba* kept printing his prose poems, and in April one of his most ambitious poems, "Springtime and Screentime Mixed," appeared in *Les Soirées de Paris*. The title points to an experiment with simultaneity: the poem "mixes" spring and the movies, pastoral and urban imagery, different scenes and different voices, and its images of modernity (apartment blocks, movies, photography, pneumatic messages, trains) flare into epiphany. Jacob was no antitechnological snob: he saw the play of light and shadow in film as yet another way for sacred vision to be made manifest; in this poem, angels appear, and the following year Jacob would receive (so he thought) another celestial apparition right in a movie house.

"Springtime and Screentime Mixed" unrolls over three and a half pages. It starts bumptiously:

> The apartment blocks are new, the glasses of water clear.
> For my health I endure a diet more severe.
> Let's go to the Park, if it feels like fun
> I meet the Muse there off and on![84]

Twirling movie plots and visions ignited from everyday scenes ("Sun! You explode the tombstones in the cemetery"), Jacob juggles a dizzying number of tones. He tosses up the absurd: "And I recall, o Panama, your isthmus. / But don' t expect me to indulge in exoticismus." For a breath, he's confessional, comparing Brittany and Paris—and opting for Paris. Suddenly, mystical realities flare:

Springtime! Springtime! The sky-blue mirrors the roof tiles,
Man is followed by an angel, and answers his appeals.

Rejecting the paparazzo glamour of vacationing royalty, the poem ends with Jacob in his Harlequin mood:

To the fancy Rialto
I prefer my room on the Rue Rataud,
I freely offer the tune of a dance
On flute or viola whimsical—
I say this without impertinence—
to my neighbors in the hospital
And the jade necklaces the swallows carve in flight.

Many of the poems Jacob was now publishing would reappear in *Le Cornet à dés, La Défense de Tartufe*, or *Le Laboratoire central*. But already, just two months after its debut in *Les Soirées de Paris*, Richard Aldington quoted "Springtime and Screentime Mixed" in his article on recent French poetry in *The Egoist*. Aldington's piece was lackadaisical, but it shows where an educated Englishman turned at the time for news of contemporary French letters: the *Mercure de France, Les Soirées de Paris*, and Jean-Richard Bloch's *L'Effort libre*.[85]

V.

IN APOLLINAIRE'S JOURNALISM in the spring and early summer of 1914, one observes daily life in the capital taking its course, by turns frivolous, solemn, witty, and blithe. On May 14 in *Paris-Journal* he celebrated Derain. The next day with bittersweet brevity he reported on Laurencin's show of watercolors from 1908—the happiest year of their love. On May 22 he announced that Vlaminck and Kahnweiler were setting off on "an important cruise" down the Seine in their sailboat, the *Saint-Matorel*, and that Vlaminck would attend a performance of the Ballets Russes that night. A world of rich charm and playfulness was fluttering invisibly toward its end.[86]

Apollinaire had a personal shock in store for him before the public crisis. Only a few days after his piece on Laurencin in *Paris-Journal*, he had an apéritif with her in a bar on the Rue Vavin, and she announced that she had news for him. He had news too, he replied. After a squabble, she told him hers: she was getting married—to the German painter Otto von Waëtjen. At first Apollinaire couldn't believe it. Then he rose, paid the bill, turned on his heel, and walked away. Laurencin and von Waëtjens were married in a small private ceremony on June 21 and left immediately for a honeymoon near Bordeaux. She never saw Apollinaire again.[87]

ON JUNE 14, Picasso and Eva left Paris for the Midi. They stayed a few days in Avignon, looking for a place to rent; in the last week of June, Picasso sent Jacob a postcard of Édouard-Antoine Marsal's kitsch painting *Apotheosis of Mistral*. (The Provençal writer Frédéric Mistral, who won the Nobel Prize in 1904, had just died in March 1914.) "I'll make your apotheosis," Picasso wrote his old friend.[88] The painters were gathering for a summer of comradely work: Derain and his wife Alice set up house near Avignon and saw Picasso and Eva often; Braque bicycled all the way from Paris, arriving by July 5 in Sorgues, where he reunited with Marcelle, rented a house, and set to work. Kahnweiler and his wife were spending their holiday in the Bavarian mountains. Vlaminck had been warning Kahnweiler that he thought war was brewing; even Derain, a few weeks earlier, had written that "the political situation seemed strange"; and Picasso had urged the dealer to take out French citizenship, in case of war. But Kahnweiler, a man of peace, a German whose life was in Paris, couldn't conceive of such a war.[89]

On June 28, 1914, at eleven-fifteen in the morning, the Bosnian Serb nationalist Gavrilo Princip shot and killed the Austro-Hungarian Archduke Ferdinand and his wife, Sophie Chotek von Chotkowa and Wognin, as they rode in an open car in Sarajevo. While Austria-Hungary maneuvered to punish Serbia, Jacob, Apollinaire, and their friends went about their summer business, oblivious to any real threat. Only Vlaminck was apprehensive and sold the two boats he owned with Kahnweiler—the *Saint-Matorel* and *L'Enchanteur pourrissant*—and sent his friend half the proceeds. Otherwise the summer seemed carefree.

The June issue of *Les Soirées de Paris* carried one of Jacob's best stories. Dedicated to Emma Hertz, "Surprised and Charmed"—by an unconscious irony that events would soon bring to light—starts by recalling Jacob's lack of military prowess and his humiliation in 1897 at being discharged from military service. Part fiction, part autobiography, the story records Jacob's discovery of his vocation as an author, a maker and a discloser of plots, and simultaneously his expulsion from his family. He simplified and to some extent mythologized the events narrated, but the story evoked Quimper, its surrounding landscape, and Jacob's old schoolmate Dr. Auguste Morvan sufficiently to enrage Morvan, who read it in *Les Soirées de Paris* and threatened to throw Jacob in the Odet River.[90]

THE JULY–AUGUST ISSUE of *Les Soirées de Paris* flew like a banner with brave insouciance. It would be the magazine's last number. Reciprocating Aldington's hospitality to French poetry in *The Egoist*, Apollinaire ran an article by F. S. Flint introducing French readers to the Anglo-American Imagists, citing Pound's famous formula, "Direct treatment of the 'thing.' "[91] It's a fascinating glimpse of the *entente cordiale* of Anglo-American and French Modernisms. Works by Léger illustrate the issue, and Max Jacob is represented by two poems that would appear later in *La Défense de Tartufe*, "Written for the S.A.F." and "The Conservatory Competition." The S.A.F. was the Société des Amis de Fantômas, a fantastical society dreamed up by Apollinaire and Jacob to celebrate the adventures of the popular fictional criminal Fantômas, the hero of a series of execrably written novels by Marcel Allain and Pierre Souvestre. Apollinaire, Jacob, Salmon, and friends used to storm around Montmartre at night pretending to be bandits and leaving Fantômas's graffiti on walls: The Bloody Hand.[92]

ONE DIDN'T SEE war coming in the French press in June and July 1914. Most newspapers teemed with news of the sensational trial of Madame Caillaux, wife of the former prime minister Joseph Caillaux; in March she had shot and killed the editor of *Le Figaro* in revenge for his campaign against her husband. (She was acquitted in July.) In the pages of *Paris-Journal,* no subject seemed too trivial. On June 5 one article described the happy accident by which the national holiday, July 14, would fall on a Tuesday, creating a very long weekend. Another, entitled "A Monstrous Jewish Wedding," gratified Christian readers with a report of a wedding of the daughter of a chief Hasidic rabbi near Czernowitz attended by eight hundred guests, a "pantagruelesque feast."[93] Business as usual: Jews continued to be an inexhaustible subject for humor. On July 22, Apollinaire wrote an article about a poor Jewish painter in a Russian province "where there are Jews and camels." The governor's wife was disturbed by the gurgling noises the camels made at night and ordered all the camels to have their tongues cut out. The next day the painter packed his bags to flee. Why? he was asked. "How can I prove I'm not a camel," he replied, and went to New York, "the biggest Jewish city in the world."[94] (*Camel* is slang in French for "bitch" or "brute.") On July 24, Apollinaire slipped in a little announcement about an upcoming show of Max Jacob's paintings.

And then all hell broke loose. On July 15, *Paris-Journal* had reported on the state visit to Russia of President Raymond Poincaré and his wife and Prime Minister René Viviani. This would hardly have been more significant than the news of an extended holiday weekend except that their long trip home, starting on July 23, gave Austria the chance to issue an unacceptable ultimatum to Serbia at a time when the allies, France and Russia, couldn't formally consult about a response. Russia had already alarmed Germany and Austria with preparations for mobilization. On July 27 the headline in *Paris-Journal* brayed, "The Austro-Serbian Conflict: Austria Said to Have Declared War." Formally, Austria declared war on Serbia the next day, July 28, and on the twenty-ninth bombarded Belgrade, the same day Poincaré and Viviani arrived at Dunkirk. On July 31 the French Socialist leader Jean Jaurès, a pacifist who had been rousing his party to try to force Germany and France to sign a peace treaty, was shot in the head and killed as he sat in a café in Montmartre. On August 1, Germany, allied to Austria-Hungary, ordered a general mobilization and declared war on Russia, Serbia's ally. France responded with a general mobilization.

The next day German troops roared into Luxembourg, and on August 3, Germany declared war on France and invaded Belgium. England, which had been resisting being drawn into a Serbian conflict, declared war on Germany on August 4.[95]

The Kahnweilers, on vacation in Bavaria, fled into neutral Switzerland and from there took a train to Rome. On August 2, Picasso accompanied Derain and Braque to the train station in Avignon; they had been called to military service. "I never saw them again," he later told Kahnweiler. He meant it allegorically. Of course he "saw" them again, but their comradeship in art had concluded, and henceforth they would work alone.[96]

Max Jacob, in Paris, imagined that he, too, might be called to the army, and he wrote Soffici in Florence asking him to return the copy of *Cinéma-Thomas* (as it was then called) while the mails still functioned.[97] To Jean-Richard Bloch, also in Florence where he had been teaching at the French Institute, Jacob wrote, "It seems there are 90,000 men at the frontier. Send me back my manuscript while the mail still works." (This was *Le Terrain Bouchaballe*.) "It seems that men like me who have been discharged will stay in Paris in municipal services. Do you see me as a postman or a street cleaner?" He signed the letter, "Max Jacob, poet-road laborer." The war had begun.[98]

CHAPTER 10

THE GREAT WAR
AND CONVERSION

I.

World War I would bring a dark frenzy to artistic life in Paris. The early phases, as seen in the French newspapers, evolved from blasts of patriotism in August 1914 through a gradual toning down in September as it began to dawn on people that the conflict wouldn't be easily concluded. Jacob quickly learned to read between the lines. To Jean-Richard Bloch, who was badly wounded, Jacob wrote at the end of September that "one has to understand their language: light retreat means bloody defeat, and great victory means a light advance."[1]

La Journée financière et politique struck the general note of defiance on August 3, just after Germany declared war on France. The memory of France's humiliation in 1870 still rankled: "*Vive la France!* The situation is serious, but not critical. . . . We have never had a greater opportunity to triumph, to erase the violence to national sovereignty inflicted in 1870."[2] *Le Journal* blared, "The Germans have crossed the frontier of France."[3] By August 11, when the Germans encountered resistance in Belgium, *L'Intransigeant* announced, "New French Success in Belgian Territory," while *Le Journal* reported on the war to the east: "The avant-garde of our right wing temporarily withdraws from Mulhouse" (which, as Jacob understood, meant that they'd been roundly defeated).[4]

Day by day the papers recounted German atrocities—many, though not all of them, true: civilians shot, houses burned, churches destroyed, wounded soldiers executed. In Paris, French flags hung from almost every building. Shops were shuttered. By August 13, alarming news filtered through: in Belgium, the Germans had occupied Liège and were bombarding the great fortress there; to the east, German armies were advancing toward Paris, and *Paris-Midi* predicted that "the principal collision of the armies will occur, it is thought, between Namur and Verdun."[5]

AT THE BEGINNING of the hostilities, Jacob left a manuscript of poems for safekeeping in the household of Sylvette Fillacier's parents, her brother, and his wife and children in Enghien, a small town a few kilometers north of Paris. As the fighting drew close to the capital, he was frantic to rescue his work. Travelers jammed the train stations. "You can get a train to Enghien," he was told at the station, "but you'll never get back!" His friend the Magus Lagnel thought he might procure him a bicycle. But in the Place Clichy, Jacob saw the tram for Enghien and hopped on.[6]

The Fillaciers had often welcomed Jacob, and now he stayed about a month with them, paying for his board. Sylvette's brother had been called to the army; his young wife, Sophie, had two children to care for, and the house was crowded. Besides Sophie and her children, it sheltered Sylvette's parents and Sophie's mother and brother. All these people, including a baby boy and a little girl, are mentioned affectionately in Jacob's letters; he clearly made himself very much at home there. He assisted the ambulance drivers who were bringing in the wounded and heard something about the fighting from the soldiers, but not much, as they'd been instructed— like schoolchildren, he said—not to recount "at home" the horrors they'd seen. Those duties didn't take up many hours each day, so he spent a lot of time in the Fillaciers' vegetable garden, reviewing his poems, choosing and recopying the three hundred best, and writing what he called "an important preface" entitled "On the Prose Poem." This selection would turn into his most celebrated book, *Le Cornet à dés*, though for the moment he called it *Poésies incomplètes*, anticipating that if he died in the war, his life work would, indeed, remain incomplete.

The garden was hardly peaceful. It resounded with the shouts of children and the weeping of mothers whose husbands were at the front. But in

September it grew noisier still. The Germans came so close that the citizens of Enghien began to evacuate, in great disorder, and Jacob almost lost all his work.[7] Even as his country was being overrun, he remained focused on his art, trying to establish an oeuvre that would outlive him. It's striking that the Germans were so close to Enghien, though at the time (according to Jacob) the papers claimed that they were several hundred kilometers to the north. The train stations were madhouses: German planes would fly over while the passengers stood around gazing up stupidly, "their noses in the air," and railway workers fired revolvers at the sky.[8]

By the end of August, bombs were falling on Paris. Though they were small explosives and don't seem to have caused much damage, they had a dramatic psychological effect. So did the news that the enemy was closing in on the capital. On August 31, *The Daily Mail* reported Clemenceau's stirring speech: "Yes, their guns are almost within earshot of Paris. And what if they are? . . . Let them burn Paris if they can. Let them wipe it out, raze it to the level of the ground, we shall still fight on."[9] At the same time, war was inflicting predictable miseries on civilians; the papers reported unemployment, poverty, and hunger (with the *Journal des débats politiques et littéraires* warning against the pernicious effects of creating revolutionary ideas in the poor by providing free meals at soup kitchens).[10]

From Jacob's letter to Bloch, we glimpse the war as experienced by civilians. The Germans had occupied the town of La Ferté-sous-Jouarre, a few kilometers to the east of Paris, and a Prussian officer and a few soldiers were quartered in a local house. The owner offered the officer a bed in his own bedroom while the soldiers slept on the floor. Accustomed to reading at night, the householder lit his candle and took up his book. The officer blew out the candle. When he heard the officer snoring, the reader lit his candle again, whereupon the officer, waking up, ordered his men to throw the book and the candle out the window. In the morning, the officer asked the householder whether he had any complaints, and shot one of his own soldiers in the head for having helped himself to wine in the dining room. (Jacob's narration leaves crucial points unclear: Had the householder complained about the wine? Did the officer shoot his own soldier to maintain discipline, or to frighten and humiliate the householder?)[11]

Even the unreliable newspapers began to suggest how desperate the struggle was becoming. On August 24, *The New York Herald* announced, "Battle of the Nations Now Raging in Belgium: Is Expected to Last for Several Days."[12] The next day, the *Herald* suggested the features of this new kind of war: the vast scale of the killing, and the paralyzing stalemate that would turn into the nightmare of prolonged trench warfare.[13] The British *Daily Mail* printed a headline that would grow grimly familiar: "Third Day of Battle—No Gain to Either Side."[14]

The military crisis provoked a political crisis, and by August 27 Jacob would have read in the French papers that the prime minister had accepted the resignation of the entire cabinet and reconstituted a "government of national defense." A few days later the news was even more dire: a proclamation that the government—the president, the prime minister, and all the ministers—had left Paris to "preserve national safety" at an undisclosed location.[15] The government established itself at Bordeaux, as everyone learned the next day.

There followed the great battle of the Marne that turned the tide of this phase of the war, pushing the Germans eastward, toward Verdun and away from Paris. The newspaper accounts reflect the terror, the suspense, and then the amazement of the French. The decisive fighting took place September 6 through 9, and at last the headlines declaring victory had a basis in fact.[16] In a famous improvisation, General Gallieni, the military commander of Paris, sent six thousand reserve troops into the fray in a fleet of six hundred Parisian taxicabs, a feat perhaps more powerful in mythology than in actual strategy, but effective nonetheless. During the next few days the Germans retreated, pursued by the French and by the British Expeditionary Force, until on September 12 they dug in along the Aisne River and—though no one could see it at the time—readied for four years of near-paralysis in the mud. Two million men fought in the first battle of the Marne, and half a million were wounded or killed. Among the dead was the poet Charles Péguy.

MAX JACOB FOUND his way back to Paris by September 10 and wrote to Sylvette Fillacier that day from his room on the Rue Gabrielle. His three brothers and his brother-in-law had enlisted. He tried to enlist, but as someone formerly discharged from military service, he was told to wait until he was called up. Life was hard. He had almost no money, since no one was buying gouaches or paying for horoscopes. He ate at a soup kitchen funded by an American lady where, he said, they ate beef without tomato and tomato without beef, and where the political discussion was so idiotic, he'd almost rather have been bombarded by real projectiles.[17] The streets were empty, he reported to Bloch, who was convalescing in Poitiers. No more hoodlums, no whores, no drunks. He spent his time drawing and reading Spinoza, Vigny, La Fontaine, and Boileau, and he received a little unemployment benefit (as a tailor!) arranged for him by his friend the Magus Lagnel, a tailor.[18] He maintained a vigorous correspondence with absent friends: Kahnweiler in Siena, Bloch in Poitiers, Maurice Raynal recovering from a wound in Quimper.

The first death to touch Jacob personally was that of his young cousin Raynal, the actor from the Comédie-Française who had visited him in Quimper in 1912 (not the critic Maurice Raynal, he assured Kahnweiler and Bloch).[19] As one of the few of the *bande à Picasso* not fighting, Jacob served as an unofficial news bureau. From his letters, we learn that Picasso was still in Avignon; Apollinaire was with the Foreign Legion at Orléans along with Serge Férat and Galanis; Canudo was a lieutenant in Lyon; Mac Orlan was wounded in the foot but returned to battle; Léger was in a regiment at Versailles; Juan Gris was trapped in Collioure (desperately poor because Kahnweiler could no longer support him); Picabia was in Bordeaux "very unhappy with military discipline"; Braque was a sergeant at Le Havre; and Derain and Poiret were at Lisieux.[20]

II.

WRITING HIS WOUNDED friends, Jacob took various tones—sympathetic, jocular, witty—that showed him reaching out to them, but at the same time separated by an unspeakable gulf. To Bloch, he wrote, "Your letter made me shiver, right down to my bones. Your surprise at the fields of oats not yet trampled, there's a scene worth all the newspaper reports!"[21] In a letter to Maurice Raynal, the Parisian wit rings strangely. Jokes were their lingua franca, but in this context they seem surprisingly insensitive. "Dear Maurice," he wrote, "I congratulate you on being wounded. And I thank you. It's good for the honor of the whole brotherhood."[22]

However flippant, Jacob's letters were acts of friendship, offering gossip and anecdotes as if to draw his traumatized comrades back to a world outside the war. In the last week of September, as he was comforting Bloch and Raynal, the Germans bombed Reims Cathedral and laid the town in rubble. The newspapers expressed stupefaction at the toll in civilian lives and the outrage of destroying one of the world's great religious monuments.[23] *The Daily Mail* described refugees streaming out of the smoking ruins of Reims, and day by day the papers reported the "furious," "enraged," "very violent" battle of the Aisne, where the vast conflict stretched from Reims to Verdun. This was not another Battle of the Marne. *L'Éclair*'s headline for September 30 presaged many headlines to come: "17th Day of Battle! The Germans renewed their attacks, all have been repulsed."[24]

Max Jacob, in Paris, was safe from burning cathedrals. While Picasso in Avignon continued to paint, Jacob kept revising his manuscript of poems. He focused on it all the more since he thought for a while that his only copy of his novel, *Le Terrain Bouchaballe*, had been lost in the mail ("So much the better!" he exclaimed to Kahnweiler); it turned up in the possession of an uncle of Bloch's in Paris, though Jacob wouldn't recover it for several months.[25] Most of his friends were away at the front or wounded. Even Reverdy had enlisted; he married his companion Henriette Bureau on September 8 as the Battle of the Marne hung in the balance, and left the next day for military training. (He would be discharged in a few months, because of his neurotic sensibility, one imagines.)[26] But in early November, Gris returned to Paris, aided by a small allowance from Kahnweiler and by gifts from Picasso and Gertrude Stein. Picasso and Eva returned in mid-November, and Serge Férat came back to work as a hospital orderly. Bit by bit, something like artistic life began to take shape again in Paris, led by foreigners like Picasso, Gris, and Férat who didn't have to fight; by those like Jacob who were free from military service; and by women patrons like Hélène d'Oettingen.

Picasso, on his return, began experimenting with representational drawings. He told Henri Mahaut that he wanted to see "if he could still draw like everyone else,"[27] and in early January he drew Max Jacob in this fashion, a psychological masterpiece, the pencil concentrating on Jacob's high-domed bald head, heavy brows, large melancholy eyes, and firm mouth. He also paid attention to the rumpled jacket, vest, and sweater, and to Jacob's lively hands—the right hand in a fist in his lap, the left resting more openly. Picasso continued to paint Cubist works during these months, but already, as Jacob wrote Raynal, "Picasso's return marks the return of a new art in which pure lines trace those of nature's vulgarity," leading Jacob to wonder if Cubism had become a school, like the school it had replaced. A few weeks later he announced to Raynal, "Picasso is giving up Cubism, in part."[28]

With so many of their friends away, Picasso, Eva, and Jacob saw even more of Serge Férat and Hélène d'Oettingen, in restaurants in Montparnasse or in the baroness's apartment where something of the old salon survived. Out in the cafés, they saw Serge and his mistress, young Irène Lagut of ethereal features and an already alarmingly rich erotic history (which included having been debauched at age fifteen, and taken off to St. Petersburg where she was "sold" to a grand duke for his orgies until she fell ill with typhoid and was shipped back to Paris).[29] Irène would soon affect Picasso's life dramatically, but for the time being she was Serge's girl, so much so that in a letter to Raynal, Jacob called her "Irène Serge" when he reported that "Jeanne Léger and Irène Serge are the Muses."[30]

AT THE END of November, Jacob confessed to Raynal about the disordered life he was leading; since he was writing to a wounded soldier, he took care to acknowledge the war and to express some sense of guilt. "We have canteens in Montparnasse which give the artistic temperament an opportunity to forget national and other sorrows at the expense of decency, even as far as dancing."[31] Dancing was the least of it. The parties lasted late into the night when the Métro no longer ran, and Jacob often found himself "in foreign beds (Swedish and Russian)," which brought scandal and then remorse. His desire to sell copies of *La Côte* kept him circulating in cafés. He described his activities with remarkable candor: "the desire to please, the vanity of showing off one's talents, the illusion of living a double life, the grinding mechanism of pleasure, the escalator that carries you farther along the route laid out by happenstance, all this pushes me to violate the codes of human respect and of military authority."[32] This confession didn't occur at random but was strategically placed to prepare Raynal for the announcement that Jacob had decided to be baptized in the Roman Catholic faith.

As with the apparition of 1909, one has to sift through various accounts and conflicting dates to arrive at a sense of Jacob's experience. And as always with Jacob, we're in the presence of a master storyteller who invented his truth as he shaped it—but then lived by that truth. His letter to Raynal, dated November 30, 1914, is the surviving document closest to the event, and the journal entries in *La Défense de Tartufe* support the dating implied in the letter. In that book, he began his initiation on what must have been Monday, November 30, 1914, then day by day described his arguments with the priest, his remorse, and his sins, until the entry dated "18 or 19 December" recorded his second apparition, a vision of Christ appearing on the movie screen in a thriller by Paul Féval.[33]

Whatever the exact dates, the main lines of the experience seem clear and were observed by everyone around Jacob. Sometime in late November 1914, he was sitting with friends at the Rotonde and mentioned that he wanted to be baptized. A Monsieur Pica (whose name suspiciously or auspiciously resembles Picasso's), a little crippled hunchback, "a very decent man," Jacob told Guiette, said it would be easy to arrange; he would send Jacob to his friend Cardinal Amette, the archbishop of Paris. Jacob replied that he didn't need so august a figure. Pica then advised him to go down the street to the convent of Notre-Dame de Sion, whose mission was the conversion of Jews.

Jacob presented himself at the convent the next day. The elderly priest to whom he was introduced, Father Schafner, almost turned away when he learned that his visitor was not the man he had been expecting, but seeing Jacob's distress, he agreed to speak with him. Jacob wept as he told his story. The priest had known other Catholic writers, Huysmans and Coppée, and told Jacob that he had more penitence than faith. "It seems I have a temperament inclined to believe, but that my reason doesn't adhere. And I, who thought I had reasoned myself into faith!"[34]

Trying to justify his decision to Raynal, Jacob listed two motivations: the apparition of 1909 ("The Jews are waiting for the Messiah! I'm no longer waiting since I've seen him!"), and a desperate desire to change his life.[35] He wouldn't become an anti-Semite, he insisted, though he fortified himself with a gross generalization: "The Jews are men of intellect; I need men of heart."[36]

He confessed his decision to Bloch a few weeks later. This confession, made to a fellow Jew and a cousin, rings differently; it is more urgent and defensive. And he asked Bloch not to tell the family, since the news might kill his (Jacob's) father. Impertinently, he asserted, "You know that God did me the honor to appear to me and my furnishings October 28, 1909, 7 rue Ravignan. He renewed this miracle before my eyes last December 17 at 10:30 p.m. on the Pathé movie screen on the Rue de Douai. Any more hesitation would be ingratitude."[37] As if this declaration wouldn't sufficiently discomfit Bloch the Jewish socialist, Jacob went on the offensive, rolling out the argument that the Jews, having fulfilled their historic mission to reject Jesus and thereby inspire the founding of a new religion, should now join that new religion. "Don't treat me as an apostate," Jacob begged his cousin. "I'm not rejecting anything: I had no religion and I'm choosing one."

La Défense de Tartufe is a painful book. Jacob would publish it right after the war, but he drew most of the material from the months immediately preceding and following his baptism in 1915. It resembles *Saint Matorel* in depicting Jacob's story as he understood it: a dissipated life, an encounter with God, the embrace of faith. But whereas *Saint Matorel* presents itself as fiction, *La Défense de Tartufe* offers the illusion of documentary autobiography. The verse poems read like bulletins from the life of the poet.

The book focuses on God's entering the poet's life, most significantly in the apparition of 1909, then in the movie theater. As we've seen, the prose poems in *La Défense de Tartufe* purporting to document the first apparition are in fact far more artificial than the fiction in *Saint Matorel*. The diary entries and the devotional exercises in *La Défense de Tartufe* intensify the realistic illusion and make of this book a confession as cunning as the *Confessions* of Jacob's hero, Jean-Jacques Rousseau.

The ideal to which Jacob devoted himself in December 1914 demanded that he reject the Judaism of his birth. This he seemed eager to do. He was casting off several versions of Judaism: his parents' provincial shopkeeping world; the grander commercial world of his Gompel cousins; and Sylvain Lévi's academic rationalism. Max Jacob wanted magic, mysticism, fantasy, love, and a personal God, and he thought he would find them in the Roman Catholic faith. In his diary, he wrote as if he had already renounced, or could renounce, his Jewishness: "I feel only friendship for the Jews, but I ought to hate them, because in my heart of hearts, there's a truly Christian temperament. I've suffered from the Jews, who only play along with those who flatter their racial pride, but since I don't gratify them, let them at least let me go where I please."[38] This passage in the diary rises to a pitch of hysteria in which the caricature of the pariah Jew resembles a twisted self-portrait: "The Jews are pariahs, noisy, deafening, famous, but pariahs, because they're deprived of the pleasure of being Christian. . . . Let them drive me out!" he exclaims as the paragraph turns into a desperate address to God. "Here I am! Here I am, Lord, and for life."[39]

Preparation for baptism required self-examination and penitence, and he struggled to align his occult ideas with the new dogma. On the very first day of instruction, he claimed to believe in God "because I've seen one," then wondered, if there was one god, why not others? He caught himself and explained that by this polytheism, he meant Jesus, the Virgin, and the saints. The following day he wondered if he could ask his instructor, Father Ferrand, for his birth date so that he could draw up his horoscope, but he sensed that this gambit would hardly square with orthodoxy. He was also eager to show off the fruits of his years of esoteric interpretation of Scripture; when he explained to the priest his theory about the zodiacal significance of Christ's washing the feet of the disciples, his mentor replied that for Christians, washing the feet meant humility.[40]

In the diary, Jacob composed a detailed self-portrait. We see him making a spectacle of himself at dinner parties. At the house of the W family, he wrote, "driven by a demon, I sang, danced, talked, joked, and ended with a harsh and mean-spirited remark. There's the apprentice Christian!"[41] In another household, he suspected the husband and wife of filching money, clothing, and tobacco pouches from their guests, and he took revenge by saying pointedly to the hostess that it was easier to take what one wanted than to ask for it, and by introducing her to his friend the professional burglar (no doubt "the King of Burglars" he mentioned to Bloch).[42]

The self portrayed in these pages is proud, humble, ostentatious, easily wounded, vengeful, weak-willed, and desperate for reformation. Instead of praying, he spent December 8, the Day of the Immaculate Conception, "in the most appalling debauchery with three women, one of whom is having a nervous breakdown."[43] On a draft of a poem in the Doucet collection, he listed his sins: "talking too much—cocaine—drank too much all night—profanity—spoke against my enemies—many lies—spoke against my friends—laziness—bad example—revenge—thoughts offensive to purity."[44] The "debauchery" with the three women was likely to have been not so much sexual as hours spent wasting himself in the other vices on his list. One of the prose poems in this section of *La Défense de Tartufe*, "God Has Abandoned Us," highlights the dissipation of Montparnasse, Jacob's struggle to detach himself, and the confusion of temporal and sacred authorities. Once again the police entered the scene; they were on the alert, not just for homosexuals "disturbing the peace" but also for more general bohemian disturbances. "God Has Abandoned Us" has an epigraph from Jacob's poem "Christ in Montparnasse," an ebullient piece placed later in the book: "Pécher, pécher, se repêcher" (To sin, to sin, to fish oneself out again).

The orgy is in the South! The orgy is in Montparnasse! in a studio, the orgy is in Montparnasse. "Who's there? Open up!" It's the priest! It's the cross! It's the banner and the procession. They've crossed the studio, and they're lined up at the back. "Who's there?" "Open up! It's the good Lord!" Everyone's terrified! Come in, my Lord. But it was only the police commissioner, a nasty belted guy with a mustache.[45]

Jacob contrasted his "debauch" with the three women to a woman whose company he preferred. This was the South African writer Emily Alice Haigh, who also went by Beatrice Hastings, and wrote under the pen name Alice Morning. He had good reason to like her: she was translating and publishing his prose poems in A. R. Orage's magazine *The New Age* in London. She had arrived in Paris in April and was living in a house in Montmartre, where her lover Modigliani was often to be found. "I've met a truly great English poet," Jacob wrote Bloch. "Miss Hastings, a drunk, a pianist, elegant, bohemian, dressed in the fashion of the Transvaal and surrounded by bandits who dabble in art and dancing."[46] Around the same time, he wrote Apollinaire that Hastings would get drunk all by herself on whiskey, a habit that appeared to him exotic.[47] If Max Jacob berated himself for his vices, he looked downright sober compared to Hastings and Modigliani, whose intoxicated fights could be heard out on the street to the tune of shouts, blows, and broken windows.

Now Jacob was torn between the frantic life of the cafés and studios and attempts at purification, confiding to his diary that during the day he listened with tears in his eyes to Father Ferrand's discourse on Christian virtues and at night fell back into huge horrors because he couldn't live without his friends, and they couldn't live without horrors.[48] The key figure looming here is, of course, Picasso. Not that Picasso endangered his own art with drink or drugs. On December 19, Jacob noted, "I ate too much at P's . . . , given over to every temptation. . . . P advises me to go see a Jewish priest: why? . . . He says my visions are more Jewish than Christian because of the Bible."[49] Picasso agreed to be Jacob's godfather and maliciously suggested that Jacob take the Christian name of Fiacre— a dense pun, since the name not only referred to a horse-drawn cab and alluded to Jacob's early poem for Picasso, "The Horse," but also recalled

Saint Fiacre's power to cure hemorrhoids and fistules, ailments not unrelated to Jacob's forms of lovemaking.[50]

||

MAX JACOB HAD celebrated film as a medium for vision in the poem "Springtime and Screentime Mixed." Now, on December 17 (or 18 or 19), God took the initiative and "materialized" before his eyes on a movie screen at ten-thirty p.m. on the Rue de Douai.[51] Christ, this time, wore a white robe and had flowing black curls and sheltered an urchin in his garment—which reminded Jacob that he had been hugged that morning by his concierge's little son, and that later in the day he had ordered the boy to apologize to his mother for being rude. Jacob addressed Christ in intimate terms, moving from the formal *vous* to the familiar *tu*: "Oh! My Lord! How I love you (*vous*)! How I love you (*te*), my dear God, my pretty God! How good you are to me!"[52] He wept in his seat, smoked (!), and went out to the street to listen to "his voices."

When Jacob related the adventure to Father Ferrand, the priest was nonplussed. Jacob recorded the exchange shortly afterward in the poem inspired by his vision, "Christ at the Movies":

> "You go to the movies, then?" with dumbfounded air
> Demanded my confessor.—Yes, Father,
> What if I did? Didn't Our Lord go there?[53]

In the diary, Jacob moved from ecstatic address to speculation about the difficulty spirits had in materializing for humans, and he decided that they needed a backdrop in order to become visible, either his red wall hanging or the movie screen. In its whimsy, this film apparition expressed the heart of Jacob's experience of the sacred: it came to him as a revelation, not separate from daily life but inextricable from its dailiness, in all its sordid, piteous misery. Jacob's Catholicism was a religion for outsiders, for sufferers, the poor, the sinful. He embedded that vision in "Christ at the Movies":

They call me crazy! Yes! I hear the reader now—
Or blasphemous, you scold with furrowed brow.
Madmen yourselves, if truth can make you laugh.
The Lord is everywhere, and with the worst riffraff.
To feel God in oneself, to hear Him, to reply,
Whether at the movies, in the street, at a café,
This common miracle shouldn't start a fuss:
Outside of church, God's everywhere, and speaks with us.

The priests repeatedly delayed Jacob's baptism, and one can imagine many reasons for their suspicion. Jacob reported to Apollinaire that he would be baptized January 20 with Picasso as his godfather and Sylvette Fillacier as his godmother. (Apollinaire was by this time in the South of France, in Nîmes, training to be an artillery officer in the French army.)[54] But Father Ferrand was called to the front, and another priest took over Jacob's instruction.[55] In February, Jacob confided to his diary that the priests held up his baptism every day: "Clearly, the Church wants nothing to do with me," he exclaimed, and added in a burst of self-pity, "No one has ever wanted anything to do with me."[56]

The date was finally set for February 18, but new obstacles appeared. Fillacier had only a civil marriage to Marcel Olin, and Picasso was living in sin with a divorcée. Near despair, Jacob wrote Sylvette to apologize. "Sir!" the priest had exclaimed. "This baptism will occur in this house, and atheists and libertines will not cross the threshold!" The Father Superior was called in. As Jacob refused to allow a monk for a godfather, they finally compromised and allowed him to have no godmother, and Picasso for his godfather. Jacob burst into tears, and the Father Superior admonished him, "Weep for your sins, my child. Baptism will erase them, but stop consorting with atheists!" The refractory initiate wrote Sylvette, "When I'm baptized, I'll consort a great deal with atheists, if only to bring them to mass."[57]

At last the solemn day arrived. Dressed ceremoniously in black, wearing dress pumps and lace socks, Jacob was so preoccupied by the etiquette of the occasion in the convent's looming, modern chapel that he didn't feel the spiritual revolution he had anticipated. Never mind: he trusted it would come later.[58] He spent the rest of the day amusing his friends in Montparnasse; in the Métro on the way home that evening, he heard a voice asking, "You who seek me, why do you chase me away?"[59] For his Christian name, he chose Cyprien. It signified "growth," he explained years later to Marcel Béalu, a meaning not traditionally associated with either Saint Cyprien of Antioch or Saint Cyprien of Carthage.[60] Both of those Cypriens lived dissolutely before being touched by grace, and both practiced magic.

But the key to Cyprien for Jacob was likely to have been the association of Venus with the island of Cyprus, and his interpretation of Venus as a goddess of growth.[61] On the day of the baptism, *The New Age* published a selection of Jacob's prose poems translated by Hastings, including this tidbit, interpreting his Christian name: "The Lenten fast is, for Catholics, the moral purification of the springtime. The body of Christ which is flesh—that is, Venus or Increase—is veiled in the churches. Is this to signify that men should return upon themselves in view of new growth?"[62] Jacob turned even the sacrament of baptism into his own mythology, and if the ceremony converted him to Roman Catholicism, it is just as true that he converted Catholicism to his own purposes.

Jacob's keenest emotion on the day of his baptism focused on Picasso. A few days earlier he had castigated himself for exploiting his intimacy with his genius friend in order to increase his own glory.[63] Now, on the day of baptism, he concluded his account by noting that Picasso had given him an inscribed copy of Thomas à Kempis's *The Imitation of Christ*. He then swerved into a direct address to his friend: "You are what I most adore in this world after God and the Saints, who already regard you as one of their own."[64] Hardly devout, Picasso took the occasion in stride, giving Max the affectionate protection he craved and at the same time acknowledging the very different meaning the rite had for him: "We were brought up in all this! It's all new for you!"[65]

If Jacob expected a magical effect from baptism, he was disappointed. And astonishingly, on the certificate of his baptism, in which he "renounced the blindness of the Jews and recognized Our Lord Jesus Christ as the

Messiah promised by the Holy Scriptures of the Old Testament," Jacob lied about his birth date. He claimed to have been born on July 11, 1876, when his real birth date, as he well knew, was July 12. He perpetuated the lie a few days later in an "Examination on Hope," writing that astrologically, his birth date July 11 predicted "hopes that will not come true."[66] Even while confessing painful truths about himself, and in a ceremony of radical redefinition of identity, he created a fable. The confessions too, in their way, were fabulous, and so was the sacrament of baptism.

III.

IN EARLY 1915, Picasso had more on his mind than Max's baptism. Eva's illness grew more serious, and in mid-January she had a second operation and spent a month in a clinic. In the fall, knowing her lover's fear of disease, she pathetically tried to hide her pallor under makeup, and she and Picasso were hardly cheered by living right over the Cimetière Montparnasse.[67] Picasso sought consolation and found it, as Richardson discovered, in a secret affair with Gaby Depeyre, a dark-eyed young woman who lived in his neighborhood. He was clearly passionate about her, fantasized about marrying her, and even sneaked away for a holiday in Provence with her. But through this dark year, he also had to care for Eva, and he managed his new love with such discretion that it seems not to have reverberated in the intensely gossipy Montparnasse.[68] He spent more time than ever in the studio since so many of his friends were away and since he found it uncomfortable, as a healthy man of military age, to relax in public. The art historian Pierre Cabanne thinks there is something decorative and stymied about Picasso's canvases in this period, and that without Braque to steady and challenge him, he lost his bearings.[69] But Richardson shows how Picasso translated his grief at Eva's dying and at the war into several small paintings and, more monumentally, in the two major paintings, the sinister *Harlequin* and the long-revised *Seated Man*, which Richardson regards as Picasso's farewell to Cubism: "This is a painting about the act of painting—a magic act, Picasso always said. The artist has done a vanishing trick; he has melted into the cosmic darkness of paint, taking Cubism with him."[70]

||

PICASSO PRACTICED PAINTING as a dark, if not a black magic. Jacob's magic was lighter in spirit. Disappointed in not experiencing a revolution in his baptism, he was gratified to find that effect in his first Communion; so gratified, that he immediately sought the same stimulation by communing again the next morning, "without consulting anyone and after a cowardly, brutal, and hasty confession."[71] This time God did not reward him.

Another kind of magic was at work, however. Though French literary publishing had almost shut down, the only ventures being propaganda such as the "anti-Boche" diatribes of *Le Mot* launched by Cocteau and the fashion illustrator Paul Iribe, Jacob's poems kept appearing in *Lacerba* (Italy not having yet entered the war). And thanks to Hastings, a generous assortment of his prose poems appeared in February and March 1915 in *The New Age*. He had also received encouraging recognition for his Quimper story, "Surprised and Charmed," in the penultimate issue of *Les Soirées de Paris* in June.[72] However much he wasted his time and his health in Montparnasse, he was also shaping his prose poems into the masterly order that would be revealed two years later in *Le Cornet à dés*.

In November, *Lacerba* published six of Jacob's prose poems, three of which would make it into *Le Cornet à dés:* "Contagion," "Preexistence of Forms," and "A Tale by Andersen." The first presents a glimpse of hell. In the second, another swipe at Romantic literature, the swan refuses the bread offered by the poet but doesn't disdain the thumping noise of the washerwomen and the quarrels of tired workmen.[73] Now, in March 1915, *Lacerba* brought out eleven more of these radical shards. In "Postcards," not reprinted, Jacob again used film as a medium for his method of fast transformations and "kinetic" vision. The three "dice" he saved for *Le Cornet à dés* combine experiments in angle of vision with a clatter of rhyme, alliteration, and assonance suggesting meanings beyond normal meaning, *hors texte*—a word for photographic plates, meaning "beyond the text." In these pieces,

Jacob cut his art down to essences of sight and sound, a deliberately marginal poetry. One needs to taste this nonsense in the original French:

> L'oiseau gaucher et bossu nommé Morguë ne fait son nid qu'avec des épis de blés et l'orne avec des capucines, par préciput et hors texte.

Capucines, "nasturtiums," puns on Capuchin monks; *par préciput* is a Latin phrase used in French law to designate an inheritance.

> The left-handed and hunchbacked bird named Morguë makes its nest only with ears of wheat and decorates it with nasturtiums, *par préciput* and in colored plates/beyond the text.[74]

The selections in *The New Age* reveal even more about Jacob's choices in *Le Cornet à dés.* On January 14, Hastings wrote appreciatively on *La Côte* and translated several of Jacob's Breton poems. Two weeks later she reported the gossip flying around Montparnasse that Picasso was "painting" a realistic portrait of Jacob. (She hadn't yet seen the drawing.) On February 18 she filled two pages of *The New Age* with thirty-one of Jacob's prose poems, to be followed by seventeen others in May. A great many of these dice poems would go into *Le Cornet à dés.*

A few of the poems from *The New Age* could be called aphorisms, sententious observations on the model of La Rochefoucauld. Suddenly, out of the lineup of maxims, poetry flashes: dramatic, imagistic, teasingly narrative, rich in sound-play. These are the dice Jacob would shake in his dice cup. Some of them occupy only one line, like the androgynous erotic line "Ses bras blancs devinrent tout mon horizon," which Hastings (herself bisexual) rendered as implicitly heterosexual: "Her white arms became all my horizon" (assuming a male speaker). Some of the poems play with the very idea of literary style, metatexts *avant la lettre,* as in the poem entitled, in Hastings's English, "Poem in a style thus [*sic*] is not mine" for a poem Jacob would entitle simply "Poem" in the book.[75] This poem, like so many others, takes its procedure from the movies, and in its dreamlike imagery would show the young André Breton, Philippe Soupault, and Louis Aragon, future Surrealists, what a poetry of the unconscious could perform: "The hail is on the sea; and night falls: 'Light up the beacon for the bovines!' "[76]

||

THE STYLISH LITTLE counterrealities of Jacob's prose poems had to contend with massive external realities. In March, German zeppelins began to bomb Paris, and Gertrude Stein and Alice Toklas were so frightened that they left to spend a year in Palma de Mallorca, depriving Picasso of two more of his friends. In March, Jacob received official word of his military discharge.[77] As usual, he bestirred himself to help others; he collected money to help Severini, who was poverty-stricken and close to death with tuberculosis; to beloved Sylvette Fillacier, he wrote about his efforts to find public assistance for the widow of a painter who had been killed in battle.[78] In May came desolating news: Braque, wounded in the head, had to be trepanned and was moved from hospital to hospital, then to the Hôtel Meurice for convalescence. (Salmon put about the rumor that Picasso never visited his old friend during this period;[79] Richardson claims that he did visit him, in spite of his terror of illness.[80]) Kisling was wounded in the same battle.

By early May, Jacob set back to work on *Le Terrain Bouchaballe*. It had taken months for him to recover the manuscript: in a long, jocose letter, Jacob described to Bloch the visit to Bloch's uncle, a wine merchant whose "ugly maid" found the long-lost parcel. Jacob clutched the manuscript to his breast and sped home on the Métro to "the bitter pleasure of disgusting" himself with his prose.[81]

LE TERRAIN BOUCHABALLE would occupy Jacob for years. Meanwhile a young man turned up in Picasso's life who would, at first, highly irritate Jacob, but who would prove one of his most loyal friends. At twenty-six, Jean Cocteau was a slender, powdered, witty, determinedly *arriviste* poet.[82] He came from a bourgeois family but made it his business to cultivate aristocrats and figures in *le beau monde*. The famous and famously homosexual actor Édouard de Max of the Comédie-Française thrust the eighteen-year-old Cocteau into high society in 1908 by staging a reading of his poems in a theater on the Champs-Élysées. Since then Cocteau had brought out two volumes of wispy verse; with Maurice Rostand (whom Jacob had cruelly parodied) he edited *Schéhérazade,* a decadent arts journal, from 1909 to 1911; and with his eye always on the main chance, he was editing the jingoistic magazine *Le Mot.* But now Cocteau decided that real glory was to be found in the avant-garde, and he set about courting Picasso. He arranged for the composer Edgard Varèse to introduce him. By the next year, he would succeed—brilliantly, it must be said—in drawing Picasso into the world of Diaghilev, the Ballets Russes, and elegant society.

SEPTEMBER BROUGHT MORE grim news from the front. On September 25, Bloch received his second serious wound, and on the same day in a different battle, Cendrars lost his right arm. Jacob followed the war not only through the newspapers and correspondence with his friends but increasingly in letters to and from soldiers whom he didn't know. Such was the case with Albert Uriet, a young painter and poet who wrote Jacob from the trenches and who introduced him, through correspondence, to a man who would become a staunch friend, Jean Paulhan. Jacob's letters to Uriet show him in the role of literary pedagogue. In early October he warned Uriet about the preciosity of the writer Jules Renard and sent him ideas about the genre of the prose poem he had already worked out in his draft of a preface for *Le Cornet à dés.* The prose poem mustn't be a parable as in Baudelaire or Wilde: "It must be a piece of sky speckled with reality. Situated far from us in order to *exist,* and reflecting us in order to interest us."[83]

Jacob recommended to Uriet the poems of Pierre Reverdy. A few weeks later he might not have done so: in October, Reverdy brought out his slim volume of prose poems entitled, simply, *Poèmes en prose,* with Paul Birault, the Montmartre printer who produced Jacob's books. This event set off a war.

Reverdy occupied a position in relation to Jacob similar to Juan Gris's relation to Picasso: initially, that of acolyte. Reverdy had arrived in Paris in 1910, after the revolution of Cubism was well under way. Gris came to Paris from Madrid in 1906 and worked as a cartoonist, but in 1910 he fell under the spell of Picasso.[84] Reverdy dramatized his relations to Jacob in

1917 in his roman à clef *Le Voleur de Talan,* whose punning title suggests "The Thief of Talent." A painfully sensitive man, Reverdy idolized Max Jacob, who befriended him in his early, anxious days in Montmartre. For a while they were neighbors in the Bateau Lavoir, and in *Le Voleur* Reverdy called Jacob a magician, "le Mage Abel." But Jacob continually needled him. When Reverdy said he was writing verse, Jacob replied, "That's all very well, but there's the prose poem." When Reverdy published his prose poems, Jacob told him, "That's all very well, your little stories, but there's the novel." And when Reverdy wrote a novel, Jacob wanted to know how many pages it was.[85] From Jacob's point of view, Reverdy scooped the model of Jacob's prose poems and rushed to publish his own volume ahead of Jacob's. In 1943, Jacob wrote that "someone he wouldn't name" had scrambled to bring out a volume that was a pastiche of Jacob's. "The gang was delighted. 'You've been buried, Max!' "[86]

From this distance, the quarrel over the prose poem can seem absurd, all the more so as Reverdy's grim disoriented parables hardly resemble Jacob's "dice." At the time, however, the stakes were high for writers and artists to be seen as inventors. From Reverdy's point of view, his mentor had impugned his artistic integrity. Years later he described the scene in Jacob's room when he had peered into the famous trunk of manuscripts and Jacob slammed the lid shut—an action that made Reverdy feel expelled, not just from Jacob's friendship but from the whole rich, intimate world of artistic Montmartre.[87]

Le Voleur de Talan depicts the two protagonists, the mysterious "thief" and the magician Abel, poignantly describing the thief's reverence for the master and dramatizing the "theft" as a scene of inspiration. When the magician has disappeared,

> Still someone lived in his room

> Plunged into the half-open trunk
> to take what remained

> And when he raised his forehead his skull had grown larger[88]

If Reverdy turned on Jacob, it was out of wounded love. He seems not to have realized that publishing his *Poèmes en prose* before Jacob's would affront the older writer. Reverdy dedicated the third poem in the book, "Envy" (or Desire), to Jacob, and it reads as a humble tribute: "He owns the stars and the beasts of the earth, the peasants and women to use as he will. The Ocean nursed him, the sea nursed me, and it's he who received all the images. Destiny, if you thought I could leave, you should have given me wings."[89]

Jacob attacked swiftly. He had been laying the foundations of an international reputation by publishing in Milan and London, and now, through the painter Francis Picabia, he had a forum in New York: Alfred Stieglitz's journal *291*, named for the address of his gallery on Fifth Avenue. Picabia, a wealthy man, had met Stieglitz the year before at the Armory Show.[90] Picabia had seen a lot of Jacob in the summer of 1914, and in the fall he held a bureaucratic position with the military in Bordeaux in connection with the displaced government.[91] He got himself dispatched to Cuba and en route stopped in New York to collaborate with Stieglitz on *291*. Jacob was delighted to be paid ("The check is chic! Chic, it's the check!" he quipped) and delighted to have his say in New York.[92]

Jacob's first article for *291* took up an entire page and featured a portrait of him by Picabia: Jacob as a flashlight on a pedestal surrounded by a laurel wreath. He had been asked for a chronicle of the arts in Paris, but Jacob had no inclination to deliver information straightforwardly. Instead, he produced "a lyrical chronicle in the style of a music hall revue."[93] Entitled "La Vie artistique," Jacob's piece hurtles through multiple voices: the Gardener of the Bois de Boulogne, the Poet, the Chronicler, the Art Critic, and "Mr. Pierre Reverdy." In this torrent of coded allusions, he really did give news of artistic Paris, but in a form comprehensible only to those already in the know. Into this potpourri, Jacob inserted two prose poems he would place later in *Le Cornet à dés*.[94] More strategically, he took revenge on Reverdy.

He has Reverdy burst into the conversation: "Were you speaking of me?" "Not at all!" replies the Chronicler. After the Poet recites Jacob's poem "On the night there are three mushrooms," Reverdy declares, "I'm not the one who wrote that poem." To which the Literary Critic replies, "But yes! In 1894, with Mr. Max Jacob's wet nurse!" The Critic sails into a discourse about Reverdy's poems, modulating to a concise statement of Jacob's aesthetic of the prose poem: "Whereas all poeticized prose gives up being in order to please, the prose poem gives up pleasing in order to be. It's something like a Cubist painting. The first condition of an existence is the space that separates it from others. You have put M. Max Jacob's sky around each of his poems." He pays Reverdy a grudging compliment, sensing in him a "horrible courage to sacrifice a thousand conventional beauties," and then, using a phrase he had recently written to Uriet, pronounces: "So one can define your poem as M. Max Jacob defined his own as a piece of sky speckled with realities." The Critic winds up with an insulting epistolary *politesse:* "Please accept, my dear colleague, with my gratitude for the exquisite work you have sent, the assurance of my perfect literary esteem."[95]

In this seriocomic piece, Jacob articulated his vision of the prose poem: its refusal of representation, its aesthetic autonomy, its move toward abstraction. He also punished Reverdy for presuming to publish his "imitations" ahead of Jacob's "originals." The two men would remain locked in a fraternal battle for the rest of their lives. Jacob came to recognize Reverdy as a poet of dark, independent integrity, and Reverdy—even while attacking his erstwhile mentor—would publish him in *Nord-Sud* and owed to Jacob his own conversion to Catholicism. The composer Vittorio Rieti, who knew Jacob well in the late 1920s and '30s, reported that Jacob spoke constantly of Reverdy.[96]

||

IN DECEMBER 1915 the war seemed static in its horror. At the same time, artistic life in Paris began to quicken. Ozenfant's exhibits at Madame Bongard's salon were one sign of the revival, along with his magazine, *L'Élan*. So was the gallery Poiret opened in the space adjacent to his fashion house, variously called the Salon d'Antin or Chez Barbazanges. In November a young woman called Adrienne Monnier, who had been working as a secretary for the journal *Annales littéraires et politiques* (and had known Reverdy there, during one of his odd jobs), took the extraordinary initiative of founding a small bookshop on the Rue de l'Odéon: her store would become a nerve center for the best in national and international literature, and she would supervise the translation of Joyce's *Ulysses* into French. At the same time, the Swiss painter Émile Lejeune opened a series of concerts, poetry readings, and art shows in his studio at 6 rue Huyghens, called Lyre et Palette. Art began to sell again as new dealers moved to take the place of the absent Kahnweiler. Léonce Rosenberg bought Picasso's large *Harlequin* and for a few months seemed poised to become the major Parisian dealer in modern art until his carelessness alienated the best painters and their supporters: Apollinaire wrote Jacob, a few months later, to say that he'd been horrified at the art displayed at Rosenberg's house: "He's too futile for us. . . . It's deplorable, the most authentic works look like junk."[97]

Eva's sufferings drew to an end in late 1915. By early November she was in a clinic at Auteuil, where Picasso visited her every day and watched her fade. She died on December 14. The funeral procession was dismal—just seven or eight friends—and Jacob behaved abominably. At this grimmest of times, he seems not to have been able to give up his role as joker. His feelings must have been complicated; he liked Eva, he adored Picasso, and he may have been subliminally jealous of Picasso's love for Eva. The effect was "sinister," Gris wrote, and pained Picasso.[98] Later Maurice Sachs would report from hearsay that Jacob had been charmed by one of the drivers of the hearse and insisted that the man pray with him at the grave and accompany the mourners afterward.[99]

IV.

THE NEXT FOUR years could be considered Jacob's period of glory. His long labors bore fruit in major books: *Le Cornet à dés* in 1917, *La Défense de Tartufe* in 1919, *Cinématoma* in 1920, and *Le Laboratoire central* in 1921. He began serious friendships and collaborations with the musicians Erik

Satie, Alexis Roland-Manuel, and Georges Auric. His friendships with actors and his practice as a mimic would flow into a number of plays, some of which were produced in Paris. His social connections began to extend far beyond Montmartre and Montparnasse, and though he didn't plunge as deeply as Picasso into high society, in his own way he became a luminary in circles that included Prince and Princesse Georges Ghika; Comte Étienne de Beaumont and his wife, Edith, splendid patrons of the arts; the wealthy American lesbian writer Natalie Barney; Misia Sert, queen of the Paris salons, arbiter of taste, and promoter of Diaghilev; and Coco Chanel.

Jacob's emerging prominence can be seen in his role as explicator of the avant-garde to the intelligentsia of New York. Stieglitz ran his second chronicle, "La Vie artistique," in the February 1916 issue of *291* (sadly, the last issue of this daring journal).[100] Jacob continued the music hall method of his first chronicle, crackling with puns and veiled gossip. Riskily, the piece starts off with a prose poem in which Virgil and Dante in the underworld meet Eve "bent over with despair though her nudity is consoled by a halo," a poem that would appear in *Le Cornet à dés* as "Judgment of Women."[101] If this was Jacob's salute to the recently deceased Eva, one is hard put to imagine a joke in worse taste. It's in the spirit, perhaps, of the grisly wisecracks about the war circulating in Paris; Gertrude Stein later quoted Picasso saying, "Won't it be awful when Braque and Derain and all the rest of them put their wooden legs up on a chair and tell about the fighting?"[102] But Jacob's article surges ahead to evoke the scandal that had just erupted in Montparnasse when the Mexican painter Diego Rivera, who had for a while adopted Picasso's Cubism, suddenly accused the master of "stealing" his method of indicating foliage with green dots.[103] As with Jacob's quarrel with Reverdy, the artists and writers jealously guarded their "discoveries." He concludes with one of the most beautiful lines from *Le Cornet à dés*, one that had already appeared in English in *The New Age*: "Ses bras blancs devinrent tout mon horizon" (His white arms became my whole horizon).[104]

In a telling sign of Jacob's visibility, the young Romanian poet Tristan Tzara, about to found Dada in Zurich, wrote to him as to an admired master. Jacob replied with one of his most often quoted letters. To the budding

Dadaist, Jacob suggested, "Decomposition enlarges art but recomposition fortifies it." He ran through the various jobs he'd held—student, tutor, art critic, janitor; claimed to have seen God on his wall in 1909; and said of Picasso, "He has been my friend for sixteen years; we've hated each other and we've done each other as much harm as good but he's necessary to my life." He concluded: "I'm a pretty good fellow; I'm pious, I try to do good rather than ill; I drink less than I used to and I try to remain chaste in my celibacy. I'm light-hearted, I like telling stories; I adore my friends, I love music and I make drawings that don't sell. I shout that I'm talented to persuade myself that I am, but I don't believe it. Send me some poems."[105]

IN THIS PERIOD, Jacob was on affectionate terms with Apollinaire. The soldier-poet, who had become engaged to Madeleine Pagès, a young schoolteacher from Algeria he had met on a train in Nice the year before, came to Paris on a short leave in February. Jacob wrote him chattily after the visit, complimenting him on his new poems, and telling about his friendship with the Russian poet Ilya Ehrenburg, a sparkling presence in Montparnasse in those days, along with the other Russians, Serge Férat, Hélène d'Oettingen, Marie Wassilieff, and Rivera's lover, the young painter Marevna. He steered clear of Montparnasse, Jacob confessed, because he sinned there "ignobly," and he avoided Poiret for the same reason.[106]

Several further friendly communications passed back and forth.[107] Then the catastrophe hit. As Apollinaire sat in his trench just north of Reims, reading—of course—the *Mercure de France,* he was struck by a shell. Splinters pierced his helmet and his skull. Four days later he wrote Jacob from the military hospital, "Dear Max, Write to me. You know I've been wounded in the head by a shell. . . . I'll be operated this morning."[108]

V.

THE EFFECTS OF the war, for Jacob, extended far beyond France. Through his friendship with the Armenian Joseph Altounian, he became imaginatively engaged with the fate of the Armenian people. The Ottoman Turks, allied with the Germans and feeling threatened in 1912 by Bulgaria and the powers of the Entente, had reacted with an outburst of violent national-ism and a policy of eliminating Christian minorities.[109] Deportation, death marches, and massacres of the Greeks in Turkey began in 1914. A year later the Turks began arresting and murdering Armenians; they marched thousands of women and children into the Syrian desert, where they died of hunger and thirst, and they conscripted men into the army and into labor camps, where they were killed. By 1916, gruesome news of the exter-minations leaped into the headlines in France.

As a newly minted Christian, Jacob took the horrors to heart. On February 14, 1916, the bishop of Orléans gave an impassioned address in Paris about the sufferings of the Armenians. That was followed by an even more rousing occasion in April, when Paul Deschanel, the president of the Chamber of Deputies, delivered a thunderous speech in the amphi-theater of the Sorbonne.[110] Max Jacob had helped Altounian on the young man's arrival in France from Smyrna in 1908, guiding him in the world of Parisian dealers. Now Altounian, already quite successful, commissioned Jacob to write a polemical poem for the Armenian cause, to be distrib-uted, not to put too fine a point upon it, as propaganda. So Jacob produced a booming poem, "The Allies Are in Armenia," He never reprinted it, though it served its purpose at the time and earned him some francs.[111]

APOLLINAIRE SPENT THE first few weeks after his operation at the Hôpital Val-de-Grâce in Paris, but he was soon moved to the Italian hospital on the Quai d'Orsay, where Serge Férat was working as a medical aide. Since Apollinaire was Serge's star, Jacob wrote a friend, "it's pretty much Apol-linaire who rules the Italian Hospital. . . . He parades his wound around Paris."[112] Cocteau, meanwhile, was serving in a fancy ambulance corps at the farthest western sector of the front. In early April, Cocteau returned to Paris on leave, and it was then that he conceived the ballet *Parade* and pre-vailed on Picasso to draw his portrait. Picasso, frustrated and lonely since Gaby Depeyre had refused to marry him, allowed Cocteau to amuse him and introduced him to Modigliani and Jacob. The bohemians regarded with suspicion this emissary from the *salons* who had styled himself "The Frivolous Prince." "Cocteau talked nonstop," said Reverdy, "the same sound as the rain beating on the skylight. Nobody paid much attention to what he said."[113] Cocteau, for his part, even though he worked hard to penetrate Picasso's world, sneered at much that he found there. In August he wrote the elegant Valentine Gross, "Nothing very new except Picasso keeps taking me to the Rotonde. I never stay more than a moment, despite the flattering welcome given me by the circle (perhaps I should say the cube). Gloves, cane, and collars astonish these artists in shirtsleeves— they have always looked on them as the insignia of feeblemindedness. . . . Max Jacob performs in dancing pumps on a slack rope. A convent gardener, slipping dirty books to the nuns. A kind of sweet, dirty jack-of-all-trades."[114] Writing to Gleizes, he was even harsher, and called Jacob "Claude Anus."[115]

Cocteau felt superior to the scruffy artists, but he maneuvered to have them paint his portrait. Along with the earlier flashy portrait of himself by Jacques-Émile Blanche, he could now boast likenesses by Modigliani and Kisling as well as Picasso's drawing. He also immortalized the day of August 12, 1916, in Montparnasse with pictures he took with his mother's camera. By this time, Cocteau had wangled a discharge from the ambulance corps. He had returned to his military duties on May 6, to endure the first shattering weeks of the Battle of the Somme in July.[116] By late July he broke down and fled to Paris, where his mother arranged a desk job for him. That is why we find him with her camera on the terrace of the Rotonde with Picasso, Picasso's current girlfriend, the fashion model Pâquerette, Max Jacob, Ortiz de Zarate, Marie Wassilieff, Henri-Pierre Roché, and Kisling. He snapped a sequence of pictures between 12:45 and 4:30, leaving a visual record of that playful artistic afternoon in Montparnasse.[117] Jacob is dressed as a natty *boulevardier* with bowler hat, starched white collar, silk ascot, and jacket with wide lapels; Picasso wears a white shirt, a loose dark tie, a floppy dark jacket, and a cap; Kisling, with his broad Slavic face and black bangs cut straight across his forehead, is also dressed up, wearing a coat and tie. After they've left the café, they clown around: Jacob places his foot, in its dress pump, up on a curb; Kisling kneels and pretends to shine it while Ortiz leans from behind to pick Jacob's pocket. (It was the very next day that Cocteau claimed never to "stay more than a moment.")

Not all the pranks of Montparnasse could keep the war at bay. On July 4, Sylvette Fillacier's husband, the actor Marcel Olin, was killed by a shell. He was awarded a military medal posthumously: he had been the first out of his trench in the attack. Picasso, Jacob, Salmon, and Gris visited Sylvette to console her for the loss of their old friend Marcel. Frédé, the owner of the Lapin Agile who had so often fed *la bande à Picasso,* offered what he could by way of comfort to Sylvette; "You have to eat beefsteaks, large beefsteaks."[118]

Boccioni, the Futurist, was killed on August 17, not in battle but trampled by a horse during military exercises. He had not been a friend of the Bateau Lavoir—far from it—but in some larger sense he was their companion in modern art. Day by day the toll mounted. At the same time, artistic life increased in tempo. On July 17 an art exhibit organized by Salmon at Poiret's Salon d'Antin opened with fanfare, featuring works by Matisse, Derain, Chirico, Severini, Segonzac, Rouault, and others. The stunner of the show was Picasso's *Les Demoiselles d'Avignon,* shown here in public for the first time. Jacob showed two little pastels of Breton landscapes. His time to shine came a few days later: on July 21, Apollinaire gave a lecture entitled "Painters and Poets" in front of *Les Demoiselles,* presenting poems by Jacob, Reverdy, Hastings, Ehrenburg, and others. Four poems of Jacob's were read aloud.[119]

AUGUST BROUGHT ROMANTIC drama. Picasso, rejected by Gaby Depeyre, had become obsessed with Irène, Serge Férat's mistress. He had carried on a clandestine affair with her since the spring, but in midsummer he decided to abduct her. Fractured versions of the story turn up in Apollinaire's novel *La Femme assise* (The Seated Woman), written the following year; Apollinaire was certainly in a position to write about it, since he helped Picasso capture Irène, and since Irène, who liked women too, had something of a romance with Jacqueline Kolb, the pretty redhead— "la jolie rousse" of Apollinaire's poem—whom Apollinaire would later marry. In early August, Picasso and Apollinaire invited Irène to lunch and meandered with her from restaurant to restaurant plying her with so much champagne she couldn't tell, afterward, how she ended up in Picasso's newly rented little house in the suburb of Montrouge, where he locked her in. Irène soon climbed out a window and returned to Serge, but only to keep enticing Picasso, so that both men seem to have been driven slightly crazy by her. In late August, in order to pry her loose from Serge, Picasso showed a picture of her in the nude to Hélène d'Oettingen, Serge's possessive foster sister, accusing Irène of being a whore; whereupon Serge became enraged and demanded that Irène leave their apartment; whereupon Irène attempted suicide by gassing herself in the kitchen; whereupon Serge forgave and rescued her . . .[120] By September, Serge had taken Irène to Brittany to rest. Jacob knew the story and wrote of it delicately to Altounian: "By his side in Bénodet Serge has the tragic Irène, the capricious Irène, the inescapable Irène—I cannot say more."[121]

VI.

JACOB'S FRIENDSHIP WITH Liane de Pougy, now Princesse Ghika, and her husband, Georges Ghika, intensified during the summer of 1916. In July, he thanked the prince in a ditty for some act of generosity, and on August 1 he wrote them from his den on the Rue Gabrielle, "It's very hot and I'm a great sinner. God sends me humiliations, I'll console myself for the horrors of mankind by going to Saint-Germain Sunday to contemplate you both." This letter included a poem imagining Cupid ruling the Ghikas' household, with Liane implicitly cast as Venus. "What can I say?" he concluded. "That I miss you, that I'm bored to death, that I love you both, since you permit it and I proclaim myself here and everywhere, your very devoted, Cyprien Max Jacob."[122] He would soon land on them for a considerably longer stay, not in Paris but at their country retreat at Roscoff on the northern coast of Brittany.

Jacob hadn't seen his family since the outbreak of war, and his father was ailing. By late August Jacob was at home in Quimper and writing to Henri-Pierre Roché, Marie Laurencin's old lover (and much later, the author of the novel *Jules et Jim*). Roché, who enjoyed "connecting" people, was a specialist in *ménages à trois*, but he also connected artists and patrons, and on August 12, when he joined Picasso, Jacob, and the others clowning for Cocteau's photographs, he seems to have mentioned to Jacob the possibility of Jacques Doucet's buying some of Jacob's books. In his letter to Roché, Jacob declared that he'd be delighted to meet Doucet and asked that copies of *La Côte* and *Les Alliés sont en Arménie*, which he had left with Picasso, be sold to Doucet and the money sent on to Jacob in Brittany.[123]

He needed money badly. His stay with his family had turned sour. For whatever reason—Jacob wasn't sure—his mother banished him from the house after a few days, saying, "You've seen your father! You've seen your friend [Serge Férat, tending to Irène in nearby Bénodet]; now it's time for you to go!"[124] Writing Picasso, Jacob wondered whether he was being expelled to save money, but noted that his sister Mirté-Léa and her son Robert had stayed on in the house; perhaps it was his Christianity that offended his mother, or the fact that he was translating the medieval Catalan mystic Raymond Lulle, or that he crept out each morning to attend mass. He'd never return to Quimper, he announced: Picasso was his only attachment in this world. Without enough money to return to Paris, Jacob took the seven-hour train ride to Roscoff and installed himself for six weeks as the guest of Prince and Princesse Ghika.

Les princes, as Jacob called the Ghikas, offered him a princely refuge. Writing to Picasso, he described Clos Marie, the farmhouse Liane had restored, with its whitewashed beams, immense library, armchairs and sofa upholstered in white with cushions designed by Poiret, black-and-white-tiled floors, and antique oak tables and cabinets. Tamarisk trees sheltered the house from the ocean. The village of Roscoff perched on the edge of a rocky bay; the coast was dotted with chapels, lighthouses, and customs houses; and artichokes grew in the fields. In the mornings Jacob attended mass and then read and wrote in the library; after lunch, the routine prescribed a siesta for everyone in the household including three black servants, the cook, and the chambermaid. Afternoons were given over to rambles in the countryside, errands in the village, or excursions in a boat around the nearby islands, and the day concluded with conversation, dinner, and more conversation around the princess's elaborate "Louis XV or Louis XVI" bed. He irritated his hosts, he confessed, by spending too much time in the bathroom. The most urgent message to Picasso came at the end of the letter, underlined: "I'll return to Paris as soon as I have the money from Doucet." And he made clear that he was not quite living up to the terms of the agreement with Doucet: "Tell him [Doucet] I have the Matorel manuscripts: it isn't true but I'll copy them from the books since he likes manuscripts." Given his recent rupture with his family, his affectionate signoff carried particular weight: "Hugs to you, my son and only father."[125]

The idyll at Roscoff ended in mid-October when Picasso sent Doucet's payment. He addressed Max warmly—"My dear godson Max"—and in his slightly Hispanicized French asked his friend to help him with his move: Picasso was now definitely leaving the cavernous apartment on the Rue Schoelcher, where he had lived with Eva, and taking full possession of the little house in Montrouge. Jacob had returned to his room on the Rue Gabrielle by October 24 when, in a sign of his complex relations with Reverdy, the two poets joined in sending "Pablo" a birthday greeting; however spiteful their attacks on one another, the members of *la bande à Picasso* still composed a clan as tightly knit by aesthetic purpose as by fraternal envy and aggression.[126]

||

"THINGS ARE STIRRING in Montparnasse," Jacob wrote the soldier Albert Uriet. "Art shows, concerts, readings, lectures . . ."[127] Apollinaire, out and very much about after his hospitalization, reassumed his role as ringleader: his fantastical narrative, *Le Poète assassiné* (The Assassinated Poet), came out in October, translating the adventures of Picasso's gang into a myth in which Picasso is the Benin Bird (a nod at African sculpture), Apollinaire is Croniamantal, and Laurencin is Tristouse Ballerinette, while the book's orphic title weirdly prefigures the author's early death. Max Jacob doesn't appear in the fable. At the same time, the young poet-editor Pierre Albert-

Birot interviewed the not-yet-"assassinated" poet for his magazine, *SIC*, a bold venture combining Futurist typography and vaguely Cubist theories. (The title is an acronym for *Son Idée Couleur:* Sound Idea Color.)

In his interview, entitled "The New Trends," Apollinaire sounded the conservative strain that would characterize his last phase: he celebrated the effect of war on art, the "male simplicity" it would bring to "a new humanism," and a reconciliation of past and future. Now naturalized as a French citizen, he asserted his patriotism. Cinema was the art of the future, he predicted, and the future theater he described sounds like *Les Mamelles de Tirésias* (Tiresias's Breasts), the "surrealist" play he would produce the following year.[128] Apollinaire further expressed his "male simplicity" by abandoning his fiancée, Madeleine Pagès.[129] She had served her purpose.

Apollinaire and Jacob played starring roles in the renaissance of the arts. Both had poems in the catalogue for Paul Guillaume's show of Derain's work in October, an exhibit the painter attended in military uniform, on leave from the front.[130] Jacob gave "The Visionary's Mass," a poem freshly composed at Roscoff and signed with his Christian name, Cyprien Max Jacob: "Stop smiling, if the end of the world has come."[131]

In November, Jacob wrote Sylvette Fillacier, asking if in spite of her mourning for Marcel Olin, she would perform his poems for a gala in his honor at the Lyre et Palette on December 3.[132] Émile Lejeune had organized a show of works by Matisse, Picasso, Ortiz de Zarate, Modigliani, and Kisling; the opening on November 19 featured music by Satie, to which Cocteau brought his flock from *tout Paris*, Comte Étienne de Beaumont, the *salonnière* and novelist Madame Aurel, and others.[133]

Jacob's grand day came on December 3, the conclusion of the show. Picasso drew his portrait for the occasion, a pencil sketch of Jacob sitting in an armchair with jacket, tie, and vest. Reproductions of the portrait were sold at the performance, along with a two-sentence prose poem: "Struck by lightning, the archangel had time only to loosen his cravat. It looked as if he were still praying."[134] Paul Dermée, a mediocre poet but assiduous adherent of the Apollinaire-Jacob circle, lectured on Jacob's poetry. Calling Jacob "the Mallarmé of Cubism," he quoted the formulations about the modern prose poem Jacob had recently published in *291*.[135]

Fillacier read Max's poems. He must have felt at last like a master, no longer "an old apprentice."

The next day, glowing, Jacob went to see Lejeune. "How do you think it went? Well, huh?" Very well, Lejeune replied, but not being well acquainted with Max's work, he wanted to know the whole poem from which the lines about the archangel had been taken. Jacob drew himself up, adjusted his monocle, and declared, "My dear fellow, that *is* the whole poem. Cyprien Max Jacob in its purest state."[136]

Jacob's triumph reached beyond the Rue Huyghens. The December 1 issue of Ozenfant's *L'Élan* devoted its entire first page to him with a reproduction of Picasso's Ingres-like portrait from 1915 and a scattering of prose poems with an art chronicle Jacob must have intended for *291*, now defunct. The prose poems all came from the sequence that would make up section four of the first part of *Le Cornet*.[137] Jacob hid them among his wisecracks as he had hidden lovely poems in the Matorel stories. Not until they appeared the following year in their own volume, *Le Cornet à dés*, would these inventive pieces show their true force.

Lifting the prose poems from their context in *L'Élan*, one glimpses the future Dice Cup, a work that has found a permanent place in French literature. "And when of the Polish lancer, his limbs cut off and his bottle broken, nothing remained but his eye, the eye sang 'The Two Grenadiers.'" "I declare myself worldwide, oviparous, a giraffe, thirsty, sinophobic and hemispherical. I drink from the sources of the atmosphere which laughs concentrically and farts at my ineptitude" (another Kabbalistic reference, in the concentric circles). "They think a man has truffles in his heart." "Mystery is in this life, reality in the other; if you love me, if you love me, I'll show you reality." "When you snore, the material world wakes the other." Into these flashes, Jacob compressed his vision of earthly life shot through with mystical radiance from a spirit world.[138]

IRÈNE LAGUT, FRESH from her suicide attempt, returned to Paris that fall and, exercising her great gift for trouble, sent welcoming signals to Picasso. By early December, just as Jacob's poetry was celebrated at Lyre et Palette, she moved into the house in Montrouge where the painter had locked her up five months earlier. There they seem to have enjoyed a cozy affair. Jacob visited them for lunch in their hideaway, as did Cocteau, with whom Picasso was now collaborating on *Parade* for the Ballets Russes, designing sets and costumes.[139] On December 23, Picasso, Jacob, and the art collector André Level had lunch with Jacob's friend the dealer Paul Guillaume. As usual, we find Max Jacob in the giddy middle of things.

Irène had the tact not to accompany Picasso to the banquet to honor Apollinaire on the last day of 1916, where she would have run into her old lover Serge Férat. Jacob, Reverdy, Gris, Cendrars, and Dermée organized this sumptuous lunch at the Palais d'Orléans. The guests represented avant-gardes new and old. Even the menu showed scars of art battles. Jacob had composed a list of dishes to celebrate his friend: "Hors d'oeuvres cubistes, Poisson du Roi-Lune, Contre-filet à la Croniamantal," and so forth, ending with "Biscuits du Mimétisme" (Mimetic Cookies). Apollinaire corrected the menu. He had ceased to champion Cubism, so the hors d'oeuvres became "Hors d'oeuvres cubistes, orphistes, futuristes, etc." No doubt remembering old accusations of having copied Jacob, he changed "Biscuits du Mimétisme" to "Biscuits du Brigadier Masqué," and he capped it all off with his famous title, "Alcools."[140]

The banquet broke into mayhem. Guests began hollering as soon as the prolix Madame Aurel began the speeches. Aesthetic rivalries erupted into food fights. Still weak from his wound, Apollinaire imposed order by reciting a poem. This hilarious occasion had the tragic coloration of the period: while the armies remained stalemated in slaughter and several of the guests were severely wounded, the poets and painters gathered in a Dionysian frolic. Domestic sorrow, too, shadowed the party; the painter Gino Severini and his wife, Jeanne, had just lost their baby to illness brought on by cold and poverty.[141]

CHAPTER II

THE DICE CUP
AND THE ARMISTICE

I.

Nineteen-seventeen began grimly. Coal and sugar were rationed; the weather was bitterly cold. In January the Seine flooded, as greenish-brown waves splashed against the arches of the bridges, covered railroad tracks, and threatened the stacked barrels and cases at the river port of Bercy.[1]

Jacob's father died on January 3, and the son made the weary trip to Quimper by train for the funeral. He had last seen his father in August, when his mother kicked him out of the house. Now he was assailed by guilt for all the disappointment he had caused; assailed, too, by nostalgia for his youth and for his native town. The rite was meager and secular, with no flowers or ceremony. But, Jacob stressed to Picasso, the "first citizens" of the town attended, along with the workers from the Jacob family shops. Jacob stood with his brothers and sisters at the grave watching the grave-diggers pitch clods of earth onto the coffin. "How many memories were buried with him!" he exclaimed to Picasso. "Everything that was dear to me before you became my all; for you sum up all my friends and my whole life aside from my family." He asked his friend to pardon him all the wrongs he might have done him.[2]

BACK IN PARIS, Jacob was carried forward in the surge of art. This would be a defining year: he would publish his masterwork, *Le Cornet à dés;* he would write an important series of letters of aesthetic reflection for his patron Jacques Doucet; and he would publish prominently in Reverdy's new journal, *Nord-Sud*.

Doucet's sponsorship freed Jacob from poverty and the need to piece together a living on the sly at the family trade of tailoring: he had been scraping together rent money by hemming buttonholes for military capes.[3] But Doucet inspired Jacob in other ways. Elderly and recovering from an illness in the South of France, Doucet wanted to be kept up to date on Parisian arts and letters.[4] Jacob's letters to his patron describe artistic developments in the capital, but even more important, they articulate his ideas just as he emerged as a modernist master.

Jacob's first letter to Doucet mentioned his father's death and then described his manuscripts, a precious summary including the collection that would become *Le Cornet à dés:* "This manuscript is very thick and preceded by a preface in which I summon Rimbaldian exasperation back to style, that is to traditional composition; I'm a reactionary. Revolutions are made only when based on the past."[5] He mentioned also a manuscript of verse poems (work that will find its way into *La Défense de Tartufe* and *Le Laboratoire central*); the play and the novel of *Le Terrain Bouchaballe;* the novel *Le Phanérogame;* the collection of story-portraits he's now calling *Cinéma Thomas;*[6] and interpretations of Scripture. Jacob made clear to Doucet that he won't gossip about Picasso, principally because the painter hates it, but also because Jacob doesn't want to be remembered only as "Picasso's friend."

A week later Jacob recounted his apparition and his conversion; discussed delivery of the manuscripts; offered to put Doucet in touch with Apollinaire; and explained why he couldn't write to order on subjects Doucet had proposed: the subject had to rise from one's deepest inward self.[7]

IN THE FERMENT of artistic life, Jacob presented Reverdy at Lyre et Palette on January 18, celebrating his rival while arguing for his own vision of the prose poem.[8] A few days earlier another explosive party took place, this one celebrating Braque who, like Apollinaire, had been wounded in the head. Picasso, Apollinaire, Gris, Jacob, Metzinger, Reverdy, Dermée,

Wassilieff, Matisse, and the Norwegian Walter Halvorsen organized the *fête* in Marie Wassilieff's studio. The banquet set off the usual bohemian drama, as Modigliani threatened Beatrice Hastings's new lover with a revolver. Marie pushed Modigliani down the stairs, Picasso locked the door, and the party continued until six in the morning. Long afterward Moricand remembered Braque and Derain dancing like savages, waving turkey bones.[9] Picasso was accompanied, not by Irène Lagut (who had returned to the long-suffering Serge Férat), but by the model Pâquerette, with whom Picasso amused himself when potential brides were out of reach. Jacob entertained everyone with imitations of Braque's mother and his colonel. Two days later Picasso left for Rome with Cocteau to work on *Parade*. When he returned in late April, he would be on a course that pulled him away from Jacob for good: his new love, the ballerina Olga Khokhlova, would detach him from old friends and launch him into the high society where Cocteau moved with such ease.

In 1917 neither Picasso nor Jacob anticipated such estrangement. Jacob continued his letters to Doucet, discreetly asking for advances, explaining his antinaturalistic principles, and more and more drawing Doucet into the publication of *Le Cornet*.[10] Meanwhile Jacob copied his manuscripts to sell to Doucet while leaving himself drafts to assemble into books.

||

IN MARCH, JACOB began preparing to publish *Le Cornet à dés* at his own expense. Picasso agreed to provide an etching for ten luxury copies; the rest would be unillustrated. With Picasso in Rome and Doucet demanding constant reports, the next few months of Jacob's life are documented with novelistic precision in his letters. He inquired anxiously about Picasso's etching; Apollinaire started holding court at the Café Flore ("It's boring"); Reverdy was launching a new journal; Picabia started a magazine in Barcelona, *391*, a reincarnation of Stieglitz's *291* but more Dadaist; he asked Jacob and Picasso for material, but at the same time attacked Picasso for backsliding into representational art.[11]

For *Le Cornet à dés,* Jacob wanted a design "without typographical gewgaws, very simple, Kahnweiler-style. I hate the Ozenfant flimflam and all the Picabesqueries."[12] He was referring to the experimental typography in Ozenfant's journal *L'Élan* and in *391.* Yet he owed Ozenfant a lot, and several of his pieces would appear in Picabia's new magazine.[13]

In February a lovely poem of Jacob's appeared in *391.* He probably wrote "Atlantide" that fall at Roscoff with the Ghikas; the poem breathes with the freshness of wind off the waves, mingling marine imagery with Parisian scenes of Sacré-Coeur, where Jacob attended mass daily when he was in the city. Though news from the fronts was somber, Jacob dreams of a new Eden after war.

> A younger continent awakes:
> After Bellona, we'll have Eve!
> A new landscape rises from the wave:
> No foam is flung yet on the rocks
> The first drop bubbling from a spring
> Hasn't yet washed a single field.
> A giant on the Eiffel Tower's crown—
> with moonlight threading through his hair—
> rejects his heavenly offspring, to give birth
> to people living upon earth.
> The lighthouse the tempest licked all night
> Is a basket of seaweed crinkled tongues
> It's tangled, and the tide brings in the heads
> Of Eves pale and rumpled in their flight.
> They're preparing the new continent up at Sacré-Coeur.
> A young man showed off the model houses there
> On a pier and our Savior's hands
> By my bed on the hill where pilgrims flock all year.
> Some fry eggs on a little camping stove
> One's got nothing left but one shoulder and his chest
> There's a Breton peasant woman.

And the young man still stays by me
In this dormitory room Our Lord is nude
He offers his wounded hands
The new continent will take work and thought
It's at Sacré-Coeur it will be wrought.[14]

The two landscapes, the seashore and Paris, "rhyme" with their towers, the lighthouse and the Eiffel Tower. Metrical verse is spliced into irregularly punctuated free verse. The postwar Eden jars with the glimpse of a cripple (maimed by war?). Erotic hints slide into a vision of Christ. The "new continent" seems both a country recovering from war and the new life promised to a convert. Jacob's faith and his poetic art align in the simple line "He offers his wounded hands." For Jacob, this redemptive work takes place at Sacré-Coeur, the basilica where he prayed and trusted to the magical power of Communion.

II.

IN LETTERS TO Picasso and Doucet, Jacob narrated a scuffle between Reverdy and the Mexican painter Diego Rivera. Léonce Rosenberg had invited "his" painters along with Jacob and Reverdy to a dinner at an elegant restaurant, after which they repaired to the still more elegant studio of André Lhote. The party gained momentum, and Reverdy—the "young and ardent theoretician of Cubism," as Jacob called him—discoursed so fervently that Rivera felt insulted and slapped him. Reverdy flew into a rage: "To slap meh! Meh!" ("*Me gifler moâ! Moâ!*" wrote Jacob, imitating Reverdy's meridional accent). Reverdy hurled himself on Rivera; other guests piled on to separate them; furniture was broken, bibelots flew, and pictures fell off the wall with a shattering of glass. Reverdy's friends pulled him outside while the Lhotes—Madame weeping—collared Rivera. "And that's the most serious event of the season," pronounced Max to Jacques Doucet.[15]

But it *was* serious. Reverdy had just brought out the first issue of his austere journal *Nord-Sud,* named for the new North-South Métro line linking the artistic neighborhoods of Montmartre and Montparnasse. The editorial stated that this was the moment to renew the arts and to rally around the central figure of Apollinaire.[16] In the first issue, Paul Dermée's obituary for Symbolism was followed by Reverdy's essay on Cubism, in which he berated johnny-come-lately imitators. Reverdy's central point, ceaselessly argued, was that Cubism was an art of nonrepresentational realism.[17]

Jacob expressed both admiration for and reservations about *Nord-Sud.*[18] But bickering aside, he found a home in its pages. The first issue carried his verse poem with the abstract title "Poem," and as its three-line epigraph, his own famously punning verse "Comme un bateau, le poète est âgé, / le poème étagé / Dahlia! dahlia! Que Dalila lia." (Like a boat, the poet has grown old / the poem in layers / Dahlia! Dahlia! That Dalila tied.) The syllables proliferate so that the poem itself becomes a multistoried structure and a flower of multiple petals of sound and sense.[19] It was followed by his story "Don Juan's Story," a pastiche of Byron in music hall lyrics. His most interesting piece for the first issue of *Nord-Sud,* however, was one he wasn't allowed to publish. The Catholic printer refused to set Jacob's poem "The Demoniac's Mass"; Jacob's confessor wouldn't allow the poem to appear in a journal but permitted it in a book (where its demoniac powers would be tempered by context?).[20] Eventually published in *La Défense de Tartufe,* "The Demoniac's Mass" dissolves the Latin hymn for the vespers service of All Saints into an astrological obscenity in French: *"Plac-are . . . , Christe . . . servulis . . . serviculis . . . beatam me dicent orifice astral."* The astral orifice suggests—however lightly—anal lovemaking, as the macaronic Latin *"Intumescitur anima mea, longitudinal"* brings to mind a swelling not just of the soul. In this black mass, Jacob's degeneration of sense recreates the sense of someone who pushed language and experience far beyond the norms of his day and tested his own faith by experimenting ironically with blasphemy. He was also exploring the alliance of sacred and profane that would characterize much twentieth-century thought.[21]

In April, in the second issue of *Nord-Sud,* Jacob expressed his experience of the war in two prose poems that would open *Le Cornet à dés,* marking that collection in its esoteric way as a document of the Great War. The first six poems of the book all concern the war: nightmares of dying as a civilian; propaganda and misinformation; the pursuit of spies and traitors. Unlike Apollinaire's exuberant vision of war as a magnificent and sexy if deadly game, Jacob's "The War" reflects terror:

> At night the outer boulevards are filled with snow; the bandits are soldiers; I'm attacked with laughter and sabers, I'm stripped; I flee only to fall into another square. Is it the courtyard of a barracks, or of an inn? So many sabers! So many lancers! It's snowing! Someone stabs me with a syringe: it's a poison to kill me; a skull swathed in black crepe bites my finger. Vague lanterns throw the light of my death across the snow.

"1914," placed first in *Le Cornet*, is still more oblique, blending a vision of Christ descending, almost naked, and wounded, with scenes of the Quimper of Jacob's childhood and an invasion of sinister "couples" who float down from the sky on black threads and occupy the family house: "Ever since, the police have been watching me."[22]

IN APRIL THE battle between Reverdy and Jacob over the prose poem continued in *Nord-Sud*. Though Reverdy gave generous space to Jacob in his pages—*Nord-Sud* no. 2 also included a story by Jacob[23]—he renewed his accusation of Jacob's appropriating the work of others (meaning Rimbaud's conception of the prose poem): "Afterward a lamp reflector was seen trying to blind the moon with its mirror. It was late. On the sky were to be seen the shadows of the *one* who had invented the new world *in books*. He had erased all the names and replaced them with his own."[24] A few days before the appearance of the April issue, Jacob gossiped to Picasso in a letter that *Nord-Sud* was gaining weight and—in a pun on the "green" in Rev*erd*y's name—quipped that "*Reverdy verdit*": "Reverdy grows green, he lives in eternal wrath and suspicion."[25]

By this time, Jacob had printed and begun to distribute subscription forms for *Le Cornet à dés*. A printer's strike held up the book; the printer lost the photographic reproduction of Picasso's 1915 portrait, and Ozenfant, who still had the original in the files for *L'Élan*, refused to lend it again. (It took the intervention of Juan Gris to release it.) Nerve-rackingly, Picasso, who had promised the etching on whose sale the whole project depended, kept delaying, preoccupied as he was in Rome with the Ballets Russes and his pursuit of Olga. (He procrastinated until the last possible moment: the unillustrated *Cornet* appeared in October 1917, the one with the 1915 portrait not until late December, and the special edition with Picasso's new etching of a Cubist Harlequin in late January or early February 1918.)

PICASSO RETURNED FROM Rome on April 24. He hovered briefly, long enough to attend the premiere of *Parade* at the Théâtre du Châtelet, the largest theater in the city. Here, in the vast dimensions of the stage, he could witness his vision realized in the monumental figures of the Managers. And he must have seen an image of his own glory, magnified by the new art form but also by the scandal that erupted during the performance, with cries of "Boches!" from some in the audience and tempestuous applause from others. Diaghilev had achieved another success, not as resonant as *Le Sacre du Printemps*, but still a major event in the history of Modernism. At the last moment, Satie and Picasso suppressed Cocteau's modern noises (sirens, trains), and Cocteau stormed around backstage in a fury. (By the time he composed an account of the collaboration for the June–July issue of *Nord-Sud*, he spun the story so that Satie's music was to have formed the background for the mechanical noises [!], and it was only through an unfortunate accident that the noises had been omitted.)[26]

Picasso was so distracted by *Parade*, and perhaps also by Olga, that he forgot to attend a dinner given in his honor by Jacob, the sculptor Jacques Lipchitz, Gris and his companion Josette, and several others. Or perhaps, as Richardson suggests, he didn't "forget" but was caught between two worlds, his old bohemian comradeship and Diaghilev's high-society glitz. Of course, Diaghilev celebrated the premiere of the ballet with a fancy dinner, and of course Picasso, as one of the creators, had to attend it. But he didn't inform his old friends, and they felt snubbed, sending a note expressing their regret, ironically signed with aristocratic names: Prince de Lipchitz, Max von Jacob . . ."[27] Then the star painter rejoined the Ballets Russes in Barcelona.

III.

IN JUNE, *SIC* pulled off a coup: a production of Apollinaire's burlesque play *Les Mamelles de Tirésias* (Tiresias's Breasts) in a small theater in Montmartre, with music by Germaine Albert-Birot, set and costumes by Serge Férat, the costume of the androgynous main character, Thérèse-Tirésias, by Irène Lagut, and Max Jacob singing in the chorus. An elaborate description appeared in *SIC* with snippets of the press coverage in succeeding issues;[28] *SIC* would print the whole text of the play separately. Apollinaire and the Birots clearly hoped to reproduce the provocation of Jarry's *Ubu Roi*. This hope was hardly realized: If *Les Mamelles* is remembered today, it is only because Apollinaire wrote it; it has none of Jarry's fabulous diction. Jacob, in his account for *Nord-Sud,* rightly hinted that Apollinaire's genius was lyric, not dramatic.[29]

In a revision of Aristophanes' *Thesmophoriazousai,* Apollinaire's main character, Thérèse, decides she's tired of being a wife; she opens her bodice and rips off her breasts (balloons) and flings them into the audience, while sprouting a beard. Assuming the name Tiresias, the Greek prophet who experienced life in both sexes, she ties up her husband and strides away. The husband then generates more than forty thousand children by himself. For all its avant-garde trappings, the play expresses Apollinaire's new conservative strain, the anxiety he shared with many French people that they were losing the war because of France's low birth rate. Reviewers were quick to take note: "Essentially, Guillaume Apollinaire is a traditionalist and beneath his hurly-burly, clowning, Grand Guignol fantasy, he demands a return to order."[30] (That phrase, "return to order," would ring more and more loudly in the postwar years.)

Les Mamelles aroused intense expectations and controversy. Apollinaire had invented the word *surrealist* in his program notes for *Parade,* but now he emblazoned it on his own play, and the word was picked up by the press.[31] Years later Georges Gabory recalled the excitement in the theater, with the Romantics in flowing cravats and flowing locks shouting "Vive Victor Hugo!" while the old anarchists protested the fertility thesis and devotees of advanced art roared their approval. Having learned about the young poet's defense of his play, Apollinaire invited him to his apartment a few days later. Gabory felt ill at ease with "this large, paunchy, pontificating man" who received visitors in his military uniform; he struck the youth as ambitious for worldly fame, coveting an academician's green robe.[32]

Max Jacob had as ambivalent a response to *Les Mamelles* as to everything else regarding Apollinaire. To consolidate his leadership, Apollinaire gave a lecture in June, "A Trend in Contemporary Poetry," in a concert hall on the Champs-Élysées. Since Reverdy and his wife had withdrawn to the South of France so the gloomy poet could write his novel about the feud with Jacob, he had left *Nord-Sud* in the hands of—who else but Jacob?[33] So it was that Jacob composed the editorial chronicle of the June–July issue, including notices of Apollinaire's lecture and of *Les Mamelles*.[34] His tone was impertinent, to say the least. About the lecture, he wrote: "Let no one reproach me for having missed the lecture by our dear and admirable poet Guillaume Apollinaire; I was playing hopscotch all day Saturday on the Rue Simon-Deureux and lost track of time. The concierge of number 12 told me the poet had been, by turns, witty, lyrical, biting, tragic, noble, gallant, ironic, eloquent, wise, tender, well-informed."[35] He took a more serious approach to *Les Mamelles*, complimenting his friend on his lyric burlesque, though not without his usual pirouettes: "Lyricism is neither attitude nor beatitude."

Jacob had sung in the chorus of *Les Mamelles*, and his poem "Périgal-Nohor" was printed in the program for the play. *Les Mamelles* was to be a "manifestation" of the new arts, and Jacob supported it. He was bitterly surprised, therefore, a few days after the performance, when he dropped in at the Café de la Rotonde and was assailed by reproaches: *he* was responsible for the flop of the play; *he* had "let Apollinaire put on his play in order to triumph at his defeat"; *he* "only praised Apollinaire in order to injure him."[36] Jacob rushed over to the Café Flore to warn Apollinaire of the rumors. Apollinaire, not surprisingly, took it very ill. He would be even more affronted when a letter of protest signed by a group of minor Cubists and, unfortunately, by Juan Gris, appeared in *Le Pays* on June 29. The painters declared that their "plastic researches" had nothing to do with "certain theatrical and literary fantasies." Apollinaire ended his friendship with Gris over this incident.[37]

Jacob had given an excellent poem to honor *Les Mamelles*. "Périgal-Nohor," entitled simply "Poem" in the program, came out also in the summer issue of *Nord-Sud*. Characteristically, it mingles traditional metrics and free verse, with irregular punctuation, clashing registers of diction, daffy allusions, puns, and clichés. It concludes:

> There was something vegetal about the sea
> In block letters laboriously I trace
> I'll always be a schoolboy in this art
> Scholar foolscap collar we wear a crown that glows
> The one who receives is worth him who bestows.[38]

The lace *coiffes*, the sailboats, and the cathedral lend a Breton tinge to the vision. In the cross-gendering of names (Madame Mirabeau, Madame Mirabelle), Jacob hints, as so often, at ambiguous sexuality. But above all, the poem celebrates poetry in its blend of humility ("I'll always be a schoolboy in this art") and the pride that turns a schoolboy's collar into a crown. Throughout, the poem balances the exalted and the lowly: azure against market share, imaginary castles against hedges, treasure against coal tar, crown against a school collar. Jacob's poetry always contains both.

IV.

THE UNITED STATES entered the war on April 6, 1917, but it would be months before the declaration translated into tangible force. In May, Apollinaire's boyhood friend, René Dalize, was killed in battle, and in July,

Jean-Richard Bloch was wounded yet again. In August, Jacob sheltered for eight days a young Breton soldier who claimed to be on leave. With his typical generosity, Jacob wrote Doucet about the young man's plight, to which Doucet responded with *his* typical generosity, sending a handout. Not long after the guest's departure, two policemen turned up at Jacob's door and informed him that he was guilty of "harboring a deserter": he spent the day explaining himself to the commissioner of police, testifying and pleading. He risked six months of prison, he complained to the art dealer André Level. But his postscript was cheerful: "Do you know, I'm selling my paintings like little buns before the war."[39]

Paris seemed empty in the summer and early fall of 1917, with Jacob's friends either wounded, fighting in the trenches, or away, Picasso in Spain, Braque at Sorgues. In late August, Apollinaire joined Irène Lagut and her occasional lover the redheaded Ruby Kolb on their vacation in Brittany; Richardson speculates that they may have entertained a *ménage à trois,* but in any case, Apollinaire would soon be engaged to Ruby Kolb, also called Jacqueline, who would become "la jolie rousse" in his famous poem.[40] On his way back to Paris, Apollinaire stopped in Quimper and visited Madame Jacob at the family store; she was flattered by the attention of this decorated military officer, "with such fine bearing."[41] Jacob wrote Henri Hertz that Paris was "an enjoyable vacation spot" because all his friends were away and he could work; he described his articles for *Nord-Sud* and the chronicles for Doucet, and he sketched the idea for a novel about a stolen watch that would turn into *Filibuth, ou la montre en or.*[42] He spent part of each day painting since the dealer Georges Aubry was now selling his gouaches. He wrote Picasso that he saw almost no one, just Gris and Reverdy from time to time. (Reverdy had finished his novel *Le Voleur de Talan.* Adrienne Monnier carried it in her bookstore; it's not clear when Jacob read it, though he must have seen it by early November, when he wrote Cocteau that he didn't want to be around Reverdy.)[43] In mid-August, Jacob and Salmon served as official witnesses to Kisling's wedding with the painter Renée Gros, but Jacob decorously abstained from the three-day orgy of drinking and dancing that followed the ceremony.[44]

||

IN THE RELATIVELY quiet period leading up to *Le Cornet à dés*, Jacob's heart was engaged with two unattainable young men: Jean Paulhan and the composer Alexis Roland-Manuel. In his letters to both he exercises his powers of seduction. He could hardly have hoped for a romantic liaison with Paulhan, a married military officer training soldiers from Madagascar in the South of France; Jacob's letters to him mingle literary criticism with expressions of affection that stay just within the bounds of epistolary correctness.

With Roland-Manuel he allowed himself to go further. Roland-Manuel was Jewish: his real name was Roland Alexis Manuel Lévy. His wife, Suzanne, a pianist, was a cousin by marriage of the young Michel Leiris, who would come to occupy an important place in Jacob's imagination. The fact of Roland-Manuel's being married didn't prevent Jacob from bringing out the heavy artillery of his charm. Roland-Manuel had set a poem of Jacob's to music, and he and Jacob now played with the idea of collaborating on an operetta (which they did indeed complete: *Isabelle et Pantalon*, performed in 1922). Jacob's letters to the composer are fireworks: erotic insinuation, hyperbolic protestations of friendship, and stylistic flourishes in the voices of other writers. On September 17 he donned the costume of the fin-de-siècle aesthete Barbey d'Aurevilly, capering through allusions to Victor Hugo: "You are my superb and generous lion" (*Hernani*, Act 5, sc. 3). "I love you and I'm dying of it," the letter concludes, with this postscript: "Give my regards to your noble parents and to your powerful and charming wife."[45]

The letters to Roland-Manuel suggest something about Jacob's literary style, like his improvisations at parties, an art of mimicry designed to express love and to seduce while at the same time veiling desire. He joked about his desires: "What a shame that *The Imitation* forbids 'inordinate affections'! I'm obliged to forbid myself the feelings I have for you, but also, what refined joy there is in this struggle with oneself."[46] In the blend of erotic and religious impulses that would characterize his relations with young men in the years to come, he prays for Manuel's conversion at the same time as he almost confesses to passion.[47]

||

LONG AWAITED, LONG delayed, the unillustrated version of *Le Cornet à dés* was finally published in October 1917. At first it didn't inspire much of a response, as Jacob noted stoically to Picasso.[48] But as weeks passed and the version with Picasso's 1915 drawing came out, reviewers began to praise the book, and its fame spread until a year later Jacob's little room on the Rue Gabrielle became, in Gabory's phrase, the Poetic Grand Central Station of the century. In that dusky room Gabory met the soon-to-be-famous writers Raymond Radiguet, Antonin Artaud, and André Malraux; he also found there the young men who would go on to found Surrealism: André Breton, Philippe Soupault, and especially Louis Aragon, who wrote a roman à clef called *Anicet ou le panorama* celebrating Jacob in the figure of the ascetic mystic Jean Chipre.[49]

Though the title, *The Dice Cup*, suggests the operation of chance, there was nothing accidental about the book's arrangement. On the contrary: Jacob gathered his dice poems from the little magazines, art chronicles, and notebooks into a rigorous composition, an order even more visible in the first edition's division of the first section into five parts.[50] In his longer preface, Jacob insisted on the conscious nature of composition. (He had been refining this preface since 1914 and had not cobbled it together at the last moment to preempt Reverdy as the latter angrily supposed.)[51] If his book courted randomness in the throw of its dice, it was in the radical methods of juxtaposition, within poems and between poems: a reordering of conventions of narrative, diction, logic of association, and argument. The book's power derives, at least in part, from the deep coherence under-girding its superficial disorder.

The reader is ushered into the volume through the first six poems concerned with the war, preceded by a "Notice" professing wartime earnestness.[52] The war glimpsed here is subjective, nightmarish, oblique, grotesque, and even, at moments, funny, as in "Fausses nouvelles! Fosses nouvelles!" (False News, New Graves!), whose punning title Jacob took from a headline in the newspaper *Paris-Journal* from July 1914.[53] "False news" appropriately describes Jacob's prose poems since the declared subject is never the real subject in these experiments in poetic abstraction: all news is false news. For these parodies of a multitude of genres—newspaper articles, Romantic lyrics, political rhetoric, crime novels, advertisements— what is really at stake is a new method of seeing represented in a new method of literary composition. "Poem," originally entitled "Poem in the Form of a Tangled Ball of Thread," gives a good example.

> It's hailing on the sea; night is falling. "Light the bull-lighthouse beam!"
>
> The old courtesan has died at the inn: everyone's laughing in the house.
>
> It's hailing and they're showing a film to the sailors in the schoolroom.
>
> The teacher has a fine face. Here I am in the country: two men are watching the bull beam shining.
>
> "Here you are, finally!" the teacher says to me. "Are you going to take notes during the film? The little bunch of assistant teachers can make room for you at the table."
>
> "Notes? What notes should I take? On the subjects of the film?"
>
> "No! You'll compress the rhythms of the film and the falling hail and also the laughter of everyone present at the death of the old courtesan to get an idea of purgatory."[54]

Jacob took from film not sequence but rather something like its opposite: film's power to juxtapose, rapidly, different scenes and images: montage. What matters is the rejection of subject matter: "What notes should I take? On the subjects of the film?"—in favor of an abstract method of composition: "No! You'll compress the rhythms of the film."[55] And as the mention of purgatory suggests, the poem insinuates a religious revelation.

Many titles in the 1917 edition, later simplified, gesture toward Jacob's conception of his dice poems as art objects that could be apprehended not in time but "simultaneously" in space: "Simultaneous Poem with Simple Superposition," or "Simultaneous Poem with Two Mobile Rollers."[56] Some of the poems style themselves as works of visual art: painting, sculpture, or film. One untitled piece reflects Jacob's long observation of Picasso at work: "When you paint a painting, at each touch, it entirely changes; it turns like a cylinder and it seems almost interminable. When it stops turning, it's finished. My last one represented a Tower of Babel as lit candles."[57]

But like Picasso's paintings, Jacob's poems are never entirely abstract. However obliquely, they depict his deep concerns. At a most obvious level, they distinguish themselves from literary forebears with titles like "Poem in a Taste That Is Not My Own" dedicated "to you, Rimbaud," or "to you, Baudelaire": the allusions propose not an "anxiety" of influence but a modernist thematics of influence acknowledged and rejected.[58] A more secret thread traces an obsession with the crossing of gender: the title of "Sir Elisabeth (Pronounce 'Soeur')" makes no secret of the game, but many other poems flip between male and female and vice versa.[59] The theme of the police recurs just as often, often in the poems of ambiguous sexuality.

Unlike the religious verse poems of *La Défense de Tartufe* and *Le Laboratoire central,* the prose poems present mystical experience only by implication. Yet mysticism infuses the whole volume. Jacob disintegrates literary and social conventions and the idea of a socially coherent self to reintegrate his part-Kabbalistic, part-Christian ecstatic sense of supranormal realities: "Mystery is in this life, reality in the other; if you love me, if you love me, I'll show you reality."[60] Such experience, for Jacob, is never entirely detached from the erotic. Nor is it detached from suffering: "As I came down the Rue de Rennes, I bit my bread with so much emotion I thought it was my own heart I was tearing open."[61] Jacob had been composing self-portraits in his prose chronicles for Doucet, but his most accurate self-portrait for this period is to be found in *Le Cornet à dés.*

He had already published his ideas about the prose poem in his attack on Reverdy in *291.* Now he consolidated those ideas in the preface he entitled

"Preface of 1916" (to distinguish it from his one-paragraph "Preface of 1906," an attack on Rimbaud's "exaltations").[62] Jacob announced the modern prose poem as an artifact of a new classicism, an art of deliberate stylization: his poetry drew material from the unconscious but was consciously constructed. The famous first sentence of the main preface declared, "Everything that exists is situated."[63] He went on to develop two related ideas, "situation" and "style." By the situation of the poem, he meant the margin that distanced it from real life: "The work of art must be detached from its subject. That's why it must be *situated*."[64] By "style," he meant the "handling of the medium" that created the separation between the person of the author, and the created work. His defense of an antimimetic art sounds like Reverdy's statements in *Nord-Sud:* "A work of art is significant in itself and not through comparison with reality."[65] But he distinguished himself from Reverdy in repelling Romantic and Symbolist predecessors. The Jacobian prose poem discarded Aloysius Bertrand's vignettes and Baudelairean and Mallarmean parables, as it disdained Baudelairean "surprise" and Rimbaud's "exaltations." "To surprise is easy; one must transplant."[66] In an odd way, Jacob's theory of impersonality and his attack on Romanticism overlapped with Eliot's espousal of literary impersonality in "Tradition and the Individual Talent," published two years later.

JACOB'S OLD FRIEND Louis de Gonzague Frick wrote one of the first reviews of *Le Cornet à dés*. In the December issue of *SIC*, Frick insisted on the personal element Jacob wanted to excise, evoking Jacob as astrologer, magus, and "one of the seven sages of the Hill of Montmartre."[67] But on the whole, though blind to the originality of the book, his review welcomed it. A far more controversial account appeared in a book at just the same time. In *The Young French Poetry: Men and Trends*, the journalist Frédéric Lefèvre demonstrated stunning ignorance of his subject, celebrating the wispy *vers libre* of Vildrac and devoting the bulk of its pages to the versifiers Vincent Muselli and Adolphe Lacuzon. His final chapter, "Literary Cubism," appalled the poets whose work it discussed. Lefèvre had been snooping around Paris, pestering Reverdy, Jacob, Apollinaire, and others for interviews, and now he produced a philistine assault on all the new poetry. He admitted outright that Reverdy and Apollinaire disputed the concept of "Cubist poetry." This made no difference to Lefèvre, who plunged ahead quoting poems out of context and deriding the new school.

Jacob excited Lefèvre's particular venom. The portrait, not untainted by anti-Semitism, occupied more than two pages: "Max Jacob is the deacon of the new Chapel. . . . His hands are as pudgy as you like and polished with leisure; in a slight deviation of ancestral adaptation, they no longer reach out with cautious rapidity to palpate precious objects and evaluate bibelots, but they stretch forth seeking friendship."[68] After a scornful description of Jacob's conversion, Lefèvre concluded in terms calculated to inflame resentment: "He has renewed—excuse me—created the prose poem. . . . At least, so he claims; and of his two students, one, Paul Dermée, confirms it; the other, Pierre Reverdy, claims the same paternity for himself."[69]

But in the appendix, Lefèvre's book doubled back on itself. When he wrote it, he had just received the proofs of Le Cornet à dés, and he seems to have been won over by Jacob's work in spite of himself. Instead of revising his nasty earlier chapter, he simply tacked on the incoherent appendix in which he admired the "marvelous intellectual discovery" of Jacob's title, and after calling the preface unnecessary, he proceeded to quote from it extensively, stating, "In our era, Max Jacob seems to have deeply understood the prose poem," and calling him "everyone's master."[70]

Reverdy was incensed. In Le Voleur de Talan he had just published a subtle account of his poetic exchanges with Jacob; now he saw himself publicly humiliated as Jacob's "student" and his work violently misrepresented. No review of Le Cornet would appear in Nord-Sud. Instead, in December, Reverdy denounced the vile book by "M. Frédéric Narcisse."[71] Though Lefèvre had presented a most disobliging portrait of Jacob, what Reverdy retained, of course, was the appendix; years later he said that Lefèvre's book was part of Jacob's revenge and that "Jacob had snookered poor Lefèvre to make him say that Jacob was everyone's master and in every genre."[72]

V.

IN 1918 THE Germans began bombarding the city with new long-range cannons and bombs from airplanes and zeppelins, at first only at night, but starting March 23, during the day as well. On Good Friday, March 29, a bomb shattered the Church of Saint-Gervais, killing seventy-five people. On the night of June 15–16 bombs destroyed Gompel's department store.[73] Jacob wrote Roland-Manuel describing his fear during a bombardment at night: he had had dinner with Henri and Emma Hertz, and at dessert, "the champagne was uncorked one hundred and twenty kilometers from Paris, or rather, right on top of Paris." While the rest of the party took refuge in the cellar, Jacob walked home, wandering the eerie streets in an artificial mist that smelled of garlic, while overhead the sky exploded with fireworks, and hoodlums scurried in the shadows, laughing. It gave him a clear conception of hell.[74] Jacob was so frightened of an invasion that he memorized a sentence in German he intended to pronounce, if attacked, while clinging to the gate of Sacré-Coeur: "Lassen sie mich, Herr General, ich bin ein armer Dichter!" (Spare me, Sir General, I am a poor poet!)[75]

Horrors accelerated. On March 15 the Turkish minister of war ordered the extermination of all Armenians over the age of five, and a few days later the Germans renewed a furious offensive on the Western Front, pushing the British Fifth Army almost to the Atlantic. Only at the end of April did the landing of American divisions begin to make a difference. Bread was rationed, coal was scarce. Yet in Paris the arts continued to thrive. On January 23, Paul Guillaume opened a show of Picasso and Matisse, and by the end of the month the deluxe editions of *Le Cornet à dés* with Picasso's etching of a Harlequin finally appeared. Jacob planned new publications: he began circulating subscription bulletins for his 1906 novel *Le Phanérogame,* and Picasso promised an etching for this book too. By August, Jacob was negotiating with the Société Littéraire de France for the commercial publication of the book he would come to call *La Défense de Tartufe.*[76]

||

PICASSO, LONG ABSENT with the Ballets Russes, had been back in Paris since late November, staying at his house in Montrouge while Olga, now his fiancée, resided at the elegant Hôtel Lutetia. But Jacob and Picasso continued to correspond, especially now that they lived at such a distance from each other. The distance was not only geographical: though Picasso continued to help his old friend with etchings for his books and would invite him to be one of the witnesses at his wedding, he was increasingly drawn into a wider social sphere. Jacob nursed the friendship with gifts of tobacco—difficult to come by in wartime—and with hilarious anecdotes. One involved a visit with Roland-Manuel to the composer's father-in-law, a director in the Ministry of Agriculture in the Office of the Suppression of Frauds, a man of imposing integrity, such integrity, Jacob discovered, that on his desk a large notebook entitled "Suppression of Fraud" was empty, and he offered them expensive cigars and liqueur, goods confiscated by the customs office.[77] Less amusing was Jacob's account of meeting his elderly cousin Sylvain Lévi on the Rue Bonaparte. The street was empty, and the two men passed, pretending not to see each other.[78]

If Jacob pretended not to recognize the old professor, he was much taken by the new novel *Et Cie* (And Co) by Lévi's nephew, Jean-Richard Bloch. A signal advance over Bloch's earlier stories, *Et Cie* narrates the saga of a family of Jewish immigrants from Germany in the mid-nineteenth century establishing themselves as minor industrialists in France. "It's the only accurate depiction of a Jewish family and it's full of intelligence and taste," Jacob wrote Paulhan.[79] To Bloch, who had been horribly wounded the previous July—his third wound in battle—Jacob wrote shyly in March, sending him a copy of *Le Cornet* and confessing that he hadn't dared write to him earlier, ashamed of being a civilian when his cousins were in the line of fire.[80]

||

THE SPRING OF 1918 brought gratifying reviews of *Le Cornet*. Henri Vandeputte called Jacob "a rich and profound soul who pours out upon the startled mind, as from a magician's cup, a thousand multicolored papers and transparent doves."[81] In the first issue of Paul Guillaume's *Les Arts à Paris*, Apollinaire pronounced that "M. Max Jacob has produced his most important book so far. In it his inspiration is infinitely varied, from irony to lyricism, blended surprisingly in his prose poems."[82] Paulhan published an enthusiastic review in *La Vie*, despite having been hospitalized with malaria and pneumonia.

IN MARCH, REVERDY brought out one of his most beautiful books, *Les Ardoises du toit* (Roof Slates), with drawings by Braque; it was followed in April by Apollinaire's *Calligrammes*, an uneven assortment of lyrics of love and war, enlivened by typographical picture-poems, or *calligrammes*, and by some truly memorable pieces, including "The Windows" celebrating Robert Delaunay, and "La Jolie Rousse." The two books produced something of a joust. Reverdy must have been pleased by Aragon's intelligent praise in *SIC:* he called Reverdy the poet of the negative, of the conditional mood, and of night.[83] But the days of Reverdy's idealization of Apollinaire had long passed. He now cultivated friendships with younger poets and expressed exasperation at Apollinaire's pretensions, writing to Paulhan, "Apollinaire suffers himself to be adored from 6 p.m. on in the restaurants of Montmartre." His irritation spilled over into new suspicions of Jacob: "This setting sun [Apollinaire] needs to gild his uniform, and it's at the feet of this new golden calf that Jacob serves mass."[84]

Apollinaire was too busy being Apollinaire to bother with Reverdy's pique. On May 2 he married Jacqueline Kolb at the Église Saint-Thomas-d'Aquin, attended only by Picasso, the journalist Lucien Descaves, Vollard, and Gabrielle Buffet, Picabia's wife. Weeks sped by, and on July 12, Jacob's real birthday, Picasso and Olga Khokhlova were married in the town hall of the seventh arrondissement, with Apollinaire and Jacob as witnesses for the groom, and for the bride, Cocteau and a Russian colonel. A religious ceremony followed in the Russian church, after which the party went for lunch to the Hôtel Meurice. Two weeks later Misia Sert treated the new couple to an elegant meal with Jacob, Apollinaire, Cocteau, and Henri Simon, a minister in colonial affairs; and two days later the newlyweds were off to Biarritz for a prolonged honeymoon.[85]

||

ONLY IN LATE July did the advantage in the fighting swing to the Allies. Finally united under the command of Foch, and strengthened by reinforcements from the United States, Canada, Australia, and the colonies, the Allies threw the Germans off balance on the Marne on July 18 and forced them back to the Somme on August 8–12. In late September, Foch opened his grand assault on the Western Front. To the southeast, Bulgaria surrendered on September 29, the Ottoman Empire on October 30.

Dodging bombardments in Paris, Jacob bustled to secure funds to publish *Le Phanérogame* and corrected proofs for it; he was also preparing the book that would become *La Défense de Tartufe* and, in October, scrambling to put *Cinématoma* in shape for publication. A publisher for it had suddenly appeared, Éditions de La Sirène, founded by Paul Lafitte with Cocteau and Cendrars.[86] In late October and early November, Jacob announced to both Picasso and Paulhan that La Sirène had asked him for a manuscript and that he was in a flurry to finish six years of work in six weeks.[87] (At first he hesitated about the terms offered, and Cocteau had to persuade him.)[88] With the help of Antonio de Barrau, Jacob was also polishing a translation of the medieval Catalan mystic known in France as Raymond Lulle, *The Book of the Lover and the Beloved*, erotic-spiritual canticles that would influence his own poetry. He continued the chronicles of the wandering watch for Doucet though his contract with that patron was concluding.

Another ending came with the closing of *Nord-Sud* in November. Worn out by aesthetic battles, poverty, anger, and depression, Reverdy stopped publishing the journal. But two greater endings now loomed. Apollinaire, who had been confidently stage-managing the arts in Paris, happy in his new marriage and in his new position at the newspaper *Excelsior,* was suddenly struck by the Spanish flu. Picasso and Jacob, his old companions, had Cocteau send his own doctor, but it was too late. Struggling to breathe, Apollinaire insisted, "Above all, don't tell my mother! I want to die in peace!"[89]

Apollinaire died in the afternoon of November 9, the day Kaiser Wilhelm abdicated. The poet's stunned friends and his widow kept vigil by his corpse. Austria had already surrendered, and on November 11 at five a.m. in Foch's railroad car, the Germans accepted defeat. The armistice was proclaimed. Paris exploded in a wild ringing of church bells, and joyous crowds thronged the streets shouting "À bas Guillaume!"— Down with Wilhelm, the Kaiser. Picasso, Jacob, and Salmon looked at one another in horror. Jacob wrote René Fauchois, "I keep watch each night over what remains of him. We've spent enough hours laughing together for me to spend a few next to him, weeping. . . . Neither the success of my friends nor the triumph of glorious France can revive in me what this death has forever blighted. I didn't know until now how much he was 'my life.' "[90] Something was broken inside, Jacob felt; it was almost as if some part of him had died. To the journalist Gaston Picard, who had asked him for an article of reminiscence, he replied that he couldn't write briefly about a man who, with Picasso, had reigned over him for years.[91]

Yet Jacob could not avoid complicated feelings about Apollinaire. As he had at other funerals, he made a spectacle of himself as the cortège wound its way to the Père Lachaise cemetery. Death brought out the carnival spirit in him. As one of the principal mourners, walking beside Salmon with Picasso just behind them, he imitated the voices of the old days at the Entrepôt Voltaire and the Bateau Lavoir, and he inspired hysterical laughter by pronouncing funeral orations for all of Apollinaire's living friends.[92] The day after the death, he wrote Salmon, "I beg God's forgiveness because I'm not grieving." Josette Gris remembered him saying, as they followed the coffin, "And now, I'll be the leader!"[93] Jacob would mourn, celebrate, and resent Apollinaire for the rest of his life. He recognized in him a true lyric poet. Years later, in *Chronique des temps héroïques,* he saluted his old friend: "I saw the sublime Guillaume Apollinaire agitated, like the human sibyls: he rocked back and forth, blushed, wept, sang, exclaimed, and drew mysterious figures. I recognized you, O Moon, when I recognized, in these mysterious figures of the Inspired One, the same signs with which magicians call to angels and demons. And he, Apollinaire, was amazed, laughed, and studied them. Golden moon, here is the finest of your sons."[94]

CHAPTER 12

THE STRUGGLE FOR THE AVANT-GARDE

I.

Military peace did not bring peace to the arts. The years immediately following the Great War would see the final spasms of Cubism and the brutal rivalry of two new avant-garde groups, each claiming more radical credentials than the other: Dada and Surrealism. Cocteau solidified his reputation in rapid-fire publications and theatrical productions. Emerging from Dada, the Surrealists did their best to eliminate competitors: Cocteau, Dada, and eventually Max Jacob. Kahnweiler returned from exile in Switzerland and started up his gallery again from scratch, since the French government had sequestered his entire stock and he had to woo the artists back from other dealers. What was at stake was nothing less than the legacy and future of Modernism, torn between Reverdy's austere aestheticism, Jacob and Cocteau's playful pluralism, the nihilism of Dada, and the prophetic claims of Surrealism. For Max Jacob, the years 1919–21 traced an arc from hope to bitter disappointment.

HE WAS STILL living in his room on the Rue Gabrielle on the ground floor at the back of the courtyard. A tall wardrobe with a full-length mirror divided the chamber, with the sleeping nook in the rear and the working and living space in front: the mirror faced outward, to the courtyard. Guests were invited to sit in the faded red velvet armchair or on two chairs with fraying straw seats; if those were taken, they perched on the table or lounged against the wall. Jacob had his "central laboratory" at the large table; here in the litter of manuscripts, cigarette butts, pastels, and tubes of gouache he composed his poems, tales, plays, and paintings. On the wall he had scrawled in large letters, "Never go to Montparnasse!"[1] He went out a good deal, sometimes to Montparnasse or to visit Prince and Princesse Ghika in Saint-Germain-en-Laye, or to readings, art openings, and theater, or to the cafés and restaurants of Montmartre, especially the Savoyarde, where he held court. Each morning he rose early to attend mass at Sacré-Coeur, returning down the street humming a canticle. As he entered the courtyard, the tiny crippled woman who lived above him, a professional beggar, hollered, "Fine goings-on! Sacré-Coeur in the morning, orgies at night!"[2]

December 1918 set the stage for literary dramas that would play out in Paris for the next few years. Tzara, in Zurich, brought out the Dada Manifesto, and it reverberated in the French capital; though Tzara and his friends had learned from the prewar avant-garde movements, their celebration of mayhem and contradiction made Cubism look like classicism and Futurism like a form of idiot optimism. "We shred the linens of clouds and prayers like a furious wind, preparing the great spectacle of disaster, fire, decomposition. . . . DADA MEANS NOTHING."[3] To these young people revolted by the war and by the corruptions that had produced it, only a clean sweep of all previous art and philosophy would suffice.

In France, André Breton was brooding his way toward a new poetry. Aged twenty-three, from a modest family, he had been a medical student and soldier for the last three years; he had worked as a stretcher bearer at Verdun and as an intern at several military hospitals. Adrienne Monnier, who ran the bookstore La Maison des Amis des Livres, described him as beautiful as an archangel, with his "massive" head, his hair thrown nobly back, and his stern gaze the color of jade.[4] His friend Aragon celebrated him in his autobiographical novel, *Anicet ou le panorama, roman*, as Baptiste Ajamais, a commanding figure with "his steely gaze, his proud lip."[5] Having just lost his idealized friend the dandy-nihilist Jacques Vaché to an overdose of opium in January 1919, Breton wrote immediately to Tzara in Zurich, in a sense inviting him to take Vaché's place, and for three years he made common cause with Dada until his search for meaningful (rather than meaningless) revolution took shape as Surrealism.[6]

Max Jacob occupied an ambiguous position for these radical young writers. On the one hand, and especially since the publication of *Le Cornet à dés*, he represented a force of renovation and subversion of official culture. On the other, he was already an elder and, as such, suspect; all the more suspect since his conversion to Catholicism. For now, the young writers courted him. Breton—who had befriended Apollinaire and Reverdy, and in other moods the classicist poet Paul Valéry—was intrigued by Jacob and in the beginning welcomed his contributions to *Littérature*, the journal he started in March 1919. But he always held him at arm's length. Louis Aragon, however, Breton's comrade at the Hôpital Val-de-Grâce and co-editor with Philippe Soupault of *Littérature*, visited Jacob often and for a time considered him a guru. In *Anicet* he cast Jacob as Jean Chipre (a version of Jacob's Christian name, Cyprien). Chipre is a mystic and a figure of exemplary poverty; some of his statements come right out of the preface to *Le Cornet à dés:* "Poverty, purity. Riches in art are called bad taste. A poem is not the display window of a jewelry shop."[7] Anicet, the Aragon character, is tempted by this sacrificial vision, but the exchange is interrupted by the arrival of the painter Bleu, a cruel caricature of Picasso, who lights an expensive cigar, announcing, "I am glory."[8]

In Jacob's room Georges Gabory met other ambitious young literary men, Raymond Radiguet, Antonin Artaud, and André Malraux, and Breton and Aragon in their sky-blue medical-military uniforms, Breton "solemn, important, pinched and dogmatic, Aragon arrogant, insolent."[9] Aragon read aloud the first chapter of *Anicet*, and Breton recited the poems he would publish later that year in his book *Mont de Piété* (Pawn Shop).

At this stage, André Breton wobbled like a compass needle between opposing literary magnetic poles. At age eighteen, just before the war, the intelligent, intransigent young man had written to Valéry, and the elder poet had generously guided him, offering him an exquisite literary education. But attracted though he was to Valéry's classicism, Breton was increasingly drawn to Rimbaud and to the sadistic *Chants de Maldoror* of Isidore Ducasse, the fictive Comte de Lautréamont, and now he was experimenting with Dada. Smelted in the furnace of war, Breton embodied his era and its contradictions: fiercely rational, he pursued techniques of the irrational (hypnosis, psychoanalysis, automatic writing); contemptuous of art, he sought forms for new art; resistant to authority, he imposed his will on others and had a genius for organizing. Flirting with nihilism, he sought revelation. Even at this stage, Gabory reports, his friends nicknamed him "Vladimir Ilitch" (Lenin).[10]

In 1919, Breton imagined he could rally the old and new literary avant-gardes in the pages of a single journal. *La Nouvelle Revue française* had ceased appearing during the war and wouldn't resume until June; Reverdy's *Nord-Sud* had folded; *SIC* and *L'Élan* were flimsy. The field lay open. In January, Henri Cliquennois invited Breton to join him in running the journal *Les Jeunes Lettres*. It's typical of Breton that he translated this invitation into a take-over, writing to Aragon, "We're thinking of invading the journal *Les Jeunes Lettres* and rechristening it. . . . Contributors will include Gide, Valéry, Larbaud, Fargue, Royère, Spire, Salmon, Billy, Max Jacob, Reverdy, Tzara, Mireille Havet, Paulhan, Giraudoux, Morand, Drieu La Rochelle, Philippe [Soupault], you, and me."[11] The list reads like a map of literary Paris; with the exception of Proust and Claudel, it includes the key writers of the period and shows not only the breadth of Breton's taste at this point but also his cunning: famous elders from *La Nouvelle Revue française* and the old days of Symbolism would attract readers to the young authors. Breton even invited Cocteau to contribute, though he loathed him.[12] The list also reveals the masculine character of French letters: the only woman, Mireille Havet, was a songwriter and an open lesbian, and so was allowed a place.

Breton's personal magnetism and the complexity of his aesthetics at this stage may be measured in his relations with Reverdy. Embittered at having had to close *Nord-Sud*, jealous of Jacob, and infuriated by the upstart Cocteau, Reverdy expressed his vision of the corrupted avant-garde in *Les Jockeys camouflés* (The Camouflaged Jockeys), a collection of poems he published in 1918. In free-floating *vers libres*, the poem "The Mechanical Jockeys" imagined a cavalcade of robot horses clattering across the sky, leaving behind nothing but darkness. The following poem, "Other

Jockeys, Alcoholic," presents a caricature of Max Jacob with false teeth, accompanied by another drunk jockey, perhaps Cocteau.[13] In August 1918, Breton, who loved making lists and ranking artists and writers, included Reverdy among his heroes: Rimbaud, Picasso, Braque, Derain, Jarry, Lautréamont . . .[14] Breton admired Reverdy's integrity, and for a while the sensitive southerner thought he had found a responsive soul and maybe even an acolyte. He was soon disabused.[15]

THE FIRST ISSUE of *Littérature* appeared in March with pieces by Gide and Valéry, a majestic opening. Salmon contributed a war poem of a certain journalistic freshness, followed by Jacob's "La Rue Ravignan," a love letter to the old Bateau Lavoir. Implicitly, the poem acknowledged a graceful kinship between two generations of Modernists. After the first two lines spoken by God, the poem takes up in verse an image Jacob had used in a prose poem in *Le Cornet a dés*, a burning house as a rose on a peacock's tail:

> To pester my Son at the hour when all repose
> To consider a hurt you think is trivial?
> The burning house is like a rose
> Open in the gray peacock's spreading tail.
> I owe you all, my sorrows and my joys.

The poem ends tenderly, evoking the days of youthful inspiration:

> L'impasse de Guelma has its corregidors
> And the Rue Caulaincourt its dealers in art
> But the Rue Ravignan is the one I adore
> For my standard-bearers' interwoven hearts.
> There, cutting designs in my beloved gems,
> My greatest faults were those in my own poems.[16]

The issue concluded with lyrical evocations by Aragon of Tzara's *vingt-cinq poèmes* and Reverdy's *Les Jockeys camouflés* and, to indicate the aesthetic position of the new venture, a review of other journals: insult to the fuddy-duddy *Mercure de France,* admiration for *Les Écrits nouveaux* (which carried Breton's essay on Jarry), and celebration of Tzara's Dada Manifesto. The final statement demonstrates Breton's strategy of containing explosive new art within the framework of the old, somehow flattering and threatening in the same breath: "We are happy to announce the forthcoming appearance under the direction of M. André Gide of *La Nouvelle Revue française,* the prewar journal that won the most esteem in the world of letters."[17] This synthesis of old and new would not last long.

II.

RAYMOND RADIGUET WAS still a schoolboy in the Lycée Charlemagne in Paris when he met André Salmon while delivering his father's drawings to the newspaper where Salmon worked as an editor. At fifteen, Radiguet was strikingly handsome, with a "Greco-Buddhist" face, proud straight nose, full lips, tousled hair, and sulky expression.[18] He was also strikingly gifted. Albert-Birot had already printed his poems in *SIC,* and Tzara had published him in *Dada.* He lived with his family in a suburb of Paris and took the train into the city for school. Salmon introduced him to Max Jacob, who took him up immediately, though probably not in a romantic sense. They seem to have met by February 1919, and within days they were using first names and addressing one another with the familiar *tu.*[19] In June, Radiguet joined other poets in a celebration of Apollinaire at Léonce Rosenberg's gallery, and there Cocteau caught sight of the young prodigy. A few days later Jacob sent the boy to call on Cocteau at 10 rue d'Anjou, where Cocteau lived with his mother, and from that encounter grew one of the most intense infatuations of Cocteau's life. Years later Jacob told Marcel Béalu, "One can't tell the truth. . . . I've been asked recently for memories of Radiguet. What do you want me to say? Radiguet was a young man whom X, I, and others killed. That's the truth."[20]

In 1918, Radiguet saw Georges Gabory almost every day. Just a few years older, Gabory was publishing his harmless poems in *SIC* and was close to Aragon, Cocteau, Jacob, Gide, and Malraux. From his memoirs, one gets a sense of the fluid sexual mores in this milieu. At fourteen, Radiguet had had an affair with a young married woman, "Alice," whose husband was off at war; the boy was said to have treated her callously, and Salmon found himself in the position of trying to comfort her.[21] Radiguet would use her as a model for the character of Marthe in his novel *Le Diable au corps* (The Devil in the Flesh), a story very like theirs narrated with chilling clarity. Gabory was having an affair with—in fact, was living in Montmartre with—a considerably older woman he called Irma, whom he had met through Max Jacob. But both young men were also, in their different fashions, attracted to men. To the distress of his parents, Radiguet would soon be carrying on in a very public way with Cocteau, who spirited him off to nightclubs, aristocratic parties, and the Côte d'Azur. (Radiguet continued, however, to have flings with women, including the much older Beatrice Hastings and the sexual sophisticate Irène Lagut.)

Gabory's sexuality seems even more complicated, and his remarkably frank account sheds light on Jacob's erotic life and on the culture of semicloseted Parisian homosexuality. Gabory objected that he would never have submitted to "the appalling Carlos" (Vautrin) of Balzac's novel *Splendeurs et misères des courtisanes* (Splendor and Misery of Courtesans) when Jacob facetiously called him by the hero's name, Lucien de Rubempré. "I'm too feminine, I preferred women," declared Gabory. "A lesbian, Uncle André [Gide], the great virile Doric [Greek] would have said, in his journal, not yet published at that period; before having read it, I had already intuited my own nature. Everyone has his own way of being homosexual."[22]

When Gabory took up with the erotically voracious Irma, Jacob "pardoned" him: after all, it was he who had introduced them. But the older writer held to a subtle code of homosexual loyalty. Once, when Gabory permitted himself "a smile a little too 'hetero' about the behavior of a friend," Max said in a pinched tone, "we know very well you're 'not a member of the club,' you!"[23] And Gabory described a scene of attempted seduction by Jacob. In his memoir, it comes right after the episode of Jacob converting his irreligious young friend and serving as godfather at his baptism in the little church of Saint-Pierre-de-Montmartre, a ritual Gabory submitted to out of passivity more than religious zeal: this would not be the last time Jacob mingled conversion and seduction. On the night Jacob made a pass at him, the two had dined at La Savoyarde, entertaining a Breton cousin of Jacob's, a clerk or accountant. Max put on a fireworks display of wit and brilliance. After they accompanied the cousin to the Métro stop at Pigalle, Jacob proposed to Gabory that they go back to his room to write a comedy about the provincial guest; to wet their whistles, Jacob bought a bottle of eau-de-vie, set the bottle on the table, and in a state of mounting excitement, arranged the chairs. Wanting no part of that initiation, Gabory said he needed to go to the bathroom. In the dark courtyard, he let himself out the main door and fled.

"You ran off last night," Jacob chided him the next day. But he forgave him. Perhaps the most interesting part of the story is Gabory's conclusion: "My prudence hadn't surprised him; at that time one still had the right 'not to belong' "—suggesting that in 1988, when he published his memoir, Gabory felt homosexual identity to have become a more rigid and exclusive category.[24]

III.

IN THE FIRST months of 1919, at the seasoned age of forty-four, Jacob had every reason to feel hopeful. He was on friendly terms with ardent younger writers, cheerfully announcing to Doucet that he would be "collaborating regularly" with *Littérature*, "little Breton's journal." His novel about a flying mystic, *Le Phanérogame*, had come out in December.[25] Three new books were about to appear, an exhibit of his paintings was planned for April, and his one-act play, *Trois Nouveaux Figurants du Théatre de Nantes* (Three New Understudies at the Nantes Theater) would be presented at the Barbazanges Gallery in June.

By this time, Jacob and Picasso saw each other only rarely. Aragon's depiction of Picasso as Bleu signaled a real social fact: Picasso's fame and his absorption in Olga's worldly life separated him from his oldest French friend, Max Jacob. Picasso and Olga were now installed in a grand apartment on the Rue la Boétie in the eighth arrondissement, a bastion of the *haute bourgeoisie*. Jacob's New Year's greeting to his "dear godfather and brother" in January 1919 sounds uncomfortably formal, and in March, when Jacob learned that Picasso had connected their names on an etching, he wrote in some surprise that he was touched and moved.[26] Picasso was preparing to leave for three months in London to design the sets and costumes for yet another ballet, Manuel de Falla's *Tricorne;* obliging, as usual, Jacob dug into the archives in Paris to send his friend material about Spanish costumes.[27] With some diffidence, he announced to Picasso the opening of a group show at the Térisse Gallery where his gouaches would be exhibited; he wrote with similar modesty to Doucet, "I neither wanted nor desired this hardly brilliant manifestation."[28]

Jacob had lived for years close to a demonic genius in art, and he had no illusions about the strength of his own little landscapes and theater scenes. But they have charm. Reviewing the show, Roger Allard wrote, "M. Max Jacob has his own originality: it's his own particular sort of compassionate sarcasm."[29] Jacob counted on making his mark with his books. On April 1, Éditions de La Sirène brought out the translation he had made with Antonio de Barrau of *The Book of the Lover and the Beloved* by the thirteenth-century Catalan mystic, philosopher, and mathematician Raymond Lulle (Ramon Llull, in Catalan). The book represented an important shift for Jacob from esoteric self-publishing to publication by a real house, and at first he complained about the terms. Cocteau remonstrated; Jacob was quickly mollified, writing, "I don't want to distress anyone. Arrange, let us arrange."[30] Cocteau arranged; in his first chat column, "Carte blanche," for the newspaper *Paris-Midi*, he announced the forthcoming publications of La Sirène: Mallarmé's *Madrigaux*, illustrated by Dufy; Cendrars's *La Fin du monde* (The End of the World), illustrated by Léger; Jacob's *Cinématoma;* and Salmon's book-length poem *Prikaz*.[31]

Lulle is recognized even today as an extraordinary figure, among other things, as a mathematical genius. His *Ars magna,* a complex mechanical system of combining ideas he invented to help in theological disputation, later inspired Giordano Bruno and, even more significantly, Leibniz. What mattered to Jacob was that Lulle had experienced visions of the Crucified

Christ, and *The Book of the Lover and the Beloved* is an ecstatic account—in short paragraphs, which Jacob could assimilate roughly to his prose poems—of the soul's mystic-erotic quest for God. Jacob would later adapt its embedded dialogues for his own love poetry. Lulle depicted the lover, or soul, as the madman of love: "Tell me, oh madman of love, what is most clearly seen, the Beloved in the Lover or the Lover in the Beloved? —And the Lover replied: It's by love that we see the Beloved; but we recognize the Lover by his sighs, his exhaustion, his anguish."[32] Lulle's psychology appealed to Jacob and reminded him of his own search for the sacred. In the philosopher's dissolution of space and mystic exchange of essences, Jacob found a pattern he would use years later in poems like "Dialogue III." Lulle: "The Lover said to his Beloved: You are everything, you are everywhere, you are everything and with everything. I want to give myself to you entirely, to possess you entirely and to be entirely possessed by you.— And the Beloved replied: You cannot have me entirely without belonging entirely to me.—And the Lover added: Have me entirely and I shall have you entirely."[33] In "Dialogue III" Jacob would write, "I love me in You. / You love me in you."[34]

Jacob had told Doucet about his forthcoming book, *Le Christ à Montparnasse*. It would appear in January 1920, retitled *La Défense de Tartufe*, but already a significant portion had come out in the April–May 1919 issue of *Les Écrits nouveaux* under the title "Le Christ à Montparnasse."[35] A postwar journal kept afloat by its director André Germain, scion of the Crédit Lyonnais bank, *Les Écrits nouveaux* welcomed authors ranging from literary journalists like Salmon and André Billy to Jacob's politically minded cousin Jean-Richard Bloch to the august Paul Valéry, and even made room for the experimental young like Breton. Such tolerance would soon be out of fashion. Gabory described Germain as "thin, tight, pinched, starched, ageless and sexless, always impeccable in a mouse-gray or dead-leaf-colored suit, wearing a blond wig." He lived in an apartment at the Hôtel Meurice, where he once treated Jacob and Gabory to a dinner of alarming sobriety, offering them only mineral water and a few sips of sauterne. Germain could be munificent in his own way: one morning Jacob startled Gabory and Irma out of bed, delivering a check for one hundred francs from Germain, payment for an article of Gabory's, and a massive bouquet of lilies and white roses.[36]

A medley of prose and verse, "Le Christ à Montparnasse" is pure Max Jacob, himself a medley of contradictions: in Rousseauian fashion, the author presents himself in a disguise of naked sincerity; professions of humility sound like boasts; self-revelations are larded with lies (the altered birth date, and the claim that he had not used drugs before his apparition in 1909).[37] But if we hold Jacob to a standard of imaginative reality rather than documentary realism, we may accept the invitation into his world of fiction, the experimental truth granted by art. For better or for worse, for better *and* for worse, in "Le Christ à Montparnasse," we watch Max Jacob inventing a myth of himself in terms of his idiosyncratic adopted Christianity. And here we find the essential threads of his story with Picasso: "February.—I'll be baptized on the 18th. P. will be my godfather."[38] Discussing pride and humility: "I helped so-and-so, I lived with him! We shared all our thoughts! And this [I tell] so that the blaze of his glory should shine on me."[39] "My godfather gave me an inscribed copy of *The Imitation of Christ*. Dear P., this new claim on my affection for you cannot increase it. You are certainly that which I love most in the world after God and the Saints who already consider you one of their own."[40]

Of the three verse poems included in "Le Christ à Montparnasse," one narrates his discomfiture at being turned away from baptism in 1909, and one, "The Eucharist," is marred by ill-digested devotional language. But the third, "Christ at the Movies," a masterpiece of wit and vision, pours through its ingenious couplets the truth that counted for Jacob, his experience of the sacred in the mixture of high and low, holy and profane: "Outside of church, God's everywhere, and speaks with us."[41]

IV.

JACOB AND HIS friends didn't pay much attention to politics, even as the world was being reshaped around them. On March 29, Raoul Villain, the assassin of Jean Jaurès, was released from prison, provoking a huge demonstration in protest, with one hundred thousand people thronging the streets of Paris. The labor unions organized a still more enormous protest for May Day; the government prohibited it; crowds marched anyway, and in the afternoon protesters confronted police, cavalry, and the Republican Guard in front of the Assemblée nationale. Paving stones flew, and the guards charged; disorder spread through the city, buses were toppled and barricades thrown up. None of this echoes in Jacob's letters; he must have stayed tucked away in Montmartre. Negotiations to prepare the Treaty of Versailles had been trundling along since April. The one hint of Jacob's being aware of the unusual times occurs in his letter in June to Picasso, who was in London for *Tricorne:* Paris was full of soldiers on horseback, he reported, and soldiers were guarding the Métro stations.[42]

Riddled with compromises, the treaty was signed on June 28, exactly five years after the assassination of Archduke Franz Ferdinand. But the great public demonstration came on July 14, when the Allies' victory parade, timed to coincide with the French national holiday, set the city in a fever. Cocteau described it in his column for *Paris-Midi:* Maréchal Foch, very pale; Maréchal Joffre's horse prancing; the different Allied contingents marching, each with its flags and band music, Belgians, British, "Hindus," Scottish Highlanders in kilts, Greeks with white stockings and black pompoms on their shoes, African blacks, Algerian *zouaves,* the clanking of tanks.[43] The wild festivities, the joyous sobbing went on all night.

While the diplomats argued and schemed at Versailles, Jacob wore himself out preparing his new books and a play that the gifted young actor Pierre Bertin was directing at the Galerie Barbazanges. At the end of May, Jacob wrote Emma Hertz to beg off from dinner: he was tired and overworked, he said, and desperate to finish the play in time for rehearsals.[44] He did finish it; not only did he write it, but he acted one of the main roles and utterly charmed the audience.

COCTEAU AND JACOB had been growing steadily closer, and Cocteau's publicity for Jacob's *Trois Nouveaux Figurants du Théâtre de Nantes* in *Paris-Midi* gave the play a boost. This friendship, untroubled by erotic complications, would prove one of the steadiest in both their lives. Both were homosexuals attracted to younger men, so there was no danger of them falling in love with each other; nor did they compete for the same lovers. Both were histrionic, liable to a strain of hysteria. By now, they understood each other well and could confide in each other with refreshing openness; their letters overflow with playful exuberance and with relief, one senses, at not having to prevaricate about whom or how they loved. They were sharing the same publishers, La Sirène and the Société Littéraire de France (which had just brought out Cocteau's fable *Le Potomak* and would bring out *La Défense de Tartufe* at the end of the year). Cocteau's initial snootiness about Jacob had passed, and Jacob had come to admire the younger man's wit, social brilliance, and seriousness as a writer, especially after *Le Potomak* showed, for the first time, Cocteau pulling something from his own dream life—the grotesque figures of the "Eugènes"— which resembled nobody else's work.[45] Now, and until Jacob's death, the two would make common cause. As would soon become clear, they had common enemies.

Cocteau's article announcing the play added to Jacob's mystique. Salmon would not have been pleased to see himself deleted from the story of the birth of Parisian Modernism: "Picasso, Georges Braque, Max Jacob, Guillaume Apollinaire, four friends of pain and glory." Cocteau presented them as inventing a new bohemia. His remarks on the new art have the acuteness of an acolyte; Cocteau had carefully studied the revolutionary art he strove to join.

On Jacob:

Many of his pals thought he was a "joker." Max amuses them. Max is a card. He makes puns. Frightful misbehavior.

Poetry is a vast pun. The poet associates, dissociates, turns over the world's syllables. . . .

Max Jacob a tightrope dancer, Max Jacob at the boardinghouse table, Max Jacob with his great Jewish melancholy, his conversion, his monkish good humor, his faith which he never exploits, his Breton imps, his cattiness, his heart of gold, I love him, I admire him, and we all owe him something. . . .

> Max Jacob lives in a little room opening on a courtyard in Montmartre. He goes to the Sacré-Coeur, writes, paints charming gouaches that bibliophiles fight over, visits painters.
>
> His neighbors call him M. Max. They're convinced that one day M. Max could have his own statue in the old Place Ravignan, the cradle of modern art.[46]

Since no text of the play survives, we owe our sense of it to Cocteau. It was a farce set in a provincial boarding school where a student falls in love with the headmaster's daughter, and the headmaster's wife falls for the assistant headmaster. In the end, the two women run off with the student to join a theatrical troupe in Nantes. Jacob's longer plays creak, but here he shone, just as he had when he danced on tables and acted out scenes at the Bateau Lavoir. Max played the headmaster, with his cane, skullcap, and snuffbox, his threats and his frightened tears, and he was able to report to Picasso that the play had pleased: "people liked it."[47]

When Jacob wrote Picasso about his play, he also described the hostilities percolating in Paris: "Everyone keeps badmouthing everyone else. There's the Reverdy clan, the Cocteau clan, and the generals don't have any soldiers, or at least the soldiers keep slipping from one clan to another."[48] The clan Jacob didn't foresee, or foresee as a danger, was the group around Breton, for now allied with Dada.

The resurrected *Nouvelle Revue française* came out in full force in June with Valéry's poem "Palm" and pieces by Claudel, Gide, and Proust. Jacques Rivière's editorial affirmed the mission: out of the ruins of war, a new classicism, a rededication to the values of intelligence and the French critical spirit.

But at *Littérature*, a different force was gathering. In June, Jacob's verse poem "Moral Death" came out in *Littérature* in good company, featured right after a previously unpublished poem by Rimbaud. It takes up the Christian apocalyptic scenario Jacob had already explored in the prose poem of nearly the same title in *Le Cornet à dés*. But whereas the prose poem imagines a fairytale sweetness at the end of the world, the verse poem projects a violent fantasy, part comic, part grotesque, of Paris turned topsy-turvy, the Eiffel Tower quenching its thirst in the river; fashionable boutiques, shirt factories, and greengrocers dripping blood; bourgeois hanging from their coatracks—all presaging Christ's triumphant appearance, naked, out of the clouds.[49] The poem's first noun, *revolution*, had a strong spiritual meaning for Jacob: it was what he had experienced in his encounter with the divine. One can imagine Breton being drawn to the apocalyptic scenario and at the same time being repulsed by the theology.

A change in the weather can be observed in the next issue of *Littérature*. Readers opening the magazine in July were struck by an eye-catching, full-page advertisement for Tzara's journal *Dada*, in brash typography that offended French canons of taste: "*LITTÉRATURE oui mais DADA.*" Not the least of Tzara's talents was as a graphic designer. The issue led off with the cynical letters of Breton's dead friend Jacques Vaché, texts Breton was now treating as holy writ.

The August issue featured another poem by Jacob, "Other Characters in the Masked Ball." Its opening lines now had an ironic relevance to Jacob's position vis-à-vis the younger generation:

> Crippled restorer of old automobiles,
> The anchorite crawls back to his nest, alone.
> Crikey! I'm old, too old to live in Paris;
> Your sharp-edged houses knock against my heels.[50]

But the warning shot to Jacob came in Vaché's letters. In August 1917, Vaché had written to Breton, "So we love neither ART nor artists (down with Apollinaire). . . . We've nothing to do with Mallarmé, without hating him, but he's dead. . . . Reverdy, amusing as poetling, boring in prose; MAX Jacob, my old joker—PUPPETS—PUPPETS—PUPPETS." In May 1918, Vaché wrote, using his Jarryesque jargon word for approval, UMOREU (UMOURASS): "Art should be amusing and a little dull—that's all—Max J—once in a while—could be UMOURASS—but, you see, he's ended up taking himself seriously, a curious intoxication."[51] No wonder Jacob began to doubt the good intentions of his young friends at *Littérature*. As he wrote to Cocteau in January 1920, "I think *Littérature* is friendly to us (??)— I doubt everything."[52]

V.

IN JUNE, COCTEAU presented a beguiling image of Max Jacob in his articles in *Paris-Midi*, and in August 1919 André Salmon's disjointed "poetic narrative" *Manuscript Found in a Hat* came out from the Société Littéraire de France with drawings by Picasso, full of romanticized memories of the Bateau Lavoir.[53] But the more widely Jacob became known, the more he had to struggle to control the portraits that began to proliferate. Writers now recognized the prewar bohemia of Montmartre as a salable topic and Jacob as one of its legendary figures. In February, Francis Carco brought out *Scenes from the Life of Montmartre*, a tawdry novel in which Jacob is portrayed as Monsieur Crabe, "the honor and scandal of the Rue Ravignan." Crabe is a grotesque, "a little man of forty, who fidgeted like a crippled mouse and carefully cultivated his legend."[54] He communes with a familiar demon named Balthazar, confesses his artistic failure to the poet-hero Coquelet, and shoots himself in the head, leaving a few paltry manuscripts that his friends publish out of charity. Aragon, reviewing *Scènes* for *Littérature*, pronounced it despicable, but Jacob had a far more personal reason to dislike the book, as he had thought of Carco as a friend.[55] He wrote Carco with stiff humility, "I think the demon speaks truly. . . . I recognize myself in him and you see it, alas! . . . The parts about aesthetics— if I say so, are the weakest. Thanks and cordial greetings all the same, Max Jacob."[56] He must have made his dissatisfaction clearer in other ways; a month later he wrote that they should not endanger their good relations for literary nonsense.[57] And he invited him to the exhibit of his paintings at the Térisse Gallery.

By late summer 1919, Jacob hadn't seen Picasso for months. The painter spent June and July in London preparing *Tricorne*, and then he and Olga withdrew to the Côte d'Azur until late September. The separation was as much social as geographical: Olga was determined to detach Picasso from his old bohemian friends. No one could take Picasso's place in Jacob's heart, but he craved companionship, and other friendships and flirtations kept him occupied. He saw a good deal of the Ghikas at Liane's grand house in Saint-Germain-en-Laye, probably not suspecting that his hostess didn't always adore him. In her diary for July 19, 1919, Liane noted that illness prevented Max's next visit; she confessed that she didn't like him: "He's a poor creature, hugely gifted, but with an ill fate that undermines him. . . . Beautiful ravaged face. . . . He's changed religion, which I'll never approve. Why deny his race? Pretext, idiocy! Anyway, he can't change his nose."[58] An immensely complicated woman whose diary teems with memories of lesbian affairs as well as adventures with wealthy men from her days as a *grande cocotte,* Liane was by this time cultivating Catholic piety along with malice, and in other moods she expressed real affection for Jacob. With her scandalous past, she remained on the margins of respectable society, and at some deep level, she and Jacob understood each other. On August 16 he visited the Ghikas with André Germain, editor of *Les Écrits Nouveaux;* because it was the day after the Assumption of the Virgin, Liane promised her diary to be indulgent to her guests, and she concluded afterward that Max had been witty and charming.[59]

From the Ghikas, Jacob made a quick trip to Brittany, saluting his mother and siblings in Quimper and continuing to the small fishing port of Douarnenez. Here he stayed with the art dealer Georges Aubry, who had helped arrange the show at the Térisse Gallery. From Aubry's balcony one moonlit night in early September, he wrote Cocteau describing the ocean and the cliffs, the voices rising up from the village street, the braying of a trombone playing a quadrille, then silence.[60] By September 10 he was back in Paris and visited the Ghikas in the clinic at Neuilly, where Georges was recovering from an operation; a month later he brought Henri Hertz to see them in Saint-Germain, a visit Liane recorded in her diary; he looked well, she said, he spoke well, and he impressed the pious ex-courtesan by remarking that Jews "had something metallic about them."[61]

||

ON OCTOBER 26, Paul Rosenberg staged an important show of Picasso's work. Jacob must have seen it and must have said something about it to his old friend; the only written communications are a note with a birthday gift of cigars on October 24; a note thanking Picasso for providing an etching for the frontispiece of his new book, *La Défense de Tartufe;* and a New Year's greeting sent in late December in which formality gives way to an ardent expression of friendship: "You always have the first place in my prayers because you have never stopped being—believe me—the only friend I have on earth and you know it well. *The others, it's the world.*"[62]

The year drew to a close with the publication of the regular edition of *La Défense de Tartufe;* the luxury edition with Picasso's etching of a sharply chiaroscuro woman's head wouldn't appear until January. The book's plurality in form—prose poems, verse poems, diary entries, spiritual exercises, and meditations—echoes the plurality of Jacob himself: visionary, sinner, artist, lover, and hypocrite. Assuming the mask of Molière's hypocrite, Tartuffe (but changing the spelling by one letter to *Tartufe*), Jacob dared his readers to test this drama of sincerity, repentance, and confession.[63] And perhaps he dared them to test their own sincerity and their convictions about stable selfhood. In a milieu of deeply ingrained anti-Semitism (one remembers Liane's comment about his nose), he employed all the resources of his art to establish, in enemy territory, a renewed and purified self: a lived myth of conversion and transformation.

La Défense de Tartufe is divided into four sections. Section one, "Antithesis," presents, in high-wire, jangling verse, the gaiety and desperation of the poet before his apparition. Shifting into prose poems, section two, "The Revelation," gives the core experience of the book (and of Jacob's life), his vision of Christ on the wall; it also provides kaleidoscopic glimpses of the poet: "The frightened monk—that's me," "The Breton—that's me." Section three, "Decadence, or Mystic and Sinner," describes the poet's disorderly life between the apparition and his baptism; lurching between remorse and debauch, it combines verse poems (including the magnificent "Christ at the Movies"), prose poems, and extracts from the diary of Catholic initiation. Section four, whose title echoes Saint François de Sales's *Introduction to the Devout Life*, mingles verse poems—some with a new folkloric naïveté that Jacob would use in later work—and meditations on traditional subjects, the Last Judgment, the Incarnation . . . One senses the strain of the Modernist Harlequin trying to find a language in which to integrate this new experience. This section is introduced by a narrative tag that proved more a statement of fantasy than of fact: "The poet, having abandoned worldly life because of its sins, finds in Catholicism that which he hadn't found in mysticism: peace!"[64]

THE OCTOBER ISSUE of *Littérature* carried Jacob's poem "A Prisoner's Complaint," an absurd, melancholy, and camp lyric. It concludes:

> Birdcage of mute fingers, jail
> The muse is a bird flying through
> The bars across my prison cell
> I saw its grace, I saw its smile
> But couldn't follow on its trail.
>
> Farewell, muse, go let people know
> This festival evening in town
> In the prisons where they keep us down
> We die from having loved them so.[65]

That issue held the seeds of future conflict. Tzara had not yet arrived in Paris, but his poem in *Littérature*, "Galvanized Nobility," sounded a revolutionary note. Inspired by Dada proclamations arriving from Zurich and by Tzara's book *vingt-cinq poèmes*, Breton and his friends were eagerly awaiting this new guru. Tzara, a Romanian, had been living in Zurich, speaking German, and spoke French poorly; his poetry has no allegiance to the deeply remembered cadences of French poetry that pulsed in the lines of Apollinaire and Jacob. Disruptive of syntax, harshly prosaic, startling in its jammed-together images, "Galvanized Nobility" contrasts violently with Jacob's lyricism:

> I sterilize myself mask slow lemon bell
> vulture goes to bed in the black and crinkled air
> if i smash the vase mow down the birds of fixed ecstasy
> among the fruits speed plays exerts the incandescence of the trident[66]

Another revolution was brewing in the same issue, in the opening chapter of Breton and Soupault's experiment in automatic writing, *Les Champs magnétiques* (The Magnetic Fields). Breton had drawn Soupault into the secret project of driving themselves—almost to the brink of madness—to take dictation from the unconscious, and they had composed in this way the prose of *Les Champs magnétiques*, texts steeped in Rimbaud but also in the young authors' personal experiences: the shocks of war, hospitals, and losses.[67] Max Jacob had been experimenting for years with dream visions and dictation from the unconscious, but Breton had his own reasons for writing him out of the story. For the rest of his life, Jacob would keenly resent the injustice.

VI.

NINETEEN-TWENTY FOUND MAX JACOB in a perturbed state of mind. On the one hand, he was enjoying more success than he had ever known: *La Défense de Tartufe* was receiving good reviews and selling well, *Cinématoma* was about to appear, the Bernheim-Jeune Gallery planned a one-man show of his paintings, the art journal *La Renaissance de l'art français* would run a long article by Salmon about his art, and Pierre Bertin was preparing the production of another of his plays. At the same time, Jacob's recent defense of Cocteau's *Le Coq et l'Arlequin* had drawn scorn from various quarters. Reverdy and Gris, he complained to Cocteau, refused to greet him.[68]

The real fireworks began with Tzara's arrival in Paris, on January 17. He turned up at the door of Picabia's mistress Germaine Everling. She had just given birth the week before (while Breton and Picabia, in their first meeting, were engaged in a conversation in the adjoining room about art and philosophy and had to be evicted by the midwife). Now Everling was asked to welcome the penniless Romanian as a guest; Breton, Éluard, Aragon, and Soupault rushed over that afternoon to greet Tzara, and for a while her apartment became the command center of Parisian Dada. The editors of *Littérature* had already planned an artistic, musical matinée for January 23 in a working-class neighborhood; by adding Tzara to the mix, they created the first of an incendiary series that introduced Dada to Paris.

The plan, before Tzara's arrival, was fairly conventional: Salmon would kick things off with a speech about post-Symbolist poetics, and Jacob's actor friends Pierre Bertin and Marcel Herrand were to recite poems by the old avant-garde, "the great ancestors" Apollinaire, Cendrars, Reverdy, and Jacob. Paintings by Léger, Gris, De Chirico, and Lipchitz would be displayed, and Les Six would play their music. Neither Reverdy nor Jacob was present. Things unrolled peacefully until Picabia's antipaintings were brought out, including *The Double World*, a scribble in black and white adorned with the inscription from Duchamp's mustachioed *Mona Lisa*, L.H.O.O.Q. (sounded out in French, "Elle a chaud au cul," She has the hots in her ass). Avant-garde art already depended on an irritable or outraged response from the public, but Dada pushed that provocation to an extreme. The audience began hooting at L.H.O.O.Q., but when Tzara himself stepped out onstage—his presence in Paris until that moment having been kept secret—things flared as he monotonously declaimed the text of a speech by the nationalist Léon Daudet while Breton and Aragon rang bells. The older artists, like Salmon and Gris, began shouting in protest, and Jacob's friend Florent Fels, the pacifist anarchist who edited the new journal *Action*, hollered, "Back to Zurich! Shoot him!"[69] (Some pacifism!)

A new force had entered the city. *Ubu Roi*, *Le Sacre du printemps*, *Les Mamelles de Tirésias*, and *Parade* had been works of art that shocked. Dada undid the very idea of art: the medium was shock itself, and a galvanized relation to the audience, which itself became part of the spectacle. As Fels's insult made clear, Dada not only created a crisis in the definition of art, it also brought out a strong strain of French chauvinism.

For now, Breton adopted Dada as his own revolution. While Tzara and his French allies followed the storm they had created on January 23 with three more Dada manifestations, Reverdy helped to organize a counter-attack: the writers whose work was read (including Reverdy, Jacob, and Salmon) signed a statement announcing that they were united in their care for a purely French art of creation, not destruction.[70] Jacob wasn't present when this reading took place, but he signed the statement, and from then on his relations with Breton's coterie rapidly deteriorated.

The Dada matinée on January 23 administered the first shock. The second occurred the next day: Modigliani, worn down by drink and hashish, died of tubercular meningitis at the Hôpital de la Charité. Two days later his pregnant girlfriend flung herself out a sixth-floor window. Jacob had never been close to Modigliani; he told Michel Manoll years later that he found Modigliani "the most unpleasant being I ever knew. Proud, furious, insensitive, mean, and rather stupid, sneering, infatuated; and all the same maybe only he and Picasso will remain as the painters of the period."[71] Jacob's poem, "To Monsieur Modigliani to Prove to Him That I Am a Poet," suggests an ongoing argument between them.[72] They had known each other for years; it was Jacob who introduced Modi to the dealer Paul Guillaume, and it was at Jacob's urging that Modigliani began to paint.[73] Whether or not the two men liked each other, they shared worlds: their Jewishness, their interest in the occult, and their love of poetry. Modigliani painted two portraits of Jacob, catching his dandy persona with a starched collar and stern mouth.[74]

Kisling and Moricand tried to make a death mask of Modigliani's handsome, ruined face and botched the job, so they brought the broken pieces of plaster, speckled with bits of hair and skin, to the sculptor Jacques Lipchitz, who created a whole mask from the fragments. Salmon, Kisling, Juan Ortiz de Sarate, and Modigliani's other dealer Leopold Zborowski took charge of the funeral, a massive spectacle parading through the streets of Montparnasse where Modigliani had often lurched, dead drunk.[75] Max Jacob followed the cortège, saying goodbye to yet another old companion.

||

IN JULY, DIAGHILEV's ballet *Tricorne* with sets and costumes by Picasso had opened to lavish applause in London, and the Paris premiere took place at the Opéra on January 27. Four days later Max Jacob carefully dressed himself in a coat and tails and an opera hat—a collapsible top hat called a *claque* specifically designed for the theater—and set off down the Rue des Martyrs to the Place Pigalle, where he intended to catch the Métro to attend the second performance.[76] In the Place Pigalle he was caught in the whirl of traffic; a large, glossy automobile knocked him down and rolled over him, then sped away. His head had been under the vehicle, witnesses reported; "I profited from seeing the underside of a car," he later quipped. A crowd gathered him up. "My left side suspender is bothering me," he said when he came to. "You aren't wearing suspenders," he was told. "Then have I broken my collarbone?"[77]

What followed was a nightmare even worse than the accident, and it produced one of Jacob's best pieces of writing. He translated the episode into the hallucinatory prose account "Hospital Nights and Dawn," and one can piece together the events from its nonchronological fragments. He was taken to the public hospital, the Lariboisière; in a delirium of pain, he was interrogated about his "respected mother's maiden name"; he was left for hours alone on a metal chair in an unheated waiting room; finally a woman attendant arrived, huffing and puffing, and with the help of a male nurse undressed him and bathed him in icy water. By this time he was in agony, with each breath torn up from his crushed lungs; as pneumonia set in, they wheeled him through freezing corridors and deposited him in a room crowded with sickbeds, air thick with tobacco smoke. Here he spent the night in such pain, he even forgot to pray. For the next several weeks he drifted in feverish hallucinations. As he slowly regained lucidity, he made friends with the patients suffering in the adjoining beds—the Arab dentist, the tubercular chauffeur, a young house painter. . . . All night long, every night, as the sick and injured groaned and tossed, the attendants refused care: no medications, not even a glass of water.

From this experience, Jacob crafted a vision of hell and a furious indictment of the indifference and institutional arrogance, the vicious collaboration of science and bureaucracy that ran the hospital. And as always for him, reality appeared on many levels at once:

> The hospital is a train station: travelers for the land of shadows! Travelers for another health! . . . Hospital, mausoleum for the living, you're between two stations, yourself a station for the departures from which no one returns. I kneel in contemplation before your threshold; I thank God who left me among the living upon the earth. . . . Oh, you people hurrying in your cars, you'll die! Olé! Sexy dogs, young and old, you'll die! Housewives and *grandes dames*, bluestockings, you'll die, my friends! Drivers of cars, listen! Listen to my death knell, I say you'll die. I just learned it at the hospital, and I cry it aloud on the Boulevard Magenta. You will die, we will die.[78]

As soon as he was well enough to receive visitors, friends flocked to his side. Picasso loyally came and exclaimed, "To think I wanted to name you Fiacre for your baptism, and here you are wounded by a *fiacre*!" "A *fiacre*? I was run over by a luxury car," Max snapped.[79] Eugenia Erráruriz, Coco Chanel, and Misia Sert took turns at his bedside, formidable ladies of fashion he had come to know in his forays into the society of the salons. (Chanel, by now one of the richest women in France, was having an affair with the somber Reverdy, a conjunction that makes sense when one remembers that they both had endured rough childhoods in the South and that both were severe perfectionists.) Liane de Pougy didn't visit but wrote at length about Jacob's accident in her diary, describing his injuries, promising herself to coddle him and to invite him for a month's convalescence in her house. She liked him better now that he was beginning to earn a living and no longer wore the cast-off garments of his friends.[80] Yet even while she sent him baskets of fruit, and while she and Georges ran around Paris buying antiques and attending the premiere of Cocteau and Milhaud's *Le*

Boeuf sur le toit, she confessed to feeling "too fragile" to venture into a hospital for the poor.[81] In late February, she and Max had one of their spats: Max complained of the food at the hospital, so Liane went out and bought pork, chicken, and beefsteak. (This meant going to three different stores, she irritably recorded.) These delicacies, roasted, were dispatched to Max in a handsome porcelain serving dish. Max protested, "But it's Lent!" and gave it all away to the other patients. "He's more Catholic than the Pope, this renegade Jew!" grumbled Liane.[82]

Jacob's reputation grew day by day even as he lay wheezing in bed. The work of many years had suddenly become visible in two utterly original books, *La Défense de Tartufe* and *Cinématoma,* and they were reviewed in the most prestigious journals. This attention marks a transition for Jacob from shabby, marginal bohemian to chic bohemian. Yet he would never really fit the Establishment: his art proved too various and peculiar, his whole person too disreputable, ever to be tamed.

In March, Henri Ghéon, Gide's close friend and a co-founder of *La Nouvelle Revue française,* praised *La Défense de Tartufe* in the pages of that journal: "M. Max Jacob renews the genre of the macaronic poem with infinite wit and the most beautiful poetic gifts." Ghéon distinguished Jacob's "refined, subtle, and desperate art" from the "cold verbal mechanics of his mediocre imitators"; noted that Apollinaire owed much to Jacob; and predicted that Jacob's real poetic power would outlive his momentary renown for "fantasy" and "potpourri." Ghéon, a homosexual whose experiences in the war had brought him back to the Catholic faith, admired the confessional prose of *La Défense de Tartufe* but especially noted the poems.[83]

Cinématoma came out on February 10. Jacob had finished this collection of radical voice-portraits in 1912 but thereafter revised it assiduously, later naming it one of his favorite books, "the one where I tried out the system of the revelation of character through diction."[84] He was fascinated by the new art of film; after all, Christ had appeared to him against the backdrop of the screen of a tawdry movie, he adored Chaplin, and in 1918 he'd written an essay for *Nord-Sud* on the revelatory power of the medium.[85] The book's title, *Cinématoma,* compresses various meanings: besides *cinema,* the syllables *toma* suggest "tome" (volume) and "atoms," with each portrait acting as an atom in the larger molecule of the book. In a typical Jacobian mixture of high and low, "Thomas" recalls Saint Thomas Aquinas, much on the mind of the recent convert, and also a tomato. In the social simultaneity of these stories, peasants, bluestockings, petit-bourgeois, lawyers, and matrons all perform their arias, redefining fiction as an art not so much of plot as of voice.[86]

Cinématoma immediately found admirers. The critic Roger Allard welcomed it at *La Nouvelle Revue française:* "With a discretion that is his alone, he [Jacob] excels in using and transposing the trivial detail and the note of bad taste. Critics have thought they'd taken the measure of his method; they haven't recognized the sorrowful poetry ill disguised by all this borrowed diction. His fantasy unfolds from a foundation of a cruel and sagacious observation."[87] In the *Mercure de France,* Jean de Gourmont, like Allard, compared Jacob to the eighteenth-century adventurer and prolix author Rétif de la Bretonne, competitor of Sade, celebrated by the Surrealists for his dreamlike *Les Nuits de Paris.* "M. Max Jacob," Gourmont wrote, "a subtle poet, possesses the truest and the rarest gifts of the novelist; the versatility of his language adapts to the most varied characters so each speaks in his own idiom with its intonations, gestures, and tics."[88]

Not everyone took to Jacob's book. In June he would see a clear sign of disapproval from *Littérature* in Aragon's cryptic review, whose first paragraph could either refer to Jacob's female characters or be read as a homophobic slur: "*Women love to talk;* this is true of women in general; thus woman here is understood in the collective sense."[89] By this time *Littérature*'s new orientation was evident: it opened with a delightfully absurd piece by Tzara. In the war of the journals, meanwhile, Jacob's supporter Allard had just attacked Aragon's first book of poems in *La Nouvelle Revue française.*[90]

IN MARCH 1920 another journal entered the lists. Two years earlier, still in uniform, Florent Fels, a young soldier who had been decorated with two crosses for valor and the Medal of Versailles, came to see Jacob, and since then they had corresponded, with Jacob advising the young man on his hopelessly earnest poems. Fels soon gave up poetry and directed his energy into founding *Action*, a journal of literature and art.[91]

Breton and his friends perceived *Action* as a direct threat. It represented a humanism they now rejected, and its contributors were drawn either from *La Nouvelle Revue française* (André Suarès, Roger Allard), or from the older avant-garde they intended to replace (Salmon, Jacob), and their bête noire, Cocteau. The March issue of *Action* featured Jacob in four verse poems and an essay about him by Henri Hertz.[92] One of those poems, "Romantic Allusions to Mardi-Gras," in its code-switching frolic, hints at the layers of disguises and of complex feelings experienced by a gay man in that (officially) straight society: "My life is a tango, my heart a Grand Guignol."[93]

||

JACOB EMERGED FROM the hospital on March 5 and stepped into a temporary aureole: his show at Bernheim-Jeune opened on March 8 and was a success in all respects, earning him three thousand francs, enough to live on for months, and also establishing him as an artist to be sought after.[94] The catalog contains one of his most often cited self-portraits, by turns whimsical and serious:

> I know dance, singing, piano, madrigals. I know the respect owed to the elderly, to scholars, to white sepulchers; joy, love, hunger, isolation, success. I have university degrees (ex-student of . . .) I believe that only in sorrow does man recognize himself as human, know and recognize other men. I'm forty-three years old, I'm almost bald, I've almost no teeth, I'm writing this in an airy and charming hospital where my pneumonia is being treated.

He described his humiliation by the art teacher in the lycée in Quimper, and his timid attempt to study painting in Paris at the Académie Julian.[95]

At the same time, Salmon wrote about Jacob's painting in the journal *Renaissance de l'art français et des industries de luxe:* he made no claim for Jacob as a master but celebrated him as a serious painter, not a poet who dabbled, and recalled the romance of their early years together in Montmartre.[96] On the evening of the show, Bertin produced Jacob's farce *Ruffian toujours, truand jamais* (Always Libertine, Never a Bum) at the Barbazanges Gallery after a concert by Auric, Stravinsky, and Satie. The audience glittered with Cocteau's aristocrat-aesthetes: Princesse de Polignac, Princesse Murat, and Comte and Comtesse de Beaumont (on whom Radiguet would model the characters of his novel *Le Bal du Comte d'Orgel,* Count D'Orgel's Ball). Picasso attended, as did Cocteau, Salmon, and Gabory. Jacob had leaped from his sickbed into the stage lights. In the next few weeks he saw the Ghikas several more times, offending Liane on one occasion by arriving late and being "impudent, demanding, and catty" and smoking at the dinner table. "In short," she concluded, "money isn't good for him." Two days later he took the train to the South of France for two months of convalescence.[97]

VII.

HE HEADED FOR Sainte-Maxime, a fishing village on the Côte d'Azur across a small bay from Saint-Tropez. Still weak from pneumonia, he settled into the Grand Hotel and wrote and painted ten hours a day, pausing only for solitary meals in the hotel dining room and short walks. It rained for two weeks, a cold wind blew, the "azure" sea looked black, and the mountains rising steeply behind the village looked blacker. So much for azure. Jacob described the dismal scene in letters to Salmon, Roland-Manuel, and others: he hated the palm trees (overgrown feather dusters), the cramped gardens, the pretentious tourists, and the equally pretentious residents who tallied the number of dukes they'd sighted.[98] But he worked well, writing the story of his stay at the hospital, and he confided to Salmon that a "horror of Paris" had pushed him to leave "the Dadas" and the throes of Cubism behind.[99] When the rain let up, he did begin to explore the coast, visiting Nice, Cannes, Hyères, and most happily, Marseille, to which he took a strong liking; it was an energetic working city, not a resort, and its blue, blond, red, and ochre colors delighted him.[100]

He hadn't forgotten Paris, nor had Paris forgotten him. Paulhan, now working part time at *La Nouvelle Revue française*, wrote to inquire about manuscripts he might have for the press and the journal. Gaston Gallimard followed up with a letter on April 19 expressing lively interest in Jacob's work.[101] Jacob replied graciously. The problem, he explained, was that he had just published two books and had promised the next one, *Art poétique*, a book of aesthetic reflections, to the publishers the Émile-Paul brothers: his cupboard was bare. But he hoped to be able to show Gallimard something soon, a book and a story.[102]

||

WHEN JACOB RETURNED to the melee on June 4, he gravitated to Cocteau's clan and to the Ghikas. Liane and her prince, by this time, served as his surrogate family, whatever their disagreements, and Liane's diary for the rest of the year records many visits from Max, sometimes accompanied by Cocteau, Radiguet, and Auric. Georges Auric was a musical prodigy from Montpellier. He had arrived in Paris at age fourteen just before the war to study composition. At the Conservatoire, he became attached to Darius Milhaud and Arthur Honegger and soon met Francis Poulenc. Intellectually brilliant, a passionate reader as well as a pianist and composer, he had a gift for friendship and was mysteriously able to stay on good terms with people who detested one another: even while joining Cocteau and the group of Les Six and writing for Cocteau's *Le Coq*, he managed to remain friendly with Breton and the clique at *Littérature*. He had come to know Max Jacob in Montmartre as early as 1918; years after Jacob's death, he preserved inscribed copies of his books.[103]

In Paris, Jacob found Kahnweiler back in business. Still a German citizen, the dealer had returned from exile in February and was patiently winning back his artists (though Picasso remained elusive). His friend André

Simon, a Frenchman, provided legal cover for the enterprise, Galerie Simon, in cavernous premises on the Rue d'Astorg on the Right Bank near the competitors Paul Guillaume and Paul Rosenberg. Jacob also found himself portrayed in two new books.

||

FROM THE HOSPITAL, Jacob had written Salmon to praise his *Manuscript Found in a Hat,* pleased to see the Bateau Lavoir evoked with such loving nostalgia.[104] In June, Salmon's roman à clef, *La Négresse du Sacré-Coeur* (published in English as *The Black Venus*), came out from the Nouvelle Revue Française. Salmon had appointed himself the recording angel of the heroic days of Cubism, and he would spend the rest of his life elaborating the tales at mind-befuddling length. In *La Négresse,* Salmon represented himself as Florimond Daubelle, a bohemian poet; Picasso as Sorgue; and Max Jacob as the saintly Septime Fébur.[105] One chapter transposes the story of Picasso and Fernande's adoption and abandonment of Raymonde. In a Dickensian scene Fébur is charged with installing the child in an orphanage; horrified by the place, he spends his last money taking her out to dinner instead and lodges her with a good-hearted woman. This isn't what happened to Raymonde, but Jacob's kindness to the child had been real, and he wrote Salmon, "S.F. saw himself a little revised but basically true. The good Septime wept real tears, calling himself a fool."[106]

Jacob found another version of himself in Apollinaire's ramshackle posthumous novel *La Femme assise* (The Seated Woman). Cobbled together from fragments, the story recycled old descriptions of Montparnasse and recounted Picasso's abduction of Irène Lagut and Apollinaire's dalliance with Ruby, "la jolie rousse": Picasso is Pablo Canouris, a Spanish-Albanian painter with blue hands; Apollinaire is Anatole de Saintariste; and Jacob turns up as Moïse Deléchelle (Moses Of-the-Ladder, a pun on Jacob's ladder), an ashen-colored man who strikes cello sounds out of his stomach.[107] In a dénouement Jacob must have read as a comic reflection on their friendship, Saintariste and Deléchelle end up shooting each other as Saintariste tries to prevent the spy Deléchelle from blowing up the Montparnasse train station with a bomb hidden in a loaf of bread.

VIII.

LA NOUVELLE REVUE FRANÇAISE first deigned to notice Dada in September 1919, when Jacques Rivière declared, "It's deplorable that Paris seems to welcome such nonsense, that comes to us directly from Berlin."[108] A few months later the powers at *La Nouvelle Revue française* changed their tune, influenced in part by their protégé Breton. The pages of the journal began to serve a double purpose: the public reflections by Gide and Rivière on the meaning of the new movement can also be read as a private argument with Breton, whose intelligent service they did not want to lose. At the same time, in the course of 1920 one can trace in the pages of *Littérature* and *Action* the abandonment of Max Jacob by the new militant avant-garde.

Jacob wasn't the only older experimental writer to risk being outflanked by the young. Gide, who had led the way in questioning the foundations of bourgeois society, now confronted the new revolution in an essay entitled simply "Dada" in *La Nouvelle Revue française* in April 1920. It's a strange piece, revealing a streak of anti-Semitism and marked by the trauma of war. Without naming Tzara, he calls him "the inventor of Dada" and observes, "I hear he's a foreigner.—I'll easily believe it. A Jew.—It was on the tip of my tongue."[109] Gide asks why foreigners should care for "our French culture"; points to Dada's destructiveness; and names the war as the machine of ruin that had inevitably produced Dada.[110] He concludes by expressing sympathy with the desire for new forms, citing Christ's injunction in Matthew 9:17 not to put new wine in old bottles but hoping "that in this cask [Dada], the best wine of youth will soon begin to feel a little smothered."[111]

A still more pointed exchange took place in the August issue of the journal, where the elders allowed Breton to have his say. In the fervent essay "For Dada," Breton celebrated the revolutionary work of Rimbaud and Lautréamont but canonized Vaché, who had distinguished himself by producing nothing. Affirming a solidarity that would soon fly apart, Breton quoted poems by Soupault, Éluard, Tzara, Picabia, and Aragon and brandished Apollinaire's word *Surrealism*. Rivière followed Breton's piece with his own, tempered "Gratitude to Dada," praising Dada for exposing a theoretical weakness in the "subjectivism" of earlier radical writing (Mallarmé, Apollinaire, and Jacob).[112] Thus did the establishment maneuver to contain the brush fire.

These debates directly affected Max Jacob. Rivière had quoted the preface to *Le Cornet à dés* several times, treating Jacob as an authority on Modernism. It was just at this moment that the tide turned against Jacob. He had already irritated Breton by his friendship with Cocteau and by signing the letter protesting Dada in February. But his sympathy for Fels's *Action* made him an outright enemy. The July issue of *Action* led off with nine prose poems by Jacob; July would also be the last month in which Jacob's work appeared in Breton's *Littérature*.

The first of Jacob's prose poems in *Action*, "My Life in Three Lines," curiously links the two antagonistic journals, because just as Breton was preparing to expel Jacob, Éluard, always more tenderhearted, singled out "My Life in Three Lines" for praise and reprinted it in his review of journals in the July issue of *Littérature*. The poem also relates to Jacob's running quarrel with Reverdy, and Reverdy would pick up the main image, the cooking pot, for his attack on Jacob in the next issue of *Littérature*. Though Jacob never collected it in a book, the poem has more than documentary interest as a meditation on originality and influence, and Jacob's painful sense of having had his art consumed by others.

MY LIFE IN THREE LINES

I dreamed I was in water boiling in a cooking pot shut with a padlock. I vaguely heard people shouting and laughing. Someone opened the pot: "Who do you want to eat you first?" The pot was opened a second time: "You want the other one to eat you, does that mean you're not my friend?" The water kept boiling and as cooks say, I

was reduced, reduced, reduced and finally I was hardly there at all.
There was nothing left of me to eat. What remained said, "Adieu!"[113]

The real twist of the knife came in September in *Littérature,* where
Breton used Reverdy against Jacob. In the group of Reverdy's prose poems
opening the issue, three attacked Jacob. The cooking pot reappeared in
"Man's Friend or Parasite" as a symbol in which the Jacob figure, an old
man with curling fingernails, a hooked nose, and bad teeth, cooks up writing from other authors' work.[114] The anti-Semitic rage continued in "The
Old Apprentice": "the same rag merchant, the same junk dealer, this line
of hooked nose and the sale of old trimmed-down books resold as new and
signed with a fake name."[115] Reverdy was turning the accusation of pla-
giarism back on his accuser: Jacob had attacked him in 1915 for imitating
Jacob's prose poems, and now Reverdy lashed out at Jacob for using the
discoveries of others. (Reverdy meant primarily Rimbaud, and the accusation was misguided; Jacob had absorbed Rimbaud, along with Baudelaire,
Laforgue, and Corbière, but he had made his own modernist art from self-
conscious and deformed allusion.)[116]

Jacob must have been hurt by Reverdy, but these days he was more
and more taken up with Cocteau and Radiguet and their crowd. Cocteau
brought out his new collection of poems, *Poésies 1917–1920,* in May. It
represented an advance; though still indebted to Reverdy, it sounded less
like everybody else. The poems veered between proclaiming radicalism
and affecting ennui.[117] Jacob wrote Cocteau a remarkable letter about it,
disguising a lesson in modern poetry as praise. Under extravagant compliments and professions of humility, Jacob condensed in a few lines his own
principles of composition. "Your book enchants me and all I want to do
now is to write like Cocteau," he claimed. And then he advised:

Exaggerate to make oneself understood.
Deceive and satisfy.
Assemble in one single passage everything relating to a sensation to
define it.

. . .

Confuse the listener for the love of a word or a legitimate attack of
madness.
Use, but not without scorn, all the old techniques . . .
Such [*sic*] would be a modern poetry if our mumblers and friends
practiced it, or enemies
but
the image is not (isn't it so?) what foolish people think
it's the spark that flies up when the hammer of Man strikes
the anvil of reality. You alone know this truth.[118]

Hardly had Jacob mailed this letter when another book arrived from
Cocteau: *Carte blanche,* his collected articles for *Paris-Midi.*[119] A book
more remarkable than either of Cocteau's also appeared in July: Radiguet's
first collection of poems, *Les Joues en feu* (Cheeks on Fire). Radiguet was
seventeen. These prose poems and short lyrics startle in their freshness
and sophistication, their sonic play, their cool intelligence; one under-
stands why people said of the boy that he had been "born forty years
old."[120] His prose poems slightly resemble Rimbaud's, and his free verse
owes something to Reverdy, but the voice is all his own and has none of
Cocteau's swagger.

Jacob's affection for Radiguet is evident in "Nocturne," a poem in
rhyming quatrains he dedicated to him and published in the summer issue
of *Le Coq* that Cocteau and Radiguet edited together. As Radiguet moved
to adopt more classical forms in both poetry and prose, part of the "return
to order" so bruited in postwar France, he and Jacob shared a deep understanding about what it meant to write a modern poem: not an explosive
device, but a cadenced enchantment carrying the older art into new space.[121]

IX.

IN THE LAST few months of 1920, Jacob committed some typical social
gaffes and some just as typical acts of generosity. He came close to breaking with his cousin Jean-Richard Bloch in August. The Nouvelle Revue

Française had just published a collection of Bloch's essays, and Jacob wrote him a firmly disapproving letter. A Socialist, Bloch was committed to the ideals of a populist art. Jacob could not have been less sympathetic. "Jean! My dear Jean! Is it possible that you, an intelligent man, dally with such twaddle?"[122] "The people," Jacob argued, don't like fake proletarian art concocted by intellectuals. They like really popular art, folklore, and even classics, when the classics have been around long enough. The only task for the artist is to "prepare future Beauty and let the people decide for itself." "Pardon the violence of this letter which doesn't exclude my admiration for your fine articles and my friendship with you," Jacob wound up. But the friendship effectively came to an end.

Jacob's relations with the Nouvelle Revue Française also came under strain. Paulhan and Gallimard had asked him for work, and he had given them the only copy of the incomplete manuscript of the collection of stories *Le Roi de Béotie*. On August 3 he wrote Paulhan complaining that they had kept it too long and he needed it back.[123] Jacob had carried the manuscript over to Gallimard's office accompanied by Gabory; in those days, publishing was so personal that Gallimard invited them to sit down, and Jacob read parts of the book aloud, to Gabory's appreciative laughter. (Gabory would later work at the Nouvelle Revue Française as a reader, and Gallimard told him that his amusement at Jacob's reading had prompted him to accept the book.)[124] The acceptance was delayed, however; the manuscript was for a time lost between Paris and Bordeaux, and it took weeks for Paulhan to sort things out. Later that month Jacob wrote Paulhan to complain: "I like you, my dear Paulhan, you know that. The Nouvelle Revue Française can go fuck itself, but I really like you."[125]

JACOB SAW THE Ghikas frequently, often not realizing how much he could irritate Liane. On August 1 he brought Cocteau and Radiguet. Liane's impressions were hardly charitable: "Oh, this parade—half-starved and tinted gray—Cocteau leading with the sharp and ravaged profile of a vicious, anxious old maid, Radiguet timid, twisting, closing his eyes and opening his mouth or vice versa as if his skin were too short for his face, Max as always with his puppet mask." She found her guests noisy and rude, scattering ashes and demanding that the dahlias be removed from the table. In the afternoon Max read from his new book (probably *Le Roi de Béotie*) that, in spite of herself, Liane found "charming" (noting that Cocteau was vexed not to hold center stage). In September, Liane dreaded the prospect of a week's visit from Max in her Breton house, Clos Marie. Jacob spent some days with his family in Quimper early in the month—peacefully this time—and menaced the Ghikas with his arrival. Liane had the flu, and though she didn't forbid his visit, she poured her grievances into her diary: Max had wretched table manners, he ate the best part of the fish, he took half the cheese off the cheese tray and helped himself to most of the cream in the pitcher; he put his muddy shoes on the white silk counterpane; he disturbed the whole house going to mass at six a.m.[126] He arrived on September 16, smiling and well dressed, bringing a Breton cake and a package of crêpes. The week passed without upheavals, and on the last evening Max read aloud from the play he had carved out of his novel, *Le Terrain Bouchaballe:* Liane found it "very amusing, not very dramatic" and decided, "He's not really a playwright." She wondered if he should become a priest!

After bustling around Brittany on more brief visits—he wrote the Kislings of traveling in "a steamboat, sleeping car [*sic*], auto car [*sic*], auto *sans quart*, tramway," and going "from city to city, village to hamlet, city to villages, dragging my laziness and my melancholy"—Jacob returned to Paris in early October.[127] There he was greeted by his first publication in *La Nouvelle Revue française*, a short story called "Good Intentions," about a grizzled little marquis who haunts churches to witness and bless weddings and funerals and inadvertently excites the jealousy of the groom in a shabby wedding ceremony. It's one of Jacob's studies in cruelty, sorrow, poverty, and moral ignorance.[128]

In December in *Littérature*, Aragon took a smack at Jacob. No longer the romanticized Chipre of *Anicet,* now Jacob was grouped with other triflers in a list under the title "Are There Still People Who Amuse Themselves in Life?" The company wasn't all bad—Aragon insulted the crew at *La Nouvelle Revue française* along with Matisse, Pierpont Morgan, and the Unknown Soldier—but Jacob saw himself consigned, here, to the ranks of the irrelevant.[129]

||

FOR ALL HIS perversities, Jacob helped a number of people. One was the deaf Catalan painter José de Togorès, recently arrived in Paris: he was poverty-stricken, and his father had just thrown away the last of the family fortune. Jacob was so moved by his work he recommended him to both Kahnweiler and Guillaume. Togorès later recalled how he stayed in his studio, shivering with cold, the day before Christmas 1920, while his father filled a taxi with his canvases and went to meet Kahnweiler. The father returned several hours later in an empty cab: the dealer had bought everything and would devote his first postwar show to Togorès in 1922.[130]

The story of Benjamin Péret's beginnings in Paris shows Jacob's special kind of generosity. The boy had been flung into the Great War at age fifteen and had spent much of the war in military hospitals. He was from Brittany, and when he came to Paris, he went to find Max Jacob, who had just emerged from his own hospital. Jacob wrote Picabia asking him to help "this lovely boy," "a staunch Dadaist." Picabia did help, introducing Péret to Breton and his friends, and Jacob again pitched in for Péret, writing to Salmon about trying to find the young man a job.[131] Even more significantly, from a moral point of view, Jacob went out of his way to help Reverdy, who had recently attacked him in such vile terms: early in 1921 he wrote Paul Budry to ask if he could expedite the publication of a story of Reverdy's for *Les Écrits nouveaux* as Reverdy was broke and needed money badly.[132] And he helped Radiguet in innumerable ways. A letter from October 1920 advised him to go see Malraux, only two years older than Radiguet and already working at the Éditions du Sagittaire; this correspondence reveals a whole network of friendships: Jacob, Radiguet, Malraux, Gabory.[133]

ON DECEMBER 9 the obstreperous Picabia, nominally a Dadaist, staged an evening that alienated Breton for good. Fully aware of Breton's loathing for Cocteau, Picabia organized a show of his own paintings—everything from his early Spanish Impressionism and portraits of women to his Dada contraptions—at the Galerie de la Cible on the Rue Bonaparte, across from the Académie des Beaux-Arts, and he invited Cocteau and his jazz combo from the nightclub Le Boeuf sur le Toit to perform: Auric and Poulenc at the piano, and Cocteau in a top hat improvising on drums, castanets, drinking glasses, the mirliton, and a klaxon. The motley guest list, too, was designed to enrage Breton: Jacob, Fargue, André Germain, Jean Hugo; the inevitable Comte Étienne de Beaumont; assorted princesses; and Picasso, Satie, Laurencin, Tzara, Aragon, Soupault and his wife. Tzara chanted his newest manifesto, with Cocteau's band punctuating each "canto."[134] Cocteau would go on to the triumph of Diaghilev's revival of *Parade* two weeks later at the Théâtre des Champs-Élysées, and Picabia and Tzara would in their different ways prevent Breton from leading Dada: Dada was, by definition, unleadable.

For Max Jacob, the year 1920 came to a peaceful conclusion. The day after Christmas, bearing an enormous box of chocolate pralines, he visited the Ghikas with Auric. They ate and chatted all afternoon and evening, and Max improvised a magical tale about the pregnant Virgin (who resembled Liane). By this time, he and the princess knew each other so well that their quarreling could be a form of intimacy, but on this holiday only good spirits reigned.[135]

X.

WRITING TO SALMON in January 1921, Jacob remarked, sadly, that he hardly saw Picasso anymore. He also mentioned that *Le Terrain Bouchaballe* would be coming out in two volumes from Émile-Paul and that he would dedicate it to Salmon. His first version of the dedication, "To André Salmon, the earliest of the modern poets," raised a cry of protest from the *habitués* of the Rue Gabrielle, so he changed it to "To André Salmon, precursor of the modern poets, my admired and respected friend." Either version was a form of logrolling; he knew perfectly well that Salmon had never initiated any poetic forms but had amiably followed the experiments of Jacob and Apollinaire.[136] He also announced the forthcoming publication of *Le Laboratoire central,* from René Hilsum's Sans Pareil, the main publisher of Dada: Hilsum kept his door open to Jacob. This book, Jacob's most significant collection of verse poems and a landmark in French poetry, would appear in April, and Jacob set great store by it. But already in February Kahnweiler ("Kahnvellum," in Jacob's joke about the expensive materials) brought out a smaller work of Jacob's in a luxury edition with four lithographs by Gris, *Ne coupez pas, Mademoiselle* (Don't Cut the Line, Mademoiselle), one of Jacob's most appealing minor pieces, a children's story-poem about a giant who seizes a city's system of telephone and telegraph wires for a wig. In the havoc of misdirected messages, it's a figure for poetry itself, if one thinks of poetry as a disruption of conventional communications.[137]

JACOB RELIED ON the Ghikas for stability in his social life during the next few months. He saw them almost every week. Liane was preparing to sell her mansion and purchase a smaller house since the prince's mother kept them on a less than princely allowance. Liane suffered from migraines; Max showed real solicitude, often turning up with flowers or a container of broth that his landlady made and that Liane found soothing. In April he found a buyer for her painting by Jean-Jacques Henner, an academic artist greatly admired in that era; the painting sold for eight thousand francs, with a 10 percent commission going to Max.[138] "The wheel of fortune has turned in Max's favor," Liane noted. He was cutting a figure in the artistic and literary world: "This pleases him, amuses him, make him giddy, avenges him."[139]

Jacob now needed friendship more than ever. On February 4, Picasso's son Paulo was born. Picasso didn't invite Max to be the godfather and didn't even send him an announcement of the birth. Jacob was deeply hurt. He complained to his old friend the dealer André Level, to Gertrude Stein, and others, but no amount of complaining could change the bitter fact. When he went to visit the new parents, he said, even the baby turned away from him.[140]

He received another blow in March from Breton and the Dadaists. The March issue of *Littérature* opened with a chart (appropriately entitled "Liquidation") ranking a long list of artists and intellectuals (and the odd politician). In a pastiche of the lycée system of grading, the rankings ran from -25 ("total aversion, or absolute indifference") to 20, the grade in each case being an average of the grades assigned by the evaluators. Of course, the colleagues graded one another generously, so that Aragon, Breton, Éluard, and Tzara emerged triumphantly. Jacob's humiliating grade of -1,27 put him in the company of Christ, Beethoven, and Gide, and higher than Homer and Virgil. Picasso emerged with a respectable 7,90, and Reverdy with 5,36. More than the insult of the average grade was the personal wound of the individual judgments. Aragon, who had come to Jacob's room at the Rue Gabrielle to learn about poetry, assigned him a 1; Breton a 0; and Péret, whom he had welcomed and helped, gave him a 4. Only Éluard, in whom the poetic instinct trumped ideology, awarded him an appreciative mark (13). Tzara gave him a paltry 3. Breton's vicious and talentless friend Théodore Fraenkel brought Jacob's average down with his -20, as did the -10 from the young novelist Drieu la Rochelle, later to distinguish himself as an anti-Semite and Vichy collaborator.[141]

From one point of view, the list could be dismissed as a juvenile prank. But the rankings mattered: they made brutally clear that some of the most talented younger writers had organized to demonstrate their contempt. A new spirit of militaristic cruelty had entered the world of the arts, very different from the playful bitchiness of prewar Paris. Nor would it have escaped Jacob's attention that Jacques Doucet had now hired Breton to produce reports on the cultural scene, taking Jacob's old role.[142] The adoption of the lycée grading system for the liquidation was presented as satire, but at some deep level it expressed Breton's serious obsession with power and hierarchy.

When Jacob visited the Ghikas in March, Liane found him ill with nerves and fatigue, though he rallied and entertained his hosts and walked with them to inspect the new little house Liane had just bought. A week later he came again, worn out from a sleepless night at a masked ball (an extravaganza given by the dancer Caryathis), agitated and dissipated, and all the more irritable for not having been able to take Communion that morning.[143] They had been "visited by a devil," Liane thought. He didn't tell the Ghikas, but he was already dreaming of an escape from Paris.

||

Le Laboratoire central came out in April. The title had a comic origin: Jacob had looked out the window of the composer Roland-Manuel's apartment on the Rue de Bourgogne and seen a sign for his friend's father-in-law's profession: "Central Laboratory for the Suppression of Fraud."[144] The book gathered poems of many years, some dating back to 1903 and 1904, some freshly composed. Like the poems in *Les Oeuvres burlesques et mystiques de Frère Matorel,* these pieces followed the arc of their creator's experience, from dissipation and sorrow through visionary crisis to acceptance of the sacred. The verses are dissonant and hybrid, mingling traditional metrics and free verse, with irregular punctuation, clashing registers of diction, and goofy allusions and clichés: by playing with and against conventions, Jacob made convention itself a theme. The versification was so sophisticated, the ironies so multiple, even readers accustomed to Modernist poetics in his day had trouble, at times, grasping what he was up to. He may have had to wait for the twenty-first century to find a hearing sympathetic to this wild mixture.

IN THESE POEMS, sound often leads sense: in "The Explorer," "Côtes, coteries, échos des côtes et des cottages / Des cottages et des boycottages!" (Coasts, coteries, echoes of coasts and cottages / Of cottages and boycottages!)[145] or in "Acidulous Music," "Boum! Dame! Amsterdam!"[146] In this central laboratory, one can trace Jacob's whole poetic development to date. Though the style is hybrid, it expresses a powerful unifying vision: this is a poet who wrings language hard to find his truth, a mystical and erotic truth.

Le Laboratoire central opens with a delicate song to Auric. But the real opening is the long, ambitious poem, partly in verse, partly in prose, celebrating Jacob's joyous stay with Picasso and Eva in Céret in the summer of 1913. Picasso, reading the book, must have recognized this appeal to their old friendship. The volume closes with the utterly unironic "Litanies of the Holy Virgin" as Jacob adjusts his free verse to the task of devotion. Devotion notwithstanding, he couldn't restrain himself from including a futile fib in the list of his publications in this volume. He claimed 1915 as the year of publication for *Le Cornet à dés*—a celebrated book that everyone knew had appeared in 1917. What motivated this childish reordering of the calendar? Nineteen-fifteen, of course, was the year Reverdy published his rival collection of prose poems. Perhaps Jacob meant the changed date not as a lie that he hoped would be believed—it wouldn't have been—but as another assertion of his claim to priority in the form. Jacob was a fabulist. It's hard to know, sometimes, how much he believed his own fables or in what sense he believed them. In dramatic contrast to the fictional date, his self-portrait, a pencil drawing reproduced as frontispiece to *Le Laboratoire central* reveals a piercing self-scrutiny: the bald, domed head; tired, malicious, riveting eyes of enormous depth; sagging nose; a wicked little smiling mouth.

On April 7 the indefatigable Madame Aurel devoted an evening to Jacob's poetry, with Henri Hertz discoursing on "Max Jacob in Ten Minutes" and three actors reciting his work. Reverdy and Gabory were among the guests, along with the perfidious Péret. Jacob wrote describing the evening to Cocteau and Radiguet, who were then vacationing in the South of France, touching also on the awkward matter of Radiguet's having agreed to write a review of *Le Laboratoire central* for *La Nouvelle Revue française* and then reneging; Radiguet excused himself, saying he was in a fever of his own poetic composition and in no mood to write critical prose (and that the only thing to say about Jacob's book was that it was "marvelous"). Jacob replied tactfully that he too found criticism burdensome but added, "Besides, this book, in spite of your compliment, seems not to have pleased you very much, it sums up twenty years and reflects twenty states of soul, often twenty styles either suffered or created by me—I have the right to say so." He went on to report that he had taken the manuscript of his book of stories to Gallimard, with whom he had a long talk about modern literature. "As you can imagine, I spoke about my friends, only my friends. Because the Dadas are playing tricks on me and I'm not a saint." Several months later, as he was leaving for the monastery, Jacob was disheartened by the cool reception of *Le Laboratoire central* and wrote to thank Cocteau for his praise: "A handshake at the cemetery gate. I've been mistaken all my life. . . . I thought I was a poet!"[147]

||

SICK OF THE turmoil and treachery of Paris, Jacob began to think seriously of retreat. Abbé Frédéric Weill, a priest he had known before the war, a converted Jew now teaching at a Catholic school in Orléans, came to see him in Paris. When Jacob confessed that he wanted to live in the country under the guidance of a parish priest, the *abbé* suggested the Benedictine abbey of Saint-Benoît-sur-Loire, where Jacob could live in the parsonage with the priest, Abbé Fleureau. Before this could be arranged, Jacob had to submit to a tough interrogation by Fleureau, who traveled to Paris to interview him, but the penitent poet managed to convince his new host to accept him, and he began to paint gouaches furiously to earn the money he needed for departure.[148]

While Jacob scrambled to extricate himself from the city, he received a few signs of goodwill. In April, *La Nouvelle Revue française* published four of his stories, a new genre he had invented called "Letters and Commentaries." These short pieces extended the studies in voice and character of *Cinématoma*, except that now the protagonists revealed themselves through writing letters, while the commentaries that followed each letter set up an ironic tension between different versions of experience. The format put into high relief all Jacob's gifts as a fiction writer: a keen eye and ear for hypocrisy, deceit, and self-delusion; perfect pitch in idiom; and economy in implying a complex situation.[149] In May, *Action* published a suite of his lyrics and prose poems, and in June the journal *Signaux* brought out a story about the romance between a nineteenth-century opera diva and a selfish composer.[150]

Among the disappointments attending his departure from Paris was the long-feared first sale of Kahnweiler's sequestered stock of paintings at the Hôtel Drouot on June 13–14. Léonce Rosenberg disgraced himself by serving as the "expert" for this mindless liquidation of the greatest collection of Cubist paintings in the world. The painters bitterly opposed it, knowing that flooding the market like this would cause prices to drop and expose modern art to ridicule. When Rosenberg walked into the room, Braque seized him by the collar and kicked him so hard he went flying into André Level. Braque, a trained boxer, continued to batter Rosenberg, and when Matisse rushed up to find out what was happening, he yelled, "Braque is right! This man has stolen from France!" The combatants were hauled off to a police station, where no charges were pressed, Braque being a decorated war hero. Back at the sale, buyers swarmed: Doucet was there; a crowd of dealers; Paulhan, Éluard, Tzara . . . and probably Jacob, who wrote about it years later in his book on Paul Guillaume.[151]

AT TIMES, LIFE proves more surreal than any aesthetic movement. At some point in the spring of 1921, Jacob acted out the Passion of Christ as a music hall routine in a café while Reverdy was present. Brought up a freethinker, Reverdy was suddenly struck by the spiritual reality Jacob was enacting; all his suffering and depression welled up in a passion of his own, and he was converted. Once again Max Jacob led the way. Reverdy was baptized on May 2 in the little church of Saint-Pierre-de-Montmartre with Jacob as his godfather. Max gave him a prayer book inscribed, "To Pierre Reverdy in memory of his baptism. May this baptism give you a new life, and give new life to our friendship. Max Jacob, Monday, 2 May, 1921." After the ceremony, Reverdy confessed the huge burden of hatred and jealousy he had been carrying, and Jacob wept.[152] Just as Max Jacob was starting his *vita nuova*, Reverdy began one of his own. The two men would be as competitive in religion as in poetry.

Among the temptations Jacob left behind in Paris was an attractive young man he had just met at the apartment of Roland-Manuel and his wife Suzanne. Twenty-year old Michel Leiris, a cousin of Suzanne's, liked to escape to her artistic domain where he could meet Ravel, Satie, and other colorful types. And there he met Max Jacob, a man who would have an immense influence on his life. A few days after that encounter, Leiris visited Jacob at the Rue Gabrielle, where the author inscribed a copy of *Cinématoma* to him: "To Michel Leiris, who strikes me as the representative of the beautiful and serious and grave and lighthearted postwar youth."[153] The friendship would not begin to take shape until November.

||

JACOB ALSO BADE farewell to Picasso. On June 4 he wrote a heart-wrenched letter to his godfather, defending himself against some unspecified accusation from gossip. Another, longer letter, on expensive stationery, summed up the history of their friendship, telling Picasso that he had been involved in all the joys and distresses of Jacob's life, that he represented the whole world of the arts for him: "You are on my horizon and you are near me, in me, and around me." If "third parties" hadn't come between them, Jacob thought, they never would have stopped being friends. "Alas! So many third parties between us!"[154] At the end of June, with something like a broken heart, Max Jacob set off for the dusty, secluded life of a village parish and a mostly empty monastery in the Loire Valley.

Picasso, that summer in Fontainebleau with his wife and son, translated his feelings into two versions of a dramatically chiaroscuro, late Cubist, majestic and funereal painting, *Three Musicians*. Theodore Reff and John Richardson have read these paintings—each with three monumental figures of a Pierrot, a Harlequin, and a monk—as portraits of Apollinaire, Picasso, and Jacob, respectively, and both works as elegiac evocations of their lost bohemian youth in Montmartre. The version now in the Philadelphia Art Museum seems the earlier; it's more colorful and more crowded, and the figures seem to be smiling. The starker work in the Museum of Modern Art in New York more obviously suggests death: either literal death, for the Apollinaire-Pierrot in his brilliant white playing-card costume, with an ominous black dog (Anubis, Cerberus) under his chair, or figurative death, for the Jacob-monk on the right, his face covered in a stringy mask that Reff reads as a Bakota mask from Gabon, and that Richardson reads as the fishnet and raffia masks worn at Carnival by transvestite *mascarones* in Andalusia.[155] Whatever the source, the effect is eerie and threatening. That July, Picasso made a large drawing of a Benedictine monk in a cowl. Max Jacob had taken his leave. For Picasso, his old friend, he was out of sight but not out of mind.

Part III

CHAPTER 13

SAINT-BENOÎT

I.

Max Jacob began his *vita nuova* in the parsonage of Saint-Benoît-sur-Loire, a squat stone building that he described as a packing trunk set among weeds.[1] He was the paying guest of the priest who had interviewed him in Paris, the *curé* Monsieur Fleureau, a man with little round, pale green eyes and his mouth hanging perpetually open. Jacob worked downstairs in a room opening onto the vegetable garden; he looked out on rose bushes in heavy blossom, lilies, geraniums, two pear trees, box hedges, pumpkins, and currant and raspberry bushes. "I've put all my hopes in my green beans," confessed Abbé Fleureau.[2]

Jacob paid four hundred francs a month for room and board, taking his meals with Fleureau and Abbé Charles Breut, the Benedictine vicar, in the red-tiled dining room with its massive antique cabinet and a heavy door ("real Louis XVI") opening onto the garden. He slept upstairs on a feather bed in a room usually reserved for the bishop on his rounds. Next to the parsonage rose the eleventh-century Romanesque basilica of Saint-Benoît, famous for its square frontal tower, the harmony of its proportions, its pale blond stone, and carved capitals that Jacob would come to know well, especially the scene of a soul torn from the grip of a demon by an angel. The relics of the saint, the founder of the Benedictine order, were guarded in a casket in the crypt.[3] The village was rigid, cold, and prosperous.[4] The central square, bordered with plane trees, remained empty except for market days, and all around stretched infinitely flat fields of wheat and barley. The broad, yellowish Loire lazed by the edge of town.

In this new quiet, where a fly buzzing in through the window over his manuscript constituted an event, Jacob once again took up *Filibuth*, the novel about the adventures of a wandering watch he had started on Doucet's monthly allowance. He was working also on a new collection of prose poems to be called *Visions infernales* (Infernal Visions), a "Catholic *Cornet à dés*."[5] At first, he felt nothing but relief. To Kahnweiler, he wrote that he had thrown himself upon peace as a man sick with fever would seize a pitcher of iced lemonade; to Roland-Manuel, he described himself as a sick whale seeking currents of fresh water in the Bay of Biscay or along the coast of Portugal.[6] He wrote Marcoussis about his apprenticeship in Catholic life and the charm of its orderliness.[7] But he missed his friends, confessing to Salmon his crazy desire to go hug them; he had long hours, days even, of solitude, during which he forbade himself to be bored.[8] Jacob had always written vivacious letters, but at Saint-Benoît he became a prodigious correspondent; his epistolary oeuvre has turned out to be a literary achievement in itself.

The monastery proper, as opposed to the parsonage, sat at the bottom of the garden, a grim building resembling a municipal school. There had been no monks there since 1792, when the Revolution suppressed religious practice; the official separation of church and state in 1905 and the expulsion of the Catholic teaching orders from France had further restricted monastic life, and the main Benedictine community was now installed at the monastery of La-Pierre-qui-Vire in the department of the Yonne, to the east. Jacob, then, was not "living in a monastery." He was living at close quarters with two priests in an active parish attached to a basilica, a national monument, and a site of pilgrimage. Abbé Breut, the Benedictine responsible for the mostly empty monastery and the upkeep of the basilica, was a Breton of peasant background, a heavy, blond man, quiet at mealtimes but talkative when he and Jacob took evening strolls along the Loire. Jacob admired these priests and wanted to learn from them, but their culture was entirely different from his. As he wrote

Théophile Briant, "I was Christian, I'm becoming clerical."[9] He woke at six-thirty to attend mass and by eight was installed at his writing table, attending afternoon services as well. On Sundays he entertained the children from the choir after vespers, playing croquet or *boules,* studying their characters: the crybaby, the little proud one (who would become a poet), the glutton, the neurotic, the clever one, the sturdy one.[10] In July the monastery suddenly swarmed with pilgrims celebrating the Feast of Saint Benedict, July 11 (the date of Jacob's pretend birthday). They crowded the monastery and filled the basilica with Gregorian chant, sometimes practicing in the garden.[11] Jacob delighted in the singing and was disgruntled by the mob.

Soon enough the idyll showed strains. Jacob became aware of subtle tensions between his two priests and within himself. As early as August 11, he wrote Georges Ghika, "I thought I'd find happiness. Alas! I've only found myself face to face with myself: impotence and stupidity!"[12] And he nearly set fire to the parsonage. He'd thrown a smoldering cigarette butt into his wastepaper basket, where it eventually burst into flame while the guilty poet was out attending the afternoon service. The housekeeper saw smoke, ran in, and tossed the basket out the window, damaging the trellis for the grapevine on the side of the house. The *curé* scolded Jacob and forbade him to smoke inside, a heavy penance. To make matters worse, Jacob was beginning to run out of money. His several publishers, the Émile-Paul brothers and Gallimard, stopped sending their monthly stipends, and he worried about having to return to Paris to sell more gouaches. After a few anxious weeks and some coquettishly diplomatic letters, the payments resumed. (Therein lay the seeds of future trouble, as Jacob considered the remittances as the sort of allowance Doucet had given him, whereas the publishers were making payments as advances on actual books.)[13]

In September, Jacob was asked to leave the parsonage and move into the old monastery; perhaps the *curé* wasn't convinced that he'd stopped smoking indoors. Jacob complained to friends that his *curé* could no longer keep him and that he now lived in a disused monastery.[14] Here he worked in a room "as big as a dormitory" with an immense table upon which he could lay out all his books and papers. He slept upstairs in a monk's cell and was frightened at night, the building was so large, spooky, and empty. He ate some of his meals at the local hotel. But he still had Sunday dinner with the priests in the parsonage, and he soon got used to his new quarters, settling in so well that he refused invitations from Roland-Manuel and his parents to visit them in their country house, and from the Ghikas to visit Saint-Germain-en-Laye. After the summer holidays, the monastery housed not only Abbé Breut but his white-haired mother, who cooked for the family; his brother "the Captain," a Breton fisherman who now occupied himself with the vegetable garden; the Captain's wife; and their daughter.[15] Eventually Jacob took most of his meals with this family, well nourished on the beefsteaks, trout, sautéed potatoes, and custard the old mother prepared. The monastery would be his home until 1928.[16]

The immense flatness of the Loire Valley played in his imagination and began to enter his poems, along with the golden fields, the sluggish river, and the pear trees in the garden. The poems of this period are like prayers, idealizing an orderly Christian life, often in terms of family: sober parents, well-behaved children, domestic arrangements that Jacob could never have endured but that represented, for now, a dream of redemption. These passages from the poem "Voyages" imagine the ideal:

Saint-Benoît-of-the-Ancient-Vine
Polinge in the land of Orléans
your calm fields and Loire benign
will erase Paris from my mind. . . .

Flat, the flat earth reflects the whole sky,
the rivers are scars streaked on the dying God,
the wheat is his Hair, fountains the Honey flow
that pours from his Heart, from his Body, in flood.

I have the photograph of the world in my head,
I want nothing but this picture of God you are to me,
I want only, God, as men, those men you made. . . .

I love well-tended children, sensible young girls,
I love the piety of mothers, fathers hard at work,
gaiety without shouting, a little wine at meals,
the young in the choir singing, Sunday at church.[17]

||

JACOB WAS PASSIONATELY affectionate, and it was hard for him to live without comrades, let alone without lovers. In September two young men showed up at the monastery during the days: Roland Moufflet, a seminary student spending his holidays with his peasant grandmother, and Moufflet's cousin, Louis Vaillant, a graduate of the elite military academy Saint-Cyr who was awaiting his first assignment as an officer. Throughout September, Jacob's letters mention these new companions, who seem to have dropped by his workroom almost every day, pleased, no doubt, to find a famous writer in the village. Moufflet would rummage among the old books and documents in the attic of the monastery, running down now and then to announce his discoveries "that demolish what we knew about the dates of Childebert, Mérovée, or Clovis II." He was "pale, thin, smiling, gentle, and mocking," and Jacob comically depicted himself trying to keep up with such erudition: "I confine myself to perfidious remarks such as, 'Esterhazy was a very old family, yes! An Austrian family.' "[18]

But it was Louis Vaillant, the young officer, who would become a life-long friend, someone Jacob profoundly respected and never tried to seduce, a "blond ephebe" who resembled an angel.[19] Vaillant, whose name (Valiant) suited him allegorically, had a brilliant record at Saint-Cyr, dabbled in painting, and read modern literature. He studied Jacob's manuscripts, appreciated his prose poems, and asked for advice about "worldly life." Jacob, famous for his gaffes, recounted with amusement to Salmon his new role as instructor in etiquette.[20] He wrote the Hertzes that his new friends interrupted his work: " 'Should a lieutenant, on his arrival in a garrison, make social calls to the wives of officers?' 'Was Philippe I, the successor to Hugues Capet, who reigned for forty-eight years, a good king, yes or no?' The white walls of my immense workroom resonate to such questions."[21]

Ever generous, Jacob went into a flurry in August trying to find money for his godson Gabory, who was hard up, even as Jacob wondered how to pay his own expenses. He hit on an ingenious solution. Having heard of Max's financial difficulties, Kisling wrote offering to pay back an old loan. Jacob refused the payment but suggested that if Kiki wanted to do some good, he could send the money in installments to Gabory. Kisling agreed, and Gabory scraped by.[22] Like so many other literary young men—they were mostly men, in those days—Gabory was trying to patch together a living from freelance editorial work, reviewing, and his poems and articles. Prodded by Jacob, Paulhan hired him as a reader for the Nouvelle Revue Française.[23] Agreeable and moderately talented, Gabory lacked the stamina, and perhaps the ruthlessness, to survive in the long term as a writer, but he paid close attention to everything around him, and his memoirs give a lively picture of the era.

Even in retreat, Max Jacob wasn't absent from the literary scene in Paris. In August, *Action* carried a sympathetic review of *Le Laboratoire central* (and advertised Paul Guillaume's gallery as selling Jacob's paintings along with those of Picasso, Derain, Vlaminck, Modigliani, and Matisse). The *Mercure de France* applauded Jacob's "laboratory": André Fontainas noted the counterpoint of "exquisite fantasy" with melancholy, of clowning exuberance with gravity, and argued that Jacob and Apollinaire were too often considered together, pointing out the difference in tone (Apollinaire more "subtle," Jacob more "sarcastic").[24] Jacob was less gratified by Henri Ther's review in the new magazine *Aventure,* edited by René Crevel, an associate of Breton's: this slightly snooty article illustrates the kind of misreading to which Jacob has often been subjected, mistaking art for personality. It's true that by this time Jacob had become a public figure, the Harlequin from the novels by Carco, Salmon, and Aragon. Ther could hardly see past the persona. While praising the "richness of expression, diversity of associations, and verbal fireworks," he preferred the sweeter, more conventional verses and was disconcerted by the puns and nonsense.[25]

December brought a long, serious review of *Le Laboratoire central* by Roger Allard in *La Nouvelle Revue française*. Like Ther, Allard began with

Jacob's legend but treated the matter more subtly, as a threat to understanding the poems and a risk to the poet. An admirer of *Le Cornet à dés*, Allard was puzzled by the variations in tone of *Le Laboratoire central*; though he praised Jacob's "fluid and brilliant style," he likened the poems to "little phials with misleading labels, so that one is never sure of the contents: bitterness, irony, sarcasm, buffoonery, satiric eloquence." In his desire "to be sure," Allard shared his era's basic assumptions; he could hardly conceive of an art of deliberate dissonance. Yet he was an intelligent and sensitive reader, and his descriptions pointed to real elements in the poems: "the feeling of a refined vengeance, reprisals the poet exacts against himself each time he finds himself guilty of a true emotion." What is a true emotion? Under their veils and masks, Jacob's poems had been examining that question for years.[26]

IN JULY, *Les Écrits nouveaux* ran a selection of Jacob's aphorisms from the book the Émile-Paul brothers would publish the following year as *Art poétique* (The Art of Poetry). Long meditated, these pronouncements— some as short as a single sentence, some in roomy paragraphs—articulate Jacob's ideas at this time of his crowning maturity. He had published or was about to publish his major works, he had reached a significant turning point in his life, and he knew what he was about. One recognizes some of the statements from letters: the paragraph about "exaggerating in order to understand" he had initially written in the letter instructing Cocteau.[27] He restated the principle of abstraction for the prose poem in terms similar to his preface to *Le Cornet à dés*, and he extended his quarrel with Jean-Richard Bloch about politicized art.[28] The renewed classicism Jacob had been discussing with Cocteau and Radiguet turned up in statements on Christian art: Jacob's antipathy to Romanticism now took the form of a claim about classicism and Christianity in terms that other conservative Modernists might recognize (one thinks of Eliot, though the two writers are in most respects wildly dissimilar): "Official art is a romantic art; romantic art is anti-Christian since it extols the passion which Christianity reprehends." The orderly detached art that Jacob now praised was "the attitude of the classical artist."[29] In his Modernist

Christian classicism, Jacob could sound Parnassian: "Painter, cut your diamond." But at the same time, like Picasso, Jacob understood emotion as the primary driving force.[30] And in a single sentence, he summed up the essence of his art, that particular quality of mystical realism that distinguishes him from all other writers: "I dreamed of recreating life on earth in the atmosphere of heaven."[31]

In October, ever faithful, Salmon cited Jacob's paragraph about exaggeration and Modernist art in his essay on Apollinaire in *Action*.[32] The same issue carried three poems by Jacob, two of which he retained for the collection *Les Pénitents en maillots roses* (The Penitents in Pink Tights). The crankiest of the three, "Boredom at Europa's Bull," mingles details from life at the monastery with elements of fantasy, fairy tale, and folk song. Daily worries are transformed into wordplay; his anxiety about remittances from publishers produced the toothsome first line, "Tant de maravédis, escarcelle des veuves!": the exotic, Spanish word for cheap coins, *maravédis*, and the obsolete *escarcelle* (wallet), turn sordid financial care into a fizz of syllables. The escapist poem that French poets had kept rewriting since Baudelaire's "Invitation au voyage" here dreamed of a distant land of idealized poetry, Persia (made more explicit in the version published in the book, where the misprint "Peste!" was corrected to "Perse!"). The poet, a beleaguered Narcissus, consoled himself in the cadences of a folk tune.[33]

IN NOVEMBER, TWO more of Jacob's fictional "Letters with Commentaries" came out in *Action* as the epistolary book *Le Cabinet noir* (The Darkroom) took shape. Once again Jacob put selfishness on stage. In "Letter from 1920" a bourgeois mother complains about her children and the insolence of the working class; the commentator, a stand-in for the author, wryly questions the mother's claims. In "A Modern Poet's Letter" a young man writes to his girlfriend, and the various commentaries (from the girlfriend, one of her older lovers, the young man's mother, and his uncle) reveal a complex network of competing egotisms.[34] These fictions sprang right out of Jacob's gifts as letter-writer and mimic. He had already used part of a letter to Cocteau in *Art poétique;* within the next few months he

Fig. 1. Jacob family living room, rue du Parc, Quimper, 1939. *Collection Gérard Zunz. Reproduction Patricia Sustrac.*

Fig. 2. Pablo Picasso, *Mademoiselle Léonie*, for Max Jacob, *Saint Matorel*. Etching, state IIa. September 1910.

Fig. 3. Pablo Picasso, *The Convent*, for Max Jacob, *Saint Matorel*. Etching, plate 2. 1910.

Fig. 4. Photograph of Picasso, 1904, by Ricardo Canals y Llambri.

Fig. 5. Anonymous photograph of Picasso, 1908, in the studio of the sculptor Ignacio Pinazo Martinez at the Bateau Lavoir.

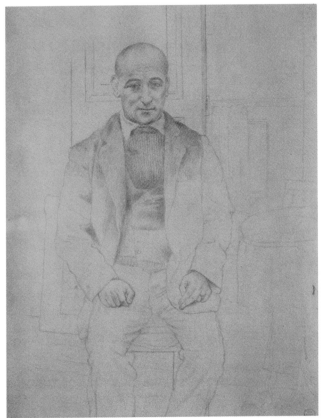

Fig. 6. Pablo Picasso, *Portrait of Max Jacob*, January 1915, pencil on paper.

Fig. 7. Jean Cocteau, Photograph of Moïse Kisling polishing Max Jacob's shoes, 2 August, 1916.

Fig. 8. Anonymous photograph of Picasso in front of the final state of *Man Leaning on a Table*, 1916, in the studio of rue Schoelcher.

Fig. 9. Guillaume Apollinaire with head bandaged, 1916.

Fig. 10. Amadeo Modigliani, *Portrait of Max Jacob*, 1916–17. *Cincinnati Art Museum.*

Fig. 11. Pablo Picasso, *Three Musicians*, oil on canvas, Summer 1921.

Fig. 12. The Basilica of Saint-Benoît-sur-Loire seen from the apse, circa 1940.

Fig. 13. Man Ray, photograph of Max Jacob, 1922.

Fig. 14. Dora Maar, photograph of Jean Cocteau, circa 1935.

Fig. 15. Photograph of Max Jacob, Paris, before 1936.

Fig. 16. Jacques Boudet, photograph of Max Jacob wearing the yellow star, May 1943.

Fig. 17. Max Jacob, portrait of Picasso, gouache, 1944.

Fig. 18. Max Jacob, *Vision of the War*, gouache, circa 1943.

would turn a whole letter written to a real person (Michel Leiris) into a story. A confessional artist, he treated everything he touched as material to be transformed.

II.

JACOB HAD MET the intense, troubled twenty-year-old Leiris in May at the apartment of the Roland-Manuels. Now in November, learning of the death of Leiris's father, Jacob wrote a letter of condolence to the young man. Michel was the youngest child of a bourgeois family from the inelegant neighborhood of Auteuil. His two elder brothers had been in the war (one as a stretcher-bearer). Michel, young enough to have escaped that hell, attended the Lycée Janson-de-Sailly (in a class with René Crevel and the future Franco-American writer Julien Green). He then moved to the less demanding École Vidal. The hardworking father he despised for his boring attire and vulgar taste in art had earned enough as an employee in a brokerage firm for Michel to explore theater, nightclubs, and bars. He was already indulging in bouts of heavy drinking; he powdered his delicately chiseled face; he dressed like a dandy and affected as much eccentric behavior as he could muster. When he met Max Jacob, he had left school and was wondering what to do with himself. In the short run, his course was clear: he had to serve two years in the army under unusually easy terms arranged by a family friend, requiring him to complete a degree in chemistry at the same time. For the long run, he was baffled. He inclined to the arts but had as yet produced nothing.[35]

For a few months it appeared that Jacob might become the young man's surrogate father. The story turned out differently, but even in the misfiring of their communications, Jacob left Leiris with essential lessons about writing, a debt his pupil would repay years later when he wrote the preface for Gallimard's 1978 edition of *Le Cornet à dés*. Even more than ideals of style, what connected the two was an instinct for confession and wordplay: all of Jacob's oeuvre can be seen as fictive autobiography, and Leiris turned out to be a preeminent ethnographer of the self, opening his book

L'Âge d'homme (Manhood) with the Rousseauian claim to speak of himself "with a maximum of lucidity and sincerity."[36] He was, he asserted, "a specialist, a maniac of confession."[37]

Jacob's first letter to Leiris, on November 18, must have struck a chord. Evoking the grief he imagined the young man to feel, Jacob took up the theme of the instructive value of sorrow—a leitmotif that recurs throughout his writing—declaring, "But sorrow is necessary, and a son would never become a man if he didn't take on the place and the responsibilities of those who preceded him."[38] Leiris, at this stage, suffered a wild insecurity as to whether he was "a man": he was attracted to women but afraid of them, drawn also to transvestites, and he had managed to make love with a woman for the first time only when he himself was dressed in female costume.[39] A hypochondriac, plagued by neurotic fears and haunted by a sense of not having proven himself in war, Leiris would, in time, distill his fears into the brilliant imagistic prose of the book called, not coincidentally, *L'Âge d'homme*.

At age twenty, he was far from considering himself a man. He must have answered Jacob's letter immediately; the next letter from Saint-Benoît is dated November 24. In this missive, Jacob moved from consolation to an attempt at conversion, presenting himself as "this old grandfather that I am for you" (though he was only forty-five). The first sentence stated dramatically, "We grow only through suffering." Leiris's half of the exchange has not survived, but we can glean it from Jacob's replies. Leiris, even at this age a self-portraitist, had written that he "despised" himself, that he was "soft," "egotistic," and "a grotesque little character." Jacob responded that this description didn't fit the person he knew; that real egotists can't know that about themselves; that far from being "a grotesque little character," Leiris struck him as being "a strong, hearty fellow of decisive gestures, a little violent."[40] Both of them were right. (Leiris was indeed subject to fits of violence, especially when he was drunk, and despite his short stature and slenderness, he provoked fights in bars. He was, as Jacob intuited, a man of definite and stubborn character.)

Jacob's letter proceeded in a direction that hardly pleased its recipient: an account of the decadence of French civilization since the Revolution, and the need for healing through the resurgence of Catholic values. The letter became downright crude in its salesmanship, listing the "material benefits" to be gained from conversion. The list reveals a good deal about what Jacob fancied he had won from his own conversion, as well as a childish, even magical faith in divine protection:

1. *absolute security*! As long as you don't sin, you're saved. If you sin, you go to confession, you're still saved.
2. The clear knowledge of good and evil laid out in the commandments of God and the Church.
3. Clarity of attitude: no more hesitation, no more doubt, no more timidity! I walk gaily, I know where I'm going.
4. A peaceful conscience.
5. The tremendous support of God and the angels, which is incontestable when one has experienced it oneself.[41]

This vision didn't square with the real complexities of Jacob's life as a Catholic: he was preaching as much to himself as to Leiris. He wound up briskly in the tone of a doctor, prescribing "a good general confession to any old decent priest" and "a good communion": "then tell me how you feel."[42] Though neither of them knew it at the time, Leiris would make "general confession" his life's work.

Leiris was a naturally gifted writer, and his letters stimulated Jacob to ever more artful responses. So artful, that he saved the text of the letter from November 24, and with minor revisions and a commentary, he published it as a fiction the following spring, much to Leiris's discomfiture. For now the correspondence remained private, and Jacob, recognizing something of his young self in his new friend, poured forth advice and cautionary tales. From letter to letter his expressions of affection heated up, though he maintained the formal *vous* until February the following year.

On December 6, Jacob was sitting at his worktable at two in the afternoon, watching winter sunlight gild the apse of the basilica and the few leaves left in the garden. A good fire burned in the woodstove. He meant to work, but Michel's letter tempted him to chat. "My only love has always been the arts," Leiris had written. Jacob took this as the "theme of his sermon." What followed was a mini-autobiography, recounting his years of penury and the humiliations of the "disguised begging" by which he sold subscriptions for his first books; even now, when he earned a living from his paintings and had advances from publishers, he lived in fear of poverty. And how did other writers survive? Through the odious and demeaning daily labor of journalism, as Salmon did, or by churning out novels for serial publication like Alphonse Daudet? "The *black bureaucracy* of authorship, what a horror!" Then he imagined an alternate career for Leiris: why not become an enlightened administrator—in any field—and write poetry and novels on the side? He cited examples: La Fontaine was an engineer of forests and waterworks, Charles-Louis Philippe was a clerk in a town hall, Benjamin Constant a state councilor. There was no need for Leiris to hurl himself into chemistry if he didn't like it; he was young; he could choose any number of professions. And then the key word reappeared: "What I advise, is [for you] to be a man of energy, of heart, of sufficient income, and to earn your living, even in a haberdashery shop."[43]

Leiris would interpret this letter in his own way. Sufficiently impressed by Jacob's picture of the "black bureaucracy of authorship," he would avoid it, but not by becoming an engineer, administrator, or chemist. On the contrary, inspired by the artists he had met through Jacob, he would throw himself into a turbulent life of Surrealist agitation. Only much later would he find his way to a version of the solution Jacob had envisioned, training as an ethnographer and working at the newly founded Musée de l'Homme from 1937 to 1971. But all this remained in the distant future, invisible in the clouded crystal ball.

A few days later Jacob wrote Leiris, "How fond I am of you! How I understand you! How I feel for your commotion!"[44] In the stream of letters of the next few months (advising Leiris to be patient in his military service, describing Saint-Benoît, reflecting on asceticism and suffering), Jacob imagined an alternate scenario for his own life. At times the discrepancy between real and ideal exploded into unwitting comedy, as when Jacob advised, "Study is a form of asceticism. Magnify what study has given you by another form of asceticism. Try chastity: you'll tell me how you feel. It's easy! Just a matter of habit."[45] Just a matter of habit. When he wrote this letter, in good conscience one assumes, Jacob had been trying chastity for about eight months. The exercise would not last much longer.

||

JACOB RARELY SAW his sister Mirté-Léa and her husband, Lucien Lévy, in Paris, where they ran a little jewelry shop.[46] Nor did he see much of his brother Jacques, the tailor, who also lived in Paris, and he had alienated the Gompel and the Sylvain Lévi cousins. But he didn't lack family feeling and was delighted when a second cousin, the eighteen-year-old Francis Gérard Rosenthal, reached out to him just before he left for the monastery. Francis Gérard, his nom de plume, was bright and educated and dreamed of being a writer; with some classmates, he founded a literary review, *L'Oeuf dur,* in the spring of 1921. He and Jacob corresponded for years. Jacob treated Rosenthal to the same ideas about Christian classicism he had relayed to Leiris, but with different emphases, Rosenthal being both a cousin and a Jew. "There are no more rules for prosody," Jacob declared gaily.[47] He tried to steer the young man clear of Romanticism,[48] claimed Heine as the source of all modern literature, and challenged Rosenthal, as he was challenging Leiris, to become "a man."[49] By becoming a man, Jacob meant demanding moral seriousness from literature. His argument grew tortured as he insisted that all great art was Catholic, dismissing in a wave of the hand the idea of Jewish or Protestant art and expressing even more impatience for Arab art or "Indo-Persian higgledy-piggledy," thus eliminating his cousin Sylvain Lévi's entire life work. He was similarly cavalier about the Greco-Roman heritage ("mortally boring"), which left him with a very narrow and almost entirely French notion of "classicism."[50] Sensing that Rosenthal was not a candidate for conversion, Jacob merely suggested that he could remain <u>a good faithful Jew</u> (his underlining) and strengthen himself by reading Christian moralists. In one of the most revealing letters, Jacob took up Rosenthal's anxiety about identity. Jacob's answer described his own ironic sense of self: "Don't worry that your personality is a disguise.

Calm down! *There's no such thing as a disguise.* I've seen costume balls and each person's costume expressed his character just as well and *better* than his normal dress."[51]

For an intelligent man, Jacob could be remarkably dim-witted (as in his vision of Catholic art). Nor was he always so contemptuous of foreign literatures; in other moods he was enthusiastic about Shakespeare, George Eliot, Dostoyevsky, Hardy, and other non-Catholic foreign authors, and in the days of the Bateau Lavoir he had been inspired by translations of Persian and Japanese poetry. This new bigotry stemmed from his new environment, his project to refashion himself as a loyal French Catholic. As the weather grew colder in autumn, his host in the monastery, Abbé Breut, took to joining Jacob in his workroom, where a fire burned all day in the stove. The priest sat reading his breviary or the extreme right-wing newspaper *Action française;* occasionally they joked and sang together or even did what Jacob called "Swedish gymnastics" (Jumping jacks? Touching toes?). On Sundays, priests from neighboring parishes might join them and Abbé Fleureau for dinner in the parsonage. For this costume ball, Jacob was trying to wear the mask of a devout provincial Catholic.[52] It would never truly fit. And in a moment of bitter lucidity, he acknowledged it, writing to Rosenthal, "Though a Christian can strengthen his spirit by trying to be Jewish, just let a Jew try the reverse: the critics will be sure to judge him irremediably Jewish."[53]

IN MID-DECEMBER AN unusual letter found its way to Jacob. An envelope from Puerto Rico reached a Parisian post office addressed simply to "M. Max Jacob, Poet, Painter, Astrologer." It happened that the clerk who was preparing to throw out undeliverable mail was René Rimbert, an amateur painter who had read Jacob's poems in literary journals and seen his show at Bernheim-Jeune. He asked around and forwarded the letter to the Rue Gabrielle with an explanatory note but (discreetly) no return address for himself. The letter, a request for an autograph, wended its way to Saint-Benoît. Jacob, in turn, wrote back to Rimbert at the improbable address "M. Postman, Painter in Montparnasse, Paris"—and Rimbert received it.

Thus was born yet another friendship.[54] Jacob sent Rimbert this disarming self-portrait: "I'm a little old man with a small, ruddy face, and big feet. I'm bald, stupid, toothless. I'm imbecile, weak in the head, absentminded, mean, pious, tearful, gossipy, chatty. I speak only of myself, I complain about everyone. I'm dirty, poorly dressed, pretentious, easily duped, jealous, incapable of sustained conversation, but fairly friendly and polite."[55] This picture in no way resembles the photographs of the forty-five-year-old Jacob, who looks distinguished, forceful, and alert. If he really felt this unlovely, perhaps it's no wonder he appealed to God for a dream of absolute love.

And Picasso? He seemed now to belong only to the past. Jacob made a quick trip to Paris in early November, mostly to see publishers, and spent a night with the Ghikas. (Liane found him "not at all sanctified" by his stay at Saint-Benoît, but embittered and worried.)[56] On that visit, he saw Picasso, reporting afterward to Kisling that it would have made him weep, the two old friends treating each other with cold politeness. "Ah! It's the death of my whole life! He's more dead than Apollinaire."[57] But he swallowed his pain and at the end of November wrote his godfather a long letter full of anecdotes in his old style. One of the stories, local gossip about a burglary and a swindle, would become material for a "Letter with Commentary" that he would publish the following year in *Le Cabinet noir*.[58]

III.

A WRITER'S LIFE risks boiling down to a list of titles and the odd love affair. If skimpy in romance, 1922 produced a literary harvest. Jacob's collection of stories, *Le Roi de Béotie*, came out from the Nouvelle Revue Française in mid-December 1921. Like so many of his books, it's unclassifiable, a gathering of monologues in the style of *Cinématoma*, short stories, three plays, and lightly disguised memoirs. The material stretches back to Jacob's youth in Quimper and the early days in Paris at Gompel's department store and the Bateau Lavoir.

Four of the tales take place in Quimper, two tracking the vicissitudes of the arts in the provinces in the adventures of pianos bought, sold, and rented in endless shenanigans. "Surprised and Delighted," first published in *Les Soirées de Paris* in 1914, cut closer to the bone. One of Jacob's best stories, composed in a supple, swift style, it presents an only slightly mythologized version of Jacob's defection from his family and his betrayal of their hopes for him, concluding, "Thus began this life of privation and suffering that is still mine today."[59]

The autobiographical strain continued in the stories set in Paris, two of them involving Picasso. In "Bohemia During the War of 1914," the painter appears as "the most recent theoretician of art and the most serious and most important producer of plastic invention"; one delicate sentence reads like a private note to his old friend, evoking their shared life and "the delicious knots that individual obligations may have loosened, alas! but have not yet entirely broken."[60] In "The Voltaire Warehouse," one of several pieces in which Jacob recreated Gompel's store, Picasso could have read an even more direct and emotional appeal to their shared past, a reminder of the weeks in 1903 when they lived together in Max's little room.[61]

Gathering stories published in *L'Élan*, *Les Soirées de Paris*, *Action*, *Nord-Sud*, and *La Nouvelle Revue française*, the volume also included the play *Chantage* (Blackmail, a pun since *chantage* contains *chant*, "song") that Charles Dullin would produce a few months later in Paris. The masterpiece of the book is the final section, "Hospital Nights and Dawn," Jacob's account of his experience in the hospital. Gallimard had asked him for a novel and hesitated when presented with this gallimaufry. In hindsight, the Nouvelle Revue Française can take pride in having published one of the most original collections of French prose of its era. In the title, Jacob presented himself in yet another sly mask; "The King of Boeotia" alluded to a lyric in Offenbach's *Orpheus in the Underworld*, always a touchstone for Jacob: the character John Styx, in the Underworld, confesses that in life he was King of Boeotia and offers his heart to Eurydice. In ancient Greece, Boeotia stood for the "sticks" (if not the Styx), a boorish province. In this guise, the urbane yet awkward poet offered his heart to the public.[62]

||

JACOB SPENT CHRISTMAS and the New Year quietly in Saint-Benoît, laboring on *Filibuth*, reading the Revelations of the mystic Anne-Catherine Emmerich, and carrying on his massive correspondence. His priests pressured him politically: both were partisans of Charles Maurras's royalist Action Française and urged him to vote for the far-right party. It was a tragedy, he complained to Cocteau; he was forced either "to vote against [his] origins" or against the Church.[63] (A few months later he would write to compliment the anti-Semite Léon Daudet, co-founder of Action Française, on his book *The Stupid XIXth Century;* Léon was the brother of Jacob's gentle friend, and Proust's lover, Lucien Daudet.)[64] There would be no end to the contortions required to maintain a Catholic-Jewish identity.

Paris now appeared to him an insane asylum, and from afar he observed young men he cared for throwing themselves away in the postwar follies of alcohol, drugs, and promiscuous sex. "Gabory is falling, will fall, has fallen; Radiguet idem," he wrote Francis Gérard Rosenthal.[65] Cocteau helped lead this dance to perdition. On January 10, 1922, Louis Moysès, who had run the Gaya, the bar where Cocteau and his musicians established their headquarters, opened his new venture, the nightclub Le Boeuf sur le Toit (The Ox on the Roof), named for Milhaud's and Cocteau's "Spectacle-Concert." It was located at 28 rue Boissy d'Anglas, the elegant street leading from the Hôtel Vouillemont at number 15, to the Hôtel Marigny, the homosexual brothel Proust had helped establish for his friend Albert Le Cuziat, the model for Jupien in *À la recherche.*[66] As in Proust's novel, the underworld was a handclasp away from *le beau monde.* And Cocteau reigned over it all, setting the tone of the new nightclub and attracting there his clan of aristocrats and snobs, making Le Boeuf the whirling center of the whirling 1920s in Paris. Not without suffering: after the inaugural party a few days before the official opening, Radiguet and Brancusi, drunk and in evening clothes, ran off on a whim to Marseille and from there to Corsica for several weeks. (This was not a homosexual escapade, since Brancusi preferred women, but part of a pattern of Radiguet's flights from his possessive mentor and lover.) As Jacques Porel remembered, by this time "everyone" was watching the handsome Radiguet wreck himself with alcohol and sleeplessness, wondering where it would lead.[67]

JACOB KEPT HIS distance from the fevers in the capital. He remained none-theless engaged in the life of the arts, writing a preface for a show of the Catalan painter Togorès. The exhibit, the first in Kahnweiler's new Galerie Simon, opened in early February.[68] Jacob's text hardly gives a sense of Togorès's sweet, stylized work, but its general statement about Spanish art seems really to be describing Picasso: a Spanish painter "never has enough of the nature of things; he's a realist through the depth of his analysis." The next step in the argument, about Spanish mystics, pertains as much to Jacob's poetry as it does to painting: "In any case, to say mystic is to say realist."[69]

Jacob's poems praising Saint-Benoît and Catholic life began now to appear in print, "Mysterious Garden" in *Les Écrits nouveaux*, and "Farewell to the Parsonage of Saint-Benoît-sur-Loire" and "Voyages" in *Action*.[70] And theatrical projects drew him to Paris at the end of March. *Isabelle et Pantalon*, the opéra bouffe he had created with Roland-Manuel, was in the works for a production at the Trianon-Lyrique. When the composer asked him to design the set, Jacob protested that it was impossible: he couldn't compete with Picasso and Derain, everyone would laugh at him. In this long letter he mentioned his affection for the young painter André Masson, who would enter the story more intensely a year later. The rest of the letter reflected on his friend the actor Pierre Bertin's abandonment by his wife, the pianist Marcelle Meyer, who had run off with Marcel Raval, the editor of *Les Feuilles libres*. Jacob blamed Bertin for letting his wife amuse herself at dance halls and consort with dubious characters like the Baroness d'Oettingen and Poiret's sister the bisexual fashion designer Nicole Groult.[71] Yet he couldn't refrain from joking: "She loves Raval! I love Raval too and plenty of people love Raval, whom I've never met. So what?"

A more immediate lure to Paris was the production of his play *Chantage* in March, directed by Charles Dullin with sets by Artaud; Jacob was eager to see Leiris, and he looked forward to meeting the mysterious artist-postman René Rimbert;[72] he promised to see his work in the Salon des Indépendants, and in answer to a question of Rimbert's about his relation to Cubism, he composed a little treatise that has often been quoted:

> I wasn't a Cubist:
> 1. because hearing of nothing else I was delighted to think about other things.
> 2. because it wasn't in my temperament.
> 3. because I would have wanted to be the best and I wasn't capable of it.
> 4. because Picasso had chosen Braque for his student, not me.
> 5. because basically I understood literature, not painting.
> 6. because I create my works from the pit of my stomach and the pit of my stomach is comic opera.
> 7. because by training I'm a forty-six-year-old man of the Impressionist period, and Cubism was an add-on to my life.
> 8. because Cubism pleased my mind and not my hand and I'm a sensual man.
> 9. because Cubism often strikes me as ugly and I love—pretty things, alas!
> 10. because I'm an old Virgilian poet.
> 11. I don't know why.
> 12. in fact, I've made many Cubist drawings.
> 13. all this is Picasso's fault.[73]

||

JUST BEFORE HEADING to Paris, Jacob sought to help Reverdy, who was desperately poor and trying to leave the city for the Abbey of Solesmes. In a letter most likely addressed to his publishers the Émile-Paul brothers, Jacob pleaded for financial assistance for his brother poet and rival.[74]

Chantage seems to have come off fairly well. It's an unpretentious farce, pitting a greedy bourgeois couple against a country cousin and his wife. In a Paris hopping with theater, most of it frivolous, Jacob's play was no worse than other lightweight entertainments; Jacob, however, complained that Dullin had "screwed up" his play, not letting the actors express "its psychology."[75] René Crevel saw the performance; though allied to Breton and Dada, Crevel never lost his sympathy for Jacob. (Nor did he share Breton's hatred for Cocteau; Crevel was bisexual, a dandy, and a creature of the night, a faithful patron of Le Boeuf sur le Toit.)

In Paris, Jacob stayed at his old room on the Rue Gabrielle and kept busy seeing publishers and friends. He had lunch with Leiris, introducing him to Antonin Artaud. Leiris, always sensitive to dress and physical appearance, was impressed by Artaud's beauty, by his pale complexion and pale gray-green suit, and the contrast between his poverty and the dignity of his bearing.[76] Jacob saw Rimbert's paintings (and recommended him to Kahnweiler, though nothing came of it) and visited the Ghikas. He struck Liane as healthy and calm, but he told her that he'd "sinned greatly" in Paris and had gone to confession at Sacré-Coeur, since it would be too embarrassing to confess such things to the priests with whom he lived.[77]

By early April he was back in Saint-Benoît, observing the fruit trees blossoming. Two of his books appeared that month: the first, short edition of Le Cabinet noir (The Darkroom) from Les Marges, and his aesthetic meditations, Art poétique, from Émile-Paul. He dedicated Le Cabinet noir to Roland-Manuel in this year of their collaboration. (The title refers to the surveillance of mail in the ancien régime as well as to the darkened room for developing film: in the darkroom of Jacob's stories, the human soul comes to light.)[78]

The figure of Madame Gagelin had already made her debut in Cinématoma, and now this savage portrait of Jacob's mother reappeared in "A Mother's Advice to Her Daughter" in Le Cabinet noir.[79] Madame Gagelin reveals every conceivable bourgeois prejudice and a hilarious materialism by which family names are melted into commercial enterprises: "I've told you a thousand times that the Bastides of Toulon are the same family as the Bastides Oils of Grasse with an excellent reputation in the region and two cars, whereas Madame Bastide of Marseille is a little stinker I've never been able to stomach, a Verdilhan from Algeria."[80] A paragraph on fashion is followed by advice about how to run a household, based on

Madame Riminy-Patience's admirable oppression of her maids, who are half-starved and allowed no outings except on the Day of the Dead. In every phrase, one feels the vengeful delight with which Jacob translates his mother.

Le Cabinet noir shows Jacob in top form. Paul Morand, the novelist-diplomat, companion of Proust, Chanel, and Cocteau, and *habitué* of Le Boeuf sur le Toit, greeted the book in *La Nouvelle Revue française,* citing lines from it that he said "would go to heaven" and concluding, "Is it necessary to repeat that Max Jacob is one of our masters and an ornament to our epoch?"[81] For all Jacob's complaining, the Nouvelle Revue Française had clearly opened its arms to him. The publishing house had just brought out his *Le Roi de Béotie,* and its magazine reviewed each of his books in this period sympathetically. In March, in an act smacking of nepotism, the magazine printed Gabory's appreciative review of *Le Roi de Béotie,* in which he singled out for particular praise the feel of "a true emotion" and "real tears" in "Hospital Nights and Dawn," and in August the editors ran Malraux's welcome to *Art poétique,* "the best justification for the literary movement called 'Cubist' that anyone has written."[82]

Les Écrits nouveaux had published excerpts from *Art poétique* the previous year, but the book as a whole has an authority one wouldn't have divined from those fragments. The fruit of twenty-odd years of poetic discipline, *Art poétique* remains a key document in Modernist aesthetics. Jacob's aphoristic style transferred to the form of the essay something of the technique of the prose poem: arguments flash from insight to insight, requiring the reader to supply logical connections. Whereas the selection in *Les Écrits nouveaux* consisted largely of "Christian Art," the weakest part, the book had five sections and emphasized more strictly aesthetic matters, presenting a definition of Modernist literature with the clarity of one who had helped to create it.

Originally dedicated to Cocteau (though published with no dedication), *Art poétique* can be read as an echo of an ongoing conversation with Cocteau and Radiguet.[83] Largely in reaction to Dada, the three had been prodding one another toward a counterideal of a classicist Modernism: "Hurrah for common sense, logic, the only classic!" Jacob had written to

Cocteau in July 1921.[84] Jacob picked up from Cocteau's *Le Coq et l'Arlequin* the anti-Romantic quip, "The nightingale sings badly," and extended it: "Some nightingales sing badly; there are others."[85] In turn Cocteau, in *Secret professionnel*, published a few months later, elaborated Jacob's image of art as a ball one throws at a wall to keep it bouncing.[86] In June, Cocteau wrote to say he loved *Art poétique;* he would carry it in his "revolver" pocket to defend him, and he described its style in a sentence he would shortly incorporate into *Secret professionnel:* "What style—what a simple way of saying complicated things—whereas people think style is a complicated way of saying simple things."[87]

In 1920, Jacob and Radiguet had collaborated on a little play, and they had recently written a story together, "Edwige or the Hero," a pastiche of *Thus Spake Zarathustra*, Greek tragedy, and Sylvain Lévi's Sanskrit erudition.[88] One of the shortest maxims in *Art poétique* is attributed to Radiguet: "Insignificance is the vice of mediocre poems in the new spirit, but significance doesn't guarantee the presence of an idea." One other maxim may or may not have come from Radiguet: "Modern poetry skips all explanations."[89] But the book is manifestly Jacob's, stocked with ideas he'd been working out for years—ideas from which Radiguet had learned, including some of Jacob's most often-quoted statements. On art and illusion: "Art is a lie, but a good artist is not a liar."[90] On selfhood: "Personality is only a persistent error."[91] On style: "The old master style is the style of a student."[92] "So well written, so well written that nothing is left."[93] In *Art poétique,* Jacob described, almost as in a recipe, what made a poem "modern": "Too-rich rhymes and the lack of rhyme, voyages, names of streets, and billboards, memories of one's reading, slang, whatever happens in the other hemisphere, unexpected events, the feeling of dream, surprising conclusions, the association of words and ideas, there's the new spirit."[94] In this book, Jacob extended his earlier argument about the incarnational nature of wisdom in his meditation on Christ's "fifth wound," the spear cut in His breast: "the physical mark of the deep intelligence."[95] Jacob's Catholic faith centered on this image and is incomprehensible without it.

||

BEFORE RETURNING TO Saint-Benoît, Jacob held court at his old haunt, the café La Savoyarde, where a group of young painters gathered round him. These included the Nietzschean Romantic André Masson, Élie Lascaux, and Jean Dubuffet. Jacob recommended them all to Kahnweiler, and two of them, Masson and Dubuffet, would become internationally famous, Masson for his Surrealist fantasias, Dubuffet for "Art Brut." But in 1922 they were young and unknown. They began to take on an identity as the group of the Rue Blomet, the street where Masson had his studio and ran a visionary commune. For a while the Rue Blomet clan considered Jacob their "bon Papa."[96] In April, Lascaux visited Jacob for several weeks at Saint-Benoît, taking over a large ground-floor room for his studio. He was charming company, Jacob reported to Kahnweiler, and worked hard, painting views of the basilica and of Max's cell and work desk in his naïf style. They, too, did "Swedish gymnastics" together, transformed by Lascaux into "violent ballets, another kind of Ballets Russes."[97] (Lascaux would soon be absorbed into Kahnweiler's circle when he married Lucie Kahnweiler's sister Berthe. Michel Leiris's life, too, would be changed when he met the painters and Kahnweiler.)

Lascaux and Jacob spent the rest of April peacefully at Saint-Benoît. The actor Pierre Bertin, at loose ends since his wife left him, stayed with them for Easter ("an abnormal Parisian presence," Jacob reported), and Jacob enjoyed the visit of his sponsor, Abbé Weill, who came to lunch one day with three priests.[98] At the end of the month, Jacob accompanied Abbé Breut on a three-day visit to the central Benedictine monastery at La Pierre-qui-Vire, in the mountainous region to the east. He loved the severe landscape with its woods, valleys, rivers, and cathedrals and found the monks peaceful and welcoming.[99] Here he tasted the Other Life, the timeless dream of Catholic peace.

May brought more travel. Jacob scuttled to Paris to deal with publishers, mainly for publicity for *Art poétique*. His brother Maurice, "the

African" who had lived for twenty-seven years as a colonial officer in Senegal, returned to France, and Jacob spent eight days in Quimper to help welcome him back. As usual, he experienced tensions at home: his family objected to his going to mass, so he had to sneak out at six each morning through the adjacent hotel, where the proprietor let him out a back door into the cathedral square at an angle invisible to his family's apartment. His sister Delphine so resented his presence that she wouldn't let him put sugar in his coffee; he took to pocketing sugar cubes from his friends' saucers at the café for use at home.[100] During this visit he showed the artist Giovanni Leonardi, an old friend from Montmartre, around Quimper, inspiring Leonardi's attachment to the town for the rest of his life.

COCTEAU'S NEW VOLUME of verse, *Vocabulaire*, appeared in April. Jacob wrote to congratulate him. It's a serious letter: Jacob was at pains to distinguish the superficial modernity of subject matter from the structural modernity of imaginative association: "It's not enough to find your comparisons in railroad stations or the Racing Club to make new images; that way, at best, one makes new comparisons, not images. Images: to imagine: to forge imaginations!"[101] In reply Cocteau, reassuring Jacob that he bore no ill will about the missing dedication to *Art poétique*, suggested that Jacob should review *Vocabulaire* for *Les Écrits nouveaux*.[102] Jacob took the hint, and his review appeared, not in *Les Écrits nouveaux* but in Maurice Raval's *Les Feuilles libres*.[103]

The poems in *Vocabulaire* hearkened back to older conventions Cocteau had spun out with such facility in his youth, now fresher in diction and imagery but still fundamentally derivative. Cocteau was making a pitch for himself as the chief poet of the fashionable "return to order" that had settled on war-weary France in the 1920s:

Anyone who used to snap at me
Seeing my features in reverse
Will suddenly understand my verse
Honored order faithfully.[104]

"Evidently order is back in style," snapped Allard in his review, noting that the visible features of the poet were not so much "in reverse" as masks for Apollinaire and Max Jacob. Yet he admitted that this was Cocteau's best book so far.[105] One of the most effective pieces was a tribute to Jacob entitled "The Poet from Quimper."

Jacob felt real affection for Cocteau and sympathized with the call for clarity and cadence. In his review ("just reading notes," "I don't know how to write an article"), he faced head-on the problem Cocteau had created for himself through his manipulation of publicity. He put his finger on Cocteau's strength, praising "the dramatist who has done nothing less than to invent a new kind of theater by combining the music hall and literary dialogue." This assessment seems fair; if Cocteau lives on, it is for his plays and his films, not for his stale verse. Cocteau was extravagantly grateful: "Divine Max, I love you, I admire you, I divine your every nuance and I savor the lightest of your pollens that fertilize our poetry."[106]

IV.

IN MAY 1922, Jacob began a friendship with a poet far more gifted than Cocteau. He had known of the French-Uruguayan poet Jules Supervielle at least since 1920, when several of Supervielle's poems appeared in *La Nouvelle Revue française*. Though brought up in Uruguay, Supervielle had attended the lycée in Paris and worked at the French Ministry of War during the war. He was thirty-five and married to the Uruguayan beauty Pilar Saavedra; they had five children and were living in Paris, comfortably sustained by the Supervielle family bank in Montevideo. He had published a pamphlet of poems at age seventeen at his own expense, and another collection in 1910. But it was the appearance in 1919 of his third book, *Poèmes*, that brought him to the attention of sophisticated French readers. He wrote to Jacob in the spring of 1922; receiving a sympathetic reply, he sent Jacob his new book, *Débarcadères* (Wharves). Jacob immediately recognized the originality of these poems in which supple free verse and amplitude of

breath opened a huge imaginative horizon. Supervielle brought the large
gestures of Paul Claudel and Valéry Larbaud to bear on his own material:
seascapes, ships, South American Pampas, gauchos, and mountains. It
wasn't the exotic geography that inspired Jacob so much as the force of the
"hallucinatory images" and the rhythmical authority, as he wrote Supervielle excitedly on May 18.[107] For a while they exchanged letters almost
daily, each reveling in the sense of having found a kindred soul, with the
added energy, on Supervielle's side, of feeling he was finally in touch with
a living master.[108] In August they exchanged photographs, and Jacob idealized the "sublime beauty" of this handsome family.[109] The two poets
wouldn't meet until the following year, but Jacob was so stirred by the
friendship that he dedicated to Supervielle six prose poems published that
summer in *Le Disque vert*.[110]

The friendship with Leiris intensified over the summer. At the end of
May, in one of many letters trying to shake Leiris out of his lethargy, Jacob
responded to the poems his young friend had sent, saying that the verses
were "pretty good" but smelled imitative.[111] For the next two years Jacob
offered detailed, and sometimes appreciative, criticism of Leiris's poems,
but he persistently encouraged him to get a practical education, whereas
the young man wanted just the opposite: advice on how to live as a writer.
Years later Leiris reflected on this mismatched friendship:

> The first modern poet I met (a man I admired at least as much as
> Apollinaire) had discouraged me over and over, pressing me to con-
> tinue my bourgeois studies without aspiring to be anything but "a
> good man" or, at most, "a distinguished amateur." I wilted under
> this judgment which appeared to me to admit no appeal; I expected
> from this man, not moral advice, but that he would share with me the
> recipe and the key, and I was almost ready to participate in his vices,
> if that had been a way to acquire his genius.[112]

A few weeks later in that spring of 1922, Leiris was disagreeably surprised to see Jacob's letter to him from the previous November published
as "Short Story with Commentary" in *La Vie des lettres et des arts*. The

text was almost identical; not even the proper name had been changed, though Jacob presented himself as a priest.[113] This was the letter sketching French culture as essentially Catholic; it contained the list of benefits to be obtained from conversion (including the promise that it would help him pass his exams in chemistry!). The first paragraph, however, eloquently expressed Jacob's belief in the value of suffering, and it must be this passage that tempted him to raid private correspondence for fiction: "We grow only through sorrow."[114]

||

IN EARLY JULY, Jacob spent a couple of days in Paris, lodging with Dubuffet at his rooming house in the Rue Berthollet in the fifth arrondissement. He wrote Madame Aurel that he couldn't see her; it was purely a business trip, dickering with publishers.[115] He missed the dreary third liquidation sale of Kahnweiler's Cubist stock at the Hôtel Drouot on July 4; nobody was beaten up; the paintings were presented derisively, upside down; and the prices were contemptible.[116] Back in Saint-Benoît for the rest of July, he worked on a history of the basilica that Abbé Fleureau had requested, enjoying puttering in old books.[117] Once again the monastery teemed with pilgrims.[118] In mid-July he expected a visit from Leiris.[119] But before Leiris's arrival, Dubuffet turned up on a motorcycle and whisked Jacob off on a three-day adventure.

The trip unfolded in a sequence of surprises worthy of Jacob's fiction and grew to an epic comedy in his letters to Cocteau and the Ghikas.[120] Jacob may have had a frisson of romantic interest in Dubuffet, but mainly he experienced the intoxication of speed, freedom, and youth. Dubuffet, in any case, aged twenty-one and just beginning to test himself as an artist, was attracted only to women.[121] They set off with Jacob on a cushion on the baggage rack to admire a mosaic in a village five kilometers away. But the weather was glorious, and they pressed on in their vagabondage, stopping to visit village priests Jacob knew, eating and sleeping in village inns all the way to Blois, 150 kilometers and three days away.[122] And here the motorcycle broke down.

After a day consulting mechanics, Jacob chugged back to Saint-Benoît by train while Dubuffet returned to Paris for a spare part. Act II: "Return of the Charming Boy" (as Jacob recounted it giddily to Cocteau) with his motorcycle and another friend, the handsome scamp of a poet, Roland Tual. They had picked up the repaired *motocyclette* (now christened "Hell" by Jacob) and ridden it back toward Saint-Benoît, but it broke down some kilometers from the village, so they pushed it the rest of the way on foot. When Leiris arrived by train on July 28, Jacob met him at the station dressed in "dark brown trousers, a white vest, a dark blue shirt and a beige silk jacket with a straw boater on his head, holding a flowered cushion."[123] Jacob was flanked by Tual and Dubuffet, in his sporting outfit. The young men stayed three days, to Jacob's joy. He was less pleased that Dubuffet left the broken motorcycle with him and in the insouciance of youth breezed off to celebrate his mother's and his grandmother's birthdays in Le Havre, bombarding Jacob with two letters a day demanding updates on the repairs. Days later the motorcycle still lay on its side in Saint-Benoît, "immobile, bulbous, square, resting in the weeds, fatal, ugly, subtle."[124] Dubuffet reappeared later and stayed for weeks, leaving only at the end of August after some days with Masson, who also showed up.[125] For a while, Jacob reigned over a little commune of young men. Masson, Dubuffet, and Tual overlapped; Jacob read Cocteau's *Secret professionel* out loud while Masson and Dubuffet painted, and Tual immersed himself in Cocteau's *Vocabulaire*. Tual returned to stay for the whole month of September. Jacob hinted to Cocteau of romantic frustration: "I have a big collection of portraits of me that they leave, that they leave behind, to make clear that this desire for my face is just a flight of their hands, not of their hearts."[126]

Leiris's visit to Saint-Benoît in July proved fateful. He and Roland Tual discovered in each other a common passion for poetry, and each recognized in the other a charismatic dandy.[127] They slept in monks' cells next to Jacob's room "cluttered with books, where the chamber pot kept company with sacred images and the unfinished novel."[128] They ate at the inn, stayed up late talking, smoking, and reading aloud, and the next day visited the basilica with Max as their voluble guide, followed by a troupe of tourists. The whole village was whipped up in a festival with bands playing every few yards. Leiris and Tual returned to Paris together that evening, reciting Apollinaire in the bus to Orléans, and the poems of Tzara and Cendrars through the streets of Orléans where they roamed until three in the morning, waiting for the train. The friendship persisted in Paris. Tual introduced Leiris to Masson, and Masson—who turned out to be the artistic guru for whom Leiris had been waiting—brought Leiris to Kahn-weiler's gallery and into the world of modern painting. At Kahnweiler's, Leiris met Picasso, who would prove a lifelong friend, and he also met his future wife, Zette (Louise), presented as Lucie Kahnweiler's sister, but actually her illegitimate daughter.

For the time being Leiris remained attached to Max Jacob. It was to Jacob that he owed his education in poetry and his initiation into Masson's magical world. Jacob was an inspired pedagogue, at times paradoxical, urging his student at once to imitate and to surpass imitation, and demand-ing musicality: "Music, Michel, music! A verse that doesn't sing is not a verse, even if it's opulence incarnate."[129] His advice echoed themes from his *Art poétique* and looked forward to the two pamphlets in the Rilkean genre of "Letters to a Young Poet" that he composed in 1941.[130] "Begin by imitating," Jacob instructed Leiris. "If you have any originality, it will declare itself." "Use the right word, the simple word, the images will come by themselves." Every so often, the teacher awarded a gold star: "Bravo! . . . I'm overjoyed to see your work coming into its own."[131]

Jacob seems to have made another hop to Paris in August, and judging from a letter he wrote Leiris, he may have attempted to seduce "mon petit Michel" during that visit. He opened forthrightly: "You have the right to talk of morality, I do not."[132] Whatever it was that Jacob did, he feared it had scandalized Leiris, but he also tried to turn the episode into a lesson: "What were you doing at the Saphir? And what was I doing at 2 a.m. at the Savoyarde? 'He that is without sin among you, let him first cast a stone.'" Jacob no longer had the courage to condemn anyone, he said. "Don't make fun of me," he begged. "I don't wish on you the pangs and the hell of a life made of follies and repentance, temptations, weaknesses, and tears."[133]

Though Jacob disciplined his affection for Leiris ("*I love you* in Our Lord"),[134] he felt deeply for him. Some of this transmuted love is audible in a poem he composed for him in 1922. He veiled "Poem: Love and Time" as a conventional lyric, a pastiche of romantic heterosexual verse. Published in *La Revue européenne* in 1923, the poem had seven stanzas and was dedicated to Leiris. By the time he reprinted it two years later in *Les Pénitents en maillots roses*, he felt betrayed by his friend and wrote on the manuscript, "Dedication deleted because Michel Leiris is a Surrealist."[135] The final stanzas of the original version contrast Apollinairian crooning with Jacob's caustic gay wit: if Venus had been born in the ocean instead of the Mediterranean, she "would have been a man." The poem speaks worlds about the pain of love that still could not speak its name.[136]

IN LATE AUGUST, Jacob wrote Leiris hinting at tensions with Dubuffet and a welling up of desire and fear of that desire. Dubuffet, bored at Saint-Benoît, was pressing Jacob to leave. Since it was on the back of Dubuffet's infernal motorcycle that Jacob had made his brief flight from the monastery, he must have felt a demon beckoning: he couldn't leave, he wailed, because "however pitiful the environment, it's still a wall against Hell and the sin which lies in wait for a poor man at every moment. Oh! No longer to sin! No longer to sin! Alas! What a wish!"[137] Jacob would continue to see a lot of Dubuffet in the next few years, not in a sexual relationship but in an artistic friendship with emotional complications. Dubuffet was the main model for the Man of Flesh in the novel Jacob wrote the following year, *L'Homme de chair et l'homme reflet* (The Man of Flesh and the Reflected Man), and sure enough, the motorcycle became part of that story. "I've developed a horror of motorcycles," announces the narrator, "ever since I suffered a breakdown, at night, in the steppes of the Beauce, twenty kilometers from any help except that of the angels."[138]

One senses the complexity of Jacob's feelings in his remarks about Dubuffet to Leiris in the next few months: Dubuffet is "adorable," "judicious, sophisticated, intelligent, honest," "highly talented."[139] It was probably at Dubuffet's departure from Saint-Benoît that Jacob wrote the poem to him entitled "The Airman's Fiancée." Once again Jacob disguised his desire as a heterosexual romance.

If you're weary of our shore,
Airman, you can fly away.
You were so calm, so prudent here
I won't regret your getaway.

The heart your wing seduced is no
Longer yours, artist of the air,
On someone else it will bestow
Its stolen good beside the Loire.

Airy is flighty, it also is
fickle, given to burglary:
if your pride is vigorous
it will retrieve our long-lost joy.

A pigeon follows as you fly
and then returns: on his feather dress
may I find the ring, design
and pledge of our forgiveness.[140]

The "fiancée" in the poem threatens to give "her" heart to someone else. The someone else at Saint-Benoît at the moment was Roland Tual, who stayed for a month. A gifted talker, steeped in poetry, Tual never managed to commit words to paper; like Masson and Leiris, he would soon pledge allegiance to Breton's Surrealism. For now, he sought inspiration from Jacob. The experiment turned out badly. Jacob proposed that they collaborate on a play, and as Tual wasn't writing anything of his own, Jacob dictated a comedy based on a skit, *The Elocution Lesson,* that he and Marcel Olin used to perform at the Bateau Lavoir. The plot turns on a drunkard trying to teach elocution to a buxom maid with a heavy Alsatian accent. Jacques Copeau of the Théâtre du Vieux Colombier had asked him for a one-act. Jacob sent a draft of *The Elocution Lesson* in mid-September; Copeau liked it, but Jacob asked for the manuscript back so he could expand it. In the first week of October, Tual disappeared (without paying his bill for room and board at the monastery), taking the manuscript with him.

Jacob was beside himself. He wrote frantically to Kahnweiler and to Gabory, asking the latter to alert Gallimard: he was afraid Tual would publish the play under his own name. Meanwhile he had to pay Tual's bill at Saint-Benoît. Like many of Jacob's dramas, this one proved overblown. Tual was unreliable but not a scoundrel, and within several weeks he had returned the manuscript, apologized, and sent Jacob money—so that by early November, it was now Jacob who was in debt to Tual.[141] And as so often in his tiffs, within ten days Jacob confessed to "dear brother Roland" his remorse at "the spider webs the devil spun between us," and promised he would "work all his life to repair the injuries."

V.

WHILE JACOB DICTATED the play to Tual, Breton's crew at *Littérature* launched a new attack. The personnel had changed. Breton had broken with Tzara, as the September issue of *Littérature* proclaimed. More surprisingly, Soupault, one of Breton's staunchest comrades, disappeared from the masthead: he disliked Breton's taking up with Picabia, and Breton disliked Soupault's taking up the direction of the more bourgeois *La Revue européenne*. The September issue of *Littérature* reverberated with recriminations against Soupault. ("Soupault the businessman," sneered Aragon. "If only you'd become a minister in the government," complained Jacques Baron.)[142] Breton called Soupault his "dear friend forever" in the editorial but declared that the journal would now celebrate Picabia, Duchamp, and Picasso and look for its future in the young contributors Baron, Desnos, Max Morise, and Pierre de Massot. (A year later Breton would break Massot's arm in a brawl over Dada.)[143]

Breton was fueled by aggression. In this issue of *Littérature* he turned savagely against his old mentor Valéry, dumping him, along with Matisse, Derain, and Marinetti, in "a ditch of ruin"; and as usual he snarled at Cocteau.[144] But the more serious challenge to Jacob and Cocteau took the form of Aragon's "Project in Contemporary Literary History," an outline of the Parisian avant-garde from 1913 on. Two years before the first Surrealist Manifesto, a history was being composed to clear the way for what would become Surrealism. Madame Aurel is tossed in the trash; Dada is dispatched ("Tzara unmasked"); and Jacob is kicked aside ("Max Jacob and his dwarves").[145] In the November issue of *Littérature*, Breton claimed the name "Surrealism" for the researches in "psychic automatism" in which he was engaged with Desnos and Crevel.[146]

Cocteau was still on the Côte d'Azur with Radiguet when he saw *Littérature* in September. He wrote Jacob of the shame he felt, and Jacob replied, consoling him but expressing his own pique: "And to think these people came to me like the Burghers of Calais to ask me for the keys to my city!"[147] But this September, Jacob was more wounded by Picasso than by Breton or Aragon. Picasso and Olga spent the summer with their son at the fashionable resort Dinard, on the northern coast of Brittany. In July, Picasso sent Max a postcard from Dinard, to which Jacob replied with elliptical courtesy: "Double and touching souvenir of the beaches of my adolescence and of the friend of my youth."[148] But in mid-September, when Picasso sent the conventional touristic gift of a package of Breton crêpes, Jacob was hurt to the quick. To his old friend, he mailed a short message of coded gratitude and reproach ("translated from a Persian poem," a reference to Matorel), but to Salmon, Cocteau, and Kahnweiler, he complained bitterly, alluding to his early story "Surprised and Delighted." "If you see Picasso," he wrote Salmon, "tell him I was very touched by his gift of Breton crêpes. Surprised and delighted, I must say." To Cocteau, he exploded: "Picasso's crêpes! I see the whole scene . . . vacation spot, expensive postcards! Dinard! Ah! He's no longer, he's no longer! He's no longer my friend! No!"[149]

A flutter of social life distracted him from his grievance. On another lightning trip to Paris in mid-September, Man Ray photographed him. It's a mischievous portrait. Jacob is seated at an odd angle, twisting to the left, his right hand in his trouser pocket, his left elegantly placed near his stomach; he gazes off to the left with enormous, darkly glinting eyes, his mouth hovering on the verge of a smile. He's dressed as a dandy in a gray textured suit, a dark vest, a dazzling white dress shirt, and a black bow tie. He seems to be about to erupt into motion. In a sense, he also took Man Ray's picture, describing him to Cocteau as handsome, with "a royal face, and eyes whose gaze is terrifying: but when evening falls, he looks ashamed."[150] The photographer gave him a print of a portrait of Cocteau, which he brought back to Saint-Benoît and tacked up on his bedroom wall.

||

FOR SEVERAL WEEKS, Jacob and Cocteau corresponded about the Daudet family. Julia Daudet, the widow of the nationally beloved writer Alphonse Daudet, had a small château near Tours where her family gathered: the elder son Léon, furious monarchist and anti-Semite, novelist, deputy, and co-founder of the movement Action Française; and Lucien, an ineffectual writer and painter. Jacob knew Lucien from Paris, and his mother had invited him to lunch.[151] Since Cocteau's mother was friendly with Madame Daudet, Jacob consulted him about etiquette: he had written to the Daudets saying he was now free to visit but had received no reply. How to interpret this? Cocteau reassured him: Madame Daudet had just received the Légion d'honneur and was simply busy in its aftermath. Eventually the invitation was renewed, and Jacob duly visited; his friend the composer Poulenc was present, along with several other guests, including the local priest. Jacob was afraid he committed frightful gaffes, but they couldn't have been so awful, as Léon sent him a copy of his new rant, *The Stupid XIXth Century*.

No wonder Jacob was beset by anxiety at the Daudets' château. A notorious bohemian, he tried to present himself as respectable to this conservative, upper-class family. A Jew, however thoroughly converted, he faced in Léon Daudet one of the most rabid anti-Semites in France. Daudet's book spewed out venomous condemnations of Romanticism, the French Revolution, democracy, liberalism, Jews, Protestants, and Freemasons, seeing them all as a single mad conspiracy. Jacob would have come across this sentence about the politician Alfred Joseph Naquet, who had crafted the divorce law: "This divorce was the work of the Jew Naquet. I knew this Jew, and I saw him at work. He was a frightful Oriental, hunchbacked like a character from the *Thousand and One Nights*, with the eyes of a sadistic *almeh* (Jewish virgin), twisted in physique, tortuous in morals, and he knew what he was doing. He inserted himself into the French family like his compatriots into French finance, and he destroyed it."[152]

Jacob wrote to thank his "dear Sir and very admired Master" for the book. In the guise of complimenting the author, Jacob tried to instruct him about Jewish mysticism. How could he have imagined that Daudet would begin to, or want to, understand? Jacob praised his ferocious satire, claimed to be reading it aloud to his priests and guests at Saint-Benoît and offered a quotation from his own *Art poétique* as if to establish common ground in rejecting Victor Hugo. At this point the letter veered into profoundly personal territory, as Jacob incorporated paragraphs from his own manuscript on symbolic readings of Scripture to persuade Daudet to study Kabbalah and demonology. After presenting the proud monarchist with these fruits of his reflection on Jewish mysticism, Jacob concluded humbly, apologizing for "emptying his satchel," adding, "I thought this observation might interest you and that I was the only one who could make it."[153]

To Cocteau, Jacob criticized Daudet's book. He agreed with the attack on Romanticism, but remarked that Daudet had learned everything from those writers. As for Jewish finance, Jacob said he was still looking for it: he didn't know a single Jewish banker except the Lazarus family, who were hardly wealthy, and nowhere near as rich as the Daudets. At the heart of Jacob's being was his belief in the continuity of Judaism and Christianity; Daudet forgot "that Christian morality is Jewish in origin. Since Our Lord, the Holy Virgin, and the Evangelists were Jews."[154]

||

A FANTASTICAL FRIEND turned up on September 18 and stayed till the end of the month. The Swiss writer and musician Charles-Albert Cingria, at thirty-nine, was a full-fledged dandy, aesthete, and eccentric. He had known Jacob from the old days in Montmartre. Born in Geneva to a Polish mother, into an Italian commercial family with a background in Turkey, Cingria was a Romantic Catholic, passionately opposed to the Calvinism of the city of his birth. Multilingual, erudite, trained in composition and church music, and a flamboyant performer on piano, organ, and spinet, Cingria traveled widely and turned in his twenties to literature. He lived in a dream of the Middle Ages, inflamed by Charles Maurras, G. K. Chesterton, and the theologian Jacques Maritain: the only politics that counted for him were the early medieval realms of Lotharingia and Burgundy. He published his lyrical travelogues in Swiss journals and in *La Nouvelle Revue française;* not until 1928 would he begin to collect them in books.

Cingria slipped right into life at Saint-Benoît, participating in Gregorian chant, playing the harmonica, discoursing with the priests, exploding in belly laughs. Like Jacob, he was a brilliant talker, and the two of them must have carried on quite a duet. As Jacob wrote to Gabory, Cingria was "stirring up the monastery."[155] The two of them helped to harvest the grapes from the arbor, clambering up and down ladders.[156] Jacob's good humor persisted after Cingria's departure; he narrated to Cocteau an episode in which Abbé Fleureau lost his flat priestly hat (*barrette*); it was discovered hanging in the branches of a peach tree. Jacob cheerfully joined in the work in the garden, digging potatoes after lunch and muddying himself pushing a wheelbarrow.[157]

VI.

IN MID-NOVEMBER, JACOB returned to Paris for the production of *Isabelle et Pantalon,* the opéra bouffe he had composed with Roland-Manuel, directed by Louis Masson at the Trianon-Lyrique. Jacob stayed with Dubuffet, a visit prolonged for two months as Jacob fell seriously ill with the all-purpose French "liver ailment." Jacob had his own room in Dubuffet's

rooming house, where the painter cared for him when he was around.[158]
Dubuffet even wrote letters for him and copied out a poem.[159]

Jacob did have enough energy to supervise rehearsals and to attend the
opening. Like *Chantage*, *Isabelle et Pantalon* had little aesthetic ambition
(Jacob called it "an imbecility"),[160] though Roland-Manuel's music gave
it a certain distinction. It's recycled commedia dell'arte with the classic
French characters, Arlequin as the lover, Pierrot as the cuckolded husband, Isabelle the sexy young wife, Pantalon the lecherous doctor, and
Zerbinette the maid. Jacob had fun with the rhymes and the farcical plot,
and Roland-Manuel's music is as frothy as it needed to be. Jacob reported
to his collaborator in mid-December that Princesse Ghika, her friend the
Duchess of Clermont-Tonnerre, and four gentlemen "courtiers" had seen
it, and that the princess found the music "delicious."[161] The play earned
Jacob a pretty sum of money (two thousand francs), so that he was able
to buy new clothes, boasting to Gabory of "my Isabelle jacket and my
Pantalon pants."[162]

But his illness took its toll. He suffered pains in the abdomen and could
hardly drag himself from bed. Cocteau sent over his own doctor, the same
Dr. Capmas who had failed to save Apollinaire.[163] Jacob was too sick to
attend the premiere of Cocteau's ambitious version of *Antigone* directed
by Charles Dullin (who had directed *Chantage*). Whereas *Chantage* had
been a minor affair in the temporary quarters of the Ursulines, Dullin
put on *Antigone* on the new stage he would make famous at the Théâtre
de l'Atelier in Montmartre, and the production, with sets by Picasso, costumes by Chanel, and music by Honegger, is still remembered as a landmark in the history of theater. Dullin played Creon, and Cocteau chanted
the choruses through a hole in the backdrop. Dullin's assistant, Denise
Piazza, a stagestruck young woman from an affluent family, described the
heckling from Breton and his gang from one side, and Raymond Duncan
and his Hellenes from the other; Cocteau shrieked from behind the curtain
that everything would come to a halt unless they quieted down. The police
evicted the hecklers, and the show went on.[164]

Sick and miserable, holed up in Dubuffet's rooming house, Jacob wrote

Cocteau to congratulate him on *Antigone*. He asked him to let Misia Sert know that he couldn't attend one of her soirées.[165] He wrote Madame Aurel to beg off from her invitations;[166] and he groaned in letters to Salmon and the Hertzes that medical bills had eaten up everything he'd earned from *Isabelle et Pantalon*.[167] He even advised the cherished Leiris not to visit.[168]

||

YET MAX JACOB had a way of springing back to life like Harlequin in the puppet theater; just when he'd been knocked out and cast aside, he popped up again. In January he alarmed Leiris with his tales of poverty. But by the end of the month, back at Saint-Benoît, his health restored, he wrote to thank Leiris for his solicitude, reporting that the operetta had cleared up his debts and that a stipend from the publisher Kra for a new novel would pay his expenses, along with several thousand francs he expected from Gallimard for *Filibuth*. He had also begun to paint his "blessed gouaches" again; Malraux had just bought a batch for 700 francs.[169]

Leiris was much on Jacob's mind. Back in the monastery, Jacob set to work on the book that would become *L'Homme de chair et l'homme reflet* (The Man of Flesh and the Reflected Man). He built the story around the two young men who most interested him at this point, Jean Dubuffet (Georges, the Man of Flesh) and Michel Leiris (Maxime Lelong, the Reflected Man). And as he had done in *Le Cabinet noir*, he plundered his astrological files to compose personality types. On February 3 he wrote Roland-Manuel to say he'd squandered the better part of a day reading his letters in the Aries file, when he'd really meant to look up "Mr. X" (unnamed) for the portrait he needed for the eighteen-year-old hero of the new novel.[170] Mr. X was Michel Leiris, Roland-Manuel's wife's cousin. Meanwhile he cautioned Leiris not to let Roland-Manuel know how much they corresponded: one senses a certain excitement in Jacob's juggling so many friendships and crushes.[171] A week later Jacob warned Leiris that he was using phrases from the young man's letters to create a character in his novel. Having already turned a real letter *to* Leiris into fiction, he took care now to ask for a kind of permission, disingenuously assuring him that the man in the novel wouldn't resemble him.[172] In fact, the egotistical Maxime Lelong, the Reflected Man, turned out to have a good deal in common with the real-life model who bore the same initials. When the novel appeared, Leiris protested (but a decade later copied a whole passage of the portrait into his journal).[173]

Jacob was so thoroughly a lover and writer, his loves flowed into his writing, and his writing flowed into his loves. At times he could hardly tell the difference.

CHAPTER 14

JACOB THE PEDAGOGUE

I.

N ineteen twenty-three brought the publication, in quick succession, of Jacob's two most important novels, *Filibuth, ou la montre en or* (Filibuth, or the Golden Watch) from the Nouvelle Revue Française, and the long-awaited *Le Terrain Boucha- balle* from Émile-Paul. The year would be rich in erotic and emotional complications; even as Jacob grounded himself more firmly in Catholic life, some part of him rebelled and launched him into increasingly trou- bled attachments. Saint-Benoît had not expelled the demons.

IN *FILIBUTH,* JACOB divided himself into two characters: the "author" (named "Max Jacob," living on the Côte d'Azur) and Monsieur Odon- Cygne-Dur (Odon-Swan/Sign-Hard), a man of letters who lives in a room on the Rue Gabrielle in Montmartre.[1] The first and third sections drew on Jacob's real circumstances: the wardrobe with the full-length mirror from the Rue Gabrielle; the beggar woman who shouted at him; his oil lamp; the hoodlums, urchins, and quarreling neighbors; his trouble with the police for harboring a deserter; and in the finale, Dur's retreat to Saint-Benoît-sur-Loire. The story revolves around the pair of Monsieur Dur and his concierge, Madame Lafleur. This promiscu- ous, wine-sotted, mean-spirited woman who constantly calls the police on her own children is a caricature of Jacob's real concierge at the Rue

Gabrielle, the mirror image in which Dur discovers himself (hence the importance of the wardrobe mirror). To the extent that the book has a plot, it tracks the gradual redemption of Monsieur Dur and, even more improbably, of Madame Lafleur. Like Jacob's other fictions, it hardly follows a sequential narrative but jolts from dialogue to dialogue: characters reveal themselves through voice, not action. The golden watch of the title, stolen, lost, coveted, traded, and finally crushed by a car, connects all the actors. Into *Filibuth*, Jacob poured his gifts of ventriloquism and his feel for his tawdry neighborhood in Montmartre. Less convincing, the middle section lets the watch pass into the hands of a luxurious courtesan and thence to Venice and Japan before it finds its way back to Madame Lafleur. Jacob may have drawn on his friendship with Liane de Pougy for the portrait of the courtesan, and her imbroglios with foreign ministers and the secret police afford him amusing material, but the section lacks the verve of Dur's story, in which Jacob offered what he did best, skewed autobiography.[2]

Though Jacob lamented the book's poor sales, it fared well critically. Jacques Porel, who loved *Le Cabinet noir,* praised *Filibuth* as an elaboration of story around the character types of the earlier work, noting Jacob's picture of "this mechanistic and bestial existence we persist in pursuing, far from God."[3] Benjamin Crémieux wrote in *Les Nouvelles littéraires* that Jacob, who had been considered a fantasist, was really "a psychologist, and a historian of manners," suppressing plot in order to reveal inwardness.[4] Philippe Soupault, Breton's ex-comrade who was now editing *La Revue européenne,* praised the way Jacob's characters overwhelmed the story, comparing them to close-ups of faces in film. The book was, he asserted, "miraculous."[5]

A DECADE EARLIER Jacob had been almost unknown except to avant-garde coteries. Now he had novels appearing from two of the most respected publishers in France, and he also found himself on the jury of an important literary prize, the Prix du Nouveau Monde. The intrigue surrounding the prize proved as outrageous as any situation in Jacob's fiction. The two main contenders were Radiguet's *Le Diable au corps* (The Devil in the Flesh), the novel in which the boy wonder coolly analyzed his affair with the fiancée of a soldier fighting at the front, and Soupault's *Le Bon Apôtre* (The Good Apostle), a coming-of-age fantasy in which the intellectual hero commits a crime, goes to prison for a few years, and returns to society as a dandy, businessman, and avant-garde poet.[6]

Radiguet's book appeared in March from Grasset in a thunderstorm of publicity. The story itself was considered shocking—André Germain asserted that nothing this immoral had been written since *Les Liaisons dangereuses*.[7] But the vulgarity of Grasset's campaign (posters, newsreel segments) struck many as even more offensive. Such griping didn't hinder the book's success: it really was a marvel of icy, stripped-down style, and the cynical story suited the country's postwar mood.

Jacob had been reading pieces of the novel as Radiguet composed it, but when Cocteau asked him in January to be on the jury, he hadn't read the whole work, and he wrote anxiously asking if it was obscene and "anti-religious." Jacob's scruple about being on the jury arose not from the fact that he was close friends with the author but from fear of offending the Church. He could easily be replaced on the jury, he wrote Cocteau on January 30. Cocteau must have replied immediately, because on February 1, Jacob wrote to reassure him: "Count on me. . . . It's very hard to do good. And to know on which side duty lies. . . . The bits of the book I've seen are beautiful."[8]

Literary juries are always subject to partisan pressures, but the trafficking for the Prix du Nouveau Monde was stupendous. Cocteau, the lover and promoter of one of the contenders, was on the jury and helped to arrange its composition.[9] Jacob didn't attend the three meetings of the jury, and he hadn't read the whole of Radiguet's novel when the vote was taken and *Le Diable au corps* won. In May he was still asking Cocteau why Radiguet hadn't sent him the book. Not until the end of the month, writing to compliment Cocteau on *his* cool analytic novel *Le Grand Écart*, did Jacob report that he'd finally read *Le Diable au corps* and considered it a masterpiece.[10] Radiguet wrote to thank him: "You have been my Master and you still are."[11]

||

FOR SOME YEARS, Jacob had been corresponding with Gabriel Bounoure, a young literary critic who had taught in the lycée in Quimper before the war. More recently he had directed the Institut Français in Barcelona, and this year, 1923, he was teaching at the lycée in Guéret, a small town two hundred kilometers south of Orléans. He and Jacob had finally met the previous year in Paris.[12] Bounoure and his wife now invited three writers to meet in Guéret over the Pentecost weekend of May 20. Jules Supervielle, the Uruguayan poet, traveled from Paris with his wife and children; Max Jacob took the train from Orléans; and Marcel Jouhandeau, a budding fiction writer who taught in a Catholic boarding school in Paris, returned for the holiday to his family home in Guéret. The Bounoures must have had a large house: besides Jacob and the Supervielles, they were hosting Domingo y Seguro, a young Spanish painter, and his fiancée, and Petito Llorens Artigas, a Catalan painter and ceramic artist.

Jouhandeau, at thirty-five, was a complex character. The son of a butcher in Guéret, he had been raised in an atmosphere of Catholic piety and had been taken up in adolescence by a local lady of extravagant religious pretentions. She bewitched the boy, taking over his life, separating him from his girlfriend and his parents, distracting him from his studies, and promising to fund his education for the priesthood. It took the shock of failing the baccalaureate exam for Jouhandeau to declare his independence. He cast off his fairy godmother and buckled down to schoolwork, narrating this adventure in diamond-faceted vignettes in his first novel, *La Jeunesse de Théophile* (Théophile's Youth), published by the Nouvelle Revue Française in 1921. Jacob hadn't yet read Jouhandeau's book, but he had come across his cruel, glittering stories in *La Nouvelle Revue française* and *Intentions,* and he wrote the younger author in April to compliment him, anticipating their meeting with Bounoure.[13]

The weekend's mixture of personalities created explosive reactions. The Bounoures picked up Jacob at the station on Friday evening. On Saturday, a rainy day, Jouhandeau joined the group, and they all gathered around the fireplace while Jacob, by far the senior figure, entertained them with stories of Montmartre and Montparnasse. He was a spellbinder at this sort of performance, and he must have felt a touch of euphoria. But from that point on, he misjudged his audience. When the weather cleared up, Domingo went outside to paint. Ignoring the young man's fiancée, Jacob followed him around, insisting on carrying his easel and brushes, and at last (according to Jouhandeau's later account) propositioned him. The painter fled back to the house and complained to Madame Bounoure; she in turn called her husband, who did his best to smooth things over.

The house party rolled on for several days with Jacob maintaining his irrepressible high spirits. The Bounoures hired a driver and what must have been a large vehicle from the local garage and took their guests to see the sights around Guéret. These included an abbey with sixteenth-century woodwork (where the *curé*, after receiving a generous tip, ran after the car demanding his pencil back), and a hill where they met a childhood friend of Jouhandeau's, a dentist named Jules Lagrange. Jacob immediately took against the dentist, who just as immediately attached himself to the famous author, insisting that he admire "the most beautiful view in the world." Jacob retorted that he hated beautiful views, staring west when he was directed east, while Jouhandeau fell over himself in courtesies to his old friend to cover his new friend's rudeness.[14] All these episodes appear later in Jacob's letters elaborated as comic fictions entitled "The Lagrange Affair" and "The Gentleman Chauffeur's Car."[15] They also appear in a missive of confession and apology to Jouhandeau: "I'm imprudent to the point of madness. . . . Bounoure tells me I lack humanity."[16] But confession was Jacob's stock in trade, as it would be Jouhandeau's. The weekend ignited their friendship rather than dampening it, and for some years their relations were almost as intense and personal as Jacob's friendship with Cocteau, especially as it became clear that Jouhandeau was a closeted homosexual; two years later they would be confiding in each other over anguishing romances. And both Cocteau and Leiris, through Jacob, would become actors in Jouhandeau's emotional theater.

A few months after the weekend in Guéret, Jouhandeau and Supervielle contributed to an issue of the journal *Le Disque vert* celebrating Jacob. Jouhandeau's piece, "The Magus," shows how powerfully Jacob had affected him. Jouhandeau saw Jacob as a magician who imagined the fates of his companions: Jouhandeau as a high-wire artist, and Madame Bounoure as eternally arranging imaginary flowers. Max's genius, he wrote, was to discover each person's hidden angel or demon. The long years of this tortured friendship would reveal demons in Jouhandeau that even the magus Jacob couldn't have divined.[17]

Supervielle also testified to Jacob's magic. In a letter printed in the issue, he commemorated their meeting in Guéret and saluted *Le Cornet à dés* for revolutionizing poetry. But it was in his poem for Jacob that Supervielle registered the troubling force of his personality. Like Jouhandeau, he intuited something demonic:

> Like a devil he wears gold-rimmed spectacles
> And his lips disturb like a tribe of bees
> But his eyes, his voice, his heart belong to a child at dawn.
> Who is this man whose soul emits solemn signals?[18]

Supervielle found Jacob so agitating that in the next line of the poem he reached instinctively for his wife: "Here's Pilar, she calms me down."[19]

||

THE PREVIOUS YEAR Gabrielle Buffet, Picabia's estranged wife, had asked Jacob for a chat piece on Picasso for *Vanity Fair*. Until now Jacob had refused such requests, not wanting to cash in on his old friendship or to anger Picasso. But this time he agreed. Perhaps the promise of generous payment was tempting; perhaps he was sufficiently distant, now, from the old heroic days, to want to recreate them in memory. The article, a tender reminiscence, appeared in May. With Matorel-like disregard for earthly time, Jacob misremembered the date of their meeting in 1901; he set the encounter in 1899. More mysteriously, he displaced the artist's birth date by a day, having him arrive on October 24, 1881, instead of October 25: that may have been carelessness, or a deliberate astrological fabulation. What feels true is the portrait of the artist in youth and in middle age: the vision of Picasso's boyish beauty, ivory skin, great black eyes, black coarse hair (now threaded with silver). True, too, are the descriptions of the Bateau Lavoir, and the fellowship of Apollinaire, Salmon, Reverdy, and Matisse. Along the way, Jacob tossed out messages in bottles for his now-distant comrade: the Spaniards "kept me for the evening and half through the night—we were friends! That was in '99—we are friends still, I trust."[20]

Though Jacob couldn't have known it directly, Picasso was tiring of his conjugal idyll and of life in the *gratin*.[21] Jacob had some inkling of it, though, from Kahnweiler, who had written him about the artist's bitterness and pessimism.[22] When *Le Terrain Bouchaballe* came out at the end of May, Jacob spent several days in Paris for book signings; he met Picasso in the street, and they greeted each other affectionately. Picasso asked to see Jacob's new books; he was ill shaven and had dust on his bowler hat. Back in Saint-Benoît, Jacob sent him one of the town's famous cheeses along with instructions for keeping it: it had to be allowed to ripen for a fortnight between two plates, "like an oyster." He gave Picasso directions to Saint-Benoît and asked Gallimard to send him *Le Roi de Béotie*, and the Émile-Paul brothers to send him *Le Terrain Bouchaballe*. The friendship itself was ripening, in its quiet way.[23]

||

DEDICATED TO SALMON, *Le Terrain Bouchaballe* was Jacob's acidic love letter to his native town, recreating its rivers, chestnut trees, seminary, barracks, cathedral, and side streets as in a diorama. He borrowed elements of real people for the characters. The Canon Rossi, his family's landlord, stars as the Canon Domnère, scheming in most worldly fashion to direct the town's spiritual life. The fictional mayor, Thomas Lecourbe, strongly resembles the real mayor, Théodore le Hars, who was elected in 1903 and ran into trouble for his amorous escapades and the project of the municipal theater. The Bouchaballe of the title is inspired by Jacob's old school fellow, Urbain Couchouren, who died young, leaving the town a bequest of land that resulted in years of feuding. For the hero, Pancrasse, the beadle-turned-architect, Jacob drew on Apollinaire. Written and rewritten, *Bouchaballe* was the only one of his books he was proud of, he told Leiris.[24] It was considered for the Prix Goncourt, and Marcel Arland wrote about it appreciatively in *La Nouvelle Revue française*.[25] It drew attention of a more unwelcome kind from the Church; a Catholic journal pronounced the book "unclean," and the Church authorities in Paris warned Jacob's priests in Saint-Benoît, who warned him.[26]

Le Terrain Bouchaballe is an auditory novel, a medley of voices. Each jargon identifies some besotted type rather than an individual; it's almost as if words, rather than people, were the actors. The word *zinzolin*, for instance: Jacob loved the absurd sound of this reddish-purple taffeta and its variations: *zinzoline, zinzolinette.* . . . Behind the satire one can hear the tones of Madame Gagelin:

—I want to embroider a table runner in zinzolin!
—In zinzolin! Quite the big spender, Angèle!
—Oh, it costs no more than anything else.
—I really like the feel of zinzolin!
—Yes, you could line it in pigeon-breast silk and backstitch all around.[27]

Money, fashion, propriety, power: they obsess the characters of Max Jacob's fiction, whatever their gender or social rank. *Le Terrain Bouchaballe* counterpoints legal, bureaucratic, academic, and political idioms with the crudest slang as the characters pursue their plots and counterplots.

THROUGHOUT THE SPRING, Jacob continued his correspondence with Leiris. His letters to "Michel darling" overflowed with advice, criticism, and praise for the young man's poems. In June, in another bounce to Paris, Jacob found Leiris in despair, trying to tear himself away from his fiancée Daisy, slashing himself with scissors and beset by suicidal fantasies. Jacob and the painter André Beaudin took Leiris on a long taxi ride around the city, trying to persuade him not to kill himself.[28] Back in Saint-Benoît, Jacob fired off urgent letters: *"Don't kill yourself! It would be idiotic."* He mixed advice for living with advice for writing poetry: for Jacob, the two could hardly be separated. Nor would they be, eventually, for Leiris. "Write yourself! Describe yourself! And I promise you that you won't suffer anymore . . . in that way. You'll suffer in a different way."[29] Three days later in Saint-Benoît, Jacob was painting a picture of the Pont-Neuf when he heard from Georges Limbour that Leiris had been tempted to throw himself off that bridge; he wrote again, urging Leiris to pray.[30]

THIS ALARM GAVE way to another, more comic. Just as Saint-Benoît was preparing for the annual celebration of the saint's birthday, Madame Aurel, the literary *salonnière,* descended on the monastery. *"Biȝarroïde,"* Jacob wrote the Ghikas as he contemplated the prospect of this invasion, calling her Marcus *Aurel*ius, or *Or*eille ("ear," because she was a little deaf). She threatened to give him "an armature."[31] At exactly this time, Jacob was writing seductive letters to a young Swiss-Italian writer, Nino Frank, who proposed to come for a literary apprenticeship at the monastery. Jacob hadn't met this eighteen-year-old fresh out of high school, but he liked his photograph and was already plying him with insinuations about love, purity, and the spirit. Two days before Madame Aurel arrived, Jacob declared to Frank, "I hardly know women. There's nothing so fine as a good and beautiful woman, but they're rare; women are foolish, bustling, illogical, demanding, unfair, hard, ignorant, and devoid of philosophy."[32] Two weeks of life at close quarters with Dame Aurel would confirm him in this judgment.

This literary lady was majestic in her incomprehension of the world around her. Jacob had obtained permission for her to rent a room in the monastery. She wrote her husband that "because of her character" (feminist? woman of letters?), she'd been given a room in the monastery, "the only female pilgrim." She and Max worked all day long in their cells, meeting for dinner downstairs with Abbé Breut and his family. One washed blasted Paris off in the company of "these simple souls," she declared. After dinner, she and Max strolled through "the adorable village."[33]

The adorable village wasn't pleased. The proprietor of the local hotel raised a stink about the monastery's siphoning off clients, with the result that the authorities charged the monastery a hotel tax, and Jacob himself was billed for "a personal and property charge."[34] Madame Aurel shocked everyone by parading around in a sleeveless dress, dyed hair, and makeup; some of the inhabitants concluded that she was having an affair with the poet. By the second week, Jacob found himself condemned on all sides, and he fled to Quimper, afraid that he'd never be able to return to his Benedictine refuge. Madame Aurel swooped back to Paris, convinced that she'd triumphed over peasant ignorance.[35]

Jacob exchanged one scandal for another. *Le Terrain Bouchaballe* had roiled Quimper: the citizens weren't happy to find their town satirized. Jacob's sister Delphine (something of a model for the miser Mademoiselle Gaufre in the novel) still made his life miserable and roused his brothers against him.[36] On his false birthday, July 11, he wrote Leiris, "You know I love you—but no one knows how ill at ease I feel everywhere, even in this dear childhood room where I write without shedding a tear."[37] He had hoped to make progress on the new novel, but he found work difficult in the family house, and the town was choked with tourists and cars.[38] By late July relations with his sister and brothers had become so unpleasant that he escaped to the Ghikas in Roscoff, confessing to Madame Aurel (with whom he maintained polite contact) that he had suffered so from his family he would never return.[39]

||

PRINCESSE GHIKA, a fairy princess, was tending to his wounds, Jacob wrote Nino Frank from Roscoff on August 2.[40] He arrived on July 28. For the first few days, Liane found him charming, and he found the refuge charming. He had his own worktable looking over the ocean, no one disturbed him except at mealtimes, and his novel advanced.[41] By August 4, Liane confessed to her diary that he was "insufferable when he was spoiled,"[42] and their old alternating current of affection and quarrels resumed. He would never be a real Christian, she thought; he was "envious, jealous, a fag, false, smug about lowly tasks, gossipy, blundering . . . possessed by all the demons."[43] Yet he amused her and Georges. A few days later he mollified her with a magnificent cake from Quimper, and for another week he kept the peace by narrating stories from his life. On her saint's day, August 14, he gave her chocolate pralines and an antique jeweled box sent in secret from the family shop in Quimper: Liane, accustomed to gifts from princes and bankers, duly recorded her pleasure at this tribute.[44] (At the same time, he complained about the money spent on gifts to hosts.)[45] Three weeks into the visit, Liane so approved of his new outfit—white linen trousers and a geranium-colored blazer—that she marched him around the village so he could be admired. Stock was reissuing *Le Cornet à dés* in a revised edition with Gabory's preface, to be dedicated to the Ghikas, a gesture Liane truly appreciated.[46]

During these quiet weeks Jacob plugged away at *L'homme de chair et l'homme reflet* and composed new prose poems; he would publish a group of twenty-five of them, a mini-*Cornet à dés*, entitled "Le Carnet à piston" (String-Pulling Log, or Horn-Tooting Log), dedicated to Liane.[47] As usual, he was stage-managing a complicated life through the mail. He disappointed Nino Frank, announcing that he wouldn't be back at Saint-Benoît until December;[48] he wrote Jean Grenier, whom he had hoped to see at Saint-Brieuc, that he couldn't abandon his jealous hosts at Clos Marie;[49] and he flattered Jouhandeau and tried to cajole him out of a state of sterility.[50]

He did venture out to visit Leiris, André Masson and his wife Odette, and the playwright Armand Salacrou and his wife Lucienne, at the village of Plestin-les-Grèves, only thirty kilometers to the west but a half day's trip on poky and ill-connecting trains. Leiris had found this village for the communal vacation. Released from his engagement to Daisy, and for the moment free from thoughts of suicide, Leiris was writing strong poems, Jacob thought.[51] He reported to Jouhandeau that they were renting rooms from the locals, "like soldiers on maneuvers." Jacob lodged at the tobacco shop and liked the pretty proprietress so much he fantasized about marrying her.[52] The group went to the beach, ate together at a cheap restaurant, and read poetry out loud at night. Masson was struggling with his painting, and they were all, Jacob lamented, suffering the influence of Rimbaud.

As *le bon Papa* of Masson's group, Jacob had introduced the painters to the master dealer Kahnweiler, and he had been advising Leiris and Salacrou on their writing. His poem to Leiris appeared that month in *La Revue européenne* along with poems to the painters Jean Dubuffet and André Beaudin. But at Plestin he saw his young charges slipping out of his grasp. They were romantic rebels, steeped in Nietzsche and Rimbaud; he was now a grumpy elder. Though the time passed festively with walks through the woods and to the beach, he felt, obscurely, their "contempt"—the word he used in a letter to Cocteau.[53]

Jacob had met the aspiring playwright Armand Salacrou and his wife Lucienne, an aspiring poet, through Dubuffet in 1922. He conceived an importunate affection for this young couple. A slender man with light hair and sharply defined features, Armand had grown up in Le Havre and was studying law in Paris. Intelligent, ambitious, and cold, he profited from Jacob's advice and connections until he no longer needed them, at which point he let the friendship lapse. The two men couldn't have been more different. Jacob poured himself out in expressions of love and flattery, which disgruntled the self-contained northerner. Armand felt manipulated into buying a gouache of Jacob's when they first met.[54] During the next few years, Jacob sometimes stayed with the Salacrous at their tiny apartment in the fifteenth arrondissement at the petit-bourgeois, western end of the Left Bank. Poor Jacob, styling himself "your old godfather" to Armand and Lucienne, had no idea how he irritated them.

Armand fended off yet encouraged Jacob's attentions, writing him elegant letters that brought more compliments: "That bastard writes splendid letters!"[55] Yet Jacob was tough in his criticism of Salacrou's early plays. That November he would write, "Your play is charming but unperformable, completely unperformable, and really a bit Hamletic."[56]

In mid-September, while the Salacrous were still part of the commune at Plestin-les-Grèves, Jacob wrote from Roscoff, embracing "the Plestin family" and mentioning that the Ghikas were expecting an English stockbroker. He professed delight: "Terrific! They'll take care of him, and I'll have a vacation from my vacation."[57] In fact, he was apprehensive, irritable, and jealous at the arrival of Liane's friend Benjy. He sulked, acted rudely, then fell ill with a liver ailment and congestion of the lungs. He had never been an easy patient to take care of. Liane brought him broth and lemonade, while Georges applied mustard plasters and entertained him. After a few days, the princess grew exasperated at his bad manners and his "bad hygiene": he bunched up her precious eiderdown quilt under his "dirty chin" and covered it with pencils, open books, soiled papers, burnt matchsticks, broth, and lemonade stains.[58] A crisis erupted when Odette Masson telegraphed from Plestin begging Max to come: André had to have an emergency operation at Morlaix for enteritis. Max felt he couldn't disturb the princely regime by leaving, but in any case he was too sick to move. Liane, who had encouraged him to stay until Christmas, now suggested that he should go to a hotel: she didn't want an invalid on her hands. Everything blew up in a quarrel over a cigarette and two mint cough drops that she didn't think he should have, and her refusal to have a fire in the fireplace in his cold bedroom. Max rose in a tantrum, packed his bags, roused the servants, and got himself driven to the station in the evening, coughing and wheezing miserably. He took the train to Chartres, where he put up in a hotel, having missed the connection to Saint-Benoît. In her diary, Liane exclaimed, "Max is gone! Finally! We'll disinfect his room."[59]

Reparations followed. From Chartres the next day, Jacob posted an apology to the Ghikas' housekeeper, not daring to address his hosts directly, and he ordered a fancy pâté to be delivered to them. He visited the cathedral (almost Cubist, he wrote Kahnweiler) before dragging himself back to Orléans and thence to Saint-Benoît by train, "half dead with cold and the fear of death."[60] Congested lungs led to pleurisy. For days, at Saint-Benoît, he stayed in bed, and then for weeks he huddled by the fire in his cell with a harsh pain in his chest, leaving only for the local clinic for cupping and the local doctor's office for sessions of cauterization, *pointes de feu*, a red-hot needle applied to the naked back.[61]

II.

IN THE LAST months of 1923, Jacob's private and public lives diverged dramatically. In public, it was a time of triumph. Two short stories appeared in print, a Rousseauian fantasia of the writer at work, "The Non-Solitary Rambler" in *Intentions*, and "The Name," dedicated to Bounoure, in *Europe*.[62] His suite of prose poems for Liane came out in *Les Feuilles libres*. Bounoure published an essay on Jacob's fiction, the first serious literary criticism his work had received, a study of the multiplicity of fictive selves in Jacob's work, and of the fictive nature of all selfhood.[63] In November the Belgian-French journal *Le Disque vert* devoted an entire issue to Jacob. Larbaud gave a talk on Jacob at Madame Aurel's salon; it was printed in both *Intentions* and *Philosophies*.[64] Kahnweiler published a luxurious edition of *La Couronne de Vulcain*, Jacob's tale for children from 1909, and Stock brought out the new edition of *Le Cornet à dés*. Jacob even had the satisfaction of a blessing from Picasso, who in an interview described Jacob, Apollinaire, and Salmon as "the inspirers of and inspired by Cubism."[65]

In private, these months were dim. Jacob's ill health affected his mood; even in December he wasn't well enough to travel to Paris to hear Larbaud's lecture. After the sophisticated company of the Ghikas and Masson's group, Saint-Benoît seemed duller than ever. "Life here is very flat," he wrote Salacrou in October, though an overnight visit from their common friend the painter André Beaudin lifted his spirits.[66] To Sylvette Fillacier, now married to a military officer in Morocco, he wrote of old age and illness: "We didn't discuss our health ten years ago, dear friend. Cuppings! Cauterizations! White hair! Old friends separate, lose each other, and if they meet again, don't know how to communicate . . . Moral and physical suffering."[67] Learning of her marital difficulties, he wrote again, delicately, asking her to let him know if she needed money.[68] He told Kisling, "No news from the old gang. Picasso is silent. Derain, it's as if we never knew each other. Only Salmon, the dear man, is loyal."[69] He reminded Jouhandeau and Leiris, each suffering in his own way, that "the only school is pain, joy teaches nothing."[70] To Salacrou he offered a minatory self-portrait, describing his lost hair, lost teeth, reddened complexion, and bowed shoulders, all due, he thought, to precocious vices. He added that he had recently seen Dubuffet, shockingly ravaged by dissipation.[71]

Bit by bit he repaired his friendship with the Ghikas. Georges expressed concern for his health; Jacob replied in a scribble from bed, begging his pardon (but clearly letting him know how much he had suffered).[72] Liane pardoned him a few weeks later, and in a sign of peace sent him a bright red vest, scarf, beret, and socks she'd knitted for him. Max was overjoyed. He proudly showed the scarf to his doctor and would wear the garments for years to come, blazons of friendship and forgiveness that became a theme in their correspondence.[73]

His friendships with new artists and writers consoled him, somewhat, for the loss of older friends. He had great hopes for the poet Georges Limbour and the painter André Beaudin; he kept corresponding with Salacrou; in spite of his irritation at Masson's romanticism, he admired his talent and praised him to Kahnweiler; he encouraged Lascaux, Jouhandeau, and Leiris; and he deplored Dubuffet's decadence and worried about him.[74]

The friendship developing with the philosopher Jean Grenier would prove one of the most solid of Jacob's life, and since Grenier spent much of his time teaching abroad, they communicated mostly by mail. Detained by the Ghikas at Clos Marie that summer, he hadn't been able to visit Grenier, but they remained in touch. Grenier's intelligence sparked Jacob's, inspiring some of his most eloquent letters. In late October, responding to Grenier, Jacob reflected on his work in a way quite removed from the Modernist ideas in *Art poétique;* the humility, the emphasis on truth and humanness, suggest some of the hard lessons he was learning. In the postscript, he advised, "Be human, uniquely human." In a postscript to his postscript, he continued, "By human I mean true feeling giving birth to other true feelings. The framework doesn't matter and style matters even less. To invent in truthfulness."[75] Jacob was circumspect about homosexuality with Grenier, whom he didn't know well at this stage; when Grenier asked if he had read Proust's *Sodome et Gomorrhe,* Jacob took a distant tone and said he hadn't read the book because the title was too scandalous for Saint-Benoît.[76]

While Jacob wheezed and coughed in the monastery, his material prospects brightened. Gaston Gallimard drove down from Paris, "pockets full of contracts." Jacob signed an agreement giving Gallimard the rights to all his future prose and committing himself to a hectic schedule of production:

he was to deliver *L'Homme de chair* in a month and start on another novel. "Jesus! Mary! Joseph!" he cried out to Liane.[77] He was also to expand *Le Cabinet noir* for a new edition. At the same time he was gathering poems for a new collection for Kra: this would be *Les Pénitents en maillots roses*. He complained to Roland-Manuel about the struggle with his poems: "Weeping, grinding of teeth, aesthetics before I die of pleurisy. I'm transforming the prose poem and the verse poem, and I open my side to the spear thrust of Longinus, *but one can't know what it is*. I've failed poetry and heaven!"[78] For all the weeping, he really did transform the prose poem: *Visions infernales*, published the following year by Gallimard, touches depths of sorrow and fear inconceivable in *Le Cornet à dés*. And *Les Pénitents en maillots roses* contains some of Jacob's most elemental lyrics.

||

NINO FRANK, the Swiss-Italian boy from Naples with whom Jacob had been flirting by letter, arrived in Saint-Benoît in early November. "I'm afraid of loving you too much," Jacob had warned.[79] Still a child in some ways, Frank landed with a trunk full of books and a determination to make himself into a writer in Italian and French. He had never encountered a homosexual and hadn't the slightest inkling about same-sex desire. On their first evening in the monastery, after he'd unpacked his books and clothing in the cell that Jacob had arranged for him, and he and Jacob plunged into their first literary discussion, Jacob said, "Poets kiss each other. Let's kiss." Whereupon Nino chastely kissed his host on the forehead. "Not like that!" protested Max. "On the mouth! Russian style! Long live Dostoyevsky!" and seizing the boy, he planted so forceful a kiss on his lips that Nino leaped out of his grasp. His distress was so evident, Jacob never renewed the experiment, and he and Nino settled down to months of amicable literary cohabitation. It didn't lack for hiccups; a note Jacob slipped under Frank's door was clearly written in the aftermath of a quarrel: "So I'm a terrible man!" Jacob repeated five times. "You take it into your head to come to Saint-Benoît and I have to accept it. . . . I'm supposed to put up with being judged, examined, observed like a strange beast. . . .

And when, always having to be hospitable, charitable, and polite, I have a moment of ill humor, I'm a terrible man. If I'm a terrible man, you have your own room, stay in it!"[80]

That quarrel was rapidly patched up, and Nino's presence cheered the last, dark months of 1923. He read aloud from Dostoyevsky's *The Idiot* while Max painted, and the two kept up running arguments about literature. Jacob studied him, using elements of his character for the Reflected Man in his novel and for the next book he was beginning to sketch, *Tableau de la bourgeoisie* (Classification of the Bourgeoisie). Nino, for his part, studied Jacob for an article for an Italian journal. Among Jacob's admirable traits was a relative lack of jealousy; seeing that Saint-Benoît was too limited an environment for the boy, he urged him to make his way to Paris, and introduced him in a letter full of gay innuendo to Cocteau, describing Nino's soft mouth, satirical smile, and Harlequin hands, his fake silk shirts and sober but elegant taste in ties.[81]

Nino enclosed his own letter to Cocteau with comic interpellations by Jacob. In mostly correct French, Nino described Jacob in terms designed to amuse Cocteau: "He's cramming my skull—*It's not true.* He's teaching me nothing—but I'm learning something (*that's not true!*). He has no respect for Dada—which pains me (*not true!*)." Frank concluded sassily, "I'll arrive at your house Wednesday [December] 12 at ten in the morning, and I count on being angry with you by noon. Please accept my respectful homage."[82]

||

IN HIS POSTSCRIPT to Cocteau, Jacob added this sarcastic message: "If Radiguet still remembers Max Jacob, let him receive the expression of my friendship." He hadn't heard from his protégé-prodigy in weeks and felt neglected. He was neglected: Radiguet was busy dying. He had spent the summer with Cocteau in Piqueÿ, a village on the Atlantic coast in the Bordeaux region, along with the alcoholic François de Gouy, Comte d'Arcy, and his boyfriend the American Russell Greeley; the painter and decorator Jean Hugo and his wife Valentine Hugo; and Auric and Poulenc.

As all these people were also Jacob's friends, their names turn up often in the summer's correspondence: "I love Auric and I love Gouy, I love Radigo," Jacob wrote blithely from Roscoff in mid-August.[83] Radiguet drank heavily but was also working on his novel inspired by the Beaumonts, *Le Bal du Comte d'Orgel*. Without realizing it, both he and Valentine Hugo caught typhoid. She traveled farther south with her husband, and when she fell ill, she was diagnosed and operated on, successfully, in the hospital in Montpellier. Radiguet and Cocteau stayed on in Piqueÿ until the end of September.[84]

When they returned to Paris, Radiguet was already quite sick. He continued his haywire existence, intoxicated by drink, drugs, and celebrity, and driven, too, by a need to escape Cocteau. In his last weeks he lived with the Polish model Bronya Perlmutter in the Hôtel Foyot near the Jardin du Luxembourg. He was determined to marry her, he told Auric, so he wouldn't "become a forty-year-old man called 'Madame Jean Cocteau.' "[85] When Radiguet fell violently ill, his body worn out by years of abuse, Cocteau sent Dr. Capmas to care for him, the same fashionable imbecile who had tended Apollinaire so ineffectually. Capmas didn't recognize the symptoms of typhoid and prescribed—of all things for a dying alcoholic—grog. By the time Coco Chanel sent her own doctor and had Radiguet hospitalized, it was too late. On December 9, Radiguet, hallucinating, told Cocteau, "Listen to something terrible. In three days I am to be executed by God's firing squad. . . . The order was given. I heard the order."[86] Radiguet died three days later, early on the morning of December 12, alone in the hospital. His mother had left, and Cocteau—terrified of catching the disease, or beside himself with grief, who knows?—wasn't at his side. Weirdly, in his bewilderment, Cocteau kept his date with Nino Frank, who arrived at Cocteau's door that morning not knowing anything about Radiguet's illness.[87]

The death of the "boy king" sent shock waves through *tout Paris*.[88] Chanel arranged the sumptuous funeral—a child's white casket, white horses, red roses—at l'Église Saint-Honoré-d'Eylau, and Misia Sert paid the bill. De Gouy and Greeley settled the hotel bill for Radiguet and Bronya Perlmutter. Moysès, the proprietor of Le Boeuf sur le Toit, where

Radiguet had consumed inhuman amounts of alcohol, wiped the slate clean of all remaining charges. A great crowd flocked the church, including Picasso, Brancusi, and the black jazz band from Le Boeuf sur le Toit. Cocteau stayed home in bed.[89] Max Jacob remained at Saint-Benoît.

Cocteau seemed mad with grief. At times, he confessed to Jacob, he felt Radiguet's ghost hovering near him. He visited his lover's family almost every day for a while, suffering because the brothers resembled Raymond. He read mystical premonitions of early death in the boy's novels, and he had what felt like prophetic dreams. He was like a drug addict or alcoholic forced into violent withdrawal, he wrote Jacob.[90] And soon enough, he would resort to real opium. Fearing for Cocteau, Jacob wrote him long, sympathetic letters, warning him against demonic derangement in mourning, begging him to see a priest and to take communion.[91] Instead of going to church, Cocteau went to Monte Carlo to see Diaghilev's productions of ballets by Auric and Poulenc, and there he began to smoke opium.

Jacob took the death hard. He wept when Radiguet's father sent him the inscribed copy of *Le Diable au corps* that Radiguet thought he had mailed but had misplaced earlier that year.[92] A couple of days before Christmas, François de Gouy and Russell Greeley drove down to see him at Saint-Benoît, surprising him at the door of his cell in their fur coats. They spoke at length of Radiguet. The visit was all the more welcome as Nino Frank had returned to Italy to visit his pregnant mistress.[93]

Jacob grieved for Radiguet and was not unaware of his role in the boy's fate. Christmas Day marked another loss, the presentiment of the death of a friendship. That month Michel Leiris stopped sending him drafts of poems and stopped responding to his epistles of moral and poetic counsel. On Christmas Day, Jacob wrote him, wondering if Leiris thought he (Jacob) disdained his work, or was tired of his despair, or didn't love him anymore. Even if they belonged to different literary generations, Jacob pleaded, that was no reason "to cut the telephone cord of friendship."[94] From then on, Leiris stayed aloof from Jacob, throwing in his lot with Masson and the Rue Blomet circle and, through them, with the Surrealists. When he published his first poem in January in *Intentions*, he didn't let Jacob know about it, and he dedicated it to Masson.[95] Jacob complained to

Jouhandeau, "As long as the dear and adored boy struggled with the Muse, I was his confidant; now that he's a poet, he's fallen silent. This behavior is hardly delicate."[96]

III.

DURING THE NEXT several years, Max Jacob led an increasingly distempered life, repeating the scandals and quarrels that had marred 1923, feeling betrayed by younger writers, and stumbling into painful romances. The title of the collection of prose poems he published with the Nouvelle Revue Française in 1924, *Visions infernales*, accurately describes his state of mind. Because he let himself fall in love with impossible young men instead of settling for the casual sex of his earlier days, he opened himself up to new forms of suffering. Not only would he find his affections exploited, but he was convinced that those affairs led to eternal damnation. The truly infernal pain awaited him after death, he believed, but some of it he began to experience in the present, an erotic and spiritual hell on earth. Now more than ever he felt his life as excruciating self-division: the penitential ideal of Saint-Benoît alongside the squalor of shameful loves. From this torment arose some of his strongest poems. "My new style: to strip my guts," he told Grenier.[97]

This new phase brought new friendships. His attachment to Jouhandeau deepened; so did his feelings for Cocteau, now in the throes of grief and addiction. He remained close to Nino Frank, who returned to Saint-Benoît in the new year, leaving his mistress in Italy. (No word about her baby.) And a new horizon opened with the founding of a journal, *Philosophies*, by a group of young intellectuals who adopted him for a time: Pierre Morhange, the political philosopher Henri Lefebvre, and Norbert Guterman. In the next two years he published essays and several poems in their pages.[98]

Morhange was Jewish, a fact that made Jacob uneasy. For now, he welcomed the attention of this intelligent young man, a driven intellectual who admired his work. Morhange spent several days in the monastery in February. In a letter to Salacrou, Jacob called him "unbearable"; to Jouhandeau, he described him as humble but likely to turn into an ogre someday and as having the fidelity of a poodle.[99] In any case, Morhange, his friend Lefebvre (who became a celebrated leftist philosopher), and the multilingual Polish Jewish intellectual Norbert Guterman drew Max Jacob into the endeavor of their new journal. They published his "Notes on the Fine Arts" in March 1924 and visited him often at Saint-Benoît, taking him on jaunts in Lefebvre's car.[100] Lefebvre remembered these excursions as madly entertaining but also, at times, as perverse. Jacob became manic in the company of smart young men, regaling them with stories and outrageous theories. On one occasion, he made them stop the car so he could urinate in a field by the side of the road. Somehow, in the operation, his ring slipped off his finger. Always poor, he considered his rings as his savings account, and he made a tremendous fuss about finding the ring, insisting that his friends grope around in the damp grass until someone finally retrieved the errant gem.[101]

||

ANDRÉ BRETON's COLLECTION of essays, *Les Pas perdus* (The Lost Steps), came out in January with an insult to Jacob: "Messieurs Pierre Reverdy and Max Jacob have mastered this form [prose poems]; too bad for them that those paper bank notes have lost their value."[102] Not till the end of the year, however, with the appearance of the first Surrealist Manifesto, would Jacob realize the full force of Breton's campaign. For now, in the spring of 1924, his work kept him almost in a frenzy. *L'Homme de chair* was about to appear from Kra, the poems *Visions infernales* in May from the Nouvelle Revue Française, and he had promised Gallimard yet another prose book for 1924, *Tableau de la bourgeoisie*. On top of all this writing, he had a contract with the Galerie Percier in Paris for his gouaches, so he was regularly sending his landscapes and theater scenes to André Level and René Mendès-France, who ran the gallery: he needed money, as Gallimard had (once again) stopped sending the monthly stipend.[103]

L'Homme de chair et l'homme reflet came out in April.[104] Though the book opens with some of Jacob's old tricks—breaking right into a monologue in the style of *Cinématoma,* with a separate author's voice maintaining a mocking commentary throughout—this novel differs from his earlier fiction. For one thing, it has more of a plot. "I got the idea in my head to write a novel like everybody else," Jacob told Jouhandeau, echoing Radiguet, who had been echoing Picasso.[105] For another, Jacob treated the autobiographical elements differently. Though Maxime Lelong, the Reflected Man, in some ways resembles Jacob's "watery" sense of himself, he is far more obviously based on Leiris, as Georges Ballan-Goujart is drawn from Jean Dubuffet.[106] In studying these two heterosexual friends, Jacob created a homosexual utopia, a male world from which women were expelled. Superficially, the story teems with women and with male-female romances: Jacob must have thought he had sufficiently masked his subject. At heart, it's a story of male bonding, and a fantasy of creating an entirely male family with the two men taking in a lost boy. When a reviewer suggested that the heroes seemed to have an "appalling" affection for the child, Jacob assumed his most respectable pose to banish any such imputation.[107] Yet the traces are all over the book.

In *L'Homme de chair et l'homme reflet,* families are presented as not just oppressive but murderous. Children are killed or abandoned by parents. Maxime Lelong's mother, *née* Gagelin (another appearance of Jacob's mother), a pretentious snob, starves Maxime's half-sister to death so she can afford her monthly society dinners; the baby Georges Ballan-Goujart, the Dubuffet character, born inconveniently two months after his parents' wedding, is handed to a midwife with the explicit though wordless instruction to kill him: a gesture of wringing the neck of a chicken, and a sheaf of banknotes. (Jacob chose Guéret, Jouhandeau's town, as the scene of this birth.) The midwife sees more profit in keeping the child alive, so he grows up to be the other hero of a plot that turns on his taking charge of yet another abandoned baby, Claude. If families are dangerous, women present a special threat. Fathers are weak and foolish. Lelong, Maxime's father, somewhat like Leiris *père,* is an ineffectual businessman; Ballan-Goujart *père,* like Dubuffet's father, is a wine merchant, though Jacob endows him with a further career as a deputy in Paris. Mothers and girlfriends are predatory, and little Claude is shuffled among Georges's lady friends until Maxime and Georges set up their household with Claude after World War I. The child grows up with these two "godfathers" in a bohemian home in Paris, where Georges—like Dubuffet—lackadaisically runs one of his father's factories and Maxime is a bookkeeper for the Folies Bergère. As the boy enters adolescence, his two "godfathers" vie for his affection and "fondle" him. In an extraordinary scene, Maxime's estranged wife Estelle returns and tries to seduce Claude; interrupted by Georges—who pulls the boy into his lap, caressing his hair—Estelle explodes, "Oh! But they're in love! How they hug! . . . Georges, you make me blush, you know, with your loves . . . your *pederastic* loves."[108] By the end, Claude escapes the jealousies of his guardians by running off to Morocco. In one of the most affecting sequences, Georges chases Claude across France, taking the night train from Paris to Marseille and dashing to the docks in a taxi, arriving just in time to see the ship leaving the port. The longing, the pursuit, and the loss all seem to echo Jacob's pain at the flight of the real young men he cared for: Leiris and Dubuffet, synthesized in the figure of Claude, the imaginary son.

In *L'Homme de chair et l'homme reflet,* no one is saved. Georges ends up with the monstrous Estelle in poverty; Maxime, the Leiris character, ends up alone and will never do anything with his life except sell tickets for the Folies Bergère and trade in crummy antiques. Claude remains a question mark, selfish and disillusioned.

What was Jacob doing in this tale? At one level, he seems to be diagnosing the ills of prewar and postwar France, a society rotten with materialism, hypocrisy, and lust. In an interview with Frédéric Lefèvre, he claimed to be illustrating the evils of free love, broken families, and the haphazard education of illegitimate children; he makes it sound like a sermon on family values by a village *curé*.[109] But the novel tells a different story. All heterosexual families, not just broken families, are doomed. In response, Jacob imagined a structure for manly love in which the roles of father and son somehow incorporate the erotic. (As the years passed, he would call his boyfriends his "sons.") And sadly, the novel recognizes, that dream could not survive, or couldn't survive French society in Jacob's era.

When he read the book, Leiris found episodes from his own life transposed into Maxime's. The night he and Roland Tual spent roaming in Orléans reciting poetry while they waited for the train to Paris; his Nietzschean illusions; his literary ambitions; his complaints about military service; and his "quest of the ideal" all turn up in Jacob's pages. He must have complained to Jouhandeau and perhaps directly to Jacob. In a letter to Jouhandeau, Jacob declared, "I've *never* portrayed Leiris in a novel; I just took two anecdotes from his letters. Nothing serious. . . . I love Leiris deeply: I've done him no wrong and no harm. I never want to see him or his writing again."[110]

To Kahnweiler, Jacob grieved over the "total, black, and stunning failure" of *L'Homme de chair*.[111] But the book had been out for only six weeks, and though it never sold well, it made its mark critically. Jacques Viot, in *Intentions*, saluted the book as "a classic."[112] In *La Nouvelle Revue française*, Marcel Arland called Jacob "the sharpest observer of our time" and praised the novel for catching "the sound of life"; Jacob, he said, had renewed the art of portraiture. John Charpentier, in the *Mercure de France*, called Jacob "a kind of genius." *Sélection* devoted an essay to "Max Jacob the Novelist," analyzing the "spoken style" of his fictions, and it ran a separate laudatory review of *L'Homme de chair*. René Lalou, in *Vient de paraître*, greeted the book as a "psychological film" and an example of "transfigured realism."[113]

Frédéric Lefèvre, the journalist who had caused so much trouble for Jacob in 1917 with his book *The Young French Poetry*, interviewed him now for his series in *Les Nouvelles littéraires*. Jacob used this forum to defend his place in literary history: he, not the Chilean Huidobro, had invented "literary cubism," and it was Lefèvre himself who had introduced the term in 1917, referring to Max Jacob.[114] In May, as promised, the Galerie Percier showed his art along with the work of Serge Férat: Jacob relied more and more on the sale of his paintings, as Gallimard's payments were irregular.[115] He had to paint, he quipped to Salacrou, "to pay my taxis in Paris and my ataxia."[116]

IV.

JACOB WENT TO Paris in mid-April, staying with the Salacrous, who made him comfortable, whatever they thought of him later. He called them his "dear godchildren."[117] Nino Frank came by for dinner with the writer Massimo Bontempelli. Jouhandeau was also present: he was just getting to know the Salacrous, and here he met Nino Frank.

Back in Saint-Benoît, even as Jacob corrected proofs for *Visions infernales*, he entertained a cheerful gang of visitors over Easter weekend: his cousin Francis Gérard, the "heroic Lascaux" (the painter), Nino Frank and Bontempelli, the nineteen-year-old Ecuadorean poet Alfred Gangotena, and the *oratoire* (aspirant to the Society of Oratorian Fathers) Pierre Robert. Of this last personage, more would soon be revealed. For the moment, Jacob thought him "a genius." He described him enthusiastically to Kahnweiler and Mendès-France, hoping to interest them in his *naïf* paintings: the young man, who had been writing to Jacob for two years, had been a sergeant in the Ruhr; was an athlete; knew English, German, and mathematics; spoke of killing and stealing and revolution; and was a Communist convert to Catholicism—"a magnificent man."[118]

IN FEBRUARY, JACOB had thanked Jouhandeau for "loving his friends" and asked for news of Leiris: it was Jacob who had introduced them. When he wrote the Salacrous on April 28 that Jouhandeau was in despair and suggested that they comfort him, he probably didn't suspect the full reason for the crisis. It was Michel Leiris.

Leiris, with his delicate face and haunted eyes, had fascinated Jouhandeau from their first encounter. Jacob served as a news agency for the floating communities he enjoyed creating, so it was natural that he should discuss Leiris with Jouhandeau in the spring of 1924. In early March, Jacob wrote Jouhandeau admiringly of Leiris's poem in *Intentions* but immediately qualified the praise, adding that he wished Leiris had more "flesh and blood": "he hasn't suffered enough, loved enough."[119] In June, he asked Jouhandeau to tell "dear Michel" that a card from him would please him

(Jacob), and he wondered what god would give Leiris "an axe-blow to the stomach to empty out what he contains" (Jacob having constantly advised Leiris, as he advised others, to write from his entrails).[120] In between these two letters, a drama unfolded in Paris that brought suffering (if not poetry) to both Leiris and Jouhandeau.

An intense friendship had been developing between these two high-strung men. After hours spent wandering in bars and nightclubs, Leiris went home with Jouhandeau on the night of March 26, when they were both extremely drunk. An emotional extremist, sexually experimental, occasionally suicidal, Leiris allowed himself to sleep with Jouhandeau. Whatever happened seems to have revolted Leiris and to have awakened his latent sadism: two days later he confided in his journal that he was "attempting the spiritual murder of Jouhandeau."[121] The tortured entanglement continued for several months.

Jouhandeau's correspondence with Jacob now took on a far more personal tone, though it's not clear how much Jacob knew about what was occurring between his two friends. In April he wrote to console Jouhandeau for something Jouhandeau was in despair about, probably—since this happened right after the evening with the Salacrous in April—his having drunk too much at that dinner and fearing disgrace.[122] The letter went on to praise Jouhandeau's stories about a creepy alter ego called Godeau. Since it was precisely during these weeks that Jouhandeau was pursuing Leiris, the drinking seems a symptom of a much deeper pain. A week later, when Jacob thanked the Salacrous for their hospitality, he added, "I've learned other things I can't write about."[123]

For the next several months, Jacob's letters to Jouhandeau abound in references to Leiris and suggest that Jacob came to know something about Jouhandeau's murdered heart. On May 26 he declared, "Leiris is unbreathable," adding in a postscript, "The little sweetheart will soon be bitter and will plunge his claws into our tender hearts." He concluded mysteriously, "I would like to tell you something else and my pen gapes in front of the black paper."[124] In early June, he wrote about Leiris needing the axe-blow; two weeks later, he told Jouhandeau, "Leiris is maladjusted and unadjustable. . . . He weeps when he should laugh, and vice versa; he has no genius, he's turned himself into a poet the way one makes oneself a glove merchant; I love him in spite of myself."[125] In mid-July, Jacob was still comforting Jouhandeau over Leiris. By August the affair seems to have calmed down, as Jacob told Jouhandeau he was happy that Leiris had "condescended to apologize" and advised, "Ah my dear, let's not keep company with the young; these hurricanes disturb everything."[126] By this time, both Jacob and Jouhandeau had other things to worry about.

In March, Jacob invited the "genius" Pierre Robert to stay at Saint-Benoît. Just released from military service, Robert turned out to be a charismatic con man with no formal education or family resources. Already in June, Jacob wrote anxiously to Jouhandeau about his disappointment in his guest. Now he saw that all the superficial expertise in foreign languages, mechanics, and algebra cloaked "an absolute lack of an inner life."[127] He soon found much worse. Like a traveling salesman, Robert charmed the priests and Abbé Breut's family with his jokes, and he set about torturing Jacob, barging into his cell at all hours, taking his paper, pens, and books, and sneering at him in company until Max felt displaced and "martyrized" in his own home. As a crowning coup, Robert had himself accepted as an oblate, an official lay associate of the priesthood—a vocation he had no intention of pursuing, but which served his immediate picaresque purpose. Aware of the hypocrisy, Jacob began treating him coldly, for which the priests condemned him. Once again, he fled Saint-Benoît and took refuge with the Ghikas at Roscoff.[128]

||

VISIONS INFERNALES, JACOB's "Christian Cornet à dés," came out in late March, two days before L'Homme de chair. In a gesture of reconciliation, he dedicated it to Reverdy. Mostly prose poems interspersed with a few vers libres, the new pieces continued the dream techniques and wordplay of Jacob's earlier poems but concentrated on the drama of damnation. Unlike Le Cornet à dés, the effect is of obsession and constriction. "One has the demons one deserves; here's my portrait!" announced the first poem, "Demonic Ethnography."[129] Jacob's demons were real to him. In these poems, they seem like comic book imps, but the terror is genuine, springing up out of the most commonplace situations where even sacred figures, angels, and ladies celebrating holy days change suddenly into monsters. Everything is morally metamorphic. And just as suddenly, words slip their moorings: Jacob's puns now carry a theological charge. "The Attack" plays on the homonym of *le foie* (liver) and *la foi* (faith, translated here as "deliverance").

At the bend in the road, a man threatens me with a knife. With amazing agility, I seize his hands, but he's entirely invulnerable. A crowd surrounds me, I remember that the policemen spoke to me and that I gave my address. No one saw Him: he was behind me, and his hands were taking my measure. Then I slumped: he thrust a blade into my side; he'd aimed for my liver or deliverance. Today I know the man with the knife.[130]

One of Jacob's most famous lines constitutes a poem all by itself:

Mes grelots! maigre lot! ce sont ceux du péché.
(Freely translated: "My jingle bells! meagre spells! the sound of sin.")[131]

As so often in Jacob's nightmares, he associates the threat of the police with a suggestion of homosexuality:

IN THE BROUHAHA OF THE FAIR

Under the arcades, two men arrived, strangers to town. "It's the police from Paris," someone said. If they were from Paris, they'd be better dressed, if they were policemen, they'd be shabbier. Their eyes were like an insult to joy. The day after a wedding, Jacques and I were holding hands, it was Sunday, the crowd was streaming out, there were scholars, but when holy water was sprinkled, the two men fled and flames shot up from the pavement where they'd been standing.[132]

Jacob had asked Picasso for an old engraving of a portrait of him for the frontispiece, but as the painter didn't respond, he used a self-portrait rendered in woodcut by Georges Aubert. For this haunted volume, Jacob presented himself as an aging peasant wearing a beret, a crumpled jacket, and a benign expression (perhaps to ward off demons). The magic, if such it was, didn't work: Jacob was about to enter one of the more demonic phases of his life.[133]

CHAPTER 15

DEMONIC LOVE

I.

Jacob now plunged into more and more turmoil.

In May 1924, Madame Aurel asked him to talk about Jouhandeau in her salon. The invitation at least diverted Jouhandeau from his suffering over Leiris, and he and Jacob consulted: Jouhandeau didn't like salons, and Jacob didn't like lecturing. In the end, Jacob compromised by writing an "outline" of a study of his friend's work, a series of condensed paragraphs we would now call bullet points. After intricate negotiations, it appeared both in *Intentions* and in *Le Journal littéraire*.[1] Jacob praised Jouhandeau's strong base in Catholic education, his austerity, "cruelty against mankind and himself," groaning laughter, the entomologist's view of people, and the combination of pride and humility. He was most excited by Jouhandeau's method of creating characters; his people weren't scarecrows but "victories in a soccer match." In *Intentions*, Jacob's essay was followed by another installment of Jouhandeau's novel, *Monsieur Godeau intime*, a blasphemous chapter in which the hero seems to develop stigmata and almost succeeds in committing suicide by ingesting poison in front of his fiancée.[2]

Jouhandeau's private crisis over Leiris gave way to a public upheaval in Guéret. His fiction was all drawn from real goings-on in the town. His first novel hadn't bothered anyone because it was centered on the experience of one boy. But the new book, *Les Pincengrain*, featured local characters as stylized grotesques, with their adulteries, frauds, and sorrows center stage. When a chapter appeared in *Les Nouvelles littéraires,* all it took was one subscriber in Guéret for the whole town to erupt. The book was published a few weeks later; a mob stormed Jouhandeau's mother's house, demolished the garden, and soiled the downstairs hallways while he and his mother huddled upstairs, burning new manuscripts.

Tucked away in Roscoff, Jacob received these shocking reports from Jouhandeau and tried to comfort him. He was reminded, he said, of the crowd of peasants attacking his family's house in Quimper in 1901, blaming the town's only Jews for the new anticlerical laws.[3] The sacrifice of the burned pages, painful as it was, should be seen as a kind of progress toward perfection; Jouhandeau would emerge all the stronger. A few weeks later he assured his friend that the town's violence, once spent, would quiet down into a vague resentment, which is indeed what happened.[4]

MEANWHILE JACOB'S OWN drama was brewing in Roscoff. His escape from Saint-Benoît echoed the scandal of the previous summer, and his stay with the Ghikas was about to degenerate in a repetition of their earlier quarrel. As usual, the first weeks passed peacefully. In mid-August, the news broke that Jacob's young friend André Malraux had been arrested for stealing statues from the temples at Angkor Wat and sentenced to three years in prison in Cambodia. The French newspapers were in a tizzy, torn between a sense of colonial privilege and respect for law. Jacob saw Malraux's act as an expression of youthful lyricism and wrote to *L'Éclair* to protest the sentence.[5] Meanwhile domestic life at Clos Marie became more complicated with the arrival of "Missy," or "Oncle Max," the Marquise of Morny, a former lover of Liane's whom Jacob took at first for a man; he even described her as a man to Cocteau.[6] He seemed to like her well enough, and the Swiss couple she brought with her; it was in her car that he took a jaunt to Saint-Brieuc, where she dropped him off so he could visit Jean Grenier. From Saint-Brieuc, Jacob went to stay for a day or so with Pierre Morhange of *Philosophies* and his family in their country house, where he was quite taken with another guest, a Polish mathematician he described to Jouhandeau as "in love, blond, brutal, tender, and with the most beautiful blue eyes I've ever seen."[7]

By the time Jacob returned to Roscoff, he and Liane had managed a month together without a fight. New guests put an end to peace. A young count arrived with his aristocratic mistress or wife (Jacob gave various descriptions); the count also had an African manservant, "shaved" cats and dogs, and a set of instruments for a jazz band. And he had on his person, unknown to Jacob, his wife's (or mistress's) fortune of twenty thousand francs. He and Jacob went out for a drink at the local hotel. They drank so much that they missed dinner at the Ghikas', and the count passed out in a bedroom at the hotel. They seem to have stayed all night; the wife/mistress was in hysterics (more about the money than about her companion's virtue, it would appear). When Jacob turned up at Clos Marie, he was locked out and his trunk was on the doorstep. He'd been expelled.[8]

II.

AFTER A FEW days licking his wounds in Quimper, Jacob returned to Saint-Benoît, where he was relieved to find that the usurper Pierre Robert had departed. Late with *Tableau de la bourgeoisie,* he received blistering remonstrances from Gallimard. Friendship gave some comfort: letters flew back and forth with Jouhandeau, Grenier, and Salacrou, to some extent with Cocteau, and increasingly with Norbert Guterman of *Philosophies.* Louis Émié, a young man from Bordeaux he hadn't yet met, also wrote him regularly. Day by day, in his cell, *Tableau de la bourgeoisie* took shape.

Surrealism emerged officially in October. When Breton opened a center for the movement on the Rue de Grenelle and published the *Manifeste du Surréalisme* with Jacob's own publisher, Kra, Jacob's bitterness knew no bounds. To Jouhandeau he exclaimed, "People marvel at M. André Breton's hallucinations of eye and ear, his work in sleep-trances and his mystic puns; I've spent my life working like this! And he gets all the credit for this discovery because he dolled it up with a word of Apollinaire's."[9] Even before the manifesto appeared, he felt despised, writing to Level, "Young people to whom I taught the ABCs of literature don't even pronounce my name. And you ask why I don't come to Paris? Ask rather why I'm still alive. There's my balance sheet! Poor, hated, erased from the arts, and sick."[10]

Disappointments piled up. Soupault begged off from dinner with him in Paris—for fear of being scolded by his Surrealist comrades, Jacob suggested. "He likes me well enough, but the others hate me for having been the witness, for being the witness, and having been dada and surrealist before they were."[11] His rancor spilled over into a tantrum with Pierre Morhange over delayed payments for his work in *Philosophies;* to Guterman, he railed about Morhange's "banditry."[12] He had looked forward to a few days in Paris and had to cancel the trip for lack of funds. Just as well: he worked doggedly, and by the end of the month he'd reached the final pages of *Tableau de la bourgeoisie.*[13] He called this work his "Summa."[14] Perhaps. It laboriously expands Jacob's method of spoken portraiture into an absurd system of classification of types: Roaring Combative Families; Roaring Succulent Families; Humiliated Chatty, Ardent, and Cruel Families; Hardworking, Accumulative, and Honorable Families; Gracious Families—Jacob's panoramic view of the godless materialism (as he saw it) of his society and his own family. His mother, as Madame Gagelin, makes another fatigued appearance. The book tired him to write and is tiresome to read.[15]

To complete the season's disappointments, Nino Frank, who had promised to spend Christmas at Saint-Benoît, never appeared, though Abbé Breut's family had prepared his bed and cooked a special meal.[16] If Jacob enjoyed any comfort in the last days of December, it lay in his correspondence with Norbert Guterman, the one member of the trio at *Philosophies* he really liked. They exchanged ideas about André Breton, lyricism, and aesthetics, and Jacob was sufficiently placated by December 10 to send all three editors a collective hug and some doggerel on their names. *Philosophies,* after all, was paying him tribute these days, not only publishing his new poems and a section of *Tableau de la bourgeoisie* but allowing him to "review" his own novel, *L'Homme de chair et l'homme reflet;* and Morhange, in a review of *Visions infernales,* called Jacob "the greatest poet of our time."[17]

III.

IN 1925, JACOB restored his spirits in a two-month trip to Italy. But the more consequential voyage was interior. On his return from Italy, he fell painfully in love with one young man, then another. At the same time, even as his friendship with the Catholic philosopher Jacques Maritain took root, Jacob found himself torn more dramatically than ever between profane and sacred loves. The shift in emphasis in the titles of the two books of this period—*Visions infernales* of 1924 and *Les Pénitents en maillots roses* of 1925—traces an evolution from a vision of sex as hell to a vision of love as penitence, from dead-end horror to suffering as a redemptive possibility. The process was slow and brought real pain. A year full of external agitation, 1925 was almost barren in poetry but fertilized the ground for the quite different work of Jacob's later years. In the turbulence, he turned increasingly to Jouhandeau.

THE YEAR BEGAN sociably enough with visits from Malraux and his wife. Released from prison in Cambodia, Malraux appeared none the worse for wear, staying with his father in Orléans before returning to Cambodia: he offered to arrange a series of lectures in China for Jacob, an invitation the poet refused.[18] Tzara swam back into Jacob's life in December, sending him a new book of poems. Now that both Tzara and Jacob had been sidelined by the Surrealists, Jacob—who had always liked Tzara—replied affectionately, calling the Romanian a true "new man" and not a "petty arriviste" (read Breton);[19] they would see each other and renew the friendship during Jacob's visit to Paris in March.[20] And in mid-January, Grenier's perceptive essay on *La Côte*, Jacob's Breton poems, appeared in *La Bretagne touristique*.[21]

The previous year Jacob had sent Maritain a copy of *L'Homme de chair* humbly inscribed "with profound respect and profound sympathy in God." In *Art and Scholasticism* (1919), Maritain had shown himself sensitive to poetry as an expression of spiritual experience. Two years later, in *Théonas*, he cited *La Défense de Tartufe* as an "extraordinary" example of conversion, and in an interview with Frédéric Lefèvre, he mentioned Jacob along with Cocteau as important aesthetic innovators.[22] Both Maritain, a convert from Protestantism, and his wife Raïssa, a convert from Judaism, were active proselytizers: it's not surprising that they should have been attracted by a convert as visible as Jacob. At this stage, Maritain remained close to Maurras and Action Française (though he would disengage in 1926 when the pope condemned the movement); in 1921, Maritain sounded like Léon Daudet, proclaiming the "necessity of a battle for public safety against Judeo-Masonic secret societies and against cosmopolitan finance."[23] Yet even in 1921 Maritain asserted that "a Catholic writer . . . owes it to his faith to avoid all hatred and contempt for the Jewish race," as "the race of the prophets" is the tree from Christianity grows.[24]

Maritain welcomed Jacob's friendship. And now Cocteau brought them into even closer association. Auric, the composer, had known Maritain for years and read Cocteau's poems aloud to him and Raïssa. The charismatic missionary priest Père Charles Henrion had given Maritain Cocteau's *Le Coq et l'Arlequin*. In June 1924, while Cocteau—still grieving for Radiguet—was playing Mercutio and dying every night on stage in his adaptation of *Romeo and Juliet*, Auric took him to Meudon and introduced him to the Maritains. Since Radiguet's death, Cocteau had dulled his grief in opium. As he wrote Maritain (with characteristic egotism), "Out of all the youths, I chose Radiguet, to make him my masterpiece. Imagine his death, and me alone, half-mad amidst the rubble of a crystal-cutting workshop."[25] In his sorrow and increasing addiction with its attendant ills—nightmares, impotence, grogginess, stomach pains, constipation—Cocteau was in a vulnerable state and began to fantasize about religious salvation. The Maritains and Reverdy, whom he saw often, gave him constant examples of faith, as did Jacob, with whom he corresponded almost daily. "My dear Max," Cocteau wrote in January 1925, "If only I could live near you and become a real Christian."[26]

Jacob came to Paris at the end of February to celebrate the engagement of the painter Élie Lascaux with Berthe Godon, Lucie Kahnweiler's sister.

He stayed for two weeks with the Salacrous and gadded about with them, Crevel, Tzara, and Jouhandeau; the latter intimacy had matured to the point of using the familiar *tu*.[27] He saw "Reverdy's dear and saintly face."[28] He also saw Picasso, no doubt at Kahnweiler's party but also at the studio where he admired a new, large painting, probably *The Dance*.[29] But one of his main activities during this visit was to help Maritain arrange an opium cure for Cocteau in a clinic. Here Cocteau would be immured for six hellish weeks of withdrawal, treated with cold showers, enemas, and "electric baths" and forbidden to see friends. Jacob wrote him every day, a lifeline Cocteau never forgot.[30] Emerging from his "cure," Cocteau suffered a *coup de théâtre* at the Maritains', meeting the tall, sunburned priest, Père Henrion, just back from the Sahara: Cocteau was smitten by this heroic male figure in a white burnoose decorated with a crimson cross rising from a crimson heart. Within five days, the Maritains and Reverdy had rushed him into confession and into taking Communion with the priest in the Maritains' private chapel. A few weeks later, in August, Cocteau retired to the Mediterranean resort Villefranche to write a pamphlet about his conversion, "Letter to Jacques Maritain." Before he finished the letter, he started smoking opium again.[31]

||

DURING HIS STAY in Paris, Jacob had a serious encounter with Judaism in the person of the Corfu-born Swiss novelist Albert Cohen. It was a tragically fruitless meeting. In Cohen, Jacob could have seen an intellectual and even mystical way of being Jewish that in no way resembled the commercial and academic worlds of his family, but he was by this time too committed to his Catholic identity to imagine any other for himself. Yet he recognized Cohen's extraordinary force and talent.

At age thirty, Cohen, from an affluent family and trained as a lawyer, had yet to make his mark as a writer, but he was editing *La Revue juive* with backing from Gallimard and an advisory board that included Einstein, Freud, and Chaïm Weizmann. He was a vigorous Zionist. He had just published a long poem of Jacob's in his magazine, "Eyes in the Stomach." In rhyming couplets, Jacob asserted the Christian revelation as a supersession of Judaism.[32]

Cohen and Jacob met in Paris in March and had so sympathetic a conversation that they forgot about lunch until early afternoon. The next day Cohen showed Jacob his manuscript of visions, which Jacob thought magnificent, writing to Paulhan that Cohen was "an unknown genius."[33] Then Cohen took Jacob to task for his conversion and went so far as to suggest that he should become a Zionist leader. Each of these passionate men had in mind to convert the other. At their appointed dinner the following evening, Jacob brought along Jouhandeau as a bulwark against "Zionism" (Jacob's word).[34] A few days later, not finding Cohen at the Hôtel Lutetia where he was staying, Jacob was writing him a warm letter at the hotel desk when Cohen appeared before him, severely. Jacob handed him the note, Cohen read it and shook Jacob's hand. They went up to Cohen's room, where he explained that he'd heard that Jacob was maligning him all over town. Since Jacob had, on the contrary, been proclaiming Cohen's genius, he was astonished. They cleared up the misunderstanding with Jacob professing his admiration for the strength of Cohen's faith, and they went downstairs and had an excellent dinner in the hotel restaurant with Cohen's friend the poet Georges Cattauï, also Jewish.[35]

Jacob judged this mild spirit ripe for conversion, and he worked on him hard. In long letters, he tried to persuade Cattauï that the Old Testament prophesied the New, that the stigmata of saints proved the presence of God, and that conversion would bring him a "spiritual revolution" as well as good luck. He desisted only the following November, saying they should set questions of "race and religion" aside.[36]

Around the time Jacob affirmed his Catholic faith in "Eyes in the Stomach," he did some fancy footwork to reconcile his occult beliefs with his adopted religion in the essay "The Key to Dreams," published in *Philosophies* in March. Taking up material he had been mulling for more than a decade, he tried to align his Kabbalistic vision of a hierarchy of heavens, corresponding to different states of the soul, with his idiosyncratic interpretation of Catholic dogma. Taking the text of Psalm 142 ("Anxiatus est super me spiritus meus": literally, "Disturbed above me is the spirit"),[37] he focused on the preposition *super,* claiming that the human "spirit" was *above* the self, *super me,* and that this meant that the spirit in a state of visionary ecstasy was free to roam from heaven to heaven, as in the visions of Anne Catherine Emmerich, the Magus Lagnel (his old friend from Montmartre), and Dante. He mentioned his own apparitions as further evidence and concluded by adding to the three categories of Catholic prayer ("vocal," "cordial," and "mental") a fourth, "visual prayer," by which he meant mystical vision. In "Eyes in the Stomach," as so often, Jacob tried to unify Judaism and Christianity, and in this essay he tried to bind together his identities as occultist and Catholic—two more instances of a life spent trying to create a whole from multiple, contradictory parts.[38]

IV.

IN APRIL, JACOB began to plan a trip to Italy for the papal jubilee in June. He had been dreaming of Italy, and his friendship with Nino Frank had sharpened his desire. To finance it, he accelerated his production of gouaches.[39] He also had to battle Gallimard, who wanted to divert a payment of 1,250 francs from the Émile-Paul brothers to himself; Jacob had promised yet another novel to the Nouvelle Revue Française but had accepted a little assignment on the side from Émile-Paul, a vignette of Montmartre for a volume called *Tableaux de Paris.*[40] He fussed about getting a passport and accepted the invitation to stay in Rome with Jouhandeau's acquaintance, Paul Petit, an attaché at the French embassy.

In the last two weeks of April, Cingria landed in the monastery again, playing the piano in a vague and scrambled manner and telling fortunes with tarot cards—treading so close to Jacob's own gifts, Jacob found him unsettling.[41] By May 11, Jacob was in Paris, where he had lunch with Albert Cohen and Cattauï before catching the train south. From Toulon, he took a detour to the coastal town of Hyères to meet a young man who had been writing to him, a Jean Vinciguerra. Whatever hopes he had nourished for this encounter were quickly quenched, as Vinciguerra, in uniform for his military service, affected an air of Wertherian disenchantment and stuffed himself with *pâtisseries* during their "sinister" lunch, though he roused himself sufficiently to take Jacob on a tour of the beaches and villas of Hyères in his car.[42] From Hyères, Jacob made his way inland to Grasse, famous for its perfume factories, and spent two days with de Gouy and Greeley in their villa perched on flowering hills, a landscape and company that enchanted him, and where he could relax with witty homosexual friends without having to fake anything.[43]

For the next six weeks Jacob traveled exuberantly through Italy. Though he initially found the northern landscape on the way to Milan dry and uninspiring, he soon fell under the spell of the crumbling colorful walls, the side streets and churches, the paintings of Tintoretto and Veronese, the ancient mosaics, the cloisters and courtyards, the ancient sculpture, and the good humor of the inhabitants.[44] He spent the week of May 16–22 with Nino Frank and his lover, the actress Nina Ronchi, at her parents' house near Lake Como, touring the lakes and mountains, and there he met the archaeologist Paolo Maggi, who would later show him around Milan (exhaustingly).[45]

From Verna he went to stay with Paul Petit in Rome: not having met the diplomat, he had demanded a description from Jouhandeau ("face, dress, social position, character!").[46] His room looked out over the Baths of Diocletian, and he darted about the city, learning the tramlines to find the churches he wanted to see to fulfill his "Christian duty," as well as museums and ruins. His letters to Cocteau are a travel diary, bubbling with detail and anecdotes: he "disqualifies himself" as a person of taste by admiring the antiquities in the Villa Borghese; he's scolded by aesthetes for not having seen this or that and for having missed the little Giotto behind the big Chamber Pot; he's unfashionable in being impressed by the Forum; he loves the little red lady's hat on Adonis's head in Tintoretto's *Venus and Adonis* . . . Paul Petit (who would become a loyal friend and would edit Jacob's *Selected Poems* for Gallimard) arranged an evening with Paul Claudel. Dinner with the august Catholic author was a little like dining with the pope, but Jacob carried it off and amused this embodiment of tradition and propriety at a restaurant on the Janiculum as they discussed French literature and compared notes on Valéry, Bourget, Morhange, Paulhan, and Jouhandeau. "Don't accuse me of angling for the Académie-Française or the Légion d'honneur," Jacob warned Cocteau.[47]

The canonization of a humble French priest, the *curé* d'Ars, gave Jacob a taste of papal drama. He had to get to St. Peter's by six in the morning and spent hours in an excitedly shoving crowd, the nuns pushing as hard as everyone else, while families opened picnic baskets to eat chocolates and sausages. They waited and waited to see the procession of cardinals ("white mitres and red capes under the tapers—beautiful!"); to hear the choirs; and finally to see Pope Pius XI himself under Bernini's great baldachin. "I adore the pope!" Jacob exclaimed to Cocteau.[48] After more adventures in and around Rome, including finding Cocteau's *Plain-Chant* in a bookstore and being told by the proprietor that their best-selling French book was his own *L'Homme de chair et l'homme reflet,* he made his way to Naples as a guest of Jean Grenier.

Grenier was now teaching French at the Institut Français in Naples. Jacob, who had confessed to Nino Frank that he loved Grenier enough to weep or become ill, seems to have enjoyed his company. He found Naples dirty and teeming with beggars, and the *pensione* where he and Grenier stayed had bedbugs and no locks on the bedroom doors. But he remained enthusiastic, visiting Pompei with Kahnweiler's brother, later writing Supervielle and Émié that he was "crazy about Italy."[49]

The journey continued through his return to Rome and visits to the Benedictine monasteries of Subiaco and Monte Cassino (where he inquired about what it would take to become a monk and was chilled by the rules of obedience). At Assisi, on May 18, a day before Cocteau was received into the faith at the Maritains' chapel in Meudon, Jacob described to his convalescent friend his own dreamy experience in the crypt, where he clutched the wall, feeling dizzy, when he thought he heard Saint Francis murmuring to him, "I know Saint-Benoît-sur-Loire. Learn my story, write my story. You have a clear style."[50] From Assisi he whisked to Florence, where he saw "two thousand pictures a day," guided by a young Mexican painter, Agustín Lazo.[51] He returned to France by way of Siena,

Pisa, and Milan, arriving in Paris in late May. He stayed there a week, dining with Salacrou and Jouhandeau on June 1. Two days later he was home in Saint-Benoît.[52]

V.

FIRED BY MEMORIES of Italy, Jacob found Saint-Benoît dull—Saint-Benoît-the-Jaundice, Saint-Benoît-the-Spleen, he called it in letters—though the monastery began to fill up as usual with pilgrims for the saint's day.[53] Gabriel Bounoure came to visit for several days in July. He had been teaching in Syria for the past year and kept faithfully in touch by mail. Now Reverdy and his wife joined them for what turned out to be a highly uncomfortable stay, Reverdy passionate in his new faith, and Jacob setting off his firecrackers of wit, erudition, and fantasy. Bounoure couldn't make peace between them. Jacob attracted a flock of oblates and, sensing that they "lacked a sense of the supernatural," set about to show them that the supernatural surrounds everyone: he narrated wild stories mixing the legends of Saint Benedict, Brittany, Montmartre, and the Kabbalah, even introducing Magus Lagnel and his "female faun" to general stupefaction. Reverdy was incensed. He took Bounoure aside to complain of Jacob's vanity and clowning. Jacob, for his part, confessed to Bounoure behind the basilica, "I've come here to flee the gaze of my censor and his icy showers of reprobation. How seriously he takes himself. It's the sin of sins."[54] On the heels of that visit arrived Claudel and three of his five children. As he had done in Rome, Jacob entertained this pious dignitary, though he complained to Cocteau that Claudel, in conversation at the meal at the monastery, acted like a general reviewing the troops.[55] Still, he recognized, as he wrote Jouhandeau, that "there's greatness in the simplicity of that man."[56] In the same letter he referred to an incident Jouhandeau had confessed, an embarrassing episode of drunkenness in which Cocteau had brought Jouhandeau home in a taxi, in pajamas (though they hardly knew each other). Jacob was about to launch into an adventure far more abject. His confidants would be Jouhandeau and Cocteau.

||

IN EARLY AUGUST, Jacob became friendly with the Frenkels, the ultrapious family of an eminent chemist who lived near Saint-Benoît. The parents, worried about their son's frivolous habits, invited Jacob to their house to "convert" him and wean him away from his life of automobile excursions and nightclubs, and the boy then accompanied Jacob back for a visit of several days at the monastery. On August 13, Jacob wrote troubled letters to Jouhandeau and Cocteau about the seeds of this affair, which already promised ill. The boy was "a real cad," Jacob acknowledged, preparing for a life of theft, pimping, and blackmail—acknowledging also that he (Jacob) found him charming and was already suffering "without rhyme or reason."[57] Pierre-Michel was blond and looked like a ruffian with dirty fingernails and grease behind his ears from tinkering with the car. He called himself "The King of Dancers"; he stayed out all night at dance halls; he boasted of sleeping with floozies, imagined he could earn money as a gigolo, and had free use of the family automobile. Jacob fell into an amorous frenzy that lasted for four months, a feverish confusion of conversion and seduction that led him on speeding car rides across the French countryside with Pierre-Michel, at one point tearing through Paris (fast, so they wouldn't be recognized) all the way to Chartres, on the boy's condition that they not visit the cathedral.

The remarkably blind parents entrusted this ephebe to Jacob for the summer, and after dropping in on the Claudels near Blois (where they alarmed Madame Claudel, who sent her daughters upstairs, her husband being absent), the odd pair hurtled off to Brittany. They spent September and the first days of October at the seaside village of Ploaré, mostly at the Hôtel Cabon at the dramatic Pointe du Raz, the cliff at the westernmost tip of Brittany, thrust out into the battering Atlantic Ocean. Jacob's letters from those weeks tell a tale of degradation, shame, and desperate desire. His love was a "slavery."[58] Instead of converting Pierre-Michel, it was Jacob who was "converted" to roaring around in a car, missing his daily mass, and neglecting his prayers, his meditations, and his work. (He was supposed to be writing a novel for Gallimard entitled *Les Gants blancs,* The White Gloves.)[59] Jacob tried to set the boy writing exercises, a pure waste of time. Instead, Pierre-Michel hovered over Jacob's writing table complaining that he was bored and they needed to go to Brest, or Quimperlé, or anywhere, as long as they were on the move.[60] Jacob was paying all the bills for hotels, meals, gas, and car repairs. "If I'm exploiting you now, I'll exploit someone else later," sneered Pierre-Michel.[61]

It's unlikely that Jacob and Pierre-Michel had a sexual relationship. It seems, rather, a case of infatuation on one part and cynical manipulation on the other, and one can well imagine the torture for Jacob at living at close quarters with a slender, muscular, adolescent male. Whatever it was, the story crashed to a halt in early October. "The King of Dancers is gone!" Jacob protested to Cocteau on October 4.[62] Pierre-Michel had gone off to England, supposedly to study English. Jacob was so worn out, physically and emotionally, he fell ill and retreated to his childhood bed in the family home in Quimper for several weeks with stomach pains so acute he was given morphine.[63] Torn to pieces by grief and shame, he compared himself to Philoctetes. He also recognized that "this sort of boy is becoming a habit."[64]

||

JOUHANDEAU, MEANWHILE, WAS suffering his own shame and grief, and by now he felt close enough to Jacob to open his heart to him. Delivered from his passion for Leiris, he had fallen in love with a young man named André Jullien du Breuil, who was, in turn, in love with a young lady (though he seems to have been flirting with Jouhandeau at the same time).[65] Jouhandeau drew Jacob into the drama, threatening suicide; now back at Saint-Benoît, Jacob wrote to du Breuil and sent a series of letters to Jouhandeau advising him to cut himself off from the torturer and turn to God. Then the story grew lurid. Jacob thought Cocteau—back in Paris, and in the religious enthusiasm of his conversion—might console Jouhandeau. Cocteau accordingly visited the sufferer. He consoled him by leading du Breuil back to him, whereupon Jouhandeau, in a fit of malevolent torment, cynically asked the young man to sleep with him. In a further fit of self-loathing, Jouhandeau then exploded in a furious letter to Jacob, accusing him of having sent Satan. Jacob's reply contains one of his most sexually explicit statements: "The fact is, fucking makes people mean." (And in a postscript: "Of course you don't fuck every night. Neither do I!") He had sent his friend Cocteau, Jacob explained, because he was afraid Jouhandeau would commit suicide. It was an act of real love, not "an abomination."[66] Jouhandeau apologized, Cocteau remained serene, and the whole episode blew over.

WHILE ON HIS bed of pain in Quimper, Jacob received a frightening letter from Gallimard demanding the new novel, saying Jacob owed him twelve thousand francs, and threatening to impede Kra's publication of the collection of poems, *Les Pénitents en maillots roses*.[67] In December, Jacob went to Paris and sorted things out with Gallimard, at least temporarily, and the poems duly appeared. The slim collection brought together poems Jacob had written at Saint-Benoît and at Roscoff. Some of them recalled *Le Laboratoire central* in their verbal playfulness; others looked forward to the more lyrical work to come. The most beautiful poem in the book, "Infernal Vision in the Form of a Madrigal," distills Jacob's experience of passion, yearning, disappointment, and guilt, and unifies in song what he suffered as agonizing division in his life:

> "Handsome knights of Alcantara
> Venus of Marnes-la-Coquette
> The nabob of Calatrara
> Offers you his private yacht
> to sail away to Guatemala."

> When I had renounced your love, oh women,
> when I had of pleasure intoned the requiem
>   and conquered Bethlehem

When I had cast off the henbane of this world
And of the Wandering Jew's eternal
      voyage the sail unfurled

When, beneath the cramped balcony, the vice
squad and its laughter ringing de profundis
      knocking as in the old days
at my door to enroll me in its militias
I had made my room a secret oasis
      or almshouse

I did not yet know the clear sky of your eyes
the snowy kingdom of your limbs in summer
nor the perfumed hell in your thick hair
nor your beauty which will be my Holy Grail
nor your soul for which I shall be Parsifal.

—Handsome knights of Alcantara
Handsome knights of Alcantara
all aboard! anchors aweigh!
—Let them rush off toward the tropics,
I have only one mystic exodus
one reliquary and its relic
I have one tender oasis only: you,
Your eyes, their forget-me-not blue.[68]

In Paris, Jacob fell for the son of the proprietor of the Hôtel Vouillemont, Robert delle Donne. This attachment brought considerable pain,
at least in the short term.[69] But Jacob's difficult loves were not over with
Pierre-Michel Frenkel and Robert delle Donne. Those affairs could be
seen as dry runs for a far more serious passion, a "mystic exodus" that
would last for years and initiate him into an entirely new realm of suffering. The new avatar of Eros was Maurice Sachs, a charming sociopath
who worked as a desk clerk at the Hôtel Vouillemont. Sachs was devoted

to Cocteau and had just imitated his conversion, abandoning his family's Judaism in a ceremony at the Maritains' chapel with Cocteau as his godfather. Jacob had heard of Sachs for some months, and now, in December, he met him. The demon, this time, arrived in the guise of a seminarian preparing to take holy orders.

CHAPTER 16

LOVES AND FEVERS

I.

Maurice Sachs was a true child of the Belle Époque: its materialism, frivolity, and frantic pursuit of pleasure. At age nineteen he had already lived tumultuously. Like Jacob, he came from a family of atheist, secular Jews. His father, Herbert Ettinghausen, had no profession; at a loss for funds, he sold the family furniture one summer when his wife and son were on vacation, and disappeared. Sachs was five years old. His mother had been abandoned at age sixteen by her mother, Alice, who left her daughter and her diamond merchant husband Georges Sachs to marry Jacques Bizet, "the son of *Carmen*"–the son, that is, of Georges Bizet, the composer of *Carmen*. Alice and Jacques soon divorced, and by the time young Maurice knew his step-grandfather, Jacques Bizet—once a great friend of Proust's—the man was a wreck: he was drunk by breakfast and spent the day giving himself injections of morphine and shooting at bibelots in his apartment with his revolver. He lived with a mistress who amused herself by tormenting him sexually.

Pudgy and unathletic, Maurice by age six developed a sensuous pleasure in theft, stealing from the handbags of his mother's lady visitors. Because his mother had no interest in raising a child, Maurice was brought up by an English nurse, and at age eleven he was sent to an English-style boarding school. There he learned the consolations of masturbation (with a deerskin wallet between his thighs: the symbolism for this lifelong thief is weirdly perfect). He was also initiated into homosexual games and may have been raped by an older boy.[1] The one subject in which he excelled was literature, and he took refuge in the fantasy worlds of novels and poems.[2]

The school was seething with sexual activity, and at the end of his third year, Sachs and several other students were expelled. Returning to Paris, he found his mother married to a journalist. Sachs was dispatched to live with his grandmother, Alice Bizet, who chain-smoked, maintained an alarmingly youthful appearance, and had no inclination to take care of anyone. On the loose in the city, Sachs lied and cheated his way through two more years of lycée, skipping classes and spending days with the decrepit Jacques Bizet, who placed his loaded revolver in the boy's mouth and instructed him to finish himself off that way when he was tired of life. Bizet's mistress found it funny to ply Maurice with cognac. When he wasn't pursuing this education, he floated around the salons frequented by his mother and his grandmother—always the displaced person, learning to survive by wit and charm.

In 1922, Jacques Bizet followed his own advice and shot himself in the head. More wounding to Maurice than his death was the fact that he left no letter or bequest to the boy who had visited him day after day. But Sachs's shaky adolescence truly caved in the following spring when his mother, heiress of the diamond business, was discovered to have written an enormous bad check. She emptied the company safe and fled to a hotel in Normandy, where Sachs and his stepfather found her, locked in her room, almost dead from an overdose. The stepfather gave Sachs eight hundred francs and vanished from their lives (except that as the husband of a convicted swindler, he spent nine years paying off her debts). To avoid a prison sentence for his mother, Sachs spirited her to London, where she would live until after World War II.

In the midst of the melodrama, Sachs did not, of course, pass his baccalaureate exam. He sold the remains of his grandfather's library and joined his mother in London for six months, working in a bookstore from which he stole books. By 1923 he returned to Paris, now seventeen and on his own. He lived in a tiny hotel room and eked out a living selling books for the Librairie de France. It was in this unsettled period that he met and charmed Robert delle Donne and his sister Marie. They invited him home, and their father hired him as a receptionist at the Hôtel Vouillemont.[3]

Just down the street from Le Boeuf sur le Toit, the Hôtel Vouillemont attracted the same clientèle of snobs and artists. It was the fashionable place to stay, or to meet and be seen in the bar and restaurant. On any given night, Pirandello, Maurice Rostand, Anna de Noailles, Francis Poulenc, and of course Cocteau could be spotted there. So could Max Jacob when he was in town. It was a palpitating, gilded environment, ruled by the Sicilian patriarch Albert delle Donne with his dyed-black, slicked-down hair parted in the middle, his pink shirt, and a dark silk tie secured by an enormous pearl.[4] Marie and Robert drifted through it as princess and prince. Marie was a beauty, with heavy Venetian blond tresses and a pale complexion (which she tended zealously, sleeping with veal cutlets on her cheeks).[5] Sachs, with his quick intelligence and taste for luxury, slipped right into this rarefied world. The delle Donnes gave him a room on the top floor and, until his formal hiring, included him in family meals. He considered them, he later said, his "only real family."[6] Marie called him "Biquette" (Kid).

Sachs had stuffed his head with literature. From Rousseau's *Confessions*, he plucked the template he would use for the rest of his life: confess shameful behavior only to excuse it. From Balzac, all he learned was the fever of ambition. From Stendhal's *Le Rouge et le noir*, he adopted Julien Sorel's heroic amorality. And now he found in Gide's *Les Nourritures terrestres* a new screed for self-invention. He was tacking a photograph of Gide up on his bedroom wall when his new friend Gérard Magistry, from the delle Donne circle, dropped in and corrected him: "There's only Cocteau."[7] A few days later Magistry took him to see the star. When they entered the room, Sachs remembered, all he saw "was Cocteau lying in black pajamas on his little Swiss hotel bed. His long, too-thin hands moved strangely. A red scarf tightly swaddled his neck; his very black hair curled in a soft aureole over his forehead."[8] Sachs was enchanted. He now transferred his devotion to Cocteau, read all his books, visited daily, and prayed before his photograph. Cocteau folded him into his clique at Le Boeuf sur le Toit, taking him to gay dance halls and introducing him to Albert Le Cuziat, the proprietor of the homosexual brothel down the street from the Hôtel Vouillemont. He also introduced him to opium.

Later, Sachs would accuse Cocteau of "a complete lack of heart" and "an almost monstrous dryness."[9] But in his early infatuation he saw Cocteau as the key to art and luxury. To play the dandy at Le Boeuf sur le Toit, he racked up serious debts, patronizing the same fancy tailor as Poulenc. And he began swindling clients at the hotel, pocketing money intended for their theater tickets and other small sums. In his memoirs, he confessed and excused this behavior in the same breath; whose fault was it, he demanded, if credit was so easy in the 1920s?[10]

When Cocteau was baptized in June 1925, the Jewish Sachs rapidly followed suit, so seducing the Maritains that he was baptized in their chapel on August 29 with Raïssa as his godmother. By this time, Cocteau was writing Jacob about the new friend and convert. Not content with baptism, Sachs decided to enter holy orders, a flamboyant move designed to earn him new protectors and (perhaps) relief from debt. It was just at this time, in December 1925, that Jacob, still shattered from the summer with Pierre-Michel Frenkel, met Sachs through Cocteau.

Denise Piazza (eventually to be Denise Tual when she married Roland) was a friend of Marie delle Donne and often visited Marie at the hotel. There she met Maurice Sachs, "the Kid." He slipped into Marie's room each evening to report to "the children" about the goings-on at the hotel, the "chamber pot report."[11] And there she met Max Jacob.

As a boy, Sachs wanted to be a girl. Now he persuaded his sponsor Maritain to force the Father Superior of the seminary to allow him to wear a cassock immediately, when the normal practice was to don it only after four years of study. Marie and Denise went shopping with Sachs for the cassock, a gift from Marie, just days before he passed through the doors of the Séminaire des Carmes by the Jardin du Luxembourg. Sachs recalled the shiver of pleasure he felt as he slipped it on: it gave him a thrill to lift the folds lightly with both hands, like a girl, as he went upstairs. He was already so well known at Le Boeuf sur le Toit that when word got

out that he'd entered a seminary, a friend thought it was a new nightclub and asked for the address.[12] This was the man who would soon rule
Max Jacob's heart.

II.

SACHS ENTERED THE seminary on January 2. At this point, Jacob hardly
knew him and was embroiled in other friendships, quarrels, and romances.
His heart was still bleeding over Frenkel, and in the first two weeks of
the New Year, he fixed on the blond Robert delle Donne as a new object
of passion. At the same time, he was managing intricate friendships with
Cocteau and Jouhandeau. To both of them, Jacob confessed his suffering
over Frenkel.

In Paris in early January he stayed with Wladimir Smirnoff, an art
critic and bank clerk. He had sprained his hand, and his liver was acting
up again, but those pains didn't keep him from the new pains of love.[13]
It was from Smirnoff's address that he wrote Robert on January 6, still
using the formal *vous*, fearing he had been indiscreet, but breaking out
in a postscript that hinted that Robert had given him some encouragement. "Believe in my friendship which was too spontaneous not to have
been, I fear, indiscreet," he protested in the body of the letter, signing
himself, "Max Jacob." The p.s. veers between conventional *politesse* and
risqué suggestion: "My compliments to Mademoiselle your sister. Robert,
my Robert, ah ah ah ah ah ah ah."[14]

A lot must have passed between the two men over the next ten days,
because when Jacob returned to Saint-Benoît on January 15, he wrote the
next day to Robert in intimate terms, begging him not to show the letter to Frenkel (to whom he had introduced him). His first letter would
be for Robert, he declared, rhapsodically repeating the dear name and
describing the "nocturnal Siberia" of snow, cold, and mud he found at
Saint-Benoît. "Robert darling," he continued, "the first day, you asked
me what *penitence* is. This is penitence! Snow, infernal darkness. Robert!
Robert! Ah! Ah! Ah ! Ah!" (The "Ah! Ah!" was the performance of a tic

of delle Donne's; Robert burst out with an "ah" of joy when the conversation turned to religion.)¹⁵

He wrote still more passionately four days later, recycling for Robert the statement he had made years before about Picasso: "Don't tell anyone that you are after God what I love most in the world." Jacob assumes his advisory role, urging Robert to do acts of charity—including taking Frenkel under his wing and prying him loose from the right-wing militant group, the Camelots du Roi. Jacob's two passions, his Christian and erotic faiths, blend in a single élan, rising to an ecstatic sexual metaphor: "Send me twenty pages of general confession. No, Robert, you are my darling Robert, you can't imagine the ravages my feelings make in me: it's painful and delicious. One must pay attention to others *truly*, mystically (mysticism is realism: one wants to see, one wants to feel God). Let us carry our electricity, our ions, our electrons, our steam, our whole astral body to others by the will to discharge our engine which would explode."¹⁶

On January 18, Jacob wrote a *de profundis* letter to Jouhandeau. He had left his heart in Paris with Jouhandeau, with Frenkel, with Robert delle Donne, he cried. "Oh cruelty against myself, infinite suffering: I'm killing myself, my art, the best of myself; I'm crucifying myself in the sight of God who doesn't listen to me." About Frenkel he scrawled in the margin: "*I love him so much I howl.*"¹⁷

Jacob's passions were not monogamous: he could entertain several attachments at the same time, including his tormented attachment to God. The same day as his cry to Jouhandeau, he wrote Sachs in the seminary, opening with the formal *vous*. But by the end the letter breaks into a confession of love for delle Donne and an appeal for shared understanding, using the familiar *tu:* "Like you, I deeply love Robert delle Donne. I'd have left Paris long ago if my heart hadn't kept me near him. . . . Here's the poor flesh bleeding everywhere, and you, Maurice, you're bleeding like me, it's what brings us together, since now a whole new friendship begins for us." As often in Jacob's letters, he thrust the essential message into a postscript: "I suffered horrendously at leaving Robert Friday. I loved him too much to stay in Paris. Only you could understand this sacrifice, this affection, because you know it and you know what we owe our Lord, the only one worthy of our adoration."[18]

Jacob had urged Jouhandeau to meet the charming delle Donne. They did meet in January, and Jouhandeau wasn't charmed; he wrote Jacob that his new friend was a scoundrel. Jacob and Jouhandeau were already in the midst of a quarrel with Paul Petit, Jacob's host in Rome, who also knew Jouhandeau and kept an apartment in Paris. The three had dined together in January, and evidently Petit accused them both of being "snake men"; he seemed to blame Jacob for corrupting Jouhandeau. Jouhandeau complained of "enchantments" as well as about delle Donne, and on January 24 Jacob wrote justifying himself and defending "the scapegoat" Robert. One senses the very different temperaments of Jouhandeau and Jacob, and the different ways in which they experienced their homosexuality. Jacob was ardent, anguished, and guilty, but he accepted the turmoil and lived it, sometimes even with a sense of humor. Jouhandeau—perhaps because he taught in a Catholic boarding school, perhaps simply because it was his defensive nature—seems to have been horrified by his homosexuality, to have gone to lengths to hide it, and to have lashed out at characters he considered threatening and unsavory.[19] Evidently delle Donne presented such a threat, so much so that Jouhandeau intimated that the police might become involved. Jacob struck back: "About the police: 1. At his [Robert's] house I've met the Marquise de Charette, Painlevé's private secretary and I've even met myself there."[20]

III.

JACOB DIDN'T LINGER long in the mud and darkness of Saint-Benoît. He had been invited to lecture in Madrid at the Residencia de Estudiantes, and he used the occasion to present his "symbolic" interpretations of Scripture. He'd been collecting notes on the subject for years and still imagined that he would write a book about it. In spite of his sprained wrist, he busily produced gouaches to pay for the trip, writing Cocteau that he was also working on an expanded edition of *Le Cabinet noir* and preparing drawings for the *Tableau de la bourgeoisie* to pay off his debt to Gallimard: he had still not begun the novel he had contracted to write for them, *Les Gants blancs*. Confiding now more than ever in Cocteau, he reported Jouhandeau's disapproval of delle Donne, and Frenkel's moral progress: the former thug was now engaged to a pious girl and was finally studying for his exams. In a rapid association of ideas, showing his attempt to sublimate that painful love, he continued, "As for me, I try to purify everything in myself; the only happiness is in God."[21]

Happiness may have been in God, but for Jacob it remained on earth too, in fleshly love. He shared with Cocteau a flexible, ironic style of living out these contradictions within an (officially) straight society, writing several days later: "A few years ago I thought *l'homme au sexuel* [homosexual, man of the sexual] was written like that, and I didn't understand it. . . . I've still not fully grasped the word."[22]

By February 4 he was in Madrid, and he delivered his talk the next day. He had hardly prepared, but with his usual brio he combined music hall clowning with exegetical fervor and held his audience rapt.[23] As reported in the Residencia's newsletter, Jacob's "lecture, his improvisation—as he called it—was a witty, delicate, airy composition with explosions of light."[24] Under the direction of the scholar Alberto Jiménez Fraud, the Residencia was the liberal intellectual center of Madrid, and the Spanish considered Jacob a Modernist celebrity. In Jiménez's villa Jacob had a ground-floor room and enjoyed a "royal" hospitality, with his own bathroom, eggs and jam with his coffee, and stacks of handsome stationery.[25] Journalists interviewed him, dignitaries paid court, he met countesses, and he visited the Prado, where he was particularly struck by the works of Bosch, Brueghel the Elder, and the "naïve" Titian. (At first he found El Greco, Picasso's idol, "sublime"; later he said he wasn't enough of a painter to weep in front of those paintings, already too well known from reproductions.)[26] Jiménez took him to Toledo to see the Escorial and the cathedral, where Jacob discovered what "treasure" really could mean. The landscape impressed him as bleak and solitary, with hardly any houses, just patches of box trees on yellowish ground cut by ravines, the sky striped gray, blue, gray, and jagged mountains beyond. It had nothing of the tenderness of Italy.[27]

He returned to Saint-Benoît by way of Lourdes and Bordeaux. Lourdes disappointed. It looked like a shabby spa town, with rows of hotels and the streets crammed with boutiques selling religious trinkets. The mountains "crushed" the dwellings.[28] He saw no crowds of pilgrims and had trouble even finding a mass being celebrated. The one he finally stumbled on took place in a chapel in a grotto; later, in the church above, he watched the new bishop of Versailles being installed. Jacob, as usual, knelt in prayer in the aisle, and when the bishop descended from the pulpit to bless one of the ecclesiastics, he mistook Jacob for the intended and blessed him instead: "Thus, a new Jacob, I stole Isaac's blessing. 'Jacob' in Hebrew means 'supplanter.' "[29] The only miracle Jacob witnessed at Lourdes was a joke he made years later: he prayed to the Virgin, and She replied, "Address yourself to my son!"[30]

Louis Émié, the young journalist from Bordeaux who had been writing to Jacob, finally had a chance to meet his famous correspondent on Jacob's homeward route. Émié was twenty-seven, living with his parents, working for a local newspaper, and trying to write poems and literary articles; he'd published two small pieces on Jacob, and over the years Jacob had sent him copies of his books. In photographs Émié looks mousy: Jacob seems never to have had a crush on him. Émié's parents were suspicious of their son's literary leanings and not inclined to support so risky a vocation. When Jacob wrote announcing that he would arrive in a few days, the young man was almost sick with worry; not only would he meet his hero face to face, but his whole future might depend on his parents' judgment of his bohemian friend.

Jacob arrived in Bordeaux in the evening during a light rain, and went to find his host at the newspaper office. Émié led him to a hotel near a church where he could attend mass in the morning; Jacob was to come to his parents' house at noon the next day. Émié was late returning home for lunch, dreading the impression the Parisian poet would make upon his parents. To his surprise, as he entered he heard a babble of voices and laughter from the dining room. Max was strutting around chatting with his father, teasing the old aunt, narrating fantastical tales; the family was spellbound. No more hotel: they moved Max to a room in a neighbor's house, and he was to take all his meals with the Émiés. The visit had been planned for a day or two; it lasted almost two weeks. He had just bewitched an audience in Madrid, and now the performance spilled over into the household in Bordeaux.[31]

It was February, Carnival season. On the first evening of Mardi Gras, the town held a costume ball Émié's parents were to attend, and Émié was to report on it for his newspaper. Jacob had no costume but turned up attired in striped pants and a frock coat borrowed from Émié *père*. He later complained to Cocteau that he'd "had to go on a binge as if we'd just survived a shipwreck. Costume ball till 6 a.m.! A horror."[32] The horror, if such it was, came retrospectively. A veteran of Parisian costume balls (and the author of the poem "Le Bal masqué"), Jacob enjoyed himself so much, he stayed up way past the midnight curfew he had set for himself (so he could attend mass at six a.m. on an empty stomach); at first he compromised by drinking no more champagne after midnight, but by two a.m., hot and thirsty, he ordered another bottle, and he and his young friends continued their "binge" until dawn, with a stream of stories, songs, and improvisations, including a prose poem Jacob jotted onto a pamphlet picked up from the floor.[33]

As Émié grew nervous about the deadline for his article, Jacob winked, told him not to worry, and dictated the opening lines in an impeccable pastiche of cultural journalese: "It would take the tender and delicate pencil of a Gavarni and the harmonious palette of an Impressionist to depict all the details of the unforgettable scene the ballrooms at the Alhambra offered, Tuesday night, to the numberless couples dancing."[34] This wouldn't be the last time Jacob dictated an article to Émié. The next exercise would turn nasty.

Jacob appeared each day at noon at the Émiés' house with flowers or a box of candy. He narrated, sang, and improvised on the piano pastiches of Donizetti, Wagner, Verdi, Massenet, and Debussy. Émié and his friends marched Jacob along the quays and showed him the Grand Théâtre ("a Cubist masterpiece," Jacob judged). Some evenings Jacob drifted with them from café to café. Other evenings, at home in Émié's room, he read his notebooks and offered literary advice. And one day they took a taxi to the village of Tabanac to visit a priest Jacob had promised to see: Émié was astounded at the poet's transition from clowning to humble devotion in the presence of the cleric. As soon as they left, Jacob switched back to smoking and joking. This was Max Jacob, wrote Émié: one had to accept him as he was, "with his reversals, his contradictions, his vertiginous multiplicity, always sincere, too sincere perhaps, in spite of himself."[35]

A scene with Émié's parents had a peculiar aftermath. At dinner one evening, Émié *père* complimented Jacob on his moonstone cufflinks. With characteristic élan, Jacob unclipped them and popped them into his host's hands as a gift. The parents objected: Jacob insisted. The problem was, it turned out months later, the cufflinks didn't belong to him: they were on loan to Maurice Sachs from Monsieur delle Donne, the proprietor of the Hôtel Vouillemont. And they were much more valuable than Jacob realized.

IV.

JACOB LANDED IN Saint-Benoît by February 20, back in the middle of stories he'd left behind: his infatuation with Robert delle Donne, complications with Jouhandeau, and ambivalence about the now-betrothed Frenkel. Waiting for him in the stack of mail at the monastery was a missive of obscene abuse from Breton and Péret; he was not the only one so favored, as the pair had written similar insults to a number of well-known authors and had smashed up the offices of *Les Nouvelles littéraires*.[36]

Jacob suffered anxieties about delle Donne, but nothing like the tortures Frenkel had inflicted.[37] Just before catching the train to Madrid from Paris, Jacob had dropped in at the Hôtel Vouillemont and kissed Robert in the presence of his father; Robert repelled the kiss with stiff coldness. Returning from Spain, Jacob found ninety-three letters "from the entire universe" but no word from Robert. Accordingly, when Jacob dashed to Paris in the first two days of March to launch *Les Pénitents en maillots roses* (at long last appearing from Kra), he hadn't dared visit the delle Donnes. Cocteau affirmed that "Robert adores you," and Robert wrote reassuringly, so that for the next few months a torrent of love letters flowed from Saint-Benoît to the Hôtel Vouillemont.[38] As for Frenkel, the little beast was getting married in Paris in April, and Jacob would be his best man. ("My real wedding," Jacob wrote delle Donne, "will be to see you, to shake your hand—since it's impossible to kiss you now.")[39]

Les Pénitents en maillots roses hardly made a splash, but it won discreet admiration. One of the most sympathetic reviews came from the Belgian Victor Moremans, who had first caught Jacob's attention in 1924 with a friendly account of *L'Homme de chair et l'homme reflet*. Now Moremans wrote a thoughtful piece about *Les Pénitents*. Though he naïvely compared Jacob to "the pure artists of the Middle Ages," he had the good sense to point to "Infernal Vision in the Form of a Madrigal" as one of the most affecting poems, and he characterized Jacob's nature as "multiple, candid, fantastical, spontaneous." Jacob, he asserted, was a magician.[40]

La Nouvelle Revue française took minuscule note of the book, in three paragraphs by Jean Cassou: "By living perpetually in the intellect, one loses contact with mankind and with all things, and even with oneself. . . . Happy and free Max Jacob, and how much fun he must have, condemning us to so much joy and so much freedom!"[41] Cassou had "dug his mole tunnels under my poor Penitents," Jacob complained to Cocteau, who had reason to commiserate, as Cassou had treated his *Poésies* snippily in 1925.[42] Robert Guiette praised *Les Pénitents* in *Sélection*, and André Fontainas wrote perceptively in the *Mercure de France*, noting its "double haunting" by circus games and religious rites.[43]

BUT JACOB WAS looking ahead. In May, *La Nouvelle Revue française* published three letter-stories, material for the expanded *Cabinet noir*.[44] Two slight poems came out in *Les Cahiers libres* in May, one of them alluding comically to his sprained wrist.[45] Far more interesting were the poems he published that summer. Five came out in *Commerce*, the journal financed by T. S. Eliot's cousin, Marguerite Caetani, Princesse Bassiano, and edited by Paul Valéry, Léon-Paul Fargue, and Valery Larbaud; all five have lyrical power, and one of them signaled an important renewal of an old direction. In "Supposedly Translated from Breton," Jacob returned to the folk inspiration of his early book *La Côte*. The long lines chanted a traditional tale of a maiden seduced and dying in childbirth: "A new song has been composed in the village of Saint-Goazec-de-Léon. / A new song has been composed: it's about this poor Jeanne Le Bolloch." Crès was bringing out a new edition of *La Côte* with aquarelles by Jacob; perhaps this stimulated him to adopt once again the mask of the folk singer. He had suggested to Julien Lanoë that they should make Lanoë's Breton journal *La Ligne de coeur* the "organ of a Celtic renaissance," and in that spirit he tossed off two Breton poems and signed them "Morven," giving his singer a name, Morven le Gaélique. In her, or him (for *morven* in Breton means "girl"), he stabilized his multiple selves in a somewhat unified persona (of uncertain gender) and excluded the razzle-dazzle of Modernist ironies.[46]

But the triumph of the spring of 1926 came in the poems for Maritain's journal, *Le Roseau d'or*. If Jacob was troubled by bad angels like Maurice Sachs, he also had good angels, foremost among whom were Maritain and Louis Vaillant. Jacob's antics shouldn't blind us to the reality of his Catholic faith, and his friendship with Maritain testifies to that faith. Reciprocally, the theologian considered Jacob one of the master poets of the age.[47] When Maritain founded *Le Roseau d'or* in 1925, he sought the "most advanced" poets who had any connection to Catholicism and even those who didn't;[48] he particularly wanted Jacob. In the second issue, Jacob's three poems appeared alongside work by the novelists Georges Bernanos and Julien Green and the essayist Henri Massis: Maritain dreamed of a Catholic Renaissance, and the journal was meant to demonstrate it.[49] The issue also featured Sachs's borrowed translation of *The Young Visitors,* a novel by the English child prodigy Daisy Ashford. True to form, Sachs grafted his translation onto the manuscript version by Jean Hugo and François de Gouy; he published it under his own name with a preface by Cocteau.[50]

Jacob's poems in *Le Roseau d'or* are melodic and dreamlike, rising out of the center of his being—the center of a cross where his sacred and profane loves intersected. The best of them, "Agonies and More," he had drafted in his notebook in Spain.[51] Fluidly rhymed in lines of seven syllables—*vers impairs*—the five-line stanzas subtly knock off balance the "marriage" of sorrow and love:

AGONIES AND MORE

I'm afraid you'll take offense
as I weigh and weigh again
in my works and in my heart
your love from which I live apart
that other love I'm dying in

What will these lines be about
God whom you nag day in day out
God his angels and his priests
or your love's infernal feasts
and their gobbling agonies

Righteous rocks old blood-soaked gods
I leave return veer close again
to my all-too-easy sin
my loves are in my pocket here
I'll sail weeping out to sea

On Edinburgh's city wall
so much sorrow marries so
much love
this evening Poetry your horse
wears a black veil[52]

V.

WHEN SACHS ENTERED the seminary, he had already been fired from the Hôtel Vouillemont, and he left massive debts behind. Inspired by the young man's sudden religious fervor, Jacob scraped together his meager resources to help pay what was owed. The Maritains—hardly wealthy— also put in a great deal of money, as creditors were knocking on the seminary door.[53] Sachs owed large sums as well to his former employer, Monsieur delle Donne—and he had "given" (more likely, sold) to Jacob the hotelier's moonstone cufflinks. He had at the same time been filching valuable objects from Cocteau's room. Cocteau spent the last months of 1924 in Villefranche-sur-Mer, fuddled with opium, and he gave Sachs letters to his mother and her cleaning lady asking them to permit his acolyte to remove things from his room: he needed the money to finance his drug habit. One can imagine the tangle of emotions with which Sachs carried off his idol's relics: theft of any kind gave him a thrill; these particular larcenies brought him closer to the absent beloved; he was sending part of the money to Cocteau. (A few years later, when adoration turned to vengeance, he stole more cynically from Cocteau, many of whose rare books and manuscripts signed by their authors, including Proust, turned up for sale in catalogues.)[54]

In his first two months as a seminarian, Monsieur l'Abbé Sachs—as he had the right to be called—seemed pleased with his new identity. The institution imposed order; he was treated with respect; he rose early and helped to serve mass, which gave him a feeling of power. He had little taste for studying theology but enjoyed the solitude of his cell, where Cocteau's poetry, Jacob's *La Défense de Tartufe,* and the works of Anne Catherine Emmerich, Aquinas, Bossuet, and Pascal kept him company. Jacob's Jewish friend Georges Cattaüi had converted and was now an older seminarian; so was the Alexandrian Jew Jean de Menasce (soon to translate *The Waste Land* and parts of *Ash Wednesday*); and the young Hungarian Baron Jean de Wasmer, who fell in love with Marie delle Donne when she visited Sachs. Sachs was allowed out on Wednesdays and weekends; he spent them with the Maritains at Meudon, happy in the swirl of sophisticated Parisians who gathered there.

By mid-February he shocked Jean Hugo with his withering imitations of the Father Superior, and by mid-March Jacob warned Robert delle Donne to tell Sachs that his conversation was scandalous.[55] Sachs was chafing at the priestly discipline. Penitential exercises—flagellation, a hair shirt, a bracelet of nails—only sharpened his appetite.[56] Now when he bolted from the seminary, he made the rounds of the salons open to him through the patronage of the Maritains and Cocteau; he went to the theater and art openings. Jacob, Cocteau, and the Maritains watched in trepidation. Maritain tried to direct his protégé's energies into proselytizing, and for some weeks Sachs excited himself by writing letters of "spiritual direction" and schemes of conversion. At the Maritains' gatherings, he preached vehemently.[57]

If Jacob worried about Sachs's vocation, he had equal reason for concern about Cocteau's fledgling faith. Early in 1926 Cocteau met another aspiring writer, Jean Desbordes, a boy of twenty, naïve and sweet-natured, besotted with Cocteau's work.[58] It's not clear what relations they had that spring, but in May, when Desbordes was called up for military service, Cocteau got him exempted so he could stay in Paris.[59] Whatever details Cocteau confessed to Jacob, he made it clear that his faith was wavering, and Jacob replied in a long letter warning that the demon was touching him. Jacob's admonitions to beware of perfectionism, to try to live his faith realistically, accepting himself and his weakness but at least recognizing his lapses for what they were—sin—give a good picture of Jacob's own tempestuous religious life. "The sense of evil isn't hypocrisy, it's the fear of God," he stated, and advised frequent confession, a practice he often described as taking an aspirin.[60] He and Maritain consulted about "Jean's" shaky faith.[61] Mixed with these Christian instructions to Cocteau were accounts of Jacob's own romantic upheavals; Jacob told of going to Paris for Frenkel's wedding in April.[62] And Jacob was expecting the visit of Robert delle Donne and his friend Alfred Ottoni, another fashionable young blade, another temptation.

Cocteau and Jacob saw themselves as a team, fathers raising a brood of literary sons whose talents, temperaments, and looks they endlessly discussed. Cocteau wrote in March, assuring his friend of Frenkel's devotion.[63] That young man and his bride visited Saint-Benoît in May and again in July. "Pierre-Michel married! Married and just the same," Jacob reported. And in the margin: "The jaguar dies still wearing his spots, says an African proverb." Far more perturbing, now, to Jacob were his feelings for delle Donne. In letter after letter, he implored him to visit. And when a visit was finally promised, Jacob replied, "Hosannah! Joy, joy, joy, *pl.d.j.*"

(shorthand for *pleurs de joie*, Pascal's amulet recording his religious revelation: "tears of joy").[64]

Jacob's illness, poverty, and fear of attacks by the Surrealists in the theater kept him from traveling to Paris for the premiere of Cocteau's *Orphée* in June, a theatrical triumph with strong homosexual overtones, a work of transfigured mourning for Radiguet. Jacob also missed Picasso's exhibit at the Paul Rosenberg Gallery.[65] And now he and Cocteau had a fresh scandal to gossip about: Georges Ghika, the prince, had fallen in love with a girl he and Liane had invited to Roscoff for the summer. "The news," Jacob announced to Cocteau. "Georges Ghika has dumped/dumped is the atmospheric word; I beg your pardon: it came spontaneously after reflection / Liane."[66]

Maurice Sachs soon put the Ghikas' scandal in the shade. The Father Superior allowed him to accompany his grandmother, Alice Bizet, for summer holidays at what she remembered as a quiet resort on the Riviera, Juan-les-Pins. By now, it had become a hot spot for the crowd from Le Boeuf sur le Toit: the Picassos, Marie Laurencin, René Crevel, the Beaumonts, Isadora Duncan, F. Scott Fitzgerald, and right nearby, in Villefranche, Cocteau and the young American novelist Glenway Wescott. Sachs fell in love with an American adolescent, Tom Pinkerton. They spent a night walking hand in hand weeping along the beach (in Sachs's account) before "succumbing to passion" and igniting a scandal all along the coast. The two paraded around together for days, Sachs using his cassock as a beach robe, sometimes lending it to Tom, who let it slither onto the sand.[67] Cocteau saw that he would be compromised by these antics and ordered Sachs to leave. Pinkerton's mother protested to the local bishop, threatening to call the police and prosecute for corruption of a minor. Sachs bustled his grandmother back to Paris; at the seminary, he confessed to the Father Superior, who counseled him to give up his priestly vocation and do his military service.[68] Tortured by longing for Tom, Sachs returned to Juan-les-Pins for weeks. Shame finally drove him away. In September he retreated for eight days to the Abbey of Solesmes, where he met Reverdy. October brought him to Saint-Benoît. His story would now entwine for several years with Max Jacob's.

VI.

ON AUGUST 4, when Jacob wrote a letter of goofy greetings to "Cher Monsieur l'Abbé, cher Maurice," with messages for Picasso, Cocteau, and François de Gouy, he had no idea of the misadventure with Tom Pinkerton.[69]

He spent August and September sociably in Brittany.[70] Ten days in Quimper passed more peaceably than usual, and Robert delle Donne and Ottoni turned up to take him on excursions.[71] He enjoyed a week at Douarnenez with the Colles; there he focused for the first time on Jean Colle's seventeen-year-old son Pierre. The boy was handsome, lazy, a chess player and fencing champion, considered disreputable because he had so many girlfriends. As he hovered over Jacob's worktable, the poet promised to take him on a jaunt in someone's car if he wrote a poem about it. They took the trip, Pierre composed two surprisingly good poems, and Jacob sent them to Julien Lanoë, who published them in *La Ligne de coeur*. Pierre was ecstatic. (He would grow up to be one of Jacob's closest friends, his art dealer, and ultimately his literary executor.)

In September, Jacob's visit to Jean Grenier in Saint-Brieuc brought him a new friend, the novelist Louis Guilloux. Like Grenier, Guilloux would prove to be one of the most intelligent of all in Jacob's large acquaintance, and he left what is probably the best portrait of Jacob in action.[72] A native of Saint-Brieuc, Guilloux had worked as a journalist for several years in Paris and had just given up that job to return to Brittany. He was twenty-seven, married, poor, and determined to be a writer. When Jacob arrived on the evening of September 13, Grenier dashed over to Guilloux's house to alert him that Max was to be found, after dinner, at the Café du Commerce. And there the three convened, at what Max baptized the "Café Machin et des Colonies"—Café Thingummy and the Colonies. Several days of hilarious literary play now unrolled. Some glimpses: Max drew something on the paper tablemat at the café. "Watch out!" he warned, covering the drawing "as if it were a dangerous animal, capable of leaping at our faces."[73] "It's Stavrogin!"[74] He tore off the drawing and gave it to

Guilloux, who kept it for years. Grenier studied the schedules for trains and buses; they were to go to Saint-Quay the next day to look for Jacob's friend Paul Sabon.

> "Who?"
>
> "Paul Sabon. . . . An exquisite creature. A flower!"
>
> "Ha!" said the resolutely heterosexual Grenier. "One of your new little friends?"
>
> Max pinched Grenier's ear. "You," he said, "you have this—" and he traced the line of Grenier's cheek with his thumb—"you have this line." Bursts of laughter.[75]

Here we see Max Jacob joyful, funny, and laughingly at ease with young men who presented no amorous possibilities, nothing but the pleasure of intelligent friendship. They clowned around all evening, leaving the café and strolling the deserted streets, Max relating his exploits in Spain and his religious interpretations.

> "People don't understand religion," said Max.
>
> "Everyone can't live with demons or afford apparitions."
>
> "But it was my guardian angel!"
>
> "Yes. You started small."
>
> "Speaking of which," said Max, "I've seen the Holy Virgin."
>
> "Oh! And how's she doing?"
>
> "Not so bad, for her age. Quite well, in fact."[76]

The whole next day carried on the three-way discharge of jokes. In the bus station, while Grenier went off to buy a newspaper, Max took Guilloux's hands and insisted that they should use the familiar *tu*. At Saint-Quay, they wandered about, couldn't find Sabon even by inquiring at the post office, and went to the beach. There Max made a semicomic scene with Guilloux, calling him *vous*, accusing him of no longer loving him—

"And how long is this farce going to go on?" demanded Guilloux.

At which Max embraced him, and said, "Ouf—I was scared. So it's settled? You're coming with me to Nantes?"

Guilloux had no idea of going to Nantes. But it was summer, they were giddy, and why not?

IN NANTES, GUILLOUX and Jacob spent the evening with Lanoë and put up in a hotel, where Jacob didn't even try to make a pass at his new friend, who so obviously didn't invite it. The next day they visited the museum— especially to admire Max's favorite Corot—and then a church, where Max took the atheist Guilloux through the Stations of the Cross. He acted them out step by step, concluding in a storm of tears and in prostration. The tears were real. The theater was real. Jacob's religion was theatrical and, like all real art, a form of truth. He and Guilloux had lunch with Lanoë at an open-air restaurant shaded by trees along the riverbank and concluded the day composing a poem together, a ditty Guilloux kept and printed in his memoir, with the date, "Nantes. September 15, 1926."[77]

VII.

JACOB RETURNED TO Saint-Benoît by way of Paris. He stayed with the Frenkels: that would have been the staid apartment of Pierre-Michel's parents, since their newlywed son was still in the army and hadn't yet set up his own household. Pierre-Michel was polite with everyone, Jacob reported to Cocteau—his main confidant—but with Jacob the good manners masked "an incomprehensible anger." Jacob was being disingenuous: he must have sensed how their escapade of the previous summer would have complicated the young man's feelings.[78] He visited Liane in Saint-Germain-en-Laye: she was salving her wounded pride in a fling with a young Italian beauty, Mimy Franchetti. Her old lover Natalie Barney and other allies were petting her and surrounding her with roses. Jacob judged the princess harshly: "She's trying to whip up her reputation as if she intended to begin all over again as Pougy at age fifty-four or what? Why?—It's grotesque!"[79] He missed a date with Robert delle Donne, now working in the hotel, doing accounts, which he hated.[80] Jacob did see Nino Frank, who was making his way as a journalist. The end of September found him back in his cell at Saint-Benoît, waiting for Maurice Sachs.

And Sachs arrived. Delle Donne and Ottoni delivered him to Jacob in Orléans.[81] He was devastated by shame and by longing for Tom Pinkerton. Here the story becomes complicated. One has to filter the distortions in Sachs's multiple accounts and set them beside evidence from Jacob's letters to Maritain and Cocteau and the hundreds of letters from Jacob to Sachs.[82] Already on October 7, Jacob wrote Jouhandeau that he suffered from the battle in his "solar plexus between all-too-real loves and the horrifying fear of hell."[83] Disappointed in Frenkel and delle Donne, he was ready to love someone, and Sachs, a wounded angel escaped from the seminary, dropped right into his lap.

Jacob undertook to cure this damaged soul. Like Nino Frank, Sachs had a cell adjoining Jacob's. He participated in the life of the monastery: meals with Abbé Breut's family, mass on Sundays, walks and gossip in the village. Jacob set him to writing: while the elder painted his gouaches and hummed his poems, Sachs poured his experience at Juan-les-Pins into a novel called *Veronica's Veil:* he transposed Tom into Thomas, the dead beloved of the heroine, Véronique, who falls in love with his identical twin and ends up killing him and herself. "Tom is finished, I've finished Tom," he claimed.[84]

Sachs's portraits of his benefactor range from the sentimental to the vicious. In *Le Sabbat,* written after their break, he at least acknowledged that Max had "almost" brought him back to life and had been something like a father to him.[85] He depicted Jacob accurately enough as a "double" character, torn between his Catholicism and his lust, his peasant simplicity and his taste for perfumes and gems, his fundamental goodness and his malice. All of this rings true. What rings patently false is the accusation of avarice—just one example of Sachs's many lies, this one particularly odious since Jacob for several years labored and deprived himself in order to provide his "son" Maurice with money to satisfy his appetites.[86]

Le Sabbat presents a fairly honest physical picture of Jacob: a stocky little man, bald, with a stubble of white hair around the edges of his scalp, a Mr. Punch nose on a head too large for his body, lively eyes . . . He wore a checkered cap, a threadbare jacket of his father's, *sabots,* and Liane's red socks.[87] The novel *Alias,* in 1935, distorted the picture in its anti-Semitic fun-house mirror image of César Blum: "On a very short and very round body, he carried his enormous head on which from a distance I observed the huge hooked nose and, when he raised his hat to greet me with such exaggerated courtesy I was embarrassed, a naked skull encircled by a few white hairs, minuscule sparkling eyes, large sensual lips and a little hand, too fat, too short, too white which marked him as a Jew."[88] Later this creature is revealed as a hideous priapic monster leaping upon the hero who defends himself with a powerful punch.

There was no such punch. On the contrary, Sachs allowed the older man to fall desperately in love with him, milked him for money, gifts, and social connections, and let him "adopt" him as a symbolic son. Of course, Jacob would have attempted to caress him, as he had with Nino Frank, Gabory, and numberless other young men. Those caresses were easy to repel. Sachs took full advantage of his friend's desire. It was only years later, in vengeful retrospect, that he turned him into such a gross caricature.[89]

After a few days in Saint-Benoît, they took off together on a picaresque ramble. Jacob wanted to meet a young admirer, a tutor in a Jesuit boarding school in Évreux, west of Paris. The travelers arrived in town in the evening, left their bags in a hotel, and climbed the hill to the school. "Oh, I hope he's handsome," panted Jacob, out of breath from the exercise. The admirer turned out to be a gangly young man with stringy hair and sad eyes. He was an orphan; he idolized Max Jacob. A reproduction of a portrait of Jacob by Picasso was tacked to his cell wall, and from under the bed he drew a trunk containing a collection of all of Jacob's books, including rare first editions. Jacob was stunned. "He's handsome, as handsome as a Van Dyck," he whispered to Sachs. He ordered dinner for the three of them in a private dining room at the hotel, called for champagne, and— Sachs having retired early to bed in his own room—spent the night with the tutor, who had overstayed the curfew at his school. Early the next morning Jacob dragged them both to confession and Communion and bade the tutor farewell at the train station. (They learned later that he lost his job; he and Jacob had confessed to the same priest. Sachs left the story there. But the tutor had a name, Joseph Pérard, and he and Jacob remained friends. Far from being ruined by the encounter, Pérard took up a literary life in Paris as a journalist and translator, and he visited Jacob often in his years at the Hôtel Nollet.)[90]

One of the connections Sachs desired was an introduction to Jouhandeau. So from Évreux the pair popped up in Paris in Jouhandeau's neat mansard rooms, Sachs dressed nattily in golfing pants buckled just below the knee, a pale jacket with long side flaps, and a wide, striped silk tie, his dark hair cut so that it stood up from his brow in a rampart.[91] Jouhandeau was horrified at the sight of this man. It turned out that he had already run into Sachs at some gay dive, and he remained silent while his guests chattered about their upcoming trip to Bordeaux to recover delle Donne's cufflinks; he turned stony when Sachs announced that he would dedicate his novel to Jouhandeau. As soon as the two departed, Jouhandeau wrote Jacob that if his name were even mentioned in the novel, he would cut off Sachs's testicles with his own hands.[92]

From Paris, the wayfarers made their way to Bordeaux, acting like gleeful tricksters, egging each other on in Odyssean inventions. By now Jacob was smitten with Sachs: the tutor in Évreux had been just a sideshow. When Jacob wrote Jouhandeau defending Sachs, he treated the story of the cufflinks as mythological exploit: "The Argonauts have brought back M. delle Donne's cufflinks with the aid of legends, as befits Argonauts." They explained to the Émiés, Jacob boasted, that the cufflinks belonged to Sachs's grandmother, or rather to his deceased grandfather, who had them as a gift from the Maréchal de Saxe.[93] So many lies proliferated around these cufflinks, it's hard to keep them straight. Louis Émié reported the grandmother story. As Jacob apologized and explained and Sachs stood bashfully beside him, Émié darted away and returned with the precious baubles. In *La Décade de l'illusion*, Sachs narrates a lie so improbable it seems designed not to be believed: that the cufflinks had been given to Jacob the year before by *his* father (long dead!), were subsequently given to Robert delle Donne, and were now needed in order to appease the father. "We invented some sweet lie that Max Jacob immediately purged in the confessional."[94]

The Émiés seem to have taken it in stride as a vagary of artists, and treated Jacob and Sachs to a hospitable week in Bordeaux. Sachs dazzled Émié with his name-dropping, a spider web of inventions and gossip from Le Boeuf sur le Toit. With Émié's friend Jean-Loup Simian they made the rounds of the city, gadded about at a fair, drank good Sauterne. And since Émié was stalled on an article he had to write about Jouhandeau, Jacob dictated it to him, cramming it with piquant details: "He's thirty years old, he's bald and ugly. . . . He resembles an entomologist or even an insect. He speaks quietly, he's gentle but sometimes troubling glints light up his eyes . . ."[95]

The adventurers returned to Saint-Benoît by way of Alfred Ottoni's mother's house near Orléans. There they spent lyrical days, Jacob "repairing his finances" by painting gouaches while Ottoni and Sachs read Balzac aloud to him. And it was probably there that Ottoni and perhaps Sachs got the idea of marketing Jacob's paintings in Paris for prices higher than the Galerie Percier was asking. The Ottonis' turreted house would turn up later in Jacob's dedication of *Fond de l'eau* to Ottoni.[96] From Touraine, unaware of the negative impression he had made during their visit in Paris, Sachs wrote Jouhandeau proposing "a disinterested friendship"; he and Jacob wouldn't discover Jouhandeau's savage letter until a few days later at Saint-Benoît.[97]

The end of October brought Sachs and Jacob back to the monastery where they passed two quiet weeks, Jacob painting and working on poems while Sachs completed his novel. Jacob was putting together the volume that would become *Fond de l'eau,* and Sachs helped with the ordering.[98] Jacob wrote Maritain thanking him for his little book on Maurras's conflict with the Church and reporting that Maurice had finished a novel and that "this absorption in work and in regular devotional exercises to God is excellent for this first-rate soul who is dear to us, isn't he?" (Well might he ask, as the Maritains had been appalled by the blowup at Juan-les-Pins.)[99]

A few weeks later he asked Maritain to help save the Ghikas' marriage.[100] These weeks with Ottoni and at Saint-Benoît may have been the happiest of Jacob's life. All his loves were balanced; he lived in the presence of God with an intelligent, gracious, witty lover-son. He was painting and writing. Inspiration flowed. It was the dream of his novel, *L'Homme de chair et l'homme reflet*.

Sachs now had to leave for military service in the Army of the Rhine in occupied Germany. On November 12, the day before the departure, Jacob wrote delle Donne a letter that was, this time, not a love letter, but a letter *about* love: his love for Sachs. He praised Sachs's writing, told how he had made Maurice work, described the "scandalous novel" that worried Cocteau and the Maritains—"I'm not for scandal, but Maurice must absolutely give forth what he has inside him." He sorrowed at the impending separation.[101] The next day Jacques Bonjean, a young jeweler Sachs knew from the Beaumonts' circle, came with his wife to pick Sachs up and escort him back to Paris, where he would catch the train to Germany. Jacob accompanied them to the station and walked the five kilometers back to the monastery alone in the night, weeping. He was deeply in love. He saw in Maurice an ideal, "a noble character," and believed in his talent as a writer. The one point to which Jacob was not entirely blind was Sachs's ambition: he described him in his last days at Saint-Benoît as "silent as ambition itself with a secret rage to triumph."[102] Missing Sachs made him feel seasick or sick with migraine; he could hardly keep from flinging himself onto his bed to sob.

VIII.

FOR THE NEXT several years, a great deal of what we know of Jacob's life and feelings comes from his letters to Sachs. Maurice was his "darling angel," his "great darling sonny." Jacob sent him money, books, magazines, gifts of food, a constant stream of news, praise, advice. During all this time, Sachs had quite other matters on his mind but kept up the pretense sufficiently not to interrupt the flow of presents. Only slowly did Jacob come to realize his "sonny's" corruption. Then the letters sparked with alarm and anguish.

Cocteau tried to warn Jacob about Sachs. The Frivolous Prince had scolded the ex-seminarian, among other things, for the debts he still owed the delle Donnes and his rudeness to them. Sachs had also written a rebellious letter to his godmother Raïssa Maritain that shocked her so much, she'd fallen ill. For the next few weeks, Jacob defended Sachs to Cocteau, outrageously blaming delle Donne for "usury."[103] Jacob was, for now, completely under Sachs's sway and adopted his mythologies. Everywhere he turned, he had to mop up confusions created by his "son."[104]

To Sachs, he wrote constantly. Every little incident went into these missives—Jacob's stepping on a tube of paint and tracking it across the floor, visits from the newly married Lieutenant Vaillant, Jacob's purchase of a sapphire ring from Bonjean, the rupture between Cocteau and Jouhandeau . . . In every letter he offered money and concluded with outbursts of affection: "I live in you, you live for me and I feel your joys in my own nerves."[105] He tried to smooth relations between Sachs and Cocteau and again and again assured Sachs of his admiration. "My darling son, I hug you on my old heart with tears of pain. Max."[106] "My greatest joy is to love you."[107]

Meanwhile he had to earn a living. Ottoni had begun hawking Jacob's paintings, thereby angering Jacob's faithful dealer André Level at the Galerie Percier.[108] In December, when Jacob's stomach trouble acted up and he took to his bed for several days, Ottoni came to care for him, and Louis Vaillant attended him almost every day (when he could wriggle free from the women who now had him in hand: his wife, mother-in-law, mother, aunt, and cousins: Jacob was always wry about the marriages of his male friends).[109] To round out the company, young Pierre Colle showed up, intoxicated with poetry since his work had appeared in *La Ligne de coeur*. He and Jacob spent a day reading Cocteau's poems aloud, along with Radiguet's collection *Les Joues en feu*, which sent Jacob into a spasm of tears.[110]

The year ended with two political events that mattered to Jacob (who usually paid no attention to politics). His friend Cingria, the belly-laughing, piano-tinkling enthusiast of the Middle Ages, was imprisoned in Rome for speaking ill of Mussolini. Jacob wrote influential acquaintances to try to get him freed: Claudel, Paul Petit, Kahnweiler.[111] On a larger scale, at least in the Catholic world, on December 29 the pope condemned Action Française and the ideas of Charles Maurras (for monarchist incitement to violence and insubordination to the Church). As Jacob reported to his devout friends the Marcel Neveus in Brittany, "We're very agitated by the decisions of the pope concerning Action Française and creating turmoil for three-quarters of Catholics."[112] The condemnation did create turmoil at Saint-Benoît: Jacob's two priests disagreed violently about how to respond, Abbé Breut insisting on loyalty to Maurras, and the *curé* Fleureau demanding obedience to the Church. To the *abbé*, who wanted him to vote for Action Française in the next election, Jacob protested, "I came to Saint-Benoît to save my own soul, not the Daudet family."[113] The crisis poisoned the air, Jacob told Maritain in exasperation. "Can't you get your tablemates to discuss something else?" Maritain replied. "Astronomy, for instance?"[114]

IX.

JACOB'S LOVE FOR Frenkel had blocked his work for months. His love for Sachs, by contrast, released a powerful current of poetry, and the poems for *Fond de l'eau* began to appear in journals. In December, three poems in *La Nouvelle Revue française* showed the range of his styles: another Breton folk poem in the manner of Morven le Gaélique, a mystical prose poem, and a delicate free verse lyric.[115] In January, *La Ligne de coeur* presented six poems, three of which would take their place in *Fond de l'eau*. These are full-throated, mysterious pieces. Two were in the voice of Morven: "A School-teacher's Hat" and "The Eckmühl Lighthouse." In their freshness and simplicity, the Morven poems would prove, not surprisingly, among Jacob's most popular works.

THE ECKMÜHL LIGHTHOUSE

The Eckmühl Lighthouse is a huge lantern.

If you've lost your way on the heath you look to right and to left and you see where Saint-Guénolé is.

Since I met you, Marie Guiziou, I've looked for your eyes on all the oceans of the world.

But your eyes turn every direction where there are lovers.

Marie Guiziou! Marie Guiziou! My life is like the heath and you are for me like the Eckmühl Lighthouse.

Marie Guiziou! My life is like the ocean around Penmarch! and if I can't see your eyes, I'll be shipwrecked on the rocks.[116]

Finally, with the publication in March in *Le Roseau d'or* of "Poem," his cry at Sachs's departure in November, almost all the poems for *Fond de l'eau* had appeared in print, and he sent the manuscript to René Laporte at the Collection de l'Horloge, a series put out by *Les Cahiers libres*.[117] It would be a book of imaginative power and rhythmical fluidity.

||

IN JANUARY, ANDRÉ Salmon produced the first book devoted to Jacob, *Max Jacob, Poet, Painter, Mystic, and Gentleman*. Written in Salmon's tediously fanciful style, it has at least the virtue of being composed by someone who had lived through the old days of the Bateau Lavoir.[118] The old hijinx of their camaraderie in Montmartre are recounted with complaisant nostalgia, even down to their poverty-stricken menus. Some of the details may be questionable, and the story is tinged with resentment at Picasso; clearly Salmon felt left behind. He seems oddly hostile to Kahnweiler, too, accusing him of driving a hard bargain when he "carried off" Jacob's Breton trunk full of the Matorel poems and (according to Salmon) demanded Picasso's painted standing screen as part of the deal.[119]

A less pleasant version of the old Montmartre days came in Francis Carco's *De Montmartre au Quartier Latin*. As he had done in *Scenes from the Life of Montmartre* in 1919, Carco played up what he knew best, the life of hoodlums, drunkards, and whores. He had never been part of *la bande à Picasso*, and his tales are lurid, often made up out of whole cloth. Jacob wrote his old friend Sylvette Fillacier to commiserate about Carco's deformed picture of Marcel Olin, her dead husband. "Marcel was the first to defend and protect me, no one spoke ill of me in his presence," Jacob recalled. "He cared for me when I was sick and helped me when and how he could. Carco's book is full of lies and horrors."[120]

X.

IN JANUARY 1927, Jacob was missing Sachs and writing him almost daily: Had he received the special cheese from Saint-Benoît? Had the money order arrived? This long-distance love didn't prevent Jacob from caressing a new boy for several days. A teenager named Robert Levesque, a student of Jouhandeau's in Paris, wrote Jacob and turned up on January 3. A high-strung, intellectual boy, he was suffering from love for a fellow student at his Catholic school and from his guilt about that love. Jouhandeau admired his writing and had already sent him to Gide, who welcomed him.

Levesque would never figure largely in Jacob's story, but they corresponded for a few years, and through his eyes we glimpse the poet's style of seduction. Jacob met his guest in the evening at the bus stop wearing the checkered cap Sachs also remembered, a monocle, thick gloves, and *sabots*. He showed Levesque to his guest cell and, observing him keenly in the lamplight, exclaimed, almost with surprise, "Well, you're nice-looking, very nice-looking, very. Let's give each other the kiss of peace." By this time, Levesque was already making plans to leave the first thing the next morning. They had dinner downstairs in the monastery, where Levesque met Abbé Breut's family—the old mother who cooked; the *abbé*'s sister-in-law, and his eighteen-year-old niece, Cécile, who kept staring at the new guest. That evening, in Jacob's cell, Levesque found his host unpleasant—"very Jewish," boasting about himself, overpraising Levesque, "acting unnatural." The poet undressed and changed into his nightshirt in front of the boy but made no advances.

Levesque was not religious. The next morning he didn't attend mass but had breakfast with Jacob and accompanied him on errands in the village and a visit to the basilica. He had lunch with the *abbé* and the family, noting that Jacob was on a diet because of his stomach trouble: applesauce, jams, vegetable soup. In this company, Jacob turned into an old bourgeois gentleman. After the meal the two walked along the banks of the Loire, and on returning to their cells, Levesque broke down, confessed his trouble, and wept in Jacob's arms. That evening, after dinner and prayers, "Max" read his new poems aloud; Levesque perched on the arm of his chair; Jacob took him in his arms and rocked him like a child. "I had to resist slightly to prevent his being indiscreet," wrote Levesque. Whatever resistance he offered sufficed. Holding the boy, Jacob tilted his head back, "a marvelous beauty, his face in adoration, like a chalice. . . . His eyes are half-closed, he's overtaken by extraordinary, unique, inspired passion and fervor." Levesque rose early the next morning for mass in the crypt. After breakfast, Jacob led him through his Stations of the Cross in the basilica, followed by recitations of psalms and litanies, and meditation. In the afternoon Jacob painted and Levesque puttered in the master's books. When he left the next day, Levesque felt he had experienced "a rest, an enchantment, being near an astonishing man in an environment of unique poetry." In the train, he was left with "the ravishment and the inquietude of love."[121]

Together Jacob and Levesque sent Jouhandeau a postcard of doggerel rhymes. Jouhandeau must have expressed anxiety about the encounter because Jacob followed up with several letters emphasizing the innocence of the visit and the boy's allegiance to his teacher. Levesque, for his part, pursued the friendship with Jacob in letters, and Jacob warned him not to inflame Jouhandeau's suspicions.[122] Soon enough Jouhandeau had a more concrete reason for anger at Jacob: Louis Émié's article about him (partly dictated by Jacob) came out in *La Revue Nouvelle*, and Jouhandeau was incensed. He stopped writing to Jacob for months. The guilty poet kept sending his own letters into Jouhandeau's silence, not exactly apologizing for Émié's piece and pretending not to know what was wrong.[123]

Jacob's meeting with Levesque bore more interesting fruit than Jou-handeau's jealousy. Answering the boy's queries about Carco's book, Jacob sent an important letter clarifying the birth of Cubism as he had observed it. Objecting to Carco's claim about "the Jewish origins of Cubism," Jacob explained that Apollinaire wasn't Jewish and anyway had nothing to do with Cubism; that Picasso had been inspired by an African sculpture he had seen, with Apollinaire and Jacob, at dinner at Matisse's house; that the very next day the painter had begun drawing the simplified, cross-hatched faces that would turn into Cubism.[124]

The history of Cubism was fresh in the poet's mind because he was just about to publish a substantial article on the subject, his second memoir of Picasso. As usual, he muddled the dates but gave the essence of the story: the meetings with Apollinaire and Salmon, their poverty, Picasso's affirmation of Jacob's poetry. The days of their youth in Montmartre had now become as much myth as history. Two sentences, in particular, were designed to offend Braque: "One evening Picasso met Braque and made him his student. It was Braque who had the assignment of exhibiting the first Cubist paintings for reasons I need not elaborate."[125]

||

MAURICE SACHS, IN Germany, was not having an easy time. Over his own objections he had been enrolled in the École des Officiers de Réserve. At Landau, during cavalry exercises in mud and snow, his horse fell, and Sachs broke his left arm. The military doctors thought it was a simple dislocation and kept trying to jam the fractured bones back into place—a treatment not only agonizing but increasingly damaging to the arm, which swelled to the size of his thigh. The injury sent him to the infirmary. Here, with his good hand, he worked at a new "novel." By the end of January the doctors realized that the arm wasn't healing; they sent him north to the hospital in the spa town of Wiesbaden, and there, after an X-ray revealed the fractures, a cast was put on. He enjoyed his convalescence mightily. "Laziness, reading, dreams of writing," he said in *Le Sabbat*, describing also the homosexual games at night in the dormitory and concerts and café life in town. And he began to drink heavily.[126]

"I love you desperately," Jacob was writing him from Saint-Benoît.[127] Jacob believed he would share his future with this promising son. A future had to be paid for, so money was a constant theme. "I'm occupied in fabricating money," Jacob wrote on January 11 (that is, painting gouaches). And several days later, reporting a two-day visit with Bonjean and his wife in Paris: "And speaking of fortune, my big sonny, perhaps you need money? I have 4000 francs, how much do you need?" In the same letter there's a glimmer of insight: "You let yourself be adored, and you don't tell me anything. It's wrong!"[128] It's striking that in all the discussion of Sachs's "need" for money, not once does the topic of paying his debts come up. Sachs's funds served his present amusements. In Jacob's mind, the money he made so painstakingly, painting by painting, was also meant to pay for the holidays he and Sachs were to take together. In February a series of letters recounted his struggles with "a Chartres cathedral" for "old man delle Donne" that had been sent back, unappreciated—"Two weeks of work!"[129] Ten days later: "Our whole fate hangs on the spires of Chartres!"[130] And in a statement bordering on abjection: "I suffer from your poverty, it seems to me I'm responsible for it and for you, and I ask your pardon."[131]

Sachs's new story, "Alphonse," provoked a remarkable letter from his lover-mentor-father. A treatise on homosexual survival, the letter shows how educated gay Frenchmen of Jacob's generation accommodated themselves to straight conventions. In a panic, Jacob admonished his "son" to play by the rules. After detailing the state of "their" finances, he turned to the novel. "Why all these pederastic tales? Ah! Maurice, Maurice! You've not been cured of Paris! . . . Little wretch!! Reflect that you're going to compromise everybody again—including me, known to everyone as your friend! Ah! Maurice! And if you create another scandal, we'll have no one to launch your book!" (Here Jacob was thinking of Sachs as a second Radiguet, whose book was so effectively "launched" by Cocteau and Grasset.) "But if you're so convinced of your purity," Jacob continued, "remove from your book anything that could cause a scandal for Maritain and Jean [Cocteau]. . . . Substitute young girls for the little boys, it will only improve the book, I assure you, pederasty no longer has any novelty: everyone's talking about it." His postscript gave even more strategic advice: "I beg you to get back in Cocteau's good graces; he's indispensable for your career as a writer."[132]

Cocteau, by this time, was entranced by his new boyfriend, Jeanjean (Jean Desbordes), and the two were seen everywhere together: Cocteau had the social prestige to get away with it. He had persuaded himself that this talentless young man was a miracle, Radiguet resurrected.[133] He wrote Jacob confessing that he was "a bad Catholic" but sure, too, that God and the Virgin Mary would pardon him because his love was as natural as the movement of atoms in the sunlight. "Don't scold me," he added.[134] Jacob replied with a disquisition on love, perhaps the clearest statement he ever made of his own erotic theology. "You say, 'Don't scold me!' to win my agreement," he replied. "I don't agree with *myself:* I struggle against myself, against you, against my heart, against everything." The core of the matter, he explained, was that those atoms in the sun had free will and could distinguish good from evil. And there were two kinds of love. There was the selfish kind—loving another for the pleasure he can give us. "But to put up with the imperfections of a child because you'll help him succeed and adapt him and adopt him, that's love according to God." This truly disinterested love, Jacob maintained, was pleasing to God. The other was Hell. (There's no doubt that he knew both kinds.) In his postscript he named names—Vaillant, Picasso, Radiguet—but left out the name that mattered most to him at the moment, Maurice Sachs.[135]

||

IN THE LESS-THAN-IDEAL world, the Ghikas had reconciled and were living together again in an uneasy truce.[136] *Fond de l'eau* came out at the end of March. "Sublime," said Cocteau. "Every line is a block of grace— marble webbed with human veins."[137] Victor Moremans welcomed it in *La Gazette de Liège,* noting Jacob's new austerity, mystic struggles, and the relative absence of demons. "If it's not yet Paradise, it's in any case the realm of the purest poetry."[138] Robert Guiette declared that the poet had never looked so deeply into himself.[139] Ottoni and delle Donne now carried Jacob off on an excursion of eight days to visit the cathedral of Bourges, the churches of Poitiers, and the châteaux of the Loire. Jacob's passion for delle Donne had subsided or had been subsumed in his love for Sachs; now he could simply enjoy the company of this "good and elegant angel." Writing Sachs, he allowed himself to observe that Ottoni—who was helping to sell Jacob's work—understood nothing about painting and walked by a Rembrandt in the museum without pausing to look.[140]

In April, Cocteau sent the ephebe Yvon Belaval to spend Easter weekend with Jacob. Nineteen years old, a university student, Belaval came from Montpellier. "After eight days of Max he'll be golden," promised Cocteau.[141] Jacob welcomed the shy young man. "You'll start by saying 'Shit' to me, and then we'll have a boxing match," he said, as he walked him from the shuttle bus stop to the monastery. He asked his birth date (for his horoscope) and advised him what to wear when he went to Paris (English style, breeches buttoned at the knee, red ties). During their evening stroll along the Loire, Jacob described his apparition and his religious life and insisted that they use the familiar *tu*. As they tiptoed barefoot up the dark stairs in the monastery to their cells, Jacob held Yvon's hand and suddenly asked, "Why are you laughing?" Yvon hadn't laughed. Feeling his way into his cell, Jacob found matches and lit the oil lamp. For a moment, Yvon didn't recognize the face he saw strangely illuminated in the dark room. "You didn't laugh?" said the host. "I believe you. Ah, well! It's the Devil loitering around here. Every time I want to do something bad, I hear that laugh."[142] That was as far as he went in seducing Yvon Belaval.

The next day Jacob led his guest on the usual tour of the village and the basilica and gave him a poetry lesson, describing how Apollinaire started by humming a tune, then finding words, and how he (Jacob) read the dictionary every day, letting words slide into one another and sharpening images: "The main thing is to avoid pathos, such as Victor Hugo." And he launched into an improvisation of Hugolian rhymes, unreeling verse after verse. Yvon stayed two days, not eight, but Jacob was charmed. Over the next few months he worked hard to convert the boy. Their friendship lasted the rest of Jacob's life.[143]

In late April, the Galerie des Quatre Chemins in Paris exhibited some of Jacob's gouaches, a show crowned by an article by Florent Fels in *Les Nouvelles littéraires*.[144] Cocteau bought a gouache.[145] But all this activity was only a prelude to the reunion with Sachs. "What will happen to Maurice Sachs when he leaves the army?" Jacob asked Cocteau at the end of February. "Surely he can't stay at Saint-Benoît until he's elected to the Academy?"[146] He must have discussed the question with his "sonny." In an idle moment Sachs seems to have proposed becoming a farmer. This idea elicited a sensible objection from Jacob: farming required specialized knowledge and long experience (not to mention hard work, for which the urbane Sachs had no taste). Already in this letter, in late March, Jacob was trying to plan their holiday. June in Quimper would be difficult because Jacob had to see his elderly mother, and bringing Sachs to the house would be impossible. Nor could Jacob afford to put him up in the expensive hotel. He proposed that they visit the Colles in Douarnenez, with Sachs boarding in a room in town and taking his meals with the Colles. (The constant problem was how to be a male couple and not attract suspicion and opprobrium.)

They were also planning to visit Reverdy in Solesmes. As usual, money presented a challenge. Jacob was beginning to see—rather late in the game—that Sachs was utterly irresponsible. Did he *absolutely* need money? Jacob asked. "In that case, there's a hundred franc note for you. But only in this last case because I prefer to keep this bit of money for our stay in Brittany. After all, if we have to start scrimping ??!!!?? we'll scrimp."[147] A few days later Jacob wrote that since they were "family," his "son" had the right to see their budget, and son of shopkeepers that he was, he presented in ledger form what he had and what he owed. In the margin: "We're poor, my big darling. Get that into your darling adored head that I kiss so sadly—If only I could shower you with gifts and buy you silk shirts, blue and pink pajamas, madapollam socks and polo shirts . . . I kiss your dear beloved face a thousand times and water it with my dirty tears.

Max."[148] On April 6, while Sachs was still at Wiesbaden, Jacob wrote more cheerfully, "My big sonny, We have 3,265 francs in the till."

It doesn't take clairvoyance to see the catastrophe building up. Jacob thought he had adopted a son-lover. Sachs saw that he had an open bank account. Under the impression that Sachs was still a devout Catholic, Jacob filled his letters with religious advice, underlining the essential: "<u>Don't forget that if confession retrieves God's grace, the sin remains, and this sin must be expiated!</u>"[149]

Jacob had good reason for his anxiety about the date. The convalescent left the hospital on April 9 and went to Paris to stay partly with his grandmother and partly with the Bonjeans, not with Jacob at Saint-Benoît. For the rest of April and through May, Jacob's letters grew increasingly worried. He doesn't seem to have traveled to Paris for his show at the Quatre Chemins in late April. On May 4 he wrote: "Your silence concerns me." On May 19: "I await your arrival."[150] In his letters to everyone else—his publisher René Laporte, Maritain, Cocteau, Lanoë—he announced that Sachs was coming to Saint-Benoît.[151] He made elaborate plans with his "son" for their visit to Reverdy at Solesmes and for the Breton sojourn, which Sachs wanted to spend on the island of Bréhat off the northern coast.[152]

Sachs was supposed to join Jacob at Saint-Benoît on June 6; from there they would go to Solesmes, north of Paris, then west to Brittany. Jacob had presented to Cocteau his theory of disinterested love; with Sachs, he had a chance to practice it. As late as June 4, he wrote Maurice a letter full of solicitude, urging him to visit the Maritains and Cocteau before leaving Paris, "without thinking that I'm waiting for you." He should also attend to his "dear grandmother." And he underlined three times: "<u>I'm not waiting for you.</u>" (He had been waiting for months.) But he informed Sachs that he (Jacob) would leave for Solesmes on June 10. "The main point is that you should feel absolutely free. Tell yourself that I don't count. I'm an old gentleman who loves you devotedly but who doesn't want and cannot and should not want or have the power to get in your way. . . . Be free and virtuous." Beneath this profession of detachment pulsed a passionate need for everything he claimed not to want. He also recognized that the only way to hold on to Maurice was to leave him free (and to fund his freedom). Jacob's more realistic fears break through in the margin: "I kiss you and pray that God not abandon you in this terrible and monstrous Paris. . . . Remember that you're a Christian and Catholic: it's all I demand."[153]

Sachs did come to Saint-Benoît, and the odd couple set off. On their way north, on July 10, they passed through Paris, apparently unaware of the political drama playing out there. At least, no mention of it turns up in Jacob's letters. His militant acquaintance Léon Daudet had been convicted of defaming the government and was sentenced to five months in prison after a series of incendiary articles in *Action française*. Refusing to submit, Daudet fortified the offices of the newspaper with barbed wire and barricades and gathered an army of five hundred Camelots du Roi, his monarchist militia. Jean Chiappe, the new prefect of police, was trying to negotiate Daudet's surrender that very night.[154]

Oblivious to this threat to French democracy, Jacob and Sachs seem to have attended a ball given by Vicomtesse Marie-Laure de Noailles and her husband Charles.[155] There Jacob met Jeanjean, Jean Desbordes, for the first time. (The boy confessed something painful about himself; Jacob suggested to Cocteau that he send him to recuperate for a few weeks in Brittany.)[156] The incident with Daudet was an early tremor in the convulsion democracy would suffer in France a decade later. Chiappe himself would reenter Jacob's story.

On the island of Bréhat, Jacob and Sachs enjoyed a three-week idyll. The island was simple: pathways cutting across moors, a few houses clustered among rocks, a church here and there. Pine trees, rose bushes, palm trees, eucalyptus.[157] They had enough money; Sachs was happy. There was nothing to do except go to the beach, take walks, fish for crawfish, and loiter in the cafés. Sachs described it as "a retreat for old painters and bon-vivants tired of the boulevards."[158] They made friends with guests in the hotel; Sachs, always on the lookout for useful connections, mentions Armand Dayot, inspector general of the Beaux-Arts and an influential art critic, who was on vacation with his wife and daughter.[159] Jacob went to mass every morning and in the hotel room made a series of drawings of Christ for his Stations of the Cross using Sachs as a model—the beloved body transfigured. Sachs had watched Ottoni marketing Jacob's gouaches and saw an opportunity in these devotional drawings: why not collect them in a fancy art book? Jacob agreed. From this collaboration would grow Sachs's abortive career as a publisher; that fall he launched a venture in art publishing with Jacques Bonjean, and their first production was an album of forty drawings, Jacob's *Visions des souffrances et de la mort de Jésus fils de Dieu* (Visions of the Sufferings and Death of Jesus Son of God), dedicated to Sachs.

In early July, Jacob and Sachs left Bréhat to visit Reverdy at Solesmes.[160] In *Alias*, Sachs gave a distorted picture of the encounter between the old adversaries but caught the essential contradictions in their friendship: jealousy, affection, clash of temperaments. Calling the Reverdy character Albert Troy, he depicts Blum-Jacob's joy at seeing his friend, the friend's standoffishness, their shoptalk ("So, are you painting?" "Of course; and you? Are you writing?"). They agree in feeling bitter about Picasso. In the midst of an affectionate stroll, a quarrel blows up out of nothing, Troy accusing Blum, "You think you're a saint, you think you're a great painter, you think you're a great man, and you're nothing but a scumbag, a hypocrite, an old fairy."[161] Who knows how much of this Sachs made up? If Reverdy didn't say it outright on this occasion, there were certainly times when he thought it.

Jacob repaired to Quimper on July 4, while Sachs seems to have returned to Bréhat for several weeks before reporting to the army.[162] Jacob's visit with his family lasted two weeks before they "threw him out."[163] He was back on friendly terms with the Ghikas and planned to visit them later in the summer; meanwhile he sent Liane a packet of Morven poems.[164] He passed a few days at the Hôtel Belle-Vue in Bénodet, migrating by the end of July to the hospitable Colles in Douarnenez, where he settled for August.[165]

AND NOW JACOB's and Sachs's stories diverged painfully. Sachs rejoined his regiment, and his captain set him to cleaning toilets, where he was discovered reading Montesquieu by the captain of another company. Lying about his baccalaureate, Sachs was appointed librarian for the officers. He spent the rest of his military service in splendid circumstances with his own bedroom, a bicycle, and plenty of time to read: he devoured Gourmont, Marcel Schwob, Proust, Gide, and Nietzsche.[166] The golden-haired barmaid from the officers' mess chose him as her sweetheart; in spite of his reluctance, the young woman insisted, and he reflected that in the barracks it was better not to be known as a *pédé,* so for the rest of his time in the army, he let Lisbeth take care of him and managed to satisfy her vigorous sexual appetite.[167] He spent his leaves in Paris with Bonjean and his wife and baby, preparing the publishing venture with Jacob's evangelical drawings: Bonjean put in all the money, Sachs the literary connections.[168] Reading Nietzsche, he determined to become "a great man." He also began to drink "enormously," as he explained in *Le Sabbat:* "It's with a bottle in my hand that I was going to open the doors of the Hell of Paris, in a drunken desire to abase myself, but thirsting, however, for a better world which I also sought in wine."[169]

"I have only you," Jacob wrote from Douarnenez in July.[170] He described life with the Colles—the father's boring conservatism, the son's lazy charm. He sensed dangers for Sachs: he should turn to God. He thanked Sachs for his zeal in promoting the album of drawings. He encouraged his friendship with Pierre Colle. Some days later Pierre himself wrote Maurice, confessing his desire to make his way in Paris, in a gallery or bookstore, after his military service; he looked up to Sachs as to a worldly elder. By late August, Sachs was giving Jacob cause for concern: "I don't understand anything!" protested the "father." "I've written two letters in the last ten days and sent a money order, you reply that you've received nothing."[171]

Life was merry with the Colles.[172] Jacob then moved north to spend September and October with the Ghikas at Roscoff. He had no opportunity to quarrel with Liane: he was too busy trying to ease the conflict between the unhappy spouses, with Liane "ripping into" Georges and constantly threatening to evict him.[173] In spite of the domestic discord, Jacob worked well, writing more Morven poems, painting gouaches, and drawing. But in every letter to Sachs, along with chatter about daily life, he advised him about living virtuously. And he sent money.

Again and again, anxiety surfaced. October 28: "My son Maurice, I won't hide from you that I'm very worried. It's at least eight days since I sent you the money order for 300 francs." On October 30 he came up with a plan to keep Maurice safe: Sachs should marry: that would settle him down.[174]

Cooped up with the Ghikas, Jacob missed his "son" and missed the jolly company of other young friends and protégés. He had at least seen Grenier in nearby Saint-Brieuc, the young philosopher resembling "Schubert without eyeglasses."[175] Now Jacob heard that Cocteau needed money for a trip with Jeanjean to the Côte d'Azur. In his most endearing manner, Jacob wrote that the Queen of Sheba once borrowed five francs from her Nubian valet "for a taxi," and that this old servant (Jacob) offered his own drop of water to the royal reservoir: he had five hundred francs extra in his bank account—could Cocteau use it?[176] Cocteau replied with deep appreciation. The emergency had passed: Gallimard coughed up some money, and Moysès, the proprietor of Le Boeuf sur le Toit, lent his car and chauffeur.[177]

Jacob spent November in Paris, but without seeing Sachs, who was still in the army. It was a sociable month leading up to the show of his drawings at the Galerie des Quatre Chemins. He stayed at first at the Hôtel Nollet, a seedy but decent place just off the Place de Clichy; here he met the composer Henri Sauguet. It seems to have been Sachs who directed him to the hotel; though Jacob couldn't know it at the time, it would soon become a home base as important as the monastery.[178] For now, in November 1927, he quickly accepted Bonjean's hospitality and passed the rest of the month in that household.

Aside from worry about Sachs, the main drama of this Parisian stay emanated from Jouhandeau. The offended novelist had cut off their relations in July. Now he sent Jacob a conciliatory note. Jacob replied immediately, inviting him to the Hôtel Nollet, promising to show him his new drawings. Entering Jacob's room, Jouhandeau passed an art dealer on the way out (probably Bonjean, perhaps Level) and found the table covered with gouaches and drawings.

"Have I ever given you a present?" Jacob asked him. On Jouhandeau's replying no, Jacob told him to choose a drawing. Jouhandeau picked what is, indeed, one of Jacob's strongest, a resurrecting Christ, naked, seen from below "like a swimmer in water," twisting at the hips, arms raised.[179] Jacob turned pale, then reddened and said, "Listen, Marcel, I love you well, but I'll love you even more if you agree to take five other drawings and leave me this one."

"No, Max. Keep this drawing and the five others. I didn't ask you for anything. I don't want to carry anything off."

They spoke for a while of other things. But as Jouhandeau said goodbye, Jacob offered him the drawing, tears in his eyes, yet smiling. Their friendship, for the time being, was resurrected. It would last until Jouhandeau's ferocious anti-Semitic attack in 1936.[180]

||

THE SHOW AT the Quatre Chemins was a triumph, earning more than fifteen thousand francs. Jacob sold drawings to Princesse Violette Murat, Conrad Moricand, Jean Dubuffet (now married and running his family's liquor business), Georges Hugnet, and others.[181] Ottoni, on the side, was drumming up sales of the gouaches. The previous March, Jacob had written to Level that Paris "frightened and horrified" him.[182] Now the city welcomed him. He saw a great deal of Cocteau and Jeanjean and was stirred by his encounters with composers, Sauguet and "a musical genius named Nabokoff."[183]

Jacob had reason for good cheer, all the more so as he spent the first two weeks of December with his beloved Lieutenant Vaillant and his bride at their little villa in Compiègne. This poky suburb resembled paradise since it housed Vaillant, the purest love of Jacob's life. In the evenings they sat by the lamp, the two men painting and smiling at each other, the young wife quietly embroidering.[184]

News from Sachs broke into this peace. It's not clear what Jacob heard, but something shocked him into writing a letter of extraordinary alarm. For the first time, he sensed something dangerous in his beloved. The letter was disturbingly prescient about the criminal turn of Sachs's later activities, in terms resembling a pronouncement made years later by a judge handling one of Sachs's scams. The judge would say, "I'm amazed that you have no innate sense of honesty." (Sachs treated that matter almost gaily. A sense of honesty? "What could I answer? I was amazed myself. I was born without one.")[185]

In December 1927, Jacob hadn't written to Sachs in days, he confessed, because he didn't want to offend him, but at last he'd decided he must open his "suffering heart" and speak the truth. He was overcome with "frightful fears." His son, his dear son Maurice, needed a "parapet" to keep him from evil. First point, underlined: "Maurice lacks a moral sense!" And this was terrible, "because without realizing it you'll do dreadful things that will carry you far." One reason for Jacob's disturbance seems to have been Sachs's calling the publishing venture with Bonjean the "Collection Maurice Sachs": Sachs undercut Bonjean in this claim and also seemed to capitalize on the scandal associated with his own name. But more serious shenanigans, not specified, terrified Jacob and gave him an inkling of what might lie in store. Second point: Jacob didn't blame Maurice's "need for luxury," but he trembled when he thought "where this alliance of need for money and lack of moral sense may lead you. There are times when I fear the police and criminal courts for you." "Maurice, watch out!" he pleaded. And in the margin, rather remarkably for the religious Jacob, he added, "It's not about God and Hell. It's about preserving yourself from the *gendarmes*." He concluded by assuring him that Bonjean loved him and that he, Max, loved him.[186]

On this occasion, Sachs managed to soothe his anxious lover. But a few weeks later Jacob pointedly mentioned that two thousand francs were missing from the gallery accounts.[187]

XI.

JACOB'S OLD LIFE in Paris was calling him back. His gouaches and drawings were selling. Editors and readers liked his Morven poems: in December the reviewer in the *Mercure de France* singled out Jacob's poem "Noël" from the November *Ligne de coeur*.[188] Picasso was warm. Jacob's other friendships flourished: Jouhandeau, Cocteau (and Jeanjean), Bertin, Kisling, Paulhan, delle Donne, and Ottoni. From Compiègne, Jacob didn't return to Saint-Benoît but went back to Paris, spending the rest of December and the first two weeks of January with the Kislings and then with Bertin. In February he wrote Level, "I've been happy in Paris in the midst of everything I love and which is my true life, all of you, and Picasso whose welcome as in the old days touched me."[189]

He returned to the monastery on January 12, but for the next several months he bustled back and forth between Saint-Benoît and the city, staying with the Bonjeans in late February and with Bertin again in March. And life in the monastery was anything but quiet. His old friend Théophile Briant visited, agitating to secure the Légion d'honneur for Jacob. More remarkably, Jacob met someone who should have been an enemy, the painter Max Ernst, Dadaist and darling of the Surrealists. Jacob reported to Sachs, "I've met Max Ernst. Love affair, we observe each other curiously as if saying, 'You're not as bad as I imagined, I like you.' He's a handsome, frank, silent, intelligent man." (With his blazing blue eyes and high forehead, Ernst was legendarily handsome.)[190] Several weeks later Cingria descended on the monastery, quite revived from his stint in Mussolini's prison.[191]

As for Sachs, he explained away whatever irregularities had terrified Jacob in December. In mid-January, Jacob wrote from Saint-Benoît, "Of course, we'll leave sermons aside. I've said what I had to say." And yet again he asked if Maurice needed money (but cautioned that he, Jacob, also had financial needs and hadn't been fully paid for the drawings he'd sold). He recalled their "sacred stay at Bréhat." And warned Sachs that Ottoni shouldn't compete "indelicately" with Level in selling Jacob's paintings.[192]

On one of his visits to Paris, Jacob had a scene with Gallimard. He had been dragging his feet for several years, putting off the novel for which he had signed a contract, *Les Gants blancs*.[193] He and Paulhan had been corresponding for a year about additional stories for an expanded *Le Cabinet noir*.[194] All those contracts stuffed in Gallimard's pockets several years earlier were now in a state of confusion. In January, Jacob threw a tantrum in Gallimard's office, calling his publisher a thug; Gallimard was pale, his assistant Roger Allard in a sweat.[195] For a few weeks Jacob made noises about a lawsuit.[196] Somehow he and Paulhan weathered the dispute and stayed friends. By March 3, Jacob had decided not to sue; nor would he write another novel.[197]

The Morven poems continued to appear and to win admirers. Clusters had come out in *La Ligne de coeur* the previous June and November,[198] and in February, *La Revue européenne* brought out six more, dedicated to Prince Ghika.[199] Even more reassuringly, three serious appreciations of Jacob appeared in April. So sensitive to slights, so easily wounded, Jacob had evidence that he was not despised. Jean Cassou, the critic who had almost dismissed *Fond de l'eau* in *La Nouvelle Revue française*, now turned his argument (that Jacob had left reality behind) into an extended compliment in his essay "Max Jacob and Freedom" in the same journal. Ranging over the whole oeuvre, fictional and poetic, Cassou saw in Jacob a spiritual revolt against bourgeois society. He celebrated Jacob's almost nonrepresentational literary art and called him "the Picasso" of poetry.[200]

Also in April, the journal *Le Mail* in Orléans dedicated a whole issue to Jacob. Reading these tributes—from the editors Marcel Abraham and Roger Secrétain, and from Hugnet, Jouhandeau, Cassou, Cocteau, Lanoë, and the mystic elder Symbolist poet Saint-Pol-Roux—one feels suddenly the mysterious difference between a man and an author. A work of art is separated from the world, Jacob had claimed in his preface to *Le Cornet à dés*, by its "style" and its "situation." The author might be said to be equally separate from his social and psychological self. The Max Jacob celebrated in the pages of *Le Mail* is a myth, a figure of enchantment, lifted out of daily life on the wings of rhyme, cadence, image, and story, and lifting others by the force of his imagination. Secrétain visualized Jacob chatting with angels in the vegetable garden of Saint-Benoît. This is not the man harassed by publishers, suffering liver ailments, and sending money to an absent, cynical lover. This is a poet who ignited poetry in others. "He's our last resource against what Nietzsche called . . . 'the spirit of heaviness,' " wrote Cassou.[201]

At the same time, Louis Thomas wrote a hagiographical article about

Jacob in *Les Nouvelles littéraires*.[202] A new world seemed to open up for him in Paris. His young friends—especially Sachs and Pierre Colle—urged him to leave the monastery. Even Abbé Weill, his old sponsor, advised him to return to his intellectual tribe in Paris. After seven years of retreat, he packed up his clothes, books, and paints and moved back to the city. "Sachs is coming on April 10," he wrote Cocteau, envisioning a shared life with his "son."[203]

Sachs was formally released from the army on April 17. But he had a different plan for his future. He didn't even mention Jacob in his account of his months in Germersheim. As he knelt in the officers' library and pronounced his resolution "to be a great man," only one name inflamed his imagination: André Gide. Arriving in the train station in Paris with forty francs in his pocket, he telephoned Gide, bought a new tie, took a cheap hotel room, and the next morning walked across the city to Gide's villa in Auteuil, determined to make a new conquest.[204]

Part IV

CHAPTER 17

THE YEAR OF CRASHES

I.

As Max Jacob and Maurice Sachs converged on Paris, they suffered parallel disappointments. Sachs's fantasy of being welcomed, perhaps even adopted, by Gide rapidly crumbled. The master received him with cold politeness: Sachs's intimacy with Cocteau and the Maritains was hardly a recommendation for the Protestant and in some ways puritanical Gide, and Sachs left the interview stricken with shame. Jacob, for his part, quickly realized that his "Sonny" intended to live his own separate life of wheeling and dealing.

In the first three months of his return, Jacob stayed at the grandly named l'Ermitage du Régent, a dim boardinghouse on the Rue Daubenton in the fifth arrondissement. "No more Saint-Benoît," he wrote Nino Frank, who had settled in Paris to escape Italian Fascism and was working for *Les Nouvelles littéraires*.[1] Jacob's new Parisian sojourn, which would last eight years, hurled him back into frenetic sociability. Other love affairs, including his last passion, replaced the absorption with Sachs, and new friendships occupied him even as several old friends drifted away, notably Cocteau and Jouhandeau. It was a worldly period. He was caught up in the entertainments of the aristocracy: the Beaumonts, Vicomte and Vicomtesse de Noailles, Prince and Princesse de Polignac. He was honored as never before, receiving the Légion d'honneur and an important poetry prize. And after the shock waves from the crash of the New York

Stock Exchange struck France, he grappled once more with poverty, resorting to lecture tours, living off his reminiscences, and performing the persona of Max Jacob.

||

IT TOOK SEVERAL weeks for Jacob, just back in Paris, to perceive that his romance with Sachs had come to an end. Arriving in the city a few days before his "Sonny," he saw a good deal of Paulhan; he met with Jean Cassou, now an ally; he dined with Jean Grenier, "superb" on his return from lecturing in Greece; he spent days with the young composer Henri Sauguet at Sauguet's furnished room, collaborating on an operetta called *Un Amour du Titien* (A Love of Titian's).[2] They worked together with gusts of laughter on the absurd scenario, another commedia dell'arte frolic like *Isabelle et Pantalon,* which he'd composed with Roland-Manuel.

Relations with Sachs must have seemed normal at first, though they weren't staying at the same address. On April 27, 1928, ten days after Sachs's return, Jacob wrote him in good humor: "My Soldier Boy, I'm at Sauguet's. . . . Come, my dears, and find Sauguet who'll have lunch with you, with the adorable Bérard."[3] Jacob and Sachs were business partners, after all: Sachs was trying to sell copies of their album, *Visions des souffrances et de la mort de Jésus fils de Dieu,* and he would soon set up as an art dealer with Pierre Colle, selling Jacob's work. On May 5, Jacob wrote his "Sonny" that he was dining that evening with the actor Marcel Herrand, and that "Philippe" had taken their albums to sell to his father.[4] (Philippe was twenty-year-old Philippe Lavastine.)

But Sachs was falling apart. Incensed at Gide's rejection, feverish in his fantasies of succeeding "in business," Sachs was turning into a lush. He knocked back three Pernods for breakfast to take the edge off the hangover of the night before; he gulped whiskey all day from his hip flask; he couldn't sit down to dinner unless he'd had ten cocktails. He gained weight, and his hair thinned out. And he began to frequent in earnest the homosexual brothel down the street from the Hôtel Vouillemont, abandoning himself to what he later called an "atrocious promiscuity" with anonymous boys.[5] It's not surprising that Jacob apologized to Paulhan for the sorrows he brought to their lunch.[6]

Otherwise Jacob's new Parisian life felt promising. He had always liked Paulhan, and now he found in him a truly steadfast friend, as Paulhan was arranging Gallimard's publication of expanded editions of both *Le Cabinet noir* and *Tableau de la bourgeoisie*. Gallimard also bought the rights to *Cinématoma*. He'd reconciled with Gallimard, Jacob wrote Émié, explaining that he wouldn't visit Bordeaux but planned to spend the summer in Brittany, adding that he'd left Saint-Benoît for good.[7] In Paris, he worked closely with Sauguet, Émié's friend from Bordeaux.

Sauguet, now twenty-seven, had earned his living since the age of fourteen as a musician in Bordeaux, playing the organ in churches and collecting the songs of the Auvergne with Joseph Canteloube. Inspired by Satie and Les Six, he had come to Paris in 1921. He studied composition with Charles Koechlin, organized a concert in honor of Satie, and through Satie came to know Diaghilev. When Jacob met him in 1927, he had just gotten his big break, Diaghilev's production of his ballet *La Chatte* in Monte Carlo. Speaking of Jacob years after the poet's death, Sauguet emphasized their strong attachment and the joy they took in collaborating. Sauguet was gay, and at this period he liked to dress in drag when relaxing with friends, but his friendship with Jacob had no romantic strain; it was based on a shared love of music. Max had an extraordinary talent as a mimic and acted out all the roles in *Un Amour du Titien*, Sauguet remembered, repeating with a kind of wonder, "Max Jacob lived in a state of perpetual creation."[8] He was struck by Jacob's "prodigious memory" and serious knowledge of music, judging that Jacob "thought like a musician, if not in music."[9] This friendship lasted until the poet's death.

Philippe Lavastine also provided comfort. "Pierre Colle and Lavastine are phosphorescent nebulae," Jacob told Paulhan.[10] Unlike Frenkel and Sachs, Lavastine was educated, the son of a professor of psychiatry, by an odd coincidence studying Sanskrit with the elderly Sylvain Lévi. Jacob met him through Cocteau and the swirl of young men around Cocteau: among others, Sachs and Henri Tracol, a classmate of Lavastine's from the Lycée Condorcet who shared his passion for India.[11] To Lanoë, Jacob praised Philippe's legs, long neck, curly hair, and pale skin, and he was so entranced that he spent part of the summer with this new friend in one of those intimacies confusing seduction and conversion.[12]

Paris welcomed the prodigal poet. Nino Frank published an article about his return, presenting Jacob in his "Roman emperor" guise.[13] In May the art dealer Jeanne Bucher exhibited Jacob's gouaches next to paintings by Picasso, Braque, Chagall, and Rouault.[14] At the opening, Jacob lectured on his central themes, "The Body of Christ" and "Religious Anatomy," unifying the religious and erotic myths by which he lived and to which he had given graphic form in his drawings of Christ's suffering for Sachs's album.

In 1923 the Belgian writer Robert Guiette contributed "Notes for a Portrait" to the Jacob issue of Le Disque vert.[15] Though they had exchanged letters, Guiette had never met Jacob and drew his notes from the fiction and poetry. But in 1927 an editor asked him for a biography of his hero, and after months of correspondence, Jacob agreed to meet him. Guiette tracked him down at l'Ermitage du Régent in April 1928, "a very modest hotel," he noted.[16] On that first visit, Jacob's room was crowded with friends. As he had done on the Rue Ravignan, on the Rue Gabrielle, and at Saint-Benoît, Jacob painted his gouacheries while listening to his friends' jokes and launching his own, all the time licking his brush, dabbing spit across the paper to lighten the color, thickening a shadow here and there with cigarette ash, and stepping back to adjust his monocle and consider the effect. Guiette was struck by Jacob's large, eloquent eyes and small chubby hands, and by the sensuous way his pencil trembled as it sketched each figure.[17]

The next day Guiette found Jacob alone, and what started as an interview turned into dictation. Guiette sat in the armchair while Jacob lay on the bed, a towel over his eyes, narrating his life with eerie precision, a life "at once real and legendary," as the scribe quickly realized. Eventually the poet rose and began painting, still recounting his story.

Each night Guiette wrote up his notes. After several days of this immersion in his own fable, Jacob called a halt, and Guiette completed the manuscript on his own. Jacob then reviewed the text, mainly approving—"No one will believe you: it's too true!"—and correcting details. By this time the original publisher had disappeared, and Guiette had trouble placing the work, but in 1934 the loyal Paulhan ran two chapters in *La Nouvelle Revue française*.[18] "Clearly he had romanticized his life," Guiette admitted. "At times, he invented it (perhaps). But this *Vie de Max Jacob* corresponded to the vision he had of himself. The Max Jacob revealed in legend was the Max Jacob he believed."[19] Which is to say, perhaps, that an artist's creative power goes into making not only works of art but his very persona.

II.

JEAN DESBORDES'S ILL-WRITTEN little book *J'adore* came out in June. Both the publisher, Grasset, and the lover, Cocteau, hoped Desbordes would be celebrated as a new Radiguet. Jeanjean had, alas, nothing in common with the boy king. His effusions circled around private erotic scenes, poorly described: "When he was very young, the first time, sexual pleasure took away both his breath and his childhood. Three white drops fell, the first, pure drops destined for the grass, light and solemn like the poppy's white blood."[20] The imaginative world in these pages is claustrophobic, restricted to the boy's sensations, with all the self-awe of adolescence.[21] The poppy, of course, announced opium. The only other person to inhabit these pages was Cocteau, master and initiator, especially into the mysteries of the drug.

Cocteau's preface to *J'adore* makes peculiar reading. It opens with a romantic reference to Nathan Leopold (of the 1924 *Leopold and Loeb* case, in which two college students in Chicago murdered a boy to prove they could get away with it): "One would have to be that young American assassin whom the birds preferred to a tree in order to speak of you, Jean Desbordes."[22] Cocteau implied that Desbordes's pantheistic onanism would be (unjustly) considered criminal. He related how the adolescent, finding Cocteau's novel *Le Grand Écart* in his provincial solitude, wrote to the author; how Cocteau inspected the incoherent manuscript, saw dreamlike possibilities in it, and took the boy under his wing. He presented Desbordes's naïveté as a sign of "genius."[23]

This smarmy book thrust Jacob into a dilemma. Cocteau was one of his closest friends. At the same time, his Catholic mentor, Jacques Maritain, was writing urgently, worried by rumors that Jacob's name would be used to promote *J'adore:* "Jean Desbordes's book, this atrocious confusion of eroticism and religion, spits in the Face of Christ. . . . Is it true that you're going to help advertise this book?"[24]

Jacob had been in affectionate correspondence with Maritain, announcing his return to Paris and assuring him that in leaving the monastery, he had not abandoned his daily devotions; he added that his life was *solitary* (a signal that he would not be living in sin).[25] Two weeks later, writing from Brittany, where he and Lavastine were staying at his old hotel in Bénodet, Jacob passionately defended Desbordes to Maritain, incorporating *J'adore* into his private mythology. Now that Jacob was living close to another attractive young man, the argument with Maritain forced him more than ever to face the contradiction between the dogmas of his faith and the promptings of his heart. Jacob answered the theologian, trying to make room in the Church for same-sex love (unnamed), presenting Lavastine as evidence of God's work: "If I was helping to 'spit in the Face of God,' He wouldn't grant me favor by converting the poet Lavastine, profoundly, through my voice."[26]

In Jacob's theology, Christ brought true intelligence to earth in the form of His sacred blood: "Desbordes's book is a monument to the new, lost, and recovered intelligence."[27] When he wrote Maritain, Jacob had already composed a defense of *J'adore* for *Les Nouvelles littéraires* and had shown the text to Cocteau, who in turn quoted from it to Maritain: "Genius is a directly divine intelligence. . . . I speak of the admirable Jean Desbordes."[28] To which Maritain replied (to Cocteau), "Let me tell you that Max's statement is perfectly idiotic."[29]

The crisis over homosexuality and faith agitated Jacob's acquaintances for weeks. Like Maritain, Reverdy was horrified by Desbordes's book and wrote Jacob to tell him so; Jacob replied to him on the same day he wrote Maritain, in an almost word-for-word copy of that letter.[30] Meanwhile he was delighting in Philippe's company in the little seaside town of Bénodet. Treating Sachs now as an affectionate accomplice (but still addressing him as "My son Maurice"), he reported Philippe's progress in faith while praising his physique:

> Philippe in a black bathing suit
> makes his golden-armed salute
> and from dawn till evening, he
> glows like an ostensory.

In the same letter he announced that Philippe had gone to confession, taken Communion, refused meat on Friday, and was likely to attend mass on Sunday.[31]

In July, Sachs brought out one of the only other books in his rickety publishing venture, Cocteau's *Le Livre blanc* (The White Book), printed anonymously. Lacking the narrative structure of Cocteau's earlier novels, this tale wanders through a series of episodes, in each of which the male hero tries to love a woman but really loves the man to whom she's attached, whether pimp or brother. Littered with drug overdoses and suicides, the book is less a story than a manifesto defending homosexuality. Without signing his name, Cocteau was declaring his rebellion against the intolerance of his Church and his society.

In Bénodet, and starting in late July in Douarnenez with the Colles, Jacob was reenacting his familiar scenario of educating a young man in faith and in life. At least this time he was more armored, and he never fell for Lavastine as he had for Frenkel and Sachs. He liked him enough, though, to dedicate to him the new edition of *Le Cabinet noir*. And he was wounded when Philippe tired of his tutelage and went off to rejoin his girlfriend on Belle-Île, an island a little farther south. Jacob, who had been paying their expenses, wrote Sachs bitterly, "The question of money is a real nuisance. As long as I had money, I was able to spoil Philippe, [but] now he's bored; he's gone off to join Liliane again and didn't hold back from snarling at me when all I ask is his progress, his own good. . . . Philippe has spoiled my vacation: 'Education, childbirth, child-lies.' " ("*Éducation, enfantement, enfant te ment:* the pun on *enfantement*, childbirth, and *enfant te ment*, the child lies to you, condenses Jacob's Socratic-erotic view of his relation to his protégés: he imagined himself their mentor-lover-father, bringing them "to birth" as whole men.)[32] Jacob expressed his distress, his need for attachment, and his ambiguous connection to Sachs in his conclusion: "You are my son Maurice, I also have my son Pierre [Colle], *I am not adopting Philippe.* I kiss you, Max."

Sachs had somewhat regained Jacob's trust by sending him a portion of the proceeds from the sale of their album. When Jacob thanked him at the end of August, he was still smarting from the loss of Lavastine. He praised Sachs for "raining manna" and added that Philippe had revealed his true egotistical nature.[33] The same day he lamented to the actor Roger Karl even more vulgarly: Lavastine "played me for a fool as long as I spoiled him and threw me over when I demanded the slightest sacrifice. . . . He's gone to meet up with his floozies." He added that his main art dealer had dropped him, angry at Jacob's selling to others.[34]

This last detail was no casual matter; Jacob depended for his livelihood on the sale of his paintings. The business of selling his art was becoming perilously bound up with his affections for young men: Sachs, Colle, and even Lavastine. The quarrel with Philippe didn't last long. Two weeks later Jacob wrote Sachs that Philippe wanted to sell his "art-junk": the word *brocanter*, "to sell junk or second-hand goods," suggests the world of the Jacob family's antique shop in Quimper.[35] But it was Sachs and Colle who undertook the serious enterprise. A number of letters in the ensuing weeks tracked the uncertainties of the venture. On September 21, from his friend Dr. Benoiste's sanatorium in Brittany, Jacob wrote his two young friends who were installed at the Hôtel Nollet in Paris and had formed a partnership. Commenting on the contract they proposed, Jacob thanked them for their "good will and affection" but stated that the contract was "just about unacceptable." "Let's stay as we are," he suggested; he would let them sell his work but gave them no exclusive rights. (Colle already had seven paintings he was supposed to place.)[36]

A week later Colle sent Jacob money from the sales, and Jacob wrote from Brittany that he planned to return to Paris on October 1 and would stay a few days at the Hôtel Nollet while he "arranged his winter" in Paris. As it turned out, he would establish his central laboratory at the hotel for six years. In *La Décade de l'illusion*, Sachs claims that he and Colle persuaded Jacob to leave Saint-Benoît and set up at the Hôtel Nollet, which is hardly the case, though Sachs's presence in Paris did help Jacob leave the monastery in some larger sense.[37]

Business relations with Sachs and Colle remained turbulent. On October 2 Jacob signed a contract with them, but a week later Sachs's shady maneuvers already threatened it, and Jacob wrote, "A contract falls of its own weight" if it's not respected. Referring to some recent blowup, he said they should leave business alone and "stay good friends."[38] Once again Sachs lured him back, and by the end of the month Jacob wrote Cocteau, who was deep in his opium affliction with Jeanjean in Villefranche, that he had a contract with Colle and Sachs and "worked only for them." One feels the power of Sachs's con-man charm in Jacob's next statement: "Maurice wants to get me decorated" with the Légion d'honneur. Sachs hadn't the ghost of a chance of doing that. But money flowed easily in those days in Paris, and Sachs was hobnobbing with Cocteau's crew, as high on dreams of fortune as Cocteau was on opium.[39]

Sachs was living in delirium. Through Cocteau, he wangled an introduction to Chanel, who was by now fabulously rich. She wanted a magnificent library for her apartment, and Sachs was known as something of a book dealer: Chanel hired him, allotting sixty thousand francs a month for his expenses. For a while, he gained her friendship and served also as a private secretary, organizing her dinner parties—which made him the object of endless solicitation. With so much money streaming through his hands, Sachs rented a swank apartment on the Rue des Eaux in the same building as the Bonjeans, while keeping a room at the Hôtel Nollet along with a studio at the Square du Port-Royal: he used the multiple addresses for escaping creditors, since even when he was lavishly funded, he spent beyond his means. At the Rue des Eaux, he had two domestic servants, a secretary, a masseur, and a taxi on call; he ate at expensive restaurants, had his clothes made by the finest tailors, and spent his evenings at Le Boeuf sur le Toit. He entertained lovers like a pasha. One of them, a young scholar of Hinduism called Alain Daniélou (brother of the future cardinal Jean Daniélou), he installed for a while in the Hôtel Nollet.[40] And he tried to break into the Faubourg Saint-Germain, the Proustian domain of highest aristocratic privilege. Through Chanel, he pried his way into the salons of the Noailles, the Luynes, the Rochefoucaulds, and the Tremoilles, whose names he recited in the memoir like a magic spell.[41] The magic quickly wore off; it took more than expensive clothing to impress these wary nobles. But in late 1928 and early 1929, Sachs thought he was "Rubempré, Julien Sorel, and Rockefeller" all rolled into one.[42]

In this intoxicated season, he and Colle organized an exhibit for Jacob at the Galerie Briant-Robert, run by Jacob's friend Théophile Briant. Picasso drew a portrait of the poet for the catalog: Jacob seen in profile as a Roman consul crowned with laurel.[43] Cocteau, Picasso, Bérard, Picabia, and Sauguet were among the luminaries attending the opening. (The poet himself didn't appear.)[44] On December 14, Jacob signed a paper giving Sachs power to conduct all his business.[45]

III.

JACOB'S FRIENDSHIP WITH Jouhandeau took a peculiar turn at the end of 1928. In the heady days in Paris before his first departure for Saint-Benoît, Jacob had been friendly with the dancer Élisabeth (or Élise) Toulemon, who styled herself "Caryathis, La Belle Excentrique." Jacob called her Carya. She was a theatrical dancer who had earned quite a reputation for her risqué performances and hung about with many of Jacob's friends—Cocteau, the actors Roger Karl and Marcel Herrand, the Beaumonts, Lucien Daudet, and Poiret. When she once criticized Jacob for seducing boys, he had thundered at her, accusing her of ignoring her own religious reality and not "having the faith of a coalman."[46] Back in Paris in 1928, Jacob sought out Carya, who had retired from the stage and was having penitential fantasies. In October, Jacob saw her so often that the two began to contemplate entering into a celibate marriage and retreating to Saint-

Benoît together. Who knows what to make of this dream, but for Jacob it represented, possibly, a retreat from bruising romances.

In mid-October, when he and Carya organized a dinner party at her apartment, he didn't know that she was falling in love with Marcel Jouhandeau. In November, Carya gave another party, supposedly to celebrate the possibility of the Légion d'honneur for Jacob (for which Paulhan was working behind the scenes). She received a mysterious letter from Jouhandeau, saying she had "turned his body into a livid flame like iron beaten on the forge," and that "the mystic spouse" would arrive at the end of the meal: she was to leave an empty chair for him. At table, Jacob objected to one of the dishes, telling her, "When we're married, Carya, you'll remember that I never eat mayonnaise." All during dinner, the guests wondered at the empty chair. At dessert, Jouhandeau marched in and asked her to marry him, setting off a bacchanalian festivity; Jacob remained imperturbable at the table, continuing a monologue. He was evidently hurt, because in several notes to Jouhandeau following the evening he pardoned, castigated, and then pardoned his friend again.[47] (The Jouhandeau ménage turned into hell on earth but was a stimulus to writing: the two furious egotists published multiple volumes cataloguing their rancors. When Jouhandeau came out with *Monsieur Godeau marié* [Monsieur Godeau Married] in 1933, an only slightly fictionalized version of his loathing for his wife, Jacob visited her to sympathize but admitted, "I had a narrow escape.")[48]

||

IN LATE DECEMBER, Sachs enticed Reverdy to Paris with the offer of a contract for a new book of poems and the loan of his studio at Square du Port-Royal. Reverdy, tired of his religious retreat at Solesmes and needing money, accepted the offer, and Sachs fetched him at the abbey and drove him to Paris, leaving Henriette behind. In Paris the improbable probable happened: through Sachs, the severe, dark-haired southern poet rejoined his old love, Chanel, the severe, dark-haired *couturière*, though one was poor (and married) and the other a multimillionaire.[49] The consequence for Sachs was less opportune. When Chanel invited the poet to inspect her library, he discovered that Sachs had filled the shelves not with bibliographical treasures but with worthless volumes picked up from the bookstalls along the Seine.[50] By the end of the summer, Sachs had lost his job and his reputation as a book dealer.

Meanwhile he was robbing Max Jacob as well as his associates, Bonjean and Colle. The correspondence makes sorry reading. At times Jacob thought it was Colle who was keeping the money from the sale of his paintings. On February 15, 1929, he wrote Sachs, thanking him for a check but asking about a commission he was expecting from one of Colle's sales.[51] In increasingly agitated letters, Jacob protested that he'd been led on by promise after promise into compromising situations, and that money was withheld so he was "dying of hunger" and couldn't pay for his room at the hotel. "Don't promise anything more! Just pay me what you owe me, as the contract says, and buy what I make! . . . I have for you what's called an unhappy love, since you scorn me and I truly love you."[52]

After a few months of these explosions, Jacob declared that things had to change. Even at this extremity, when he announced that he (Jacob) was no longer bound by the agreement and was finding his own clients, he still maintained the attachment: "You are my son in spite of everything because the heart is not a wallet, and vice versa."[53]

Before being fired by Chanel, Sachs branched out into what he called "the traffic in paintings" with artists who commanded much higher prices than Jacob, and as his book business dried up, he relied more and more on dealing in art. Before the stock market crash, fortunes could be made in the works of the École de Paris, and Sachs especially liked Soutine and Utrillo, though on occasion he found himself selling Picassos, Derains, and Segonzacs (painters he later attacked). In this business, too, he soon turned to crime, dragging friends into shady deals, contracting debts, and sometimes stealing.[54]

Jacob's own life these days was peripatetic. Visitors flocked to his room; he didn't have an hour to himself.[55] One meeting would have enormous consequence: among the innumerable young men who sent him poems was Pierre Andreu, a law student bored with law, vaguely studying philosophy, and mad about literature. Andreu and two friends sought out Jacob at the Hôtel Nollet in the winter of 1929. The boys—they were hardly more than boys—were starting a literary magazine, *La Courte Paille*, and asked Jacob for a contribution. He obliged. The ditty "For My New Young Friends" came out in the first issue, March 1929, followed by another poem, "Bélisaire," in the April issue.[56]

Andreu was becoming a fascist. As he recounts in his memoir *Le Rouge et le blanc* (The Red and the White), he was growing up in a time of economic crisis and political breakdown and was repulsed by what he took to be the decadence of democracy and "capitalist consumer society." Inspired less by the old monarchist Action Française than by Emmanuel Mounier and the mystic radicalism of the journal *Esprit*, and even more by the syndicalist journal *L'Ordre nouveau*, he and his friends were filled with enthusiasm for what they vaguely conceived as "revolutionary countries": Italy, Germany, the Soviet Union.[57] After the war he wrote a biography of his friend Pierre Drieu La Rochelle, chronicling the novelist's proud collaboration with Vichy and the Nazis and his suicide as the war ended. Andreu looked back on his youthful illusions with a fair degree of lucidity, and his memoir is a useful document for anyone trying to understand antidemocratic ideas in France. In spite of his fascist sympathies, he was no anti-Semite. He remained loyal to Jacob, and he wrote the first full-scale biography of the poet France would come to regard as one of its martyrs.

But Jacob didn't only see obscure young men. He attended fancy costume balls, like the one given by Vicomte and Vicomtesse de Noailles that lasted till breakfast time.[58] In April he made a quick trip south, hopping off the train to attend mass in Marseille and then proceeding east to Grasse to visit de Gouy and Greeley.[59] At the end of May he confessed to Cocteau that his life was "completely crazy": he had just returned to Paris from a four-day jaunt by car with Pierre Colle, Bébé (Bérard), and the Bonjeans; in Le Havre they had visited Dubuffet, who was running his family's liquor business.[60] With relief, he withdrew to Brittany for the summer, though his life there hardly quieted down: he spent June in the little wind-battered *pension* Ty-Mad in the port village of Tréboul, surrounded by artists, including his old friend Marcoussis and his wife Alice Halicka. Cingria also turned up. In July, Jacob settled at the Hôtel Belle-Vue in Bénodet, almost a second home.

||

BY THIS TIME, Jacob's literary life advanced almost on its own. Galli-mard brought out in quick succession three editions of earlier books. The expanded *Le Cabinet noir,* now dedicated to Lavastine, appeared in September 1928. Victor Moremans greeted it in *La Gazette de Liège,* as he could be relied on to do, praising the huge social panorama in these imaginary letters and the author's moral penetration.[61] Jacob thanked this earnest admirer in a letter designed not to disturb his peace of mind: "I haven't lost the hope of becoming a passable Christian."[62] The expanded *Tableau de la bourgeoisie* came out in June, followed by *Cinématoma,* which Jean Cassou reviewed thoughtfully, associating it with the self-betraying letters of *Le Cabinet noir:* in these two books, he claimed, Jacob descended into the hell of bourgeois greed and self-righteousness made real in the "implacable naturalness" of gabble. The author was a "visionary genius."[63]

But Jacob was bringing out new work as well. In January 1929, Kra served up his potboiler, appropriately entitled "Gluttony," a chapter in the anthology *Les Sept Péchés capitaux* (The Seven Deadly Sins); in his section, Jacob gathered characters from his earlier works (including his mother, yet again, as Madame Gagelin) and let them rattle on.[64] New poems popped up here and there. The handsome pages of *Commerce* presented twenty new poems by Morven le Gaélique: these faux-naïf songs unified at least one element of Jacob's complex persona in their pathos, lyricism, and directness.[65]

More poems sprouted in the Swiss journal *Raison d'être;* in *Jazz;* in Andreu's *La Courte Paille;* and in *Les Feuillets inutiles.* "Description of Ecstasy" in *Raison d'être* would find its place in Jacob's collection *Sacrifice impérial,* the slim volume the Émile-Paul brothers would publish in 1929. In unrhymed free verse, this passionate lyric signaled the new (and final) phase of Jacob's poetry: religious, visionary, intimate works that leave *Saint Matorel*'s music hall ironies far behind.[66]

||

IN THE *PENSION* Ty-Mad in Tréboul, in June, Jacob found new joy in the company of Christopher (Kit) Wood. A young English painter rapidly absorbing the lessons of Modernism, Wood was a bisexual who had become friendly with Cocteau and his entourage and had fallen under the spell of opium. He had exiled himself to Tréboul in an attempt to break free of addiction.

His good looks were almost supernatural: with his high, narrow forehead, straight nose, and chiseled cheekbones and lips, he looked like a dream of the perfect Englishman. Cingria said he was "neither a soul nor a body; rather, it was like a light, a fine transparent glow of alabaster—one was taken aback by his presence as by a privilege."[67] He had come to France at twenty in 1921, taken up first by the banker and art collector Alphonse Kahn, then by the Chilean diplomat Tony de Gandarillas, the nephew of Picasso's friend Eugenia Errázuriz. Picasso took an interest in Wood's work; so did Cocteau. And through Cocteau, Wood had one of his few affairs with a woman, becoming enamored, for a while, with the boyish beauty of Cocteau's friend Jeanne Bourgoint.

But in Tréboul in 1929, Kit Wood was accompanied by his new mistress, the Russian Froska Munster. Jacob called them the "runaway lovers," as Wood hid from Gandarillas in a rented cottage with Froska and painted for hours a day. He and Jacob became close; he learned from Jacob the trick of adapting compositions from postcards, and Jacob adored Wood's scenes of the fishermen, sailboats, peasant women with long black dresses and *coiffes,* and the whitewashed houses, slate roofs, and stony streets of Tréboul, where life centered on the port and the life of the sea, and on peasant Catholicism with its pardons, saints' parades, and festivals. The skeletal structures of new boats being built rose like dinosaur exhibits at the water's edge. Jacob and Wood recorded that now-vanished world in their paintings.

||

JACOB'S FRIENDSHIP WITH Picasso had settled into amicable conventions. Jacob would have had no way of knowing—and almost no one
else knew—that since early 1927 Picasso had been carrying on an affair
with an adolescent girl, Marie-Thérèse Walter, whom he maintained in an
apartment in Paris (and hid in a *pension* in Dinard during summer holidays
there with his family). Jacob made a ritual visit to the Picassos at the Rue
La Boétie at each New Year to bring a gift to their son. From time to time
he dropped in at the studio, as Olga had made it clear that he wasn't welcome in her elegant home.

But this August granted the two old comrades a sweet if modest
renewal. Accompanied by Olga and Paulo, Picasso traveled down from
Dinard in his shiny chauffeur-driven car to visit Jacob in Quimper, spending the night in the local hotel. On this occasion at least, Jacob's family
was proud of him: the most famous painter in the world came to see them
and express his loyalty to their wayward Max. Picasso treated everyone
graciously and took photographs of Madame Jacob, Delphine, and Gaston
in front of their shop. Prudence Jacob, now a dignified lady with white hair
drawn back from her wide brow, presses her right hand to her mouth, half-
covering a shy grin. Delphine and Gaston stand proudly together. Jacob's
elder sister, a handsome woman with the large Jacob eyes and strong nose
and jawline, wears a string of pearls and a cardigan over her blouse and
skirt; portly Gaston, with rounder features and a distinctly more jovial
expression, wears a three-piece suit, a starched white shirt, and a tie. They
are the picture of French respectability.

Several days after the visit, Picasso sent copies of the pictures to Jacob,
who wrote to thank him.[68] But between Picasso's visit and this note of
thanks, Jacob's speedy life crashed. On August 19, as he returned with
Pierre Colle in Colle's father's car from a visit to Lanoë in Nantes, a tire
burst, and they smashed into a tree. While Colle emerged unharmed,
Jacob was severely injured, with multiple fractures in his left leg, his left
shoulder dislocated, his whole left arm paralyzed, and his right hand damaged.[69] Treated with chloroform and morphine, his left leg in a cast, he was

immobilized on his childhood bed in Quimper for the next three months. Willy-nilly, his family had to care for him. In the first few weeks he had difficulty writing at all. He did manage to signal to Maritain, a month after the accident, that he could hardly hold a pen, but that he thanked God for having arrested him in his "too ostentatious and too frivolous" life.[70]

The Roaring Twenties were also crashing. For Sachs, the catastrophe came when Chanel fired him at about the same time as Jacob's accident. At first he was too ashamed to tell Jacob. In a letter to Robert delle Donne, Jacob wrote from Quimper, "I kiss you as well as Maurice. . . . (He's making a big mistake not to write to me about everything, for he has no better friend than me.)"[71] When Sachs finally did confess, complaining that his "fair weather friends" had abandoned him, Jacob replied with customary generosity: "Whatever happens, I'll never consider your tacking off course to avoid shipwreck as anything but tacking. And in any case, words carry weight: *fair weather friends* doesn't mean 'friends.' I flatter myself that I am your friend and will remain so."[72]

On October 29 the New York Stock Exchange fell. The American banking system and economy were shattered, though it would take months for the effects to hit France and rattle the whole structure of patronage, publishing, and art markets that supported Jacob and his friends. As a footnote to this season of disasters, the beautiful, neurotic Jeanne Bourgoint, the sister of Cocteau's sometime lover Jean Bourgoint and the model for the sister in Cocteau's novel *Les Enfants terribles* (The Holy Terrors), committed suicide on Christmas Eve 1929 with an overdose of barbiturates.

IV.

WORD OF JACOB'S accident spread quickly. Letters of comfort flooded in. Robert and Marie delle Donne wrote him from Monte Carlo, where they were on holiday with Marie's husband, and Ottoni, and the wretched Sachs. Supervielle sent him a dozen novels, and Paulhan shipped package after package of books.[73] Friends kept the local shops busy delivering flowers and baskets of fruit. Jacob had always lived intensely through correspondence, but now it was his lifeline. Gradually, as he regained the use of his hand, he was able to reply. On a postcard, he declared to Kit Wood, "You know, Kit! You know that after certain looks, certain thoughts, certain words we're friends forever."[74] By the end of September, he was able to sit by the fireplace for two hours each afternoon, and a talented masseur was "hastening his recovery."[75] He spent his days in an orgy of reading. When Robert delle Donne asked for advice about books, Jacob's reply would fill a library: he had consumed Jouhandeau's new novel *Astaroth*, Cassou's *La Clef des songes*, Gide's *L'École des femmes*, and Malraux's *Les Conquérants*, and he was absorbed in Freud's *Introduction to Psychoanalysis* ("Fascinating!"). He went on to recommend Turgenev, Gogol, Conrad, Bernanos, Gómez de la Serna, Byron, Shaw, Gobineau— a map, if only a partial one, of Jacob's mind.[76]

One consequence of his forced immobility was the deepening friendship with a remarkable young man, Pierre Minet, perhaps the purest bohemian Jacob was ever to know. Born in Reims in 1909, the boy idealized revolt and attached himself to a group of older students with literary ambitions who called themselves "Les Simplistes." He left school at thirteen and ran away to Paris in 1925, just as he turned sixteen, to live in the streets, sleeping in doorways and under bridges. But he kept writing. Blond, blue-eyed, with an appealing face, he lived off handouts from friends and strangers and by selling his drawings. It was he who found a patron for his friends in Reims, the editor Pierre Léon-Quint, who helped them start their journal, *Le Grand Jeu,* in the spring of 1928 (with several of Minet's poems). (The Surrealists felt so threatened by the mysticism of *Le Grand Jeu* that they instigated a "trial" against it.)[77] After months on the streets, Minet also found a patron for himself, Lilian, an American painter twenty-five years older than he, with whom he had a tumultuous affair that lasted for years.

This untamable young man met Jacob in 1925, introduced, no doubt, through Minet's brother-in-law René Gaudier; at that time, the boy's insolence infuriated Jacob.[78] But in the spring of 1929, Minet really got to know Jacob, seeking him out at the Hôtel Nollet. Minet was then recovering from a two-month stay in a hospital, his health damaged by exposure, poor nutrition, and alcohol. That spring he fell ill again, and in the fall he developed coxalgia, a tubercular condition in the hips that confined him in a sanatorium on the northern coast of France.

By this time, Minet had published a chapbook of poems and a novel with the Nouvelle Revue Française; a second novel would appear in 1930. Imprisoned in a cast at Berck, Minet wrote to Jacob, similarly imprisoned in plaster in Quimper. At this point they hardly knew each other. But Jacob mobilized to help him. Over the years, even in his own severe poverty, Jacob often split the little he had, sending half to Minet. And now he tried to find people to send books to the young invalid.

Bit by bit, Jacob healed. On December 10 he wrote Vaillant that he was taking his first steps, not "in the vast universe" but from the bed to the fireplace and over to the window.[79] He let Paulhan know that he was walking with two canes.[80] In early January he reported to Minet that he was hobbling and had even managed to descend the stairs and venture out to the café.[81] He took up painting again, as his finances demanded.

One of the books Jacob read as he mended was Gertrude Stein's *The Making of Americans* in Georges Hugnet's abbreviated French version.[82] Jacob and Stein had never been close, but now they were drawn together in a shared nostalgia. "Dear friend from the Rue Ravignan," Jacob greeted her. He praised the power and gaiety of her book; certain passages, he said, were worthy of Swift. He saluted "our good, dear, and precious memories of the time when we were making so many things (nobody knows what it was like)."[83]

Jacob relived an even deeper past in an article by his classmate from the lycée, René Villard, now a professor of English at the lycée at Saint-Brieuc. Jacob had remained closer to René's brother Abel, a painter in Quimper. But for several years René had been collecting information about Jacob with a view to writing about him; now René published a memoir of their school days, describing the triumvirate of Jacob, Raoul Bolloré, and Villard, their outlawed literary journal, and their collaboration on *Le Cahier des maximes*.[84] "Your article is charming!" Jacob exclaimed, praising his friend's truthfulness and "firm, earthy" natural style.[85] Villard's article stirred up the old grief at Bolloré's suicide. Soon Jacob would have a new suicide to mourn.

As he regained strength, Jacob thought he might be able to return to Paris in March. "Dear Son Maurice," he wrote Sachs on January 26. "Life here is sad, slanderous, calamitous. . . . Where is joy? I hope with you."[86] For once, he received a reply from the hardly joyous Sachs, and Jacob in turn responded," Your letter gave me enormous joy. 'Where is joy?' I asked, and I answer, 'In your letter!' "[87]

His joy was tested a few days later: he slipped on the sidewalk and refractured his leg. He was condemned to a new cast and another three months of immobility. "The adorable Maurice Sachs" now wrote him frequently, amusing him with gossip from Paris.[88] Jacob and Minet exchanged letters from one sickbed to another as Jacob campaigned to find sponsors to send Minet books, and at the same time he tried to train his roughnecked young friend to thank the people who helped him. He also sent him news: "Pierre Reverdy is no longer with Mlle Chanel," he gossiped.[89] He kept in touch with the Catholic poet Henri Ferrare and with Paulhan, who brought out another handful of Morven le Gaélique's poems in *La Nouvelle Revue française*.[90] A lawyer helped him prepare a suit against Colle's insurance company, seeking compensation for his injuries in the accident. (The case, which took the form of an "amiable" suit against Colle, would drag on for years but eventually produced the modest pension on which Jacob lived for the rest of his life.)[91] It wasn't until mid-April that his leg healed sufficiently to free him from bed again; by April 22 he was "trotting" and attended the Easter service at the cathedral.[92]

V.

STILL FRAGILE, JACOB escaped his family in May 1930 and established himself at the Grand Hôtel in Bénodet. He didn't entirely escape; they insisted on managing his finances, intercepting payments for his paintings and poems to place in a savings account. "I have to *ask* for my money. It's atrocious. They're making me save," Jacob complained to Minet.[93] Minet had also escaped his confinement and was convalescing in nearby La Trinité-sur-Mer. Jacob read Minet's new autobiographical novel, *Histoire d'Eugène*

(Eugene's Story), reporting that he had sinned in doing so: it reminded him of the Marquis de Sade. "Eugène's" sexual adventures—mostly with women but occasionally with men—shocked Jacob. But at the same time he complimented Minet on his "undeniable talent" and on the achievement of the illusion of truthfulness.[94]

These Breton days were happy, though Jacob now felt like an old man, with one hand almost numb and a crippled foot, "no longer able to run with fortune or after her," he told Félix Maillols.[95] When Cingria visited, he found Jacob in high spirits. Buoyed by a contract with the Galerie Georges Petit in Paris, no longer bound by his agreement with Sachs and Colle, he painted for hours a day. In mid-June he moved from Bénodet to the little *pension* Ty-Mad in Tréboul, where Cingria and some spirited architects joined him.[96]

Amid a cluster of village houses, the *pension* Ty-Mad rose on a hill, its glassed-in dining room opening on a broad ocean view. But at low tide the water was invisible; it retreated beyond the line of rocks and pine trees embracing the bay, leaving an immense expanse of black, oozy mud and seaweed from which small mired sailboats poked up. Children trudged through the muck, looking for coins and even banknotes (which flew from tourists' tables in the wind).[97] Jacob attended mass at the tiny fifteenth-century Gothic church abutting the hotel garden.[98] Kit Wood and Froska returned. Life was cheerful, passionately focused on painting, with friends from Quimper popping in and out, and Pierre Colle offering excursions in the redoubtable automobile. News of trouble arrived muted by distance: the suicide of the painter Pascin in Paris. Jacob shocked Cingria by acting out an imitation of Pascin's Bulgarian accent during a rainy day at Ty-Mad before Cingria knew of the artist's death; it was announced that evening by one of the architects fresh from Quimper. "What?" Jacob asked Cingria. "Didn't you know Pascin had died?"[99] In other troubled news from afar, Jacob learned that Sachs, to escape his creditors, had arranged with a doctor friend to be hospitalized in a clinic in Paris for a pretend appendicitis: Jacob invited him to come "recuperate" in Brittany.[100]

Froska didn't stay long, so for weeks Kit Wood occupied his two rooms at the hotel by himself.[101] He took all his meals with Jacob, and during the days he threw himself into his painting, using thick house paint and carving with his brush to create the rough seas and thrashing cypress trees he loved. He had not broken free of opium. Because he had a meager supply and couldn't afford much more, he scraped old residue from his pipe and smoked that, giving himself an even more poisonous dose. Jacob wrote Sachs that sweet-natured Kit was now "caustic, bitter, mocking," and Cingria, when he joined them, described Wood as white as a corpse, sprinkled with opium ash.[102] Jacob's pencil portrait of Wood, dated July 20, 1930, shows a sad, haunted face.[103]

Wood left Ty-Mad in mid-August. "Dear darling Max," Cocteau wrote, "I'm happy about your friendship with Kit. He's pure."[104] But by this time Jacob had his doubts about Cocteau's own "purity" and about his effect on others.

Jacob had not, however, given up faith in his "Sonny." In May he'd written Maritain that he thought Maurice had entered a better phase and that he had resolved to pay his debts. On August 10 he wrote Maritain from Tréboul that he was expecting Sachs any day.[105] At least he had Minet for company: Pierre Colle drove Jacob to La Trinité-sur-Mer to pick up Minet, who stayed for a month at Ty-Mad, rude at table but artistically serious.[106] It wasn't Sachs who arrived a few days later, but a letter from him with a newspaper clipping reporting Kit Wood's death on August 21 under the wheels of a train in Salisbury Station.

Jacob was devastated. His response to Sachs is incoherent with grief. Everyone at the hotel was weeping, he said. He begged Sachs to swear never to kill himself. Though the report had been ambiguous, Jacob took it for granted that Wood had committed suicide. In letters to Minet, he said Wood's brutal death had made him ill; he'd been suffering and could hardly write. He blamed opium.[107]

EVEN AS JACOB waited for Sachs in Tréboul, his "Sonny" came up with a new scheme. Rousing himself from his alcoholic torpor, he befriended a young man whose father sold antiques and wanted to expand into the business of modern art in New York. Sachs, a proficient English-speaker with fancy social connections, seemed just the man for the job. On August 13 he bade farewell to the Maritains; the ever-hopeful Jacques wrote him a few days later that "a whole new life would open up" for him in America.[108] Jacob advised that he'd still be "a good little Christian" if he'd been satisfied with that, and the sacraments would have cured him of his "adventures" better than his "excessive cassock" or psychiatry. (For a while, Sachs had seen the psychoanalyst René Allendy, who also treated Anaïs Nin.)

"Try America, it'll be a new chapter in the astonishing story of your life, dear Maurice. . . . I kiss you, beloved beloved son."[109] On September 7, Sachs sailed on the *Paris* with his young colleague and a stock of art treasures paid for by his new employer (two Goyas, a Renoir, a Manet, some early Picassos), and a few pieces that he had "borrowed"—including drawings by Jacob and Modigliani that he'd lifted from Gérard Magistry, who would never see them again.[110]

||

JACOB GRIEVED FOR Kit Wood for months. He mentioned him in all his letters, crying out to Jean Colle, "Kit! Kit! Dear, dear Kit. I'm inconsolable."[111] To Froska Munster, he wrote a long letter of condolence, praising Kit and expressing his bewilderment: it's almost as if he were asking for consolation from her rather than offering it.[112]

By mid-September, the Ty-Mad emptied out and Jacob remained alone after a short visit from Yvon Belaval. The weather was foul: thunderstorms, days of relentless rain. In October the Ghikas were to pick him up for a stay in Roscoff, but they canceled, both because of Liane's ill health and because of the imminent death of Jacob's older brother Maurice, "the African." Maurice had retired to Châlons-sur-Marne; he had been ill for years and died quietly on October 22.[113] November found Jacob back in Paris at the Hôtel Nollet. He would limp for the rest of his life.

CHAPTER 18

THE HÔTEL NOLLET

I.

For a few months, back in Paris, Jacob lived in the past. In Tréboul he had been especially moved by Stein's portrait of Picasso in her new book, *Ten Portraits*, and even more enthralled when Fernande Olivier began to publish installments of her memoir.[1] But a triumphant show of his gouaches at the Galerie Georges Petit in December pulled him back into the present. A glittering assembly of aristocrats and artists turned out to celebrate his recovery, along with Picasso, Cocteau, and Salmon. Eight paintings were sold that evening, "and as they sell for 4500 francs what they buy for 1200, they're thrilled," reported Jacob.[2]

THE HÔTEL NOLLET, at 55 rue Nollet just off the Boulevard de Clichy, is a drab five-story building with gray metal shutters. It hasn't changed since the 1930s, according to Vittorio Rieti, though now it's a clinic, not a hotel.[3] The street has a grimy decency. Here for the next five years Jacob would live in a hive of poetry, art, and music, his room bustling with visitors who watched him paint, humming to himself, a cigarette dangling from his lips. Occasionally he would put down his brush and dart over to the wall to add a line of verse to the drafts he had pinned up there. He always had two or three paintings going at the same time. His room was in the back, its single window looking out over a courtyard; Rieti's room was also in the back, and from it the composer could hear Sauguet playing the piano in the room just above his. For several years, Rieti, Jacob, and Sauguet ate lunch together every day at the hotel, with other friends often joining them; even, at times, Princesse Ghika.[4]

Vittorio Rieti was an Italian Jew, born and brought up in Alexandria and educated in Milan. A craggily handsome man, he won attention early for his music; Alberto Casella was his teacher, Berg and Schoenberg admired him, and he soon formed friendships with Stravinsky, Prokofiev, Hindemith, Les Six, and Sauguet, and he wrote ballet music for Diaghilev. In 1931 he was just founding the chamber music group La Sérénade with his close friend (and lover), the violinist Yvonne de Casa Fuerte, who also lodged at the Hôtel Nollet. Jacob called her "the Marquise," and she was indeed a marquise; her husband, Illan Álvarez de Toledo, Marquis de Casa Fuerte, a friend of Proust, Montesquiou, Debussy, and Les Six, also lived at the hotel, at least off and on. Rieti's Italian wife Elsie and their small son were established in Rome, and the composer moved easily among the European capitals where his music was performed.

In a letter to Elsie, Rieti described an early encounter with Jacob. One evening just before dinner, a band of "young men" invaded his room: Boris (Kochno), Bérard, Sauguet, and Jacob.[5] Sauguet was dressed in a red crêpe de chine dress, with pearls and face powder (apparently a normal routine for him). Max cast everyone's horoscopes amid general chatter and joking. But that was just the hors d'oeuvre. When the others left, Jacob invited Rieti to dine at the hotel and then up to his room, where he established an atmosphere of "opium" (Caporal cigarettes) and through the smoke drew his new friend into a discussion of men, women, love, painting, age, priests, provincial life, and hell, and narrated his life, his conversion, and his sins. He fussed to make his guest comfortable in the armchair, then lay down on the floor "to see him better." "You're very sweet, may I kiss you?" he asked suddenly, and planted a firm kiss ("not exactly paternal") on Rieti's cheek. The composer broke out into imbecile laughter. But the evening continued with no discomfort; Jacob assured Rieti that he could see right away he wasn't "a member of the club," that he was a ladies' man. "And this is what it's like to be stuck in the Hôtel Nollet," Rieti told Elsie, to whom he remained deeply attached in spite of his affair with La Marquise.[6]

Rieti set four of Jacob's poems to music. "All that is just for the rhyme!" he chuckled over Jacob's poem "Monsieur le Duc," "What on earth does it mean?"[7] Rieti translated Jacob's medley of tones into sophisticated dissonances, a play of major and minor notes and rapidly shifting tempi. Poulenc set two groups of Jacob's poems, and the young American composer Virgil Thomson set Jacob's "Stabat Mater" for soprano and string quartet, his first published work.[8] To François de Gouy, Jacob described the musical effervescence at the hotel with Sauguet, Rieti, and "a little eighteen-year-old genius," Igor Markevitch (who would eventually make his name as a conductor). Yet again Jacob brought up the sorrow of Kit Wood's death: Tony Gandarillas is "inconsolable," he said, "and so am I."[9]

"Whom did Max Jacob love, really love, romantically?" Rieti asked Sauguet, long after their friend's death as the two old men sat together. "He never had one stable love," replied Sauguet. "But he always loved Picasso."[10] Be that as it may, Jacob fell in love easily and suffered for it. In February 1931 a new crush caused him considerable pain. Writing to Minet, Jacob described the agitation inspired by the Argentinian count Reggie de Sablon-Favier (known as something of a wastrel and even, it was bruited, a gigolo). "Reggy [*sic*]. Pericordial anguish, sensation of emptiness in the stomach. Vertigo, sadness with no cause. . . . But it's over." After other gossip—the arrival at the Hôtel Nollet of a peasant godson of Jacob's—he returned to the theme of love. His health was good, but his morale was destroyed by worries and perhaps by "odious, senile" love. He'd dragged some friends to a café in the hope of seeing Reggie—who was there, closely watched by a lovelorn lady, herself closely watched by an aspiring suitor. Vaudeville, observed Jacob. But lucidity proved no balm.[11]

For the next few years Minet was one of Jacob's main confidants. Neither charming nor easily charmed, Minet presented to Jacob no romantic possibility: his roughness broke through the older man's affectations and performances, making room for a rare frankness.[12] Jacob's letters to him abound in details of life at the hotel: the peasant godson has been employed as a dishwasher but stole Sauguet's piggy bank (*tirelire*, another pun: *tire-lyre*, "pull-lyre"); a magazine has asked Jacob for an article on "The Call of Sex"—"Which one?" Jacob shot back. He gave them Minet's name: "That will teach them to disturb me in my psychoanalytic meditations." But in a letter from March 1, 1931, we learn that Jacob's affair with Reggie had taken on more substance.[13] He concluded with a line from one of his own earlier poems of troubled romance: "And there spread the immense, blank ennui of a moonless night."[14]

In April he was still suffering over Reggie but over others as well. At the hotel, he said, they were living "in music and sin."[15] He didn't always manage to sin as much as he'd like; he told Rieti that the hotel should be named "Nollet me tangere."[16]

He also described to Minet his quick trip to Quimper for the trial to determine the insurance payments from his accident. His family was good to him, he acknowledged, but he couldn't stand "the silences, the drivel, the authoritarianism, the polite and obligatory social visits, the over-familiar and boorish old pals." The trial itself resembled a "posthumous consecration": copies of his books, photographs, and attestations were solemnly circulated. Jacob hoped for a considerable award from this exercise—as much as fifty thousand francs. As it turned out, he would receive much less, and that sum in turn attracted the attention of the tax authorities.[17]

II.

PARIS ALSO BROUGHT disappointments. Since Paulhan had asked him for a series of chronicles for *La Nouvelle Revue française,* Jacob produced a fantasia of characters from the Hôtel Nollet.[18] Paulhan professed to like it, and Jacob imagined that he'd have another source of income.[19] But in April, Paulhan had to tell him that *La Nouvelle Revue*—which essentially meant Gide—didn't like the work. It offered a kill fee for the second chronicle, which Jacob proudly refused.[20] The disappointment was compounded by Gallimard's reluctance to publish a volume of the Morven poems that Jacob had been collecting at Paulhan's request. He had never felt comfortable in the offices of *La Nouvelle Revue française;* now he felt rejected and despised.[21]

||

FRANCE WAS IN the grip of economic depression. Don't come to Paris, Jacob advised Minet, who was chafing at life in Reims. Everyone was poor. Even the rich no longer paid their bills. No one took taxis. Jacob had only the twelve hundred francs he needed to pay the month's rent at the hotel; Pierre Colle lived entirely on credit.[22] When François de Gouy commissioned a sequel to *Le Cornet à dés* as a private manuscript, Jacob produced it and was rewarded with a bouquet of flowers plucked from a vase in de Gouy's hotel. "Here's the lovely silvery light of the Île de France," said the gentleman, presenting the blooms. "It's not only light that's silvered," replied Jacob. Whereupon the count began lamenting the sorry state of his finances. A few nights later he showed Jacob an antique watch, a family heirloom studded with amethysts. "It's yours," said de Gouy. "You gave me a princely gift, I'm giving you a royal one." This watch would end up in a pawnshop.[23]

The hotel weathered a crisis of another sort: Jacob's godson—who had been fired from one menial job after another, stole from guests, and tried to seduce a chambermaid—now attempted suicide by swallowing iodine. This produced chaos in the hotel, arrival of a doctor and the police, a trip to the hospital. When the young man's stomach had been pumped, Jacob took him to the train station, purchased a ticket, and guarded him until he saw him safely packed off to Toulouse.[24]

Jacob's bitterness in 1931 permeates his prose. *Le Figaro artistique illustré* asked him for a reminiscence of Montmartre, no doubt expecting a sentimental postcard view of bohemia. They received instead an essay in ferocious realism. Opening with a famous line from *The Aeneid*, "Unspeakable the sorrow, O Queen, you ask me to renew," Jacob now saw Montmartre of the glory days as sordid and criminal. He remembered Utrillo sitting drunk in the gutter with spittle and blood dribbling from his lips; he remembered the Lapin Agile, where he used to dance on tabletops, as "a dusty place, a dark meeting place of poverty, pathetic tunes, silence, and drunken noise." He remembered being called out into the street by hoodlums and being knocked to the ground. He remembered that Picasso (unnamed) always carried a revolver. Somehow, he said, "the brave and pure artists that we were" managed to survive this environment without being soiled. In his last lines, he attacked Carco (unnamed) as a "sub-Murger" (a pun on Murger, author of *La Bohème*): "Let them suppress everything that perpetuates the so-called tender memories that you call bohemia and I call wretchedness, let all the sub-Murgers shut up."[25] This self-revision was all the more remarkable considering that for the next few years Jacob would increasingly draw on those memories for his livelihood.

The bitterness turned even more personal in his self-portrait for the *Dictionnaire biographique des artistes contemporains 1910–1930*. After telling his familiar tale of encounters with Picasso, Apollinaire, and God, he concluded: "Here I am in Paris, called 'master' by some, 'imbecile' by others. I'm neither one nor the other; I'm a hardworking man, not as saintly as some say, nor as depraved as some believe. A few of my books are known; I don't have the courage to write any more; I haven't enjoyed the success I expected from writing, and my painting has unexpectedly succeeded. Probably death will find me at my station with my gouaches or coming out of daily mass. I imagine a lot of people will attend my burial; they will be of all possible castes, of all worlds."[26]

||

IN JUNE, JACOB returned to Quimper, but to avoid squabbles with his family, he rented two large rooms on the Place de La Tour d'Auvergne: he had a little money and expected more from the outcome of the trial. He filled the chambers with manuscripts, smashed pastels, legal documents, and the proofs of his new collection of poems, *Rivage* (Shore). His windows looked out over linden trees; he could hear the trumpet playing reveille from the nearby barracks and the whistles of locomotives. It had been raining, he wrote his new friend Léon Merle de Beaufort, "for six thousand years."[27] The trial dragged on. His family was more irritable than ever: the depression had cut into the sale of antiques; it rained continually; and his cousin

Henri Jacob, who lived off investments, now declared himself "ruined" and Jacob was afraid he'd have to support him.[28] In spite of Jacob's "magnificent" rooms, he found Quimper more and more oppressive.[29] By August, his old stomach ailment flared up again. The real reason, he confided to de Gouy, was the constant struggle with "the madness" of family.[30]

He was still feeling ill when he returned to Paris at the end of September, and financial anxiety hardly improved his digestion. The real blow fell in November: the Galerie Georges Petit didn't renew his contract. He worried about being able to pay for his room at the hotel and could no longer afford taxis.[31] Cingria, too, was hard up: at lunch with Jacob at the hotel, he grandly refused the offer of a loan of five francs but accepted ten *sous*. (Later he borrowed hundreds of francs from Jacob and grandly refused to repay him.)[32]

Yet Jacob soldiered on. He had lunch every day with Rieti and Sauguet, he kept painting, he wrote poems, and friends flocked to his room, including new recruits like Lavastine's friend the journalist Henri Tracol, Jacob's young cousin Didier Gompel, and a young priest, Abbé Morel.

Maurice Morel would prove to be one of Jacob's sweetest friends. When the *abbé* sought him out at the hotel and showed him his poems, "You're not a poet," Jacob pronounced. "You're made for painting." They visited museums together, and Jacob invited him to paint next to him in his room. Morel would turn up as Jacob was finishing lunch, and the two would go upstairs to paint or out to see art. This friendship provided an education: Morel would go on to paint but, even more seriously, to write art criticism, to befriend painters, and to collect work (including Picasso, Rouault, and Léger). "As a priest, I sensed the conflicts in Jacob, and I tried to help him triumph over them," Abbé Morel said, speaking of his old friend forty years after the poet's death. "Jacob accepted the whole Christian premise. He lived in the constant memory of the apparition of Christ. 'I saw Him,' he said, in his worst moments. The Stations of the Cross counted enormously for him." Jacob had a horror of abstraction, the *abbé* remembered. "He needed the concrete, the baroque, the burlesque."[33]

But Jacob's main joy in December 1931 came from music, in "concerts of mutual admiration" with Rieti and Sauguet.[34] Poulenc set five of the

Morven poems, then created what would become one of his favorite pieces, the "profane cantata for baritone and chamber orchestra," *Le Bal masqué* (The Costume Ball), arranging four poems from *Le Laboratoire central*.[35] Poulenc loved the peasant simplicity of the Morven poems but was seduced even more by the "violence, truculence, and humor" in Jacob's "The Costume Ball"; he found in it the spirit of the cheap colored prints of the Parisian weeklies of his childhood, and they inspired his own "strange carnival music."[36]

In December 1931, René Laporte brought out Jacob's slender penultimate collection of poems, *Rivage*. The individual dedications reflect Jacob's current life: poems offered to Lavastine, Markevitch, and Sauguet, and one not dedicated to Sachs but originally mailed to him in a letter (appropriately entitled "The Widower," which is how Jacob must have felt in relation to Sachs).[37]

Rivage opens with a rhyming, self-deprecatory self-portrait, "You're No Longer Writing?," that Poulenc would set to music years later. Some of the poems are pierced with dreamlike images: "I'm dressed up in smoke," he declares in "The Widower." "Slowly they go, indolently slow / The forms of extinct desires," he murmurs in "The Wedding of the Blind."[38] "The trees and their green stomachs, all covered with scars," he notes in the untitled "The striking army of images."[39] The book was hardly noticed. In one of the few reviews, the Breton poet Pierre Guéguen noted Jacob's transformations of comic verse into "a crystalline river of subtle lyricism." He particularly praised "The Widower" as "a poem of interior tragedy."[40]

In December, Jacob's feelings about himself may be gauged by the cruel self-portrait, "Max Jacob's Own Public Confession or Caricature," illustrated with five reproductions of his paintings; he presented himself kaleidoscopically. "Yes, doctor!" he exclaims. "A bourgeois can be evolved, suffering, hypersensitive, and wrathful. A bourgeois is a man who isn't human: so I'm like a stone (there are stones that weep)." Jacob had called a version of himself Monsieur Dur (Mr. Hard) in *Filibuth;* here again he saw himself as "hard"; also as contradictory, stupid, dogmatic, and insecure. The style is rapid and hard-edged; it's one of his better pieces.[41]

III.

JACOB NOW ENTERED a phase of frightening poverty and glamorous sociability. In January 1932 he described for the Ghikas what they must have noticed for themselves: poor people on every street corner, rich people firing their servants, and factories laying off thousands of workers. He thanked the Ghikas for their Christmas gift of a wallet; he didn't tell them that he had almost nothing to put inside it.[42] His painting didn't prevent him from dying of hunger, he informed Paulhan.[43] The tax authorities were pursuing him, Colle's insurance company was appealing the decision for his compensation, the Hôtel Nollet wanted to evict him, and the art market had collapsed.[44] A few days later, he wrote de Gouy, he at least staved off expulsion from the hotel by selling two gouaches; as for the tax agents, *le Fisc*, they could come and seize what they wanted, but there was hardly anything to grab, and the gouaches were officially worthless because he had no gallery. What he really begged de Gouy and Greeley to do was to visit Reggie, sick with pneumonia in a hotel in Cannes.[45]

By March, a friendly politician managed to extricate Jacob from his tax troubles: an influential acquaintance had pulled strings. It came out that Jacob had never declared his income from his paintings, so had never paid taxes; the lawsuit had attracted *le Fisc*.[46] The arrangement removed the immediate threat of seizure but didn't relieve his poverty. He pawned his rings and his watch; he couldn't afford a taxi to visit Minet, now in the Hôpital Saint-Louis; he told Cocteau that he lived on credit and debt.[47] The poet Henri Ferrare, in Geneva, of whom Jacob had inquired if he knew any "fat cats" who might help, responded with a banknote of his own and persuaded a priest to send a small sum.[48] Jacob was friendly with Natalie Barney, often attending her salon; she pressed seven hundred francs into his hand, murmuring, "I've been told you're struggling; accept this, you can pay me back later."[49]

For Jacob did go out in "society." He had to: it was the only way to find "clients" to buy his paintings. He saw Cocteau's film *The Blood of a Poet* and found it beautiful. He gossiped to François de Gouy about an evening with Prince and Princesse Edmond de Polignac: Cocteau's old friend the poet Anna de Noailles had been lifting her flounces to show off her legs, proclaiming "I'm Beauty, Grace, and Genius" in "an apocalyptic torrent." Jacob said it was terrifying, how she and Cocteau resembled each other: they were doubles, "same magician's hands, same gaze, same smile, same gestures, same opinions, same conversation, same eternal illnesses."[50] Colette was also present, and Jacob professed to be "in love so far as marriage, suicide, etcetera" with the society novelist Violet Trefusis;[51] he broke off the letter to rush out to lunch with Jules Supervielle, Natalie Barney, and Marie-Louise Bousquet, the Parisian agent for *Harper's Bazaar*.

||

AND YET IN the "terrible winter" of 1932, as Jacob described it to Grenier, and the terrible spring and summer following it, some successes bolstered him.[52] Poulenc's premiere of *Le Bal masqué* was received enthusiastically at the concert at the Noailles' villa in Hyères. At the end of April, Jacob published yet another memoir in *Les Nouvelles littéraires*. Rich in detail, the essay remains one of the liveliest accounts of the brave little avant-garde of Picasso, Apollinaire, Jacob, and Salmon, describing the laundry hanging from the windows of the neighboring apartment buildings, and how Picasso, gazing at them, pronounced, "Napoli." The old scenes lived once more: Picasso's dog Frika clanking her chain on the studio floor, "the geological precipices of Montmartre over the ocean of Paris," the meeting with Salmon at Picasso's door, the meeting at the Austin Fox bar with Apollinaire. As he had explained to Robert Levesque, Jacob insisted that Cubism was born from Picasso's examination of an African statuette Matisse showed him. None of the painter's friends understood what he was doing: "I didn't understand Cubism. Guillaume sang about it without grasping it. Salmon hated it. None of those who would become famous in the Cubist parade knew Picasso in 1906. Picasso is the sole creator of this way of painting."[53] To which Picasso is reported to have said, "It's very true."[54]

In his article, Jacob alluded to Fernande Olivier's memoirs that had been appearing in *Le Soir* and the *Mercure de France* and that would be published as a book the following year. Rumor had it that Picasso had halted the series in *Le Soir* and was trying to oppose Stock's publication of the book. But Fernande was destitute. Jacob had always liked her; now he went to Picasso and asked him, point-blank, to help his old lover. The painter remained silent. Fernande had betrayed him years ago; that finished the story.[55]

The Galerie Georges Petit held an immense retrospective of Picasso in June. Jacob must have had complicated feelings as he walked through the rooms where his own small exhibit had opened two years earlier. Picasso's triumphant canvases commanded the walls, paintings from as early as *La Vie* from 1903, many of the key works of Cubism, and the two versions of *The Three Musicians* of 1921 where Jacob may or may not have recognized himself in the black-robed, masked Pierrot. The show was "a genial torture," he wrote de Gouy.[56]

Also in June, Gallimard brought out a cheaper version of *Tableau de la bourgeoisie*, retitled *Bourgeois de France et d'ailleurs* (Bourgeois of France and Elsewhere). The book was widely reviewed. The fantasist poet Franc-Nohain, whose comic verse had inspired Jacob in his early years, praised it in *L'Écho de Paris*,[57] *Le Quotidien* welcomed its humor, and the faithful Moremans took the book as an occasion, once again, to celebrate Jacob's radical religious morality.[58]

Jacob wasn't publishing much poetry in these months: he seemed more engaged in collecting older work. But he did bring out two new poems in September, a prose poem called "Eternal Current Events" and a haunting lyric appropriately named "Convalescence" from this period in which he tried to heal from the car accident and from financial and emotional shocks. It contained these lines:

CONVALESCENCE

O day that strikes me down! O life stolen from me
I want to be cured of my courage
and not die of my ennui.

. . .

O God who repairs worlds
look at the world I am!
open my rib cage, touch my loins
with the finger that wrote in the sand a mystery
when you pardoned the woman accused of adultery.[59]

||

DURING THIS SEASON when Jacob couldn't afford to leave Paris, he had a suggestive encounter in letters. The eighteen-year-old Albert Camus, through his teacher Jean Grenier, wrote to Jacob from Algeria and received from the author "a reply that did me a great deal of good." He felt "a profound sympathy" for Jacob, he told Grenier. "Life has been hard for him."[60]

In the summer of 1932, Max Jacob was in a bleak mood; life did seem hard. *Rivage* was a failure.[61] He had won his lawsuit, but *le Fisc—le Fixe, le Fiche*—would claim most of the award, so he would end up with only a tiny pension since *le Fisc* had "*confisc*ated" so much.[62] His cousin Henri, the one who was not entirely "ruined," was dying in Quimper, and Jacob wanted to see him. But Henri died precipitously, and the inheritance, such as it was, was divided between Gaston and Delphine, Jacob's brother and sister who lived in Quimper; Jacob arrived in time only for the funeral. To de Gouy and to his new friend Andreu, he frankly called his siblings "robbers" and described the grotesque scene of the funeral cortege meeting the handcarts already transporting the cousin's linens and blankets to the Jacob household.[63]

IV.

MAX JACOB MET the last serious love of his life, a law student named René Dulsou, in October 1932 at the house of his friends the Léon Merle de Beauforts in Paris, the kind of cultivated businesspeople Jacob genuinely liked, not the creeps of his *Bourgeois de France et d'ailleurs*. An executive at a Parisian insurance company, Léon was a sophisticated man who appreciated the arts. René Dulsou, too, had a taste for the arts.

Dulsou also came from a Parisian business family and knew the Merle de Beauforts through his parents. A cousin of Jacob's friend the sculptor René Iché, he also knew François de Gouy and Russell Greeley, which suggests that he was already somewhat familiar with the Parisian artistic homosexual milieu. He was twenty-three and studying law in Nice, though spending a considerable amount of time in Paris, supposedly preparing for exams. In a memoir published in 1969 under the pseudonym "Sinclair," he described himself at twenty-three as "numb, mixed-up, inhibited"; he was both timid and insolent; he imagined himself, looking back, as "perfectly odious."[64] He already knew he was homosexual and had had a number of erotic encounters, all purely physical. He also recognized that what he called "homophilia" still had "the odor of sulfur" about it and had to be hidden. Max Jacob, he said, firmly believed in such discretion. But with Jacob, Dulsou was thrilled to meet "the homophiliac intelligentsia of the era." And he found in his older lover, even more than a "pederast," a pedagogue.[65]

Jacob fell for Dulsou immediately. In an early move, he sent him a "fiancée" poem, a barely disguised invitation:

Return again despite the note
A demon wrote to you from me
You'll climb in across the window ledge
If you don't have the key.[66]

The affair lasted for three years. But because Dulsou was often away in Nice or with his parents in Paris (or in the house they rented in a Parisian suburb), a rich account of the romance survives in Jacob's letters, some of which took the form of a fictive diary he called *Le Roman du Pélican* (The Novel of the Pelican)—a pelican, perhaps, because that bird was mythologically supposed to feed its young with blood from its own breast. This, Jacob discovered too late, was what happened with Dulsou. *Le Roman du Pélican* details the minutiae of Jacob's life, an almost hour-by-hour record of his frenetic socializing, his artistic and poetic struggles and triumphs, and his passion. The main characters are "the hero" (Jacob), "X" (Dulsou), an Italian gigolo named Guglielmo Pacifico (Dondi), Marie and Robert delle Donne, Jacob's new friend Baron Marc de Nicolas du Plantier, the actor Marcel Herrand, Dubuffet (who had returned to Paris and was painting again), and Pierre Colle. It was a time of jarring contradictions, as Jacob began to achieve fame—the Légion d'honneur was finally awarded in 1933, a spectacle in his honor was held at Le Boeuf sur le Toit, concerts celebrated his poems, his poetry was enshrined in Marcel Raymond's influential book, *De Baudelaire au Surréalisme*—yet he endured the continual humiliation of poverty. Jacob's love for Dulsou inspired some beautiful poems, a late lyric flowering. And in 1934 democracy in France began to shatter.

In a letter to Dulsou from November 1932, a few weeks after their meeting, Jacob changes from *vous* to *tu* in midstream. This was a "pedagogical" letter, instructing René to find his proper "desert" for self-reflection, but also reporting that he's sold a gouache for five hundred francs, and saying that if René had been there, they would have dined gaily on the sum.[67] In December, Jacob explained the Crucifixion—the vertical of the Cross signifies will and reason, the horizontal signifies the world.[68] In December he invited him to a fancy soirée. In January 1933 a short note addressed to "My beloved son René" expressed despair: "You saw it, I'm morally sick. . . . You know my affection for you and you won't blame me. *I want to die.* I kiss you. Max Jacob. P.S. I have no ambition except to die, die, die."[69]

JACOB USHERED IN the New Year 1933 in a night of partying with Dulsou that threatened to have serious consequences for Jean Dubuffet. As Jacob related it, Dubuffet's wife was suing "Jeandub" for divorce, accusing him of pederasty and Jacob of pimping. Dubuffet, Dulsou, and Jacob had spent the night carousing and ended up sleeping at Dubuffet's apartment in his wife's absence, Jacob and Dulsou on the couch. "Mme Jeandub" discovered a watch cover and a monogrammed handkerchief belonging to Dulsou, and a fur coverlet stained and scented with perfume; forcing open a drawer of her husband's desk, she found pages of a fantasy about

Germans and dogs. Madame Merle de Beaufort came to the rescue, testifying that everyone knew that Jeandub, Dulsou, and Jacob had celebrated the New Year together in perfect innocence and had slept in the Dubuffets' apartment because they were tired. There was perfume on the coverlet because Jacob used perfume. Madame Jeandub withdrew her demand for divorce (though the marriage fell apart later). "That'll teach Jeandub to write fantasy literature and elucubrations about Germany and dogs," concluded Jacob.[70]

The news from Germany, however, wasn't funny. On January 5 it became known that Hitler and the German vice-chancellor Franz von Papen had made a secret agreement to oust Chancellor Kurt von Schleicher. On January 30, Hitler alone became chancellor. Jacob was filled with dread. He wrote Minet that they were living in an atmosphere of vague anguish, something like the time of the French defeats in 1915. He promised to send Minet a money order—"from one poor man to another"—and, true to his word, mailed him small sums throughout the year, though he himself barely scraped by. As for private life, he told Minet, he was "torn up, in love, ignorant," and the priests were refusing him absolution.[71]

Jacob's social life was feverish. When he wasn't playing with Dulsou, he saw everyone else, old friends and new. He had become close to the younger poet (and lawyer) Jean Follain, whom he considered "the best in modern poetry."[72] Now he and Follain became enthusiastic about Georges Schehadé, a Lebanese poet who had just arrived in Paris.[73] After refusing to meet Robert delle Donne's friends "those du Plantiers" in February, he ran into them in March and became "best friends" (to delle Donne's stupefaction).[74] His letters to Dulsou recount a dizzying round of parties, with the Paulhans, Hugnet, Marcoussis and Alice Halicka, Natalie Barney, and the Merle de Beauforts, as well as the lunches with Sauguet and Rieti and the endless stream of visitors at the hotel.

He was ravaged by his love for Dulsou. And now the strange personage of Dondi, the gigolo, entered their lives. One afternoon Dulsou telephoned Dondi in Jacob's presence and made some arrangement that Jacob found disturbing; to "expiate," Dulsou stayed with Jacob for dinner. Dondi turns up all the time in *Le Roman du Pélican*. And at least once Jacob resorted to Dondi's services when he was lonely for Dulsou, as he confessed in *Le Roman*, afterward suffering "atrocious remorse."[75]

René Dulsou was a cynical fellow, eager for the social contacts Jacob provided but at the same time determined to pursue his own pleasures. If he wanted glory, he came into Jacob's life at the right time. He wasn't present, however, for one of Jacob's most splendid occasions, a "Max Jacob evening" at Le Boeuf sur le Toit, a performance of his poems in settings by Roland-Manuel, Nicholas Nabokoff, Poulenc, Rieti, and Sauguet. Pierre Guéguen recited Jacob's poetry; the poster for the show featured Picasso's portrait of his friend as a Roman consul. An enormous crowd attended. Jacob drank champagne until two in the morning and attended mass at seven-thirty. All in all, he was pleased.[76]

He remained in the public eye that spring. In April he published yet another reminiscence of Montmartre, managing to introduce new stories, remembering how he had run through the streets at night with Picasso and Apollinaire shouting "À bas Laforgue, vive Rimbaud!" and how Picasso threatened to shoot someone who spoke slightingly of Cézanne.[77]

In July 1933 Paulhan's scheming finally paid off, and Jacob was named a chevalier de la Légion d'honneur. Anatole de Monzie, the minister of education, signed the papers, and André Salmon (already a chevalier) came to the hotel to deliver the declaration and the red ribbon with the medal. The award was widely reported in the press, but Jacob felt obscure hostility from Quimper; as he told René Villard, his fellow citizens wanted him to fail. They had predicted that he'd lose his lawsuit, and now they were jealous of the Légion d'honneur.[78] "At least it'll make my mother happy," he quipped.[79]

Meanwhile he was suffering about Dulsou. To Liane, he confessed that he'd been afflicted by a love the Church condemned, a love that chewed him up while the Church refused him absolution. At the same time, he had to struggle like a raw beginner to place his writing and sell his paintings.[80] "I'm completely drunk on wine, alcohol, and illness," he wrote Dulsou. "I'm in love and want only to talk about the object of this love."[81] Remembering this torment a year or two later, he composed "Ballad of the Night

Visit," which he disguised by backdating it to 1929 and by marking the beloved as female. A chant in versets rather than a prose poem, repetitive, rich in internal rhyme and assonance, dreamlike, baroque, it expressed this dolorous passion in fuller cadences than he had ever allowed himself.[82] The poem recalls a December night when Jacob skidded his way in a taxi (which he could hardly afford) through a blizzard to keep vigil under the beloved's window.[83]

As he had done with Frenkel, Jacob cultivated Dulsou's parents. Somehow these respectable parents saw, or chose to see, only an affable, famous, and pious writer taking an interest in their sons. By June 1933, Jacob was spending weeklong visits at the Dulsous' holiday house in Le Vésinet, and in August he wrote an eloquent letter of condolence to Dulsou *père* in sympathy for his father's death.[84]

||

JACOB WAS NOW engaged in an epistolary friendship with an unusual woman, the scholar Marguerite Mespoulet. Educated in Paris and Oxford, she had taught French literature at Wellesley College since 1923, and in 1933 she had just taken a professorship at Barnard. It was to her that Jacob wrote in August that he would go to Lourdes for the jubilee on September 2, then spend a month with friends near Narbonne.[85] These friends were the Dulsous, who also had a house in the South. Jacob pawned his rings again to pay for the trip, so desperate was he for René's company.[86] He left Paris on August 30, hurtling after his lover, supposedly to stay a month.[87]

Lourdes was only a pretext: Jacob wanted to be with Dulsou. As he had feared, the visit was curtailed, and by September 3 he was heading north by train to see René Villard in Quimper.[88]

||

MAURICE SACHS REAPPEARED in France in October after three picaresque years in the United States. The gallery business in New York had crumpled, gutted by the Depression. But Sachs moved fast in New York society and easily charmed the gullible natives; in short order he found himself giving lectures in fancy salons, and then on NBC radio, where he was welcomed as an authority on politics and culture. An agent snapped him up and booked him for a transcontinental lecture tour, in the course of which he met Gwladys Matthews, the daughter of a Presbyterian minister in Seattle. Sachs had already converted once; to do it again was easy, and in the blink of an eye "the famous French economist," as he was billed, married into the respectable Matthews family.[89] The marriage lasted eight months, just enough time for Gwladys to translate her husband's slapdash lectures that Knopf published as *The Decade of Illusion*.[90] (The young lady must have lost illusions enough to last a lifetime.)

Bidding Maurice bon voyage in 1930, Jacob had predicted "a new chapter in the astonishing story of your life," but not even he could have foreseen quite how astonishing it would prove. In February 1933, Sachs fell in love with Henry Wibbels, a twenty-year-old American he met in Hollywood. Leaving scandal in his wake once more, he abandoned his wife and sailed with Wibbels to France, arriving in early October. Once again Sachs applied to Gide for support. This time the master was more welcoming, impressed, it seems, by Sachs's tales of success in America. Sachs and Wibbels holed up in a flea-ridden hotel, but Gide lent them money and helped Sachs to a position at the Nouvelle Revue Française, directing an imprint of "adventure stories."

The "adventures" continued. Sachs began stealing rare autographed books from Cocteau. Called on the carpet by Gaston Gallimard, he whipped out a forged letter from Cocteau granting him authority to sell the works. "I pardon Jean," he announced, and set fire to the letter in front of his employer—who was so taken aback, for the moment, he refrained from sacking him.[91]

By this time, Sachs no longer had Jacob in his sights: he had more to gain from Gide, Cocteau, and Gallimard. As Sachs said of Jacob with spectacular understatement in *La Décade de l'illusion*, "In Paris, life began to separate us a little." Indeed it did.[92]

But in 1934 Jacob was obsessed with Dulsou. He saw the usual whirl of people: Dulsou when he was around, Marc du Plantier and his wife, Conrad Moricand (now an astrologer), Frenkel, and Dubuffet.[93] At the same time he entertained monastic fantasies, announcing in November that he was planning a retreat in the Jesuit monastery outside Paris. (A few days later he jubilated to René, "Nollet Bollet Nollet!": he lasted only one day in the cold and dark.)[94]

And he remained a public personage. On December 11, in a "Gala de Musique Moderne," Rieti played the piano for his settings of four poems by Jacob in a program that included Poulenc, Honegger, Auric, Milhaud, and Debussy (whose *Sonata for Violin and Piano* was performed by Rieti's lover Yvonne de Casa Fuerte, with Poulenc at the piano).[95]

V.

IN DECEMBER 1933 a financial scandal broke. Alexandre Stavisky, "Handsome Sasha," a Polish Jew who had become a French citizen, was discovered to have operated an immense Ponzi scheme out of the city of Bayonne through a network of pawnshops. Hundreds of millions of francs had disappeared; politicians at all levels were compromised—including the mayor of Bayonne and ministers in the Radical Socialist government. It turned out that for years Stavisky had been protected from earlier prosecutions for fraud. Léon Daudet and Action Française and other right-wing parties were already seething, but when Stavisky was found dying of gunshot wounds to the head in an Alpine chalet on January 8 and died the next day, the country went into a frenzy. Many accused the government of murdering the swindler in order to silence him. Monarchists and fascists seized the opportunity to try to bring down the government; the Camelots du Roi marched in the streets and fought with police on January 11 and again in the week of January 22–27. Anti-Semitism flared. The prime minister resigned, replaced by another Radical Socialist, Édouard Daladier. On February 3, Daladier fired the right-wing prefect of the Parisian police, Jean Chiappe, and Chiappe refused to go. On February 6 the supporters of the right rioted: police and National Guard fired on the crowd, killing fifteen people. Three days later the Communists rioted in response. Daladier resigned, and the elderly Gaston Doumergue, who had been president of the Republic from 1924 to 1931, now established a conservative "government of national unity."

It was a running joke in Paris that Jacob resembled Chiappe: they were both bald and short, with large dark eyes, pudgy cheeks, and a prominent nose. Pierre Colle was completing his military service doing office work in the École Militaire; he began inviting Jacob to lunch in the cafeteria, where the poet charmed the soldiers by reading their palms and telling horoscopes. Word got around that Jean Chiappe was visiting once a week as the lunches stretched out at greater and greater length and celebrities joined the party: Cocteau, Sauguet, Dullin, and Milhaud. Only when the military governor read in the newspaper that the fanciest place to lunch in the city was his cafeteria did the charade come to an end.[96] But Jacob was mistaken for Chiappe all over the place. When Marcoussis and Alice Halicka invited him to an evening with Romanian friends, one of the guests, the former Romanian ambassador, astonished everyone by greeting the poet, "What a pleasure, my dear Chiappe, to find you here!"[97] In January 1934, just weeks before the riots of February 6, Jacob published a comic poem, "La T.S.F." (*Télégraphe sans fils,* or radio), dedicated to "M. the Prefect of Police in Paris."[98] In the days after the riot, Jacob found himself bizarrely implicated in the national disorder: everywhere he went, on the Métro, in the street, and in restaurants, people stared and sometimes greeted him, taking him for the bold prefect of police who had stood up to the government.[99] There was a delicious irony to this doubling since Jacob had so often been harassed by the police in his ragamuffin days.

THE VIOLENCE OF February 6 shocked the country. Jacob's old friend Carya (Élise), now Madame Marcel Jouhandeau, witnessed it firsthand with her husband and in some sense participated. United in their intensifying anti-Semitism if in little else, the couple moved with the protesters to the Place de la Concorde to confront the Chamber of Deputies. As Élise described it, around ten p.m. a shot was fired (by whom?), killing a woman leaning out a window of the Hôtel Crillon; the crowd shouted insults to the government; the National Guard responded with machine-gun fire. Characteristically, Élise Jouhandeau mentioned what she was wearing: when a guardsman whacked her with his truncheon, the blow was softened by the thickness of her fur coat.[100] Blundering through the battle, the Jouhandeaus came face to face with Drieu La Rochelle.

By now a famous novelist, Drieu was no friend of Jacob's. Attracted to absolute solutions, he had been steadily moving toward the radical right, like Jacob's friend Pierre Andreu. In his biography of Drieu, Andreu described the guards firing on the crowd on February 6 and Drieu (who had fought and been wounded three times in the Great War) "running under the bullets" in the thick of the fray. "The next day, he was a fascist." Drieu, Andreu, and their comrades had lost faith in democracy and saw Mussolini's "fascist socialism" as a model. They were seeking, Andreu explained, "a way toward socialism that wouldn't take the mediocre path" of democracy; "they were against everything, against rotten parliamentarianism and against the thieves of capital."[101]

Many French citizens shared the fantasy of a strong leader who would rescue the country: the soil of the Vichy government was already being prepared in 1934. Liane was not alone in admiring Mussolini.[102] Jacob's allegiance was to God rather than to any earthly leader, but his article of astrological predictions on January 2, 1934—five weeks before the riots of February 6—reveals his idiosyncratic view of European politics. (How seriously he took the article is hard to say: he told Dulsou it was a "vulgarization.")[103] He predicted the approaching death of Hitler; more convincingly, he predicted strikes and riots in France in January and claimed that "the terrible year for the whole earth" would be 1941.[104]

||

IN THE WINTER and spring of 1934, Dulsou was in Nice studying for a law exam, his second try. Jacob wrote him almost every day. These letters mix observations of the crises in the streets with news of Jacob's own life and advice for René. "They're firing Chiappe because he's a nuisance for Daladier," he reported on February 4. The day after the shootings, he wrote indignantly, "The Chamber [of Deputies] revealed itself: inferior to contemporary standards, unworthy of Paris, of modern France, stupid, cowardly, ferocious, idiotic. They tossed Chiappe out on purpose to *terrify* Paris: robbers become assassins when their burglaries are interrupted."[105] Paris was empty; taxis were on strike; people were scared. He feared a dictatorship by the minister of the interior.[106] The Jewish theme surfaced more and more frequently in his letters: reports of conversations at dinner parties where he found himself defending Jewish respect for ancient tradition; and an evening with Kisling (who was Jewish) at Moricand's sumptuous apartment, where Kiki wanted to know why everyone had it in for the Jews. Jacob offered the standard Catholic line that suffering was "useful for preserving God's chosen people"—which Kisling said explained nothing, and which Max Jacob would have reason, in a few years, to test in a very personal fashion.[107]

Jacob dined out almost every night, with his younger Gompel cousins, with Moricand, Dubuffet, Cingria, Frenkel (now running a private detective agency!), the Jouhandeaus, the Paulhans, and *tutti quanti*.[108] Reggie was still in the picture, though not amorously. Dondi threaded his way through these weeks; Dulsou seemed now to distrust him, so Jacob broke off with the gigolo.[109] In side news, the romance between Rieti and the marquise created drama in the hotel: the marquis was nowhere to be seen; the marquise owed the management three hundred francs and had her key confiscated and her baggage seized, and took refuge weeping in Jacob's room. Somehow she paid the bill the next day, and she and Rieti left the hotel for good, depriving Jacob of his companionable lunches. (Sauguet had already moved out.)[110]

But Jacob's main theme, in his hundreds of letters to Dulsou, was love. He wept in front of René's photograph.[111] René was his adopted son.[112] When Dulsou made it clear that he wanted to pursue other affairs, the elder lover, desperate to please, made plans for such a life: "We'll adopt the style of life which you desire, which I desire. But don't deprive me of your dear presence," he pleaded.[113] There would be "falls," but as long as René was morally conscious of them as falls, they could manage.

Other tremors besides René's desire for freedom rattle these letters. René was seeing quite a bit of a poet called Jean Le Louët, a fellow just

Dulsou's age. In a few months he would become a more significant actor in the play. And it was becoming clear that René's father was seriously ill, probably with tuberculosis. Throughout that spring and into the summer, Jacob wrote Madame Dulsou and René with sympathy and medical advice.

VI.

WHILE THE COUNTRY jolted along, Jacob's private life was anything but peaceful. The du Plantiers drove him to Rouen on Easter Monday, and when he returned to the hotel, his diamond ring had disappeared. Detectives came and interviewed the clientele and staff; everyone was furious; the diamond (Jacob's form of a savings account) was gone for good. A few days later a taxi crashed into Jacob's taxi; he was wounded in the head, mouth, hands, and chest. For at least a week he was bedridden, cared for by a kind lady called Henriette Belcourt, "very sweet and ugly," who had accosted him in the Métro one day, "crazy about arts and letters," and liked to help him.[114]

In July, fully restored, Jacob spent two weeks with his beloved Louis Vaillant in Toul, describing for Dulsou the captain's garden, the peacefulness of the little family, Madame Vaillant's stupidity, and the captain's patience with her. Dulsou had been called to military service; Jacob asked Vaillant to pull strings to make things easier than usual. As he traveled between Toul and Quimper, he dashed through Paris especially to see René.[115]

Jacob's stay of several weeks with his family in Quimper passed without incident. He painted, trying to earn enough to pay his bill at the Hôtel Nollet. All year he had been sending small sums to Pierre Minet; finally free from the hospital and walking with crutches, Minet needed still more convalescence, so Jacob arranged for him to spend several months near Quimper at the sanatorium run by his old friend Dr. Benoiste. In late July he spent a night there to visit Minet and the Benoiste family; the young author was determined to read to his friend the manuscript of his new "Gidian" novel celebrating incest. Jacob put the reading off for hours, preferring conversation, a walk, and the family lunch. But in the afternoon, Minet sat in Jacob's room and started reading. After a few pages Jacob had had enough: he couldn't listen to any more of these horrors. Minet plowed ahead. After a few more pages, Jacob exploded, attacking the prose, pointing out redundancies and "stinking academicisms." Minet protested but soon backed down. Years later he said that that was when he began to learn to write.[116]

Jacob spent late August and the first half of September at the Hôtel Nollet, and it was there that his young cousin Didier Gompel visited him and asked what he was doing, receiving the reply that Jacob was preparing his "impromptu lectures" for Switzerland.[117] But Jacob could no longer afford the hotel. Even as he wrote to console Moricand, who lost his fortune that fall and became practically indigent, Jacob faced his own crisis and left the hotel to move in with Pierre Colle, on the Rue de Duras in the eighth arrondissement. As he wrote the poet René Lacôte, "Here I am installed with Pierre Colle, an art dealer with no deals. We fight more effectively as a team."[118]

||

IN JUNE, JACOB thanked Paulhan for "the beautiful MXJB issue" of *La Nouvelle Revue française*.[119] It really was a Jacob issue. To Guiette's biographical sketch, Paulhan added Bounoure's dithyrambic appreciation of *Les Pénitents en maillots roses*, *Visions infernales*, *Fond de l'eau*, and *Rivage*—not so much a review as an evocation of the essential Jacob, seen as a Celtic elf fallen among humans to release a fountain of "new poetry from clichés and gossip, concierge chat, our humble confessions of sin, our many turpitudes, and even our good feelings." He judged *Fond de l'eau* Jacob's "most beautiful book" and emphasized his union of "Talmudic intelligence" and Kabbalistic inventions" with "the generosity of the Christian heart and Celtic grace."[120]

Under the title "Actualités éternelles," Paulhan ran eleven poems by Jacob, some in metrical rhyming verse, some in free verse, some prose poems. Paulhan chose well. Religious and, in flashes, mystical, these poems avoid the tone of village catechism that weighs down much of Jacob's religious poetry. By turns witty and ecstatic, they hold together in rhythm what Jacob had so much trouble harmonizing in his life.[121]

NINETEEN THIRTY-FOUR WAS a fertile year for Jacob. In February, *Le Figaro artistique illustré* brought out another story-letter in the genre of *Le Cabinet noir*.[122] With Moricand, he published an astrological essay, "The Spiral and the Serpent," arguing that the mechanistic view of the universe as a product of centrifugal and centripetal forces is simply a restatement of ancient symbolic wisdom.[123] Every few weeks *Les Nouvelles littéraires* presented a column of his poetry. Four poems came out in *Le Journal des poètes* in February, including "The Two Loves," a poem arising directly from his agony with Dulsou.[124] In May, Gallimard bought the rights to the three Matorel books from Kahnweiler, and in May and September the Spanish journal *Cruz y Raya* ran translations of texts Jacob seems to have composed from his improvised lectures in Madrid in 1926.[125] More "mystical" poems appeared in *Le Beau Navire* in December.[126]

The year 1934, however difficult, closed on a hopeful note. He had made peace with Michel Leiris; the old Surrealist battles lay far behind them, and Leiris had calmed down, establishing himself as an author and ethnographer with the publication of *L'Afrique fantôme* (Phantom Africa), his memoir of a two-year expedition across Africa from Senegal to Ethiopia. Jacob excitedly recommended the book to Dulsou, and in December he wrote the young Raymond Queneau, whose novel *Gueule de pierre* (Gob of Stone) he admired, that he looked forward to meeting him at the home of his "astonishing friend" Michel Leiris.[127] The year ended with a Christmas present from the literary establishment: he was awarded the "Noël du poète" Prize. He needed the money, and the honor would stand him in good stead as he embarked on his new career as lecturer.

VII.

IN THE FIRST few months of 1935, Jacob lived in a counterpoint of excitement and grief. Émile Heubi, a Swiss impresario based in Lausanne, arranged a six-week lecture tour that would hurtle Jacob around Switzerland and into the South of France. He was the central act of a troupe that included an actress, a female dancer, and a tired, much-yelled-at male pianist. But while the tour was in full swing, Dulsou announced in a telegram that his father was dying, and the next day a telephone call confirmed the death. From Lausanne, Geneva, Grenoble, Lyon, and Bienne, day by day, Jacob sent letters of condolence and sorrow to René and his mother, while being hauled by car from one city to another, and rehearsing the show, performing, and entertaining admirers at receptions. Between these exhausting forays they had only a few days to rest in Lausanne before taking to the road again.

Jacob was truly pained at Émile Dulsou's death and worried about its effects on René. He feared the young man didn't yet have the "armor" he needed for life.[128] He felt guilty at amusing himself and sightseeing while René and his mother grieved.[129] "My son, don't give way to grief," he advised, and, oddly, "Keep your feet warm." He feared that the family might become poor, and he vowed to work to support them.[130]

At the same time, Jacob was proving a success on the stage. He had been acting for years in cafés and drawing rooms: now he was doing it professionally. He loved the curtain calls. He'd been called back four times, he boasted, describing how he swept off his hat to bow, then held it to his heart or stretched out away from his body. He performed in a black suit, a pink shirt, a colorful tie, and a white scarf, and he held a cane: his act sounds a bit Chaplinesque. But the lectures were pure Jacob—a medley of reminiscences of Montmartre and Montparnasse, evocations of his famous comrades and the birth of modern art. From Switzerland and Grenoble, the troupe blazed its way south to Nîmes, Perpignan, Montpellier, Béziers, and Toulouse. The cabaret singer Charles Trenet, a friend, came all the way from Paris to Perpignan to watch the show.[131]

In March, Hubert Fabureau published his book *Max Jacob, son oeuvre* (Max Jacob's Achievement). It contributed to Jacob's fame, but it was an unpleasant work, highly anecdotal, stressing the poet's Jewishness in a patronizing way. Ostensibly, however, it treated Jacob as a major French writer. Thus consecrated, Jacob had barely time to catch his breath in Paris after his tour when he and Pierre Colle moved to a new apartment, a large studio at 17 rue Saint-Romain in the sixth arrondissement, and then he set off for more lectures, this time on his own.

Dulsou stayed in Paris that spring, and he and Jacob saw a lot of each other. From Angers, in May, where Jacob gave a lecture at the Catholic University, he wrote Dulsou a long, novelistic letter, describing the trip, his hosts, and a reunion with the novelist Louis Guilloux. Jacob concluded with a greeting that sounded a note of danger: "Friendly regards to Jean Le Louët, whom I like in spite of his laugh the other night."[132]

JACOB HAD OCCASIONALLY been troubled by Dulsou's frivolity. Early in the affair, he asked why René had "no profound moral ambition." "Your life has no purpose," he pointed out. "Are you going to remain a pretty little witty gentleman who gads around in automobiles, shines in conversation and yacks about the latest movies?"[133] From time to time Jacob renewed these admonitions. But on the whole he smothered his worries. His passion was mingled with guilt at leading the boy astray.[134] And like any older lover, he was painfully aware of the difference in their ages—a quarter of a century, in this case. Still, he had enough to offer, in celebrity, devotion, and sheer fun, that he believed in the stability of this love and in Dulsou's essential goodness.

The scales fell from Jacob's eyes at the end of June. Dulsou was in love with Le Louët. Worse, speaking to Le Louët, he sneered at Jacob and at his work. This scene took place by telephone, when Jacob overheard Dulsou talking to the new boyfriend. Jacob broke off the affair in a furious letter, with this message scrawled over the top of the page: "You will receive no more letters from me. *You can rest assured.* This is the last one." He listed his grievances: Dulsou constantly preferred tennis or card games or the company of little assholes to being with him; he had sacrificed the heart of an artist by denigrating his work; he resented Jacob's interest in his life, whereas Jacob was entirely devoted to him. From now on, Jacob's door would be closed to him.[135]

It was one thing to claim not to love anymore; it was quite another to tear such a love out of his heart by the roots. Jacob felt almost anni-hilated by Dulsou's treachery. For the young man to have another affair was normal, and Jacob had trained himself to expect it. But to degrade the love they had shared was unpardonable. To Paulhan, three weeks later, Jacob wrote that he felt like a poisoned rat. He was living alone; he had "liquidated all the traitors, spies, ungrateful monsters and thieves" who surrounded him. (This must have meant people like the du Plantiers and perhaps the Merle de Beauforts, who were also friends of Dulsou's and who must have seen Dulsou's affair with Le Louët developing.)[136]

Nor did Jacob tear Dulsou out of his heart. Paris had become intoler-able. In August he made another quick trip to lecture in Lausanne. From that picturesque landscape ("mountains like waves"), he wrote his new friend, Jean Fraysse, who was launching the journal *Les Feux de Paris* and knew Dulsou, that he would appreciate news of René.[137] From Lau-sanne, he also wrote René's cousin, the sculptor René Iché, curtly, that he didn't know where René was and no longer saw him.[138] In October he wrote Madame Dulsou a dignified explanation of his rupture with her son.[139] When the poet Henri Vandeputte, who had known him for years, published a flattering article about him, Jacob replied that he no longer recognized his own face in that portrait.[140] The experience with Dulsou had shattered him.[141]

PICASSO, TOO, WAS in crisis. Olga had long since discovered his romance with Marie-Thérèse. Though humiliated and furious, she put up with the adultery for several years when she saw that the girl had no ambition to replace her as the legitimate wife.[142] But now that Marie-Thérèse was preg-nant and Picasso wanted to leave this unhappy marriage, Olga refused to grant a divorce: a fortune, a château, and vast publicity would be involved in the crack-up. Olga moved out with Paulo, leaving Picasso alone in the apartment on the Rue La Boétie.[143] At this moment when the edifice of his life was toppling, Picasso turned to his oldest French friend, Max Jacob, and invited him to join him in a bachelors' household. Jacob replied to his "brother Pablo" that he was touched by the invitation, but he couldn't accept. Picasso had too much influence over him. Nor would Jacob tolerate it when another lady friend entered the picture—as one inevitably would—and he would either have to put up with her or leave. He had heard that Picasso was writing and expressed interest in seeing it.[144] (The faithful friend who did come to tend to Picasso was Jaime Sabartés, who didn't mind playing the role of attendant and courtier.)

TO ESCAPE PARIS, Jacob spent several weeks in September renting a room on the outskirts of the capital from a couple named Moré who didn't even know why he'd been given the Légion d'honneur.[145] He was looking for peace in which to work on a new commission, he explained to Jean Fraysse, a preface for a book about his old friend the art dealer Paul Guillaume. Guillaume had died the year before, and his widow, Juliette, wanted to secure his reputation and her own position with this work.[146] The real reason for Jacob's hiding in Boussy-Saint-Antoine was to avoid the horror of Paris.

That horror was compounded on October 9, the day Maurice Sachs's roman à clef *Alias* appeared, with its portrait of Jacob as César Blum, the lascivious hypocritical Jew. Just the year before, Jacob and Sachs had exchanged affectionate letters; Jacob thought they had "a solid friendship."[147] It's hard to imagine why the Nouvelle Revue Française would have published such a book, or why Paulhan would have permitted it. But Paulhan didn't run the Nouvelle Revue Française by himself, and Gide, who was the power there, protected Sachs these days. If they thought they would make money on Sachs's nasty gossip, they were disappointed. The book received only one minuscule review, a contemptuous dismissal in the very pages of *La Nouvelle Revue française:* perhaps Paulhan's way of defending Jacob was to assign the book to a reviewer he could count on to be hostile. Sachs never forgave him.[148]

The critical review was no comfort to Jacob, who now felt monstrously betrayed. He had loved Sachs even more devotedly than he loved Dulsou;

he had supported and defended him for years. He fled to Quimper. He burrowed in there, working on the Guillaume memoir and turning to God. He wrote Liane about his flight from a city where he'd been "robbed, robbed, insulted in speech and in writing (read Maurice Sachs's book *Alias*)," a city where he'd been abandoned "without a protector, without a friend, (except poor Pierre Colle)."[149]

In Quimper, he learned of the death of his scholarly cousin, Sylvain Lévi. He had suffered enough now to feel remorse for the insolent way he'd treated the old man, and he wrote his widow, Désirée Bloch Lévi, that he hadn't passed a day of his painful life without thinking of Sylvain with "the greatest affection"; he asked God's blessing on her children and grandchildren (without specifying which God).[150] He confessed his remorse to Kahnweiler (who wrote consolingly that both he and Picasso thought he shouldn't take on so, and that Lévi had never "recognized your importance").[151] Holed up with his family, he listened with growing dread to the news on the radio, afraid of war.[152]

And he continued to grieve over Dulsou, sending René's mother a message for her son: that despite René's hatred, he (Jacob) hoped he would find what he desired, a true path and success.[153] To Fraysse, he predicted that Le Louët would soon experience his own heartbreak when René dropped him.[154]

IN THIS SEASON, Jacob turned even more urgently to God, sneaking out of the family house in his stocking feet for early morning mass.[155] He was comforted by old friendships (Paulhan, Liane, the Kahnweiler clan with Leiris and Lascaux), and new ones (Jean Fraysse, Raymond Queneau). In July, Paulhan had asked him for prose poems for *Mesures*, a new journal he was helping to edit. Jacob provided twenty-one "mystical poems" dedicated to Louis Massignon, the scholar of Islamic mysticism. Human love, Jacob now believed, would only disappoint. In these poems he recalled his God on the wall and addressed Him. "I'm the witness of the Invisible," he exclaimed. "Burn my body to destroy the love in it, the ashes will move to trace Your Name."[156] He would devote his last years to this vision.

Part V

CHAPTER 19

SAINT-BENOÎT, AGAIN

I.

J acob's family hardly made him feel at home in Quimper. In early January 1936, disoriented, fearful, he cleared his desk, packed his trunk, and tied his manuscripts in bundles, preparing to return to Paris, the city where he now experienced only shame and despair.[1] Would Le Louët and du Plantier, Dulsou's friends, even want to see him? he asked Jean Fraysse. He took the train on January 4, moving back in with the faithful Pierre Colle on the Rue Saint-Romain. For the next several months he braved the capital, often not opening the door to visitors and not using the telephone, the instrument of Dulsou's betrayal.[2] The Merle de Beauforts did break with him, the husband forbidding his wife to communicate with him. (She wrote him in secret.)[3] Saint-Benoît began to seem the only possible refuge.

Inwardly, Jacob's last years would prove a time of healing and restoration. As he absorbed the loss of René Dulsou, his energy flowed into friendships with new young poets and one young painter. These were generous attachments, untainted by lust and disappointment: Jacob was at last growing into the experience of love as *philia*, not *eros*. Reintegrated into the parish of Saint-Benoît, he began to live his faith as a communal as well as a private daily practice, engaging fully in the rituals of the Church. He started each day by helping the priest serve mass in the dark, chilly basilica at six-thirty a.m., and he threw himself into the life of the village: baptisms, first communions, weddings, funerals, and church excursions.

His writing began to take the form of daily religious meditations that he often sent to friends. The outside world, meanwhile, blundered toward war and chaos.

||

JACOB METABOLIZED HIS grief for Dulsou in three quite different poems, all with similar titles, written in Quimper in the autumn of 1935. He sent "Buried Love" to the young Egyptian poet Edmond Jabès in 1935, entitled "Cain and Abel" in the draft; of these three poems mourning Dulsou, it's the one that most obviously fantasizes revenge, displaced into animal fables.[4] A related poem, "Novel of Buried Love" adopts a gentler tone, presenting the beloved—as Jacob almost always did—disguised as female, here draped in medieval robes. *Amour phosphorescent* (phosphorescent love) rhymes with *mort récent* (recently dead) as Jacob meditates the experience with Dulsou, its radiance, and its abrupt conclusion.[5]

The work of mourning took yet another shape in the third poem of buried love, which Jean Fraysse published in January in *Les Feux de Paris*. In a double metaphor, the lover "undresses himself" from the waters of his love as if from a garment, and describes directly the youthful body he has lost:

> I forget the long secrets of your little ear,
> your childish smile, mayfly I daren't kiss,
> your eyelids blinded by my lips.[6]

||

HOWEVER DISCREETLY HE hid on the Rue Saint-Romain, Jacob couldn't ignore the political upheavals around him. On February 13 the Socialist deputy Léon Blum was beaten bloody by an anti-Semitic mob as he left the Chamber of Deputies.[7] Three days later the city was engulfed in a massive demonstration of the allied Leftist parties that made up Blum's Front Populaire. Pierre Colle, who had by now established his own art gallery with Maurice Renou, was showing Picasso's drawings at just this time; when Jacob wrote the painter to praise the "enormous power" of his art, he remarked that the gallery wasn't crowded: the riot was elsewhere.[8]

Thanks to Julien Lanoë, three of Jacob's gouaches were now exhibited along with paintings by Bonnard, Braque, Picasso, and Laurencin in a show in the Museum of Nantes, where Lanoë was the president of the Friends of the Museum. Lanoë's journal, *La Ligne de coeur*, had folded in 1928, and Lanoë was occupied raising a large family and running his family's company buying and selling metals. But he stayed actively concerned with literature; he wrote reviews for *La Nouvelle Revue française*, encouraged young poets, and remained a stalwart friend of Jacob's. Through his good offices, the museum not only showed Jacob's paintings in 1936 but bought one for the permanent collection.[9] As Jacob rebuilt his world after the catastrophe of Dulsou, Lanoë emerged as one of the main figures of loyal decency.

To fund the move back to Saint-Benoît, Jacob accepted an invitation from the cabaret theater Les Noctambules. Once again he performed a version of his legendary self. This time he didn't lecture on art or narrate memoirs. Instead, he peered into the audience and introduced himself: "Ladies and Gentlemen, you don't know me. Nobody knows me. But I'm in the *Larousse*." Then he read letters from *Le Cabinet noir*, bits of *Le Cornet à dés*, and lyric poems. He was a hit. Here was the old Max who had danced on tabletops in Montmartre, and the director signed him on for an extra week. With his natural ebullience, he made friends with the popular singer Marianne Oswald, whose act followed his each night.[10]

But the performances exhausted him, and he was tired of playing the clown. His mind was set on Saint-Benoît. He needed to flee Paris, give up publishing, and give up seeing his friends—the one heartbreak about leaving the city, he wrote René Lacôte, a tubercular young poet he had known and encouraged since 1934, now in a sanatorium.[11] As he tore up his roots in the capital for the last time, he felt wretched, writing Cingria that he was unworthy to see him—but invited him to visit "with compassion for my weakness."[12] As so often, Jacob in these weeks suffered from a painful rift between his inner sense of self and his social persona: inwardly wounded and ashamed, he had just won acclaim on the stage, and eleven of his poems, all from *Visions infernales,* appeared that spring in the august *Anthologie des poètes de La Nouvelle Revue française* with a preface by Valéry.[13]

But more than anything, leaving Paris meant cutting his last ties—however spectral—with René Dulsou. In late March he asked Fraysse to lure the boy to a gathering by telling him that Le Louët and du Plantier would be there, without mentioning Jacob. There's no evidence that Fraysse obliged or that Dulsou came.[14] Jacob also patched things up with Marc du Plantier and his wife, inviting them to his show at the Noctambules and thanking them for pardoning his rage at Dulsou.[15] He asked du Plantier to organize a lunch where he could see René, and when this didn't work, he begged him to arrange one last meeting—"if only for a moment," adding in a hardly convincing postscript that he had for René now only "the most benevolent, paternal, and gently sorrowful feelings."[16]

Nor did he obtain this last glimpse.

On May 4 the Front Populaire won a definitive victory in the national legislative elections, and Léon Blum was poised to become the first Socialist prime minister of France and the first Jew to occupy that position. On May 25, Jacob moved out of Paris for good, leaving one last message for Dulsou with Fraysse: "Amitiés."[17]

II.

JACOB REENTERED SAINT-BENOÎT in grim conditions. He wasn't welcome in either the presbytery or the monastery: the *curé* didn't want him because he received too many guests and smoked, and the presbytery itself had lost its charm, now hemmed in by tourist billboards and the *curé*'s hideous new garage.[18] Jacob took lodgings in the local hotel run by an antipathetic couple, the Roberts. "My aureole has fallen into a ditch," he told Nino Frank.[19] He inhabited two bare whitewashed rooms in a one-story annex in the back, its windows opening onto a dreary courtyard and another garage. His finances were so tight, he could afford only one meal a day at the hotel. "I live in a bistro-hotel," he wrote François de Gouy, and to

Nino Frank he described the fire of damp wood and said he hoped to leave the house soon. He would stay there for four years.[20]

"Here lies Max Jacob," he wrote Pierre Colle, "dead on the field [of battle], in the fields, in song" (*mort au champ, aux champs, au chant*).[21] He told Paulhan, in a letter headed "Saint-Benoît s/Loire (forever)," that he was buying a grave plot in the village cemetery and had made his will. From the monastery he retrieved old boxes of letters he had left behind in 1928; it was like opening coffins, finding the signatures of old friends and lovers—some of them now enemies. (He had Sachs principally in mind, one imagines.)[22] But he didn't need the written record to stimulate his memory; his own sense of the past was heavy enough.[23] His last years in Paris now seemed to him crazy and stupid, and in this penitential mood he unpacked his books, pinned his gouaches to the walls of the Hôtel Robert, and set to work correcting the proofs of *Morceaux choisis* (Selected Works).[24] "I came here to work," he told Raymond Queneau, writing to compliment him on his new novel, *Derniers jours* (Last Days), whose hero steals a copy of *Le Cornet à dés;* "But it's the inner life one needs to change, not the *décor.*"[25]

For over a year, Jacob had been laboring half-heartedly on the preface for a book about the art dealer Paul Guillaume he had promised Guillaume's widow. Because Fraysse had an interest in the book and proposed to publish excerpts, Jacob kept him informed about his progress (and his lagging). But he complained along the way to other friends, especially Moricand and Kahnweiler. In the quiet of Saint-Benoît, he trudged forward with the account and brought it to a close in January 1937.[26] Jacob had helped Guillaume start his business back in 1915. But the text he produced had nothing to do with Guillaume. Jacob turned the assignment into a Cubist memoir, an intricately fractured, nonchronological, private tribute to Picasso, Apollinaire, and Salmon.[27] In its pages, initiates recognized descriptions of Apollinaire's enormous laugh; Marinetti roaring around in his sports car; the Baroness d'Oettingen serving her poor artist friends roast beef sandwiches; and Picasso brandishing his revolver. Jacob portrayed the fervor of the prewar avant-garde and its crash in the still-resonating Great War.[28]

||

JACOB CONCEIVED HIS second retreat to Saint-Benoît as a withdrawal from "the world." He arrived, he told Edmond Jabès, in a state of exasperation, and in that state he fired off a furious letter to the Egyptian poet; Jabès seemed to take him for a placement bureau or agent and contacted him only when he needed a favor. Jabès had sent him poems, asking for help with publication; what rankled was the young man's claim not to have time to write a letter. "I don't have time to write either," retorted Jacob. (But he sent the poems anyway to Fraysse for *Les Feux de Paris*.)[29] A few days later he apologized.

This new retreat was hardly solitary. Within a few weeks, he started making friends in Orléans, where he bought painting supplies and browsed in bookstores, and in the smaller town of Montargis he came to know several doctors, one of whom, the Hungarian Jew Robert Szigeti, would become a mainstay of his last years. And it was in Montargis that he made friends with the intellectual hatmaker Marcel Béalu, who wrote poems and novels. (Jacob mentioned Béalu in a letter to Paulhan in October 1936; in the next year Béalu and his wife Marguerite became a kind of extended family for him, carrying him off once a week for excursions in their car and for overnight visits in Montargis.)[30]

Parisian friends also began finding their way to Saint-Benoît. In the summer, Jean Fraysse came almost every Sunday, and in early August he visited for several days accompanied by the enterprising young poet Roger Lannes, the novelist Pierre Lagarde, and the painter Jean Oberlé.[31] At the end of August Fraysse and Lannes returned and stayed for a week. Lagarde, who had known Jacob since 1932, wrote up his visit in a sentimental article for *Comoedia* presenting the poet meditating under the plane trees, no longer wearing the uniform of a Parisian dandy (monocle and rings) but dressed as a peasant in a Breton beret, rough velvet trousers, a black vest, and spectacles. (Jacob found Lagarde irritating and complained that his guest had bothered him for two weeks, pumping him for stories about the village and showing "insolent disregard" for anything that didn't fit the story he wanted to tell.)[32]

Of the young men now hovering around Jacob, Lannes was one of the most coldly manipulative. He had made Jacob's acquaintance in Paris in 1934; Jacob in turn introduced him to Cocteau, and Lannes, quick to seize opportunities, joined Fraysse and Le Louët in a vague orbit around Cocteau, but for a few years he kept close to Jacob as well. His diary shows that he approached literary life like a business plan. On November 16, 1934, on his second visit to Jacob, he noted with impatience that the master, dressing for an evening out, feigned disorder, needed help, was "affected, sincere, pleasant, charming, and ironic." Lannes had been unable to bring up his own requests. Perhaps sensing his visitor's ambition, Jacob had just been teasing. A month later he persuaded Robert Denoël to dedicate a whole issue of *L'Année poétique* to Lannes's poems, and he wrote the preface for them. In 1938 he would enlist Denoël for the publication of Lannes's novel. Lannes duly recorded all these interventions in his diary. (And when in 1939 Jacob declined an invitation to travel to Paris to participate in an evening celebrating him, Lannes just as carefully recorded that he'd "communicated his displeasure" to Jacob—from whom he then distanced himself, drawing closer to Cocteau and his new lover, the young actor Jean Marais.)[33]

By September, Jacob had so many visits, he needed an escape from his escape, and he accepted the invitation from an admirer, Hughes Panassié, to hide in his château for two months.[34]

Along with friends who turned up physically in the village, Jacob maintained his usual bustle of social life in letters. In this period he drew close to the Swiss astrologer Conrad Moricand, whom he'd known as a rich boy dabbling in the arts back in Montparnasse. Moricand had lost his fortune and had had to sell his town house in Paris; he had retreated to a dingy hotel in Pigalle, awash in self-pity, trying to make a living by selling horoscopes. Ever generous, Jacob sent him clients and even asked Paulhan if "poor Moricand" couldn't write an astrological chronicle for *La Nouvelle Revue française*. Paulhan's answer: no.[35] (Two of Moricand's best clients were Anaïs Nin and Henry Miller.) With Moricand,

Jacob could expatiate on his occult beliefs so frowned on by the Church. "Saturn is in Aries!!" Jacob warned on January 5, 1936. "Misfortune for France, England, Palestine, the Jewish people."[36] The two men kept up an intense correspondence for the rest of Jacob's life and collaborated on a fanciful book about astrology (not published until 1949, with Moricand—persona non grata in France since the war—signing as Claude Valence). Dr. Szigeti, when he met Moricand, judged him "ignoble," and others who had dealings with the astrologer—including Henry Miller—eventually became troubled by his pathological egotism (even without knowing of his pedophilia). But Jacob overlooked Moricand's more repulsive qualities and honored his astral expertise and fallen elegance. It may have been easier to sustain the friendship since he hardly ever saw him. In letters, he confided about the interpretation of dreams, astrological predictions, the Kabbalah, and the value of suffering; he chatted about his daily life; he advised Moricand on survival.[37]

Jacob nursed happier epistolary friendships with the poets René Lacôte and Edmond Jabès and the novelist Raymond Queneau. He had known Lacôte since 1934 in Paris, when the twenty-one-year-old sent him a copy of his first book of poems. Jacob had encouraged him; now cooped up in a Swiss sanatorium being treated for tuberculosis, Lacôte needed encouragement more than ever. Jacob sent letters predicting his recovery (correctly, in this case), criticizing poems and poets, and relaying anecdotes. In August he sent him a copy of *Saint Matorel,* the three Matorel books Gallimard had just gathered into one volume. Replying to Lacôte's appreciation, Jacob described the state of "passive receptivity" in which he had composed the first Matorel narrative in the surge of inspiration following his apparition, and he prodded Lacôte to trust his own inspirations. In his friend's poems he found symbols from "the very Sacred Land of dreams," a testament to Jacob's real faith in a Christianized occult from which his poetry sprang.[38]

After their contretemps in June, Jacob and Jabès steadied their friendship and kept it on an even keel in letters until war broke out—Jabès and his wife safe in Alexandria, Jacob more and more at risk in Saint-Benoît. Jacob was his only master, Jabès has said. Before their first meeting in Paris in 1935, Jabès had sent Jacob a manuscript of poems. Facing the young aspirant as they sat together, Jacob tore it up and dropped the shreds in the wastebasket. "So they won't bother us," he said. "Now we can begin."[39] His letters to Jabès abound in pedagogy, and as an old man Jabès could still recite the lessons. *Cut away, concentrate*, Jacob kept urging. *Find the essential emotion.* "There where there's unfathomable depth, I mean the word that comes from a man's very entrails, there's beauty," he declared. "Otherwise it's just arty knickknacks."[40] But he also warned against mere sincerity: it wasn't enough. Use concrete words: *table, chair, tongs.*[41] *Your poems feel too easy*, he warned; they're like "<u>lyric impressions jotted down day by day</u>" (underlined). "Do you think, spoiled child of the sun, that poetry turns up the ace of hearts like love? Double or nothing? For great poets, poetry has been research into suffering."[42]

At times, the acolyte felt almost crazed by the advice. When Jabès composed a poem of 120 pages, he sent one copy to a renowned critic, another to Jacob. The critic replied first, accepting many of the sections for the journal he edited. Four days letter Jacob's letter arrived. "You're on the wrong track," he admonished. "It's not good, not good at all." "This guy is going to make me insane!" Jabès burst out, and he replied, nettled, that the elder hadn't understood. Jacob wrote back at once, humbly, saying, "The young are always right, go ahead." But the more Jabès considered his manuscript, the more fault he found with it. He withdrew it from the journal and burned it, writing to Jacob that he had made "a splendid funeral" for the poem. Jacob wrote back that he "knew those funerals."[43] It would take the horrors of the war and Jabès's exile as a Jew from Egypt in 1956 for him to find the sources of his own suffering. By then, Jacob's lesson had ripened within him, and with *Je bâtis ma demeure: Poèmes 1943–1957* (I Built My Dwelling: Poems 1943–1957), Jabès emerged as one of the towering writers in French of the twentieth century.

ONE OF THE most promising of Jacob's new friends was René Guy Cadou, a sixteen-year-old in Nantes who wrote to Jacob in July 1936.[44] The blue-eyed, curly-haired adolescent was the son of a provincial schoolmaster, and his sensibility was formed by village life in the Brière region on the

Atlantic coast, just south of Brittany. His father had moved from the hamlet where Cadou was born to positions in the nearby larger towns, Saint-Nazaire and then Nantes. It was while wandering in the streets of Nantes that the boy stumbled on an obscure bookshop and made friends with the lanky proprietor with tobacco-stained fingers, the poet Michel Manoll. At twenty-five, Manoll was an elder. They adopted each other. From Manoll, Cadou absorbed an education in poetry and, as Manoll put it solemnly, an idea of his "responsibilities as a poet." This meant devouring poetry of the past but also seizing on new work, most prominently the work of Max Jacob. Manoll was a sentimentalist, and his book about Cadou—who died at thirty-one—drips with embarrassing effusions.[45] Cadou had the intelligence to make Manoll's reading list his own while avoiding his kitsch. In Manoll's store he met Julien Lanoë (known as "the Jean Paulhan of Nantes"). When Cadou wrote Jacob in 1936, he received immediate encouragement: "Find your heart and change it into an inkwell."[46]

III.

THE ALLIED FORCES pulled out of the Rhineland in 1930, five years earlier than the Treaty of Versailles had specified. On March 7, 1936, Hitler's troops marched in. France didn't respond. The next month Léon Blum's left-wing coalition, the Front Populaire, swept the national elections, and on June 6, Blum was sworn in as prime minister with an ambitious program of social and economic reform: public works, a grain board, pensions, expanded unemployment benefits—all calculated to lift the country from Depression. (Surprisingly, most of Blum's reforms would survive in the conservative governments that followed.) In early June strikes broke out across the country, and workers occupied factories, while antidemocratic militias marched and threatened. Blum's reforms met many of the workers' demands, and he disbanded one of the most aggressive of the right-wing groups, Colonel de la Rocque's Croix de Feu. But the country had been rubbed so raw by economic crisis and ideological conflict that the reforms, while easing distress, also stirred furious opposition. One deputy, Xavier Vallat, expressed the views of many fellow citizens when he fulminated that "this ancient Gallo-Roman country will be governed . . . by a Jew."[47]

On June 10, 1936, Jacob sent Fraysse a letter with the heading "Saint-Benoît s/Loire (azure, flowers, sun, little birds, absolute silence)." Commenting on the political turmoil, the conservative Jacob crowed, "What good luck the Communists are in power! They're the ones who stopped the strikes!!" (He was needling Fraysse, who had a position in the Ministry of the Interior.)[48] What he hadn't yet taken in was that France, "governed by a Jew," was about to be engulfed in a wave of newly roiled anti-Semitism. In November the urbane Daniel-Henri Kahnweiler suddenly discovered that politically "he was a Jew."[49] Max Jacob discovered it in October.

Since Jouhandeau's marriage in 1929, he and Jacob had been drifting apart, Jouhandeau more and more absorbed in battles with his wife and Jacob often away from Paris. They kept writing friendly (if sometimes prickly) letters, however. But the days of mutual confession and consolation had long since vanished. In 1928, Jouhandeau had contributed to the special issue of *Le Mail* a small piece celebrating Jacob's mysterious faith, pondering his friend's claim that if he'd sinned, the next day before dawn he followed the Stations of the Cross on his knees, sobbing, beating his breast, making such a scene that "in the end, God is tricked."[50] In 1928, Jouhandeau found this little drama intensely moving, "a desperate and ravished tenderness," a more serious engagement with God than most Christians were willing to risk.

Jacob was at Panassié's château when he read Jouhandeau's article "How I Became an Anti-Semite" in the October 8, 1936, issue of *Action française*. It reveals much about the condition of France that this heinous piece by an eminent novelist should have been published and considered normal. Vicious, explicit anti-Semitism was not a fringe movement in 1936. Jouhandeau described how he came to the revelation that Jews were "the worst enemy of my country," and to illustrate, he presented three exemplary odious Jews. The first two, Maurice Sachs and "the Jew Benda," he named. The third, unnamed, was Max Jacob.

Jouhandeau had loathed Sachs for years. It was not difficult to do: Sachs was loathsome. But Jouhandeau made him a representative of the entire Jewish people. After describing a scene in which Sachs disgraced himself in company, Jouhandeau attacked the intellectual Julien Benda, in particular a recent article by Benda in which the author honored his Jewish forebears for their attachment to France—an attachment that was principled, not "instinctive, carnal, irrational." Jouhandeau seized on that phrase as evidence that no Jew could truly be a patriot. "M. Blum, M. Benda, and M. Sachs are not from my home and they've made themselves at home here," snarled Jouhandeau. He concluded with the most damning case: the Jew who pretended to be Christian. "I still hear him whispering in my ear (after his contortions), 'And in the end, God is tricked.' " All Jews should be escorted to Palestine, he said: "I vow to point them out to the vengeance of my people, as long as a single one remains in France who has not been subjected to a special legal status."[51] The Vichy government would soon oblige.

Jacob was shocked. For at least a decade, he and Jouhandeau had been literary brothers. To Marcel Moré, in late November, Jacob wrote that he'd considered answering the attack but judged it futile. In this letter, he addressed Jouhandeau's accusations point by point: as for "contortions" and "tricking God," they consisted in serving mass at six a.m. in a freezing church while Jouhandeau was curled up cozily in bed. For once, Jacob identified himself as a Jew: "It's we [the Jews] who invented the religion of suffering. . . . Let's learn to suffer with the grandeur implicit in the high destiny of our people," he underlined. He was ready to be martyred as a Jew *and* as a Catholic. Only in his postscript did the anger burst out: the Jewish tradition was far older than Jouhandeau's, this little renegade peasant seminarian and religious *nouveau riche*.[52] But it was to Paulhan, also Jouhandeau's publisher, that he revealed his pain most directly: he sensed around him such an atmosphere of mockery that he felt "paralyzed" (underlined), and was afraid to publish. He developed further the idea of Jewish suffering as a special destiny, "the sugar that preserves."[53]

IV.

JACOB DID FEEL paralyzed by Jouhandeau's assault. He was dead to the world, he announced to correspondents. Perhaps he even believed what he told Nino Frank, that the newspapers had orders not to speak of him.[54] (In a few years, under Vichy, it would be true.) But this season produced two major publications, albeit of earlier work, and the small essay "The Purge" for the Catholic journal *La Revue doloriste*. Into the essay, composed before the blow from Jouhandeau, he condensed years of idiosyncratic meditation on Christianity. Because human beings needed to be "purged" of their impurities, suffering was God's greatest gift. And what God wanted, Jacob argued, was "you yourself." This thesis was a far cry from his earlier Modernist fancy of a dispersed and multiple self but was its logical complement: to survive the fractured self in time, some core being needed to be acknowledged. For Jacob, this acknowledgment came in the image of Christ's suffering and love, the union of earth and heaven, human and divine.[55]

Gallimard's combined edition of the Matorel books came out in July 1936, dedicated to Picasso, "For what I know he knows, for what he knows I know." Jacob had been living imaginatively in this past friendship for years, lecturing on it and most recently writing about it in the Guillaume preface. Reviewers hardly noticed this landmark Modernist book. But on January 1, 1937, Picasso himself stepped out of the past, turning up unannounced in Saint-Benoît accompanied by his chauffeur, his sixteen-year-old son, and someone Jacob described as "a pretty Etruscan lady" (Dora Maar). Picasso said, "It's New Year's Day. Whom should I see, if not family?" "You're mistaken," replied Jacob. "It's the Day of the Dead." But he scurried out to the local shops to rustle up food for dinner, which they ate in Jacob's rooms at the Hôtel Robert under a barrage of teasing from Picasso. At midnight, the painter proposed to carry Jacob back to Paris to live with him. And once again, Jacob refused. As he explained to Salmon, he couldn't tolerate the Surrealists and Communists around his old friend. So they parted.[56]

Jacob's *Morceaux choisis* came out in late November 1936, selected by Paul Petit, Jacob's host at the French embassy in Rome and now a diplomat in Denmark. The book gives a sense of the sweep of Jacob's production, from the early nonsense poems and *Le Cornet à dés* and a generous ladling from *La Défense de Tartufe* and *Le Laboratoire central,* through the later books, including the beautiful poem "Agonies and More" from *Fond de l'eau* and a lot of the Morven poems. The last section featured prose from *Cinématoma, Le Cabinet noir,* and even extracts from the novels. In the preface, Petit called Jacob "the living and comforting symbol of inextinguishable poetry."[57] Jacob must have felt proud holding the volume in his hand, and he was perhaps surprised at the long list of titles of his other works on the first page, nine of them from the Nouvelle Revue Française. He had sometimes made fun of Petit, but he recognized now that the diplomat, who was also a serious scholar and translator of Kierkegaard, had done him a noble service. Petit's full nobility would be revealed a few years later in his acts of resistance to the Vichy regime. They would cost him his life.

||

DEAD TO THE world, Jacob was not. One person who made sure that he stayed visible was Julien Lanoë. In January, as president of the Friends of the Museum of Nantes, he asked Jacob to send gouaches for yet another exhibit. Jacob replied that he couldn't slap paintings together and mail them in fifteen days, but he proposed to lecture instead, so he stayed with Lanoë and his family and gave two talks on the same day, February 27, a marathon performance. The first, "Reflections on the Fine Arts: Thirty Years of Paintings," resembled his Swiss talks, a mixture of autobiography, art gossip, and serious presentation of the founding ideas of Modernism. Art should not be representational; a work of art should be a "general unity," not an assembly of details. Turning to poetry, he discussed "the unfathomable," the quotient of mystery that distinguishes the truly lyrical, quoting Nerval and Apollinaire. As with painting, representation is not the aim. After dinner, he delivered the second talk, on his pet subject, his mystical interpretation of Scripture.[58]

V.

ON THIS TRIP to Nantes, Jacob met the poet Michel Manoll with the tobacco-stained fingers, the proprietor of the little bookshop. His real name was Michel Laumonier. Jacob liked him but found him a bit listless and thought his poems sounded too much like Reverdy's. But the more he got to know him, the more he admired his seriousness and intelligence, and he felt for the man's poverty. Manoll was "a poet in his very marrow," he reported to Lacôte.[59] Manoll would soon emerge as one of the members of the École de Rochefort, a group including some of Jacob's new friends and a few older ones: Cadou, Béalu, Jean Rousselot, Maurice Fombeure, Émié, and Follain. Jacob wasn't particularly interested in groups, but he was always on the lookout for new talent, and these younger writers gathered around him in his last years, offering companionship, admiration, and scope for his pedagogy.

On the return from Nantes, Jacob paid a helter-skelter visit to Quimper, where he found his mother sadly weakened by age. He stopped to see the Benoistes in Kerpape and other friends in Angers; it's remarkable that he could travel at all, as storms battered the region and roads and fields were flooded.[60]

Back in Saint-Benoît, just as he was complaining to Moricand and to Liane that he was "disgusted by the world," a whole new horizon of friendship opened.[61] His old companion from *Philosophies,* the philosopher Henri Lefebvre, now teaching at a private high school in Montargis, wanted to invite Jacob to lecture. On a sunny Sunday in April, Lefebvre dragged a colleague from the school, the poet Henri Barrelle, and Marcel Béalu, the poetic haberdasher, and his wife, on an excursion to Saint-Benoît in the Béalus' tiny car, planning to leave his friends by the basilica while he consulted the penitent poet. But Jacob exploded the plan. Emerging with Lefebvre from the Hôtel Robert, he commandeered the day. They all piled into the car—Jacob wedged in front between Béalu and his wife—and they gallivanted off through the countryside, stopping to walk in a wooded park, and dining on the terrace of a restaurant in Gien. Jacob had never been close to Lefebvre, and Barrelle didn't interest him, but with the Béalus he struck up an immediate friendship. At the restaurant he acted out the characters from his *Bourgeois de France et d'ailleurs* with such energy that his hat fell off and rolled along the sidewalk. The evening concluded at the Béalus' house in Montargis with Jacob and Lefebvre arguing about Hegel. To make him feel even more at home, he discovered his own *Morceaux choisis* on the bookshelf next to Salmon's book about him. Marguerite made up a bed for him on the sofa. The young couple drove him back to Saint-Benoît the next afternoon after a torrent of literary conversation. From that day until the end of his life, he saw them almost every week.[62]

Brought up as a craftsman, Béalu now ran his own shop and employed others, a passionate autodidact. His poems, Jacob thought, had energy but "no taste, no aesthetic sense." He undertook to "spiritualize" and educate this new friend. They began exchanging letters almost daily; it's a mark of the strength of the friendship that Jacob allowed Béalu to challenge him. "You judge me!" he protested. "You judge me without knowing anything of my character"—and he described the austerity of his monk's life, insisting that he'd left everything behind: "success, money, love, the bare minimum of comfort."[63]

A month later Jacob met the other close friend of his last years when in Orléans, in the window of the art store where he bought his supplies, some brightly colored paintings caught his eye. They were by eighteen-year-old Roger Toulouse. As he had done on that consequential day at Vollard's gallery in 1901, Jacob left a note for the unknown artist. A day or so later the young man replied and came to see him in Saint-Benoît. Thus was born Jacob's last, intense artistic friendship. Roger Toulouse had been painting since boyhood and studied at the École des Beaux-Arts in Orléans. He had a long, narrow face, a straight nose, and full lips, and with his round dark eyes behind round spectacles, he had the look of a nineteenth-century intellectual. His painting was rapidly evolving from the Cubistic decorative exercises of his youth to the portraits and still lifes Jacob admired in the shop window: Expressionist work, delicately drawn, in the figurative mode of the École de Paris—shades of Pascin and Kisling.

Toulouse was hungry for guidance and for an opening into a larger world, Jacob for talented protégés. He advised Toulouse but also treated him as a colleague, someone with whom he could discuss technique as he himself began to focus more on painting than on poetry. Years later Toulouse spoke with awe of the eruption into his life of this astonishing mentor. They became friends instantly. Unlike Jacob's earlier tutorials, where flirtation muddied the instruction, his letters to Toulouse show a simple joy in the young man's gift and a desire to foster it. Within a week of their encounter, Jacob wrote him eloquently about "the inner life," the quality of constant attentiveness to the present moment it demanded: "Where am I? What's happening to me? A car passes, a child speaks to me, I'm in front of a house. . . . In this way, through attention, you'll enlarge the precious sensibility that is your fortune and your patient future. . . . Consider yourself a speck of the cosmos."[64]

But Jacob also shaped the young man's destiny in concrete ways. He introduced him to the Béalus, who befriended him and bought work; on his recommendation, Dr. Benoiste purchased a painting. Far more significantly, he sent the boy to Paris to meet Kahnweiler, Picasso, and Gertrude Stein. These giants received him kindly. Kahnweiler recommended him to Georges Maratier at the Galerie de Beaune; Maratier took him on, put his work in group shows, and gave him a one-man exhibition the following year. Stein traveled to Orléans to visit his studio and bought paintings. Jacob wrote Toulouse excitedly, "You don't realize that you've just been placed in the center of the universe."[65] And a few days later, of Stein, "Gertrude is the Louvre of the Moderns. I consider you *a success*." (But he warned him to continue his "disinterested explorations.")[66] To Béalu, Jacob wrote that Toulouse had met Picasso and Kahnweiler, "as much as to say, he's met the pope and the emperor."[67]

||

IF FRANCE WAS AGITATED, Spain had descended into civil war. Hostilities had broken out the year before, and now, on April 26, 1937, Hitler's Luftwaffe Condor Legion, supported by Mussolini's air force and coordinated by Franco's nationalist command, bombed the Basque town of

Guernica. The massive raid lasted all afternoon and into the evening, wave after wave, a shocking display of savagery. The town was almost entirely destroyed.

Action française had been reporting on the Spanish war since the beginning, in full sympathy with Franco. And André Salmon, who had worked as a journalist for twenty years for the right-wing *Le Petit Parisien*, was now its war correspondent in Spain, giving the nationalist slant. Guernica was far from Saint-Benoît, but soon enough Jacob would witness aftershocks from the assault.

In June 1937 he returned to Brittany for the summer. Staying with his family in Quimper, he found himself suddenly confronted by the Spanish war. Hundreds of refugees arrived each day by boat, to be housed by the local government in schools and in empty summer camps. Some slept on the ground. Many lacked shelter. Many were sick. There wasn't enough water or enough milk for baby bottles. Day after day, shocked by the suffering, Jacob made the rounds of the camps with the departmental medical officer, his friend Dr. Tuset. He was shocked, too, by the rapacity of some local merchants who profited from the emergency, selling supplies at exorbitant prices; but other Bretons and aid organizations offered "sublime charities." He also worried about the refugees' politics; according to the departmental prefect, there were Communists among them stirring up revolution; the police were keeping watch.[68] In later June and through July, at Dr. Benoiste's sanatorium at Kerpape, installed in a peaceful room by the sea studying Paul Vulliaud's tome on the Kabbalah, Jacob kept thinking about the refugees' plight. And he was anxious about politics. As a conservative Catholic, he was instructed to hate Communists and support Franco. Writing Salmon to compliment him on his new poems, he added that he'd quarreled with people about Franco and about Salmon's reporting.[69] He was uncomfortably aware that Picasso would take a very different view of the war. In this very month, July, Picasso's masterpiece, *Guernica,* was displayed in Paris at the Spanish pavilion of the International Exposition. A few months later Jacob heard that the painter had refused to shake hands with his old comrade Salmon.[70]

Back in Quimper for a few days at the end of July, Jacob relished once more the colorful folklore of his childhood: the old world paraded before his eyes, a procession of the faithful in the elaborate brocaded traditional costumes in which the Jacob store had specialized.[71] Stopping in Nantes on the way home to Saint-Benoît (but where was home? he was at home "nowhere, nowhere, nowhere"), he missed Lanoë, who was away on vacation, but found the tormented Manoll—"a born poet, a bundle of fibers, who will suffer much."[72] At Saint-Benoît he resumed his village sociabilities, enlivened by guests from the outside world: Pierre Lagarde and Michel Perrin came in August, Lanoë in October. And he made weekly excursions to Montargis to see the Béalus and Dr. Szigeti ("a Jewish doctor who looks like Titian's self-portrait, proud and so humble at the same time!").[73] With Béalu he had now established an intense tutorial, criticizing his poems, providing introductions to Parisian writers, warning him about the traps and illusions of literary life.[74]

And day by day, the miasma of hatred of Jews thickened. He couldn't give the lecture in Montargis that Lefebvre had requested, he told Lacôte, because his "situation as a converted Jew" required prudence. It was easy to be compromised or hated; some people were already shunning him because he had accepted an invitation to lunch at a Jewish lady's house. (The friendship with Szigeti somehow seemed to be immune.) "We live in a partisan era, and I just want to die in God, that's all."[75] The air was so poisoned, even reasonable people seemed infected. When Paulhan confessed to Jacob (with what degree of irony it's hard to tell) that he was afraid he was part Jewish, Jacob assured him—partly joking, partly not—that the Jews are a stiff-necked people while Paulhan's neck was flexible; Jews are brutal, Paulhan refined. Not a drop of Jewish blood in his veins, Jacob pronounced. Perhaps Spanish. In 1937 it was still possible to be flippant about such matters.[76]

VI.

IN NOVEMBER, JACOB returned to Paris to give the closing lecture at the "Mardis littéraires" of the International Exposition, staying with the

Béalus in Montargis the night before the trip. In the morning, after mass, he practiced his speech while shaving, gesturing in the air with his razor. "Poetry is an invented dream," he declared. (It would be the title of his address.) One must learn to find the mysterious center of one's being and translate it into the fiction, the "invented dream" of art. "But how to reconcile the lie with the sincerity that is the power of all great works?" he wondered, then interrupted himself to ask Béalu, "But come, Marcel, how do you manage to have such smooth cheeks?" while splashing himself with eau de cologne. Dr. Szigeti drove him to Paris and attended the talk. It was a solemn occasion, with Valéry presiding, and four other speakers. Only for Jacob did the audience rise in a standing ovation.[77] (Picasso's *Guernica* was the foremost work of art exhibited at the exposition, which was just closing. There's no record of Jacob's having seen it.)

A week later Michel Manoll dropped in at Saint-Benoît. He had closed his bookshop, he was ill, and Jacob wondered how he would support himself and his wife. But he was still publishing his little literary magazine, *Le Pain blanc:* one of Jacob's Morven poems, "The Little Thief," had appeared there in September.[78] "People should support poets," Manoll insisted in a letter; to which Jacob replied, "with a burst of laughter from the orchestra: Life will teach you otherwise."[79] As usual, Jacob tried to help, writing a doctor he knew in Nantes to see if he would treat Manoll, and arranging a visit to Dr. Szigeti. He and Manoll were with Szigeti in Montargis when a telegram arrived announcing that Jacob's mother was gravely ill. The doctor drove them to Saint-Benoît, where they dropped off Manoll (he would stay in Jacob's rooms, looking through his papers for poems); then Szigeti took Jacob to the train station in Orléans, Jacob weeping as they drove. He arrived in Quimper at midnight.[80]

For a week, the poet hovered at his mother's bedside, taking turns with Delphine and Gaston. His mother was groggy from morphine and opium, but she understood what was happening. "Ah yes! Madame Gagelin," she said, at the sight of her writer son. He was stricken when she added, "I didn't know you were so good."[81] "I hope my success has made you happy," the son almost pleaded. "I should be pleased," she replied, which he interpreted to mean that she was beyond caring.[82] He steadied himself, in this week of vigil, by working on a gouache that had been troubling him, three cows in a landscape. "I found my cows!" he reported to Szigeti.

His mother was emaciated, but her hands were swollen. Jacob wept in private while his sister Delphine cared for their mother with rough devotion and was rude to everyone. "Only the men in this family weep," she sneered. "She knows she won't last long," she declared in front of the dying woman. Horrified, Jacob wrote the Béalus to describe this "bourgeois death." "No drama, no crying out! My mother is failing. Nobody weeps, but what devotion and what good fires in the fireplace!"[83]

Prudence Jacob died at four a.m. on November 19. Jacob was with her, holding her hand, and feeling that she held his. Some sort of reconciliation seemed to occur. He was filled with remorse, thinking how hard he had made things for her. But he had the sense, too, that she was proud of him: she cared for glory, he told Jabès, and he had won some for her.[84]

The next few days were too flurried to allow much grieving: papers had to be signed at the town hall; the undertaker dealt with; the funeral arranged; neighbors notified; the citizens of Quimper trooped through the house to pay final respects to the old lady who had run the Jacob store for as long as anyone could remember. Jacob's old school friend Abel Villard attended the funeral with his son, and in a gesture that particularly touched Jacob, he stayed behind after the burial to speak privately with him.[85]

Jacob stopped briefly in Nantes to see Lanoë on his way back to Saint-Benoît. For weeks, in letters to all his friends, he wrote of his sorrow as he gradually took in the fact that Madame Gagelin could no longer disapprove of him. In the poem "Face," which he had sent to Lanoë in August, Jacob had imagined his own face at death, his multiple personae at last stabilized in God's love: "My lifelong studies they'll read on my face at death." It was his mother's final face he had now to contemplate.[86]

||

IN APRIL, ON his jaunt with the Béalus, Lefebvre, and Barrelle, Jacob had dressed as a dandy in Barrelle's flowing black cape and black fedora and struck a worldly pose for the photograph they took. Pleased with the picture, his young friends had copies made. Barrelle was a conservative Catholic. It was he, Béalu implied, who passed the photograph to *Occident*, the newspaper representing Franco's party in France. On Christmas Day 1937, Jacob's portrait appeared prominently at the top of a page across from a picture of Generalissimo Francisco Franco, with Jacob's poem "Suffering" in the center. A versification of Jacob's theology of suffering as a gift from God, "Suffering" must rank as one of his worst poems, pseudo-Vigny alexandrines hard to distinguish from pastiche. Béalu and Andreu were convinced that Jacob hadn't intended to contribute so publicly to Franco's cause; on the whole, he tried to avoid political quarrels, and he professed to be surprised, even disturbed, at the publication.[87] He knew it would jeopardize his relations with Picasso. But two months later he signed a manifesto of French intellectuals in support of Franco. Claudel had organized it, and as a loyal French Catholic, Jacob put his name to the document.[88] He described it carelessly to Roger Toulouse: "Someone asked me to sign a thingamajig for Franco. Claudel's name was on it. So I signed."[89] The least one can say is that, politically, Jacob was a complete naïf. And he did not yet understand the full meaning of suffering.

||

EVEN AS JACOB rooted himself more firmly in Saint-Benoît, he made several professional forays out of the region. In January 1938 he was invited to give the inaugural lecture at a show dedicated to Apollinaire at the Bibliothèque Sainte-Geneviève in Paris. By now an old hand at lecturing, Jacob was unprepared for the fiasco that broke out. The lecture, widely publicized, was attended of course by Apollinaire's old friends: Salmon, Picasso, Billy, and André Rouveyre. When Jacob declared—as he had done at Nantes—that Apollinaire's father was Madame de Kostrowitzky's lover, the gambler Jules Weil, Rouveyre stood up and protested; others vociferated; a very Parisian scandal erupted. To claim that Weil was Apollinaire's father was not only absurd in terms of timing (Weil being only a decade older than the poet); it offended the mythology surrounding the dead poet, who was rumored to be the son of a cardinal or even a pope.

Worse still, it insinuated that Apollinaire was part Jewish. Jacob had been able to pass off such a statement in the provinces. He couldn't get away with it in the capital.

It's odd that Jacob cared about the claim, but he stubbornly insisted upon it in the days and weeks that followed. On a long-ago visit to Le Vésinet, he had heard Madame Kostrowitzky introduce Monsieur Weil as the father of her sons, and he clung to this evidence. The controversy was reported in the press; even Paulhan mentioned it in *La Nouvelle Revue française*.[90] As late as 1943, Jacob told Belaval that he'd had "the misfortune to speak the truth about Apollinaire's birth" and had thereby made himself "one hundred mortal enemies, not to mention the scandal."[91]

He retreated to Saint-Benoît where he immediately had to give another speech, this one in honor of the *curé*. This talk, at least, provoked no protest. With relief, Jacob settled down in his two little rooms with his smoky wood fire, his letters, his daily written religious meditations, and his unfinished gouaches.[92]

He had been out of touch with Cocteau. The previous April, in a letter to Liane, he asked, "Cocteau? . . . And who is that?"[93] Cocteau, more and more afloat on opium, had been in some sense out of touch with himself. He had dropped Jean Desbordes and was occupied writing newspaper articles and plays to finance his drug habit. His profession now was being Jean Cocteau: a celebrity. As a sideshow he had managed the comeback of a talented black boxer, Al Brown. But for the past year he had come under the helpful influence of his new lover, Jean Marais. And now, in February 1938, he and Marais turned up in Montargis, of all places, at the imaginatively named Hôtel de la Poste, so Cocteau could buckle down and write yet another play, *Les Parents terribles*.

Roger Lannes, as part of Cocteau's entourage, drove to Saint-Benoît with Marais and the painter Josiah Adès to pick up Max Jacob.[94] Meeting at the hotel in Montargis, Jacob and Cocteau embraced each other; all their distance fell away. For a month, Jacob visited often, and in front of the dazzled provincials—Béalu, Toulouse, Dr. Szigeti—the two poets relived the old days and sparred in wit until midnight, when Cocteau expelled the audience. The doctor treated these evenings as research into "literary and artistic homosexuality." He was fascinated by this other world, free from the worries of family life—though he noted that Cocteau "worried" about how to replenish his supply of opium. He noted, too, how bits of conversation turned up later, transformed, in works of literary art. In one conversation in Cocteau's room, Jacob asked his old friend, "You still believe in pure hearts?" and, pointing to Dr. Szigeti, declared, "Just ask any country doctor." Szigeti later found the phrase transposed in Cocteau's play: "Just ask any country priest."[95] In a scene Marais never forgot, Jacob composed the actor's horoscope and warned him that he was a "Lorenzaccio" (the murderous hero of Alfred de Musset's romantic drama). Underlining the words twice in blue pencil, Jacob wrote, "Be careful not to commit murder." Marais thought this was a warning about theatrical roles, but during the Occupation, as he was preparing in earnest to go kill a journalist who had written viciously about Cocteau, Marais found Jacob's horoscope and changed his plan. Max Jacob, he thought, had saved his life.[96]

||

IN HIS CONSTANT exchange of letters with Moricand, Jacob urged the astrologer to convert to Catholicism. Over and over he tried to impress on his pagan friend the benefits to be derived from prayer. The devil ruled this era, he argued. The universe was composed "like an onion" of all the spiritual layers described by Kabbalah, but the Christian heaven of the Holy Spirit "envelops all of them and can penetrate them astrologically," he explained in one of the clearest indications of how he reconciled his apparently contradictory beliefs.[97] In August 1937 he proposed that Moricand should come live with him in the Hôtel Robert, undertake a Catholic education, and be baptized; he warned him, though, not to get the local girls in trouble, and not to discuss astrology with the priests.[98] (Jacob was lucky that his lugubrious friend didn't accept this invitation.) In this proselytizing mood, Jacob made one of his most outrageous statements about Judaism, in a letter to Moricand in February 1938, with his mother's death and his sister's harshness in mind: "A Christian is not asked not 'to live.' *On the contrary*! The Catholic religion is a schooling in sensibility. A Christian is a man capable of all feelings, while the Jew is abstract and lacks all human feeling."[99] What is one to make of such a fantasy? Perhaps just that: that in this choking atmosphere of anti-Semitism, Jacob so identified with the dominant religion that he projected everything he feared and disliked about himself (and about his family) onto a fantastical, caricatured Other he dreamed he could reject.

In this month, February 1938, Jacob published a little prose poem called "War" along with a drawing of a tortured, galloping goat (scapegoat?).

> When the sun is angry, the ocean waves speed up, the clouds in the sky rush. The Sage's eyes bulge. The Buddha's bellybutton was an empty cup: now that cup overflows.[100]

The poem must have seemed prophetic. On March 12, Hitler's troops invaded Austria. Two days later, in France, Léon Blum, who had resigned as prime minister the previous June, formed another government with a majority of the Front Populaire. It would last barely three weeks. The Buddha's belly button was flooding over.

In Saint-Benoît, Jacob tried to keep living normally. He struggled with his gouaches, for the moment occupied with a Visitation: the face of the Virgin Mary was giving him trouble, he confessed to Szigeti, as he'd never been on very good terms with her.[101] And now new patrons entered his life: the doctor Jean-Robert Debray and his wife Nelly, Parisians whom he met through Szigeti. For a couple of years they visited him often in Saint-Benoît and bought paintings. He saw a good deal of them, and his letters to them contain detailed descriptions of his paintings. Something of an artist herself, Nelly did a drawing of Jacob that the doctor framed and hung in his office.[102]

Normal life included gratitude for friendship: he wrote Toulouse that the young artist had reinspired his love of painting.[103] It also included more biography. In April, Théophile Briant's journal *Le Goéland* published René Villard's essay on Jacob's school days.[104] And that month Jacob published "Ballad of the Night Visit," a poem that was immediately recognized as a haunting and unusual work, the one he had composed about his romance with Dulsou. He later wrote that he liked the poem so much, he could hardly believe he'd written it.[105]

Late April took him on another trip, two weeks with his beloved Captain Vaillant and the captain's family in Toul. In a sign of his pleasure in his new friendship with the Debrays, he now wrote them every few days. As usual, he and the captain painted together. While he wrote, it was snowing and raining; the captain was out at the barracks; the little boys were at school; Madame was in the kitchen baking cookies for a tea Jacob dreaded. Every syllable of the letter glows with his happiness at being included in this affectionate household, tea parties or not.[106]

From Toul, Jacob passed through Paris to visit the Debrays, then proceeded to Quimper in preparation for lectures he was to give at Brest and Morlaix. The Debrays had expressed interest in visiting Brittany; Jacob made arrangements for them in a hotel in Quimper and for a stay at the shore, and he introduced them to Breton friends he thought they'd like (including the medical doctor and graphologist Dr. Tuset, in whom Jacob had an almost mystical faith). His letters to the Debrays from Quimper mingle details about hotels with theological-mystical meditations and a separate letter for Nelly of advice about painting: she should study the Golden Section, the great "secret" of proportion in art.[107]

After a peaceful week with his sister and brother, Jacob traveled to the western tip of Brittany to the port towns of Brest and Morlaix to lecture on art. In these talks he regained his aplomb. He made of them not vaudeville but a testimony of his fundamental beliefs, the imaginative unity he crafted from religious faith, mystical practice, and artistic composition (painting or poetry). For him, they were completely interpenetrating endeavors. Notes for the talk survive; it was an orderly presentation, though no doubt embellished with riffs. "Lyricism," he claimed, was mystical levitation; jazz; irrational; and "an interior conflagration." In the second section, he addressed the question of artistic truth: not scientific, not anecdotal, but eternal. The third section amalgamated Pythagorean themes: a work of art—painting or poem—is ordered by numbers and proportion, like the universe of the Kabbalah and God's notebook. In the final section, he laid out principles he had enunciated since *Le Cornet à dés* and *Art poétique:*

"placing the voice"; concreteness; establishing a "margin" between the artwork and reality; precision. He concluded with the religious allegories he lived by: love and suffering meet in Christ; art is the image on Saint Veronica's veil.

This was not a clown act. On the contrary, it was the coherent profession of faith in art-making as an embodied quest for spiritual reality.[108]

Jacob enjoyed this trip, and his two talks were received enthusiastically. He was well paid, housed comfortably by a local patron of the arts, and taken sightseeing by the inspector of historic monuments. A group of painters and architects entertained him in Brest.[109] He also visited his friend the elderly poet Saint-Pol-Roux "Le Magnifique" at his rugged manor house in Camaret, where they conversed with the poet Paul Pelleau and the young, artistic subprefect of Châteaulin, Jean Moulin—the man who would become one of the heroes of the Resistance, using the code name "Max."[110] At dusk, as they walked along the beach before dinner, Le Magnifique placed his hand on Jacob's shoulder: "I see them again," Pelleau wrote later, "both of them, so great and so good, both destined for crucifixion."[111]

From Morlaix, Jacob traveled east and spent a week in Saint-Brieuc with the novelist Louis Guilloux (the brilliant Louis Guilloux, Jacob called him). He had recovered his zest, and for the next few weeks his life was a blur of automobile rides, conversation, sightseeing, and friendship. It wasn't all frivolous: Guilloux was engaged in succoring Spanish refugees in the camps around Saint-Brieuc. Just the opposite of a Tartuffe, Jacob judged: Molière's hero pretended to virtue and practiced vice, while Guilloux derided virtue—or virtue publicly displayed—and devoted himself to helping the needy.[112]

In the last few days of May and until June 10, Jacob made Quimper his home base but mainly gadded about seeing friends. The Debrays joined him for several days; he saw the painter Fernand Léger and his wife; as usual, he visited Dr. Benoiste at Kerpape.[113] From Quimper, he wrote his cousin, Désirée (Dédé) Bloch Lévi, Sylvain's widow, a letter saturated in contrition for the impudent way he'd treated the old scholar. Not too late, he hoped, he expressed remorse for his behavior, even going so far as to call Sylvain "the only saint I ever knew," which was laying it on a bit thick.[114] But the letter shows Jacob's effort to reconcile past and present, and his Jewish and Catholic identities.

By June 10 he had returned to Saint-Benoît and resumed painting.

VII.

IN APRIL, JACOB had written to Debray that he was correcting proofs for a collection of poems that would shock him (and all Christendom), though they were less shocking than Mauriac, Claudel, or Ghéon—other professedly Catholic writers.[115] More a chapbook than a book, *Ballades* came out in late May from a small press, the last book Jacob would publish in his lifetime. It's hard to see it as shocking. But it's powerful work, in a different vein from his earlier collections; even in what now felt like his old age, at sixty-two, he was experimenting with new forms. The lyric liftoffs he had described in is lectures flutter these pages. The "Ballad of the Night Visit" sets the tone for all eight poems. In long lines of free verse—at times more versets than lines—these poems move in sumptuous cadences, rich in repetition, assonance, and alliteration. While not in the voice of Morven, they have a folkloric quality, exploring scenes of love, sorrow, and jealousy that seem to rise out of a collective reservoir of story: a fantasia on Philip II and his son Don Carlos, a doomed romance between a servant girl and a count, a nightmare parable of a train fleeing across Siberian wastes. If Jacob imagined that the poems might shock the devout, perhaps it was in the oblique but passionate eroticism of "To Have Loved You to the Point of Sacrilege"— his experience with Sachs and Dulsou—and in the more openly romantic "Ballad of the Night Visit."

||

LIFE IN SAINT-BENOÎT now reabsorbed the poet. He knew everyone, and everyone knew the little old literary gentleman. When he limped out on errands to the post office and the tobacco shop, he greeted the carpenter, the mechanic, the carter, and the shoemaker in the local patois. He painted the scenery for the *abbé*'s play, to be acted by the parishioners. He attended all the weddings, baptisms, and funerals. And since he took his main meal each day in the hotel restaurant, which also served as a bar and meeting place for the village, he kept up with the local gossip.[116]

He was absorbed, too, in circles in Montargis and Orléans. On June 20 he was a witness in Roger Toulouse's wedding in Orléans, a rite he described to the devout Debray as a secular "modern" ceremony.[117] Toulouse and his bride, Marguerite Texier, then disappeared on a honeymoon in the South of France. In July, as usual, Saint-Benoît filled with pilgrims and tourists. Someone bought the *Visitation* he'd labored on.[118] Toulouse's Parisian dealer Maratier sold a drawing of Jacob's to an American.[119] The poet Jean Aurenche and his lady friend swooped in from Paris in a fancy car, flush from their work in the movies, and took Jacob to dinner in Châteauneuf-sur-Loire.[120] In early September, Jacob spent a week in Montargis as a guest of Dr. Szigeti's family: they ate well, and he painted, but despaired of converting the Jewish doctor.[121]

Life was buzzing along like this when Hitler made his next big move. On September 30, 1938, Neville Chamberlain and the French prime minister Édouard Daladier signed the Munich Agreement with Hitler, ceding the Sudetenland (part of Czechoslovakia) to Germany. But even before the agreement was signed, Europe was shaken. Jacob was not so wrapped up in astrology that he couldn't see that trouble loomed. Already Czech refugees were finding their way to little Saint-Benoît, and the Hôtel Robert suddenly had unexpected guests: a Czech grandmother and a sixteen-month-old baby.[122] On September 23, Jacob wrote Lanoë in horror at the abandonment of Czechoslovakia and the selfish attitudes he encountered around him: anything to keep my slippers warm; who cares about Czechoslovakia? "France will be what *Mein Kampf* proclaims," Jacob predicted, and for once his political instinct wasn't wrong.[123] Two days later—on September 25, 1938, five days before the signing of the accord—France was already rationing gas and calling up reserve soldiers. Debray telephoned to tell Jacob that he and his wife couldn't visit. Young men in the reserves in Saint-Benoît were leaving to join their regiments, including a man who was to have been married the following Monday; he went off to war knowing nothing of marriage except betrothal. A young priest with whom Jacob had become friendly, a captain in the reserves, came by to return books he had borrowed. He was stiff, calm, and "reserved," but he asked the poet to hug him as he departed. Alone in his room, Jacob wept. He spent the rest of the day finishing a painting he called *The End of the Republic*.[124]

Three weeks later the sense of crisis had dissipated, at least in Saint-Benoît. Jacob reported to Debray that the last Parisians who had flocked in panic to the village had left, and that he was trying to get back to work.[125] He took up again his local duties, publishing an article in the parish newsletter about a church gathering, and participating in a ceremony honoring Abbé Fleureau's twenty-five years of service as *curé*. He published an excruciatingly pious poem in the parish newsletter, "The Ball," about a naughty little girl who bounced her ball into porcelain figurines of Christ and the Virgin in the family living room; it was discovered only after her death. "Your ball, my child, was itself a prayer," the poet opined. Was he deliberately crucifying his art to create the kind of kitsch he knew the locals would like, the equivalent of Saint-Sulpice holy images? Jacob could mimic anything; in "The Ball" he mimicked rubbish.[126]

Jacob concluded this troubled year with a burst of resilience. Rheumatism pained his right foot, and he had sore throat and a cough, but he was still visited by visions: to the religious poet Alain Messiaen (brother of the composer Olivier Messiaen), he described the pyramid-shaped crown studded with rubies he'd "seen" on an emaciated prismatic face.[127] In a more down-to-earth postscript, he added that when he died, he wanted to be buried in the cemetery at Saint-Benoît. It was snowing; it was difficult to get even a pail of hot water for shaving from the hotel. But he had just painted a *Cheerful Workman:* his symbol, he told Debray.[128]

VIII.

AS 1939 OPENED, Jacob was reading his beloved mystic, Sister Anne Catherine Emmerich, and Vulliaud on the Kabbalah. He continued to scribble away at his book of symbolic interpretations of Scripture. Gallimard wouldn't publish it, he told Queneau, who had by now published three wildly imaginative novels with the Nouvelle Revue Française and was a member of Gallimard's reading committee.[129] Queneau smoothed relations with the publisher so that a few weeks later Jacob thanked his young friend for making peace.[130] The war would make that book impossible, but Jacob had the temporary satisfaction of telling Debray in March that he was writing a book on the Holy Scriptures for Gallimard.[131]

In May, Jacob, who felt that he lived in hiding, received incontrovertible evidence that he was not lost to the world. The writer Jean Denoël was invited by a journal in Morocco called *Aguedal* to edit an entire issue devoted to Jacob. The table of contents of this dignified tribute includes some of the weightiest names in contemporary French letters: Gide, Claudel, Cocteau, and Stein (if Stein can be counted in French letters). It also featured appreciations by old friends like René Villard, Salmon, Clifford-Barney, Grenier, and Cingria, and by newer friends like Lanoë, Manoll, Messiaen, and Lannes. Gide compared Jacob to Heine and praised his style: "He never lets the word run beyond the emotion and the thought; his expression wraps them closely without any effect of drapery." Gide got lost somewhat in Jacob's novels, he confessed; but he read and reread the poems and *Tartufe,* and quoting one of the best-known lines from *Le Cornet à dés*—"Mystery is in this life, reality in the other: if you love me, if you love me, I'll show you reality"—he concluded that the way to understand Jacob *was* to love him.[132] Cocteau's contribution was an aphoristic love letter. "A poet is posthumous," he declared. His work devours him and seeks to get rid of him. "Max" had accomplished the miracle of disappearing into his work. "Dear Max—I love you in eternity," declared this elusive friend.[133]

Jacob was especially touched by the minibiography composed by a young poet he'd never met but with whom he had corresponded since 1936, the Corsican Michel Levanti. Tuberculosis had halted his military career, and at age twenty he'd been confined to a sanatorium, where he'd fallen in love with literature, and where his friend Jean Denoël put him in touch with Jacob. In 1937 he rejoined his parents in their retirement in Morocco; even more bored with colonial life than with the sanatorium, Levanti continued writing, and he and Jacob constructed a formidable friendship in letters.[134] Jacob's most revelatory letter about Brittany is one he sent Levanti ("This is a country of eclipses . . .").[135]

Jacob wrote to Denoël and Levanti in passionate gratitude for the tribute in *Aguedal*. It wasn't the praise that so stirred him but this testimony of friendship—their leaning out to extend a hand to a "living cadaver." And the cadaver sat up, though he still felt wounded by Jouhandeau's attack, by the silence of reviewers, and by the uproar over the Apollinaire lecture.[136] To Debray, he wrote that he feared the issue of *Aguedal* would only attract more enemies.[137] Meanwhile he and Jabès had been arguing about the relation of Judaism to Christianity. Years later Jabès claimed that Jacob was deeply connected to Jewish tradition and had a Jewish sense of the mystical power in words, a tradition of commentary elaborating on sacred texts, and a belief that in chanting one empties the name of God so that one can enter the sacred space and establish "one's relation to the divine."[138] As hatred of Jews combined with rising totalitarian powers, Jacob tried to persuade his young friend of the continuity between Judaism and Christianity.[139] Jabès was having none it, though he knew the arguments well: Georges Cattauï, Jacob's Jewish friend who had converted to Catholicism, was Jabès's wife's cousin. "I wrote him a pretty harsh letter," Jabès said; "I told him he had no idea what was happening."[140] Jacob replied that "this question of racism" was in the hands of the pope, the cardinals, and the bishops who were intervening with Hitler and Mussolini. Jacob considered himself both Jewish and Christian and was prepared to sacrifice himself. "It's possible you will scorn me, and that's all right," he wrote. "But I pray each morning for the martyred Jews and Catholics. . . . I embrace you, if you still permit it, and send my greetings to your wife."[141] In his last letter to Jabès, dated May 1, 1939, Jacob announced that he was "out of this world" and prepared for martyrdom. "I thank you for not condemning me, and I am your friend," he concluded. At the bottom of the page he marked a large black cross.[142]

||

IN MAY, JACOB received a cheering visit. Accompanied by his teenaged son, a powerful Jewish banker, Robert Zunz, sought him out at Saint-Benoît. Zunz was already disposed to purchase work by Jacob, but the scale of his patronage astounded the poet-painter: that day Zunz bought eight gouaches, along with drawings and a literary manuscript, for the enormous sum of six thousand francs, and commissioned Jacob to create two private albums for him gathering gouaches, drawings, and texts: one was to be on the Catholic theme of the Stations of the Cross, and the other on Brittany.[143]

Why a Catholic theme? Robert Zunz's family history and his own life story strangely resembled Jacob's in some respects. The Zunz patriarch had moved from Frankfurt to Paris in the mid-nineteenth century and set up a profitable money-changing business; his son Robert, an atheist Jew and a Freemason, returned to Paris after an early commercial venture in Brazil, completed his military service, and joined his elder brother working in the stock exchange. But in the army in the Great War, he fell under the influence of his Catholic captain. In 1926, through rapid intervention with his friend Émile Moreau, the head of the Banque de France, Zunz seems to have averted a major financial crisis for the country and staved off the collapse of the franc.[144] By 1932, concluding that the liberal government was irreparably corrupt, Zunz joined the far-right movement the Croix de Feu; met and spoke with the Catholic Existentialist Gabriel Marcel; read Maritain, Péguy, Ramón Fernández (later a Nazi sympathizer), Léon Bloy, and Léon Daudet; and in 1937 he rejected the Front Populaire and actually met with the Comte de Paris, the pretender to the throne of France. Somehow he imagined that the anti-Semitism so coded into the ideology of the French extreme right could be sublimed away, leaving an enlightened monarchy. In his diary, on October 15, 1937, he wrote,

"Starting as a Jew, I've been atheist, agnostic, Christian, and now I think Catholic; will I be baptized?"[145]

This was the man who presented himself to the Jewish-Christian poet-painter in Saint-Benoît. From the perspective of postwar France, such an intellectual evolution may seem incredible, yet Zunz was far from alone. Many French Jews had such confidence in their French nationality and even in a quasi-Catholic identity that the Vichy legislation and the Nazi Occupation took them completely by surprise.

The banker's son took photographs of Jacob, and in the days following the visit, Jacob wrote twice to the adolescent, inviting him to return. But the bulk of his correspondence was with Jean's father, his new patron. They consulted in detail about the two albums, which were to be bound by bookbinders in Montargis. Back and forth went the letters, determining the layout of the texts and drawings, the quality of the endpapers, the way a gouache was to be set into the cover of each album.[146] Jacob and Robert Zunz never met again in person, but they became friends through this collaboration and even more through Robert Zunz's conversion, in which Jacob guided him, and in both men's suffering during the war.

For now, in 1939, Jacob became intensely engaged in the preparation of the two albums. These were far more than commercial productions.[147] He created the religious album, *Méditations sur le chemin de croix* (Meditation on the Stations of the Cross) just as he was trying to pull together a lifetime of notes and lectures on Scripture for Gallimard. All the passionate Stations of the Cross on which he had led his friends and that he had illustrated in the album for Sachs now took visible shape in this private book for Zunz: thirty-seven pages of text and forty-seven drawings. These pages present Jacob's theology in its most concentrated form. It's a world of symbols focused on anatomy: the hands represent earthly intelligence, and the feet celestial intelligence, while the head stands for creation, meditation, and judgment.[148] Suffering is the key to revelation (Fifth Station): "God gave us suffering as a way to find Him, to find ourselves."[149] We are all Judas when we turn away from God (First Station).[150]

In the Breton album, Jacob created another highly personal universe.

Fearful of war, sensing that he had accomplished his life's work, Jacob looked back and established a record of his life: drawings and paintings of Breton scenes, photographs of his family's house, autobiographical scraps like receipts for rent, even his identity card for elections in Quimper. Though this work was destined for a private collector, Jacob was well aware that important collections of "treasures" end up in museums and libraries, "these luminous pathways into eternity."[151] "Ancient tombs are sometimes opened," he wrote Robert Zunz. "I do not lose hope that the tomb of my albums might share the destiny of the Egyptian pharaohs." Jacob was constructing his own funerary monument.

||

IN ANOTHER ACT of autobiography, Jacob composed an account of his conversion for Abbé Foucher, a priest in Montargis. The *abbé* had asked for this document, and Jacob obliged, dictating it to the *abbé*'s friend Paul Frizot. In contrast to the fragmented versions of his apparition he had presented in *Saint Matorel*, this "Account of My Conversion" expanded the one-page description from *La Défense de Tartufe*. Jacob now looked back at his ecstasy from the perspective of years of struggle to make personal sense of this alien theology; to adopt it as his own; to live it, day by day. "Conversion is one thing, the casting off of the old man is a long and meticulous labor."[152] Jacob's tone here is sober and humble. If this version lacks the drama of the Matorel sequence and of *La Défense de Tartufe*, it gives a mature account of Jacob's belief that God broke into his life and utterly changed his direction. Reviewing his childhood in a secular Jewish family in the heart of picturesque Breton Catholicism, he described the stages leading up to his baptism and his retreat to Saint-Benoît. In one of the most interesting asides, he noted that he still had visions from time to time, though nothing of the intensity of the old days. One has the feeling that Jacob is reciting a story so often repeated, it has become the architecture of his truth. It concludes with a reflection on parish life, the importance of the structure of prayer in common and the practice of charity.[153] Jacob was speaking from the reality of Saint-Benoît he had finally made his own.

||

THROUGHOUT JUNE 1939 Jacob saw Roger Toulouse and the Szigetis; not so much the Béalus, as Marcel had gone off to try his luck in Paris, leaving Marguerite running the hat shop.[154] Cingria and the Légers came by on July 9. On July 12, like a homing pigeon, Jacob returned to Quimper. But the next day he took flight for Saint-Brieuc to spend a week with Guilloux. He arrived in time for the national holiday, July 14, celebrated this year with special fervor: the 150th anniversary of the French Revolution. He and Guilloux sauntered through the streets observing parades of marchers dressed up as revolutionary soldiers, raucous dancing in the streets to band music, and jostling crowds. They joked and talked of literature. In 1944, Guilloux would write in his diary: "Monday, July 17. Five years ago—in '39—Max was here. I didn't suspect, then, that I was seeing him for the last time. And even less that he would die as he was made to die."[155]

Back in Quimper, Jacob fell into an elegiac mood. The proprietor of the Jacobs' apartment building where the family had lived and run their store for three generations had given notice that when the current lease was up, he intended to demolish the house. It was as if his parents were dying again, Jacob wrote René Villard.[156] He carried copies of all his books, clippings of reviews and articles, photographs, and paintings in boxes to the municipal library of Quimper. He had a sinister sense that the family house might be destroyed and all his literary documents lost; he also foresaw war and wanted his legacy protected.[157]

Before returning to Saint-Benoît, Jacob had a last visit with Saint-Pol-Roux, the fierce old poet, on the terrace of the Hôtel de L'Épée where they had often met in past years. Now the atmosphere had darkened. Tourists were leaving, the annual art show had been canceled. Everyone expected a general mobilization. But though the crisis interrupted the exhibit, the artists and local dignitaries held their banquet as usual at the hotel, and the deputy mayor of Ploaré tried to cheer up the guests: "Mobilization doesn't mean war!" At that, the painter Jean Caveng saw Jacob exchange an anguished look with Saint-Pol-Roux. "A whole world is coming to an end," pronounced Le Magnifique. Jacob remained quiet. He looked intensely at the chestnut trees, the Odet River, the trees on Mont Frugy "with an almost desperate tenderness," remembered Paul Pelleau, who sat near the two old poets. When they rose to say goodbye, they embraced in a long hug.[158]

ON SEPTEMBER 1, Hitler invaded Poland. Two days later France and England declared war on Germany. Anticipated, feared, and denied for so long, the Second World War began.

CHAPTER 20

THE OCCUPATION

I.

The French called it the Phony War, or the "Funny" War, *La Drôle de guerre*. Hitler's troops subdued Poland, then for months launched no new assault. The French armies massed along the Maginot Line to the east. After the half-hearted Saar offensive, in which they captured a few German villages, they withdrew and sat down. "You wouldn't call this war 'funny' if you saw the letters I receive," Jacob told René Villard. He began to write to soldiers at the front—as many as fifty pen pals.[1] Jacob was a writer, and in these last, fraught years of his life, his writing took the form of letters, daily religious meditations, a diary of the invasion, scattered poems, and two notebooks, one of poetic, one of ethical advice. Month by month, the noose tightened around the Jews in France.

"MY LORD ROBERT boasts of having driven me away," Jacob wrote to his new friend Count François de Montalivet in November.[2] The Roberts had abruptly told him they were closing the hotel and gave him a week to find other lodgings. After some anxious searching, Jacob moved to the rosy brick house of Madame Persillard, a doctor's widow, where he occupied a furnished room on the second floor with two windows opening on the Place du Martroi. She cooked for him (though he complained of her heavy hand with the salt and was aghast at her mixing salt with sugar); he spread out his books, papers, paints, and an ashtray on the large worktable in his room and felt at home with this kind but nosy woman who didn't scruple to read his mail when he was out.[3]

The war may have appeared "droll" to civilians, but its effects weren't invisible. Jacob saw empty cars being driven in long lines north from Orléans toward the fronts.[4] Children sent by their parents to the village for safety were being sheltered in the recreation hall of the hospice, the old people's home run by the Church across from Madame Persillard's house.[5] On September 10, Jacob wrote Roger Toulouse of the "horrible calm"— the calm of hell where you can't hear the cries—but he remarked, reassuringly, that France wasn't yet in danger. Later that day he learned that Toulouse had been called up for assessment for military service and that gas would be rationed.[6]

On September 29, Germany and the Soviet Union divided Poland, and on November 30 the Soviets invaded Finland. On December 13, Jacob's old school fellow René Villard collapsed with a stroke as he was leaving his house in Saint-Brieuc to lecture on Jacob; he would die six weeks later, and Jacob couldn't attend the burial in Quimper because the trains and buses now ran so irregularly.[7] Almost out of sight of the general population, French soldiers were defending the borders in a limited way; Jacob's friend Alain Messiaen, the Catholic poet who had been taken prisoner and then released, wrote of the suffering of the troops. Debray, Toulouse, Cadou, Follain, and Queneau were called to the army.[8]

II.

WITH THE ARRIVAL of spring, real fighting broke out. Germany invaded Denmark and Norway on April 9. Denmark fell in a day; Norway, defended by Britain, held out until early June. On May 10 one German army rolled over the Netherlands while another smashed into Belgium. Even supported by the British Expeditionary Force and two French armies, the Dutch and Belgians couldn't resist the German tanks and air assaults. On May 13 the Germans crossed the Meuse and charged into France. By May 19 they were in Amiens, the next day in Abbeville. Belgium surrendered.

The British evacuated from Dunkirk, while the Germans concentrated on France; on June 7, Rommel's army occupied Rouen, and two days later it crossed the Seine; on June 12 the French commander informed his government that he would have to surrender. Parisians began fleeing their city in any way they could: in cars, in carts, on bicycles, in wheelbarrows, on foot, joining the flood of eight to ten million people surging south to escape the Germans.[9] On June 14 the Germans marched into Paris.

The French government retreated to Tours. With the resignation of Prime Minister Paul Reynaud on June 16, Maréchal Philippe Pétain, the eighty-four-year-old hero of the Great War, took over as head of state and requested an armistice. It was signed on the evening of June 22 in the forest of Compiègne, in the same railway car in which France had imposed the terms of German surrender in 1918.[10] The French Third Republic died with that signature. The new government, headed by Pétain and established in the spa town of Vichy, was an authoritarian state, L'État Français, and on July 10 the parliament voted to dissolve itself, placing all power in the hands of Pétain, the leader of the National Revolution whose task was to impose order and to collaborate with the Germans.

||

THE FRENCH ARMIES had disintegrated, deserters roamed the countryside, and two million men had been taken prisoner.[11] Jacob's friends, of course, were caught up in the catastrophe. The Maritains, in Toronto for Jacques's lectures in late 1939, stayed in North America, moving to New York City for the duration of the war. The Paulhans and some of the Gallimard family made their way from Paris to Carcassonne.[12] Pierre Colle had been taken prisoner; he escaped, reached Nantes, and with Lanoë's help managed to join his parents in the unoccupied zone in the South. The Jewish Kahnweiler fled Boulogne with his wife on back roads to take refuge with his brother-in-law the painter Élie Lascaux, deep in southwestern France.[13] Vittorio Rieti, also Jewish, was nearly trapped in Paris. Only the day before the Germans entered the city, the painter Jean Hugo, who held a minor post in the government, procured a visa allowing him to travel south and board a ship for New York, where he joined his wife and their young son.[14] On the night of June 22—just as Pétain signed the armistice—a drunken German soldier attacked the lonely manor house on the Breton coast where the old poet Saint-Pol-Roux lived with his daughter Divine. The soldier shot the old maidservant in the mouth, raped Divine, and beat the old man so savagely that he died three months later.[15]

By June 11, Saint-Benoît was jammed with vehicles escaping Paris. The next night the relics of the saint were secretly moved from the crypt to the bishop's palace in Orléans. And now Max Jacob became another sort of writer: from June 11 to August 29, he kept a journal of the war, a remarkable document mixing occult speculation and notes of dreams with brutally down-to-earth reporting. Through his eyes, we see France fall apart.[16]

In early June, the war wasn't over: the Germans were bombing the roads, bridges, and towns of the Loire Valley all around Saint-Benoît. On June 15 the *curé* told Jacob that they were evacuating the hospital, children, and the elderly: Jacob would have to go. "I'm neither a child nor elderly," Jacob protested, and refused to leave, preferring to die in his bed than on the road.[17] He took notes. A gentleman, his wife, and their daughter tried to commit suicide by slitting their wrists; they were taken to a doctor, but "a Spaniard" drove off with their car and all their "fortune."[18] French soldiers descended on Madame Persillard's house, and Jacob heard several of them plotting to rape a seventeen-year-old girl who had lost her parents; he was blamed for being prudish in advising her not to accept a ride with them; others stepped in to protect her. At night, from his bedroom, he heard French soldiers calling out to one another: they had lost their regiments. On the side of the road, in daylight, he saw wrecked caissons in a ditch, a dead horse, a dying horse struggling to rise. Refugees crowded the parsonage. A Monsieur Beauvais, who had a million francs in his satchel, tried to persuade the *curé* to keep it for him; on Abbé Fleureau's refusal, the millionaire slept with his fortune clutched to his chest and walked around embracing it all day long.[19] The mayor and many inhabitants had fled. Those who remained slept and cooked in the crypt of the basilica—though Jacob spent his nights in the hospice, now converted to an infirmary, helping to tend the wounded, returning by day to Madame Persillard's. And at her house, to his surprise, his old tormentor Pierre-Michel Frenkel knocked on the door one morning: he was a soldier and had lost his regiment. To complete the surprise, Captain Vaillant called out to Jacob from the square, footloose with a fat, white-haired general who had lost his troops.[20]

The remaining citizens of Saint-Benoît organized a food committee to scavenge supplies, capturing and butchering cows and agreeing on prices for meat. "No more mail! No telephone! No telegrams! What peace!" Jacob declared. Hardly: the Germans were bombing the nearby towns. While Sully-sur-Loire, Châteauneuf-sur-Loire, and Gien burned, the Germans bombed the bridges and roads crowded with fleeing civilians. Corpses bobbed in the Loire; roads were blocked with the charred remnants of cars; bullets crackled across the roof of the hospice. An old couple was murdered in their farmhouse. On June 17 three German soldiers arrived in the village on bicycles; looking "cunning, determined, intelligent, and scornful," they tried to say that they wouldn't harm anyone, and left. But that evening more Germans marched in and installed themselves in abandoned houses. They broke into the cellar of the monastery, seized stored food, and dug up potatoes from the fields. Saint-Benoît was now officially occupied.[21]

FOR MONTHS, JACOB had been acting as the guide to the basilica, since the Benedictine vicar had been called to the army.[22] Several groups of Germans had already visited when, on June 29, an officer Jacob called "a Gestapo" pointed to him and declared, "You're a Jew!" "I'm Catholic," Jacob replied. The *curé* of Germigny, who was showing the Germans around, insisted that Jacob was Catholic and Breton. "You can tell the race by the nose," said the German. At the parsonage, the officer accused Abbé Fleureau of having a Jew for a guide. "He's a good Catholic," said the priest. "A Jew . . . You like Jews?" Abbé Fleureau answered that he didn't like "subtleties" and that men should help one another out of charity. "We'll see about that," said the officer. Thenceforth Jacob no longer showed the basilica, which was now guarded day and night by a policeman.[23]

||

TO JEAN FOLLAIN, who had written to him about poetry from his regiment, Jacob replied that he was talking to a deaf-mute.[24] He made the same protest to Béalu: he wasn't thinking about poetry, he was thinking about sudden death in a bombing. It wasn't dying he was afraid of, but being caught in a state of sin.[25] And it wasn't only the masses of people in flight that horrified him, the lost soldiers, the suicides, people driven mad by trauma, German military music blaring in the town square every Thursday—but "the Jewish question" that threatened to drive him out upon the roads as a vagabond.

In June, Jacob thought the end of the world had come.[26] His cousin Noémie Gompel, widow of old Gustave Gompel of the department store, committed suicide in Biarritz in despair.[27] By early August, Jacob wrote Manoll that he'd regained his balance, thanks to painting and mainly to God.[28] But it was hard to maintain such resilience; three weeks later he wrote that his life was finished and advised Manoll, "Let us love one another in God! Deepen yourself! Dig in your breast, not in your brain."[29] Even before the Vichy government imposed its anti-Jewish laws, Jacob felt tracked, writing to Lanoë that in this "terrible atmosphere of anti-Semitism," he couldn't move, but was staying in Saint-Benoît where he felt protected.[30] He explained the same thing to Jean Colle, who had invited him to Brittany. As evidence that he was protected in Saint-Benoît, he cited an incident where a Gestapo officer checked to see if "the Jew Jacob" was at the basilica; the *curé* sent a messenger to warn Jacob to hide.[31]

By the end of October, the Germans demanded a census of all Jews in the occupied zone, and Jacob wrote again to Lanoë, this time asking if he could recommend an old people's home where he could finish his days in peace. He considered himself not so much in danger as financially needy, now that the war had interrupted the sale of paintings.[32]

Jacob had protested to Follain that he couldn't think about poetry. But poems came as naturally to him as breathing. In his letter to Lanoë in early September, he included "Fioretti," poem-shards of a single line each, expressing religious terror and desolation.[33] But later that month he produced a long, ambitious poem, "Report from June 1940."

As its title suggests, "Report" draws its material from Jacob's diary: dying horses, incinerated cars, bewildered refugees, and lost soldiers all turn up in its declamatory lines. It's a bad poem, interesting for what it tells us about Jacob's conception of a public poem in a time of national crisis. He had always been an artist of burlesque and pastiche. In 1916 he had set his own art aside to write propaganda in defense of the Armenians, and he had made a similar sacrifice recently, the pious tripe of "The Ball" in the parish newsletter. Now he produced a serious war poem in Hugo's rhyming alexandrines, decked out in classical and biblical allusions, just the sort of philistine grandiloquence he had spent his life attacking.

What had happened? Jacob seems to have intended "Report from June 1940" as a genuinely patriotic offering. He wrote it in an idiom that any lycée student could identify as Official Poetry. Realistic observations— "carcasses of cars," clothing, letters, photographs, purses scattered along the roads, wounded horses—jostle with allegories. The bare facts no longer sufficed: Monsieur Beauvais's million francs swelled to one hundred million, and as if the bombed bridges flinging corpses into the river weren't gory enough, Jacob added a dog devouring a baby in front of its mother. The myth of Pyrrha and Deucalion renewing the human race after a flood blends with Noah and the Magi, and metaphors cross each other out.

It concludes:

A white horse trotted, spilling blood in streams,
His head high, holding death between his teeth.

At least, that's where the poem ended when Jacob sent it to Paulhan and to Paul Petit. Paulhan wanted to publish it, but *Mesures* had folded, and *La Nouvelle Revue française* had been handed over to the Nazi puppet Drieu La Rochelle.[34] Paulhan seems to have sent the poem to René Tavernier, who was editing *Confluences* in Lyon, and there the poem appeared, two years later.

But Jacob wanted his reportage to serve a clear, patriotic purpose, so he added a final quatrain in the versions he sent Lanoë and François de Montalivet:

Star, may your blood pour down as Wisdom's rain
and Noah of Ancient Greece, Deucalion,
after this deluge, sow in our sodden earth
renascent virtue, Reason revived, and Faith.

At least two readers criticized the poem. Lanoë called it a "rhymed chronicle," and Manoll objected to its old-fashioned style, accusing Jacob of aping the seventeenth-century classicist Nicolas Boileau. To which Jacob replied that language had to be adapted to its subject, and that for this kind of narrative, Boileau's language was appropriate.[35] From the point of view of practical rhetoric, Jacob calculated adroitly. For political, not poetic reasons, "Report from June 1940" became one of his most frequently anthologized poems. It's easy—too easy—to understand. After its author's death, it appeared in several versions in at least four anthologies dedicated to poetry of the Resistance.[36]

III.

MARCEL JOUHANDEAU, in his anti-Semitic mania, had attacked Jacob in 1936. Early in 1940 he seems to have suffered remorse for wounding his old friend and asked Pierre Minet to attempt a reconciliation. In a mood of penitential forgiveness bordering on abjection, Jacob replied to Minet that he had "deserved the lesson"; he would be delighted to receive a letter from Marcel.[37] Jouhandeau accordingly sent a private apology. Jacob replied: "My dear Marcel, I thank you / and I shake your hand. Max Jacob."[38] A few days later he wrote a much longer letter recalling their first meeting and their years of friendship; he described his present life of renunciation and humility, serving as a guide to the basilica, receiving tips he turned over to the *curé*. There was a vague plan for Jouhandeau to visit. Then Germany invaded. This was the last communication between the two men.[39]

The Vichy government lost no time in establishing its ideal Christian state. No sooner had Parliament granted Pétain dictatorial power than the gratified anti-Semites leaped into action: without any prodding from the Germans, on July 22 the French annulled citizenship for over fifteen thousand people who had been received into the country since 1927—mostly Jews fleeing persecution. A week later Vichy suspended the Marchandeau Decree of 1939 prohibiting public racism and anti-Semitism: now the newspapers bubbled with vile anti-Jewish propaganda. On October 3, Vichy passed the first anti-Jewish law, using a racial definition of "the Jew": anyone with three Jewish grandparents (or two Jewish grandparents, if the person had a Jewish spouse). Jews were expelled from the professions of teaching, journalism, film, theater, and radio. The next day another law ordered the confinement of foreign Jews in the camps already set up for Spanish- and German-Jewish refugees: by the end of 1940, these camps held fifty thousand people.[40]

In early October, Jacob was ordered to register as a Jew at the subprefecture of Montargis. And he'd heard about the camps. Reports were more and more alarming: he thought he might at any moment be thrown into a "concentration camp" where he would "have the leisure to expiate" his sins. He signed his letter to Montalivet "from the ghetto of St-Benoît s/Loire."[41] There's a touch of wit in these phrases: the outlandish words *concentration camp* and *ghetto* still felt at this point like a sinister joke to Jacob, a devout French Catholic decorated with the Légion d'honneur. But the fear was real. Nor was the trip to Montargis easy: with buses no longer running, he had to take ill-connecting provincial trains and spend hours to travel forty-five kilometers.[42] The officials in Montargis were embarrassed when Jacob presented them with his identity card from the Légion d'honneur: they didn't want to stamp JUIF in red letters upon it. Jacob insisted that they do so.[43] Years later one of the clerks, Madame Valadon, remembered the encounter: "I said, 'Oh, no, M. Jacob, not on the card of the Légion d'honneur!' And he replied, 'But yes! Besides, the honor is Jewish.' "[44]

||

OTTO ABETZ, GERMAN ambassador to Vichy, named the three principal nonmilitary aims of the Occupation: to control Communism, the banks, and *La Nouvelle Revue française*.[45] The first move, on October 9, was to close down the journal. But seeing a greater tactical advantage in keeping it open as an instrument of Nazism, the Propaganda-Staffel started it up again a few days later with the anti-Semitic novelist Drieu La Rochelle at the helm. Paulhan withdrew to the shadows but remained at the journal in the background, quietly active as an editor, using the position to work as a kind of double agent. For he did, immediately, join the army of shadows, as the Resistance came to be known: he was a key member of the Resistance network at the Musée de l'Homme.[46]

The Germans now seized French publishing, and some publishers, like Robert Denoël and Bernard Grasset, embraced the chance to expand their markets, Denoël developing a line of anti-Semitic books and Hitler's speeches, while Grasset affirmed that at last France would no longer be "suffocated" by Jewish snobbism and could "really be French."[47] Gallimard was harder to persuade, but since he wanted to protect both his journal and his publishing house, he made a deal with Gerhard Heller, the newly appointed *Sonderführer* at the Propaganda-Staffel, to eliminate Jews from his staff and from his list of authors, and he was back in business by Christmas. Heller, who fancied French literature, would enter Jacob's story in its last, bitter days. Now in the autumn of 1940, new to his job of censorship and propaganda, Heller felt both drunk with happiness and "anguished" at being perceived as an enemy of France; he was "highly sensitive," he insisted, "so events like this touch me deeply."[48] But even before Heller arrived in early November, the Propaganda-Staffel hadn't neglected its work; on October 4, 1940, Otto Abetz published "the Otto list," the document naming 1,060 books to be removed from circulation.[49]

The effects hit Jacob immediately. As a Jew, he could no longer publish, he wrote Lanoë. And he asked, did *La Nouvelle Revue française* now belong to Drieu? And would Lanoë keep publishing his poetry chronicle there? (The answer was no: Lanoë reappeared in the pages of *La Nou-velle Revue française* only after the war.)[50] Jacob complained of solitude: no more conversations about painting with Toulouse, no more sessions on poetry with the young fellows from Montargis. He was haunted by the destruction around him: Gien was a pile of stones like Vesuvius, and Sully-sur-Loire looked like the ruins of Pompeii.[51] By Christmas, life had become truly difficult; the winter was unusually cold; food was rationed; beefsteak was impossible to find; at best, one could obtain a rare fish for a high price; one had to beg to purchase firewood. He muddled along, sell-ing just enough paintings to pay his bills. When François de Montalivet bought a gouache in December, Jacob thanked him: now he could afford firewood. (But the wood was damp and smoked and hardly burned.)[52] One had to use ration cards even for soap; potatoes were expensive.[53] In October, Paul Petit had been sending Jacob small checks. Now Petit wrote from Paris that he and his family were "dying of hunger," and Jacob mailed him packages of food, even though he himself had gone without bread for three days.[54]

The anti-Jewish laws struck at the livelihood of the Jacob family. In October the Germans slapped a sign across the window of the shop in Quimper: JUDE. A few days earlier, Delphine and Gaston had posted their own sign, all too prophetic: LIQUIDATION: PROFIT FROM THE LAST DAYS. But it was the Vichy authorities, not the Germans, who confiscated their stock. The Jacobs lost the lease on the building and withdrew to live in an obscure apartment near the railway station. In Paris, Vichy agents took over Jacques Jacob's tailor shop.[55] Lanoë, meanwhile, helped Jacob by buy-ing his painting, and Jacob went to great trouble to send him a gouache, packing paper being in short supply.

By January 1941 the grim reality of the Occupation had settled upon France. "Ah! Gide admires Hitler!" Jacob exclaimed in a letter to the old painter Jacques-Émile Blanche. "Shame on the geniuses of evil!"[56] Gide, safe in the South of France, was wondering if Hitler's dream wasn't worldwide harmony.[57] Jacob, in Saint-Benoît, made his way painfully through the village across ice and mud, steadying himself with a cane.[58] Madame Persillard wept at the gift of a bar of soap from François de Montalivet.[59]

IV.

JACOB'S FRIEND JEAN GRENIER taught philosophy in a lycée in Algiers, and it was at his prompting that his student Albert Camus had written to Jacob some years before. Now Camus's school-fellow Max-Pol Fouchet reached out to Jacob. A Socialist with Catholic inclinations, Fouchet had lived in Algeria since boyhood and was assistant curator of the National Museum in Algiers; he had been in touch with Jacob since 1939, the year he took over a little literary journal, *Mithra*, and renamed it *Fontaine*. Fouchet was an indomitably free spirit. Under his direction, *Fontaine* became a key journal of the Resistance. In 1943, Fouchet set up an office in London and created a miniature edition designed to be parachuted into occupied France along with medicine and weapons.[60] Jacob's friend Jean Denoël was on the editorial board, and one isn't surprised to find the work of Jacob's young friends in *Fontaine:* Cadou, Rousselot, Béalu. In these free pages appeared some of the poems Jacob was able to publish in the last three years of his life.[61]

Meanwhile Jacob's epistolary friend the scholar Marguerite Mespoulet, of Barnard College, proposed to publish a selection of his poems. In the same spirit of preservation in which he sent his publications to the library in Quimper and compiled the albums for Robert Zunz, Jacob sent Mespoulet poems and directed her to the articles about him. He also mailed her drawings and wrote out an approximate bibliography of his work: once again he was building his own funerary monument.[62] Replying to her questions, he defined the three main "tendencies" in his work as love, humor, and the exploration of the unconscious. The drafts of poems he sent her are far more substantial than "Report from June 1940." Rich in alliteration and assonance, "Blood-Spirit" converts the pagan Dionysian maenad into the priestess of a Christian rite:

It's raining, raining, Jesus's blood
man's in the street, the gods up above. . . .
I've sung, sung the livelong day
but came the maenad and a thousand cupping glasses.
Maenad managing the promenades
Maenad managing Adam in the crowd.[63]

||

IN NOVEMBER 1940, Jacob wrote Lanoë that he had two guardian angels, Lanoë himself and Paul Petit; he was delighted that his angels had met each other.[64] Lanoë was indeed protecting Jacob. Their letters of the winter and spring of 1941 concern the gouaches Lanoë had bought, some to keep, some to sell for Jacob. In January he sent a money order for two thousand francs, and in June he courageously exhibited Jacob's paintings in Nantes without naming "the Jew Jacob" as the artist.[65] "Dear, beloved Julien, You're a door opening on the infinite," Jacob told his friend.[66] Many of these letters describe the difficulties of finding food; he mentioned that he sent packages of food to Paul Petit. And because of Petit, Jacob was now reading Kierkegaard's *Concluding Unscientific Postscript to Philosophical Fragments* in Petit's translation, just published by Gallimard. Had Lanoë seen the book? Jacob wanted to know.[67]

In April, Jacob was waiting for a visit from Petit; he wanted his advice on paintings he proposed to mail to Nantes. In a postscript to Lanoë, Jacob added cryptically, "Speak to P.P. I have the same fears as you."[68]

The reference had to remain cryptic, as mail might be opened by agents of Vichy or the Germans. Jacob and Lanoë were right to be worried. On December 12, 1940, Petit—taking to heart Kierkegaard's lessons about the authentic life of faith realized in action—published two open letters accusing Cardinals Suhard and Baudrillart of collaboration. On March 20, 1941, Petit went further and printed a tract attacking the hypocrisy of the Vichy regime's claim to protect Catholicism.[69] In June, with three friends, Petit started a clandestine journal, *La France continue*, in which he elaborated the condemnation of Vichy, gave lucid analyses of the political and military situation, and invited help in resisting.[70]

When Petit visited Saint-Benoît in late April, Jacob found him pale, yellow, thin, and sickly, but they enjoyed arguing about Kierkegaard: Jacob judged the Dane egoistic and un-Christian, while Petit tried to teach Jacob to read him dialectically.[71] But the writer who truly surprised him in the spring of 1941 was Kafka.[72] He wrote Manoll excitedly about this discovery, advising him to sell his last shirt to buy "The Metamorphosis." Kafka had made Surrealism irrelevant; he had something of the humor of Dostoyevsky, "but it's more modern, more rare, even crazier, in being less crazy. In fact it's not crazy at all, it's very realistic."[73] Between Kierkegaard and Kafka, Jacob hadn't chosen badly in the spirits to sustain him during the nightmare of the Occupation.

||

"MY FRIENDS ARE my native land," Jacob wrote in 1942 to the young Breton poet Louis Guillaume.[74] Guillaume had sent Jacob his first two books before the war. They met, finally, in 1941, at the Béalus' in Montargis, and Guillaume then visited Saint-Benoît. For Jacob, the young man represented Brittany, smelled like Brittany, sounded like Brittany, and filled him with homesickness. He called him Breton nicknames: "Laumick bihen" (little Guillaume), or "Laouïc," the diminutive of Louis. Guillaume joined the loose commonwealth of Jacob's friends, a network all the more precious in these years of deprivation and danger. The war had "annihilated" everything within him that inspired him to write, Guillaume later recalled, and it was Jacob who rescued him. "I owe it to you to have clambered out of that abyss in which you, alas, were lost," Guillaume later wrote in commemoration.[75]

A new friend turned up in May 1941. Jacques Mezure was finishing his studies in ceramics at the art school in Vierzon, in central France, when his friend Jean Semence told him of visiting the poet of Saint-Benoît, a little old man with spectacles, a beret on his head, a crumpled cigarette at his lips, and a most extraordinary gaiety. Semence described the poet's room: the worktable crowded with manuscripts and an overflowing ashtray, a painting table covered with tubes of paint and brushes sticking out of jars, an easel, a packing trunk full of papers.[76] Facing graduation and not knowing what to do with himself, Mezure wrote the master of his perplexities. To his astonishment, a letter from Saint-Benoît reached him three days later. From that day until just a few weeks before Jacob's death, they wrote each other almost every week. They were well suited: Mezure was an ardent Catholic as well as an artist and dabbled in poetry; Jacob advised him on all fronts. In his first letter, he initiated the young man into his "Kabbalistic" reading of the Bible—"It's a Jewish book, full of symbols," he asserted.[77] And as he had with Béalu and countless others, he tried to teach him about the inner life: "One can suffer (one *must* suffer) at the sight of a chair, a table, a penholder. It's about being *separated* enough from things, events, people, to be wounded or delighted."[78] With the difficulties of wartime, they never managed to meet; Mezure went north to work in ceramics in Paris, and later hid in the South to escape the conscription of French laborers to Germany. But in Jacob's letters one feels the pulse of a true friendship.

Michel Levanti, another friend Jacob never met face to face, at least came geographically closer in the spring of 1941. Levanti, the Corsican poet living with his parents in Morocco, was finally able to rejoin his lover, Gabrielle Thomassin, in France and to see his baby son for the first time. When his tuberculosis flared up again, he and Thomassin retreated with their baby to the Auvergne, in central France, where at least they had enough to eat. "My son Michel" is how Jacob addressed this poet he would never see but whom he cherished.[79]

Though persecuted, Jacob was not lonely under the Occupation once his friends returned from the fractured army. Through letters and even through occasional visits, he stayed in touch with his large tribe. Paulhan sent him a copy of Pindar ("At last! Poetry!"), and to him Jacob mentioned "the storms of anti-Semitism" he was facing.[80] He carried on an affectionate correspondence with Louis Émié (who urged him to take refuge in

Bordeaux);[81] with Toulouse, François de Montalivet, Jean-Robert Debray, Moricand, Zunz, and the young schoolteacher Maurice Métivier. His table overflowed with letters.

But he was most intensely involved, these days, with the provincial poetic Renaissance for which he became the godfather, the École de Rochefort. Jacob had always liked connecting people. Now, in the suffocation of the Occupation, connections became lifelines.[82]

The network centered on Jacob. "We created a cult around him," Manoll said.[83] It was Jacob who put Cadou in touch with Béalu in February 1941.[84] The two young poets seized on each other as brothers, and poems sped back and forth between Béalu in Montargis and the various rugged villages where Cadou worked as a substitute teacher.[85]

They were young men, in a fever of lyricism and self-importance. They had all published slender volumes. Jean Follain was the outlier. Born in 1903, he was a lawyer in Paris where he had known Jacob since the days of the Hôtel Nollet. He'd been recognized early as a poet; in 1941 he brought out his fifth book, *Ici bas* (Here Below). His poems have a mysterious simplicity and solidity; they make no flashy moves, no grand claims, yet endow their commonplace objects with an eerie grandeur. He was devoted to Jacob. Jacob, in turn, appreciated Follain's "enlargement of the real."[86] A Norman, Follain sympathized with the youngsters of the École de Rochefort and with their effort to ground themselves in lived language, lived experience.[87]

The Rochefort poets were enthusiastic, often ignorant, and intelligent. They considered themselves post-Surrealist, proudly embracing the role of provincial outsiders. They had a lot to learn, Jacob decided.[88] Part of teaching them required his smacking them down from time to time, which they tolerated. In May 1941, Jean Bouhier, a literary pharmacist in Rochefort-sur-Loire, organized them formally into a group with a plan to publish their work in the *Cahiers de Rochefort;* the *école* would include Cadou, Béalu, Rousselot, Fombeure, Émié, Follain, and Guillaume. They sometimes quarreled, but they also sustained each other. Manoll at first seemed suspicious but joined. "It's better to raise up than to scorn," Jacob advised.[89] The *Cahiers*—each one just a page folded into quarters—began appearing in May 1941, and Jacob recommended them to Paulhan.[90]

V.

WHILE THE POETS of Rochefort encouraged one another, the Germans and the functionaries of Vichy tightened their grip on the country. On May 14 the French rounded up 3,700 foreign Jews in Paris and sent them by train to the camps of Pithiviers and Beaune-la-Rolande in the Loire Valley, near Saint-Benoît. This was the *rafle des billets verts,* the round-up of the green "identity papers" that foreign Jews were instructed to pick up.[91] On June 2, Vichy passed its second anti-Semitic law, now defining as Jewish anyone belonging to the Jewish religion (not "race") and having two Jewish grandparents. It demanded a census of Jews all over France, even in the unoccupied zone, and it banned Jews from still more professions: finance, the stock exchange, law, and publishing were now closed to them. Soon afterward severe quotas were imposed on Jewish doctors, pharmacists, midwives, and dentists.[92]

Jacob felt the strangulation. He even felt it, irrationally, as a somehow legitimate judgment, writing to Paulhan that he'd been mistaken about himself. Now he aspired only to be forgotten (that wouldn't take long, he added).[93] To Pierre Minet, now working for the collaborationist Radio-France, he wrote, "I loved Poetry; (she didn't reciprocate this love)."[94] He began suffering from a painful infection in the middle ear, and vertigo; the physical pain reflected the psychic vertigo of living in a country that had welcomed monsters and declared war on its own people.[95] Jacob interpreted this larger vertigo symbolically, reading Hitler into the wicked king of the north in the Book of Daniel: "Neither shall he regard the God of his fathers, nor the desire of women, nor regard any god: for he shall magnify himself above all" (Daniel 11:37). But he took comfort in the last verse of Daniel 11: "Yet he shall come to his end, and none shall help him."[96]

To increase the vertigo, Jacob was now in a panic about his brother Jacques. The tailor shop in Paris had been seized, the proceeds from the forced sale had been confiscated, and Jacques and his wife were destitute. Jacob frantically tried to produce and sell more paintings to help them.[97] As one more sign of the times, the Germans arrested the "old, wise, erudite, and hunchbacked" archivist in Quimper, Henri Wagner.[98]

||

ON AUGUST 20, 1941, occurred the second roundup of Parisian Jews, even more shocking than the *rafle* in May because this time many of the victims were French, not foreign. The Germans initiated the action, informing the French police only two days ahead of time that they were expected to carry out the operation, and commanding the Prefecture of the Seine only on August 19 to organize the prison camp at Drancy, the so-called Cité de la Muette: clothing, bedding, food, and medicine for over four thousand men. (*Muette* here does not mean "mute" but is a deformation of the word *muete*, a kennel for hunting dogs, though once the place became a prison, the allegory of muteness was inescapable.)

At dawn on August 20, the whole eleventh arrondissement of Paris was blockaded and the Métro stations closed. Reinforced by German soldiers, the French police captured about three thousand men on the first day, and by the conclusion of the exercise four days later, 4,320 bewildered Jewish men between the ages of fourteen and seventy-two had been seized, hauled by bus to Drancy, and dumped into the vast courtyard of the former housing development six kilometers north of Paris.[99]

Max Jacob had at this point probably not even heard of Drancy, the camp where he would die. If the Cité de la Muette was known outside its working-class borders, it was as a triumph of utopian Modernist urbanism, celebrated in international architectural journals and in shows at the Musée d'Art Moderne in Paris and at the Museum of Modern Art in New York. Inspired by Le Corbusier, the architects Eugène Beaudouin and his uncle Marcel Lods had designed and built for Drancy the first skyscrapers in France, five stark rectangular towers, fourteen stories high, completed in

1935, rising at the back of a "comb" of ten long apartment blocks, two or three stories high. These were "HBM," *habitations bon marché*, low-income housing. The complex extended to the west in an enormous courtyard, eighty by two hundred meters, in the form of a horseshoe, bounded to the east, north, and west by barracks-like structures four stories high whose interiors had not been completed. The south end was open. All that was needed to turn this utopia into a kennel for human beings, or concentration camp, was to string barbed wire across the southern end and to build a watchtower at each corner.[100]

As a housing development, the Cité de la Muette proved disappointing. The first inhabitants—employees of the train and bus companies, and eight hundred Republican Guards and their families—moved in in September 1938 but had to be evacuated in December because of burst pipes; the elevators stalled; the heating failed. The French government had seen how efficiently this dire space could serve as a camp during the Drôle de Guerre, when it imprisoned Communists there. The Germans, on the very day they entered Paris, took over Drancy, christening it "Frontstalag 111," and used it to hold French, Canadian, and British prisoners of war. But by August 1941 those men had all been dispatched to Germany, and Drancy stood open to receive thousands of Jews.

The men flung into the unfinished buildings of the "horseshoe" had no beds, no bedding, and had to sleep on grooved concrete floors; there was hardly any running water; the toilets were in a shed in the courtyard; there was no toilet paper; the prisoners were forbidden to communicate with the outside world; they were fed two servings of watery soup, 200 grams of bread, and 200 grams of vegetable per day. When the cold set in, there was no heat. They suffered from fleas, lice, diarrhea, dysentery, and flu. Some men were too sick to reach the toilets, so the hallways were encrusted with excrement and stank. By November, some men had lost sixty-six pounds. At least forty had died.[101]

VI.

BECAUSE THE PRISONERS at Drancy had no way to send messages and because for some weeks even the Red Cross wasn't allowed in, no one on the outside had any idea of the hell behind that barbed wire. Even the earlier roundup of foreigners, in May 1941, and their imprisonment in camps near Saint-Benoît had been kept fairly quiet. Jacob was more aware of immediate dangers: the loss of his family's property, the difficulty of travel, harassments by the Gestapo, and the need to support his brother Jacques.[102]

But poetry and friendship sustained him. In mid-June he spent a couple of days in Montargis, visiting Dr. Szigeti and other doctor friends, where he met a seventeen-year-old medical student, Jacques Évrard, whose parents wanted their son to cultivate the poetic talent they supposed him to possess. Jacob hardly knew the young man and had seen none of his writing. The encounter took place at lunch with the parents, and Jacques later professed to remember little about it; he seemed none too eager for instruction.[103] But Jacob took the assignment seriously, and in a lined school notebook with a red cover, he composed his new *Art poétique, Conseils à un jeune poète,* and sent it to Évrard on June 23.[104]

Évrard objected to several of Jacob's formulations, especially one about the importance of "feeling" in poetry, which elicited a patient two-page letter from the poet trying to make his ideas still more clear. Évrard replied with a rather rude letter insisting on his—as he later put it—"impassible and icy dandyism." At which point Jacob broke off the correspondence. But Béalu, who knew Évrard, requested the notebook, typed it up, and passed the text along to the Rochefort poets; Jacob sent a copy to Lanoë, and Manoll wanted to publish it. (Gallimard brought it out posthumously in 1945.)[105] Jacob admired Rilke's poetry and the *Letters to a Young Poet,* but his *Conseils* are entirely his own. Some of the maxims share in the spirit of his *Art poétique* of 1922, but now, instead of abstraction, he emphasized the contemplative state from which poetry springs. The notebook began: "I'll open a school of the inner life, and on the door I'll write: art school."[106] He gathered here all the themes from his innumerable letters to young poets: the poet should be "permeable"; lyric is a "conflagration"; poetry isn't made of ideas or descriptions; the poet should honor mystery, vary syntax, be concrete, cherish words, avoid clichés, "exteriorize," and learn solitude.

On August 25, the final day of the monstrous roundup of Jews in Paris and their incarceration in Drancy, Jacob knew nothing about the crisis. He was worried about his friend Moricand's health. Living hand to mouth in Paris, Moricand was earning a bit working for Nazi propaganda at Radio-France, but he was ill with phthisis, which seemed to be an early form of tuberculosis, and for weeks Jacob had agitated for him to come to Montargis and be cared for by Dr. Szigeti. The doctor, a Jew, was beginning to experience his own difficulties, but he agreed to treat Moricand, and Jacob went to great pains to meet his friend in Montargis and help him settle in. The astrologer stayed for two weeks with the Szigetis, demonstrating his usual stunning selfishness. Even Jacob, who admired him, was shocked, writing Manoll that this friend with whom he corresponded so affectionately had seemed "a stranger."[107] More seriously, he thanked Manoll for taking in two little Jewish girls. (The children Manoll sheltered did survive the war, and so did Manoll.)[108]

Jacob enjoyed happier visits than Moricand's. Many Parisians who wanted to escape the city but couldn't reach the seashore in wartime chose Saint-Benoît for their holidays, and for a few weeks Jacob had so much company, he could hardly find time for painting. The only hotel in the village was inconveniently located right next to Madame Persillard's house, so Jacob was often called on to amuse people he hardly knew. But he also saw real friends. The singer and actor Charles Trenet visited in September. The artist-postman René Rimbert stayed for two weeks with his wife and met Roger Toulouse: the three painters walked, painted together, and discussed art—Jacob urging Rimbert to respect geometry, the golden rule.[109] Louis Guillaume turned up with Béalu.[110] To Yvon Belaval, Jacob reported cheerfully that he read Kierkegaard every day and sent him an analysis of Belaval's handwriting by his friend the graphologist Raymond Trillat. (The following year Éluard showed Trillat some handwriting by

Picasso without revealing the identity of the writer. "Loves intensely and kills what he loves," judged the graphologist.)[111]

VII.

IN OCTOBER 1941 the Société des Gens de Lettres (Society of Authors) canceled all Jacob's rights: he could no longer claim copyright for his work or collect royalties.[112] He would publish no more, he wrote Mezure bitterly; he would no longer set foot in "the void and mud called the life of an artist."[113] He reported the blow to Robert Zunz; to François de Montalivet, he wrote of living in Saint-Benoît in mud and garbage, being called "a Jew and a clique," "rich and lazy."[114]

On November 4 a Gestapo officer accompanied by a German soldier marched into Jacob's room at Madame Persillard's. Jacob put on the performance of his life. "Police," announced the officer. "*Enchanté*," replied the poet, and invited the guests to warm themselves by his little stove. Asked what he was writing, he said he was sorry he didn't have his books to show, but then, seizing a copy of *Ballades* from the table, he offered it to the officer: "Should I inscribe it for you? What's your name?" As the interrogation proceeded, Jacob interrupted politely, showing Fabureau's biography of him: all the information was in there, he assured the man. The officer picked up a stack of letters Jacob had ready to mail and demanded that he open them and explicate each line; he marked down the names and addresses (including Paul Petit's). (Thenceforth Jacob destroyed all letters he received and asked his correspondents not to use his last name.) After terrorizing Madame Persillard, the Germans left, carrying Fabureau's biography. Jacob thought he was safe.[115]

More deaths followed. The sweet young Corsican poet Michel Levanti died of tuberculosis on November 13, and Jacob sorrowed at this loss of a friend he had known only through letters: Levanti had asked his priest especially to notify Jacob.[116] But now came griefs and horrors on a larger scale.

On December 13, Jacob's brother-in-law Lucien Lévy, the jeweler, husband of his favorite sister Mirté-Léa, was arrested in Paris as part of a third, massive roundup of Jews. This one, the *rafle des notables*, focused on affluent and professional men and was carried out mainly by the SS, with support by the French police. When he wrote François de Montalivet on December 29 asking for help, Jacob still didn't know where Lucien Lévy had been taken; his cousin, Roger Gompel, heir and director of the department store and a serious art collector, had also been picked up.[117] When Jacob wrote Lanoë two days later, he learned that Lucien had been taken to the camp at Compiègne. Lucien was a veteran of the Great War, Jacob insisted, and his father a veteran of 1870; the newspapers were being careful not to report such news "so as not to provoke the indignation of reasonable people."[118] What Jacob couldn't yet know was the appalling treatment of prisoners as Compiègne, a regime of starvation. Nor did he know—though it soon became clear—that with this third roundup, German strategy had changed. In response to the United States entering the war and to the increasing attacks by the Resistance, the Nazis had started deporting thousands of Jews "to the East." They also started executing hostages. Ninety-five hostages, some from Compiègne, some from Drancy, were shot on December 15.[119]

To his shock, the banker Robert Zunz, Jacob's patron, was arrested and taken to Compiègne on December 12. This highly conservative Frenchman, a monarchist and quasi-Catholic, a veteran of the Great War who had helped to save the French economy in 1926, resembled many other respectable Jews who suddenly found themselves hurled into oblivion. Even in the barbarity of Compiègne, Zunz didn't lose his faith in France. In the talks set up by prisoners desperate to maintain a semblance of normal life, he lectured approvingly on Vichy economic policy, a corporatist structure meant to replace capitalism. He intended to proceed with his own baptism and that of his wife and children. He was lucky. Powerful Catholic friends managed to liberate him from the camp on March 25, 1942, just two days before the first deportation of 1,112 Jews from France to Auschwitz.[120]

||

THE CATARACT OF misfortune kept plunging. In January 1942, two anonymous letters warned Jacob to hide. Louis Émié had been urging him to retreat to Bordeaux, but Jacob hid for a month closer to home, in Orléans, with Roger Toulouse's in-laws, the Texiers. He stayed with this kindly couple from January 13 to February 16, during which time Roger painted his portrait, and Jacob in turn painted portraits of his hostess Madame Texier and of Roger's wife Marguerite. But he was tormented by anxiety for his family and returned to Madame Persillard's so he could receive mail and news. He was "assured" of being protected, he told Lanoë.[121]

Everyone to whom Jacob turned for help in freeing his brother-in-law professed helplessness. He even appealed to Claudel. "Dear Max Jacob," replied this Catholic eminence. "What painful news! I'll do what I can, but I won't hide from you that my credit is slender."[122] Indeed it was. The former ambassador had taken a risk, publishing a letter to the chief rabbi of France expressing the "disgust, horror, and indignation" felt by "all good French citizens and especially Catholics" at the evils visited upon their "Jewish compatriots."[123]

In February, Dr. Szigeti and his family escaped to the unoccupied zone, where they would survive the war.[124] Other friends participated, to varying degrees, in the Resistance. Paulhan had organized the first literary resistance as soon as France fell, and along with Jean Cassou and Michel Leiris, he belonged to the network of the Musée de l'Homme. He was arrested in February 1942; his collaborationist colleague Drieu La Rochelle managed to get him freed, while seven members of the group were shot.[125] On February 26, Jacob wrote Moricand that Paul Petit had been arrested, and begged Moricand to pull strings to save him: as the astrologer worked for Nazi propaganda, Jacob imagined that he had influence. Moricand replied that he could do nothing.[126] Over the next few months of Petit's imprisonment at Fresnes and then in Germany, Jacob followed his case in anguish.[127]

On March 8, Lucien Lévy died in the hospital at Compiègne, of gangrene. (He may be considered fortunate: he was spared the trip to Auschwitz.) His wife, Mirté-Léa, was "mad" with grief. Jacob took the train to Paris and Compiègne for the miserable funeral; he and his brother Jacques found Lucien's "anonymous cadaver" in the hospital morgue and followed the coffin through "interminable" drab suburbs, "alone as two rats." Too devastated to accompany them, Mirté-Léa lay at home in bed, sick, howling.[128]

From time to time, Jacob's friends tried to help him escape. Szigeti, from the South, sent him a woman border-crossing guide to try to persuade him to leave Saint-Benoît and try to make it to America. Jacob refused. The effort was too great; he couldn't imagine surviving in America without patrons, clients, and friends; his family in France needed him.[129]

||

THE FIRST TRANSPORT of Jews left Drancy for Auschwitz on March 27, 1942, in train cars provided by the SNCF, the French national railroad.

||

JACOB'S FAMILY MAY have needed him, but it was rapidly diminishing. On April 15 his sister Delphine died suddenly in her sleep in Quimper— of a broken heart, Jacob thought. There was some suggestion of suicide. "I'm hard and staunch," Jacob wrote Belaval. "Too hard, and not so staunch."[130] He took the train to Quimper and saw her on her deathbed in the cramped apartment to which she and Gaston had retreated. Her face, in life so stern, had a "paradisal beauty," Jacob wrote to Madame Marcel Neveu, the genteel, pious friend of long standing who lived in a small château outside Quimper. (Her husband had died in August 1940 in what Jacob called "a surprising and desolating atrocity," perhaps a suicide.) In spite of her harshness, Delphine had kept in touch with her bohemian brother; in a recent letter she had recounted a dream in which she and a "translucid angel" walked in Concarneau listening to deli- cious music. "That was a vision of Paradise, which you deserve," her brother told her. Delphine rejected the notion angrily, but Jacob insisted: she would go to heaven. Quimper was beautiful that April, its bridges decked in flowers, the chestnut trees in bloom. Jacob walked by the old family shop, now closed, and by the villa that had once belonged to his aunt and uncle, now a "casino" for German officers.[131] It was the last time he saw his native city.

Gaston, alone in Quimper, deaf and frail, didn't ask his brother to come live with him. Jacob was relieved: he wouldn't have been able to refuse such a request. He assured Madame Neveu that he himself was safe. "I'm told I'm protected in high places," he told her. "In higher places than people realize." (He seemed to mean both his friends who had dealings with the Germans, like Cocteau and Moricand, but also God.)[132]

ON HIS WAY back from Quimper, he stopped in Nantes to spend the night with Lanoë and his family, and repaired the gouache whose surface had cracked. By April 21 he was back in Saint-Benoît. And it was there that the new edict struck him; after June 6, when they appeared in public, all Jews were to wear a yellow star.

Still worse news arrived. On July 9, Paul Petit was deported to Germany, to the prison at Saarbrücken: he would be tried and shot in August 1944.[133] On July 16 and 17 came the worst roundup yet, the infamous Vel d'Hiv, in which German and French police spread out across Paris, capturing 13,152 Jewish men, women, and children. They were shut up in mass confusion in savage heat in the bicycle racing stadium without food or water, then shipped to Auschwitz. As French Christians saw babies and children torn from their mothers, public disapproval began to simmer, all the more as such scenes multiplied in cities across France.[134] For Jacob, the disaster took an intimate form: on July 16 poor doddering old Gaston was arrested in the public garden in Quimper; he had broken the rule forbidding Jews to use public spaces.

Once again Jacob wrote Moricand for help. His brother was in prison in Quimper, he reported. And the Parisian police had ordered the gendarmes in Saint-Benoît to verify that Max Jacob was wearing the yellow star. He was.[135]

||

YET JACOB WASN'T crushed. Poetry gave him a core of resilience and helped him to "resist." So did his religious faith and his cult of friendship. He made the yellow star his own in the poem "Neighborly Love."

> Who has seen the toad crossing the road? It's a tiny man. He drags along on his knees: as if he were ashamed . . . ? No! It's just rheumatism! One leg trails behind, he brings it forward! That's how he advances. Pygmy clown, has he crawled from the sewer? Is he going there? No one has noticed the toad in the street. Before, no one noticed me in the street: now children are amazed by my yellow star. Happy toad! You don't have a yellow star.[136]

Jacob dedicated it to his new friend Jean Rousselot. Poet and police commissioner, young Rousselot managed to maintain a delicate political equilibrium: he served in the Vichy police force, first in Vendôme, then in Orléans, but at the same time he participated in the literary Resistance (and later actively joined the *maquis*). He was on the editorial committee of *Fontaine,* which defied Vichy censorship; he was in touch with Béalu and the other Rochefort poets and got himself transferred to Orléans to be near them. He and Jacob had been corresponding for about a year when they met in late April 1942.

The encounter took place in a café in Orléans in the company of Béalu, Manoll, and Toulouse. A group of Jacob's poems had just appeared in *Fontaine,* signed "a parishioner of Saint-Benoît": religious poems in which scenes of Christ's arrest, torture, and crucifixion clearly reflected the suffering of France.[137] Rousselot was astonished by Jacob's performance. Instead of the penitential old man he expected, he found a dashing raconteur tossing off jokes and innuendos, tilted back in his chair, emitting great puffs from the fat cigar he'd been given; he looked to Rousselot like a man of the world, "an American businessman," or a spoiled, successful artist. Only when the poet stood up did Rousselot perceive the worn shoes, the frayed coat, the limp, and underneath the frantic gaiety, the anguish. Turning to make his way to the bus back to his village, Jacob carefully pocketed the stub of the cigar.[138]

Jacob soon dropped the cabaret act with Rousselot, who became one of the steadfast friends of his last two years. Alas, Rousselot's position in the police proved no bulwark against the Gestapo. Nor did the authority of the mayor of Saint-Benoît, who told a Gestapo officer once, "Leave this man alone: he's a scholar."[139]

Through all the grief, Jacob remained spirited and welcomed new friends. One recruit was Henri Dion, a minor government administrator and deeply religious young man who met Jacob on July 12, the celebration of Saint Benoît. Dion first saw the poet at the vespers service in the basilica, seated in the last row, half-hidden, wearing the yellow star.[140] Dion, behind his sober demeanor something of a mystic, lived in ecstatic celebration of the Virgin Mary; he recognized in Jacob someone who also lived in two worlds.[141]

Paul Éluard might have been considered Jacob's enemy during the heyday of Surrealism, but he now sought out the beleaguered poet. He'd been writing to him for several weeks when he turned up in Saint-Benoît on July 13, and they spent the day together. Among other things, Éluard brought copies of Jacob's books for him to sign and illustrate. Thus one old wound was healed.[142] Another healed in the affectionate letters he and Reverdy began to exchange, a reconciliation brought about by Jacob's old sponsor, Abbé Weill.[143]

Jacob was so well attended, so supported by friends new and old in Saint-Benoît, that the visits brought trouble. Someone warned him that the police suspected him of "a Jewish plot" because of all his guests. Already in late July he wrote Mezure that he might have to flee precipitously.[144] Yet four days later he wrote Lanoë that the frontiers were guarded, and that he would stay on, "protected" at Saint-Benoît.[145]

VIII.

FAR FROM THE VILLAGE, artistic life in the capital flourished in a seedy way. Cocteau, during the Occupation, was mainly occupied by theater and film, annoyed to find these "serious matters" interrupted by "the dramatic frivolity of the war."[146] He was friendly with Gerhard Heller in the Propaganda-Staffel; Otto Abetz, the German ambassador, invited him to plays and parties; he dined with the German novelist Ernst Jünger; he was particularly friendly with Hitler's favorite sculptor, Arno Breker. On the front page of *Comoedia*, on May 23, 1942, Cocteau rhapsodized about the bloated bronze figures Breker was exhibiting at the Orangerie. In capital letters, Cocteau announced, "I SALUTE YOU, BREKER. I SALUTE YOU FROM THE HIGH FATHERLAND OF POETS."[147] But precisely because of Cocteau's intimacy with the Germans, it was to him that Jacob would turn in his last days.

André Salmon made his living in these years in a collaborationist log-orrhea, writing in Vichy newspapers like *Panorama* and *Révolution nationale*. They make surreal reading. Throughout 1943, from *Panorama*'s pages stuffed with articles on theater and fashion, one would barely know that a war was going on. Salmon filled his columns with cute recollections of Montmartre and blather about artists who had proven friendly to Vichy and even to the Germans: Derain, Dufy, Van Dongen, or those who were safely dead, like Juan Gris. *Révolution nationale* was more political. Vichy France saw itself as resisting two imperialisms—one Capitalist, one Communist—and "between the two monstrous gluttons, the only option is a European Socialism, without democracy and without Jews."[148] Salmon's chitchat provided a reassuring fiction of continuing Frenchness for this savage ideology.

||

THE ALLIES LANDED in North Africa on November 8, and the Germans responded by occupying all of France. Jacob's brother Gaston, who had been released in September, was arrested again on December 16. Jacob was frantic. The first incarceration, in Quimper, had been relatively mild; the old family maidservant had been able to bring Gaston food and clean clothes. Now he utterly disappeared. Two weeks later Jacob received vague news that Gaston was "in Germany."[149] He eventually learned that Gaston was imprisoned in Compiègne. He never knew that he had been transferred to Drancy and on February 11, 1943, shipped to Auschwitz, where he went immediately to the gas chamber.[150] In a particularly sadistic episode, Jacob was told by someone "high in the police" that "he shouldn't fret about his brother: he would see him sooner than he imagined." (This, when Gaston was already dead.)[151]

War gripped the country. The Germans seized more and more Frenchmen, shipping them to labor in German factories: every day Jacob said goodbye to friends being sent off to work. The Germans also seized horses; from his window, Jacob could hear their hoofbeats on the paving stones as they were led away.[152] He was mailing food to Jacques and Mirté-Léa in Paris; at the same time, he had difficulty finding even potatoes.[153] On March 23, the Allies bombed Nantes. In September, a bomb fell in the courtyard of Julien Lanoë's house but, miraculously, did not explode. Cadou barely eluded death in that attack.[154] Jacob asked if Lanoë knew where Jean Fraysse, of *Les Feux de Paris,* had gone; he'd carried off a packet of Jacob's manuscripts, and Jacob hadn't heard from him in over a year. He also wrote Szigeti to ask about Fraysse. Fraysse had, in fact, disappeared. For many years his vanishing remained a mystery; it now seems that he was murdered in 1941, trying to escape into Spain.[155]

||

IN LATE DECEMBER 1943, Jacob went to Orléans and Montargis to buy Christmas gifts for the children of Saint-Benoît. He stayed for five days in Montargis, a guest in the family of one of his doctor friends, Dr. Lesage. Here he enjoyed the warmth of a cheerful family: the doctor's daughters played the piano, and the son, fifteen-year-old Jacques, was the special confidant for whom Jacob had composed a notebook of ethical advice, a practical guide to life.[156] Jacob returned to Saint-Benoît for Christmas—the mass celebrated in the basilica, the crèche with its plaster figures brought out year after year—followed by days of writing letters of New Year's greetings and making ceremonial visits in the village. When he reported all this to Jacques Mezure on January 5, 1944, he didn't yet know that his sister, Mirté-Léa, had been arrested.[157]

Mirté-Léa was seized on January 4 and taken to Drancy. Jacob was beside himself. He threw himself into a campaign to save her, writing to everyone he imagined might have influence with the Germans: Cocteau, Marie Laurencin, Minet (now working for Radio-France), Moricand, Misia Sert, Sacha Guitry, the Bishop of Orléans, the Archbishop of Sens. He consulted Lanoë about whether to ask Chanel, who had a German lover.[158] His letters were heart-wrenching. He described his little sister, the "companion of his childhood," her suffering as a widow, her devotion to her mentally handicapped son. "Dear friend, permit me to kiss your hands, the hem of your dress. . . . I beg you, do something," he implored Misia.[159] Sacha Guitry replied that he couldn't help "some unknown Jew." If it had been Max, he said, "he could do something."[160]

Drancy now contained men, women, and children.[161] Transports to Auschwitz were leaving almost every week. Even as her brother sent his desperate appeals, Mirté-Léa was shoved into a train car on January 20; she went immediately to the gas chamber on her arrival. Max Jacob never knew what became of her.[162]

IX.

WHEN HE WASN'T writing letters to save his sister, Jacob was reading Gongora. Better than Mallarmé, he told Béalu.[163] On the freezing Sunday morning of February 20, Dr. Castelbon, one of the Montargis doctors, drove the Béalus to Saint-Benoît to visit Jacob. They clustered in his room, warming themselves at his stove, and admired the drawings he was working on. They had lunch together in the restaurant of the little hotel. "At least they can't take this away from me: I've loved," said Jacob.

He confessed to Dr. Castelbon, "You know, you can't always believe me: I make things up. I know it's wicked, and I confess it every morning to the priest—and then start up again." They visited the basilica as they had done so many times before. Jacob, who hadn't signed his name in the visitors' book for years, added his signature, and the dates 1921–1944. They spent the afternoon chatting; they dined together. Madame Persillard gave the Béalus the bedroom next to Jacob's while the doctor slept at the hotel. Jacob stayed up late with Béalu, patiently going over his new manuscript of poems.

The next morning Jacob rose early in the brutal cold to help the vicar, Abbé Hatton, serve mass in the chapel in the hospice; then he returned to his room, lit his fire, and wrote his daily meditation. When he rejoined his friends, he was in a jolly mood, trilling a verse: "J'suis l'bouquet, j'suis l'bouquet, j'suis l'bouc émissaire" (a pun on *bouquet* and *bouc*, scapegoat: "I'm the bouquet, I'm the bouquet, I'm the scapegoat"). After lunch, the doctor drove them to Sully—still half in ruins from German bombs—where the Béalus would catch the bus to Montargis. They planned a visit for the following Sunday. "Au revoir, les enfants!" called Max, waving at them as the bus pulled out.[164]

On Tuesday, Jacob dined with friends in the village, Dr. Georges Durand and his wife Rolande; he left early to attend a parish meeting. Next day was Ash Wednesday: Jacob received this mark of death on his forehead that morning at the rite in the crypt of the basilica. On Thursday, February 24, he rose at dawn to write his meditation and to help Abbé Hatton serve mass. He was back in his room, writing letters and expecting a visit from Roger Toulouse, when a gray car from Orléans marked "P.O.L." drove up, and three Germans in trenchcoats got out.[165] They rang the bell, climbed the stairs to his room, and arrested him.

Madame Persillard dashed over to the parsonage to rally the priest and the vicar, but they were busy. ("They could have come!" she protested later. "It was a little funeral of no importance whatsoever!")[166] One of the monks from the basilica hurried to the scene, as did Dr. Castelbon, still at the hotel: he had time to thrust a flask of alcohol and a pair of his own woolen long johns into Jacob's hands. "Keep his things here for when he returns," ordered the Germans. Madame Persillard made him take a quilt. "A shame," said Jacob. "You'll never get it back." She erupted, "You see! Fat lot of good it did you to pray so much!" Jacob stayed calm; before stepping into the car, he shook hands with the small group of villagers who had gathered. At the bistro next door, when the car had driven off, Dr. Castelbon heard a neighbor say, "That man, he couldn't do no harm: he wasn't writing anymore." "He wrote with his paintings," said his companion.[167]

At noon, when he had returned from the funeral, the Canon Fleureau sent Abbé Hatton on a bicycle to Orléans to alert Toulouse, who called Béalu and Rousselot. Those three sounded the alarm, calling on Jean Denoël, Salmon, and Cocteau. "I'll do the impossible," Cocteau assured Béalu.[168] Tolouse leaped onto a train to Paris to enlist the aid of Albert Buesche, the German art critic for *Pariser Zeitung* who had met Jacob and knew his work.

In Orléans, Jacob was incarcerated with sixty-five other Jews, men, women, and children, in a filthy, freezing military cell, ten by ten meters square. They had straw mats to sleep on, already soaked in urine. They were given soup at noon, a little Camembert at night.[169] And among the prisoners Jacob discovered his friend Georges Dreyfus, a converted Jew. He managed to dispatch a message to Rousselot: "Perhaps your title will permit you to bring me some tobacco and matches. Let Cocteau know. In friendship, Max Jacob. Man of Letters, Chevalier of the Légion d'honneur."[170] But Rousselot didn't receive the message in time.

In the prison in Orléans, Jacob exercised his famous gifts: perhaps they had never been so useful. He told jokes, sang, recited verses, cast horoscopes; he tended the sick, applying cupping glasses (from two jars) on a woman suffering from pneumonia; he soothed the desperate. On February 26 the wretched group was trucked to the station, packed into a train, and hauled to the Gare d'Austerlitz in Paris. From the train, Jacob was able to send a few appeals for help. To Cocteau he wrote, "Dear Jean. I write you in a train car, courtesy of the gendarmes who guard us. We'll soon be at Drancy. That's all I have to say. Sacha [Guitry], when asked to help my sister, said, 'If it was Max, I could do something.' Well, it's me. Kisses, Max."[171] To the Canon Fleureau at Saint-Benoît, he wrote,

"Dear Monsieur the *curé*, Please excuse this letter from a drowning man, written courtesy of the gendarmes. I would like to tell you that I'll soon be at Drancy. I have some conversions in progress. I trust in God and in my friends. I thank Him for the martyrdom that has begun. Max Jacob. I forget no one in my continual prayers."[172] To Moricand, he wrote, "Dear Conrad, I write you from the train car carrying me to Drancy. Let God's will be done. The gendarmes are charming. Max."[173] He asked his brother Jacques to alert Salmon and Minet.[174]

From Paris, buses carried the prisoners to Drancy. In the ritual of arrival, Jacob passed, with his companions, from one table to another in the courtyard to be processed. He gave up his 5,520 francs and his gold watch; those effects were duly registered. He gave his personal information. At the registration table, one of the clerks, Madame Bloch, a prisoner herself, recognized Jacob as a friend of her mother, Madame Léon, also detained in the camp.[175] He was assigned to the fourth floor of stairway nineteen, given the number 15,872, the letter "B," and a green sticker— symbols of those to be deported in the next transport. He was scheduled to leave for Auschwitz in transport 69, March 7.[176]

||

OUTSIDE DRANCY, JACOB'S friends bestirred themselves. Cocteau pulled every string he could reach. Advised by Guitry and Sert, he made a plan with Georges Prade, a wealthy businessman who ran the collaborationist newspaper *Les Nouveaux Temps:* Prade owned a gouache of Jacob's and had already been called on to help Mirté-Léa. Cocteau composed a letter of appeal for Jacob's release, which Prade took to the counselor Hans-Henning von Bose at the German embassy.

> I would call Max Jacob a great poet if it weren't a pleonasm. One should just say poet—because poetry dwells in him and escapes from him, from his hand, whether he wills it or not.
>
> With Apollinaire he invented a language that soars above our language and expresses the depths.

He was the troubadour of this extraordinary tournament in which Picasso, Matisse, Braque, Derain, Chirico confront each other with their colorful coats of arms.

For years now, he has renounced the world and hides in the shadow of a church. He lives there (in Saint-Benoît-sur-Loire) the exemplary existence of a peasant and a monk.

The youth of France loves him, addresses him familiarly, respects him, and observes his life as a model.

As for me, I salute his nobility, his wisdom, his inimitable grace, his secret prestige—his "chamber music," to borrow a phrase from Nietzsche.

May God come to his aid.

Jean Cocteau

p.s. I add that Max Jacob has been a Catholic for twenty years.[177]

As Patricia Sustrac points out, however, von Bose had no authority to release prisoners. Only the Gestapo could do that. There is no record of Cocteau's letter and von Bose's request having been sent from the embassy to Gestapo headquarters.[178]

With Jouhandeau, Cocteau also sought help from Gerhard Heller, the "sensitive" officer for Nazi propaganda. Heller's later account of the affair is nauseating. His "failure" to save Jacob, he says, still pains him. The passage starts with a lie: Jacob was not arrested, as Heller claims, by the French police. As soon as Heller heard from Cocteau and Jouhandeau, he called the German embassy and even met with Otto Abetz, the ambassador, who told him, "Do what you can; I'll cover for you." But the embassy had no authority over the Gestapo. All these "initiatives," Heller says, took several days. When he finally obtained permission to visit Jacob at Drancy, "Alas! I learned that Max Jacob had died of pneumonia. . . . Empty-handed at the gates of this abominable camp, I desired nevertheless to make one final gesture; I went to a florist shop to buy a rose and returned to throw it over the wall of the camp."[179] This was not, apparently, Heller's attitude in 1944. When Youki Desnos went to him to try to save her husband and expressed anger at the death of Max Jacob, Heller replied, "Max Jacob is a Jew, Madame, those people are vermin."[180]

BY SOME MYSTIC coincidence, Jacob's old friend the composer Henri Sauguet had begun to tinker with some poems from Jacob's *Pénitents en maillots roses* in February, when Pierre Colle called with news of the poet's arrest. He and Colle went to find Picasso at lunch at his customary bistro, Le Catalan, near his studio on the Rue des Grands Augustins. Picasso was in a lousy mood, Sauguet recalled. Whether he knew of Jacob's arrest was unclear. He did say, "Max is an angel. He can fly over the wall by himself."[181]

This incident is perhaps the most widely known story about Max Jacob and is the one thing many people think they know about him. It provides several satisfactions: that of showing a famous artist to be a monster, and his lost friend as a victim. But the situation was far more complex. Picasso, it's true, was no hero; he betrayed Apollinaire back in 1911, when they were interrogated about the theft of the Mona Lisa. But though German authorities did visit Picasso's studio during the Occupation, the painter was vulnerable: he was a resident alien in Vichy France, and to be deported to Franco's Spain would have been catastrophic. When he heard about Cocteau's appeal, Picasso went to Prade and offered to sign it. Prade dissuaded him, arguing that the signature would carry no weight with the Gestapo and would only make Picasso's position in Paris more delicate than ever. The wisecrack itself was in the cruel *lingua franca* of the Bateau Lavoir.[182]

Moricand approached the Gestapo directly. It may be the only decent act of his indecent life. In a letter to Théophile Briant written on March 5— the day of Jacob's death, though Moricand didn't know it—Moricand described the maneuvers by which he was trying to stimulate Prade and the Germans to effective action. He "flung himself into the water," he said, going to see the Hauptsturmführer Rodje (*sic*: he meant Röthke), who had taken over as head of Jewish affairs in France and was hell-bent on deporting as many Jews as possible.[183] Moricand's effort bore no fruit and was in any case too late. Sacha Guitry, who had been able to free Tristan Bernard, did nothing that can be documented to help Jacob.[184] As for Misia Sert, her claim that her husband moved heaven and earth to save Jacob and obtained an order for the poet's release must remain in the realm of mythology. Patricia Sustrac has definitively shown that there is no record of any order of liberation; nor is there a record of any such transaction in the Spanish or German files.[185]

||

ON HIS STRAW mat on the fourth floor, Jacob shivered in the cold and began to cough violently. Word spread through the camp that a famous poet had arrived, and prisoners slipped past guards to see him. On the first day, he could still speak; he entertained guests in his old way, narrating tales. Madame Bloch's mother, Madame Léon, whom Jacob had known in Paris, came to see him.[186] Julien London, a prisoner who survived Drancy, described these playful sessions, rare moments of fantasy in the halls of hell. But by the next day Jacob was racked with pain in his chest; he could hardly breathe and began to vomit. He was transferred to what passed for an infirmary, and there he was cared for by several Jewish doctors who were fellow prisoners.

Max Jacob was dying of pneumonia. There was no medicine. All that could be provided was a cot, relatively clean sheets, and most of all, kindness. The several accounts of his last hours seem contradictory, but one can imagine that all are true, reflecting different phases of his agony. One witness who lived to report the scene was a Jewish doctor who claimed that Max Jacob died peacefully. He said, "I'm with God," and already seemed far away. He expressed only one desire: to die as a Catholic. He made this request tactfully, apologetically, not wanting to offend his fellow Jews: "You understand, I've given my life to this passion."[187] Another Jewish doctor who attended him, Raymond Weille, remembered that Jacob kept asking for a priest. There was no priest in the camp, but a few Jewish Catholic prisoners, converts like Madame Léon, recited the prayers for the dying over him.[188]

Others witnessed a more agonized death. Jacob hallucinated, he cried out. He saw trees marching and tried to seize them. The cold was crawling up his legs, he groaned. But his last words seem to have been peaceful: "You have the face of an angel," he told the doctor leaning over him.[189] He died at nine p.m. on March 5. Madame Bloch, her sister, and two nurses laid out the body in a little room near the entrance to the camp.[190]

TRANSPORT 69, CARRYING 1,501 people, left without him on March 7, for Auschwitz.

X.

MAX JACOB WANTED to die as a Catholic. As well as they could without a priest, his fellow prisoners tried to make that come true. Georges Dreyfus, Julien London, and several other Jewish Catholics bribed a guard and crept into the small room where the body lay; they crossed his arms over his breast, placed his rosary between his fingers, and recited prayers.[191]

The official wheels turned slowly. The death was registered by the police commissioner in Pantin on March 6 and the next day at the town hall in Drancy: all punctilious and according to the rules.[192] Meanwhile Jacob's friends had no idea that he had died: they had been encouraged to think he would soon be free. On March 9, Roger Toulouse, who had received a politely optimistic response from the art critic Buesche, gave free rein to his hopes and called the monks at Saint-Benoît, announcing Jacob's forthcoming release.[193] Toulouse, Béalu, and Rousselot pooled their money to buy Jacob a welcome-home gift and began to plan a party for him. At about the same time, on March 11, Jacob was buried in the municipal cemetery at Ivry-sur-Seine.[194]

Only on March 13 did Jacob's death certificate reach the mayor's office in Saint-Benoît. And only then did his friends learn that he had died. The mayor called Salmon, Rousselot, and Canon Fleureau; Rousselot called Béalu and Toulouse; the news spread. At first they couldn't believe it.[195] Even Prade was under the impression that an order of liberation had been signed; he called Cocteau to tell him so on March 14, only to learn the truth the next day. So convinced were Jacob's friends that they had succeeded in freeing him that a rumor circulated, which soon hardened into a myth, that the Gestapo had signed an order of release but had done so maliciously when they already knew the poet was dead. Cocteau was stunned: Prade had just told him that Jacob would be released.[196]

Pierre Colle, who learned of the death from Salmon, wrote his father on March 16 with the news. He had also learned that Jacob had named him his heir and literary executor; he prepared to go to Saint-Benoît to gather up Jacob's belongings. Already, right after the arrest, Jacob's neighbor Dr. Durand had gone into his room with the village notary to rescue manuscripts and paintings, which they deposited in two boxes and gave to the *curé* for safekeeping; Béalu and Toulouse had the same idea and filled the poet's trunk with other papers, books, and paintings on February 27 and gave them to Dr. Castelbon in Montargis to keep. Among other things, they discovered on Jacob's table an unfinished gouache, a portrait of Picasso.[197] When Pierre Colle arrived in Saint-Benoît, he found Max's room so familiar in its disorder and the smell of tobacco, he hardly dared touch anything, so strongly did he feel the presence of his old friend. Canon Fleureau gave him the boxes of papers that Dr. Durand had saved. Colle kept Jacob's rosary for his father and eventually gave Dr. Szigeti the copy of *The Imitation of Christ* inscribed to Jacob by Picasso on the day of his baptism.[198]

On Sunday, March 19, Pierre Colle went with Abbé Morel, Minet, Prade, Salmon, and Sauguet out to Ivry to wander among the graves and try to locate their friend's resting place. They found it: 44th division, 24th line, 27th grave. Colle had a cross placed upon it, and the following Sunday, Abbé Morel returned to bless it formally.[199] (In 1949, on the anniversary of Jacob's death, his body would be transferred to the cemetery of Saint-Benoît, where he wanted to leave his last mark upon earth.)

In a final contretemps, there was a mix-up about the mass Jacob's friends arranged for him at the Église Saint-Roch in Paris. A first, muddled communication brought some of them to the church on March 18, Moricand, Derain, Dora Maar, and Reverdy among them. Picasso went but lingered at the door of the church, afraid of the Gestapo.[200] On Thursday, March 21, the proper mass was celebrated at Saint-Roch, a ceremony kept quiet in order not to attract the wrong kind of attention. About fifty people gathered to pay their respects to the irrepressible spirit who had been extinguished. Picasso came. So did Cocteau, Éluard, Reverdy, Mauriac, Salmon, Derain, and Braque, old enemies, old comrades, brought together, momentarily, in a common loss.[201]

Jacob's last painting, left unfinished, was a portrait of Picasso, older, stocky, glancing over his left shoulder with his huge dark eyes. And when Michel and Louise Leiris presented a reading of Picasso's play, *Le Désir attrapé par la queue* (Desire Caught by the Tail), at their apartment two days before the final mass, a drama acted and attended by the intellectual aristocracy of Paris—Picasso, Dora Maar, Camus, Beauvoir, Sartre, Queneau—the rite took place in front of Picasso's 1915 pencil drawing of Max Jacob. The portrait was set up in the place of honor. Quizzical, taut, pensive, a little rumpled but gentlemanly, Max Jacob contemplated his best friend's madcap play and held his breath.[202]

ACKNOWLEDGMENTS

It has taken me many years to write this biography. The research took much longer than I had originally anticipated, and the work was interrupted by life as a full-time teacher and mother, by illness in the family, and by other books. But I don't regret the long period of gestation. Since I started in 1985 many scholars have worked on Jacob, and I've benefited from their research and from the increasing sophistication of critical debate about his work. A biography is inevitably a collective enterprise. I owe debts of gratitude to many people. The work would not have been possible without the support of Sylvia Lorant-Colle and Béatrice Saalburg, Jacob's faithful literary executors and the daughters of Jacob's friend and dealer Pierre Colle. Nor would it have been possible without the help of Patricia Sustrac, a foremost Jacob scholar and president of the Association des Amis de Max Jacob, endlessly generous with her suggestions and responses to questions, and active in keeping Jacob's memory alive. Among those who have enormously enlarged our knowledge of Jacob are the scholarly editors of Jacob's correspondence, especially Anne Kimball, who published the letters of Jacob to Cocteau, Nino Frank, Jouhandeau, Pierre Minet, Jean Paulhan, and Julien Lanoë; and Patricia Sustrac, who edited Jacob's letters to Jacques Mezure, to Roger Toulouse, and to Robert Zunz, and contributed to *Max Jacob écrit: Lettres à six amis*, the collection of six correspondences edited by Anne Kimball. Sustrac is also responsible for the most up-to-date research on the arrest and death of Max Jacob.

In 2005, Béatrice Mousli published a thorough biography of Jacob in French; I didn't consult it while writing my own, since I had started long before and consulted the same archives, and I didn't want to seem to be following in her tracks. After finishing my book, I was free to consult and admire hers. Antonio Rodriguez has extended Max Jacob's afterlife with his meticulous edition of Jacob's *Oeuvres* in the Gallimard Quarto edition, and among the scholars who are guiding discussion of Jacob these days, Alexander Dickow stands out.

Liliane Ziegel, a professional researcher who helped many scholars in her long life, oriented me in the libraries of Paris and often sent me books and articles when I was in the United States and needed material. I had come to her through my friend Francis Steegmuller, and she in turn became one of my closest friends, my French godmother, and an important guide to Jewish life in France. She died in 2015. Her great-niece, the writer and translator Aude Pivin, also a dear friend, helped track down illustrations and obscure articles and consulted about translation.

I owe thanks to my French friends for their hospitality and generosity: Anne Atik, Sybille Friedel, Edith de la Héronnière, Marie-Odile Masek, and Marie Mislej. And certainly anyone working on Jacob must be grateful to Maria Green, author of the *Bibliographie des poèmes de Max Jacob parus en revue,* and translator (with Moishe Black) of Jacob's short fiction in the collection *Hesitant Fire.* Maria spent her life working tirelessly on Jacob and amassed a private library of his works, many of which are scattered in obscure avant-garde publications and hard to find elsewhere. I spent a week living in her house in Saskatoon, Canada, copying from those publications and talking with her. She and I corresponded for years. Hélène Henry, another scholar who has given her life to Jacob, kindly met with me and shared photographs and documents: she is a specialist on Jacob's Breton life. Olivier and Gérard Zunz have been generous in sharing the diaries of their grandfather, Robert Zunz, and the albums he commissioned from Jacob. Fabio Rieti graciously showed me his father's letters and scores.

Anyone working on Jacob must also be grateful to Hélène Seckel, curator of the magnificent show *Max Jacob et Picasso* at the Musée Picasso in

Paris and author of the accompanying catalogue, a masterpiece of documentation. I have also relied on the emerging, monumental biography of Picasso by John Richardson. I am grateful to Sophie Annoepel-Cabrignac, curator at the Musée Picasso in Paris, and to the librarians of the Bibliothèque Littéraire Jacques Doucet, especially Paul Cougnard. When I started this work in 1985, I conducted my research with the benevolent permission of the director, François Chapon, whose own works on Jacques Doucet and on artists' books are crucial to understanding the century; now I thank the current director, Isabelle Diu.

The librarians at the Bibliothèque Nationale have been equally helpful, especially Anne Mary and Jérôme Villeminoz, responsible for the Fonds Max Jacob, as have been the librarians at the Médiathèque d'Orléans: Marie Maignaut, Olivier Morand, and Romuald Goudeseune. I am grateful as well to François Rosfelter, director of the Médiathèque des Ursulines in Quimper, and to Sandrine Koullen, the librarian in charge of the Max Jacob collection there. The Beinecke Library at Yale University, the Houghton Library at Harvard University, the New York Public Library, the Firestone Library at Princeton University, and the Rare Book and Manuscript Library at Columbia University have also been invaluable resources.

I could not have written this book without the support of several foundations that allowed me to travel back and forth between the United States and France: grants from the Guggenheim Foundation and the American Council of Learned Societies came like manna from heaven. The Committee on Social Thought at the University of Chicago has helped generously with the costs of preparing the manuscript in its final stages, as have my research funds provided by the University of Chicago. Katell Sevestre-Leyshon provided crucial assistance in collecting permissions for images and texts. Nor would the book have been possible without the affectionate help of a number of babysitters. Betsy Rodman accompanied me and my baby girls to Paris in 1985, to live with us in our dark hole near the Bibliothèque Nationale and take care of them while I burrowed in the archives. Ruth Dudding accompanied us to Brittany that summer. Over the years, Edith Loumingou, Delphine Perrin, Mathilde Boursiac, Aicha

Bah, and Yaël Pustilnicov helped to care for the children so that I could work: my gratitude knows no bounds.

Various friends have read and criticized chapters over the years, and to them as well I am immensely grateful. Roger Shattuck, Donald Carne-Ross, Christopher Ricks, Richard Howard, Rika Lesser, Ken Gross, Mary Ann Caws, Katherine Jackson, David Stang, Anka Muhlstein, Louis Begley, Peter Hawkins, Megan Marshall, Robert Pinsky, and Louise Glück all gave generously of their time and attention to the adventures of Max Jacob. So did the editors of several journals in which some of these chapters first appeared in shortened form: to Ann Kjellberg of *Little Star*, to Archie Burnett and Saskia Hamilton of *Literary Imagination*, to Emily Nemens of the *Paris Review* online, and to Jackson Lears of *Raritan*, my fervent thanks. Isabelle Faton meticulously reviewed the manuscript for errors; any mistakes that remain are my fault. Four friends heroically read the whole manuscript as it neared completion: Alexander Dickow, Adina Hoffman, Anne Kimball, and Richard Sieburth: I am greatly in their debt.

I record my gratitude to Boston University and to the University of Chicago for leaves that permitted the completion of the book.

Jill Bialosky, my editor at W. W. Norton, has watched with saintly patience as this book grew, and her advice, along with the advice of her assistant Drew Weitman, has been precious. To my agent Kathleen Anderson, I owe the whole idea of the book.

But my deepest thanks go to my family. My children grew up with Max Jacob and put up with their mother's obsession for years. My former husband Stephen Scully was similarly patient and understanding. My companion Joel Cohen has endured a *ménage à trois* with Jacob with remarkable good grace.

UNLESS OTHERWISE NOTED, the translations of prose and poetry are my own. Some of the poems referred to in the text may be found on my website, rosannawarren.com, along with the expanded version of the notes.

REFERENCES

CORRESPONDENCE

Jacob, Max. *L'Amitié: Lettres à Charles Goldblatt*. Edited by André Roumieux. Paris: Le Castor Astral, 1994. Cited in notes as *Goldblatt*.

————. *Les Amitiés et les amours*. Edited by Didier Gompel-Netter. Nantes: Éditions du Petit Véhicule, 2003; Paris: L'Arganier, 2005, 2007. 3 vols. Cited in notes as *AA* 1, 2, and 3.

————. *Une Amitié de Max Jacob: Lettres de Max Jacob à Robert Levesque*. Edited by Pierre Masson. Mortemart: Rougerie, 1994. Cited in notes as *Levesque*.

————. *Correspondance*. 2 vols. Edited by François Garnier. Paris: Éditions de Paris, 1953. Cited in notes as Garnier 1 and Garnier 2.

————. *Les Propos et les jours*. Edited by Didier Gompel-Netter and Annie Marcoux. Paris: Zodiaque, 1989. Cited in notes as Gompel/Marcoux.

————. "36 Lettres de Max Jacob à Jean-Richard Bloch, 1re partie," ed. Michel Trebitsch, *Europe* 62, no. 662–63 (June–July 1984), and "Lettres à Jean-Richard Bloch, 2e partie," no. 666 (October 1984). Cited in notes as Bloch 1 and Bloch 2.

————. *Lettres 1920–1941*. Edited by S. J. Collier. Oxford: Basil Blackwell, 1966. Cited in notes as Collier.

————. *Lettres à un ami: Correspondance 1922–1937 avec Jean Grenier*. Paris: Le temps qu'il fait, 1982. Cited in notes as *Grenier*.

————. *Lettres à Jean Colle*. Edited by Sylvia Lorant-Colle and Maurice Dirou. Douarnenez: Mémoire de la Ville, 1996. Cited in notes as *Colle*.

————. *Lettres à Bernard Esdras-Gosse*. Paris: Seghers, 1953. Cited in notes as *Esdras-Gosse*.

————. *Lettres à Florent Fels*. Edited by Maria Green. Mortemart: Rougerie, 1990. Cited in notes as *Fels*.

————. "Lettres à Henri Ferrare, 1929–1934." Edited by René Plantier. *CdR*, no. 1 (1978). Cited in notes as "Ferrare."

————. *Lettres à Nino Frank*. Edited by Anne Kimball. New York: Peter Lang, 1988. Cited in notes as *Frank*.

————. *Lettres à Edmond Jabès*. Alexandria: Éditions du Scarabée, 1945. Cited in notes as *Jabès*.

————. *Lettres à un jeune homme 1941–1944*. Edited by Patricia Sustrac. Paris: Bartillat, 2009. Cited in notes as *Jeune homme*.

————. *Lettres à Marcel Jouhandeau*. Edited by Anne Kimball. Geneva: Librairie Droz, 1979. Cited in notes as *Jouhandeau*.

————. "Lettres de Max Jacob à René Lacôte (1934–1944)," ed. Béatrice Mousli, *CMJ*, no. 11–12 (2012). Cited in notes as "Lacôte."

————. *Lettres à Julien Lanoë, 1925–1944. Avec poèmes et textes inédits de Max Jacob*. Edited by Anne Kimball. Geneva: Droz, 2019. Cited in notes as *Lanoë*.

————. *Lettres à Michel Leiris*. Edited by Christine Van Rogger Andreucci. Paris: Honoré Champion, 2001. Cited in notes as *Leiris*.

————. *Lettres à Michel Levanti*. Edited by Lawrence Joseph. Mortemart: Rougerie, 1975. Cited in notes as *Levanti*.

————. *Lettres à Michel Manoll*. Edited by Maria Green. Paris: Rougerie, 1985. Cited in notes as *Manoll*.

————. *Lettres à Pierre Minet*. Edited by Anne Kimball. Quimper: Calligrammes, 1988. Cited in notes as *Minet*.

————. Letters to Conrad Moricand, in Moricand, BnF 24919. Cited in notes as Moricand BnF.

————. "Lettres à Raymond Queneau." *Cahier de l'herne*, no. 29 (1975). Cited in notes as "Queneau."

————. *Lettres à René Rimbert*. Edited by Christine Van Rogger Andreucci and Maria Green. Mortemart: Rougerie, 1983. Cited in notes as *Rimbert*.

————. *Lettres aux Salacrou*. Paris: Gallimard, 1957. Cited in notes as *Salacrou*.

————. *Lettres à Togorès*. Terrassa, Spain: Fundació La Mirada, 1998. Cited in notes as *Togorès*.

————. *Lettres à Roger Toulouse*. Edited by Patricia Sustrac and Christine Van Rogger Andreucci. Troyes: Librairie Bleue, 1992. Cited in notes as *Toulouse*.

————. *Lettres à René Villard*. Edited by Yannick Pelletier. Mortemart: Rougerie, 1978. Cited in notes as *Villard*.

————. "Lettres de Max Jacob à Robert Zunz: Correspondance inédite 1939–1944." Edited by Patricia Sustrac. *Revue d'histoire littéraire de la France* 109, no. 4 (2009): 909–35. Cited in notes as *Zunz*.

————. *Max Jacob écrit: Lettres à six amis*. Edited by Anne Kimball. Rennes: Presses universitaires de Rennes, 2015. Cited in notes as *Jacob écrit*.

Jacob, Max, and Jean Cocteau. *Correspondance 1917–1944*. Edited by Anne Kimball. Paris: Paris-Méditerranée, 2000. Cited in notes as Jacob/Cocteau.

Jacob, Max, and Jacques Maritain. *Correspondance 1924–1935*. Edited by Sylvain Guéna. Brest: Centre d'études des correspondances, CNRS, 1999. Cited in notes as Jacob/Maritain.

Jacob, Max, and Jean Paulhan. *Correspondance*. Edited by Anne Kimball. Paris: Éditions Paris-Méditerranée, 2005. Cited in notes as Jacob/Paulhan.

Jacob, Max, and Salomon Reinach. *Lettres à Liane de Pougy*. Paris: Plon, 1980. Cited in notes as *Pougy*.

Oxenhandler, Neal. *Max Jacob and Les Feux de Paris*. Berkeley: University of California Press, 1964.

Picasso, Pablo, and Guillaume Apollinaire. *Correspondance*. Edited by Pierre Caizergues and Hélène Seckel. Paris: Gallimard, 1992. Cited in notes as Picasso/Apollinaire.

MEMOIRS AND OTHER PRIMARY SOURCES

Apollinaire, Guillaume. *Les peintre cubistes, Méditations esthétiques*, ed. L.-C. Breunig and J.-Cl. Chevalier. Paris: Hermann, 1980.

Assouline, Pierre. *L'Homme de l'art: D.-H. Kahnweiler 1884–1979*. Paris: Gallimard, 1988. English version: *An Artful Life*, translated by Charles Ruas. New York: Grove Weidenfeld, 1990.

Béalu, Marcel. *Dernier visage de Max Jacob*. Paris: E. Vitte, 1959.

Belaval, Yvon. *La Rencontre avec Max Jacob*. Paris: Libraire Philosophique Vrin, 1974.

Carco, Francis. *Bohème d'artiste*. Paris: Albin Michel, 1940.

———. *Scènes de la vie de Montmartre*. Paris: Fayard, 1919.

Cousins, Judith. "Documentary Chronology." In William Rubin, *Picasso and Braque: Pioneering Cubism*. New York: Museum of Modern Art, 1989.

Dorgelès, Roland. *Bouquet de Bohème*. Paris: Albin Michel, 1947.

Émié, Louis. *Dialogues avec Max Jacob*. Paris: Corréa, 1954.

Faure-Favier, Louise. *Souvenirs sur Guillaume Apollinaire*. Paris: Grasset, 1945.

Fillacier, Sylvette. *Chante cigale*. Paris: Table Ronde, 1960.

Frank, Nino. *Mémoire brisée*. Paris: Calmann-Lévy, 1967.

Gabory, Georges. *Apollinaire, Max Jacob, Gide, Malraux & Cie*. Paris: Jean-Michel Place, 1988.

Jacob, Max. *Advice to a Young Poet*. Trans. and ed. John Adlard. London: Menard Press, 1976.

———. "The Early Days of Pablo Picasso." *Vanity Fair* (May 1923): 62–63, 104.

———. "L'Inédit de Max Jacob sur Picasso: Fox." *Lettres françaises* 1051, no. 22–28 (October 1964): 1, 11.

———. "Je suis né à Quimper . . . ," in René Édouard-Joseph, *Dictionnaire biographique des artistes contemporains 1910–1930*. Paris: Art et édition, 1931, 2:212.

———. "Jeunesse." *Nouvelles littéraires*, April 22, 1933.

———. "Montmartre." *Le Figaro artistique illustré*, June 1931.

———. "Naissance de cubisme et autres." *Nouvelles littéraires*, April 30, 1932.

———. "Présentation de l'auteur par lui-même." *Gouaches et dessins, Max Jacob*, catalogue Exposition Max Jacob, Galerie Bernheim-Jeune, Paris, March 8–20, 1920.

———. "Souvenirs sur Picasso contés par Max Jacob." *Cahiers d'art* 2, no. 6 (1927): 199–202.

————. "Le tiers transporté: Chronique des temps héroïques." *Les Feux de Paris*, no. 7–8, January 12, 1937.

Leiris, Michel. *Journal 1922–1989*. Edited by Jean Jamin. Paris: Gallimard, 1992.

Mollet, Jean. *Les Mémoires du Baron Mollet*. Paris: Gallimard, 1963.

Moricand, Conrad. *La Vie horrifique et sublime de Conrad Moricand, alias Claude Valence, dit Coco l'Etoile, homme de lettres et de dessins*, unpublished manuscript. Copy of original in ms. BH M 5226 (1–2), Archives départementales du Loiret.

Olivier, Fernande. *Picasso et ses amis*. Paris: Stock, 1933.

————. *Souvenirs intimes: Écrits pour Picasso*. Paris: Calmann-Lévy, 1988.

Pougy, Liane de. *Mes cahiers bleus*. Paris: Plon, 1977.

Reverdy, Pierre. *Le Voleur de Talan*. 1917; reprinted Paris: Flammarion, 1967.

Sachs, Maurice. *La Décade de l'illusion*. Paris: Gallimard, 1950.

————. *Le Sabbat*. Paris: Gallimard, 1960.

Salmon, André. *Manuscrit trouvé dans un chapeau*. Paris: Société Littéraire de France, 1919.

————. *Max Jacob, poète, peintre, mystique et homme de qualité*. Paris: René Girard, 1927.

————. *Souvenirs sans fin*. 3 vols. Paris: Gallimard, 1955–1961.

Seckel, Hélène. *Max Jacob et Picasso*. Paris: Réunion des Musées Nationaux, 1994.

Severini, Gino. *La vita di un pittore*. Milan: Edizioni di Communità, 1965.

Tual, Denise. *Au Coeur du temps*. Paris: Carrière, 1987.

BIOGRAPHIES AND HISTORIES

Adéma, Pierre-Marcel. *Guillaume Apollinaire, le mal-aimé*. Paris: Plon, 1952.

Andreu, Pierre. *Le Rouge et le blanc*. Paris: Table Ronde, 1977.

————. *Vie et mort de Max Jacob*. Paris: Table Ronde, 1982.

Armel, Aliette. *Michel Leiris*. Paris: Fayard, 1997.

Fabureau, Hubert. *Max Jacob, son oeuvre*. Paris: Nouvelle Revue Critique, 1935.

Flam, Jack. *Matisse and Picasso: The Story of Their Rivalry and Friendship*. Boulder, Colo.: Westview Press, 2003.

Guiette, Robert. *La Vie de Max Jacob*. Paris: Nizet, 1976.

Martinoir, Francine de. *La Littérature occupée: Les années de guerre, 1939–1945*. Paris: Hatier, 1995.

Peyre, André. *Max Jacob quotidien*. Paris: José Millas-Martin, 1976.

Richardson, John. *A Life of Picasso*, 3 vols. New York: Random House, 1991–2010.

Steegmuller, Francis. *Apollinaire: Poet Among Painters*. New York: Farrar, Straus & Giroux, 1963.

————. *Cocteau*. Boston: Atlantic–Little Brown, 1970.

Winock, Michel. *La France et les juifs: De 1789 à nos jours*. Paris: Éditions de Seuil, 2004.

LIST OF ABBREVIATIONS

RB   *Le Roi de Béotie*
SM   *Saint Matorel*
TB   *Le Terrain Bouchaballe*

ARCHIVES

BLJD   Bibliothèque Littéraire Jacques Doucet
BnF   Bibliothèque Nationale de France
Orléans   Médiathèque d'Orléans

COLLECTED ARTICLES

CdR   *Centre de recherches Max Jacob*
CMJ   *Cahiers Max Jacob*

NOTES

PREFACE

1. The Revolutionary Assembly voted in a new penal code in 1791, removing "sodomy" and other sexual acts "against nature" from the category of crime. But Napoléon's penal code of 1810 multiplied laws against offenses to public morals, sexual assault, and corruption of minors. These laws and the penalties they specified (fines and prison terms) increased in severity as the century advanced. Though the laws contained no language outlawing homosexuality, they were phrased broadly enough to allow the police wide freedom in persecuting and prosecuting homosexuals. The nineteenth-century police in Paris kept detailed records of homosexuals who had been arrested for soliciting or engaging in sexual acts in public, and they routinely raided cafés, public baths, and *passages* where homosexuals were known to gather. See Jeffrey Merrick and Michael Sibalis, *Homosexuality in French History and Culture* (New York: Haworth Press, 2010), and Marc Daniel, "Histoire de la législation concernant l'homosexualité," *Arcadie* 8 (1961): 618–27, and *Arcadie* 9 (1962): 10–29.

CHAPTER I: BRITTANY

1. Madame Jacob borrowed a room in the house of a friend at 18 rue du Parc.
2. "Un acteur en tournée," CI, in O, 814.
3. TB, in O, 1257.
4. "Récit de ma conversion," in O, 1474.
5. Hélène Henry, "Max Jacob et Quimper," *Cahiers de l'Iroise* 3, no. 35 (July–September 1962): 133.
6. MJ, "Récit," in O, 1475.
7. Andreu, *Vie et mort*, 15.
8. Guiette, *Vie*, 31.

9. Ibid., 33. Julie Bloch was the daughter, not the sister, of Samuel Alexandre.

10. Michael Marrus, *The Politics of Assimilation* (Oxford: Clarendon Press, 1971), 31.

11. Simon Schwarzfuchs, *Les Juifs de France* (Paris: Albin Michel, 1975), 213.

12. Andreu, *Vie et mort*, 21.

13. BF, 211. The character is Madame Gagelin.

14. Leon Poliakov, *The Aryan Myth* (New York: New American Library, 1977), 206.

15. Ibid., 83.

16. Ernest Renan, *Souvenirs d'enfance et de jeunesse,* 17th ed. (Paris: Calmann-Lévy, 1893), 125.

17. F. M. Luzel, *Gwerziou* (1868–1890; reprinted Paris: G. P. Maisonneuve & Larose, 1971), 2:31–36.

18. René Plantier, *Max Jacob et Quimper,* collectif avec des articles d'Hélène Henry, Alain Le Grand-Vélin, Jean Caveng et des documents (Quimper: Calligrammes, 1984).

19. Guiette, *Vie,* 34.

20. Ibid., 33.

21. Louis Ogès, "Les Souvenirs d'Abel Villard," in Plantier, *Max Jacob et Quimper,* 27.

22. Andreu, *Vie et mort,* 20.

23. Ibid.

24. Ibid.

25. TB, in O, 1145.

26. Ogès, "Souvenirs," 30.

27. *Villard,* 11.

28. René Villard, "Max Jacob, à Quimper, Histoire d'une classe de lycée," *Correspondant,* 10 January 1930, 79.

29. *Villard,* 12.

30. Ibid., 13.

31. Ibid., 79.

32. Ibid., 114.

33. Ibid., 104.

34. Ibid.

35. Ibid., 78.

36. Pierre Allier, "Max Jacob Quimpérois," in Plantier, *Max Jacob et Quimper,* 20.

37. MJ, "Présentation," n.p.

38. Guiette, *Vie,* 39.

39. Ibid., 22.

40. Ibid., 35.

41. Peter Gay, *Freud: A Life for Our Time* (New York: W. W. Norton, 1988), 49.

42. Georges Guillain, *Jean-Martin Charcot, sa vie, son oeuvre* (Paris: Masson et Cie, 1955), 31.

43. Poliakov, *Aryan Myth,* 284.

44. Gay, *Freud,* 50.

45. Guillain, *Charcot,* 35.

46. Ibid., 137.

47. MJ to Lanoë, May 8, 1942, in *Lanoë,* 471.

48. DT, in O, 460.

49. Guiette, *Vie,* 35.

50. Ibid., 37.

CHAPTER 2: THE GATES OF THE CITY

1. Michael Meyer, *Strindberg* (New York: Random House, 1985).

2. CTH, 14.

3. HCHR, 26.

4. Ibid.

5. Kenneth Cornell, *The Symbolist Movement* (1951; reprinted New York: Archon, 1970).

6. Stéphane Mallarmé, "La Musique et les lettres," in *Oeuvres complètes,* ed. Henri Mondor and J. Jean-Aubry (Paris: Gallimard, 1965), 643.

7. "Déplacement avantageux" as "Le Fonds littéraire," in *Figaro,* August 17, 1894; and in *Revue blanche,* October 1894; Stéphane Mallarmé, *La Musique et les lettres* (Paris: Perrin et Cie, 1895).

8. MJ to Jean-Jacques Mezure, June 1, 1942, in *Jeune homme,* 89.

9. Maurice Maeterlinck, *Serres chaudes* (1889; reprinted Brussels: P. Lacomblez, 1895), 8.

10. Jules Romains, *Souvenirs et confidences d'un écrivain* (Paris: Fayard, 1958), 17.

11. CD, Preface, in O, 349.

12. Andreu, *Vie et mort,* 23.

13. François Caron, *France des patriotes* (Paris: Fayard, 1985), 453.

14. Bernard Lazare, *L'Antisémitisme, son histoire et ses causes,* cited in Denis Bredin, *The Affair,* trans. Jeffrey Mehlman (New York: Braziller, 1986), 570.

15. Hippolyte Taine, *Les Origines de la France contemporaine: La révolution, le gouvernement révolutionnaire, le régime moderne* (Paris: Robert Laffont, 1986), 753.

16. William Chambers Morrow, *Bohemian Paris of Today* (Philadelphia: J. B. Lippincott, 1900), 34ff.

17. Roger Shattuck, *The Banquet Years,* rev. ed. (New York: Vintage, 1968).

18. Patricia Leighton, *Reordering the Universe* (Princeton, NJ: Princeton University Press, 1989), 50.

19. Jean Maitron, *Le Mouvement anarchiste en France* (Paris: François Maspero, 1975), 206.

20. Ibid., 207.

21. Ibid., 235.

22. Ibid.

23. Salmon, *Souvenirs,* 1:167.

24. Guiette, *Vie,* 39.

25. Andreu, *Vie et mort,* 29.

26. MJ, "Poeme," CD, in O, 46.

27. Hélène Henry to author, n.d.

28. *Villard*, 15.

29. *Villard*, 78.

30. Guiette, *Vie*, 40.

31. MJ, "Surpris et charmé," RB, in O, 857. "Surprised and Delighted," in *Hesitant Fire: Selected Prose of Max Jacob*, ed. and trans. Moishe Black and Maria Green (Lincoln: University of Nebraska Press, 1991), 82.

32. Ibid.

33. *Levanti*, 68.

34. MJ, "Plainte du mauvais garçon" and "Le Départ," LC, in O, 564, 561.

35. Jacob's Breton album was commissioned in 1939 by Robert Zunz. Private collection Gérard Zunz, unpublished.

36. C, 23.

37. MJ, "La Croix d'or," RB, in O, 847.

38. Jacques de Cambry, *Voyage dans le Finistère*, ed. Roger Dupuy (Brest: J.-B. Lefournier, 1836), 98.

39. Albert le Grand, *La Vie des saints*, quoted in Hersart de la Villemarqué, *Barzaz-Breiz* (1867; reprinted Paris: Perrin, 1959), xxi.

40. MJ, "La Fille de fontaine," PMG, in O, 1617.

41. Hélène Henry, "Dans l'ombre de Max Jacob: Le Quimpérois Pierre Allier," *CdR*, no. 1 (1978): 43; Hélène Henry, "Max Jacob aux archives du Finistère," *CdR*, no. 10 (1988): 45.

42. Andreu, *Vie et mort*, 34.

43. Guiette, *Vie*, 40.

44. Andreu, *Vie et mort*, 31.

45. MJ to Kahnweiler, c. 1910, in Garnier 1:52–55.

46. Garnier 2:22, 23.

47. Guiette, *Vie*, 41. *Villard*, 64.

48. *Guiette*, 41.

49. Guiette, *Vie*, 43.

50. Pierre Birnbaum, *The Anti-Semitic Moment*, trans. Jane Marie Todd (1998; reprinted New York: Hill & Wang, 2003), 257.

51. Ibid., 270.

52. Guiette, *Vie*, 43.

53. Marie-Joseph Louy, *Léon Bloy et son époque, 1870–1914* (Paris: Desclée de Brouwer, 1944), 49.

54. DT, in O, 459.

55. Ibid., 462.

56. One, Café Biard, near the Place Pigalle, was a famous place for gay rendezvous.

57. On Dreyfus as scapegoat, see Léon Bloy, cited by Pierre Vidal-Naquet, "Jacques Maritain et les juifs: Réflexions sur un parcours," in Jacques Maritain, *L'impossible antisémitisme* (Paris: Desclée de Brouwer, 1994), 24.

58. CA, 10.

59. Guiette, *Vie*, 44, 45.

60. CA, 32.

61. Ibid., 21.

62. Ibid., 23. Simon's work can be seen at the Musée des Beaux-Arts in Quimper.

63. Ibid., 45.

64. Ibid., 56.

65. Ibid., 52, 107, 124.

66. Ibid., 53, 124.

67. Guiette, *Vie*, 45.

68. Andreu, *Vie et mort*, 44.

CHAPTER 3: MEETING PICASSO

1. Jean Valmy-Baysse, "Souvenirs sur Max Jacob," *Aguedal* 4, no. 2 (May 1939): 169–72.

2. Ibid., 170.

3. MJ, "Présentation," n.p.

4. Peyre, *Jacob quotidien*, 49, Andreu, *Vie et mort*, 208, Oxenhandler, *Jacob and Les Feux*, 243.

5. MJ, "Présentation."

6. MJ, *Le Christ à Montparnasse*, ms. 7198–92, BLJD.

7. Ibid.

8. Final version of "Mille regrets," in LC, in O, 564.

9. "En famille," Garnier 1:13. Revised in *Soirées de Paris* (November 15, 1913): 26, LC, in O, 623.

10. Giovanni Léonardi, "Le Poète Max Jacob: Souvenirs quimpérois," *CdR*, no. 8 (1986): 29.

11. MJ, "Plainte du mauvais garçon" and "En famille," in *Soirées de Paris* (November 15, 1913), LC, in O, 564.

12. Seckel, *Jacob et Picasso*, 35n24.

13. MJ to Kisling, January 28, 1924, in Garnier 1:22–23.

14. The café closed in 1897 but had established a new genre of cabaret.

15. *Le Sourire*, no. 2 (April 14, 1900).

16. Jacques Chastenet, *La République triomphante* (Paris: Hachette, 1955), 187.

17. Henri Dion, "Les Logis de Max Jacob," *CdR*, no. 5 (1983): 71.

18. Guiette, *Vie*, 51.

19. Béalu, *Dernier visage*, 54; Hélène Henry, "Bouchaballe 'un' ou La comédie retrouvée," *CdR*, no. 5 (1983): 5–12; Henry, "Max Jacob aux archives du Finistère," *CdR*, no. 10 (1988): 33–48; Henry, "Surprises d'une topographie jacobienne," *CdR*, no. 3 (1980): 13–50; Henry, "La Donation Couchouren"; *CdR*, no. 3 (1980): 13–50, N.a., "Documents photographiques et cartes postales pour voir *Le Terrain Bouchaballe*," *CdR*, no. 3 (1980): 54–67; Hélène Henry and Max Jacob, "La Première 'Nouvelle de Guichin' en 1910," *CdR*, no. 7 (1985): 18–29.

20. Guiette, *Vie*, 51.

21. Ibid., 52.

22. Ibid.

23. Berthe Weill, *Pan! Dans l'oeil!* : Orné des aquarelles et dessins de Raoul Dufy, Pascin et Picasso (Paris: Librairie Lipschutz, 1933), 55.

24. Alfred Cobban, *A History of Modern France* (Harmondsworth, England: Penguin, 1965), 3:58–66.

25. Guiette, *Vie*, 40; Christian Zervos, *Pablo Picasso: 1895–1906* (New York: E. Weyhe, 1932), 1:xxiv.

26. "Histoire de la cloche qui ne va pas à Rome," ms. 3, Fonds Max Jacob, Médiathèque des Ursulines, Quimper.

27. The most sinister character was Abbé Boullan, accused of ritual infanticide and portrayed by Huysmans as "le Docteur Johannès" in *Là-Bas*.

28. Rosanna Warren, "A Metaphysic of Painting: The Notes of André Derain," *Georgia Review* 32, no. 1 (Spring 1978): 123, 138.

29. *Le Zohar*, trans. Jean de Pauly, preface by Edmond Fleg (Paris: Éditions du Chant Nouveau, 1946).

30. Pierre Abraham, *Les Trois frères* (Paris: Editeurs Français Réunis, 1971), 45, 46.

31. No branch of the family, practicing or nonpracticing, was spared the Nazi horror.

32. Abraham, *Trois frères*, 45, 46.

33. Typical jumbled treatment of the Kabbalah appears in *Anthologie de l'occultisme*, ed. Blaise Cendrars for Grillot de Givry (Paris: Éditions de La Sirène, 1922).

34. MJ to Michel Levanti, n.d., in *Levanti*, 60.

35. "Thus it is written (Psalm cxix, 18): 'Remove the veil that covers my eyes, that I may behold wondrous things out of thy law.' " *Zohar*, trans. Pauly 1:145b.

36. Ibid., 3:152a.

37. MJ, "Chrétiens et païens," DT, in O, 514; DT, in O, 485. "Pensées," *Philosophies* (March 15, 1924): 57–160.

38. MJ to Levanti, October 27, 1938, in *Levanti*, 72.

39. Belaval, *Rencontre*, 45.

40. Richardson, *Life*, 1:148.

41. *Picasso's Notebooks* (catalog) (New York: Jan Krugier, 1995).

42. Weill, *Pan!*, 65–67.

43. MJ, "Le tiers transporté," in Seckel, *Jacob et Picasso*, 1.

44. Weill, *Pan!*, 76.

45. Richardson, *Life*, 1:198, 199.

46. MJ, "Souvenirs sur Picasso," in Pierre Daix, *Picasso Créateur: La Vie intime et l'oeuvre* (Paris: Seuil, 1987), 15; Richardson, *Life*, 1:25.

47. MA, 139ff.

48. The relevant memoirs are Max Jacob, "The Early Days of Pablo Picasso," *Vanity Fair*, May 1923, 62–63, 104; "Souvenirs sur Picasso contés par Max Jacob," *Cahiers d'art* 2, no. 6 (1927): 199–202; "Naissance du cubisme et autres," *Nouvelles littéraires*, April 30, 1932, 1, 2; and "Le tiers transporté: Chronique des temps héroïques," *Les Feux de Paris*, no. 7–8 (January 12, 1937). The posthumously published memoirs

are *Chronique des temps héroïques* (Paris: Louis Broder, 1956) and "L'Inédit de Max Jacob sur Picasso: Fox," *Lettres françaises,* no. 1051 (October 22–28, 1964): 1, 11.

49. The year was 1901, and Picasso was nineteen.

50. MJ, "Souvenirs sur Picasso," 199–202.

51. MJ, "Early Days," 62.

52. MJ, Lecture at Nantes, in Seckel, *Jacob et Picasso,* 243.

53. Ibid.

54. Ibid., 243–44.

55. Simon Mondzain, "Max Jacob et Montparnasse," *Arche* 1, no. 4 (1944): 107–14.

56. MJ, Lecture at Nantes, in Seckel, *Jacob et Picasso,* 244.

57. Ibid.

58. Seckel, *Jacob et Picasso,* 3, 4.

59. The lecture at Nantes collapses the first meeting with Picasso in 1901 with events from the second phase of their friendship sixteen months later. Seckel, *Jacob et Picasso,* 244.

60. MJ, "Je suis né," 2:212.

61. MJ, "Souvenirs sur Picasso," 200.

62. MJ spent the end of 1901 in Quimper and wouldn't have followed the career of his portrait in a period when Picasso painted over many canvases.

63. MJ, "Souvenirs sur Picasso," 199.

64. MJ, "Inédit," 1, 11.

65. Jaime Sabartés, *Picasso: Portraits et souvenirs* (Paris: Louis Carré, Maximilien Vox, 1946), 81.

66. Christian Zervos, *Pablo Picasso* (Paris: Cahiers d'art, 1932), 1:xxix.

67. Richardson, *Life,* 1:201.

68. Abraham, *Trois frères,* 45.

69. Ibid.

70. MJ to Charles-Louis Philippe, December 12, 1901, in Garnier 1:21.

71. Marcel Béalu, "Propos, souvenirs, et anecdotes de Max Jacob," *Boîte à clous,* no. 10 (February 1951): n.p.

72. Ibid.

73. "L'Enterrement," in Andreu, *Vie et mort,* 304–5.

74. Andreu, *Vie et mort,* 43.

75. MJ, "Je suis né," 212.

76. Fabureau, *Jacob, son oeuvre,* 16.

77. Seckel, *Jacob et Picasso,* 9.

78. Ibid. Richardson, *Life,* 1:218, 219.

79. Weill, *Pan!,* 76.

80. Richardson, *Life,* 1:248.

81. Ibid., 1:254.

82. Weill, *Pan!,* 85.

83. "Sisket" may have been the sculptor Auguste Aguero. Richardson, *Life,* 1:254; Seckel, *Jacob et Picasso,* 11.

84. Richardson, *Life*, 1:258.

85. Seckel, *Jacob et Picasso*, 20.

86. MJ, "Souvenirs sur Picasso," 200.

87. Andreu, *Vie et mort*, 37.

88. Seckel, *Jacob et Picasso*, 17.

89. MJ, "Entrepôt Voltaire," RB, in O, 862.

90. Seckel, *Jacob et Picasso*, 20.

91. MJ, Lecture at Nantes, in Seckel, *Jacob et Picasso*, 244.

92. Louis Aragon, *Anicet ou le Panorama* (Paris: Nouvelle Revue Française, 1921), 66; Richardson, *Life*, 1:262.

93. MJ, "Souvenirs sur Picasso," 200.

94. Seckel, *Jacob et Picasso*, 25n12.

95. CTH, 91.

96. Richardson, *Life*, 1:266.

97. Olivier, *Picasso et ses amis*, 20.

98. Seckel, *Jacob et Picasso*, 12, 13.

99. Ibid., 15.

100. MJ, "Souvenirs sur Picasso," 200.

101. Richardson, *Life*, 1:266.

CHAPTER 4: ROMANCE

1. Guiette, *Vie*, 59.

2. Seckel, *Jacob et Picasso*, 26n26. Picasso referred to her as "Geneviève"; see Seckel, *Jacob et Picasso*, 24; Richardson, *Life*, 1:261.

3. M, 113.

4. MJ, "A la Chaudière!" LC, in O, 601.

5. Mss. N.a. fr. 15951, BnF.

6. MJ, "Fantaisie sur le baiser inattendu," OBM, in O, 290.

7. Guiette, *Vie*, 59; Seckel, *Jacob et Picasso*, 24.

8. Andreu, *Vie et mort*, 38.

9. Guiette, *Vie*, 54.

10. Ibid., 55.

11. SM, in O, 327.

12. Richardson, *Life*, 1:21.

13. Seckel, *Jacob et Picasso*, 23.

14. Richardson, *Life*, 1:260.

15. Salmon, *Jacob, poète*, 25; Seckel, *Jacob et Picasso*, 25n5.

16. SM, in O, 195.

17. Seckel, *Jacob et Picasso*, 5.

18. MJ, "Réponse à une question . . . ," *Minotaure*, no. 3–4 (1933): 110.

19. Jacob was on the payroll at Paris-France from February 5 to November 23, 1903.

20. SM, in O, 192.

21. Ibid., 194.

22. RB, in O, 874.

23. Guiette, *Vie*, 56.

24. Ibid., 56.

25. Jacob moved to 33 boulevard Barbès at some point in late winter or early spring 1903. Seckel, *Jacob et Picasso*, 25.

26. Guiette, *Vie*, 59.

27. Seckel, *Jacob et Picasso*, 23.

28. Guiette, *Vie*, 60.

29. Ibid., 60, 61. The untitled prose poem is MJ, "La pauvre Bérénice," OBM, in O, 314.

30. MJ, "Historique de ce livre (si on peut dire)" (1943), *CMJ*, no. 1 (1951): 11.

31. Garnier misdates to 1903 Jacob's letter to Apollinaire about an engagement. Garnier 1:27); MJ to Bloch, c. 1913, in Bloch 1:146.

32. MJ, "Le mariage du poète," OBM, in O, 292.

33. SM, in O, 237.

34. Guiette, *Vie*, 61.

35. Ibid., 62.

36. Gabory, *Apollinaire*, 30.

37. MJ, *Le Christ à Montparnasse*, ms. 7198–92, BLJD.

38. MJ, "Historique de ce livre," 11.

39. Guiette, *Vie*, 64.

40. HRK, in O, 115.

41. Guiette, *Vie*, 65; MJ, "Historique de ce livre," 11.

42. Guiette, *Vie*, 67.

CHAPTER 5: THE BATEAU LAVOIR

1. Alexander Dickow, "*Le Géant du soleil*, un conte retrouvé de Max Jacob," *CMJ*, no. 15–16 (2015): 31–35.

2. "Publishing in 1921 a work that had been conceived in 1903." *Jouhandeau*, 91.

3. Hélène Henry, "Le Théâtre des hostilités," unpublished manuscript.

4. Hélène Henry, "Bouchaballe 'un' ou La comédie retrouvée," *CdR*, no. 5 (1983): 9.

5. Ibid., 33.

6. Seckel, *Jacob et Picasso*, 27, 34n3.

7. Ibid., 27.

8. "La Prime de la Sarahmitaine," *Sourire*, no. 113 (January 30, 1904).

9. MJ, "Invitation au voyage," LC, in O, 614.

10. Seckel, *Jacob et Picasso*, 22, 23.

11. Ibid., 27.

12. MJ, Lecture at Nantes, ibid., 244.

13. Olivier, *Picasso et ses amis*, 24.

14. Salmon, *Manuscrit*, 86.

15. Ibid., 32; Richardson, *Life*, 1:296.

16. Salmon, *Manuscrit*, 87.

17. MJ, "L'Inédit," 47–49.

18. Olivier, *Picasso et ses amis*, 49.

19. Salmon, *Souvenirs* 1:171.

20. Seckel, *Jacob et Picasso*, 29, 34n17.

21. Ibid., 30.

22. Ibid., 29, 30.

23. Ibid., 31.

24. Salmon, *Souvenirs* 1:119.

25. Dorgelès, *Bouquet*, 63.

26. CTH, 38.

27. Olivier, *Picasso et ses amis*, 26.

28. MJ, "Souvenirs sur Picasso," 202.

29. Richardson, *Life*, 1:351.

30. MJ, "Souvenirs sur Picasso," 202.

31. Guiette, *Vie*, 69.

32. Maurice Martin du Gard, *Les Mémorables* (Paris: Flammarion, 1957), 105.

33. Reverdy attacked the concept of Cubist poetics in "Notes et extraits," *Nord-Sud*, no. 13 (March 1918). But Jacob saw his poetry in pictorial terms. Michel Décaudin and Etienne-Alain Hubert, "Petit historique d'une appellation: 'Cubisme littéraire,'" *Europe*, no. 638–39 (June–July 1982): 7–25.

34. MJ, "Écrit en 1904," LC, in O, 582. The Algerian military leader Abd-el-Kader (1818–1883) held off the French forces for years.

35. Émié, *Dialogues*, 38.

36. Tatiana Greene, "Notice, en préambule aux lettres de Max Jacob à Marguerite Mespoulet," *CdR*, no. 4 (1981): 40.

37. MJ, "Comme Marie-Madeleine," LC, in O, 632.

38. Ms. Na fr. 15951, Fonds Max Jacob, BnF.

39. Seckel, *Jacob et Picasso*, 32.

40. Richardson, *Life*, 1:302–7.

41. Olivier, *Picasso et ses amis*, 25.

42. Ibid., 26.

43. Olivier, *Souvenirs intimes*, 185.

44. Olivier, *Picasso et ses amis*, 33.

45. MJ, "La Bohème pendant la guerre de 1914," RB, in O, 849.

46. Different memoirists insist on dates ranging from 1903 to 1905, and scholars have argued for both October 1904 and February 1905.

47. Guiette, *Vie*, 71. The crucial memoirs are Salmon, *Souvenirs*, 1:164–68; Jean Mollet, *Les Mémoires du Baron Mollet* (Paris: Gallimard, 1963), 55; Jacob, "Souvenirs sur Picasso," 199–202; Jacob, "Le tiers transporté"; and Guiette, *Vie*, 71.

48. Pierre-Marcel Adéma suggested an Italian army officer, Francesco Flugi d'Aspermont, as Apollinaire's father. See Adéma, *Apollinaire, le mal-aimé*. Steeg-

muller, *Apollinaire*, 11–19, presented as well Anatol Stern's proposal that the father might have been the son of Angelica's elder cousin Melanie Kostrowitzky and Napoléon II, Napoléon's son.

49. Mollet, *Mémoires*, 36.

50. Ibid., 37.

51. Ibid., 37, 38.

52. Seckel, *Jacob et Picasso*, 36, 244; Mollet, *Mémoires*, 55. Austin's went by many names. Officially it was Austen's Railway Restaurant, Hotel and Bar; also called Austen (or Austin) Fox's Bar, or Austin's Fox Bar, or L'Austin's Fox, or Le Fox. Steegmuller, *Apollinaire*, 133.

53. Brassaï, *Conversations with Picasso*, trans. Jane Marie Todd (Chicago: University of Chicago Press, 1991), 229.

54. MJ, Lecture at Nantes, in Seckel, *Jacob et Picasso*, 244. Translation in Steegmuller, *Apollinaire*, 134.

55. Guiette, *Vie*, 72.

56. MJ, "Souvenirs sur Picasso," 202.

57. In this chapter in Guiette, *Vie*, Salmon enters only as an adjunct to Apollinaire's funeral. Guiette, *Vie*, 73.

58. MJ to Tristan Tzara, February 26, 1916, in Garnier 1:116.

59. The word *verges* puns on *verge*, "rod," "wand," or "penis," and *vierge*, "virgin." Also on the legend of Saint Ursula and the eleven thousand virgin martyrs.

60. Richardson, *Life*, 1:305.

61. Picasso/Apollinaire, 47.

62. MJ, "Souvenirs sur Picasso," 202.

63. "Spectacle" became "Crepuscule"; "Les Saltimbanques" retained its title but lost two stanzas. Picasso/Apollinaire, 35, 36.

64. Steegmuller, *Apollinaire*, 153.

65. Guillaume Apollinaire, *Le Poète assassiné*, ed. Michel Décaudin (Paris: Gallmard, 1979), 62.

66. Salmon, *Souvenirs*, 1:166.

67. Seckel, *Jacob et Picasso*, 37.

68. Guiette, *Vie*, 74.

69. Ibid., 75.

70. Salmon, *Souvenirs*, 1:164.

71. Ibid., 1:171.

72. This postcard has fueled the controversy about dates. Richardson, *Life*, 1:327; Seckel, *Jacob et Picasso*, 37.

73. Salmon, *Souvenirs*, 1:174.

74. Olivier, *Picasso et ses amis*, 41, 42.

75. Guiette, *Vie*, 76.

76. MJ, "Jeunesse," 1.

77. Salmon, *Souvenirs*, 2:96.

78. Ibid., 97.

79. Salmon, *Manuscrit*, 84.

80. Olivier, *Picasso et ses amis*, 61.

81. Richardson, *Life*, 1:373.

82. Olivier, *Picasso et ses amis*, 68, 69.

83. Andreu, *Vie et mort*, 52.

84. Guiette, *Vie*, 77.

85. CTH, 55.

86. MJ, "Montmartre," 20.

87. Salmon, *Souvenirs*, 1:186.

88. MJ, "Jeunesse," 1; Salmon, *Souvenirs*, 1:186.

89. Olivier, *Picasso et ses amis*, 38.

90. Richardson, *Life*, 1:362.

91. Ibid., 362.

92. CTH, 48, 49.

93. Richardson, *Life*, 1:367.

94. Jacob/Cocteau, 401.

95. Olivier, *Picasso et ses amis*, 63.

96. Ibid., 44, 45.

97. Adéma, *Apollinaire, le mal-aimé*, 80.

98. MJ, "Le Cheval," *Lettres modernes*, no. 2 (May 1905): 16. The other poems are "Nombril dans le brouillard," "Bielles," "La Gale," and "Calvitie de la Butte Montmartre."

99. Salmon, *Souvenirs*, 1:181n1019, 104–15.

100. MJ, "Grand récitatif pour salons," OBM, in O, 265.

101. Seckel, *Jacob et Picasso*, 45n32.

102. MJ, "Variation d'une formule," OBM, in O, 268.

103. Ibid., 270.

104. MJ, "La Leçon de musique," OBM, in O, 271.

105. Ibid.

106. Alexander Dickow, "Max Jacob et le Symbolisme," *Europe* 92, no. 1019 (2014): 104–15, for discussion of Jacob's debt to Mallarmé.

107. The composition of *Illuminations* presents one of the most controversial problems in nineteenth-century French literary history. See Arthur Rimbaud, *Oeuvres complètes,* ed. André Guyaux (Paris: Gallimard, 2009), 939ff.

108. Paul Claudel, "Ma conversion," in *Oeuvres en prose,* ed. Jacques Petit and Charles Galpérine (Paris: Gallimard, 1965), 1008–14.

109. Suzanne Bernard, *Le Poème en prose de Baudelaire jusqu'à nos jours* (Paris: Librairie Nizet, 1959), 490.

110. MJ to Norbert Guterman, November 24, 1924, in Box 1, ms. 0528, in Guterman, Rare Book and Manuscript Library, Columbia University.

111. Andreu, *Vie et mort*, 48.

112. Guiette, *Vie*, 144.

113. MJ, "Poème simultané avec superposition simple," CD, in O, 357. In the 1922 edition, it is entitled "Idylle." In the 1923 edition, and in O, it is "Poème." The Greek is wrong.
114. Picasso/Apollinaire, 31.
115. Ibid., 32.
116. Richardson, *Life*, 1:348, 349.
117. Seckel, *Jacob et Picasso*, 40.
118. Ibid., 37.
119. Ibid.
120. MJ to Maurice Raynal, July 19, 1905, in Garnier, 1:29.
121. MJ, "Le Chevalier de la Barre," OBM, in O, 262.
122. Olivier, *Souvenirs intimes*, 192.
123. Richardson, *Life*, 1:346, 382–87.
124. Richardson disagrees with Rebecca Rabinow's "Discovering Modern Art: The Steins' Early Years in Paris, 1903–1907," in Janet Bishop, Cécile Debray, and Rebecca Rabinow, *The Steins Collect: Matisse, Picasso, and the Parisian Avant-Garde* (New Haven, Conn.: Yale University Press, 2011), about when Leo purchased the first two works by Picasso.
125. Richardson, *Life*, 1:398, 399.
126. Fernande's maiden name, from her adoptive mother, was Bellevallée. Seckel, *Jacob et Picasso*, 42.

CHAPTER 6: TOWARD CUBISM

1. Seckel, *Jacob et Picasso*, 46.
2. Ibid.
3. Picasso/Apollinaire, 45.
4. Seckel, *Jacob et Picasso*, 47.
5. Ibid., 49.
6. Richardson, *Life*, 1:428–53.
7. Seckel, *Jacob et Picasso*, 48; MJ, "Avenue du Maine," OBM, in O, 269.
8. Seckel, *Jacob et Picasso*, 48.
9. Salmon, *Souvenirs*, 1:354.
10. Seckel, *Jacob et Picasso*, 49.
11. Catherine Coquio, "Max Jacob et Mecislas Golberg, Polichinelles et Charlots," in *Max Jacob poète et romancier*, ed. Christine Van Rogger Andreucci (Pau: Publications de l'Université de Pau, 1995), 228.
12. Seckel, *Jacob et Picasso*, 35n24.
13. Guillaume Apollinaire, *Journal intime*, ed. Michel Décaudin (Paris: Éditions du Limon, 1991), 142, 145.
14. Olivier, *Picasso et ses amis*, 125.
15. Guiette, *Vie*, 61.

16. Apollinaire, *Journal intime*, 142.

17. Richardson, *Life*, 1:352.

18. Mollet, *Mémoires*, 57; Richardson, *Life*, 1:352.

19. Apollinaire, *Journal intime*, 142.

20. Adéma, *Apollinaire, le mal-aimé*, 83.

21. Guillaume Apollinaire, *Anecdotiques* (Paris: Gallimard, 1955), 43, 290.

22. Olivier, *Picasso et ses amis*, 135.

23. MJ to Levesque, January 29,1927, in *Levesque*, 16–19.

24. André Salmon, *La Jeune peinture française* (Paris: Albert Messein, 1912), 41–44.

25. Seckel, *Jacob et Picasso*, 207.

26. MJ to Levesque, January 29, 1927, in *Levesque*, 16–19. The main texts are Jacob, "Early Days"; MJ's 1927 letter to Levesque; Jacob, "Souvenirs sur Picasso"; Jacob, "L'Inédit"; Jacob "Jeunesse"; and Jacob, Lecture at Nantes, in Seckel, *Jacob et Picasso*, 246.

27. Richardson, *Life*, 1:474.

28. Ibid., 429.

29. Richardson, *Life*, 2:17.

30. Pierre Cabanne, *Le Siècle de Picasso*, 4 vols. (Paris: Gallimard, 1992), 1:283–302.

31. Richardson, *Life*, 2:23.

32. On Picasso's denial of African influence, see Richardson, *Life*, 1:451, 2:24–27; Seckel, *Jacob et Picasso*, 63n10 and 11; Salmon, *Souvenirs*, 3:253; and Flam, *Matisse and Picasso*, 32–34.

33. MJ, "L'Inédit," 1, 11.

34. André Salmon, *Propos d'atelier* (Paris: Crès, 1922), 16.; Seckel, *Jacob et Picasso*, 59; Salmon, *La Jeune peinture française*, 41–44.

35. Seckel, *Jacob et Picasso*, 59.

36. Andreu, *Vie et mort*, 17.

37. Seckel, *Jacob et Picasso*, 59; William Rubin, "La Genèse des *Demoiselles d'Avignon*," in Hélène Seckel, ed., *Les Demoiselles d'Avignon*, catalogue for exhibition at the Musée Picasso, January 26–April 18, 1988 (Paris: Ministère de la culture et de la communication: Éditions de la Réunion des musées nationaux, 1988), 364–487.

38. MJ, "Naissance," 7.

39. Richardson, *Life*, 1:396.

40. Richardson, *Life*, 2:45. Flam, *Matisse and Picasso*, 37–48; Yve-Alain Bois, *Matisse and Picasso*, catalogue for the exhibition *Matisse and Picasso: A Gentle Rivalry*, Kimbell Art Museum, Fort Worth, Tex., January 31–May 2, 1999 (Paris: Flammarion, 1998), 29–30.

41. MJ, *Le Phanérogame* (reprinted Charlieu: Éditions Bartavelle, 1996).

42. P 9. The name *Tropgrandglaïeul* conflates the three final words in Mallarmé's poem "Prose, pour des Esseintes."

43. Remy de Gourmont, *La Physique de l'amour: Essai sur l'instinct sexuel* (Paris: Mercure de France, 1903).

44. P 20.

45. Dickow observes that the professor of botany Gaston Bonnier, who accepted Jacob's story "Le Géant du soleil" for publication in 1904, was the author of a scientific book entitled *Phanérogames*. Alexander Dickow, *"Le Géant du soleil*: Un conte retrouvé," *CMJ*, no. 15–16 (2015): 31–35.

46. P 43.

47. P 181.

48. P 190.

49. MJ, "Métempsychose." Catherine Coquio, "Max Jacob et Mécislas Golberg," in *Max Jacob, poète et romancier,* ed. Alain Faudemay (Pau: Université de Pau, 1995). For comparison, see CD, in O, 408.

50. Coquio, "Jacob et Golberg," 228.

51. Émié, *Dialogues*, 197–98.

52. Olivier, *Picasso et ses amis*, 56–57.

53. Dorgelès, *Bouquet*, 300–1.

54. Guillaume Apollinaire, *Petites merveilles du quotidien*, ed. Pierre Caizergues (Montpellier: Bibliothèque artistique et littéraire, 1979), 22.

55. Pierre Abraham remembered Jacob's clothes "reeking" with ether several years earlier. Abraham, *Trois frères*, 54.

56. Carco, *Bohème*, 277.

57. Olivier, *Souvenirs intimes*, 242–43.

58. Salmon, *Souvenirs*, 1:188.

59. Olivier, *Picasso et ses amis*, 104.

60. Ibid., 106.

61. Richardson, *Life*, 2:60–63.

62. Apollinaire, *Les peintre cubistes*, 93.

63. Marie Laurencin, *Le Carnet des nuits* (Geneva: Pierre Cailler, 1956), 40.

64. Olivier, *Picasso et ses amis*, 72.

65. Apollinaire, *Journal intime*, 143.

66. Flam, *Matisse and Picasso*, 54.

67. Salmon, *Souvenirs*, 2:329.

68. Henri Hertz, "Contribution à la figure de Max Jacob," *Europe*, no. 489 (January 1970): 137–41; Seckel, *Jacob et Picasso*, 64n39.

69. Richardson, *Life*, 2:47.

70. Ibid., 2:50.

71. Salmon, *Souvenirs*, 1:378.

72. Olivier, *Picasso et ses amis*, 65, 66.

73. Ibid., 66.

74. Dorgelès, *Bouquet*, 116.

75. Salmon, *Souvenirs*, 1:160.

76. Jules Romains, *La Vie unanime*, 2nd ed. (Paris: Mercure de France, 1913), 17.

77. Peyre, *Jacob quotidien*, 124.

78. *Le Dernier cahier de Mécislas Golberg* (Paris, 1908); Mécislas Golberg, "Invocation à Louis Le Cardonnel," 91; Louis Le Cardonnel, "Jour perdu," 93; MJ, "Scène

d'intérieur," 193, in LC as "La Dame aveugle" in the sequence "Autres personnages du bal masque," in O, 625.

79. Maurice Parturier, *Max Jacob: Notes biographiques* (Paris: Le Divan, 1954), 6.

80. Apollinaire, *Journal intime*, 142.

81. MJ, "Souvenirs sur Picasso," 202.

82. CTH, 62.

83. Seckel, *Jacob et Picasso*, 65.

84. Vittorio Rieti, interview by author.

85. Jean Cocteau, *Le Passé défini* (Paris: Gallimard, 1983), 1:62.

86. Guillaume Apollinaire, "La Phalange nouvelle," in *Oeuvres en prose complètes*, ed.
Pierre Caizergues and Michel Décaudin (Paris: Gallimard, 1991), 2:894.

87. Olivier, *Picasso et ses amis*, 191; Francis Carco, *De Montmartre au Quartier Latin*
(Paris: Albin Michel, 1927), 32.

88. Andreu, *Vie et mort*, 54.

89. Guillaume Apollinaire, "Les Trois vertus plastiques," in *Chroniques d'art 1902–
1918*, ed. L. C. Breunig (Paris: Gallimard, 1960), 71–72; Apollinaire, "Le Brasier,"
in *Oeuvres poétiques*, ed. Pierre-Marcel Adéma and Michel Décaudin (Paris: Gallimard, 1965), 108.

90. Richardson, *Life*, 2:87.

91. Dorgelès, *Bouquet*, 48.

92. Ibid., 48, 49; Salmon, *Souvenirs*, 2:23.

93. Jules Romains and Guillaume Apollinaire, *Correspondance*, ed. Claude Martin
(Paris: Jean-Michel Place, 1994), 131–35; Salmon, *Souvenirs*, 1:376.

94. Seckel, *Jacob et Picasso*, 69.

95. *André Salmon on French Modern Art*, trans. Beth S. Gersh-Nešic (Cambridge: Cambridge University Press, 2005), 166n17. Vauxcelles wrote of "cubes" in his review
of Braque's exhibition in 1908, but Charles Morice was the first to write the word
cubism, reviewing the Salon des Indépendants of 1909 in the *Mercure de France*.

96. Adéma, *Apollinaire, le mal-aimé*, 102.

97. Salmon, *Souvenirs*, 2:24.

98. Ibid., 2:247–48.

99. Olivier, *Picasso et ses amis*, 78.

100. Salmon, *Souvenirs*, 2:49.

101. Rimbert, 58.

102. Ibid., 107n70.

103. Salmon, *Souvenirs*, 2:58.

104. Olivier, *Picasso et ses amis*, 81.

105. Geneviève Laporte, *Un amour secret de Picasso. Si tard le soir . . .* (Monaco: Editions
du Rocher, 1989), 54.

106. Richardson, *Life*, 2:110.

107. Salmon, *Souvenirs*, 2:58.

108. Seckel, *Jacob et Picasso*, 70.

109. Ibid.

110. MJ to Apollinaire, June 23, 1909, in Garnier 1:34–36.
111. Olivier, *Picasso et ses amis*, 230.
112. Apollinaire, "Poème lu au mariage d'André Salmon," in *Oeuvres poétiques*, 83.
113. MJ, "Souvenirs sur Picasso," 202.
114. Olivier, *Picasso et ses amis*, 163.
115. Ibid., 167.
116. Jacob/Cocteau, 455.
117. Guiette, *Vie*, 86.

CHAPTER 7: CHRIST AND THE DRUIDS

1. Red is associated with the planet Mars and its god. SM, in O, 229.
2. DT, in O, 471. "Récit," in O, 1476.
3. MJ, "Récit de ma conversion," dictated in 1939 to Paul Frizot, *La Vie intellectuelle*, March 1951, 54–66. Reprinted, modifed, in *Réalités secrètes*, October 1951, DT, in O, 1473.
4. André Guyon, "Un copain de Romains," in *Max Jacob à la confluence: Actes du colloque de Quimper* (Quimper: Bibliothèque Municipale, 2000), 85.
5. MJ, "Différents états d'esprit, ou portrait de l'auteur au travail," in ms. 7198–92, BLJD.
6. "Enquête," *Minotaure*, no. 3–4 (1933).
7. DT, in O, 136, 157, 160.
8. MJ, "Récit," in O, 1471, M 117.
9. MJ to Maurice Raynal, November 30, 1914, in Garnier 1:105.
10. MJ, "Le Christ au cinématographe," DT, in O, 488.
11. MJ to Jean-Richard Bloch, c. January 1915, in Bloch 2:145.
12. Andreu, *Vie et mort*, 56; Seckel, *Jacob et Picasso*, 73n13; Didier Gompel-Netter, *La Vie spirituelle* (May–June 1980), 402.
13. Blanchet's chapter on Jacob in *La Littérature et le spirituel* (Paris: Aubier, 1959) is the same text as the two articles he wrote under the pseudonym André Vendôme, "La Conversion de Max Jacob," *Études*, January–February 1948, 16–91 and 166–93, respectively.
14. SM, in O, 218.
15. Ibid., 233.
16. Ibid. Prose poem "Visitation," DT, in O, 472. The Hebrew letter Tet, *T*, corresponds to the number nine. Matorel asserts that the number eight represents equilibrium, intelligence, and humanity, and that God is one (SM, in O, 233, 236). Therefore the Cross equals humanity plus God, 8 + 1.
17. DT, in O, 291; Henri Dion, "Les Logis de Max Jacob," *CdR*, no. 5 (1983): 71.
18. MJ, "La Clef des songes," *Philosophies*, no. 5–6 (March 1925): 573–83.
19. Guyon, "Un copain," 85.
20. MJ, "Différents états d'esprit."
21. MJ, "La Clef des songes," 573–83.

22. Salmon, *Jacob, poète*, 17.

23. OBM, in O, 328.

24. MJ, "Poèmes mystiques," *Mesures*, October 15, 1935, 50.

25. MJ, "Récit," in O, 1477.

26. MJ, "À un prêtre qui me refuse le baptême," DT, in O, 479.

27. MJ, "Récit," in O, 1477.

28. DT, in O, 474.

29. MJ, "Récit," in O, 1477. Saint François de Sales's *Introduction à la vie dévote* presents Christian life adapted to worldly circumstances.

30. Seckel, *Jacob et Picasso*, 181.

31. Guiette, *Vie*, 87.

32. MJ, "Mes fleurs dans mes mains" and "Le Golfe de la plage," in Jules Romains, "La Génération nouvelle et son unité," *Nouvelle Revue française*, no. 7 (August 1909): 30–39. "Mes fleurs dans mes mains" became "Véritable poème," CD, in O, 414.

33. Jules Romains, "La Poésie immédiate," *Vers et prose*, no. 19 (October–December 1909): 90–95; Jules Romains and Guillaume Apollinaire, *Correspondance*, ed. Claude Martin (Paris: Jean-Michel Place, 1994), 140–49.

34. Seckel, *Jacob et Picasso*, 71.

35. Guiette, *Vie*, 119.

36. Seckel, *Jacob et Picasso*, 73; Salmon, *Jacob, poète*, 28.

37. MJ, "La Couronne de Vulcain," *Pan* 2, no. 12 (December 1909): 243–55; Galerie Simon, 1923; in *CMJ*, no. 5, 49–60; and RB, in O, 143.

38. MJ to Tzara, February 26, 1916, in Garnier 1:115.

39. Seckel, *Jacob et Picasso*, 84.

40. *Jeune homme*, 45.

41. SM, in O, 191.

42. Ibid., 183.

43. Ibid., 210.

44. Ibid., 187.

45. Ibid., 201.

46. Ibid., 227.

47. "The Cult of the Sacred Heart, the spear-cut or the fifth wound is the cult of the physical mark of the deepest intelligence." AP, in O, 1349.

48. SM, in O, 190.

49. Ibid., 195.

50. Ibid., 245.

51. Ibid., 235.

52. Ibid., 193.

53. Seckel, *Jacob et Picasso*, 76; Garnier 1:40.

54. Seckel, *Jacob et Picasso*, argues for 1910, instead of 1911 as proposed in Gompel/Marcoux, 32. Andreu, *Vie et mort*, 86.

55. Gompel/Marcoux, 32; Seckel, *Jacob et Picasso*, 77.

56. MJ to Salmon, April 16, 1910, in Garnier 1:41.

57. Ibid., 1:45; Pierre-Marcel Adéma, "Max Jacob et quelques oeuvres d'André Salmon de 1904 à 1940," in *André Salmon*, ed. P.-M. Adéma et al. (Paris: Nizet, 1987), 12.

58. MJ to Salmon, May 1910, in Garnier 1:45.

59. Hélène Henry and Alexandre Jacob, "Lettre de 1866," *CdR*, no. 9 (1987): 44.

60. Hélène Henry, "Max Jacob aux archives du Finistère," *CdR*, no. 10 (1988): 34; Guyon, "Un copain," 86.

61. MJ to Kahnweiler, c. 1910, in Garnier 1:50.

62. Ibid., 1:51.

63. Henry, "Jacob aux archives," 35. Hélène Henry, "Bouchaballe 'un' ou La comédie retrouvée," *CdR*, no. 5 (1983): 10.

64. Allier never came to much as a writer. Hélène Henry, "Dans l'ombre de Max Jacob: Le Quimpérois Pierre Allier, 1887–1959," *CdR*, no. 1 (1978): 35–56.

65. Ibid., 38.

66. Pierre Allier and Max Jacob, "Main basse sur la ville, ou 'Kemper Cancans,' " *CdR*, no. 5 (1983): 83–87.

67. Garnier 1:51, 53.

68. François Chapon, *Le Peintre et le livre* (Paris: Flammarion, 1987), 102–4.

69. Guillaume Apollinaire, *Petites flâneries d'art*, ed. Pierre Caizergues (Montpellier: Bibliothèque artistique et littéraire, 1980), 71.

70. Reverdy, *Voleur de Talan*, 164.

71. Ibid., 22.

72. Ibid., 38.

73. Ibid., 165.

74. "Lettre de Max Jacob à Charles Vildrac," *Création* 5, no. 13 (1974): 13–14.

75. MJ, "On ferme," "L'Histoire," and "Parenthèse," *Nouvelles de la république des lettres*, October 1910, 26.

76. The new title for "Tristesse" suggests the covert way in which Jacob dramatized his feelings. Renamed "Aveu" in OBM, in O, 290.

77. MJ, "Histoire des Prisonniers," "La Mère et la fille repenties," and "Nouvelles de Guichin," *Pan*, October–November 1910, 656–62.

78. Seckel, *Jacob et Picasso*, 87.

79. Ibid., 89.

80. Ibid.

81. "Jacob et Picasso vivent de compagnie / L'un peignant des tableaux et l'autre divaguant / Pablo emmerde sa toile Max va m'encaguant, / L'un d'eux a sa manière et l'autre sa manie." Seckel, *Jacob et Picasso*, 86. Encaguer is slang for "shitting, to annoy."

82. Ibid., 86, 89n9. "Ne dites pas Jacob pédé / N'aime pas le con."

83. Palmer White, *Poiret* (New York: Clarkson, 1973), 53.

84. Salmon, *Jacob, poète*, 33.

85. Olivier, *Picasso et ses amis*, 177; Olivier, *Souvenirs intimes*, 240–44.

86. MJ to Bloch, June 7, 1911, in Bloch 1:131.

87. Ibid., 133. The reference is to three Unamist plays: *L'Inquiète* by Jean-Richard Bloch; *L'Armée dans la ville by* Jules Romains; and *La Lumière* by Georges Duhamel.

88. Pierre Jakez Hélias, "*La Côte*, ou Max Jacob collecteur de lui-même," *CdR*, no. 7 (1985): 11.

89. Ibid., 6, 7.

90. René Plantier, "Max Jacob, Luzel, et la Bretagne: Étude des sources de *La Côte*," *CdR*, no. 1 (1978): 7–34.

91. C, 40.

92. Hélias, "*La Côte*, ou Jacob," 11, 12.

93. MJ to Tzara, February 16, 1916, in Garnier 1:116. Fort's *Ballades françaises* are saccharine.

94. Jacob/Paulhan, 39.

95. MJ to Grenier, September 21, 1924, in *Grenier*, 37.

96. Jean de L'Escritoire, *Paris-Midi* (June 1911), n.p. Pen name for André Billy.

97. Richardson, *Life*, 2:181.

98. Seckel, *Jacob et Picasso*, 87.

99. Steegmuller, *Apollinaire*; Richardson, *Life*, 2. The *Mona Lisa* was stolen by an employee of the Louvre, Vincenzo Peruggia; he was apprehended in 1913.

100. Steegmuller, *Apollinaire*, 223.

101. MJ to Kahnweiler, September 12, 1911, in Garnier 1:60.

102. Paul Poiret, *En habillant l'époque* (Paris: Grasset, 1930), 153.

103. MJ to Dunoyer de Segonzac, August 5, 1911, in Gompel/Marcoux, 31. MJ to Maurice Raynal, September 1911, in Garnier 1:61.

104. MJ to Kahnweiler, October 6, 1911, Garnier 1:66.

105. N.a., "École Druidique," *Hommes du jour*, no. 189 (September 2, 1011).

106. Octave Béliard, "Le Barde Druidique," *Hommes du jour*, no. 195 (October 14, 1911).

107. MJ to Kahnweiler, October 6, 1911, in Garnier 1:64.

108. "À Quimper-Corentin," *Cri du people*, October 28, 1911, 3.

109. Cousins, "Documentary Chronology," 380.

110. Daniel-Henry Kahnweiler with François Crémieux, *My Galleries and Painters*, trans. Helen Weaver (New York: Viking, 1971), 40–43. (Translation of *Mes galeries et mes peintres*, Gallimard, 1961.); Assouline, *L'Homme de l'art*, 166; Richardson, *Life*, 2:211.

111. Apollinaire's occasional journalism: *Petites Merveilles du quotidien*, ed. Pierre Caizergues (Montpellier: Bibliothèque Artistique et Littéraire, 1979), and *Petites Flâneries d'art*, ed. Pierre Caizergues (Montpellier: Bibliothèque Artistique et Littéraire, 1980). Apollinaire's signed journalism: *Oeuvres en prose complètes*, ed. Pierre Caizergues and Michel Décaudin (Paris: Gallimard, 1991), vol. 2.

112. *André Salmon on French Modern Art*, trans. Beth S. Gersh-Nešic (Cambridge: Cambridge University Press, 2005), 57; Cousins, "Documentary Chronology," 380; Richardson, *Life*, 2:212.

113. Apollinaire, *Oeuvres en prose complètes*, 2:318.

114. Apollinaire, *Anecdotiques*, 47.

115. Mary Ann Caws, *Manifesto* (Lincoln: University of Nebraska Press, 2001), 185–89.

116. MJ to Salmon, January 11, 1911, in Garnier 1:59. Francis Carco was the pseudonym of François Carcopino-Tusoli.

CHAPTER 8: BOHEMIA RISING

1. See Chapter 3 for discussion of the Doucet manuscript. MJ, *Le Christ à Montparnasse*, ms. 7198–2, BLJD.

2. MJ to Kahnweiler, April 28, 1910, in Garnier 1:43.

3. MJ to Kahnweiler, October 4, 1911, in Garnier 1:62.

4. Ibid., 1:63.

5. MJ to Kahnweiler, October 6, 1911, in Garnier 1:64–67.

6. Ibid.

7. MJ, "Grand récitatif dramatique pour salons," OBM, in O, 265.

8. MJ, "Variation d'une formule," OBM, in O, 268; "La leçon de musique," ibid., 271; "Avenue du Maine," ibid., 269.

9. MJ, "Statue fêlée," OBM, in O, 271, 272.

10. Ibid., 277.

11. MJ, "Situation des gens de lettres," ibid., 285.

12. MJ, "Le cheval sauvage et gai . . . ," OBM, in O, 293. Wrongly listed as "unpublished" in Maria Green and Christine Andreucci, *Bibliographie des poèmes de Max Jacob parus en revue* (Saint-Étienne: Université de Saint-Étienne, 1991), 34.

13. MJ, "Paysages," OBM, in O, 292; "Les poissons sont des yeux . . . ," ibid., 302.

14. MJ to Kahnweiler, October 6, 1911, in Garnier 1:64.

15. *Villard*, 71.

16. Seckel, *Jacob et Picasso*, 85n10.

17. Garnier 1:68.

18. MJ to Kahnweiler, December 2, 1911, ibid.

19. MJ to Marcel Olin, December 1911, in Gompel/Marcoux, 34.

20. Ibid.

21. MJ to Bloch, end of December 1911, in Bloch 1:134.

22. MJ to Tzara, February 26, 1916, in Garnier 1:115.

23. MJ to Michel Leiris, December 6, 1921, in *Leiris*, 36.

24. Seckel, *Jacob et Picasso*, 90.

25. MJ to Bloch, end of December 1911, in Bloch 1:134. MJ had already read several of the stories in *Effort* and *La Nouvelle Revue française*.

26. Apollinaire, *Oeuvres en prose complètes*, 2:407.

27. Ibid., 2:410.

28. Apollinaire, *Anecdotiques*, 16, 64.

29. On March 7, 1914, Apollinaire published Cravan's statement withdrawing his allegation. *Soirées de Paris*, no. 22 (February 1914): 131.

30. Ardengo Soffici, *Il Salto vitale: Autoritratto d'artista italiano nel quadro del suo tempo* (Florence: Vallecchi, 1954), 3:564.

31. Henri Hertz, "*La Côte*," *Phalange*, no. 1–7 (April 1912): 329–32.

32. MJ to Bloch, spring 1912, in Bloch 1:137–38.

33. Picasso/Apollinaire, 93.

34. Ibid., Richardson, *Life*, 2:221–33.

35. Severini, *Vita di un pittore*, 125–26.

36. Ardengo Soffici, *Autoritratto di artista italiano nel quadro del suo tempo*, vol. 4, *Virilità* (Florence: Vallecchi, 1955), 270.

37. Cousins, "Documentary Chronology," 391–93; Assouline, *Homme d'art*, 173–76.

38. Richardson, *Life*, 2:260.

39. Picasso/Apollinaire, 94–99.

40. Cousins, "Documentary Chronology," 399; Seckel, *Jacob et Picasso*, 95n31.

41. MJ to Bloch, August 2, 1912, in Bloch 1:142.

42. Cousins, "Documentary Chronology," 395.

43. MJ to Bloch, August 2, 1912, in Bloch 1:142.

44. Seckel, *Jacob et Picasso*, 92.

45. MJ to Kahnweiler, c. August 2 and 20, in Garnier 1:71.

46. MJ to Kahnweiler, c. August 1912, in Garnier 1:74.

47. Guillaume Apollinaire, *Oeuvres en prose complètes*, ed. Pierre Caizergues and Michel Décaudin (Paris: Gallimard, 1993), 3:124; Seckel, *Jacob et Picasso*, 90n32.

48. MJ to Kahnweiler, c. 1912, in Garnier 1:87. Letters out of order.

49. Ibid., 1:88.

50. MJ to Bloch, c. January–March 1913, in Bloch 1:145; MJ to Kahnweiler, December 9, 1912, in Garnier 1:82.

51. It was reprinted in 1929 by the Nouvelle Revue Française.

52. Frédéric Lefèvre, "Une heure avec M. Max Jacob, poète, romancier, et humoriste," *Nouvelles littéraires*, April 12, 1924, 1–2.

53. Béalu, *Dernier visage*, 54.

54. Saul Bellow adored Jacob's short fiction. Interview by author.

55. CI, in O, 722.

56. Ibid., 727.

57. Ibid., 719, 720, 722.

58. Guiette, *Vie*, 55.

59. CI, in O, 740, 742.

60. Jacob described the infanticide in the album created for Robert Zunz in 1939. Breton album is in the private collection, Gérard Zunz.

61. MJ, "Tablettes attribuées à un empereur romain," CI, in O, 793–96.

62. Hélène Henry, "Bouchaballe 'un' ou La comédie retrouvée," *CdR*, no. 5 (1983): 12.

63. MJ to Kahnweiler, c. October 1912, in Garnier 1:78.

64. Seckel, *Jacob et Picasso*, 93.

65. MJ, Doucet ms., *Le Christ à Montparnasse*, ms. 7198–92, BLJD. The draft turned into the poem "Pas encore," DT, in O, 481.

66. Hélène Henry, "Dans l'ombre de Max Jacob: Le quimpérois Pierre Allier, 1887–1959," *CdR*, no. 1 (1978): 41.

67. MJ, "Mille autres regrets" (early version), *Phalange*, no. 86 (August 1913): 125; "Mille regrets" (final version), LC, in O, 564.

CHAPTER 9: ART WARS

1. Assouline, *L'Homme de l'art*, 180; Steegmuller, *Apollinaire*, 235; Apollinaire, *Les Peintres cubistes*, 25. On Raynal's article, see Mark Antliff and Patricia Leighten, *A Cubism Reader: Documents and Criticism 1906-1914* (Chicago: University of Chicago Press, 2008), 333–40.

2. Seckel, *Jacob et Picasso*, 93, 95n32.

3. Ibid., 96.

4. Artemisia Calcagni Abrami and Lucia Chimirri, "Sodalizii di genio," *Le edizioni de Daniel-Henry Kahnweiler* (Florence: Biblioteca Nazionale Centrale, 1995), 45.

5. Guillaume Apollinaire, *Correspondance avec les artistes, 1903–1918*, ed. Laurence Campa and Peter Read (Paris: Gallimard, 2009), 87–88.

6. Meryle Secrest, *Modigliani: A Life* (New York: Knopf, 2011), 170.

7. Reverdy, *Voleur de Talan*, 168.

8. Apollinaire, *Oeuvres en prose complètes*, 2:537.

9. Ibid., 2:538.

10. Seckel, *Jacob et Picasso*, 96.

11. Fillacier, *Chante cigale*, 292.

12. MJ to Bloch, c. January–March 1913, in Bloch 1:145.

13. André Salmon, *Tendres canailles* (Paris: Ollendorff, 1913).

14. Peyre, *Jacob quotidien*, 90.

15. Picasso/Apollinaire, 102.

16. Apollinaire, *Oeuvres en prose complètes*, 2:1508; Assouline, *L'Homme de l'art*, 211–17.

17. Cousins, "Documentary Chronology," 416.

18. Ibid., 417.

19. Ibid., 416.

20. Seckel, *Jacob et Picasso*, 97–98.

21. Garnier 1:91–95. Letters misdated.

22. Ibid., 93.

23. Richardson, *Life*, 2:276–78.

24. Cousins, "Documentary Chronology," 417.

25. MJ, "Honneur de la sardane et de la tenora," LC, in O, 558. Richardson mistakenly calls it a prose poem. Richardson, *Life*, 2:280.

26. Picasso/Apollinaire, 102–5.

27. MJ to Apollinaire, in Garnier 1:94.

28. MJ to Kahnweiler, ibid., 94.

29. Apollinaire, *Oeuvres poétiques*, 39.

30. The word *ancien* being pronounced as three syllables, as the rule of dieresis permits.

31. Faure-Favier, *Souvenirs*, 47.

32. Apollinaire, "Palais," *Oeuvres poétiques*, 61.

33. Steegmuller, *Apollinaire*, 250.

34. Faure-Favier, *Souvenirs*, 103–5.

35. MJ to Alfred Vallette, June 1913, in Garnier 1:96.

36. Cousins, "Documentary Chronology," 418.

37. Seckel, *Jacob et Picasso*, 104–6.

38. Ardengo Soffici, *Autoritratto d'artista; Fine di un mondo* (Florence: Vallecchi, 1955), 4:196–203.

39. Marinetti never lived in France for any extended period, but he had been educated in French in Alexandria. Soffici lived for years in Paris.

40. Jean-François Rodriguez, "Su alcune lettere inedite di Max Jacob a Soffici," *Sodalizi del genio: Le edizioni di Daniel-Henry Kahnweiler*, ed. Artemisia Calcagni Abrami and Lucia Chimirri (Florence: Biblioteca Nazionale Centrale, 1995), 45–48.

41. MJ, "L'Établissement d'une communauté au Brésil," *Lacerba* 1, no. 12 (June 15, 1913): 126; LC, in O, 573.

42. Luciano de Maria, *Marinetti e i futuristi* (Milan: Garzanti, 1994), 78–85.

43. Filippo Tommaso Marinetti, "L'immaginazione senza fili e le parole in libertà," *Lacerba* 1, no. 12 (June 15, 1913): 121–24.

44. Ardengo Soffici, "Max Jacob," *Lacerba* 1, no. 12 (June 15, 1913): 126.

45. In the story "Le Haschischin," Reverdy describes Jacob's being locked up overnight. Reverdy, *Risques et périls* (Paris: Flammarion, 1972), 137.

46. Richardson, *Life*, 2:281.

47. MJ to Bloch, September 28, 1913, in Bloch 1:148.

48. Giovanni Papini, "Introibo," *Lacerba* 1, no. 1 (January 1, 1913): 1.

49. Umberto Boccioni, "Per l'ignoranza italiana, sillabario pittorico," *Lacerba* 1, no. 16 (August 15, 1913): 179.

50. Giovanni Papini, "Il massacro delle donne," *Lacerba* 2, no. 7 (April 1, 1914): 97.

51. "L'ANTITRADITION FUTURISTE" in Steegmuller, *Apollinaire*, 262–65.

52. Rodriguez, "Su alcune lettere," 47.

53. "Le Divan de Monsieur Max Jacob," *Lacerba* 1, no. 14 (July 15, 1913): 157. Poems printed, out of order, in *Poésie présente*, no. 77 (December 1990): 57–98.

54. "Mille autres regrets" and "Prière," *Phalange*, no. 86 (1913): 125–26.

55. Henri Hertz, "Contribution à la figure de Max Jacob," *Europe* (January 1970): 138–39.

56. Severini, *Vita di un pittore*, 93.

57. Ibid., 153–56; Billy Klüver and Julie Martin, *Kiki's Paris* (New York: Abrams, 1989), 50–51.

58. "République et révolutions chinoises," *Lacerba* 1, no. 21 (November 1, 1913): 74–76.

59. MJ to Bloch, October 8, 1913, in Bloch 1:150.

60. Moricand, *La Vie*, n.p.

61. "Boute-en-train," *Soirées de Paris*, no. 18 (November 15, 1913): 25–26. MJ, *L'Échelle de Jacob: Recueil d'inédits*, ed. Nicole and José-Emmanuel Cruz (Paris: Bibliothèque des Arts, 1994), 29.

62. A *message téléphonique* was a telegram-like innovation by which the person dictated a message at his post office, which then passed it to the recipient's post office by telephone.

63. Brilliantly translated by Alexander Dickow in his unpublished manuscript, *Selections from* Le Laboratoire central.

64. MJ, "Le Bal masqué," "Quelques personnages du bal masqué: I, Malvina; II, Marsupiau," *Soirées de Paris*, no. 19 (December 15, 1913): 29–32. "Le Bal masqué" is reprinted in LC, in O, 620; "Malvina" in LC, in O, 624, lacking original ninth line; "Marsupiau," LC, in O, 622, revised.

65. Apollinaire, *Oeuvres en prose complètes*, 766; Klüver and Martin, *Kiki's Paris*, 54–55.

66. Guillaume Apollinaire, "Chronique mensuelle," *Soirées de Paris*, no. 18 (November 15, 1913): 2, 3.

67. Umberto Boccioni, "Simultaneità futurista," *Lacerba* 2, no. 1 (January 1, 1914): 12.

68. François Chapon, *Le Peintre et le livre* (Paris: Flammarion, 1987), 134–37, 308.

69. Blaise Cendrars, *Du monde entier au coeur du monde* (1977; reprinted Paris: Gallimard, 2006), 58; Apollinaire, "Les Fiançailles," *Oeuvres poétiques*, 132.

70. Blaise Cendrars, "Apollinaire," *Montjoie!* 2, no. 4, 5, 6 (April–June 1914): 4.

71. Faure-Favier, *Souvenirs*, 109–11.

72. Guillaume Apollinaire, "Nos amis les futuristes," *Soirées de Paris* 3, no. 21 (February 1914): 78.

73. MJ, "Poème simultané avec superposition simple," and "Poème simultané à deux rouleaux mobiles," in CD 1917. In later editions, both appear as "Poème." CD, in O, 357.

74. MJ, "La Rue Ravignan de Montmartre," in "Extracts from Unpublished Volumes," trans. Alice Morning, *New Age*, February 18, 1915, 432. French original: *Soirées de Paris* 3, no. 21 (February 1914): 115.

75. CD, in O, 376.

76. Different accounts of the auction give different names for Picasso's paintings and cite different prices. André Level, *Souvenirs d'un collectionneur* (Paris: Alain Mazo, 1959), 17ff.

77. Cousins, "Documentary Chronology," 317, 424; Seckel, *Jacob et Picasso*, 110.

78. Picasso/Apollinaire, 110–11.

79. Seckel, *Jacob et Picasso*, 110.

80. Sylvette Fillacier, "Parmi vos lettres, Max," *Europe* 36, no. 348–49 (April–May 1958): 79–80.

81. Richardson, *Life*, 2:299.

82. Ibid., 2:292–94.

83. Cousins, "Documentary Chronology," 424.

84. MJ, "Printemps et cinématographe mêlés," *Soirées de Paris* 3, no. 23 (April 1914): 219. DT, in O, 455.

85. Richard Aldington, "Some Recent French Poets," *Egoist* 1, no. 12, (June 15, 1914): 221–30.

86. Apollinaire, *Petites Flâneries d'art*, 56, 58, 71.

87. Faure-Favier, *Souvenirs*, 113–14.

88. Seckel, *Jacob et Picasso*, 112.

89. Assouline, *L'Homme de l'art*, 227–28.

90. MJ, "Surpris et charmé," *Soirées de Paris*, no. 25 (June 1914): 328–33; RB, in O, 857; Hélène Henry, "Max Jacob aux archives du Finistère," *CdR*, no. 10 (1988): 33–48.

91. Pound composed the manifesto, but published it under Flint's name in *Poetry*, March 1913. Reprinted under his own name in "A Retrospect," *Pavannes and Divisions* (1918), and in *Literary Essays of Ezra Pound*, ed. T. S. Eliot (New York: New Directions, 1968), 3.

92. Salmon, *Souvenirs*, 2:233; "Écrit pour la S.A.F.," *Soirées de Paris*, no. 26 (July–August 1914): 402–8; DT, in O, 462.

93. "Une noce juive monstre," *Paris-Journal*, July 5, 1914.

94. Guillaume Apollinaire, "Le Pauvre peintre juif et les chameaux," *Paris-Journal*, July 22, 1914.

95. Christopher Clark, *The Sleepwalkers: How Europe Went to War in 1914* (New York: HarperCollins, 2013).

96. Assouline, *L'Homme de l'art*, 230.

97. Rodriguez, "Su alcune lettere," 50.

98. MJ to Bloch, n.d. 1914, in Bloch 2:141.

CHAPTER 10: THE GREAT WAR AND CONVERSION

1. MJ to Bloch, September 29, 1914, in Bloch 2:142.

2. *Journée financière et politique*, August 3, 1914, 1.

3. *Journal*, August 3, 1914, 1.

4. *L'Intransigeant*, August 11, 1914, 1; "Notre Effort en Haute-Alsace," *Journal*, August 11, 1914, 1.

5. "La Grande bataille," *Paris-Midi*, August 12, 1914, 1.

6. MJ to Fillacier, September 10, 1914, in Gompel/Marcoux, 39.

7. MJ to Bloch, September 29, 1914, in Bloch 2:143. MJ to Kahnweiler and Maurice Raynal, in Garnier 1:96–103.

8. MJ to Bloch, September 29, 1914, in Bloch 2:143.

9. "France Will Fight On: An Interview with M. Clemenceau," *Daily Mail*, August 31, 1914, 1.

10. "La Misère est proche," *Journal des débats politiques et littéraires*, August 31, 1914.

11. MJ to Bloch, September 29, 1914, in Bloch 2:143.

12. *New York Herald*, August 24, 1914, 1.

13. *New York Herald*, August 25, 1914, 1.

14. *Daily Mail*, August 26, 1914, 1.

15. "Proclamation du gouvernement au people français," *L'Éclair*, September 3, 1914, 1.

16. *L'Éclair*, September 9, 1914, 1.

17. MJ to Fillacier, September 10, 1914, in Gompel/Marcoux, 39. MJ to Bloch, September 29, 1914, in Bloch 2:142.

18. Jacob spelled his name sometimes Lagnel, sometimes Laignel. Andreu, *Vie et mort*, 96.

19. MJ to Kahnweiler, September 22, 1914, in Garnier 1:97; MJ to Bloch, September 29, 1914, in Bloch 2:142.
20. Garnier 1:97–101.
21. MJ to Bloch, September 29, 1914, in Bloch 2:142.
22. MJ to Raynal, September 23, 1914, in Garnier 1:100.
23. "Nos Armées ont progressé entre Reims et l'Argonne," *L'Écho de Paris*, September 2, 1914, 1.
24. *L'Éclair*, September 30, 1914, 1.
25. MJ to Kahnweiler, September 22, 1914, in Garnier 1:96–99.
26. Reverdy, *Voleur de Talan*, 169.
27. Pierre Cabanne, *Le Siècle de Picasso*, 4 vols. (Paris: Gallimard, 1975), 2:447.
28. MJ to Raynal, n.d., 1914, in Garnier 1:107–8; MJ to Bloch, c. late December 1914, early January 1915, in Bloch 2:144.
29. Richardson, *Life*, 2:396–97.
30. MJ to Raynal, November 30, 1914, in Garnier 1:103–7.
31. Ibid.
32. Ibid., 104.
33. DT, in O, 486. Narrative telescoped in Guiette, *Vie*, 89.
34. DT, in O, 482.
35. MJ to Raynal, November 30, 1914, in Garnier 1:103–7.
36. Ibid.
37. MJ to Bloch, c. late December 1914, early January 1915, in Bloch 2:145.
38. DT, in O, 485.
39. Ibid., 486.
40. Guiette, *Vie*, 90.
41. DT, in O, 484.
42. MJ to Bloch, c. late December 1914, early January 1915, in Bloch 2:145.
43. DT, in O, 484.
44. Andreu, *Vie et mort*, 97–98.
45. MJ, "Dieu nous a abandonnés," DT, in O, 480; "Le Christ à Montparnasse," DT, in O, 491.
46. MJ to Bloch, c. late December 1914, early January 1915, in Bloch 2:145.
47. MJ to Apollinaire, January 7, 1915, in Garnier 1:110.
48. DT, in O, 484.
49. Ibid., 490.
50. Ibid., 485.
51. MJ to Bloch, c. late December 1914, early January 1915, in Bloch 2:145.
52. DT, in O, 486.
53. "Le Christ au cinématographe," ibid., 488.
54. MJ to Apollinaire, January 7, 1915, in Garnier 1:110.
55. Andreu, *Vie et mort*, 101.
56. DT, in O, 501.
57. MJ to Fillacier, n.d., in Gompel/Marcoux 42.
58. DT, in O, 507.

59. MJ, "Le Christ à Montparnasse," *Écrits nouveaux* 3, no. 16–17 (April–May 1919): 70–82. DT, in O, 505–8.

60. MJ to Béalu, March 28, 1941, in Béalu, *Dernier visage*, 223.

61. MJ, *Le Siège de Jérusalem*, in *Saint Matorel* (Paris: Gallimard, 1936), 111.

62. MJ, "Extracts from Unpublished Volumes," trans. Alice Morning, *New Age*, February 18, 1915, 431.

63. DT, in O, 501.

64. Ibid., 507.

65. MJ to René Villard, August 13, 1924, in *Villard*, 26.

66. DT, in O, 508.

67. Cabanne, *Siècle de Picasso*, 2:446.

68. Richardson, *Life*, 2:363–67.

69. Cabanne, *Siècle de Picasso*, 2:447–51.

70. Richardson, *Life*, 2:416.

71. DT, in O, 508.

72. Garnier 1:104.

73. "Contagion," "Préexistence des formes," and "Conte d'Andersen," *Lacerba* 2, no. 23 (November 1914): 308–10; "Contagion" in 1922 CD (O, 417) as "La Contagion ou les imitateurs"; "Préexistence des formes" (O, 438) appears in 1922 CD but not in 1923; "Conte d'Andersen" as "Certains dédains et pas les autres," in CD, in O, 406.

74. MJ, "Poèmes," *Lacerba* 3, no. 11 (March 1915): 83; "Le périscope de Mentana," "L'oiseau gaucher," and "Alleluia! Sous les thuyas," CD, in O, 364.

75. MJ, "Poème," CD, in O, 359.

76. "Extracts from Unpublished Volumes," trans. Alice Morning, *New Age*, February 19, 1915, 431–32; "Unpublished Extracts," trans. Alice Morning, *New Age*, May 6, 1915, 15–16; MJ, "Poème," CD, in O, 359.

77. MJ to Bloch, May 14, 1915, in Bloch 2:146.

78. Garnier 1:114; Severini, *Vita di un pittore*, 186–89; MJ to Fillacier, March 14, 1915, in Gompel/Marcoux, 43–44.

79. Cabanne, *Siècle de Picasso*, 2:449.

80. Richardson, *Life*, 2:429.

81. MJ to Bloch, May 14, 1915, in Bloch 2:145–46.

82. Cocteau's social climbing was so egregious that Gide presented him in *Les Faux-monnayeurs* as Robert de Passavant (Robert Pushahead).

83. Jacob/Paulhan, 26.

84. Richardson, *Life*, 2:282.

85. Reverdy, *Voleur de Talan*, 174–75.

86. MJ to Paul Bonet, cited in catalogue, Hôtel Drouot, Exposition, December 1, 1989, item 215. Reprinted as "Petit historique du *Cornet à dés*" in CD 15 (1967).

87. Reverdy, *Voleur de Talan*, 176.

88. Ibid., 93.

89. Pierre Reverdy, "Envie," in Reverdy, *Plupart du temps, 1915–1922* (Paris: Nouvelle Revue Française, 1969), 30.

90. Picabia loved fast cars and took several epic journeys across France with Apollinaire in 1912, including one to the Alps, where the poet is supposed to have found the title to his poem "Zone." Gabrielle Buffet, "Apollinaire," *Transition Fifty*, no. 6 (1950): 110–25; George Baker, *The Artwork Caught by the Tail: Francis Picabia and Dada in Paris* (Cambridge, Mass.: MIT Press, 2007), 1–8.

91. MJ to Kahnweiler, September 22, 1914, in Garnier 1:98.

92. MJ to Albert Uriet, January 2, 1916, in Jacob/Paulhan, 33.

93. Ibid.

94. MJ, "O mon ange gardien," CD; "Il y a sur la nuit," as "Poème de la lune" in CD, in O, 375.

95. MJ, "La Vie artistique," *291*, no. 10–11 (December 1915–January 1916), in Beinecke Library, Yale University (YCAL mss. 85, Box 99).

96. Vittorio Rieti, interview by author.

97. Seckel, *Jacob et Picasso*, 128.

98. Ibid., 121.

99. Sachs, *Décade*, 205.

100. MJ, "La Vie artistique," *291*, no. 12 (February 1916): 4.

101. MJ, "Jugement des femmes," CD, in O, 419.

102. Steegmuller, *Cocteau*, 182.

103. In the draft in the Beinecke, the Art Critic addresses "Ribera." Beinecke, YCAL mss. 85, Box 99.

104. CD, in O, 361.

105. MJ to Tzara, February 26, 1916, in Garnier 1:115–17.

106. MJ to Apollinaire, n.d. 1916, in Garnier 1:117–19.

107. Seckel, *Jacob et Picasso*, 137.

108. Ibid., 128.

109. *Paris-Midi*, through October and November 1912, reported the Balkan uprisings against the Turks.

110. Germana Orlanda-Cerenza, "Les Alliés sont en Arménie," in *Max Jacob et la création*, ed. Arlette Albert-Birot (Paris: Jean-Michel Place, 1997), 29–34.

111. "Les Alliés sont en Arménie," reprinted as a brochure in 1976.

112. Sylvain Laboureur, *Catalogue complet de l'oeuvre de Jean-Émile Laboureur* (Neufchâtel: Ides et Calendes, 1991), 3:303–4.

113. Reverdy, *Voleur de Talan*, 170.

114. Steegmuller, *Cocteau*, 163–64.

115. Richardson, *Life*, 2:388.

116. Steegmuller, *Cocteau*, 157.

117. Klüver and Martin, *Kiki's Paris*, 74–75.

118. Fillacier, *Chante cigale*, 377–78.

119. Michel Decaudin and Étienne-Alain Hubert, "Petit historique d'une appellation," *Europe*, June–July 1982, 10, 11; Cabanne, *Siècle de Picasso*, 2:408; Seckel, *Jacob et Picasso*, 128–29.

120. Richardson, *Life*, 2:395–405.

121. Ibid., 2:402.

122. MJ to Ghikas, July 7, 1916, in Gompel/Marcoux, 46; MJ to Ghikas, August 1, in *AA* 1:57.

123. Seckel, *Jacob et Picasso*, 130.

124. Ibid., 131; Jacob/Paulhan, 44.

125. Seckel, *Jacob et Picasso*, 131.

126. Ibid., 131–32.

127. MJ to Albert Uriet, December 15, 1916, in Jacob/Paulhan, 48.

128. Guillaume Apollinaire, "Les Tendances nouvelles," *SIC,* no. 8–9–10 (August–September 1916): 1.

129. Steegmuller, *Apollinaire,* 308.

130. Faure-Favier, *Souvenirs,* 139.

131. MJ, "La Messe du visionnaire," DT, in O, 495.

132. MJ to Fillacier, c. November 1916, in Gompel/Marcoux 47.

133. Cabanne, *Siècle de Picasso,* 4:464.

134. CD, in O, 366.

135. "La Vie artistique," *291,* no. 10–11 (December 1915–January 1916).

136. Seckel, *Jacob et Picasso,* 134.

137. Until recently it was thought that the series of prose poems in CD following "Le Coq et la perle" all belonged under that title. It is now clear that those poems constitute section four and do not belong to "Le Coq et la perle." O, 1760n21.

138. *Élan,* no. 10 (1 December 1, 1916): 1; "Et quand, du lancier polonais" and "Que te manque-t-il," CD, in O, 361; "Croient-ils donc," in revised form in CD, in O, 367; "Le mystère est dans cette vie," CD, in O, 371; "Il arrive quand tu ronfles," CD, in O, 363.

139. Richardson, *Life,* 2:401–5, 419–33.

140. Seckel, *Jacob et Picasso,* 140n65; Richardson, *Life,* 2:426.

141. Severini, *Vita di un pittore,* 203–5.

CHAPTER 11: *THE DICE CUP* AND THE ARMISTICE

1. *Le Bonnet Rouge,* January 13, 1917, 2.

2. Seckel, *Jacob et Picasso,* 140–41.

3. Andreu, *Vie et mort,* 105.

4. Richardson, *Life,* 2:304–5.

5. MJ to Doucet, January 11, 1917, in Garnier 1:120–3.

6. Poiret published a piece from *Cinéma Thomas* in his fashion journal *Almanach de Martine.*

7. MJ to Doucet, January 17, 1917, in Garnier 1:123–27.

8. "Présentation de Pierre Reverdy a 'Lyre et Palette,'" *Pierre Reverdy 1889–1960* (Paris: Mercure de France, 1962), 16–18.

9. Moricand, *La vie.*

10. Garnier 1:123–40.

11. "Penitent Picasso has decided to enroll in the École des Beaux-Arts." Francis Picabia, "Picasso repenti," *391,* no. 1 (January 25, 1917), 1; MJ to Picasso, 1917, in Seckel, *Jacob et Picasso,* 140–48.

12. Seckel, *Jacob et Picasso*, 144.

13. MJ to Doucet, March 7, 1917, in Garnier 1:144.

14. MJ, "Atlantide," *391* 2, no. 3, (February 10, 1917), 23. LC, in O, 599.

15. MJ to Doucet, March 22, 1917, in Garnier 1:145–46; MJ to Picasso, in Seckel, *Jacob et Picasso*, 144.

16. MJ, "La guerre se prolonge . . . ," *Nord-Sud*, no. 1 (March 15, 1917): 2; reprinted in *Nord-Sud, Revue Littéraire 1917–1918* (Paris: Jean-Michel Place, 1980).

17. Pierre Reverdy, "Sur le Cubisme," *Nord-Sud*, no. 1 (March 15, 1917): 6; Pierre Reverdy, "Essai d'esthétique littéraire," *Nord-Sud*, no. 4–5 (June–July 1917), 4–6.

18. MJ to Doucet, March 22, 1917, in Garnier 1:145–46; MJ to Picasso, same day, in Seckel, *Jacob et Picasso*, 144.

19. MJ, "Poème," *Nord-Sud*, no. 1 (March 15, 1917): 12; LC, in O, 581. The epigraph is a prose poem in CD, in O, 368.

20. MJ, "Histoire de Don Juan," *Nord-Sud*, no. 1 (March 15, 1917): 13; Seckel, *Jacob et Picasso*, 144.

21. MJ, "La Messe du démoniaque," DT, in O, 510.

22. MJ, "La Guerre" and "1914," *Nord-Sud*, no. 2 (April 15, 1917): 11; CD, in O, 351–52.

23. MJ, "Note sur la vie de Rosalie Fromager, Femme Gaëtan," *Nord-Sud*, no. 2 (April 15, 1917): 12–15, reprinted in RB, in O, 875.

24. Pierre Reverdy, "Entre autres choses," *Nord-Sud*, no. 2 (April 15, 1917): 15.

25. Seckel, *Jacob et Picasso*, 145.

26. Jean Cocteau, "La Collaboration de *Parade*," *Nord-Sud*, no. 4–5 (June–July 1917): 29–31; Richardson, *Life*, 2:419–24.

27. Seckel, *Jacob et Picasso*, 145; Richardson, *Life*, 3:44.

28. "Le 24 juin, 1917," *SIC*, June 1917, n.p.; "Extraits de presse concernant la representation des *Mamelles de Tirésias* le 24 juin 1917," *SIC* (July–August 1917), n. p.

29. "*Les Mamelles de Tirésias*," *Nord-Sud*, no. 4–5 (June–July 1917), 3.

30. Guillory de Saix, in *La France* (June 29, 1917), quoted in *SIC* (July–August 1917), n. p.

31. For Apollinaire, *surrealist* simply meant a rejection of realism.

32. Gabory, *Apollinaire*, 13–19.

33. Reverdy, *Voleur de Talan*, 177.

34. The chronicle is unsigned, but the draft in Jacob's handwriting is in RDY 386, BLJD; MJ, "Chronique mensuelle," *Nord-Sud*, no. 4–5 (June–July 1917): 2–3.

35. "Conférence Guillaume Apollinaire," *Nord-Sud*, no. 4–5 (June–July 1917): 3.

36. MJ to Doucet, August 4, 1915, in Garnier 1:155.

37. Seckel, *Jacob et Picasso*, 159n76, in Richardson, *Life*, 2:426–27.

38. "Périgal-Nohor," *Nord-Sud*, no. 4–5 (June–July 1917), 19; LC, in O, 590.

39. MJ to Doucet, August 27, 1917, in Garnier 1:160–61; MJ to Level, n.d., in Garnier 1:162–63.

40. Richardson, *Life*, 2:396.

41. Seckel, *Jacob et Picasso*, 152n88.

42. MJ to Hertz, August 27, 1917, in *AA* 1:60–61.

43. MJ to Cocteau, November 9, 1917, in Jacob/Cocteau, 37.

44. MJ to Doucet, August 27, 1917, in Garnier 1:161.

45. MJ to Roland-Manuel, September 17, 1917, in Garnier 1:163–66.

46. MJ to Roland-Manuel, c. early 1918, ibid., 167.

47. Raynal: "Max Jacob prays for me too, it's a refrain he serves to anyone and everyone." Jacob/Paulhan, 56n4.

48. Seckel, *Jacob et Picasso*, 147.

49. Gabory, *Apollinaire*, 26.

50. O, 344 .

51. Reverdy, *Voleur de Talan*, 180; Seckel, *Jacob et Picasso*, 152n92.

52. "Notice," CD, in O, 351.

53. "Attention aux fausses nouvelles," *Paris-Journal*, July 31, 1914.

54. MJ, "Poème," originally "Poème en forme de peloton de fil embrouillé," CD, in O, 359.

55. Hastings published her translation in *New Age*, February 18, 1915, 432.

56. "Poème simultané avec superposition simple" became "Poème," O, 357. "Poème simultané avec deux rouleaux" also became "Poème," O, 357.

57. Hastings's version in *New Age*, February 18, 1915, 431; CD, in O, 362.

58. MJ, "Poème dans un goût qui n'est pas le mien," CD, in O, 353, 355.

59. MJ, "Sir Elisabeth (Prononcez Soeur)," CD, in O, 390; MJ, "L'Âme de la Joconde," CD, in O, 393; MJ, "Roman d'aventures," CD, in O, 393; And the frankly hermaphroditic MJ, "Ruses du demon pour ravoir sa proie," CD, in O, 420.

60. CD, in O, 371.

61. Ibid., 363.

62. Jacob wrote the "1906 Preface" only after the publication of Reverdy's *Poèmes en prose* in 1915.

63. CD, in O, 347.

64. Ibid., 348.

65. Ibid., 349.

66. Ibid.

67. Louis de Gonzague Frick, "M. Max Jacob et son *Cornet à dés*," *SIC*, no. 24 (December 1917): n.p.

68. Frédéric Lefèvre, *La Jeune poésie française: Hommes et tendances* (Paris: Georges Crès & Cie, 1918), 198.

69. Ibid., 200.

70. Lefèvre, *Jeune poésie*, 241–52.

71. Pierre Reverdy, "Un livre!," *Nord-Sud*, no. 10 (December 1917): 2.

72. Reverdy, *Voleur de Talan*, 180; Seckel, *Jacob et Picasso*, 152n92.

73. Seckel, *Jacob et Picasso*, 155, 165n20.

74. MJ to Roland-Manuel, c. early 1918, in Garnier 1:167–68.

75. Gabory, *Apollinaire*, 28.

76. Seckel, *Jacob et Picasso*, 160, 166n60.

77. Ibid., 161; Armel, *Leiris*, 148–49.

78. Seckel, *Jacob et Picasso*, 160.

79. MJ to Paulhan, April 16, 1918, in Jacob/Paulhan 66.

80. MJ to Jean-Richard Bloch, March 19, 1918, in Bloch 2:148–49.

81. Henri Vandeputte, "Le Cornet à dés," *Carnet critique* (February 15, 1917–November 15, 1918); cited in Victor Martin-Schmets, "L'Amitié de Max Jacob et de Henri Vandeputte," in *Max Jacob à la confluence: Actes du colloque de Quimper* (Quimper: Bibliothèque Municipale, 2000), 109–10.

82. Seckel, *Jacob et Picasso*, 164n9.

83. Louis Aragon, "*Les Ardoises du Toit*," *SIC*, May 1918, n. p.

84. Pierre Reverdy, *118 Lettres inédites* (Paris: Nouvelle Revue Française, 1976), 47.

85. Seckel, *Jacob et Picasso*, 157–58.

86. Scholars disagree about the founding of La Sirène: Seckel, *Jacob et Picasso*, 167n99; Miriam Cendrars, *Blaise Cendrars: La vie, le verbe, l'écriture* (Paris: Denoël, 1993), 359; Jacob/Cocteau, 40.

87. Jacob/Paulhan, 71.

88. Cocteau to MJ, November 1, 1918, in Jacob/Cocteau, 39.

89. CTH, 76.

90. MJ to René Fauchois, November 12, 1918, in Garnier 1:177.

91. Jean-Pierre Goldenstein, "Gaston Picard, le prince des enquêteurs," *Études littéraires* 5, no. 2 (August 1972): 317.

92. Salmon, *Jacob, poète*, 15; Moricand, *La Vie*.

93. Seckel, *Jacob et Picasso*, 164.

94. CTH, 20–21.

CHAPTER 12: THE STRUGGLE FOR THE AVANT-GARDE

1. Gabory, *Apollinaire*, 22.

2. Ibid., 26.

3. Tristan Tzara, "Dada Manifesto," in Mary Ann Caws, *Manifesto: A Century of Isms* (Lincoln: University of Nebraska Press, 2001), 297–304.

4. Adrienne Monnier, *The Very Rich Hours of Adrienne Monnier*, trans. Richard McDougall (New York: Scribners, 1977), 88.

5. Louis Aragon, *Anicet ou le panorama* (1921; Paris: Gallimard, 1949), 133.

6. Mark Polizzotti, *Revolution of the Mind: The Life of André Breton* (New York: Farrar, Straus & Giroux, 1995), 170; Henri Béhar, *André Breton: Le grand indésirable* (Paris: Calmann-Lévy, 1990), 127; Michel Sanouillet, *Dada in Paris*, trans. Sharmila Ganguli (Cambridge, Mass.: MIT Press, 2009), 233–53.

7. Aragon 1921, 103.

8. Ibid., 106.

9. Gabory, *Apollinaire*, 26, 54.

10. Ibid., 55.

11. Béhar, *Breton*, 73.

12. Ibid., 74.

13. "Les Jockeys mécaniques" and "Autres jockeys alcooliques." Andrew Rothwell, "Reverdy's *Les Jockeys camouflés*: From Aesthetic Polemic to 'art poétique,'" *Nottingham French Studies* 28, no. 2 (Autumn 1989): 26–44.

14. Béhar, *Breton*, 64.

15. Pierre Reverdy, "Trente-deux lettres inédites à André Breton, 1917–1924," ed. Léon Somville, *Études Littéraires* (Québec) 3, no. 1 (April 1970): 97–120.

16. "La Rue Ravignan," *Littérature* 1, no.1 (March 1919) : 15; LC, in O, 585.

17. *Littérature* 1, no. 1 (March 1919): 24.

18. Gabory, *Apollinaire*, 56.

19. Garnier 1:183.

20. Béalu, *Dernier visage*, 56; Steegmuller, *Cocteau*, 248–49.

21. Steegmuller, *Cocteau*, 249; Nadia Odouart, *Les années folles de Raymond Radiguet* (Paris: Seghers, 1973), 34–54.

22. Gabory, *Apollinaire*, 26; On Gide's distinction between Doric and Ionic art, see Roger Martin du Gard, *Notes sur André Gide* (Paris: Gallimard, 1951), 104. Code for homosexuality.

23. Gabory, *Apollinaire*, 37.

24. Ibid., 42–43.

25. P: luxury edition with Picasso's etching of a Harlequin.

26. Seckel, *Jacob et Picasso*, 168.

27. Richardson, *Life*, 3:111.

28. MJ to Doucet, April 26, 1919, in Garnier 1:189.

29. Seckel, *Jacob et Picasso*, 171n9.

30. MJ to Cocteau, c. November 1919, in Jacob/Cocteau 41.

31. Jean Cocteau, *Carte blanche* (Paris: Éditions de La Sirène, 1920), 8, 9.

32. Raymond Lulle, *Le Livre de l'ami et de l'aimé*, trans. Antonio de Barrau and Max Jacob (Paris: Éditions de La Sirène, 1920), 6.

33. Ibid., 30.

34. "Colloque III," FE, in O, 1413.

35. MJ, "Le Christ à Montparnasse," *Écrits Nouveaux* 3, no. 16–17 (April–May 1919), 70–88.

36. Gabory, *Apollinaire*, 44–45.

37. False birth date: July 11.

38. MJ, "Le Christ à Montparnasse," 70.

39. Ibid., 71.

40. Ibid., 82.

41. "L'Eucharistie," DT, in O, 497; "Le Christ au Cinématographe," DT, in O, 488.

42. Seckel, *Jacob et Picasso*, 170.

43. Cocteau, *Carte blanche*, 86–92.

44. MJ to Emma Hertz, May 26, 1919, in Gompel/Marcoux, 62.

45. MJ to Cocteau, May 1919, in Jacob/Cocteau, 44.

46. Cocteau, *Carte blanche*, 70–74.

47. Ibid., 80; Seckel, *Jacob et Picasso*, 170.

48. Seckel, *Jacob et Picasso*, 170.

49. MJ, "La Mort morale," CD, in O, 401; MJ, "Mort morale," *Littérature*, no. 4 (June 1919): 4; LC, in O, 572.

50. MJ, "Autres personnages du bal masque," *Littérature*, no. 6, (August 1919): 4; LC, in O, 625.

51. "Lettres de Jacques Vaché," *Littérature*, no. 6 (August 1919): 10–16.

52. MJ to Cocteau, January 1920, in Jacob/Cocteau, 53.

53. Salmon, *Manuscrit*. See Chapter 5 for Salmon's description of the Bateau Lavoir.

54. Carco, *Scènes*, 54.

55. Louis Aragon, "Francis Carco: *Scènes de la vie de Montmartre*," *Littérature*, no. 9 (November 1919): 27.

56. MJ to Carco, April 5, 1919, in Garnier 1:186.

57. MJ to Carco, April 22, 1919, ibid., 188.

58. Pougy, *Mes cahiers*, 36.

59. Ibid., 46.

60. MJ to Cocteau, September 4, 1919, in Jacob/Cocteau, 46.

61. *AA* 1:66; Pougy, *Mes cahiers*, 71.

62. Seckel, *Jacob et Picasso*, 170–71.

63. The word *tartufe* spelled with one *f*, meaning "hypocrite," seems to have entered the French language in the seventeenth century.

64. DT, in O, 517.

65. MJ, "Plaintes d'un prisonnier," LC, in O, 592.

66. Tristan Tzara, "Noblesse galvanisée," *Littérature*, no. 8 (October 1919): 11.

67. André Breton and Philippe Soupault, "Les Champs magnétiques," *Littérature*, no. 8 (October 1919).

68. MJ to Cocteau, c. January 1920, in Jacob/Cocteau, 53.

69. Sanouillet, *Dada in Paris*, 102–5.

70. Paul Éluard and Jean Paulhan, *Correspondance 1919–1944* (Paris: Éditions Claire Paulhan, 2003), 78.

71. MJ to Michel Manoll, January 9, 1943, in *Manoll*, 123.

72. MJ, "À Monsieur Modigliani pour lui prouver que je suis un poète," LC, in O, 568.

73. Peyre, *Jacob quotidien*, 93–94. But Peyre's book is full of errors.

74. The portrait from 1916 is in the Kunstsammlung Nordrhein-Westphalen collection in Düsseldorf; the 1920 portrait is in the Cincinnati Art Museum.

75. Jacques Lipchitz, *Amedeo Modigliani 1884–1920* (New York: Abrams, 1954), 1–5.

76. It must have been January 31. RB, in O, 945; Seckel, *Jacob et Picasso*, 173.

77. MJ, "Nuits d'hôpital et l'aurore," RB, in O, 944.

78. Ibid., 942–43.

79. Florent Fels, *L'Art vivant de 1900 à nos jours* (Geneva: Pierre Cailler, 1956), 29.

80. Pougy, *Mes cahiers*, 98.

81. Ibid.

82. Ibid., 103.

83. Henri Ghéon, "*La Défense de Tartufe*, par Max Jacob," *Nouvelle Revue française*, no. 78 (March 1920): 452.

84. Frédéric Lefèvre, "Une heure avec M. Max Jacob, poète, romancier, et humoriste," *Nouvelles littéraires*, April 12, 1924, 1–2.

85. "Théâtre et Cinéma," *Nord-Sud*, no. 18 (February 1918): n.p.

86. Saul Bellow admired the work. For an extended discussion of CI, see Chapter 8.

87. Roger Allard, "*Cinématoma*, par Max Jacob," *Nouvelle Revue française*, no. 83 (August 1920): 327.

88. Jean de Gourmont, "*Le Cinématoma*," *Mercure de France* 31, no. 141 (July–August 1920): 182.

89. Louis Aragon, "Max Jacob, *Cinématoma*," *Littérature* 2, no. 14 (June 1920): 29.

90. *Feu de joie* (Fire of Joy).

91. Gabory, *Apollinaire*, 74–81; *Fels*, 10.

92. MJ, "Le Damasquineur, "Plus d'astrologie," "Don Quichotte voyage en mer," "Allusions romantiques à propos de Mardi-Gras," *Action* 1, no. 2 (March 1920), 24–28; MJ, "Plus d'astrologie," LC, in O, 587; MJ, "Allusions romantiques à propos de Mardi-Gras," LC, in O, 595.

93. MJ, "Allusions romantiques au Mardi-Gras," *Action* 1, no. 2 (March 1920); LC, in O, 595.

94. Seckel, *Jacob et Picasso*, 174–76.

95. MJ, "Présentation," n.p.

96. André Salmon, "Un peintre nouveau, Max Jacob," *Renaissance de l'art français de des industries de luxe*, no. 3 (March 1920): 119–27.

97. Pougy, *Mes cahiers*, 215.

98. Garnier 1:209–17.

99. MJ to Salmon, April 14, 1920, ibid., 210.

100. MJ to Roland-Manuel, April 1920, ibid., 215.

101. O, 829.

102. Jacob/Paulhan, 78–79.

103. Georges Auric, *Quand j'étais là* (Paris: Grasset, 1979).

104. MJ to Salmon, February 15, 1920, in Garnier 1:205.

105. André Salmon, *La Négresse du Sacré-Coeur* (Paris: Nouvelle Revue Française, 1920).

106. Seckel, *Jacob et Picasso*, 176.

107. Guillaume Apollinaire, *La Femme assise* (1920; Paris: Gallimard, 1977), 27–28.

108. Jacques Rivière, "La Revue critique," *Nouvelle Revue française*, no. 72 (September 1919): 636.

109. André Gide, "Dada," *Nouvelle Revue française*, no. 79 (April 1920): 477.

110. Ibid., 479.

111. Ibid., 481.

112. André Breton, "Pour Dada," *Nouvelle Revue française*, no. 83 (August 1920): 208–15; Jacques Rivière, "Reconnaissance à Dada," ibid., 216–37.

113. MJ, "Ma Vie en trois lignes," *Action* 1, no. 4 (July 1920): 23; reprinted by Éluard in "Revue des revues," *Littérature* 2, no. 15 (July–August 1920): 23.

114. Pierre Reverdy, "L'Ami de l'homme ou parasite," *Littérature* 2, no. 16 (September–October 1920): 1.

115. Pierre Reverdy, "Le Vieil apprenti," ibid., 2.

116. Strangely, Reverdy reprinted these poems in 1929 after reestablishing his friendship with Jacob.

117. Jean Cocteau, *Poésies 1917–1920* (Paris: Éditions de La Sirène, 1920), 8.

118. MJ to Cocteau, July 4, 1920, in Jacob/Cocteau, 56–57. AP, in O, 1373.

119. Ibid., 58.

120. Steegmuller, *Cocteau*, 257.

121. MJ, "Nocturne," *Le Coq parisien*, no. 3 (July–August 1920), n.p.; LC, in O, 564.

122. MJ to Bloch, c. late 1920, in Bloch 2:151.

123. MJ to Paulhan, August 3, 1920, in Jacob/Paulhan, 79.

124. Gabory, *Apollinaire*, 91–92.

125. MJ to Paulhan, August 1920, in Jacob/Paulhan, 81.

126. Pougy, *Mes cahiers*, 131–32.

127. MJ to Kisling, September 28, 1920, in Gompel/Marcoux, 77.

128. MJ, "Bonnes intentions," *Nouvelle Revue française*, no. 85 (October 1920): 489–95; RB, in O, 903.

129. Louis Aragon, "Y a-t-il des gens qui s'amusent dans la vie?" *Littérature* 2, no. 17 (December 1920): 3.

130. *Togorès*, 26; MJ to Salmon, n.d. January 1921, in Gompel/Marcoux, 84.

131. MJ to Salmon, Gompel/Marcoux, 84.

132. MJ to Paul Budry, early 1921, ibid., 90.

133. MJ to Radiguet, October 22, 1920, ibid., 78–79.

134. Sanouillet, *Dada in Paris*, 165–67; Steegmuller, *Cocteau*, 260–61; Auric, *Quand j'étais là*, 173–74.

135. Pougy, *Mes cahiers*, 142.

136. MJ to Salmon, January 1921, in Gompel/Marcoux, 84.

137. NCP, n.p.

138. Pougy, *Mes cahiers*, 153; Seckel, *Jacob et Picasso*, 177n10.

139. Pougy, *Mes cahiers*, 152.

140. Georges Hugnet, *Pleins et déliés: Souvenirs et témoignages* (Paris: Guy Authier, 1972), 177.

141. "Liquidation," *Littérature* 3, no. 18 (March 1921): 1–7.

142. Béhar, *Breton*, 123.

143. Pougy, *Mes cahiers*, 150–51. Caryathis was the stage name of Elisabeth Toulemon. *Jouhandeau*, 45.

144. Armel, *Leiris*, 148.

145. MJ, "L'Explorateur," LC, in O, 575.

146. MJ, "Musique Acidulée," LC, in O, 606.

147. MJ to Cocteau, March 29, mid-April, and June 10, 1921, in Jacob/Cocteau, 64–67.

148. Guiette, *Vie*, 93–94; Andreu, *Vie et mort*, 136–40.

149. MJ, "Lettres avec commentaires," *Nouvelle Revue française*, no. 91 (April 1921): 385–400, 971–78, 97; CN, in O, 971–77, 994–99.

150. MJ, "Contes de fées," *Action* 2, no. 7 (May 1921): 13–18; MJ, "Étude Romanesque," *Signaux de France et de Belgique* (June 1921): 59–72, in O, 955–64.

151. Assouline, *L'Homme de l'art*, 321–29.

152. Christine Andreucci, "L'Amitié entre Pierre Reverdy et Max Jacob," *Centenaire de Pierre Reverdy* (Angers: Presse de l'Université d'Angers, 1990), 287.

153. Armel, *Leiris*, 148–49.

154. Seckel, *Jacob et Picasso*, 181.

155. Theodore Reff, "Picasso's *Three Musicians*: Maskers, Artists, and Friends," *Art in America*, December 1980, 124–42; Richardson, *Life*, 3:197–99; Seckel, *Jacob et Picasso*, 180–84.

CHAPTER 13: SAINT-BENOÎT

1. MJ to Marcoussis, August 13, 1921, in Garnier 2:26.

2. MJ to Kahnweiler, c. June 1921, in ibid., 15.

3. Fr. Jean Evenou, notes, in Gompel/Marcoux, 516; *AA* 1:82.

4. MJ to the Ghikas, June 25, 1921, in *Pougy*, 23.

5. MJ to Roland-Manuel, August 5, 1921, in Garnier 2:2.

6. MJ to Kahnweiler, c.June 1921, in Garnier 2:15; MJ to Roland-Manuel, November 18, 1921, in Garnier 2:46.

7. MJ to Marcoussis, August 13, 1921, ibid., 26.

8. MJ to Salmon, August 18, 1921, ibid., 31; MJ to Roland-Manuel, August 5, 1921, ibid., 20.

9. Garnier 2:14; Théophile Briant, "Itinéraires de Max Jacob," *Goéland*, August 1946.

10. MJ to Pougy, September 23, 1921, in *Pougy*, 28.

11. MJ to Cocteau, July 8, 1921, in Jacob/Cocteau, 68–9.

12. MJ to Georges Ghika, August 11, 1921, in Gompel/Marcoux, 104.

13. Gompel/Marcoux 105. *AA* 1:82; Frank, *Mémoire*, 141.

14. MJ to Neveu, September 28, 1921, in n. acq. fr. 16799, BnF.

15. Seckel, *Jacob et Picasso*, 188n37; Frank, *Mémoire*, 134–35.

16. MJ to Salmon, September 15, 1921, in Garnier 2:42; MJ to Roland-Manuel, September 5, 1921, in Garnier 2:37; MJ to Gabory, July 28, 1921, in *AA* 1:83.

17. "Voyages," *Action* (March–April 1922); PMR, in O, 674.

18. MJ to Roland-Manuel, September 5, 1921, in Garnier 2:37.

19. Ibid., 2:38.

20. MJ to Salmon, September 15, 1921, in Garnier 2:43.

21. MJ to Henri and Emma Hertz, September 29, 1921, in Gompel/Marcoux, 110.

22. MJ to Kisling, August 4, 1921, in Gompel/Marcoux, 101; August 16, in Garnier 2:29; September 12, in *AA* 1:89; MJ to Gabory, July 28, in *AA* 1:82.

23. MJ to Paulhan, September 15, 1921, in Jacob/Paulhan, 92.

24. André Fontainas, "Le Laboratoire central," *Mercure de France*, no. 149 (August 1921): 739–40.

25. Henri Ther, "Livres," *Aventure*, no. 1 (November 1921): 31–32.

26. Roger Allard, "*Le Laboratoire central*" and "*Dos d'Arlequin*, par Max Jacob," *Nouvelle Revue française*, no. 99 (December 1921): 743–46.

27. MJ, "Art poétique," *Écrits nouveaux* 8 (July 1921): 308, in O, 1373.

28. Ibid., 1374.

29. Ibid., 1373.

30. Ibid., 1377.

31. Ibid., 1379. The editors of the *Oeuvres complètes* of Radiguet have claimed that Radiguet wrote AP with Jacob. There are no grounds for such an assertion. O, 1344–45.

32. André Salmon, "Gazette de l'Étoile," *Action* 2, no. 9 (October 1921): 11.

33. MJ, "Ennui sur le taureau d'Europe," *Action* 2, no. 9 (October 1921): 18; Corrected, PMR, in O, 679.

34. MJ, "Lettres avec commentaires," *Action* 2, no. 10 (November 1921): 1–6; CN, in O, 1032–36.

35. Michel Leiris, *L'Âge d'homme* (Paris: Gallimard, 1939), 89–90.

36. Ibid., 10.

37. Ibid., 157.

38. *Leiris*, 31.

39. Armel, *Leiris*, 141.

40. MJ to Leiris, November 24, 1921, in *Leiris*, 33–35.

41. Ibid., 35.

42. Ibid., 34–35.

43. MJ to Leiris, December 6, 1921, ibid., 37–40.

44. Ibid., 40.

45. MJ to Leiris, February 7, 1922, ibid., 51.

46. Their son, Robert, born in 1909, was mentally handicapped, and eventually resided in a psychiatric hospital.

47. MJ to Rosenthal, June 3, 1921, in Gompel/Marcoux, 93.

48. MJ to Rosenthal, July 23, 1921, ibid., 97.

49. MJ to Rosenthal, September 2, 1921, ibid., 106.

50. Ibid., 106–7.

51. MJ to Rosenthal, October 15, 1921, ibid., 114.

52. MJ to Kisling, December 14, 1921; MJ to Fillacier, December 24, 1921, in Gompel/Marcoux, 117–19; MJ to Picasso, November 27, 1921, in Seckel, *Jacob et Picasso*, 186.

53. MJ to Rosenthal, October 15, 1921, in Gompel/Marcoux, 114.

54. *Rimbert*, 7–9.

55. MJ to Rimbert, December 27, 1921, ibid., 17.

56. Pougy, *Mes cahiers*, 163.

57. MJ to Kisling, February 21, 1922, in Garnier 2:90.

58. Seckel, *Jacob et Picasso*, 186–87.

59. "Surpris et charmé," *Soirées de Paris*, no. 25 (June 1914): 326; RB, in O, 857.

60. "La Bohème pendant la guerre de 1914" RB, in O, 849.

61. MJ, "Entrepôt Voltaire," *Action* 1, no.1 (February 1920): 27–48; RB, in O, 862–74.

62. MJ to Cocteau, February 3, 1922, in Jacob/Cocteau, 79.

63. Ibid., 78.

64. MJ, *Échelle de Jacob: Recueil d'inédits*, ed. Nicole and José-Emmanuel Cruz (Paris: Bibliothèque des Arts, 1994), 183–86; Léon Daudet, *Le Stupide XIXème siècle* (Paris: Nouvelle Librairie Nationale, 1922).

65. MJ to Rosenthal, March 10, 1922, and April 17, 1923, in Gompel/Marcoux 133, 160.

66. Sachs, *Sabbat*, 194–201; Benjamin Taylor, *Proust: The Search* (New Haven, Conn.: Yale University Press, 2015), 133–34.

67. Steegmuller, *Cocteau*, 277–78, 281–82.

68. Seckel, *Jacob et Picasso*, 189.

69. *Togorès*, 124–26.

70. MJ, "Jardin mystérieux," *Écrits nouveaux*, no. 4 (April 1922): 3, in PMR, in O, 698. "Adieux au presbytère de St.-Benoît-sur-Loire" and "Voyages," *Action* 3, no. 12 (March–April 1922): 13–16, in PMR and MC, in O, 674.

71. Nicole Groult had left her husband to have an affair with Marie Laurencin. MJ to Roland-Manuel, February 23, 1922, in Gompel/Marcoux 130–31; MJ to Cocteau, February 3, 1922, in Jacob/Cocteau, 77–78.

72. MJ to Leiris, February 17, 1922, in *Leiris*, 53.

73. MJ to Rimbert, c. March 1922, in *Rimbert*, 20.

74. John Ashbery discovered this letter in a first edition of CD.

75. MJ to Cocteau, September 21, 1922, in Jacob/Cocteau, 125; RB, in O, 887–900.

76. Armel, *Leiris*, 160.

77. Pougy, *Mes cahiers*, 171.

78. Three of the tales had come out in *La Nouvelle Revue française*.

79. Jacob confirmed more than once that Madame Gagelin was based on his mother: *Levanti* 66; *Autobiographie pour Paul Petit*, in O, 1780n3.

80. MJ, "Conseils d'une mere à sa fille," CN, in O, 978.

81. Paul Morand, "*Le Cabinet noir* de Max Jacob," *Nouvelle Revue française*, no. 109 (October 1922): 489–90.

82. Georges Gabory, "*Le Roi de Béotie*, par Max Jacob," *Nouvelle Revue française*, no. 102 (March 1922): 347–48; André Malraux, "Art poétique," *Nouvelle Revue française*, no. 107 (August 1922): 227–28.

83. Jacob planned to dedicate AP to Cocteau. Cocteau's friends objected to the phrase "my young friend." Jacob/Cocteau, 82–83.

84. MJ to Cocteau, July 8, 1921, in Jacob/Cocteau, 69.

85. AP, in O, 1358; Note on Radiguet, 1786.

86. O, 1359; Jean Cocteau, *Poésie critique* (Paris: Nouvelle Revue Française, 1959), 64–65.

87. Cocteau to MJ, June 24, 1922, in Jacob/Cocteau 85–86.

88. MJ and Raymond Radiguet, "Edwige ou le héros," *Écrits du Nord* 1, 2nd ser., no. 2, December 1922: 42–51. For the play, see Hélène Henry, "Chronologie du théâtre de Max Jacob," *CdR*, no. 9 (1987): 46.

89. AP, in O, 1352n4, 1786.

90. O, 1348.

91. Ibid., 1349.

92. Ibid., 1353.

93. Ibid., 1355.

94. Ibid., 1352.

95. Ibid., 1349.

96. Armel, *Leiris*, 168.

97. MJ to Kahnweiler, April 21, 1922, in Garnier 2:98.

98. Ibid.

99. MJ to Cocteau, May 1, 1922, in Jacob/Cocteau, 81–82; MJ to Leiris, May 7, 1922, in *Leiris*, 59–61.

100. Giovanni Leonardi, "Le poète Max Jacob, souvenirs quimpérois," *CdR*, no. 8 (1986): 29–31.

101. MJ to Cocteau, May 1, 1922, in Jacob/Cocteau, 81.

102. Cocteau to MJ, May 22, 1922, ibid., 83.

103. *Les Feuilles libres* published a chunk of TB and his poems for Poulenc; "Dimanche à Guichen," *Feuilles libres* 4, no. 26 (April 1922): 92–99; "Poèmes burlesques," *Feuilles libres* 4, no. 28 (August–September 1922): 47, 63–67. PMR: "Poésie," " 'Le Petit pot de fleurs," "La Belle Attitude," "Hortense," and "Cécile," O, 687–90.

104. Jean Cocteau, "M'entendez-vous ainsi?" in Cocteau, *Vocabulaire, Plain-Chant, et autres poèmes, 1922–1946* (Paris: Gallimard, 1983), 103.

105. Roger Allard, "*Vocabulaire, Poèmes*, par Jean Cocteau," *Nouvelle Revue française*, no. 105 (June 1922): 745–47.

106. Cocteau to MJ, August 16, 1922, in Jacob/Cocteau 103.

107. Sophie Fishbach and Patricia Sustrac, "Max Jacob–Jules Supervielle, Correspondance croisée (1922–1935)," *CMJ*, no. 13–14 (2013): 220.

108. Ibid., 222.

109. Ibid., 226.

110. "Monnaie de couleurs," *Disque Vert* 1, no. 3 (July 1922): 1.

111. MJ to Leiris, May 30, 1922, in *Leiris*, 62.

112. Leiris, *Âge d'homme*, 187.

113. "Réponse de l'Abbé X . . . à un jeune homme découragé," *Vie des lettres et des arts*, no. 10 (June 1922), in CN, in O, 1075.

114. MJ to Leiris, November 24, 1921, in *Leiris* 32; CN, in O, 1075.

115. MJ to Madame Aurel, July 4, 1922, in Gompel/Marcoux, 138.

116. Assouline, *L'Homme de l'art*, 345; Assouline, *Artful Life*, 179.

117. MJ to Cocteau, June 28, 1922, in Jacob/Cocteau, 88; MJ to Leiris, May 30, 1922, in *Leiris* 62n90.

118. MJ to Leiris, July 12, 1922, *Leiris*, 64.

119. Ibid., 63.

120. MJ to Cocteau, July 28, 1922, in Jacob/Cocteau, 97, 103; MJ to the Ghikas, July 31, 1922, in Gompel/Marcoux, 139.

121. Jean Dubuffet, *Biographie au pas de course* (Paris: Gallimard, 2001), 20.

122. MJ to Cocteau, July 28, 1922, in Jacob/Cocteau, 98.

123. Leiris to his mother, in Armel, *Leiris*, 157–58.

124. MJ to Cocteau, August 19, 1922, in Jacob/Cocteau, 108.

125. MJ to Cocteau, August 29, 1922, ibid., 111, 112.

126. MJ to Cocteau, September 5, 1922, ibid., 114.

127. Armel, *Leiris*, 158.

128. Ibid.

129. MJ to Leiris, October 26, 1922, in *Leiris*, 78.
130. Both pamphlets were published posthumously.
131. MJ to Leiris, September 1 and 28, 1922, in *Leiris*, 69–73.
132. MJ to Leiris, August 21, 1922, ibid., 66.
133. Ibid., 66–68.
134. Ibid., 69.
135. O, 667.
136. "L'Amour et le temps," *Revue européenne* 6, no. 2 (July–August 1923): 20; PMR, in O, 705.
137. MJ to Leiris, August 1922, in *Leiris*, 69.
138. HCHR, 57.
139. MJ to Leiris, November 10, 1922, in *Leiris*, 81.
140. "La Fiancée de l'aviateur," *Revue européenne* 6, no. 2 (August 1923): 22; PMR, in O, 685.
141. Jacob/Cocteau 123–28; MJ to Gabory, October 6, 1922, in *AA* 1:113; MJ to Kahnweiler, October 10, 1922, in Garnier 2:126–27; *Leiris*, 81; MJ to Roland Tual, October 20, 1922, in Tual, *Au Coeur*, 150–54.
142. Louis Aragon, "Projet d'histoire de littérature contemporaine," *Littérature*, new ser., no. 4 (September 1922): 6; Jacques Baron, "Philippe Soupault, *Westwego*," ibid., 23.
143. André Breton, "Clairement," *Littérature*, new ser., no. 4 (September 1922): 1–2; Mark Polizzotti, *Revolution of the Mind: The Life of André Breton* (New York: Farrar, Straus & Giroux, 1995), 191; Sanouillet, *Dada in Paris*, 278.
144. Breton, "Clairement," 2.
145. Aragon, "Projet d'histoire," 3–6.
146. André Breton, "Entrée des Médiums," *Littérature*, new ser., no. 6 (November 1922): 1–2.
147. Jacob/Cocteau, 126–31. Jacob mixed up the story of the Burghers.
148. Seckel, *Jacob et Picasso*, 190.
149. MJ to Salmon, September 21, 1922, in Garnier 2:124–26; MJ to Cocteau, September 28, 1922, in Jacob/Cocteau, 128–29.
150. MJ to Cocteau, September 18, 1922, in Jacob/Cocteau, 119.
151. Jacob had borrowed an Arab robe from Lucien for a costume party given by the dancer Caryathis in 1921.
152. Daudet, *Stupide XIXème siècle*, 181.
153. MJ, *L'Échelle de Jacob*, 183–86.
154. MJ to Cocteau, September 21, 1922, in Jacob/Cocteau, 124–25.
155. MJ to Gabory, September 28, 1922, in *AA* 1:110.
156. MJ to Cocteau, September 28, 1922, in Jacob/Cocteau, 128.
157. MJ to Cocteau, October 6, 1922, ibid., 137.
158. MJ to Leiris, c. November or December 1922, in *Leiris*, 85.
159. Jean de Palacio, "Max Jacob 2: Romanesques," *Revue des lettres modernes*, new ser., no. 474–78 (1976): 67.

160. MJ to Cocteau, August 16, 1922, in Jacob/Cocteau, 105.

161. MJ to Roland-Manuel, c. December 1922, in Gompel/Marcoux, 148.

162. MJ to Leiris, January 28, 1923, in *Leiris*, 86; Gabory, *Apollinaire*, 47.

163. MJ to Cocteau, December 4, 1922, in Jacob/Cocteau, 145.

164. Tual, *Au Coeur*, 59–60.

165. MJ to Cocteau, December 1922, in Jacob/Cocteau, 146.

166. MJ to Madame Aurel, December 1922, in Gompel/Marcoux, 148.

167. MJ to Hertz, January 5, 1923, in Garnier 2:139. MJ to Salmon, c. January 1923, in *AA* 1:118.

168. MJ to Leiris, c. January 1923, in *Leiris*, 85.

169. Ibid., 86.

170. MJ to Roland-Manuel, February 3, 1923, in Gompel/Marcoux, 152.

171. MJ to Leiris, October 9, 1922, in *Leiris*, 75.

172. MJ to Leiris, February 17, 1923, ibid., 89.

173. *Leiris*, 22–24; Frank, *Mémoire*, 143.

CHAPTER 14: JACOB THE PEDAGOGUE

1. The name puns on *cygne/signe*, "swan/sign."

2. Pougy, *Mes cahiers*, 191.

3. Jacques Porel, "Filibuth," *Intentions*, no. 16 (June 1923): 28–29.

4. Benjamin Crémieux, "Les Lettres françaises," *Nouvelles littéraires*, April 28, 1923, 2.

5. Soupault, *"Filibuth," Revue européenne*, no. 4 (June 1923): 102–3.

6. Jacob is Maxime Lévy in Soupault's novel.

7. André Germain, "Raymond Radiguet, *Le Diable au corps*," *Revue européenne*, no. 4 (June 1923): 67.

8. MJ to Cocteau, January 30 and February 1, 1923, in Jacob/Cocteau, 148–50.

9. Steegmuller, *Cocteau*, 305–7; Jacob/Cocteau, 149n1.

10. MJ to Cocteau, May 26, 1923, Jacob/Cocteau, 157.

11. Steegmuller, *Cocteau*, 307.

12. MJ to Grenier, c. May 1922, "a gentleman coming from Spain," probably Bounoure. *Grenier*, 9.

13. MJ to Jouhandeau, c. April 1923, in *Jouhandeau*, 46.

14. Ibid., 51.

15. MJ to Jouhandeau, December 6, 1923, ibid., 83.

16. MJ to Jouhandeau, May 31, 1923, ibid, 52.

17. Marcel Jouhandeau, "Le Mage," *Disque vert* 2, no. 2 (November 1923): 60.

18. Jules Supervielle, "Apparition de Max Jacob," *Disque vert* 2, no. 2 (November 1923): 54; "Apparition" in Jules Supervielle, *Oeuvres poétiques complètes*, ed. Michel Collot (Paris: Nouvelle Revue Française, 1996), 163.

19. MJ described the visit, writing to the Ghikas, May 27, 1923, in Gompel/Marcoux, 166.

20. MJ, "Early Days,", 62–64.

21. Richardson, *Life*, 3:219. *Olga Picasso*, ed. Emilia Philippot, Joachim Pissarro, and Bernard Ruiz-Picasso (Paris: Gallimard, Musée National Picasso, 2017).

22. MJ to Kahnweiler, April 17, 1923, in Garnier 2:152.

23. MJ to Kahnweiler, June 4, 1923, in Seckel, *Jacob et Picasso*, 193; MJ to Kisling, June 15, 1923, in Gompel/Marcoux, 170.

24. MJ to Leiris, June 23, 1923, in *Leiris*, 102.

25. Marcel Arland, "*Le Terrain Bouchaballe*, par Max Jacob," *Nouvelle Revue française*, no. 119 (August 1923): 228–30.

26. MJ to the Émile-Paul brothers, October 30, 1923, in Gompel/Marcoux, 196; MJ to Jacques Dyssord, December 25, 1923, in Gompel/Marcoux, 202–3; MJ to Jouhandeau, December 9, 1923, in *Jouhandeau* 87; MJ to Cocteau, December 2, 1923, in Jacob/Cocteau, 173.

27. TB, in O, 1107.

28. MJ to Leiris, June 22, 1923, in *Leiris*, 100–3; Leiris, *Journal*, 207; Armel, *Leiris*, 171.

29. *Leiris*, 103.

30. MJ to Leiris, June 22, 1923, ibid., 103–4.

31. MJ to Ghikas, May 27, 1923, in Gompel/Marcoux, 166.

32. MJ to Nino Frank, June 23, 1923, in *Frank*, 26.

33. Madame Aurel to her husband, July 7, 1923, in Gompel/Marcoux, 174–75.

34. MJ to Cocteau, August 16, 1923, in Jacob/Cocteau, 166.

35. Ibid., 166–67. MJ to Nino Frank, August 2, 1923, in *Frank*, 30.

36. MJ to Ghikas, July 17, 1923, in Gompel/Marcoux, 175–76; Pougy, *Mes cahiers*, 193.

37. MJ to Leiris, July 11, 1923, in *Leiris*, 104–5.

38. MJ to Kisling, July 15, 1923, in *AA* 1:123.

39. MJ to Madame Aurel, August 1, 1923, in Gompel/Marcoux, 181.

40. MJ to Frank, August 2, 1923, in *Frank*, 30.

41. MJ to Madame Aurel, August 1, 1923, in Garnier 2:191.

42. Pougy, *Mes cahiers*, 193.

43. Ibid., 194. "Fag" in French is *tapette*.

44. Ibid., 195.

45. *Salacrou*, 15.

46. Pougy, *Mes cahiers*, 194.

47. *Leiris*, 109; "Le Carnet à piston," *Feuilles libres*, no. 33 (September–October 1923): 157–65.

48. MJ to Frank, August 15, 1923, in *Frank*, 32.

49. MJ to Grenier, September 14, 1923, in *Grenier*, 18.

50. MJ to Jouhandeau, September 12, 1923, in *Jouhandeau*, 67.

51. MJ to Ghikas, August 25, 1923, in *Pougy*, 39.

52. MJ to Jouhandeau, September 12, 1923, in *Jouhandeau*, 70. MJ to Cocteau, August 29, 1923, in Jacob/Cocteau, 171.

53. Ibid., 170.

54. Armand Salacrou, *Dans la salle des pas perdus* (Paris: Gallimard, 1974), 135.

55. MJ to Salacrou, January 16, 1924, in Salacrou 31.

56. MJ to Salacrou, November 28, 1923, ibid., 27.

57. MJ to Salacrou, September 13, 1923, ibid., 13.

58. Pougy, *Mes cahiers*, 197.

59. Ibid., 197. MJ to Kahnweiler, September 24, 1923, in Garnier 2:212; MJ to André Lefèvre, December 25, 1923, in Garnier 2:259–61.

60. MJ to Kahnweiler, September 24, 1923, in Garnier 2:211. *Pougy*, 42.

61. MJ to Ghikas, October 25, 1923, in *Pougy*, 46.

62. MJ, "Le Promeneur non solitaire," *Intentions*, no. 17 (July–August 1923): 1–5, in O, 1332. *Le Nom* (Liège: À la Lampe d'Aladin, 1926); "Le Nom," *Europe*, no. 8 (September 1923): 385–96, in O, 1325.

63. Gabriel Bounoure, "Max Jacob, romancier," *Intentions*, no. 18 (September–October 1923), 4–21.

64. Valery Larbaud, "Hommage à Max Jacob," *Intentions*, no. 20 (December 1923): 1–3. Valery Larbaud, "Valery Larbaud, 13 décembre 1923," *CdR*, no. 1 (1978): 88–89.

65. Florent Fels, "Propos d'artistes: Picasso," *Nouvelles littéraires*, August 4, 1923, 1.

66. MJ to Salacrou, October 14, 1923, in *Salacrou*, 18.

67. MJ to Fillacier, October 21, 1923, in Gompel/Marcoux, 189.

68. MJ to Fillacier, November 14, 1923, ibid., 197.

69. MJ to Kisling, November 1, 1923, in Garnier 2:234.

70. MJ to Jouhandeau, December 24, 1923, in *Jouhandeau*, 89; also 80 (early November), and 86 (December 9, 1923). MJ to Leiris, December 2, 1923, in *Leiris*, 121.

71. MJ to Salacrou, November 5, 1923, in *Salacrou*, 23–24.

72. MJ to Georges Ghika, September 26, 1923, in Gompel/Marcoux, 187.

73. MJ to Ghikas, October 25 and December 16, 1923, in *Pougy*, 46, 49, 51, 54. *Frank Memoire*, 130.

74. *Leiris*, 116; MJ to Salacrou, November 11, 1923, in Garnier 2:240–42.

75. MJ to Grenier, October 28, 1923, in *Grenier*, 20–21.

76. MJ to Grenier, September 3, 1923, ibid., 15.

77. MJ to Ghikas, October 25, 1923, in *Pougy*, 45.

78. MJ to Roland-Manuel, October 28, 1923, in Garnier 2:222.

79. MJ to Frank, August 2, 1923, in *Frank*, 30.

80. Garnier 2:248; *Frank*, 155.

81. MJ to Cocteau, December 2, 1923, in Jacob/Cocteau, 172–73.

82. Frank to Cocteau, December 2, 1923, ibid., 174.

83. MJ to Cocteau, August 16, 1923, ibid., 167.

84. "Paris killed him." MJ to Louis Dumoulin, July 12, 1941, in *Jacob écrit*, 205.

85. Steegmuller, *Cocteau*, 314.

86. Ibid., 314–15.

87. Frank, *Mémoire*, 146–48.

88. Jacob called Radiguet "l'enfant roi"; Jacob/Cocteau, 79.

89. Steegmuller, *Cocteau*, 314–17; Jacob/Cocteau, 177n9.

90. Cocteau to Jacob, December 25, 1923, Jacob/Cocteau, 170.

91. Jacob/Cocteau, 175–83.

92. Jacob/Cocteau, 176. MJ to Pougy, December 23, 1923, in *Pougy*, 50.

93. MJ to Cocteau, December 23, 1923, in Jacob/Cocteau, 175–77.

94. MJ to Leiris, December 25, 1923, in *Leiris*, 121–23.

95. Michel Leiris, "Désert de mains," *Intentions* 3, no. 21 (January–February 1924): 23–26.

96. MJ to Jouhandeau, February 25, 1924, in *Jouhandeau*, 92.

97. MJ to Grenier, October 2, 1924, in *Grenier*, 41.

98. T. S. Eliot considered *Philosophies* one of the most intelligent journals in France. Eliot to Lady Rothermere, April 27, 1924, in *The Letters of T. S. Eliot*, ed. Valerie Eliot and Hugh Haughton (New Haven, Conn.: Yale University Press, 2011), 2:383–85.

99. MJ to Salacrou, February 11, 1924, in *Salacrou*, 35; MJ to Jouhandeau, June 2 and early July 1924, in *Jouhandeau*, 106, 120.

100. MJ, "Notes à propos des Beaux-Arts," *Philosophies* 1, no. 3 (March 1924): 1–5.

101. "In converting, he tried to create another identity, which wasn't his own. He remained profoundly Jewish." Henri Lefebvre, interview by author.

102. André Breton, *Les pas perdus* (1924; reprint Paris: Gallimard, 1969), 79.

103. MJ to René Mendès-France, February 4, 1924, in Gompel/Marcoux, 211; MJ to André Level, from 1923 through 1928, Médiathèque des Ursulines in Quimper (Fonds Max Jacob, ms. 22) and BnF; MJ, *Lettres à André Level*, ed. Bernard Duchatelet (Quimper: Bibliothèque Municipale, 1994).

104. By the publishing house Kra, run by Simon Kra and his son Lucien.

105. MJ to Jouhandeau, May 26, 1924, in *Jouhandeau*, 101–2; Radiguet, in Cocteau, *Oeuvres complètes* 11:457–58: " 'We have to write poems and novels like everybody else,' that is to say, like nobody." Picasso, in 1915, wanted "to see if he could still draw like everybody else": Henri Mahaut, *Picasso* (Paris: Crès, 1930), 12.

106. Frank, *Mémoire*, 142–43.

107. MJ to Edmond Jaloux, May 3, 1924, in Garnier 2:287.

108. HCHR, 233. Italics in original.

109. Frédéric Lefèvre, "Une heure avec Max Jacob," *Nouvelles littéraires*, April 12, 1924, 102, in Gompel/Marcoux, 229–33.

110. MJ to Jouhandeau, July 3, 1925, in *Jouhandeau*, 199, 200.

111. MJ to Kahnweiler, May 13, 1924, in Garnier 2:289.

112. Jacques Viot, "L'Homme de chair et l'homme reflet," *Intentions* 3, no. 25 (June 1924): 54–55.

113. Marcel Arland, "*L'Homme de chair et l'homme reflet*, par Max Jacob," *Nouvelle Revue française*, no. 129 (June 1924): 747–48; John Charpentier, *Mercure de France*, September 15, 1924, 764–65; Georges Thialet, "Max Jacob romancier," *Sélection*, no. 8 (June 1924): 209–17; Gille Anthelme, "*L'Homme de chair et l'homme reflet*," *Sélection*, no. 8 (June 1924): 279–80; René Lalou, "*L'Homme de chair et l'homme reflet*," *Vient de paraître*, September 1924, 445–46.

114. Lefèvre, "Une heure avec Max Jacob," 1–2.

115. MJ to René Mendès-France, February 4, 1924, in Garnier 2:275–76.

116. MJ to Salacrou, April 28, 1924, in *Salacrou*, 40.

117. MJ to Salacrous, April 28, 1924, ibid., 40–42.

118. MJ to Mendès-France, June 6, 1924, in Gompel/Marcoux, 220–21. MJ to Kahnweiler, May 13, 1924, in Garnier 2:289–91.

119. MJ to Jouhandeau, March 8, 1924, in *Jouhandeau*, 94.

120. MJ to Jouhandeau, June 2, 1924, ibid., 107.

121. Entry for March 30, 1924, in Leiris, *Journal*, 34.

122. MJ to Jouhandeau, April 20, 1924, in *Jouhandeau*, 99.

123. MJ to Salacrous, April 28, 1924, in *Salacrou*, 40.

124. MJ to Jouhandeau, May 26, 1924, in *Jouhandeau*, 101–2.

125. MJ to Jouhandeau, June 19, 1924, ibid., 113–14.

126. MJ to Jouhandeau, August 24, 1924, ibid., 128; *Lettres de Marcel Jouhandeau à Max Jacob*, ed. Anne Kimball (Paris: Droz, 2002), 38, 62.

127. MJ to Jouhandeau, June 2, 1924, in *Jouhandeau*, 106.

128. MJ to Jouhandeau, ibid., 126, 134; MJ to Salacrous, in *Salacrou*, 55–56; MJ to Ghikas, in Pougy, *Mes cahiers*, 204.

129. MJ, "Ethnographie du démon," VI, in O, 643.

130. MJ, "L'Attentat," VI, in O, 662.

131. Ibid., 648.

132. MJ, "Dans le brouhaha de la foire," ibid., 657.

133. Seckel, *Jacob et Picasso*, 195; MJ self-portrait in O, 640.

CHAPTER 15: DEMONIC LOVE

1. MJ, "Titres des chapitres pour une étude approximative sur Marcel Jouhandeau," *Intentions* 3, no. 26 (July–August 1924): 1–2.

2. Marcel Jouhandeau, "Monsieur Godeau et les Parques," *Intentions* 3, no. 26 (July–August 1924): 3–19.

3. MJ to Jouhandeau, August 5, 1924, in *Jouhandeau*, 131.

4. MJ to Jouhandeau, August 11 and 28, 1924, ibid., 137–39.

5. Pougy, *Mes cahiers*, 206.

6. MJ to Cocteau, August 17, 1924, in Jacob/Cocteau, 197.

7. MJ to Jouhandeau, August 28, 1924, in *Jouhandeau*, 138–40.

8. Grenier, 33. *Jouhandeau*, 142.

9. MJ to Jouhandeau, October 12, 1924, in *Jouhandeau*, 151–53.

10. MJ to Level, September 9, 1924, in ms. 22, Fonds Max Jacob, Médiathèque des Ursulines, Quimper.

11. MJ to Jouhandeau, November 1924, in *Jouhandeau*, 158–60.

12. MJ to Norbert Guterman, September 9, 1924, in Guterman Papers, Ms. 0528, Box 1, Rare Book and Manuscript Library, Columbia University.

13. MJ to Salacrous, November 30, 1924, in *Salacrou*, 77–80.

14. MJ to Jouhandeau, December 31, 1924, in *Jouhandeau*, 170.

15. Sections published in *Philosophies*, no. 4 (November 1924), and in *Sélection* (December 1924). Published in 1929.

16. MJ to Nino Frank, December 28, 1924, in *Frank*, 70.

17. MJ, "Visions infernales supplémentaires," *Philosophies* 1, no. 3 (September 1924): 339–40; MJ, "Psychologies," *Philosophies* 1, no. 4 (November 1920): 373–79. Jacob "reviewed" HCHR in *Philosophies* 1, no. 3 (September 1924): 335.

18. MJ to Salacrou, January 7, 1925, in *Salacrou*, 87.

19. MJ to Tzara, December 8, 1924, in Garnier 2:345–46.

20. MJ to Salacrous, March 18, 1925, in *Salacrou*, 105.

21. Jean Grenier, "Max Jacob, poète breton," *Bretagne touristique*, January 15, 1925, 6–7.

22. Jacob/Maritain 22.

23. Jacques Maritain, "À propos de la question juive," *Vie spirituelle* 2, no. 4 (July 1921); Jacques Maritain, *L'Impossible antisémitisme*, ed. Pierre Vidal-Naquet (Paris: Desclée de Brouwer, 1994), 62.

24. Maritain, *L'Impossible*, 64.

25. Steegmuller, *Cocteau*, 338.

26. Cocteau to MJ, c. January 1925, in Jacob/Cocteau, 205.

27. *Jouhandeau*, 177.

28. MJ to Cocteau, March 19, 1925, in Jacob/Cocteau, 211.

29. Seckel, *Jacob et Picasso*, 199.

30. Steegmuller, *Cocteau*, 339–43.

31. Ibid., 348–48.

32. MJ, "Les Yeux au ventre," *Revue juive* 1, no. 1 (January 15, 1925): 31–35; *Le Nom*, 1926, dedicated to Albert Cohen, in FE, without dedication, in O, 1416.

33. MJ to Paulhan, April 3, 1925, in Jacob/Paulhan 101.

34. Already an anti-Semite, Jouhandeau at this point regarded Jacob as a Catholic.

35. MJ to Cocteau, March 21, 1925, in Jacob/Cocteau, 213; MJ to Salacrou, March 18, 1925, in *Salacrou*, 104–7.

36. Seven letters to Cattauï, ms. 3253, BLJD.

37. "And my spirit is in anguish within me," in the Douay Rheims.

38. MJ, "La Clef des songes," *Philosophies*, no. 5 (March 1925): 573–83.

39. Giovanni Leonardi, "Le poète Max Jacob, souvenirs quimpérois," *CdR*, no. 8 (1986): 31.

40. MJ to Paulhan on April 3, 1925, in Jacob/Paulhan, 100; MJ to Jouhandeau, April 6 and 17, 1925, in *Jouhandeau*, 184, 191.

41. MJ to Cocteau, May 1, 1925, in Jacob/Cocteau, 270–72.

42. MJ to Cocteau, May 13, 1925, ibid., 288–89.

43. MJ to Cocteau, May 16, 1925, ibid., 290–91.

44. MJ to Cocteau, May 16, 1925, ibid. MJ to de Gouy and Greeley, in *AA* 1:151.

45. MJ to Frank, May 26, 1925, in *Frank*, 89–90.

46. MJ to Jouhandeau, April 1925, in *Jouhandeau*, 188, 69–71.

47. MJ to Cocteau, May 26, 1925, in Jacob/Cocteau, 298.

48. MJ to Cocteau, June 1, 1925, ibid., 304–6.

49. Sophie Fishbach and Patricia Sustrac, "Max Jacob—Jules Supervielle, Correspondance croisée (1922–1935)," *CMJ*, no. 13–14 (2013): 236; Émié, *Dialogues*, 55–56.

50. MJ to Cocteau, June 18, 1925, in Jacob/Cocteau, 316.

51. Andreu, *Vie et mort,* 181.

52. There has been confusion about the date of Jacob's return from Italy. Kimball shows that he stayed for eight days in Paris before returning to Saint-Benoît on July 3; see *Frank,* 95.

53. MJ to Frank, July 20, 1925, in *Frank,* 97; MJ to Jouhandeau, August 13, 1925, in *Jouhandeau,* 209.

54. Gabriel Bounoure, "Pierre Reverdy et sa crise religieuse de 1925–27," in *Pierre Reverdy, 1880–1960* (Paris: Mercure de France, 1962), 204–12.

55. MJ to Cocteau, July 18, 1925, in Jacob/Cocteau 326.

56. MJ to Jouhandeau, July 18, 1925, in *Jouhandeau* 202.

57. MJ to Cocteau, August 13 to September 23, 1925, in Jacob/Cocteau, 338–51; MJ to Jouhandeau, August 13 to October 8, in *Jouhandeau,* 209–33.

58. MJ to Jouhandeau, October 8, 1925, in *Jouhandeau,* 217.

59. MJ to Frank, March 16, 1925, in *Frank,* 79; MJ to Paulhan, April 3, 1925, in Jacob/Paulhan, 100.

60. MJ to Cocteau, October 4, 1925, in Jacob/Cocteau, 352–53.

61. MJ to Jouhandeau, October 8, 1925, in *Jouhandeau,* 220.

62. MJ to Cocteau, October 4, 1925, in Jacob/Cocteau, 352–53.

63. MJ to de Gouy and Greeley, October 16, 1925, in *AA* 1:157.

64. MJ to Cocteau, August 22 and October 13, 1925, in Jacob/Cocteau, 342, 355.

65. Marcel Jouhandeau, *Carnets de l'écrivain* (Paris: Gallimard, 1957), 203–4.

66. MJ to Jouhandeau, December 5, 1925, in *Lettres de Jouhandeau à Jacob,* 235–38. Cocteau to Jacob, December 8 or 9, 1925, in Jacob/Cocteau, 373; Jacob's reply, ibid., 374–77.

67. MJ to Salacrou, October 19, 1925, in *Salacrou,* 130–31.

68. MJ, "Vision infernale en forme de madrigal," PMR, in O, 702.

69. O, 77.

CHAPTER 16: LOVES AND FEVERS

1. Henri Raczymow, *Maurice Sachs ou Les travaux forcés de la frivolité* (Paris: Gallimard, 1988), 35.

2. Sachs, *Sabbat,* 29–41; Raczymow, *Maurice Sachs,* 31–41.

3. Sachs's memoirs are riddled with untruth. Raczymow presents the main story.

4. Tual, *Au Coeur,* 74.

5. Sachs, *Sabbat,* 79; Tual, *Au Coeur,* 72.

6. Sachs, *Sabbat,* 80.

7. Ibid., 78.

8. Ibid., 82–83.

9. Ibid., 89.

10. Ibid., 95.

11. Tual, *Au Coeur,* 73.

12. Sachs, *Sabbat,* 128, 122.

13. *Salacrou*, 140.

14. MJ to Robert delle Donne, January 6, 1926, in *AA* 1:159.

15. MJ to Jouhandeau, January 24, 1926, in *Jouhandeau*, 249.

16. MJ to Robert delle Donne, January 20, 1926, in *AA* 1:162–63.

17. MJ to Jouhandeau, January 18, 1926, in *Jouhandeau*, 244–45.

18. MJ to Sachs, January 18, 1926, in ms. 2579, Correspondence Max Jacob, Maurice Sachs, Orléans.

19. Jouhandeau was more open about his sexual life in *De l'abjection* (1938).

20. MJ to Jouhandeau, January 24, 1926, in *Jouhandeau*, 248.

21. MJ to Cocteau, January 25, 1926, in Jacob/Cocteau, 381–83.

22. MJ to Cocteau, January 29, 1926, ibid., 386–89.

23. Ibid.

24. Marie-Claire Durand-Guiziou, "Max Jacob et l'Espagne: Introduction," *CMJ*, no. 7 (2007): 16.

25. The trip had been arranged by José Bergamín and Philippe Datz, a young insurance agent Jacob had met the year before in Milan. MJ to Cocteau, June 25, 1925, in Jacob/Cocteau 320.

26. MJ, "Manuscrit," ed. Francis Deguilly and Patricia Sustrac, *CMJ*, no. 7 (2007): 48; MJ to Cocteau, February 21, 1926, in Jacob/Cocteau, 390–91.

27. Ibid.

28. MJ, "Manuscrit," 53.

29. MJ to Mezure, July 24, 1942, in *Jeune homme*, 94–95.

30. Ibid.

31. Émié, *Dialogues*, 60–81.

32. MJ to Cocteau, February 21, 1926, in Jacob/Cocteau, 390–92.

33. Émié, *Dialogues*, 65.

34. Ibid., 66.

35. Ibid., 70.

36. MJ to Cocteau, February 21, 1926, in Jacob/Cocteau, 390–92.

37. Ibid.

38. *AA* 1:172–77.

39. MJ to Robert delle Donne, March 1926, ibid., 172–73.

40. Victor Moremans, "Max Jacob, *Les Pénitents en maillots roses*," *Gazette de Liège*, March 25, 1926.

41. Jean Cassou, "*Les Pénitents en maillots roses*, par Max Jacob," *Nouvelle Revue française*, no. 152 (May 1926): 619.

42. Cocteau to Jacob, May 2, 1925, in Jacob/Cocteau, 274; Jacob to Cocteau, May 1926, ibid., 414.

43. André Fontainas, "Les Poèmes," *Mercure de France* 188, no. 672 (June 15, 1926): 671–72.

44. MJ, "Un nouveau Cabinet noir": "Lettre sans commentaires," "Lettre de 1814 pour se plaindre d'un frère," and "Lettre d'une bonne," *Nouvelle Revue française*, no. 152 (May 1926): 526–36; CN, in O, 1022–26, 1030–31, 1043–4.

45. MJ, "Sur la foulure de mon poignet droit" and "Conseils," *Cahiers libres* 4, no. 13 (May–June 1926): 3–4.

46. He sometimes spelled *Morven* as *Morwen*. MJ, "Madrigal du diable ermite," "Automne," "Sommeil," "Paysage," "Censément traduit du Breton," *Commerce*, no. 8 (Summer 1926): 63–71. As "Jeanne Le Bolloch," PMG, in O, 1665.

47. On Maritain's view of Jacob as an exemplary poet, see his *Art et scolastique* (Paris: Librairie de l'art catholique, 1927); *Frontières de la poésie* (Paris: Louis Rouart et fils, 1935); and *L'Intuition créatrice dans l'art et dans la poésie* (Paris: Desclée de Brouwer, 1966).

48. Jacob/Maritain, 24.

49. Ibid., 19.

50. Raczymow, *Maurice Sachs*, 123.

51. The first stanza is scrawled in the Spanish notebook. MJ, "Manuscrit," 57.

52. MJ, "Angoisses et autres," *Chroniques: Le Roseau d'or* 2, no. 10, 1926, 44–45. In FE, in O, 1413–14, stanzas three and four are run together.

53. Raczymow, *Maurice Sachs*, 122.

54. Jean Cocteau, *Journal d'un Inconnu* (Paris: Grasset, 1953), 102–3; Raczymow, *Maurice Sachs*, 93, 147.

55. MJ to Robert delle Donne, c. mid-March 1926, in *AA* 1:173–74.

56. Sachs, *Sabbat*, 135–36.

57. Ibid., 138. Raczymow, *Maurice Sachs*, 119.

58. Steegmuller, *Cocteau*, 382.

59. Jacob/Cocteau 417n4.

60. MJ to Cocteau, May 1926, ibid., 414–17.

61. Jacob/Maritain 39–41.

62. MJ to Cocteau, May 16, 1926, in Jacob/Cocteau, 419–20.

63. MJ to Cocteau, July 8 and 19, 1926, ibid., 430, 435; Cocteau to Jacob, c. March 1926, ibid., 402–4.

64. MJ to Robert delle Donne, c. early June 1926, in *AA* 1:185.

65. MJ to Cocteau, March 8, 1926, in Jacob/Cocteau, 400–1; Seckel, *Jacob et Picasso*, 201.

66. MJ to Cocteau, July 8, 1926, in Jacob/Cocteau, 429–31; Pougy, *Mes cahiers*, 226–39.

67. Sachs, *Sabbat*, 141–43; Raczymow, *Maurice Sachs*, 128–30.

68. Sachs, *Sabbat*, 143.

69. Seckel, *Jacob et Picasso*, 203.

70. MJ to Jouhandeau, August 26, 1926, in *Jouhandeau*, 266.

71. MJ to Cocteau, September 24, 1926, in Jacob/Cocteau, 441–43.

72. Louis Guilloux, *Absent de Paris* (Paris: Gallimard, 1952), 146–87.

73. Ibid., 152.

74. MJ to Cocteau, September 24, 1926, in Jacob/Cocteau, 441–43.

75. Guilloux, *Absent*, 154.

76. Ibid., 157.

77. Ibid., 175–78.

78. MJ to Cocteau, September 24, 1926, in Jacob/Cocteau, 441.

79. MJ to Cocteau, November 22, 1926, ibid., 454–56, and in Pougy, *Mes cahiers*, 229–37.

80. MJ to Robert delle Donne, October 2 and 7, 1926, in *AA* 1:191–93.

81. MJ to Kahnweiler, November 4, 1926, in Jacob/Cocteau, 444n1.

82. MJ's letters to Sachs, ms. 2579, Orléans.

83. MJ to Jouhandeau, October 7, 1926, in *Jouhandeau*, 274–75.

84. MJ to Cocteau, c. November 1926, in Jacob/Cocteau, 458–61.

85. Sachs, *Sabbat*, 149.

86. Ibid., 145.

87. Ibid., 145–47.

88. Maurice Sachs, *Alias* (1935; reprinted Paris: Gallimard, 1962), 186.

89. Already, at sixteen, Sachs had exploited the lust of an older writer, the academician Abel Hermant. Maurice Sachs, *Chronique joyeuse et scandaleuse* (Paris: Corrêa, 1948), 21–25; Raczymow, *Maurice Sachs*, 64–68.

90. Sachs, *Décade*, 207–22; Sachs, *Alias*, 210–19; Raczymow, *Maurice Sachs*, 136–38.

91. He was wearing the same outfit a few days later in Bordeaux. Andreu, *Vie et mort*, 96, photo.

92. Marcel Jouhandeau, *Carnets de l'écrivain* (Paris: Gallimard, 1952), 316.

93. MJ to Jouhandeau, November 2, 1926, in *Jouhandeau*, 278–80.

94. Sachs, *Décade*, 213.

95. Émié, *Dialogues*, 92. The article appeared in *La Revue nouvelle*, February 15, 1927.

96. FE, in O, 1409.

97. Raczymow, *Maurice Sachs*, 142–43.

98. MJ to Cocteau, November 14, 1926, in Jacob/Cocteau, 449–53.

99. MJ to Maritain, November 4, 1926, in Jacob/Maritain, 44–45.

100. MJ to Maritain, December 7 and 10, 1926, ibid., 46–48.

101. MJ to Robert delle Donne, November 12, 1926, in *AA* 1:193–95.

102. MJ to Cocteau, November 14, 1926, in Jacob/Cocteau, 449–51.

103. MJ to Cocteau, c. November 1926, ibid., 456–61.

104. Cocteau to Jacob, November 20, 1926, ibid., 453–54; Jacob to Cocteau, November 22, 1926, ibid., 454–56.

105. MJ to Sachs, November 24, 1926, in Orléans.

106. MJ to Sachs, December 2, 1926, ibid.

107. MJ to Sachs, December 8, 1926, ibid.

108. MJ to Robert delle Donne, November 12, 1926, in *AA* 1:193–94.

109. MJ to Cocteau, January 15, 1927, c. November 1926, in Jacob/Cocteau, 481, 458–61. MJ to Sachs, November 24, 1926, in Orléans.

110. MJ to Cocteau, December 27, 1926, in Jacob/Cocteau, 466–68.

111. MJ to Cocteau, December 29, 1926, ibid., 471–73.

112. MJ to Neveus, December 27, 1926, in ms. n. acq. fr. 16799, n. 26, BnF.

113. MJ to Jouhandeau, January 7, 1927, in *Jouhandeau*, 287–89.

114. Jacob/Maritain, 48–51.

115. MJ, "Allégorie," "Ils attendent le voyageur," "Paysage mobile," *Nouvelle Revue française*, no. 159 (December 1926): 697–99; MJ, "Allégorie," PMG, in O, 1659.

116. MJ, "La Nuit," "Sur la mort," "Méditation," "Changement de temps," "Un Chapeau d'instituteur," "Le Phare d'Eckmühl," *Ligne de coeur* 3, no. 8 (January 15, 1927): 16–18; MJ, "La Nuit," "Sur la mort," and "Méditation," FE, in O, 1422, 1411, and 1423; MJ, "Un Chapeau d'instituteur" and "Le Phare d'Eckmühl," PMG, in O, 1619 and 1618.

117. MJ to Paulhan, February 7 and 15, 1927, in Jacob/Paulhan, 121–12.

118. Salmon, *Jacob, poète*.

119. Ibid., 28.

120. MJ to Fillacier, July 26, 1927, in Gompel/Marcoux, 283.

121. Robert Levesque, "Journal: Trois jours à Saint-Benoît (avec Max Jacob)," *Nouvelle Revue française*, no. 292 (April 1977): 30–36.

122. MJ to Jouhandeau, January 17 and 19, March 11, 1927, in *Jouhandeau*, 287–94; MJ to Levesque, February 23, 1927, in *Levesque*, 24.

123. MJ to Jouhandeau, March 25, 1927, in *Jouhandeau*, 295; MJ to Cocteau, April 17, in Jacob/Cocteau 532–34.

124. Seckel, *Jacob et Picasso*, 206; MJ, "Une lettre de Max Jacob à Robert Lévesque," *CdR*, no. 6 (1984): 59–62.

125. MJ, "Souvenirs sur Picasso," 199–202.

126. Sachs, *Sabbat*, 156–57.

127. MJ to Sachs, January 3, 1927, in Orléans.

128. MJ to Sachs, January 17, 1927, ibid.

129. MJ to Sachs, February 16, 1927, ibid.

130. MJ to Sachs, February 27, 1927, ibid.

131. MJ to Sachs, February 16, 1927, ibid.

132. MJ to Sachs, March 3, 1927, ibid.

133. Steegmuller, *Cocteau*, 382.

134. Cocteau to MJ, c. April 1927, in Jacob/Cocteau, 524–25.

135. MJ to Cocteau, April 12, 1927, ibid., 526–29.

136. MJ to Cocteau, March 23, 1927, ibid., 517.

137. Cocteau to MJ, April 27, 1927, ibid., 530.

138. Victor Moremans, "Max Jacob, *Fond de l'eau*," *Gazette de Liège*, June 9, 1927.

139. Robert Guiette, "Max Jacob, *Fond de l'eau*," *Échantillons*, January 1928.

140. MJ to Sachs, March 24, 1927, in Orléans; MJ to Cocteau, March 22, 1927, in Jacob/Cocteau, 515–17.

141. Cocteau to MJ, c. April 1927, in Jacob/Cocteau, 524–25.

142. Belaval, *Rencontre*, 22–24.

143. MJ to Cocteau, April 27, 1927, in Jacob/Cocteau, 532–34.

144. Florent Fels, "Max Jacob, Peintre et poète," *Nouvelles littéraires*, April 30, 1927, 1.

145. Cocteau to MJ, c. April 1927, in Jacob/Cocteau, 531.

146. MJ to Cocteau, February 26, 1927, ibid., 499–501.

147. MJ to Sachs, March 24, 1927, in Orléans.

148. MJ to Sachs, c. late March 1927, in Orléans.

149. MJ to Sachs, April 6, 1927, ibid.

150. MJ to Sachs, May 4 and 19, 1927, ibid.

151. MJ to Laporte, May 9, 1927, in *AA* 1:208; MJ to Maritain, May 17, 1927, in Jacob/ Maritain, 48–49. MJ to Cocteau, May 21, 1927, in Jacob/Cocteau, 537; MJ to Lanoë, May 29, 1927, in *Lanoë*, 114.

152. MJ to Sachs, May 24, 1927, in Orléans.

153. MJ to Sachs, June 4, 1927, ibid.

154. Lucien Zimmer, *Un Septennat policier* (Paris: Fayard, 1967), 11–23.

155. Marie-Laure de Noailles, *née* Marie-Laure Bischoffsheim, was the granddaughter of Comtesse Adhéaume de Chevigny, born Laure de Sade, Proust's La Duchesse de Guermantes.

156. MJ to Cocteau, July 5 1927, in Jacob/Cocteau, 548–49.

157. MJ to Pougy, June 21 1927, in *Pougy*, 91.

158. Sachs, *Décade*, 216.

159. Ibid., 216–17.

160. MJ to Fillacier, July 26, 1927, in Gompel/Marcoux, 283. MJ to Pougy, July 8, 1927, in *Pougy*, 92; MJ to Cassou, September 13, 1927, in *Jacob écrit*, 124; MJ to Lanoë, July 14, 1927, in *Lanoë*, 122.

161. Sachs, *Alias*, 204.

162. On July 21, Jacob wrote to him at Bréhat. Orléans.

163. MJ to Sachs, July 21 1927, in Orléans.

164. From Quimper he sent "La fille des fontaines," "Chanson du clerc," and "Plaintes d'un mort." PMG, in O, 1617; *Pougy*, 93–95.

165. The Colles' house still stands on a hill over the Bay of Douarnenez.

166. Sachs, *Sabbat*, 158–59.

167. Ibid., 163–67.

168. Raczymow, *Maurice Sachs*, 159–60.

169. Sachs, *Sabbat*, 168.

170. MJ to Sachs, July 2 1927, in Orléans.

171. MJ to Sachs, c. August 1927, ibid.

172. MJ to Cocteau, August 20, 1927, in Jacob/Cocteau, 554; MJ to Sachs, c. September 1927, in Orléans.

173. MJ to Cocteau, October 16, 1927, in Jacob/Cocteau, 557; MJ to Sachs, October 19, 1927, in Orléans.

174. MJ to Sachs, October 30, 1927, in Orléans.

175. MJ to Cocteau, October 13, 1927, in Jacob/Cocteau, 553–54.

176. MJ to Cocteau, October 1927, ibid., 555–56.

177. Ibid., 557.

178. Sachs, *Décade*, 219.

179. MJ to Cocteau, August 20, 1927, in Jacob/Cocteau, 551–53.

180. Jouhandeau, *Carnets*, 315–16.

181. MJ to Sachs, December 8, 1927, in Orléans.

182. MJ to Level, March 26, 1927, in ms. 8491–9 to 8491–23, BLJD.

183. Nicholas Nabokov (as his name is written in English) was a composer, in exile from the Soviet Union like his cousin Vladimir Nabokov.

184. MJ to Pougy, c. December 1927, in *Pougy*, 97–98; MJ to Sachs, December 8, 1927, in Orléans.

185. Sachs, *Sabbat*, 24.

186. MJ to Sachs, December 15, 1927, in Orléans.

187. MJ to Sachs, January 23, 1928, ibid.

188. MJ, "Revue de la Quinzaine," *Mercure de France* 200, no. 708 (December 15, 1927): 664–65.

189. MJ to Level, February 8, 1928, in ms. 22, Fonds Max Jacob, Médiathèque des Ursulines, Quimper.

190. MJ to Sachs, February 15, 1928, in Orléans.

191. Ibid.

192. MJ to Sachs, January 16, 1928, ibid.

193. Palacio, "Max Jacob 2," 280.

194. Paulhan to MJ, c. February 1927, January 17 and 18, 1928, in Jacob/Paulhan, 130–33.

195. MJ to Sachs, January 23, 1928, in Orléans.

196. MJ to Gaudier, February 8, 1928, in Gompel/Marcoux, 297.

197. MJ to Cocteau, March 3, 1928, in Jacob/Cocteau, 563–65.

198. MJ, "Fête de la Très Sainte Vierge," "Genveur l'ivrogne," "Marie Kerloch," "Noces de Cana," *Ligne de coeur* 3, no. 10 (June 1927): 12–16; PMG, in O, 1636, 1625, 1624, 1635. MJ, "Chanson de clerc," "La Fille de fontaine," "Mon chien noir," *Ligne de coeur* 3, no. 11 (November 1927): 3–5; PMG, in O, 1617, 1632; And MJ, "Tentations de l'esprit," *Ligne de coeur* 3, no. 11 (November 1927): 35.

199. MJ, "Les conscrits," "Veille des cataclysms," "Le Tailleur maigre," Baptême," "Demande en marriage," and "Juliette Gallic," *Revue européenne*, January–February 1928, 61–66; MJ, "Demande en marriage," PMG, in O, 1678.

200. Jean Cassou, "Max Jacob et la liberté," *Nouvelle revue française*, no. 175 (April 1928): 454–63.

201. Jean Cassou, "Max Jacob parmi nous," *Le Mail*, special no. 5, April 1928, 241–42.

202. Louis Thomas, "Max Jacob," *Nouvelles, littéraires*, March 17, 1927, 5.

203. MJ to Cocteau, March 3, 1928, in Jacob/Cocteau, 563–65.

204. Sachs, *Sabbat*, 169–70; Raczymow, *Maurice Sachs*, 160–61.

CHAPTER 17: THE YEAR OF CRASHES

1. MJ to Nino Frank, c. April 1928, in *Frank*, 144.

2. MJ to Paulhan, April 19, 1928, in Jacob/Paulhan, 134.

3. MJ to Sachs, April 27, 1928, in Orléans. The plural "dears" probably includes Pierre Colle, who was joining Sachs in art dealing. Christian Bérard was "Bébé," the painter and set designer.

4. MJ to Sachs, May 5, 1928, in Orléans.

5. Sachs, *Sabbat,* 193–201.

6. MJ to Paulhan, April, 1928 n.d., in Jacob/Paulhan, 137.

7. Émié, *Dialogues,* 130.

8. Henri Sauguet, interview by author.

9. Henri Sauguet, "Max Jacob et la musique," *Revue Musicale,* no. 210 (January 1952): 151.

10. MJ to Paulhan, May 17, 1928, in Jacob/Paulhan, 138.

11. Tracol found Sachs "amusing," with "a gift for using other people." Interview by author.

12. MJ to Lanoë, May 26, 1928, in *Lanoë,* 159.

13. Frank, "Retour de Saint-Benoît de Max Jacob," in "Malles et Valises," *Nouvelles littéraires,* April 28, 1928.

14. "Oeuvres originales et graphiques de quatorze peintres contemporains," in Jacob/Paulhan, 135.

15. Guiette, "Notes pour un portrait," *Disque vert* 2, no. 2 (November 1923): 53–55.

16. Guiette *Vie,* 11; Jacob, *Lettres à Robert Guiette,* ed. Michel Decaudin (Paris: Éditions des Cendres, 1996).

17. Guiette, *Vie,* 13.

18. The book appeared in 1976.

19. Guiette, *Vie,* 21–22.

20. Jean Desbordes, *J'adore* (Paris: Grasset, 1928), 16.

21. Ibid., 41.

22. Ibid., 5.

23. Ibid., 9.

24. Maritain to MJ, 30 June, 1928, in Jacob/Maritain, 57.

25. MJ to Maritain, June 25, 1928, ibid., 56.

26. MJ to Maritain, July 9, 1928, ibid., 58.

27. Ibid., 58.

28. "Courrier littéraire," *Nouvelles littéraires,* August 1, 1928, 113, in Jacob/Cocteau, 615.

29. Jacob/Maritain 59n3.

30. MJ to Pierre Reverdy, July 9, 1928, in Gompel/Marcoux, 303.

31. MJ to Sachs, July 13, 1928, in Orléans.

32. MJ to Sachs, August 13, 1928, in Orléans.

33. MJ to Sachs, August 30, 1928, in Orléans.

34. MJ to Roger Karl, August 30, 1928; MJ, "Lettres à Roger Karl," *Lettre ouverte* 5 (March 1961): 61–63.

35. MJ to Sachs, September 16, 1928, in Orléans.

36. MJ to Sachs and Colle, September 21, 1928, in Orléans.

37. Raczymow, *Maurice Sachs* (168), states that Sachs and Colle "went to pick him up at Saint-Benoît in the car they borrowed from Jean Desbordes and they installed him in the Hôtel Nollet." But Jacob moved to Paris on his own in April 1928.

38. Andreu, *Vie et mort,* 214–15; MJ to Sachs and Colle, c. October 1928; Orléans.

39. MJ to Cocteau, October 31, 1928, in Jacob/Cocteau, 566–68.

40. Raczymow, *Maurice Sachs,* 168–70.

41. Sachs, *Sabbat,* 206–7.

42. Ibid., 204–5.

43. Seckel, *Jacob et Picasso,* 214.

44. Théophile Briant, "Itinéraires de Max Jacob," *Goéland,* August 1946.

45. MJ to Sachs, December 14, 1928, in Orléans; Raczymow, *Maurice Sachs,* 173.

46. Élise Jouhandeau, *Le Spleen empanaché: Joies et douleurs d'une belle excentrique* (Paris: Flammarion, 1960), 157.

47. MJ to Jouhandeau, November 20, 27–29, 1928, in *Jouhandeau,* 320–21.

48. Élise Jouhandeau, *Le Lien de ronces, ou le marriage* (Paris: Grasset, 1964), 36–39, 123.

49. *Pace* Raczymow, Sachs didn't "introduce" Reverdy to Chanel. They had had a serious romance from 1921 to 1924.

50. Raczymow, *Maurice Sachs,* 172–73.

51. MJ to Sachs, February 15, 1929, in Orléans.

52. Raczymow, *Maurice Sachs,* 175.

53. Ibid.

54. Ibid., 211–14.

55. MJ to Charles Goldblatt, April 27, 1929, in *Goldblatt,* 67–68.

56. MJ, "Pour mes nouveaux jeunes amis," *Courte Paille* 1, no. 1 (March 1929): 22–23. MJ, "Bélisaire," *Courte Paille* 1, no. 2 (April 1929): n. p.; AE, 146.

57. Andreu, *Le Rouge et le blanc,* 68–77.

58. Maurice Sachs, *Au temps du Boeuf sur le Toit* (Paris: Nouvelle Revue Critique, 1939), 230–31.

59. MJ to François de Gouy, April 12, 1929, in *AA* 1:238.

60. MJ to Cocteau, May 23, 1929, in Jacob/Cocteau, 570.

61. Victor Moremans, "Max Jacob: *Le Cabinet noir,*" *Gazette de Liège,* January 3, 1929.

62. MJ to Moremans, January 1929; Lambert Joassin, "L'amitié de Max Jacob et de Victor Moremans," *Marginales,* no. 107–8 (June–July 1966): 41.

63. Jean Cassou, "Poésie: Max Jacob, *Cinématoma,*" *Nouvelles littéraires,* July 27, 1929.

64. MJ, "La Gourmandise," *Les Sept péchés capitaux* (Paris: Éditions Kra, 1929), 115–46.

65. Morven le Gaélique, "Poèmes," *Commerce,* no. 22 (Winter 1929): 7–43.

66. MJ, "Description de l'extase," *Raison d'être* 2, no. 2 (February 1929): 7; SI, in O, 1433.

67. Charles-Albert Cingria, *Ossianide* (October–November 1949), 84; Françoise Steel-Coquet, "Christopher Wood and France," in *Christopher Wood: A Painter Between Two Cornwalls,* ed. André Cariou and Michael Tooby (London: Tate Gallery, 1996), 13.

68. MJ to Picasso, August 25, 1929; Seckel, *Jacob et Picasso,* 216.

69. MJ to Fillacier, November 1929, in Gompel/Marcoux, 317–18; MJ to Paulhan, September 21, 1929, in Jacob/Paulhan 140. MJ to Ghikas, October 6, 1929, in *Pougy,* 100–1.

70. MJ to Maritain, September 22, 1929, in Jacob/Maritain, 61–62.

71. MJ to Robert delle Donne, October 28, 1929, in *AA* 1:245.

72. MJ to Sachs, November 1929, Orléans; Raczymow, *Maurice Sachs*, 176.

73. MJ to Paulhan, November 12, 1929, in Jacob/Paulhan, 144.

74. MJ to Kit Wood, September 18, 1929, in Françoise Coquet, "Portraits d'amis: Max Jacob et Kit Wood en Bretagne," *Adam, International Review*, no. 487–92 (1988): 48.

75. MJ to Fillacier, September 27, 1929, in Fillacier, *Chante cigale*, 330.

76. MJ to Robert delle Donne, October 30, 1929, in *AA* 1:247–49.

77. Béhar, *Breton*, 217; *Minet*, 16.

78. MJ to René Gaudier, February 4, 1925, in Gompel/Marcoux, 238. Gaudier married Minet's sister.

79. Joseph Daoust, "Causerie sur les revues," *Esprit et vie*, September 13, 1984, 489–94; letters of Jacob to Louis Vaillant.

80. MJ to Paulhan, c. December 1929, in Jacob/Paulhan, 147.

81. MJ to Minet, January 8, 1930, in *Minet*, 33.

82. Gertrude Stein, *Morceaux choisis de La Fabrication des Américains: Histoire du progrès d'une famille*, trans. Georges Hugnet (Paris: Éditions de la Montagne, 1929).

83. MJ to Stein, December 6, 1929, in Annette Thau, "Max Jacob's Letters to Gertrude Stein: A Critical Study," *Folio*, no. spec. 9 (October 1976): 47–54.

84. René Villard, "Max Jacob à Quimper: Histoire d'une classe de lycée," *Correspondant*, new ser. 282 (January 10, 1930): 76–97.

85. *Villard*, 35–36.

86. MJ to Sachs, January 26, 1930, in Orléans.

87. MJ to Sachs, February 3, 1930, ibid.

88. MJ to François de Gouy, February 24, 1930, in Gompel/Marcoux, 327.

89. MJ to Minet, February 26, 1930, in *Minet*, 34–35.

90. Morven le Gaélique, "Poèmes," *Nouvelle Revue française*, no. 203 (August 1930): 166–69; MJ, "Au Marché," "Le Mariage," "Chanson du berger," "Jeunes filles modernes à Douarnenez," PMG, in O, 1639, 1638, 1668, 1640.

91. MJ to Minet, March 12, 1930, in *Minet*, 36–37.

92. MJ to Ferrare, April 22, 1930, in "Ferrare," 63.

93. MJ to Minet, c. summer 1930, in *Minet*, 46.

94. MJ to Minet, June 2, 1930, ibid., 42–43.

95. MJ to Maillols, July 22, 1930, in *AA* 1:256.

96. MJ to Ferrare, June 14, 1930, in "Ferrare," 66.

97. Charles-Albert Cingria, "Survie de Max Jacob," *Labyrinthe*, no. 1 (October 15, 1944), 85.

98. The hotel survives, and so does the church.

99. Cingria, "Survie de Jacob," 85.

100. Raczymow, *Maurice Sachs*, 182.

101. She was there on July 8. MJ to Cingria, in *AA* 1:254.

102. Steel-Coquet, "Christopher Wood and France," 20.

103. Coquet, "Portraits d'amis," 47. Wood painted Jacob, seated. Musée des Beaux-Arts in Quimper.

104. Cocteau to MJ, c. summer 1930, in Jacob/Cocteau, 574.
105. MJ to Maritain, May 22 and August 10, 1930, in Jacob/Maritain, 64–65.
106. Minet to Lilian, August 8, 1930, and MJ to Minet, August 3, 1930, in *Minet*, 48–49.
107. MJ to Minet, September 5 and 12, 1930, ibid., 50–51.
108. Raczymow, *Maurice Sachs*, 182.
109. Ibid.
110. Ibid., 184; Philippe Schmitt-Kummerlee, *Max Jacob au Grand Quartier general Nollet* (Paris: Al Manar, 2007), 36.
111. MJ to Minet, September 5 and 12, 1930, in *Minet*, 50–51; MJ to Cingria, c. October 1930, in *AA* 1:259. MJ to Goldblatt, September 16, 1930, in *Goldblatt*, 78; MJ to de Gouy, January 2, 1931, in *AA* 1:261; MJ to Jean Colle, c. fall 1930, in *Colle*, 25.
112. MJ to Froska Munster, October 10, 1930, in Coquet, "Portraits d'amis," 49.
113. MJ to Ghikas, October 8, 1930, in Gompel/Marcoux, 337.

CHAPTER 18: THE HÔTEL NOLLET

1. Annette Thau, "Max Jacob's Letters to Gertrude Stein: A Critical Study," *Folio*, no. spec. 9 (October 1976): 50–51.
2. Seckel, *Jacob et Picasso*, 220; Pierre Lazareff, "Le retour de Max Jacob a été fêté au cours d'une nuit parisienne," *Paris-Midi*, December 5, 1930, 2.
3. Vittorio Rieti, interview by author.
4. Ibid., Vittorio Rieti to Elsie Rieti, December 13, 1930, courtesy Fabio Rieti.
5. Rieti simply called him "Boris"; it must have been the librettist Kochno.
6. Rieti to Elsie, November 21, 1930, courtesy Fabio Rieti.
7. Rieti interview; Vittorio Rieti, *Quatre Poèmes de Max Jacob* (Hastings-on-Hudson: General Music Publishing, 1975); MJ, "La Crise," "Le Noyer fatal," "Soir d'été," and "Monsieur le Duc."
8. MJ, "Stabat Mater," *Commerce*, no. 22 (Winter 1929); PMG, in O, 1637.
9. MJ to François de Gouy, January 2, 1931, in *AA* 1:260–61.
10. Rieti interview.
11. MJ to Minet, February 26, 1931, in *Minet*, 55–59.
12. Ibid., 20.
13. MJ to Minet, March 1, 1931, ibid., 60–61.
14. MJ, "Allusions romantiques à propos du Mardi-Gras." LC, in O, 595.
15. MJ to Minet, April 3 and 6, 1931, ibid., 66–67.
16. Rieti to Elsie, December 13, 1930, courtesy Fabio Rieti.
17. MJ to Minet, March 12, 1931, in *Minet*, 62–63.
18. MJ, "J'en passe et des meilleures," "J'en passe et des meilleures," *Nouvelle Revue française*, no. 211 (April 1931): 593–97.
19. MJ to Minet, March 12, 1931, in *Minet*, 62.
20. February 25–May 21, 1931, in Jacob/Paulhan, 160–69.
21. MJ to Paulhan, April 22, 1931, ibid., 167.
22. MJ to Minet, April 12, 1931, in *Minet*, 68.

23. MJ to Minet, April 28, 1931, ibid., 69–70; MJ to Esdras-Gosse, July 10, 1931, in *Esdras-Gosse*, 25.

24. MJ to Minet, April 28, 1931, in *Minet*, 69–70.

25. MJ, "Montmartre," 19–21.

26. MJ, "Je suis né," 210–12.

27. MJ to Léon Merle de Beaufort, July 26, 1931, in Gompel/Marcoux, 345–46.

28. MJ to René Laporte, July 8, 1931, in *AA* 1:261–62.

29. MJ to Minet, July 26, 1931, in *Minet* 75.

30. MJ to de Gouy, August 21, 1931, in *AA* 1:263–65.

31. MJ to Minet, November 8 and 21, 1931, in *Minet*, 76–78; MJ to Esdras-Gosse, November 8, 1931, in *Esdras-Gosse*, 27.

32. MJ to Minet, April 6, 1931, in *Minet*, 67.

33. Abbé Morel, conversation with author.

34. MJ to Ghikas, December 6, 1931, in *Pougy*, 111–12.

35. Francis Poulenc, *Correspondance 1910–1963*, ed. Myriam Chimènes (Paris: Fayard, 1994), 354.

36. Francis Poulenc, *Mes Amis et moi*, ed. Stéphane Audel (Paris: La Palatine, 1963), 98–107.

37. "Le Veuf," with variants: MJ to Sachs, October 30, 1927, in Orléans; R, in O, 1442.

38. MJ, "Vous n'écrivez plus?" R, in O, 1441; MJ, "Noces d'aveugles," R, in O, 1443.

39. MJ, "L'Armée frappante des images," R, in O, 1449.

40. Pierre Guéguen, "Actualités poétiques," *Nouvelles littéraires*, April 23, 1932, 5.

41. MJ, "Confession publique ou caricature de Max Jacob par lui-même," *Renaissance*, December 1931, 331–33.

42. MJ to Ghikas, January 6, 1932, in *Pougy*, 114–15.

43. MJ to Paulhan, January 27, 1932, in Jacob/Paulhan, 173.

44. MJ to Yves Gérard Le Dantec, January 29, 1932, in *AA* 1:270.

45. MJ to de Gouy, February 5, 1932, ibid., 1:270–71.

46. MJ to Paulhan, March 10, 1932, in Jacob/Paulhan, 176–77.

47. MJ to Minet, November 8, 1931, in *Minet*, 76; MJ to de Gouy, c. April 1932, in *AA* 1:274; MJ to Minet, April 16, 1932, in *Minet*, 79; MJ to Rimbert, April 11, 1932, in *Rimbert*, 65; MJ to Cocteau, April 13, 1932, in Jacob/Cocteau, 576.

48. MJ to Ferrare, June 1932, in "Ferrare," 66–68.

49. Pougy, *Mes cahiers*, 270.

50. MJ to de Gouy, c. April 1932, in *AA* 1:274–75.

51. Trefusis was Violet Keppel, daughter of Edward VII's mistress, Alice Keppel.

52. MJ to Grenier, June 21, 1932, in *Grenier*, 83.

53. MJ, "Naissance," 7.

54. Seckel, *Jacob et Picasso*, 225n3.

55. Paul Léautaud, *Journal littéraire*, no. 9 (Paris: Mercure de France, 1960), 211–12; Seckel, *Jacob et Picasso*, 225n3.

56. MJ to de Gouy, June 21, 1932, in Gompel/Marcoux, 360–61.

57. Franc-Nohain, "Les Livres nouveaux, *Bourgeois de France et d'ailleurs*," *Écho de Paris*, July 14, 1932, 4.

58. Fortunat Strowski, *Quotidien*, July 5, 1932; Victor Moremans, "Max Jacob: *Bourgeois de France et d'ailleurs*," *Gazette de Liège*, July 27, 1932.

59. MJ, "Convalescence," *Feuillets inutiles*, September 30, 1932, 10; *Nouvelle Revue française*, no. 250 (July 1934): 21–22; HC, 84.

60. Camus to Grenier, May 20 and August 25, 1932, in Moishe Black, "Non récupérables: Camus et Max Jacob," *Les Trois Guerres d'Albert Camus*, ed. Lionel Dubois (Poitiers: Actes du Colloque International de Poitiers, 1995), 250–64.

61. To Grenier, June 21, 1932, in *Grenier* 83–84.

62. MJ to Minet, August 1932, in *Minet*, 82–83; MJ to de Gouy, June 21, 1932, in *AA* 1:360–61.

63. MJ to de Gouy, August 13, 1932, in Gompel/Marcoux, 362–63; Andreu, *Vie et mort*, 221.

64. Sinclair, "Sur Max Jacob," *Arcadie*, no. 192 (December 1969): 573–77.

65. Ibid., 574–75.

66. MJ, "La Lettre de la fiancée," to René Dulsou, c. October 1932, in *AA* 1:280–81.

67. MJ to Dulsou, c. November 1932, ibid., 1:281–82.

68. MJ to Dulsou, c. December 1932, ibid., 1:284.

69. MJ to Dulsou, c. early January 1933, ibid., 1:285–86.

70. MJ to Dulsou, March 31, 1933, ibid., 1:297–99.

71. MJ to Minet, February 20, 1932, in *Minet*, 89–90.

72. MJ to Laporte, November 11, 1931, in *AA* 1:267.

73. MJ to Paulhan, March 11, 1933, in Jacob/Paulhan, 189–90.

74. MJ to Marie delle Donne, March 7, 1933, in *AA* 1:287.

75. MJ to Dulsou, April 6, 1933, ibid., 1:303–4.

76. MJ to Dulsou, April 4, 1933, ibid., 1:302–3.

77. MJ, "Jeunesse," 1–2.

78. *Villard*, 50.

79. Oxenhandler, *Jacob and Les Feux*, 243. Oxenhandler mistakes the date: it was not November 23 but July 13, 1933.

80. MJ to Pougy, May 22, 1933, in *Pougy*, 119.

81. MJ to Dulsou, March 26, 1933, in *AA* 1:291.

82. MJ, "Ballade de la visite nocturne," *Point*, April 1938; B, in O, 1461.

83. Sinclair, "Vie et mort de Max Jacob," *Arcadie* (May 1982): 316.

84. MJ to Émile Dulsou, August 5, 1933, in *AA* 1:313.

85. Tatiana Greene, "Notice, en préambule aux lettres de Max Jacob à Marguerite Mespoulet," *CdR*, no. 4 (1981): 32.

86. *Villard*, 43–44.

87. MJ to Minet, August 30, 1933, in *Minet*, 95.

88. Villard 45.

89. Sachs, *Sabbat*, 223.

90. Sachs, *Décade*.

91. Raczymow, *Maurice Sachs*, 213–18.

92. Sachs, *Décade*, 220.

93. MJ to Minet, November 1, 1933, in *Minet*, 96–97.

94. MJ to Dulsou, c. November 5, 1933, in *AA* 1:315.

95. Program, Société des Amis de la Bibliothèque Littéraire Jacques Doucet, *Gala de Musique Moderne*, December 11, 1933.

96. André de Richaud, "Max à l'École Militaire," *Cahiers des saisons*, no. 16 (Spring 1959): 679.

97. Alice Halicka, *Hier, souvenirs* (Paris: Éditions du Pavois, 1946), 129.

98. MJ, "La T.S.F.," *Année poétique* 2, no. 2 (January 1934): n.p.

99. MJ, "Le tiers transporté: Chronique des temps héroïques," *Les Feux de Paris*, ns. 7-8, 12 January, 1937; Seckel, *Jacob et Picasso*, 241.

100. É. Jouhandeau, *Lien de ronces*, 144.

101. Andreu, *Le Rouge et le blanc*, 67.

102. Pougy, *Mes cahiers*, 284–85.

103. MJ to Dulsou, April 14, 1934, in *AA* 2:55–56.

104. MJ, "Astrologie 1934," *Intransigeant*, January 2, 1934, 3.

105. MJ to Dulsou, February 4–7, 1934, in *AA* 2:15–19.

106. MJ to Dulsou, February 11, 1934, ibid., 2:23–27.

107. MJ to Dulsou, March 1, 1934, ibid., 2:41.

108. Of the Gompels, he was especially close to Thérèse Gompel and Yvonne Netter, daughter of Gustave Gompel, mother of Didier Gompel.

109. MJ to Dulsou, February 10, 1934, in *AA* 2:46.

110. MJ to Dulsou, March 7, 1934, ibid., 2:41–5.

111. MJ to Dulsou, February 16, 1934, ibid., 2:29–30.

112. MJ to Dulsou, March 18, 1934, ibid., 2:50–51.

113. MJ to Dulsou, March 13, 1934, ibid., 2:48–49.

114. MJ to Dulsou, April 11 and 14, 1934, ibid., 2:54–59. February 25, 1934, ibid., 2:35–37.

115. MJ to Dulsou, July 4–19, 1934, ibid., 2:63–75.

116. *Minet*, 102–3.

117. *AA* 2:113.

118. Andreu, *Vie et mort*, 225; MJ, letters to René Lacôte, in Orléans.

119. MJ to Paulhan, June 29, 1934, in Jacob/Paulhan, 202.

120. Gabriel Bounoure, *"Les Pénitents en maillots roses, Visions infernales, Fond de l'eau, Rivages par Max Jacob,"* *Nouvelle Revue française*, no. 250 (July 1934): 109–18.

121. MJ, *"Actualités éternelles,"* ibid., 20–27.

122. MJ, "Toudoux, Ginette, et les parents," *Figaro illustré*, February 1934; *AA* 3:179–80.

123. MJ, "La Spirale et le serpent," *Nouvelles littéraires*, February 10, 1934.

124. MJ, "Les Deux amours," "Une nuit de Verlaine, "La Conscience est bien gênante," and "Fin du jour au carnaval," *Journal des poètes*, February 18, 1934; *AA* 3:140–43.

125. Philippe Schmitt-Kummerlee, "Un manuscrit retrouvé: Vrai sens de la religion catholique," *CMJ*, no. 7 (2007): 92; MJ, "El verdadero sentido de la religion católica," *Cruz y Raya*, no. 13 (May 1934); MJ, "Las Plagas de Egipto y el dolor," *Cruz y Raya*, no. 18 (September 1934); Trans. José Bergamin.

126. MJ, "Crucifixion" and "Prière," *Beau Navire* 1, no. 2 (December 10, 1934): 20–21. AE 168, 251.

127. MJ to Dulsou, April 23, 1934, in *AA* 2:61; MJ to Queneau, c. March 1935, in "Queneau," 215.

128. MJ to Dulsou, January 22, 1935, in *AA* 2:86.

129. MJ to Dulsou, January 26, 1935, ibid., 2:88–89.

130. MJ to Dulsou, January 31, 1935, ibid., 2:89–91.

131. MJ to Dulsou, January 2 and February 13, 1935, ibid., 2:85–96.

132. MJ to Dulsou, May 24, 1935, ibid., 2:102–4.

133. MJ to Dulsou, April 12, 1933, in *AA* 1:308–9.

134. MJ to Dulsou, c. February 1934, in *AA* 2:10–12.

135. MJ to Dulsou, July 1, 1935, ibid., 2:107–9.

136. MJ to Paulhan, July 19, 1935, in Jacob/Paulhan, 211.

137. Oxenhandler, *Jacob and Les Feux*, 242.

138. MJ to René Iché, July 31, 1935, in *Jacob écrit*, 160.

139. MJ to Madame Dulsou, October 14, 1935, in *AA* 2:111.

140. Henri Vandeputte, "Max," *Beaux-Arts* 5, no. 171 (August 1935): 20–21; *Max Jacob à la confluence: Actes du colloque de Quimper* (1994; Quimper: Bibliothèque Municipale, 2000), 121–25.

141. MJ to Vandeputte, September 24, 1935, in Gompel/Marcoux, 398–99.

142. Richardson, *Life*, 3:418–19.

143. Pierre Cabanne, *Le Siècle de Picasso*, 4 vols. (1975; Paris: Gallimard, 1992), 2:739–40.

144. Seckel, *Jacob et Picasso*, 235.

145. MJ to Fraysse, September 19, 1935, in Oxenhandler, *Jacob and Les Feux*, 243–44.

146. Suspicion later emerged that Juliette was responsible for her second husband's death.

147. MJ to Paulhan, September 2, 1934, in Jacob/Paulhan, 205.

148. Raczymow, *Maurice Sachs*, 237–38.

149. MJ to Pougy, November 3, 1935, in *Pougy*, 132–33.

150. Lyne Bansat-Boudon and Roland Lardinois, *Sylvain Lévi (1863-1935): Études indiennes, histoire sociale* (Turnhaut, Belgium: Bibliothèque de l'École des Hautes Études, Sciences Religieuses, 2003), 285.

151. Seckel, *Jacob et Picasso*, 235–36.

152. MJ to Fraysse, November 15, 1935, in Oxenhandler, *Jacob and Les Feux*, 245.

153. MJ to Madame Dulsou, December 12, 1935, in *AA* 2:114.

154. MJ to Fraysse, December 27, 1935, in Oxenhandler, *Jacob and Les Feux*, 253; Andreu, *Vie et mort*, 228.

155. MJ to Marcel Moré, December 25, 1935, in Gompel/Marcoux 400.

156. MJ, "Poèmes mystiques," *Mesures*, no. 4 (October 15, 1935): 49–55.

CHAPTER 19: SAINT-BENOÎT, AGAIN

1. MJ to Fraysse, January 3 and 9, 1937, in Oxenhandler, *Jacob and Les Feux*, 253–54.
2. MJ to René Laporte, April 5, 1936, in *AA* 2:122.
3. MJ to Charles Oulmont, May 12, 1940, in *Jacob écrit*, 60.
4. MJ, "L'Amour enterré," *Feuillets inutiles*, February 15, 1936, n.p. MJ, "Caïn et Abel," to Jabès, c. Autumn 1935, in *Jabès*, 29–30; HC, 57.
5. MJ, "Roman de l'amour enterré," *Feuilles vertes*, October–November 1935, 88–89; HC 25.
6. MJ, "Amour enterré," *Feux de Paris*, no. 2 (January 12, 1936), n.p.; Oxenhandler, *Jacob and Les Feux*, 275. HC, 59; DP, in O, 1573.
7. Winock, *France et les juifs*, 193.
8. Seckel, *Jacob et Picasso*, 238.
9. MJ to Lanoë, January 29, February n.d., and February 24, 1936, in *Lanoë*, 281–88.
10. MJ, "Pourquoi j'aime Marianne Oswald," *Marianne Oswald* (Paris: An. Girard, 1936), n.p.
11. René Lacôte, "Max Jacob à St.-Benoît-sur-Loire," *Lettres françaises*, May 14, 1959, 2.
12. MJ to Cingria, c. April 1936, in *AA* 2:122.
13. MJ's poems in the *Anthologie des poètes de La Nouvelle Revue française* (Paris: Nouvelle Revue Française, 1936): "Ethnographie du démon," "Formidables erreurs du mysticisme," "Années pourries," "Après la méditation sous un arbre," "Exhortation," "Pensée d'automne," "Éducation laïque," "Séjour," "Voyage," "Voisinage," "Jamais plus!" All are from VI.
14. MJ to Fraysse, March 26 and April 28, 1936, in Oxenhandler, *Jacob and les feux*, 255, 259.
15. MJ to du Plantier, March 21, 1936, in Gompel/Marcoux, 402.
16. MJ to du Plantier, April 26, 1936, ibid., 403–5.
17. MJ to Fraysse, May 24, 1936, in Oxenhandler, *Jacob and les feux*, 261.
18. Andreu, *Vie et mort*, 231; Béalu, *Dernier visage*, 13.
19. MJ to Frank, September 5, 1936, in *Frank*, 159–60.
20. MJ to de Gouy, January 15, 1937, in *AA* 2:135; MJ to Frank, November 7, 1936, in *Frank*, 165.
21. Seckel, *Jacob et Picasso*, 239.
22. MJ to Paulhan, September 20, 1936, in Jacob/Paulhan, 225–26.
23. Belaval, *Rencontre*, 42.
24. MJ to Marcel Moré, May 31, 1936, in Gompel/Marcoux, 408.
25. MJ to Queneau, June 2, 1936, in "Queneau," 218–19.
26. MJ to Fraysse, November 7 and December 1935; January 9, April 7, and June 10, 1936, in Oxenhandler, *Jacob and Les Feux*, 244–62; MJ to Moricand, c. May 1936, August 23, and December 5, 1936, January 23, 1937, in Moricand BnF. Some in Collier.
27. Seckel, *Jacob et Picasso*, 239.
28. MJ, "Le tiers transporté: Chronique des temps héroïques," *Feux de Paris*, no. 7–8 (January 12, 1937). Oxenhandler, *Jacob and Les Feux*, 287–302.

29. MJ to Jabès, June 4, 1936, in *Jabès* 30–33; MJ to Fraysse, June 10, 1936, in Oxenhandler, *Jacob and Les Feux,* 261–65.

30. MJ to Paulhan, October 8, 1936, in Jacob/Paulhan, 227–28.

31. Anne Mary, "Lettres de Max Jacob à Roger Lannes, La Tige et l'orchidée (1935–1943)," *CMJ,* no. 11/12 (2012): 80n38.

32. MJ to Moricand, August 23, 1936, in Moricand BnF.

33. Mary, "Lettres de Jacob à Lannes," 53–84.

34. Jacob spent only October there. MJ to Rimbert, c. September 1936, in *Rimbert* 71–72. MJ to Frank, October 18, 1936, in *Frank,* 36.

35. MJ to Paulhan, October 8, 1936, in Jacob/Paulhan, 227–28.

36. MJ to Moricand, January 5, 1937, in Moricand BnF.

37. Robert Szigeti, interview by author.

38. MJ to Lacôte, August 20, 1936, in "Lacôte," 26–28.

39. Edmond Jabès, interview by author.

40. MJ to Jabès, February 13, 1936, in *Jabès,* 38–39.

41. MJ to Jabès, c. January 1938, ibid., 49–53.

42. Ibid., 52.

43. MJ to Jabès, March 8, 1937, ibid., 40–42; Jabès interview.

44. Michel Manoll, *René Guy Cadou* (Paris: Seghers, 1954), 77.

45. Ibid., 35.

46. Ibid., 77.

47. Winock, *France et les juifs,* 194.

48. MJ to Fraysse, June 10, 1936, in Oxenhandler, *Jacob and Les Feux,* 261–63.

49. Assouline, *Artful Life,* 278.

50. Marcel Jouhandeau, "La Prière de Max Jacob, ou le jongleur de Notre Seigneur," *Le Mail,* no. 5 (April 1928): 60.

51. Marcel Jouhandeau, "Comment je suis devenu antisémite," *Action française,* October 8, 1936, 1, 4.

52. MJ to Marcel Moré, November 26, 1936, in Gompel/Marcoux, 421–22; MJ to Queneau, December 10, 1936, in "Queneau," 220–21.

53. MJ to Paulhan, January 13, 1937, in Jacob/Paulhan, 229–31.

54. MJ to Frank, November 15, 1936, in *Frank,* 167–68.

55. MJ, "La Purge," *Revue doloriste,* December 1, 1936, 3–5.

56. MJ to Pougy, January 19, 1937, in *Pougy,* 146; MJ to Leiris, January 22, 1937, in *Leiris,* 129–30; MJ to Pierre Colle, February 7, 1937, in Gompel/Marcoux, 431.

57. MC, 14.

58. Seckel, *Jacob et Picasso,* 241–49.

59. MJ to Lacôte, March 3, June 22, and September 27, 1937, in "Lacôte," 33–37.

60. MJ to Giovanni Leonardi, March 27, 1937, in Hélène Henry, "Correspondance Max Jacob–Giovanni Leonardi 1920–1944," *CdR,* no. 8 (1986): 67–68; MJ to Roger Lannes, March 28, 1937, in Mary, "Lettres de Jacob à Lannes," 61; MJ to Pougy, April 5, 1937, in *Pougy,* 147–49.

61. MJ to Moricand, April 4, 1937, in Moricand BnF; MJ to Pougy, April 5, 1937, in *Pougy,* 147–49.

62. Béalu, *Dernier visage*, 27–30.

63. MJ to Béalu, October 16, 1937, ibid., 129–30.

64. MJ to Toulouse, June 4, 1937, in *Toulouse*, 20–21.

65. MJ to Toulouse, November 7, 1937, ibid., 26.

66. MJ to Toulouse, November 14, 1937, ibid., 27.

67. MJ to Béalu, November 7, 1937, in Béalu, *Dernier visage*, 131.

68. MJ to Toulouse, June 8, 1935, in *Toulouse*, 21; MJ to Béalu, June 8 and later in June 1937, in Béalu, *Dernier visage*, 110–11.

69. MJ to Salmon, c. June 1937, in *AA* 2:140–42.

70. Seckel, *Jacob et Picasso*, 249.

71. MJ to Béalu, July 19, 1937, in Béalu, *Dernier visage*, 123.

72. MJ to Béalu, June 8, 1937, ibid., 110–11; MJ to Lanoë, August 17, 1937, in *Lanoë*, 323.

73. MJ to Levanti, May 31, 1937, in *Levanti*, 52–53.

74. Tips about Parisian cafés are in Béalu, *Dernier visage*, 112–14.

75. MJ to Lacôte, April 24, 1937, in "Lacôte," 34–35.

76. MJ to Paulhan, January 26 and 31, 1937, in Jacob/Paulhan, 232–37.

77. Béalu, *Dernier visage*, 38. Peyre, *Jacob quotidien*, 68; MJ, "La Poésie? Un rêve inventé," *Nouvelles littéraires*, November 6, 1937, 1, in O, 1523.

78. MJ, "La Petite voleuse," *Pain blanc*, September 1937, 2–3; PMG, in O, 1619.

79. *Manoll*, 36–37.

80. MJ to Béalu, November 12, 1937, in Béalu, *Dernier visage*, 131–32.

81. MJ to Szigeti, in Peyre, *Jacob quotidien*, 66–67.

82. MJ to Béalu, November 12, 1937, in Béalu, *Dernier visage*, 131–32.

83. MJ to Béalu, c. November 1937, ibid., 132–33.

84. MJ to Jabès, December 18, in *Jabès*, 46–47.

85. MJ to René Villard, December 2, 1937, in *Villard*, 77.

86. MJ, "Face," HC, 45; *Poésie vivante*, no. 16 (1966): 17.

87. Andreu, *Vie et mort*, 238; MJ, "Douleur," *Occident*, December 25, 1937, 8; HC 66.

88. MJ, "Pour l'Espagne," *Occident*, February 25, 1938, 8.

89. Peyre, *Jacob quotidien*, 102.

90. Jacob/Paulhan, 248n1.

91. Belaval, *Rencontre*, 58.

92. MJ to Béalu, January 31, 1938, in Béalu, *Dernier visage*, 135.

93. MJ to Pougy, April 5, 1937, in *Pougy*, 148.

94. MJ, *Adès* (Paris: Éditions du Chronique du Jour, 1933).

95. Peyre, *Jacob quotidien*, 58–59.

96. Andreu, *Vie et mort*, 245.

97. MJ to Moricand, May 24, 1937, in Moricand BnF.

98. MJ to Moricand, August 14, 1937, in Collier, 76.

99. MJ to Moricand, February 13, 1938, ibid., 80–81.

100. MJ, "La Guerre," *Point* 3, no. 13 (February 1938): 21.

101. MJ to Szigeti, February 14, 1938, in Robert Szigeti, "Max Jacob," *Documents du Val d'Or*, no. 47 (March–April 1947): 10.

102. MJ to Jean-Robert Debray, April 20, 1938, in *AA* 2:103.

103. MJ to Toulouse, March 17, 1938, in *Toulouse*, 32–33.

104. René Villard, "Max Jacob collégien," *Goëland*, April 1, 1938, in Gompel/Marcoux, 447–49.

105. MJ, "Ballade de la visite nocturne," *Point*, no. 14 (April 1938): 81–82; B, in O, 1461.

106. MJ to Debray, April 30, 1938, in *AA* 2:164–65.

107. MJ to Debrays, May 17, 1938, ibid., 2:166–68.

108. Charles Estienne, "Notes prises par le critique Charles Estienne lors d'une conférence faite à Brest par Max Jacob en mai 1938 sur le *lyrisme*," *CdR*, no. 8 (1986): 37–38.

109. MJ to Debray, May 22, 1938, in *AA* 2:168–69; MJ to Moricand, June 21, 1938, in Moricand BnF.

110. Hélène Henry, "La Ville engloutie et la chute de la maison Jacob," *Cahiers de l'Iroise*, no. 30 (1983): 86–91.

111. Paul T. Pelleau, *Saint-Pol-Roux le crucifié* (Nantes: Éditions du Fleuve, 1946), 120.

112. MJ to Cingria, c. end of May 1938, in *AA* 2:170–71.

113. MJ to Toulouse, August n.d. and 25, 1938, in *Toulouse*, 33–35.

114. Lyne Bansat-Boudon and Roland Lardinois, *Sylvain Lévi (1863–1935), études indiennes, histoire sociale* (Turnhout, Belgium: Brepols, 2003), 285.

115. MJ to Debray, April 5, 1938, in *AA* 2:161.

116. Béalu, *Dernier visage*, 17–21.

117. MJ to Debray, June 21, 1938, in *AA* 2:175.

118. MJ to Debray, July 26, 1938, ibid., 2:178.

119. MJ to Toulouse, c. August 1938, in *Toulouse*, 34–35.

120. MJ to Debray, July 4, 1938, in *AA* 2:176–77.

121. MJ to Debray, September 10, 1938, ibid., 2:184.

122. MJ to Toulouse, October 4, 1938, in *Toulouse*, 37–39.

123. MJ to Lanoë, September 23, 1938, in *Lanoë*, 348.

124. MJ to Debray, September 25, 1938, in *AA* 2:185.

125. MJ to Debray, October 17 and 26, 1938, ibid., 2:186–87.

126. MJ to Debray, November 23, 1938, ibid., 2:189–90; MJ, "La Balle," *Documents du Val d'Or*, November 1938. DP, in O, 1562.

127. MJ to Alain Messiaen, December 8, 1938, in *AA* 2:192.

128. MJ to Debray, December 27, 1938, ibid., 2:193–94.

129. MJ to Queneau, January 2, 1939, in "Queneau," 223.

130. MJ to Queneau, January 24, 1939, ibid.

131. MJ to Debray, March 2, 1939, in *AA* 2:198.

132. André Gide, "Max Jacob," *Aguedal*, 1939, 101.

133. Jean Cocteau, "Signe à Max," ibid., 155.

134. MJ to Michel Levanti, October 27, 1938, in *Levanti*, 72–74.

135. MJ to Levanti, March 23, 1938, ibid., 68–69.

136. MJ to Levanti, June 13, 1939, ibid., 77–78.

137. MJ to Debray, c. May 1939, in *AA* 2:200–1.

138. Jabès interview.

139. MJ to Jabès, January 1938, in *Jabès*, 59–60.

140. Jabès interview.

141. MJ to Jabès, January 1938, in *Jabès*, 59–60.

142. MJ to Jabès, May 1, 1939, ibid., 61. Jabès's last letter to Jacob (February 1944) was returned marked "Deceased." Jabès, "Preface," Jacob, *Advice to a Young Poet*, 5.

143. Receipt, May 6, 1939. Private collection, Olivier Zunz.

144. Olivier Zunz, "Note sur Robert Zunz et le monarchisme," unpublished essay, 4.

145. Ibid., 7.

146. *Zunz* 909–35.

147. MJ to Toulouse, May 16, 1939, in *Toulouse*, 46–47; MJ to Villard, May 15, 1939, in *Villard*, 85; MJ to Debray, c. May 1939, in *AA* 2:200–1. Gompel identifies the banker as André Lefèvre. It was Robert Zunz.

148. 11th Station, in O, 1503.

149. 5th Station, ibid., 1498.

150. Ibid., 1491.

151. MJ to Robert Zunz, June 15, 1939. "Egyptian pharaohs": MJ to Robert Zunz, March 26, March 1940. Private collection, Olivier Zunz.

152. MJ, "Récit de ma conversion," in O, 1473.

153. O, 1479.

154. MJ to Toulouse, May 16, 1939, in *Toulouse*, 46.

155. Louis Guilloux, *Carnets 1921–1944* (Paris: Gallimard, 1978), 392.

156. MJ to René Villard, January 4, 1939, in *Villard*, 81.

157. MJ to François de Montalivet, July 28, 1939, in *AA* 2:208–9.

158. Pelleau, *Saint-Pol-Roux*, 160–61; Jean Caveng, *Max Jacob et Quimper* (Quimper: Calligrammes, 1984), 50.

CHAPTER 20: THE OCCUPATION

1. MJ to René Villard, September 13, 1939, in *Villard*, 89.

2. MJ to François de Montalivet, November 8, 1939, in *AA* 2:217.

3. MJ to Louis Vaillant, August 24, 1938, in *Jacob écrit*, 106; MJ to Szigeti, November 7, 1939, ibid., 260n5; MJ to René Cadou, June 8, 1941, in *CMJ*, no. 13–14 (2013). MJ to Lanoë, January 6, 1942, in *Lanoë*, 459.

4. MJ to François de Montalivet, September 15, 1939, in *AA* 2:211–12.

5. MJ to Minet, October 6, 1939, in *Minet*, 109–10.

6. MJ to Toulouse, September 10, 1939, in *Toulouse*, 51–52.

7. MJ to Lanoë, March 21, 1940, in *Lanoë*, 369.

8. MJ to Jean-Robert Debray, January 12, 1940, in *AA* 2:228. MJ to Levanti, January 24, 1940, in *Levanti*, 85–86; MJ to Manoll, July 20, 1940, in *Manoll*, 61; Martinoir, *Littérature occupée*, 121.

9. Theodore Zeldin, *France 1848–1945: Anxiety and Hypocrisy* (Oxford: Oxford University Press, 1977, 1981), 340.

10. David Thomas, *France: Empire and Republic, 1850–1940* (New York: Harper & Row, 1968), 357.

11. Renée Poznanski, Denis Peschanski, and Benoît Pouvreau, *Drancy: Un camp en France* (Paris: Fayard, and Ministère de la Défense, 2015), 30.

12. Jacob/Paulhan, 252.

13. Assouline, *L'Homme de l'art*, 515.

14. Vittorio and Fabio Rieti, interviews.

15. MJ to Divine, December 30, 1940, in "Lettres à Saint-Pol-Roux," *Poésie présente*, no. 44 (1982): 13–15; Jacob/Paulhan, 275–76.

16. Hélène Henry, "Une paperasserie inestimable," 59–61; Francis Deguilly, "Présentation du manuscrit," 61–62; Francis Deguilly, "Note sur l'édition," 62; and Max Jacob, "Journal de guerre"1940. Manuscrit 2244 in the Médiathèque d'Orléans, 63–88; all in *CMJ*, no. 6 (2006).

17. MJ, "Journal de guerre," 72.

18. Ibid.

19. Ibid., 77.

20. Ibid., 73–75.

21. Ibid., 78–79.

22. Abbé Breut left Saint-Benoît in 1929—see *Jacob écrit*, 80n3. Saint-Benoît had a new vicar.

23. MJ, "Journal de guerre," 79.

24. MJ to Follain, July 16, 1940, in *AA* 2:243–44.

25. MJ to Béalu, June 10, 1940, in Béalu, *Dernier visage*, 193–94.

26. MJ to Manoll, August 21, 1940, in *Manoll*, 65–66.

27. Béatrice Mousli, *Max Jacob* (Paris: Flammarion, 2005), 423.

28. MJ to Manoll, August 2, 1940, in *Manoll*, 63–64.

29. MJ to Manoll, August 21, 1940, ibid., 65–66.

30. MJ to Lanoë, September 2, 1940, in *Lanoë*, 375.

31. MJ to Jean Colle, October 18, 1940, in *Colle*, 35–36; MJ to Salmon, March 19, 1941, in François Garnier, "Une creation permanente: Le courrier de Max Jacob," in MJ, *Max Jacob et la Création: Colloque d'Orléans, Inédits de Max Jacob*, ed. Arlette Albert-Birot (Paris: Jean-Michel Place, 1997), 150.

32. A week later Madame Persillard agreed to keep him. MJ to Lanoë, October 7, 1940, in *Lanoë*, 381.

33. MJ to Lanoë, September 2, 1940, ibid., 375.

34. MJ to Paulhan, October 10, 1940, in Jacob/Paulhan, 249.

35. MJ to Manoll, November 22, 1943, in *Manoll*, 137–39.

36. MJ, "Reportage de juin 1940," *Confluences* 2, no. 12 (July 1942): 7–10; DP, in O, 1557.

37. MJ to Minet, January 10, 1940, in *Minet*, 111.

38. MJ to Jouhandeau, May 3, 1940, in *Jouhandeau*, 349.

39. MJ to Jouhandeau, May 9, 1940, ibid., 350–52.

40. Winock, *France et les juifs*, 218–21.

41. MJ to Montalivet, October 4, 1940, in *AA* 2:247–48; MJ to Louis Dumoulin, November 4, 1940, in *Jacob écrit*, 193.

42. MJ to Queneau, January 3, 1940, in "Queneau," 225–26.

43. MJ to Jean Colle, November 4, 1940, in *Colle*, 37–38.

44. *Jacob écrit*, 242.

45. R. O. Paxton, O. Corpet, and C. Paulhan, *Archives de la vie littéraire sous l'occupation: À travers le désastre* (Paris: Hatier, 1995), 34.

46. Ibid., 12–13; Martinoir, *Littérature occupée*, 32–35.

47. Martinoir, *Littérature occupée*, 32–33.

48. Gerhard Heller, *Un allemand à Paris* (Paris: Seuil, 1981), 26–27, 42–45.

49. Paxton, Corpet, and Paulhan, *Archives,* 110–11.

50. MJ to Lanoë, October 23, 1940, in *Lanoë*, 385.

51. MJ to Maurice Gouchault, November 19, 1940, in *AA* 2:254.

52. MJ to "Mme L," December 26, 1940, in "Deux lettres inédites de Max Jacob," *Cahiers de l'Iroise* 17, no. 2 (April–June 1970): 71–72.

53. MJ to Queneau, January 3, 1940, in "Queneau," 225–26.

54. MJ to Lanoë, January 1940, in *Lanoë* 403.

55. MJ to Jean Colle, November 14, 1940, in *Colle* 37–38.

56. MJ to Jacques-Émile Blanche, January 3, 1941, in Georges-Paul Collet, "Max Jacob et Jacques-Émile Blanche: Une confluence inattendue," in *Max Jacob à la confluence: Actes du colloque de Quimper* (1994; Quimper: Bibliothèque Municipale, 2000), 137.

57. Martinoir, *Littérature occupée*, 59.

58. MJ to Lanoë, February 4, 1941, in *Lanoë* 411.

59. MJ to Montalivet, February 5, 1941, in *AA* 2:260.

60. Paxton, Corpet, and Paulhan, *Archives,* 288–95.

61. François Vignale, "Max Jacob, Max-Pol Fouchet, et la revue *Fontaine*," *CMJ*, no. 9 (2009): 96.

62. MJ to Mespoulet, April 20, 23, and 24; May 14 and 16, 1940, in Tatiana Greene, "Notice, en préambule aux lettres de Max Jacob," *CdR*, no. 4 (1981): 35–45.

63. MJ, "Sang-Esprit," ibid., 41; HC, 35.

64. MJ to Lanoë, November 22, 1940, in *Lanoë*, 389.

65. MJ to Lanoë, April 12, 1941, ibid., 417.

66. MJ to Lanoë, February 4, 1941, ibid., 411.

67. Ibid.

68. MJ to Lanoë, April 12, 1941, ibid., 417.

69. Mgr. Charles Molette, *Résistances chrétiennes à la nazification des esprits* (Paris: François-Xavier de Guibert, 1998), 85.

70. *La France continue*, no. 7 (October 1941): n.p.

71. MJ to Lanoë, May 1 and 14, 1941, in *Lanoë*, 420–25.

72. MJ to Montalivet, March 20, 1941, in *AA* 2:267.

73. MJ to Manoll, March 19, 1941, in *Manoll*, 81–83.

74. Louis Guillaume, "Max Jacob, le Quimpérois," *Simoun*, no. 17–18 (1955): 52.

75. Ibid., 50.

76. *Jeune homme*, 8.

77. MJ to Mezure, May 27, 1941, ibid., 31–33.

78. MJ to Mezure, June 19, 1941, ibid., 40–42.

79. *Levanti*, 21–22.

80. MJ to Paulhan, May 1941, May 20 and June 21, 1941, in Jacob/Paulhan, 251–57.

81. Émié, *Dialogues*, 160–61.

82. Michel Manoll, *René Guy Cadou* (Paris: Seghers, 1954), 54.

83. *Manoll*, 22.

84. Marcel Béalu and René Guy Cadou, *Correspondance 1941–1951* (Limoges: Rougerie, 1979), 15.

85. Ibid.

86. MJ to Follain, May 30, 193, in *AA* 1:311.

87. Follain's work is in the anthology *Another Republic,* ed. Mark Strand and Charles Simic (New York: Ecco Press, 1976).

88. MJ to René Lacôte, April 24, 1937, in "Lacôte," 34–35; MJ to Louis Dumoulin, March 9, 1943, in *Jacob écrit*, 226–27.

89. MJ to Manoll, May 10, 1941, in *Manoll*, 86–87.

90. MJ to Paulhan, June 12, 1941, in Jacob/Paulhan, 255.

91. Annette Wieviorka and Michel Lafitte, *À l'intérieur de camp de Drancy* (Paris: Perrin, 2012), 23.

92. Winock, *France et les juifs*, 222–24.

93. MJ to Paulhan, May 7, 1941, in Jacob/Paulhan, 251.

94. MJ to Minet, May 20, 1941, in *Minet*, 115–16.

95. MJ to Mezure, May 31, 1941, June 19, 1941, in *Jeune homme*, 40–42; MJ to Cadou, June 1, 1941, in *CMJ*, no. 13–14 (2013): 276.

96. MJ to Mezure, June 19, 1941, in *Jeune homme*, 40–42; MJ to Paulhan, June 19, 1941, in Jacob/Paulhan; MJ to Montalivet, June 21, 1941, in *AA* 2:276.

97. MJ to Montalivet, June 10, 1941, ibid., 2:274–75.

98. MJ to Montalivet, April 30, 1941, *AA*, 2:238. The arrest took place in 1941.

99. Wieviorka and Lafitte, *À l'intérieur*, 19–27.

100. Poznanski, Peschanski, and Pouvreau, *Drancy*, 15–27; Wieviorka and Lafitte, *À l'intérieur*, 11–17.

101. Wieviorka and Lafitte, *À l'intérieur*, 36–45.

102. MJ to Lanoë, June 9 and 10, 1941, in *Lanoë*, 426–29.

103. O, 1692.

104. Ibid., 1713. Évrard got into trouble, after the war, for collaborating with Vichy. He gave his account of his exchanges with Jacob years later in Jacob, *Advice to a Young Poet*, 34–39.

105. MJ to Manoll, June 1941, July 16, 1941, in *Manoll*, 94–97; MJ to Lanoë, July 12, 1941, in *Lanoë*, 433.

106. MJ, *Conseils*, O, 1695.

107. MJ to Moricand, September 2, 1941, in Collier, 130.

108. MJ to Manoll, September 3, 1941, in *Manoll*, 98–99.

109. MJ to Rimbert, September 19, 1941, in *Rimbert*, 83–84.

110. Béalu and Cadou, *Correspondance 1941–1951*, 49; Guillaume, "Jacob, le Quimpérois," 51.

111. Seckel, *Jacob et Picasso*, 262.

112. *Jeune homme*, 58n37.

113. MJ to Mezure, October 8, 1941, ibid., 57–58.

114. MJ to Robert Zunz, November 22, 1941, in *Zunz*; MJ to Montalivet, October 8, 1941, in *AA* 2:288–89.

115. MJ to Lanoë, November 14, 1941, in *Lanoë*, 452; MJ to Montalivet, December 29, 1941, in *AA* 2:290–91; MJ to Cocteau, April 5, 1942, in Jacob/Cocteau, 588–90.

116. MJ to Béalu, November 29 and December 3, 1941, in Béalu, *Dernier visage*, 250–51; MJ to Lanoë, November 29, 1941, in *Lanoë*, 455.

117. MJ to Montalivets, December 29, 1941, in *AA* 2:290.

118. MJ to Lanoë, December 31, 1941, in *Lanoë*, 457.

119. Poznanski, Peschanski, and Pouvreau, *Drancy*, 58–59.

120. Wieviorka and Lafitte, *À l'intérieur*, 122. Oliver Zunz: "Note sur Robert Zunz et le monarchisme," unpublished.

121. MJ to Métivier, February 17, 1942, in *Jacob écrit*, 285–86; MJ to Texiers, n.d., in *Toulouse*, 67; MJ to Lanoë, February 11, 1942, in *Lanoë*, 462; MJ to Moricand, February 16, 1942, in Collier, 133; Moricand BnF.

122. *Jacob écrit*, 286n9.

123. Poznanski, Peschanski, and Pouvreau, *Drancy*, 94.

124. MJ to Moricand, February 16, 1942, in Collier, 133.

125. Paxton, Corpet, and Paulhan, *Archives*, 264.

126. Moricand to MJ, February 28, 1942, in Moricand BnF.

127. MJ to Lanoë, July 30, 1942, in *Lanoë*, 481.

128. MJ to Moricand, March 18, 1942, in Collier 134–35.

129. MJ to Moricand, March 26, 1942, ibid., 135–36.

130. Belaval, *Rencontre*, 53.

131. MJ to Salmon, April 30, 1942, in O, 96.

132. MJ to Madame Neveu, c. April 1942, in ms. n. acqfr 16799, BnF.

133. The articles in Wikipedia erroneously claim that Petit was beheaded.

134. Wieviorka and Lafitte, *À l'intérieur*, 151; Poznanski, Peschanski, and Pouvreau, *Drancy*, 154.

135. MJ to Moricand, July 18, 1942, in Collier, 137.

136. MJ, "Amour du Prochain," *Éternelle revue*, no. 1, new ser. (December 1, 1944): 37, entitled "L'étoile jaune des juifs." With variations: "L'Amour du prochain," DP, in O. 1599.

137. Seven of the poems were collected in AE.

138. Jean Rousselot, *Max Jacob: L'homme qui faisait penser à Dieu* (Paris: Laffont, 1946), 29–34.

139. Ibid., 16.

140. Henri Dion, "Témoignage: Max Jacob et la basilique de Saint-Benoît-sur-Loire ou 'La Maison de Dieu,'" *CdR*, no. 5 (1983): 39–44.

141. Henri Dion, interview by author.

142. MJ to Frank, December 1942, in *Frank*, 186–87; MJ to Lanoë, June 3, 1942, in *Lanoë*, 477.

143. MJ to Lanoë, February 11, 1942, in *Lanoë*, 462.

144. MJ to Mezure, July 26, 1942, in *Jeune homme*, 96.

145. MJ to Lanoë, July 30, 1942, in *Lanoë*, 481.

146. Jean Cocteau, *Journal 1942–1945* (Paris: Gallimard, 1989), 335.

147. Jean Cocteau, "Salut à Breker," *Comoedia*, May 23, 1942, 1.

148. Lucien Combelle, "Les Jeux sont faits," *Révolution nationale*, July 17, 1943, 1.

149. MJ to Madame Neveu, December 1942 (no. 57); December 27, 1943 (no. 58). MJ to Lanoë, December 31, 1942, in *Lanoë*, 487.

150. O, 97.

151. MJ to Métivier, June 8, 1943, in *Jacob écrit*, 298.

152. MJ to Louis Dumoulin, March 9, 1943, in *Jacob écrit*, 226–27.

153. MJ to Manoll, January 9, 1943, in *Manoll*, 123–24.

154. MJ to Lanoë, October 9, 1943, in *Lanoë*, 502; Béalu and Cadou, *Correspondance 1941–1951*, 100.

155. *Jacob écrit*, 228n4.

156. MJ, *Conseils à un étudiant*, in O, 1717–19.

157. MJ to Mezure, January 5, 1944, in *Jeune homme*, 130–31.

158. MJ to Lanoë, January 25, 1944, in *Lanoë*, 511.

159. MJ to Cocteau, January 20, 1944, in Jacob/Cocteau, 597–98; MJ to Sert, n.d., in Arthur Gold and Robert Fizdale, *Misia* (New York: Knopf, 1980), 283; MJ to Minet, January 25, 1944, in *Minet*, 116–17.

160. MJ to Cocteau, February 2, 1944, in Jacob/Cocteau, 599; MJ to Szigeti, February 2, 1944, in Patricia Sustrac, "Étapes des persécutions contre Max Jacob et sa famille 1940–1944," *CMJ*, no. 9 (2009): 121; Béalu, *Dernier visage*, 332–33.

161. Wieviorka and Lafitte, *À l'intérieur*, 165.

162. Sustrac, "Étapes des persécutions," 121.

163. MJ to Béalu, February 2, 1944, in Béalu, *Dernier visage*, 332–33.

164. Ibid., 74–81.

165. Pierre Andreu, "Les derniers jours de Max Jacob," *Cahiers de l'Iroise* 23, no. 1, new ser. (January–March 1985): 8.

166. Béalu, *Dernier visage*, 82.

167. Ibid., 81–83; Rousselot, *Max Jacob*, 159.

168. Cocteau's letter, ms. 2513, in Orléans; Sustrac, "Étapes des persécutions," 122.

169. *Goldblatt*, 37.

170. Rousselot, *Max Jacob*, 160.

171. MJ to Cocteau, February 29 (actually February 28), 1944, in Jacob/Cocteau 600.

172. *Goldblatt*, 38.

173. MJ to Moricand, February 28, 1944, in Moricand BnF.

174. Seckel, *Jacob et Picasso*, 274.

175. Sustrac, "Étapes des persécutions," 122.

176. *Goldblatt*, 38.

177. Seckel, *Jacob et Picasso*, 274.

178. Patricia Sustrac, "La Mort de Max Jacob: Réalité et représentations," *CMJ*, no. 9 (2009): 105. Seckel, *Jacob et Picasso*, 276–77n28.

179. Heller, *Un allemand à Paris*, 183.

180. Seckel, *Jacob et Picasso*, 278n38, quoting Youki Desnos, *Confidences de Youki* (Paris: Fayard, 1957), 217–18.

181. Henri Sauguet, interview by author; Andreu (*Vie et mort*, 292–93) put it in the worst possible light.

182. Seckel, *Jacob et Picasso*, 275.

183. MJ to Briant, March 5, 1944, in Collier, 150–52.

184. Sustrac, "Mort de Jacob," 105.

185. Sert's claim was repeated by Gold and Fizdale, *Misia*, 283; Sustrac, "Mort de Jacob," 105.

186. Sustrac, "Mort de Jacob," 126n24.

187. Yvette Delétang-Tardif, "La Mort d'un poète," *Poésie* 44, no. 20 (October 1944). Cited in Andreu, *Vie et mort*, 294; and *Goldblatt* 44. The narrative seems romanticized; it is not true that fellow prisoners had no idea who Jacob was.

188. Dr. Weille to Hélène Henry, February 22, 1993, in Archives of Les Amis de Max Jacob; Sustrac, "Mort de Jacob," 127n29.

189. Julien J. London, "Témoignage sur l'agonie d'un poète," *Candide*, October 19–26, 1961.

190. Sustrac, "Mort de Jacob," 123.

191. Sustrac, "Étapes des persécutions," 123.

192. Sustrac, "Mort de Jacob," 106.

193. Dr. Albert Buesche to Roger Toulouse, March 4, 1944, in *Toulouse* 101.

194. Sustrac, "Étapes des persécutions," 123.

195. Rousselot, *Max Jacob*, 166–68; Sustrac, "Étapes des persécutions," 123.

196. Jean Cocteau, *Journal 1942–1945* (Paris: Gallimard, 1989), 486–87.

197. Seckel, *Jacob et Picasso*, 273 and 279n51.

198. Seckel, *Jacob et Picasso*, 118; Pierre Colle to Jean Colle, March 16 and 21, 1944, in *Colle*, 70–72.

199. Pierre Colle to Jean Colle, March 21, 1944, *Colle*, 71–72.

200. Andreu, *Vie et mort*, insisted that Picasso hadn't come. See Seckel, *Jacob et Picasso*, 276.

201. Andreu, *Vie et mort*, 293, accused Picasso of not attending. But many witnesses reported Picasso's presence. Seckel, *Jacob et Picasso*, 276.

202. Seckel, *Jacob et Picasso*, 276.

ILLUSTRATION CREDITS

1. Cliché Patricia Sustrac.
2. © RMN-Grand Palais / Art Resource, NY. Artwork : © 2020 Estate of Pablo Picasso / Artists Rights Society (ARS), New York.
3. © RMN-Grand Palais / Art Resource, NY. Artwork : © 2020 Estate of Pablo Picasso / Artists Rights Society (ARS), New York.
4. © RMN-Grand Palais / Art Resource, NY.
5. © RMN-Grand Palais / Art Resource, NY.
6. © RMN-Grand Palais / Art Resource, NY. Artwork : © 2020 Estate of Pablo Picasso / Artists Rights Society (ARS), New York.
7. Image courtesy Comité Jean Cocteau.
8. © RMN-Grand Palais / Art Resource, NY. Artwork: © 2020 Artists Rights Society (ARS), New York / ADAGP, Paris.
9. © Ministère de la Culture / Médiathèque du Patrimoine, Dist. RMN-Grand Palais / Art Resource, NY.
10. ©Cincinnati Art Museum, Ohio, USA. Gift of Mary E. Johnston. Bridgeman Images.
11. Digital Image © The Museum of Modern Art/Licensed by SCALA / Art Resource, NY. Artwork: © 2020 Estate of Pablo Picasso / Artists Rights Society (ARS), New York.
12. The Archives of the Abbaye de Fleury.
13. ©CNAC/MNAM/Dist. RMN-Grand Palais / Art Resource, NY. Artwork: © Man Ray 2015 Trust / Artists Rights Society (ARS), NY / ADAGP, Paris 2020.
14. ©CNAC/MNAM/Dist. RMN-Grand Palais / Art Resource, NY. Artwork: © 2020 Artists Rights Society (ARS), New York / ADAGP, Paris.
15. © Albert Harlingue/Roger-Viollet.
16. Orléans, Musée des Beaux-Arts © Christophe Camus.
17. Private Collection.
18. Orléans, Musée des Beaux-Arts © François Lauginie.

TEXT CREDITS

The following poems by Max Jacob from *Max Jacob, Oeuvres, Quarto,* Éditions @Gallimard 2012, are quoted by kind permission of Éditions Gallimard:

"Colloque III"
"Agonies et autres"
"Reportage du juin 1940"
"Amour du prochain"
"Le Phare d'Éckmühl"
"Convalescence"

The poem "Envie" by Pierre Reverdy from *Plupart du Temps I* © Editions Gallimard 1969 is quoted by kind permission of Éditions Gallimard.

Extracts from André Salmon's *Souvenirs sans fin I et II* © Editions Gallimard, 1955, 1956 are quoted by kind permission of Éditions Gallimard.

All Max Jacob texts not covered by Gallimard are quoted with the kind permission of Sylvia Lorant-Colle and Béatrice Saalburg, literary executors of the Estate of Max Jacob. All rights reserved.

Max Jacob Correspondence in Didier Gompel-Netter and Annie Marcoux, *Les Propos et les jours.* Reprinted by permission of Groupe Elidia, all rights reserved.

Max Jacob Correspondence in Didier Gompel-Netter, *Les Amitiés & les amours,* vols. I and II. Reprinted by kind permission of the Association des Amis de Max Jacob.

Anne Kimball, ed., *Max Jacob et Jean Cocteau, Correspondance.* Reprinted by permission of Max Milo Editions.

Anne Kimball, ed., *Max Jacob: Lettres à Marcel Jouhandeau.* Reprinted by permission of Librairie Droz, (c) 1979.

Christine Van Rogger-Andreucci, *Lettres de Max Jacob à Michel Leiris.* Reprinted by permission of Éditions Honoré Champion.

Hélène Seckel, *Max Jacob et Picasso*. For letters of Max Jacob and Picasso: © 2020 Estate of Pablo Picasso / Artists Rights Society (ARS), New York. For Cocteau letter in Seckel: © Adagp / Comité Cocteau, Paris, Artists Rights Society (ARS), New York / ADAGP, Paris 2020.

INDEX